Selling

ALL-IN-ONE

FOR

DUMMIES®

D1221950

Selling

ALL-IN-ONE

FOR DUMMIES®

**by Tom Hopkins, Dirk Zeller,
Ralph R. Roberts with Joe Kraynak, and
Michael C. Donaldson, with Meg Schneider**

WILEY

John Wiley & Sons, Inc.

Selling All-in-One For Dummies®

Published by
John Wiley & Sons, Inc.
111 River St.
Hoboken, NJ 07030-5774
www.wiley.com

Copyright © 2012 by John Wiley & Sons, Inc., Hoboken, New Jersey

Published simultaneously in Canada

No part of this publication may be reproduced, stored in a retrieval system or transmitted in any form or by any means, electronic, mechanical, photocopying, recording, scanning or otherwise, except as permitted under Sections 107 or 108 of the 1976 United States Copyright Act, without the prior written permission of the Publisher. Requests to the Publisher for permission should be addressed to the Permissions Department, John Wiley & Sons, Inc., 111 River Street, Hoboken, NJ 07030, (201) 748-6011, fax (201) 748-6008, or online at http://www.wiley.com/go/permissions.

Trademarks: Wiley, the Wiley logo, For Dummies, the Dummies Man logo, A Reference for the Rest of Us!, The Dummies Way, Dummies Daily, The Fun and Easy Way, Dummies.com, Making Everything Easier, and related trade dress are trademarks or registered trademarks of John Wiley & Sons, Inc., and/or its affiliates in the United States and other countries, and may not be used without written permission. All other trademarks are the property of their respective owners. John Wiley & Sons, Inc., is not associated with any product or vendor mentioned in this book.

LIMIT OF LIABILITY/DISCLAIMER OF WARRANTY: THE PUBLISHER AND THE AUTHOR MAKE NO REPRESENTATIONS OR WARRANTIES WITH RESPECT TO THE ACCURACY OR COMPLETENESS OF THE CONTENTS OF THIS WORK AND SPECIFICALLY DISCLAIM ALL WARRANTIES, INCLUDING WITHOUT LIMITATION WARRANTIES OF FITNESS FOR A PARTICULAR PURPOSE. NO WARRANTY MAY BE CREATED OR EXTENDED BY SALES OR PROMOTIONAL MATERIALS. THE ADVICE AND STRATEGIES CONTAINED HEREIN MAY NOT BE SUITABLE FOR EVERY SITUATION. THIS WORK IS SOLD WITH THE UNDERSTANDING THAT THE PUBLISHER IS NOT ENGAGED IN RENDERING LEGAL, ACCOUNTING, OR OTHER PROFESSIONAL SERVICES. IF PROFESSIONAL ASSISTANCE IS REQUIRED, THE SERVICES OF A COMPETENT PROFESSIONAL PERSON SHOULD BE SOUGHT. NEITHER THE PUBLISHER NOR THE AUTHOR SHALL BE LIABLE FOR DAMAGES ARISING HEREFROM. THE FACT THAT AN ORGANIZATION OR WEBSITE IS REFERRED TO IN THIS WORK AS A CITATION AND/OR A POTENTIAL SOURCE OF FURTHER INFORMATION DOES NOT MEAN THAT THE AUTHOR OR THE PUBLISHER ENDORSES THE INFORMATION THE ORGANIZATION OR WEBSITE MAY PROVIDE OR RECOMMENDATIONS IT MAY MAKE. FURTHER, READERS SHOULD BE AWARE THAT INTERNET WEBSITES LISTED IN THIS WORK MAY HAVE CHANGED OR DISAPPEARED BETWEEN WHEN THIS WORK WAS WRITTEN AND WHEN IT IS READ.

For general information on our other products and services, please contact our Customer Care Department within the U.S. at 877-762-2974, outside the U.S. at 317-572-3993, or fax 317-572-4002.

For technical support, please visit www.wiley.com/techsupport.

Wiley publishes in a variety of print and electronic formats and by print-on-demand. Some material included with standard print versions of this book may not be included in e-books or in print-on-demand. If this book refers to media such as a CD or DVD that is not included in the version you purchased, you may download this material at http://booksupport.wiley.com. For more information about Wiley products, visit www.wiley.com.

Library of Congress Control Number: 2011945564

ISBN 978-1-118-06593-8 (pbk); ISBN 978-1-118-22237-9 (ebk); ISBN 978-1-118-23629-1 (ebk); ISBN 978-1-118-24669-6 (ebk)

Manufactured in the United States of America

SKY10021113_091020

WILEY

About the Authors

Tom Hopkins: Tom Hopkins is the epitome of sales success. After starting out as a failure in sales at age 19, he achieved millionaire status by the age of 27. This was accomplished through study, perseverance, and a lot of trial and error. Tom is now chairman of Tom Hopkins International, one of the most prestigious sales-training organizations in the world. Tom's selling strategies have been proven effective in hundreds of cultures, in all types of economic cycles, and for products ranging from A to Z. Tom has written 15 books, including *Selling For Dummies, Sales Prospecting For Dummies,* and *Sales Closing For Dummies* (all published by Wiley), as well as the best-selling *How to Master the Art of Selling* (Business Plus), which has sold more than 1.6 million copies.

Dirk Zeller: Dirk Zeller, CEO of Sales Champions and Real Estate Champions, is one of the world's most published authors on success, time management, sales, and productivity. As a speaker and lecturer, he has presented before large audiences on five different continents. His tools, systems, and strategies for success are used in more than 97 different countries worldwide.

Ralph R. Roberts: Ralph R. Roberts's sales success is legendary. He has been profiled by the Associated Press, CNN, and *Time* magazine, and was once dubbed by *Time* "the best selling Realtor® in America." In addition to being one of the most successful salespeople in America, Ralph is also an experienced mentor, coach, consultant, and author. He has penned several successful books, including *Flipping Houses For Dummies* and *Foreclosure Investing For Dummies* (both published by Wiley), *Sell It Yourself: Sell Your Home Faster and for More Money Without Using a Broker* (Adams Media Corporation), *Walk Like a Giant, Sell Like a Madman: America's #1 Salesman Shows You How To Sell Anything* (Collins), *52 Weeks of Sales Success: America's #1 Salesman Shows You How To Close Every Deal!* (Collins), *REAL WEALTH by Investing in REAL ESTATE* (Prentice Hall), and *Protect Yourself from Real Estate and Mortgage Fraud* (Kaplan). Although Ralph has many varied skills and interests, his true passion is selling . . . and showing other salespeople how to boost their sales and profits. In *Selling All-in-One For Dummies,* Ralph reveals the practical sales tips and tricks he's gathered over the course of his more than 30-year career and challenges you to put them to work for you. To find out more about Ralph Roberts, visit www. ralphroberts.com.

Joe Kraynak: Joe Kraynak is a freelance author who has written and coauthored dozens of books on topics ranging from slam poetry to computer basics. Joe teamed up with Dr. Candida Fink to write his first book in the *For Dummies* series, *Bipolar Disorder For Dummies* (Wiley), in which he showcased his talent for translating the complexities of a topic into plain-spoken practical advice. He then teamed up with Ralph R. Roberts to write the ultimate guide to flipping houses, *Flipping Houses For Dummies,* and delivered an encore performance in *Foreclosure Investing For Dummies* (both published by Wiley). His other *For Dummies* titles include *Food Allergies For Dummies, Clarinet For Dummies,* and *Financing Real Estate For Dummies* (all published by Wiley). To find out more, visit www.joekraynak.com.

Michael C. Donaldson: Michael C. Donaldson is a founding partner of Berton & Donaldson, a Beverly Hills, California, firm specializing in entertainment and copyright law, with an emphasis on the representation of independent film producers. He is the author of *Do It Yourself! Trademarks & Copyrights* and *Clearance & Copyright — Everything the Filmmaker Needs to Know;* he also wrote the introduction to *Conversations with Michael Landon.* Donaldson earned his law degree in 1967 at the University of California, Berkeley. He is a member of the Beverly Hills Bar Association (where he was once co-chairman of the Entertainment Section), the Los Angeles County Bar Association, the State Bar of California, and the American Bar Association. He is listed in the current edition of *Who's Who in American Law.* He is also a member of the Los Angeles Copyright Society.

Meg Schneider: Meg is an award-winning writer with more than two decades of experience in journalism and public relations. She has authored or coauthored several books, including *Stem Cells For Dummies* and *Business Ethics For Dummies* (both published by Wiley). Meg's journalism honors include awards from the Iowa Associated Press Managing Editors, Women in Communications, the Maryland-Delaware-D.C. Press Association, Gannett, the New York State Associated Press, and the William Randolph Hearst Foundation. She recently returned to her native Iowa after 16 years on the East Coast.

Dedication

We dedicate this book to you, the reader. May your career in sales be long and fruitful!

Publisher's Acknowledgments

We're proud of this book; please send us your comments at http://dummies.custhelp.com. For other comments, please contact our Customer Care Department within the U.S. at 877-762-2974, outside the U.S. at 317-572-3993, or fax 317-572-4002.

Some of the people who helped bring this book to market include the following:

Acquisitions, Editorial, and Vertical Websites

Compilation Editor: Tracy L. Barr

Project Editor: Elizabeth Kuball

Acquisitions Editor: Tracy Boggier

Copy Editor: Elizabeth Kuball

Assistant Editor: David Lutton

Editorial Program Coordinator: Joe Niesen

Technical Editor: Steve Dailey

Senior Editorial Manager: Jennifer Ehrlich

Editorial Manager: Carmen Krikorian

Editorial Assistants: Rachelle S. Amick, Alexa Koschier

Art Coordinator: Alicia B. South

Cover Photos: © iStockphoto.com / Richard Cote

Cartoons: Rich Tennant (www.the5thwave.com)

Composition Services

Project Coordinator: Sheree Montgomery

Layout and Graphics: Lavonne Roberts, Corrie Socolovitch, Christin Swinford

Proofreaders: Jessica Kramer, Christine Sabooni

Indexer: BIM Indexing & Proofreading Services

Publishing and Editorial for Consumer Dummies

    Kathleen Nebenhaus, Vice President and Executive Publisher

    Kristin Ferguson-Wagstaffe, Product Development Director

    Ensley Eikenburg, Associate Publisher, Travel

    Kelly Regan, Editorial Director, Travel

Publishing for Technology Dummies

    Andy Cummings, Vice President and Publisher

Composition Services

    Debbie Stailey, Director of Composition Services

Wiley Publishing Sales

    Michael Violano, Vice President, International Sales and Sub Rights

Contents at a Glance

Table of Contents

Introduction

Welcome to *Selling All-in-One For Dummies,* your one-stop guide for everything you need to know about selling products and services to businesses and consumers. Because selling is both a science and an art, we don't stop with the simple nuts-and-bolts information, like how many prospects you need to call to generate the right number of follow-throughs, or what resources you can tap into to gather the information you need, or what kinds of things your sales presentation needs to cover. This book also delves into the art of selling, which is the key difference between good (or even very good) salespeople and great ones.

So, what is the art of selling? It's people skills. After all, knowing how to get along well with others is a vital skill — especially if your career involves persuading them toward ownership of your ideas, concepts, products, or services. To be successful in sales, you must be able to cooperate, have good listening skills, and be willing to put others' needs before your own.

If you have in your arsenal the selling skills covered in this book, you'll have more happiness and satisfaction in *all* areas of your life, not just in your selling career (although your selling will certainly benefit, too).

About This Book

Selling All-in-One For Dummies can help you get more happiness and contentment out of your life right now by helping you gain more respect, more money, more recognition for the job you do, more agreement from your friends and family, more control in negotiations, and, of course, more sales. Above all, this book is a reference tool, so you don't have to read it from beginning to end. Instead, you can turn to whatever chapter contains the information you need when you need it.

Each book focuses on a particular topic and is divided into chapters that deal with the various aspects related to that topic. For example,

✔ If you struggle with prospecting in general, you can read any of the chapters in Book II.

✔ If you have a presentation coming up and want to make sure it goes smoothly, head to Book III, Chapter 3.

✔ If you're looking for a variety of closing techniques, head to Book IV, which is devoted to that topic.

✔ If you have a negotiation coming up and want to bone up on your negotiating skills, look no further than Book V.

✔ If you sell in an industry like biotech or financial services, you can find chapters specific to those, as well as other specialized industries, in Book VI.

✔ To find out how to tap into social media as a way to beef up sales, go to Book VII, Chapter 7.

The point is, you can keep coming back to this book over and over as you need to throughout your selling career.

Conventions Used in This Book

To help you navigate this book, we use the following conventions:

✔ **Boldface** highlights key words in bulleted lists and key instructions in a numbered list.

✔ New terms and emphasized words appear in *italic*.

✔ Web addresses appear in `monofont`. If a web address breaks across two lines of text, no extra spaces or hyphens have been added. Just type in exactly what you see as though the line break doesn't exist.

✔ We tried to alternate the genders of pronouns used to refer to both salespeople and customers, but we didn't take out a calculator and tally them up, so rest assured that if you notice an imbalance, it wasn't intentional.

What You're Not to Read

Because this book is a reference, you really need to read only what you want to read, which means that you can skip everything else. If you're in a hurry or are a "just the facts, ma'am" type of person, you can easily identify information that, although interesting and helpful or enlightening, isn't strictly necessary in order to understand the discussion at hand:

✔ Anything marked by the Anecdote icon

✔ Sidebars, those shaded boxes that you see sprinkled throughout the book

Foolish Assumptions

In putting this book together, we made some assumptions about you:

✔ **You're either already in sales or considering going into sales.** It doesn't matter whether you're selling corporate jets or cookies, the basic selling strategies apply simply because you're selling to *people*.

✔ **You like people in general and enjoy working with them.** In other words, you're not a hermit or a recluse, you don't have an extreme case of *anthropophobia* (fear of people), and you aren't painfully shy.

✔ **You want to be a better salesperson.** Whether you're brand-new to sales and find yourself struggling or you're an experienced salesperson who already makes a decent living, you're committed to becoming even better.

✔ **You're interested in learning and willing to experiment and apply the strategies in this book.** If you're not serious about at least trying something new to get different results than you're getting now, you might as well give this book to someone else. This book contains answers, strategies, and tactics for successfully selling products and services, but they won't work unless you put them to work.

How This Book Is Organized

Selling All-in-One For Dummies is organized into eight books, each dealing with a particular sales-related topic. Each book is divided into chapters that deal with specific subjects related to that topic. Here's a quick preview of what to expect from each book in this All-in-One so that you can turn to the one that interests you the most.

Book 1: Laying the Foundation for Selling Success

Every industry or business requires that its professionals have a solid foundation. If you want to be a physician, for example, your foundation would be in the anatomy of the human body and its processes. The foundation for electricians is built on the general properties of electricity, wiring, and circuitry.

A solid foundation in sales means understanding the selling cycle and knowing what you need to know about your product or service. Read this book to bone up on (or review) the basics.

Book II: Prospecting for Gold

Very few sales professionals will tell you that *prospecting* (finding the right buyers for the product or service and selling them on their need for your product or service) is their favorite part of the job. And it may never be *your* favorite part of the job. But it's a vital part of the selling cycle, and it's why we've devoted an entire book to it.

To prospect well, you need to know where to look for potential customers and how to approach them. Perhaps even more important, you need to remember that prospecting isn't about waylaying some poor unsuspecting Joe or Josephine and talking that person into buying whatever you're selling (an all-too-common perception). Prospecting is all about finding someone who has an actual need that your product or service can really, truly, honestly meet. In this book, you find all the strategies and advice you need to prospect with confidence.

Book III: Turning Prospects into Customers and Clients

Prospecting is just the beginning of a selling cycle. Now you have quite a job in front of you: turning that person into an actual customer or client. Doing so requires a series of steps: qualifying that person (making sure he has a real need for what you're offering and the authority and resources to make the buying decision), presenting your product or service to him, and addressing any concerns he may have. This book tells you everything you need to know to accomplish each of these tasks in a way that leads you closer to your ultimate goal: the closing.

Book IV: Closing Like a Champ and Getting Referrals

"So, you ready to sign your life away?" is not a good closing strategy. Nor is "Let's get this thing done" or "That's all I got. Whadaya think?"

In fact, no matter how beautifully you execute all the other steps in the selling cycle up to this point, if you handle the close poorly or too quickly, you can lose the sale in a heartbeat. Even if you approach the close well, the potential client may still be resistant to making that final decision to invest in your product or service. So, not only do you need to know the best time and the best way to approach a close, but you also need to know multiple closing strategies.

In this book, you find out how to determine the best time to approach the close, specific closing strategies to use depending on the particular scenario, and how to avoid the traps that too many salespeople fall into. This book also includes information on getting referrals, because one of the best times to ask for referrals is at the conclusion of a successful close.

Book V: Negotiating Skills Every Salesperson Should Have

Face it: As a salesperson, you often find yourself in situations where you have to negotiate. But the truth is, many people lack the negotiating skills that could help them be more successful when trying to close a deal. Most people assume that they know a great deal about negotiating because they've done it so often, but that isn't the case. For this reason, this entire book is dedicated to the fundamental skills, the key strategies, and the good advice every person in a negotiation situation should know.

The mission of this book is to help you negotiate from strength. Understanding the structure of every negotiation in which you're involved transforms you into a confident and successful negotiator. After you've mastered the basic skills of negotiating and achieved this position of strength, every tough situation you encounter becomes easier to analyze and conquer.

Book VI: Selling in Specialized and Growing Fields

No matter what you sell, the information, instructions, and advice shared throughout this All-in-One are applicable, but in certain industries, you may need to adapt or refine your approach. If you sell pharmaceuticals, for example, your prospect pool is more targeted than if you sell washing machines. Selling in the biotech industry requires that you be aware of any controversies that may impact your products.

This book provides targeted information for selling in several specialized and growing industries.

Book VII: Becoming a Power Seller

Inside every great salesperson is a power seller just waiting to come out. A power seller is a great salesperson who is a money-generating machine. Becoming that salesperson requires not only having mastered all the components of your profession, but going beyond and thinking creatively about how you can maximize your impact and reach.

This book shows you how to reach the pinnacle of your career. We cover how to exploit change to your advantage; how to expand your influence through self-promotion, personal partnering, and branding; how to use the latest technologies and social media to expand your reach; and more.

Book VIII: The Book of Tens

The short chapters in this book are packed with quick ideas and advice that can help you avoid common mistakes, boost your skills, break your slumps, and more. Go to this book when you need a quick recharge or refresher.

Icons Used in This Book

This book uses *icons* (those little pictures you see in the margins throughout this book) to draw your attention to specific kinds of helpful and interesting information. Here's a list of the icons used in this book and what they signify.

This icon points you to stories from top salespeople who've been in your shoes and who encountered challenges you're likely to encounter. Although interesting and illuminating, these personal anecdotes are not strictly necessary reading. Feel free to skip them if you're in a rush or on a mission.

When you see this icon in the margin, the paragraph next to it contains valuable information on making the sales process easier or faster.

Some things are so important that they bear repeating. So, this icon — like a string tied around your finger — is a friendly reminder of crucial pieces of information and skills you'll want to commit to memory and use throughout your sales career.

An important part of achieving success is simply eliminating the mistakes. And the information marked by this icon — which highlights those things you want to avoid — helps you do just that.

We live in a global world, and knowing how to accommodate the expectations and traditions in cultures other than your own can help you meet the needs of a broader customer base. To find information that gives you insight and strategies to use when you're in a culturally diverse environment, look for this icon.

Despite all the more-advanced technology that lets people communicate remotely (think video conferences, social-media platforms, even the no-longer-newfangled capabilities of e-mail), many sales tasks still involve the good old-fashioned telephone. This icon highlights advice on how to make your business calls effective (and keep them legal).

Where to Go from Here

Because this is a reference book, you get to decide where you want to go. If you're looking for general topics, glance through the table of contents or the index. Or you can simply flip the pages until something catches your eye.

To make the most effective use of the material in this All-in-One, do a little self-analysis to see where you're the weakest and then go to those areas first. Doing so will bring you the greatest amount of success in the shortest amount of time. Not sure what your weakest area is and don't want to take any time figuring it out yourself? Then think about this: Studies by Tom Hopkins International have shown that most traditional salespeople lack qualification skills. They waste a lot of time presenting to people who can't truly make decisions on what they're selling. So, why not try that topic first? You can find it in Book III, Chapter 2.

Still not sure? Then start at the beginning and read through to the end. We promise you'll find lots of good information from the very first page to the very last.

Book I
Laying the Foundation for Selling Success

The 5th Wave   By Rich Tennant

SALES REP
WANTED

FUNTMAN
NOVELTIES
• Joy Buzzers • Joke Books
• Wax Lips • Magic Tricks
• Party Balloons • Explo
• Squirting Flowers

"Oh, I think we've found our man."

In this book . . .

Whether you're just starting out in sales or you've been at it since the beginning of time, Book I provides great information you can use to strengthen your foundation of selling skills. Here you find the seven steps of the selling cycle and discover how to put these steps to work for you. This book also fills you in on what you need to know about your product and your potential clients, as well as how to find that information.

Chapter 1

The Seven-Step Selling Cycle

Selling breaks down neatly into seven steps. After you master these seven steps, you may be inclined to think of selling as a cycle because, if you do it correctly, the last step in the cycle (getting referrals) leads you back to the first (making contacts for new prospects). Your new, happy client or customer will give you the names of other people he feels would benefit from your product or service, and then you have your next lead or prospect to work with.

The seven steps in this chapter are an overview of what you'll find available in greater detail throughout the rest of this All-in-One. Each step is equally valuable and plays a critical role. Rarely can you skip a step and still make the sale. But if you perform each step properly, it leads you to the next step in a natural, flowing manner — and that leads to sales success.

Step 1: Prospecting for the Next Potential Client or Customer

Prospecting means finding the right potential buyer for what you're selling. When considering your product or service, ask yourself, "Who would benefit most from this?" and then look for ways to make contact with those people. Consider these examples:

✔ **If the end-user is a corporation, you need to make contacts within corporations.** Usually, a purchasing agent is assigned to make buying decisions on behalf of the company, so you need to find a way to get in touch with that person. And if the purchasing agent isn't the decision maker, keep looking until you find the person who is.

✔ **If your end-user is a family with school-age children, you need to go where families are (for example, soccer games, grocery stores, dance classes, the park, and so on).** Alternatively, you can acquire a list from a credible source (turn to Book II, Chapter 2 for more information on that strategy) and start contacting those prospects at home.

The following sections provide a very general overview of how to prospect for clients and customers. Head to Book II for more detailed information.

Don't start prospecting until you have something of value to share with your prospects — something you're confident is worth their while to investigate and, hopefully, purchase. To determine whether you're ready to begin *any* selling cycle, take a few moments to put yourself in the shoes of the other person. Look at the entire situation through the buyer's eyes. If you were the buyer, what would motivate *you* to invest your valuable time reading a letter about this product or taking this salesperson's call? If you can't come up with solid answers, you may not have enough information about your product to even be selling it in the first place. Or you may not know enough about your potential audience to sell to them. If either is the case, spend some additional time studying both areas until you're comfortable being in the buyer's shoes.

Prequalifying your prospect

To make an informed decision about which prospects to approach, you need to find out some information about the people or companies you've chosen as possibilities. Do some research about any prospective client company at the local library or online. This legwork is sort of a prequalification step in prospecting. You'll do even more qualification when you meet a prospective client, but why waste time on an appointment with a company or person who wouldn't have a need for your offering?

Prequalifying your prospects helps you in the same way that market research helps companies determine their target markets. In fact, one of the best places to begin your research in finding the most likely candidates for your product or service is your company's marketing department. The marketing department has done research during the product development stage to determine what people want in the product or service you sell. Study their results, and you'll get a handle on where to begin.

Finding — and taking advantage of — a variety of prospecting resources

If your company engages in advertising to promote your products, you'll likely receive *leads* (names of people who called or otherwise contacted the company for more information about the product). Treat any client-generated contact like gold! What better person to contact than one who has called you for information first?

Other valuable assets are your friends, relatives, and business acquaintances. Tell them what type of product or service you're selling. Listen to the ideas and suggestions they come up with. Who knows? One of them just may know people at one of your prospect companies who would be happy to talk with you. If something good is going on, people are always willing to share their stories with others.

Getting through to prospects

If you ever face challenges getting through to potential clients, you may need to take a somewhat unusual approach to get their attention or bring about a positive response. Think creatively about how you can catch the prospect's attention. Here are some ideas:

- ✔ **Enclose a photograph of your warm, smiling, professional self.** If your goal is to arrange to meet with these people in their homes, they'll need to make some sort of connection with you other than seeing your John Hancock on a cover letter.

- ✔ **Enclose a tasteful comic about the situation your potential clients find themselves in without your product or service.** Your prospect will recognize the relief or benefit the product provides much sooner.

- ✔ **Add a clever quote or anecdote to the bottom of your cover letter.** You can find books that have quotes for nearly any occasion. Check out BrainyQuote (www.brainyquote.com) to find just the right quote online. Taking a few moments to find this kind of attention getter can make your letter stand out from the rest.

- ✔ **Use letters in place of numbers for your telephone number to make it easier to remember.** If your telephone number is 344-6279 and your name is Mary, you can use the alphabet on the telephone pad to ask your prospects to call 344-MARY. (If your name is Agamemnon, this approach won't work for you.) Use PhoneSpell (www.phonespell.org) to find out what your phone number spells.

These ideas may be a bit gimmicky if you're selling corporate jets, but they can work for salespeople marketing everyday products and services to the average consumer. The idea is to open your creative mind to unusual ways of reaching people and capturing their attention.

To ensure that your name gets in front of the prospective client more than once, send a thank-you note the day you make your first contact. Thank-you notes always are read, and if the prospect hasn't had the time to review your letter and/or brochure when she receives your thank-you note, don't you think she'll go looking for your name among the stacks of other mail she's received? You'll have made a positive first impression that will very likely bring you closer to getting an appointment.

Step 2: Making Initial Contact

You've found the right people to be your potential buyers. Now you actually get to meet them. To persuade another person to give you his valuable time, you need to offer something of value in return. For example, to gain entrance to someone's home, you may want to offer a free estimate or gift in exchange for his opinion on the demonstration of your product. With a business-to-business appointment, getting an appointment may be a bit easier because you're often working with a purchasing agent whose job it is to meet with and gather information from people like you. If you offer anything remotely like a product that her company may use, her duty is to investigate what you have to offer.

Because your goal is to make agreeing to an appointment as easy as possible, give your prospect two options with regard to dates and times. Say something like, "I have an opening on Tuesday at 9:30 a.m., or would Wednesday at 3 p.m. be better for you?" This makes the prospect look at her calendar and consider the open blocks of time in her schedule. Whereas, if you just say, "When can we get together?" she's likely to look at how busy she is and hesitate to commit.

When you get a commitment, confirm all the details, such as the following:

✔ **Where the meeting will take place:** Get directions if you haven't been there before. Sure, you may be able to get directions from an online map site or by using a GPS device, but only the people who drive there every day will think to tell you whether the street in front of the prospect's home or building is under construction and you have to take an unusual route.

✔ **Who will be present:** If you sell products to consumers and you know you need to have the agreement of both spouses, for example, confirm that they'll both be present. If you're talking with a young, single person, he may decide to have a parent or other adult present to help him make his decision.

✔ **Any necessary login information, such as access codes and passwords:** If you meet via phone, video, or web conferencing, be sure all attendees have the correct phone number or web address and any necessary login information (such as an access code or password). Also, be sure to confirm the time zone for the meeting.

When you visit with a potential client, be sure to appear at ease so your prospect is comfortable with you. After all, the number-one need of people is the need to be comfortable. If you're uncomfortable, chances are, unless you're a really good actor, your discomfort will show, and it may make your prospect uncomfortable, too.

Overcoming any tension at this point in the selling cycle is very important because if you don't get past the tension, you can end up turning a potential win-win situation into a lose-lose one. You won't make the sale, and the potential client will miss out on having your talents and fantastic product to benefit from. So, what can you do to avoid or break any tension? Consider the following guidelines:

✔ **Consider how you look to your prospect.** This item appears first on this list because it's so important. We all know the old saying "You never get a second chance to make a good first impression." When in doubt about what to wear to an appointment, err on the side of conservatism. Your goal is to be dressed like someone your potential client turns to for advice. So, if you're selling farm equipment, pass on the business suit; jeans or khaki slacks and boots may be perfectly appropriate. If, on the other hand, you're selling to a corporation, you'll want to choose more formal attire.

You want to look your best, but remember to be comfortable. If your new shoes are too tight or they squeak, you'll be conscious of that fact, and you won't be able to put all your concentration into the visit.

In a prospective client's mind, any shabbiness in your appearance translates into shabbiness in work habits or a lesser-quality product or service.

✔ **Think twice before you wear your favorite cologne or perfume.** Subtlety is the motto here. You never know if you'll meet someone who is allergic to your added scents. If the potential client opens the window, goes into a sneezing frenzy, or just plain keels over, you went a bit heavy on the fragrance — and you probably lost the sale.

✔ **Avoid distracting jewelry.** If your jewelry is attractive, that's great. But if it could be considered distracting, like a diamond tiara, that's bad. You don't want to be remembered as that person with the humongous earrings or the gold chains. You want your prospect to remember your competence and professionalism.

✔ **Avoid distracting backgrounds.** If you're video-conferencing, examine the background of your office environment and get rid of any items that may be distracting or cause the participants to question your professionalism. Similarly, if your office is in your home, eliminate disruptions from pets, children, and so on.

✔ **Be prepared to shake hands, make eye contact, and build rapport.** After all, this is a business situation, and building rapport is the getting-to-know-you stage that comes with any new contact. You must immediately begin building trust. People buy from people they like and trust. You want your prospects to feel your trustworthiness as early as possible during the initial contact.

See Book III, Chapter 1 for more details on getting an appointment and putting prospects at ease.

Step 3: Qualifying Prospective Clients or Customers

When you finally sit down with your prospect, you need to find out whether she's qualified to be your client. In selling, *qualifying* your prospects means finding out not just who they are but also what they do, what they have, and what they need in order to confirm that your product or service is a good fit for them and they have the resources to invest in it.

You don't have to take on every client who qualifies for your product or service. If Mr. Big Bucks could become your biggest client, you'll likely be investing a large amount of your time with him. If you can't stand the guy after your first meeting, consider how well you'll really serve his needs and whether someone else may be better suited to the potential stress this client could cause you.

If you've done your homework and looked up information about the prospect, you'll know what questions to ask. You'll eventually have to know a lot of information about the prospect, providing you get the account, so if you're truly convinced that this is a good match for you, you may as well ask questions now. The more specific your questions, the more impressed your potential client will be with your expertise. Asking pertinent questions shows that you're interested in more than just a closed sale and that you're looking into the future as a valued business partner with your client.

Book I

Laying the
Foundation
for Selling
Success

Your prospects will be qualifying you, too. So, be aware of what you're showing them. Most clients are looking for people who are dependable, loyal, trustworthy, intelligent, competent, and even a little fun. Do your prospects see that when they look at you? If you need to communicate a trait that's difficult to see, short of wearing your scout uniform, figure out how you can bring those images to mind in the answers you give to their questions and the information you offer in your discussion of their needs.

The goal of your qualification discussion is to determine how well suited your product or service is to their situation — whether they can afford it and who the real final decision makers are. Ask questions to get them talking about what they have now, how it's not fulfilling their current needs, and how much of a budget they have for making an improvement. These questions are the same whether you're selling to a business or an individual consumer. (Flip to Book III for the full scoop on the qualification process.)

Step 4: Winning Over Prospects with Your Presentation

Your presentation of your product, service, or idea requires the most preparation. In your preparation, practice your answers to common questions with a family member or fellow salesperson. Make a list of the benefits you think are your strongest persuaders in placing your product. Then figure out a way to work those points into responses to the common questions that potential clients ask.

For example, suppose you're selling a brand-new service where busy people can dial up a number to hear all of this week's grocery sale items at their favorite store. Then they can speak into the phone the quantity they'd like of each item (whether on sale or not) and have the items delivered to their homes. Because the service is new, you don't have a track record of success to brag about. So here's where you may start:

> PROSPECT: Well, it sounds like a good idea, but how can I be sure I'll get the items I ask for? I'd hate to be a guinea pig and end up having to do my shopping anyway because it didn't work out.

> SALESPERSON: Because this is a new service, we're paying special attention to the orders that come in. In fact, we have two people who listen to the recording of each call to confirm that your verbal request is what shows up on our shopping list. One of them will even give you a quick call to let you know that your list was received in good order, ask whether you'd like to add anything else, and arrange the best delivery time for you.

The real issue is not that the service is new but that the client doesn't feel he would have the time to shop if the service didn't end up working out. By showing that you have backup systems in place to ensure that the order is handled properly, you've answered the quality-control question that triggered the prospect's "guinea pig" reference.

Your clients buy more than your product — they buy you. To demonstrate personal dependability and trustworthiness, tell the prospective client an anecdote from another client situation or even from an outside activity of yours. For example, if you were an Eagle Scout as a kid, that says a lot about you, doesn't it? Even if you didn't make Eagle Scout but were active in scouting for a number of years, that fact presents a positive image, one that says you stick to things and honor your commitments. Find a way to bring up those kinds of activities.

Amazing things can happen during the rapport-establishing phase of a meeting. Consider the story of the salesperson who, during an initial meeting, noticed a small golf figurine on the prospective client's desk. She asked whether the decision maker liked to play golf — a fairly general and safe question. The guy gave her a brief answer that didn't carry the conversation too far in that direction. Then she remembered a brand-new type of golf club that her husband had talked about. She asked her prospect whether he had ever heard of these new clubs and briefly explained why she was asking: Because her husband was so crazy about them, she wanted to get him a set for his upcoming birthday. It just so happened that the prospect's son was a co-founder of the company that developed and marketed those particular clubs. Suddenly, this prospective client was very interested in hearing the salesperson's husband's thoughts on the clubs, and a deeper level of rapport was established.

Check out Book III, Chapter 3 for additional pointers on making winning presentations.

Step 5: Addressing Prospective Client or Customer Concerns

How do you handle any negative comments or concerns your prospect may raise during or after your presentation? Answer in simple, unemotional terms and have recommendations in mind. For example, if your product is available only in certain colors, and none of them quite fits the décor of your prospect's office, be prepared to point out the least offensive color as being somewhat complementary to his décor. In fact, when you get around to discussing the colors, suggest something like this: "Based on your color scheme, the Sunrise Blue would best complement your décor." That way, you've already seen and addressed the objection before the prospect brought it up.

If you sidestep obstacles during your presentation, there's a good chance they'll come back to haunt you if you do get the sale. Find a way to bring up and elaborate on any concerns about fulfilling the needs of the buyer as early in the presentation as is appropriate. Don't let unfulfilled expectations bring your potential for a long-term relationship with a prospect to a bitter end. Cover all her concerns and make sure that she understands how those concerns will be handled — and that she's comfortable with it.

The most common concern you'll encounter in your entire selling career is the good old standby stall: "I want to think it over." When someone says he wants to think it over, that means he's interested in owning your product. He wouldn't waste his time objecting if he had no interest in it at all, would he? And if he's interested, you need to strike while the iron is hot. Find out exactly what he wants to think over. Sometimes, he needs a little more information or some clarification of the finer points of your presentation.

In the majority of cases, however, you'll find that the client is stalling because of the money. Surprise, surprise! Everyone wants a bargain. Unless your product or service is severely underpriced, most of your potential clients will want to negotiate or will hesitate just to see whether you'll offer to include something else to get them to buy. This and other aspects of addressing client concerns are covered in more detail in Book III, Chapter 4.

Step 6: Closing the Sale

If you've researched your prospect properly, given yourself enough valuable preparation time, and handled all the previous steps in a professional manner, you'll likely close the sale. Closing should follow naturally and smoothly after you address your prospect's concerns. But if your prospect doesn't automatically pick up a pen to approve your paperwork or write a check, don't panic. You don't have to turn into Joe Typical Salesperson and apply pressure to get what you want. Getting your prospect's business can be as simple as saying, "How soon do we start?" At this point, if you're confident about being able to give her what she needs, you should begin taking verbal ownership of your future business relationship with assumptive statements and questions.

You also may want to use analogies, quotes from famous people, or today's news to persuade people to go ahead and do it today. Use similar-situation stories about other clients who got involved with your product or service and are happy they did. Be prepared to show the potential client how she can afford this product or service if that's her area of hesitation. Often, that's just a matter of doing the math to show her how affordable the item is compared to the benefits she'll receive.

When it comes time to close, you've hopefully reduced any sales resistance the person had early on and increased her level of sales acceptance so that it's just a matter of agreeing on the details of startup or delivery dates and/ or financing arrangements. You can find many methods of getting that final agreement in Book IV.

Step 7: Getting Referrals

After you close the sale, take a moment to ask for referrals. Getting referrals can be as simple as asking, "Because you're so happy with this decision today, would you mind if I ask you for the names of other people you know who also may be interested in learning about this product?" If the client has mentioned other family members in the area, ask, "Who in your family would also enjoy the benefits of our fine lawn service?" or, "Which of your neighbors takes the most pride in his yard?"

In a corporate situation, ask about other departments within the company that may need your same service. Then ask about other office locations that the same company has. Finally, ask about associates of the purchasing agent who may work at noncompeting companies.

When you're given the name or contact information of a new potential client, always ask for an introduction to the new party — by phone or in person. If the client seems uncomfortable with doing that, at least get a quick letter of introduction that you may use when you contact the person.

If for some reason you and the prospective client find that this isn't the best time to go forward with the sale, instead of just walking out the door and saying goodbye, make the contact a part of your network of people who can help you find *more* people who may benefit from your product or service. For example, another department in your prospect's company may have people who could benefit from your product or service. Or the prospect may know of other companies needing your product. Don't ever just walk away from an opportunity to network.

Immediately upon leaving the premises, drop a thank-you note in the mail to the person. This note guarantees that your discussion stays fresh in his mind for at least a few days. During that time, the right lead for you may come his way, and if you've left a good impression with your thank-you note, he'll be more likely to give you the referral.

Turn to Book IV, Chapter 8 for additional information on getting referrals.

Chapter 2

Understanding and Connecting with Potential Clients

. . . .

In This Chapter

▶ Gaining the information you need about your potential customers

▶ Responding effectively to your clients' personalities, backgrounds, and cultures

▶ Using language that lets you connect with prospective clients

▶ Listening your way to successful interactions

. . . .

*N*ow's the time to jettison any inclination you may have to follow the old adages "Ignorance is bliss" and "What you don't know can't hurt you." Although these maxims may have made sense in people's personal lives during simpler times, they have *never* been sage advice for people who were trying to sell or persuade others. In fact, the loss of sales and the personal career damage caused by ignorance can be so disastrous that some people give up on selling altogether. Fortunately, this trap is easy enough to avoid. In the world of selling, preparation is key.

In this chapter, we provide strategies that help you learn what you need to know about your clients and customers so that you can serve them better. Of course, learning as much as you can about the product you're selling is just as important; head to the next chapter (Book I, Chapter 3) for more information on that.

Getting to Know Your Clients

You research your prospective clients and their businesses so that, at the moment of truth — when you're giving a presentation or getting ready to close the sale — you aren't tripped up by lack of knowledge. The purpose of all your research is to prepare for that final moment when your prospect has to make a decision to okay your product and start building a long-term relationship with you — or not.

Suppose, for example, that you sell air-treatment systems to homes and businesses. By learning about the unique needs of each of your prospective clients, you can tailor your conversations to highlight that potential customer's needs and demonstrate how your product can meet them.

Imagine that, in the course of your research, you discover the following bits of information about one of your potential business customers:

✔ **The company must manufacture its products according to exacting standards.** With this info, you know that the company must have a high level of concern for cleanliness and precision. And your air-treatment system can help the company get there.

✔ **The company is growing, but it hasn't expanded its work site.** In this case, you can probably count on the fact that the company's employees are working in close proximity to one another. And the closer the proximity, the greater the likelihood that germs can be spread rapidly from one employee to the next. No employer can afford to have its people taking a lot of sick time, so your air-treatment system can help.

✔ **The company's financial reports show solid growth and explosive future plans.** With this information, you know that the company is poised for change and probably open to new ideas. Show the company that your air-treatment system is state of the art and expandable, and you'll be more likely to get its interest.

As this example illustrates, researching a potential client or customer not only gives you myriad opportunities to show how your product or service can meet a multitude of the customer's needs, but it also reinforces your own standing as a competent, knowledgeable professional worth building a relationship with.

The same principle that you use when you sell to businesses applies when you sell to individuals or families: The more you know about their background, the better. People will warm up to you faster when you talk about their hobbies, jobs, and kids than they will if you know nothing other than their addresses and phone numbers. Using the preceding scenario — you sell air-treatment systems — if you know that one of their children has allergies or asthma (information you gleaned through a survey-type phone call or purchased through a list broker — see the section "Getting information about individuals or families," later in this chapter), you can use that knowledge in your arsenal of benefits when you present your product.

To be successful at selling, you must be constantly on the prowl for information. What type of information? Everything and anything about your product, your company, your competition, and, most important, your prospect. And with the Internet just a mouse click away, you really have no excuse for not being well informed. An abundance of information is available, quite literally, at your fingertips. All you need is the commitment to locate and internalize it. The following sections offer advice on where to look to find the information you need.

Gathering information

The most important thing to remember when you're selling is the benefit of being able to walk in someone else's shoes. You can't be of any help to a prospective client with what you're offering him until you truly understand what he needs and where he's coming from.

So, where do you begin in your quest to walk in your prospects' shoes? Not at the shoe store. Instead, you need to do some basic research into your prospective clients and their goals. The following sections tell you how.

Getting info about businesses

A lot of information is available about potential business clients. You just have to know where to look. Start by following these tips:

- ✔ **Gather as much literature and other information as possible on a company before approaching it with your offering.** You want to be as prepared as possible before you make that first approach; that way, you're starting off on the right foot from the very beginning.

- ✔ **Visit the business's website.** Pay particular attention to the business's online product catalog (if one is available) and look for press releases so that you're up to date on the most recent news related to the business. Look for an About Us link on the website; the information you find here often gives valuable insight into the management team and their backgrounds. And who knows? You may find out that you know someone who works at that company or you know someone who knows someone there. You also can find valuable info by clicking the Contact Us link (such as the location of the company headquarters, the number of offices, and so on) or the Media Relations or Public Relations link (such as annual reports, mission statements, and future plans).

- ✔ **Get copies of the company's product brochures and/or catalogs.** Talk with one of the company's customer-service representatives about what the company offers. *Remember:* Being familiar with the products that your prospective client sells enables you to better sell her *your* product.

- ✔ **Go to the library or surf the web and look up past news articles on the business or its industry.** Being familiar with what's been happening in the industry in the past few months lets you work that information into your conversations with the people you'll be contacting. Being able to converse competently about the customer's industry gives the prospect the sense that you're knowledgeable not only about her industry but also about your own products. And that's exactly the impression you want to make.

✔ **Check out the business's financial report, if it's available.** Get the names of the company president and other key people, and find out how to pronounce and spell their names. For the pronunciation, simply call the company and ask the receptionist for that information. Pronouncing names correctly is vital to making a good first impression (see the section "Getting names right," later in this chapter, for more information).

Getting information about individuals or families

If your prospective clients are individuals or families, you need to gather information in a less formal manner. If you're learning about someone by referral, ask as many questions about the potential customer as you can without seeming overzealous or intrusive. You can certainly ask for his contact information, where he lives, how the referrer knows him (through their kids' school, church, another social venue, and so on), and what brought him to mind. It could very well be that the last time they spoke, the subject of getting a new car or having the house painted came up.

You also can use a *list broker*. List brokers often have enough information about a potential client that you can find out what types of pets she has, which cleaning products she purchases, and whether she makes a lot of long-distance phone calls. How do these brokers get this information? Think about it. Have you ever filled out a survey about the products you use in order to receive free grocery coupons? Do you send in for rebates on products? The companies that ask for that information don't just send your coupons or rebates and toss your reply card. They store that valuable purchasing information about you in their databases for future reference.

Finding a good list broker may take a fair amount of legwork. Getting a referral from someone in a noncompeting business would be great. But if you don't know anyone who's used a list broker, start by asking for suggestions from a local quick-print company. These companies, which offer economical printing of postcards and possibly even mailing services, may have clients who've had great success with particular list companies.

Readily available public sources of personal information include social-networking sites like LinkedIn (www.linkedin.com) and Facebook (www.facebook.com). And don't forget to Google the person's name to find other sources (websites, articles, and so on) in which that name appears.

Considering different personality types

To successfully connect with a prospective customer or client, you need to know a little about that person's style. There are ten basic personality types of buyers; we cover them in the following sections. Identifying the personality type of the person you want to sell to enables you to respond appropriately so that you can work successfully with whomever you encounter.

Your delivery style must be flexible enough to relate to all the different personality types. Never settle for having one presentation style. Having only one style severely limits the number of people you can serve.

Note: These personality types are exaggerated for the purpose of example, and they're not limited to any particular gender; nor do people you meet in the real world fit into boxes quite as neatly.

Buyer #1: Believing Bart

Believing Bart is already sold on your company or brand. He knows just what to expect from your products — and he likes their reliability. He's easy to work with, and, after you convince him of your personal competence, he'll remain loyal to you and your product. If he *isn't* convinced that you're competent, Bart won't hesitate to call your company and request another representative.

To this personality type, don't short-sell the product or service just because he's already sold on its quality. You need to exhibit great product knowledge to garner his trust and belief in your ability to meet his needs. Providing dependable service and follow-up helps you close the sale and gain Bart's repeat business (and referrals from him).

Buyer #2: Freebie Freddie

Freebie Freddie is a real wheeler-dealer, the guy who won't settle until he thinks he has the upper hand and you've agreed to give him something extra. Today's market is full of these types of buyers. If you give Freddie any extras in order to consummate the sale, he'll probably brag to and upset others who may not have received the same benefit.

To handle this type, let Freddie know that he's important and special — that he drives a hard bargain and that you admire his business savvy. If you think Freddie's business is worth giving something extra to, consult with your manager or the business owner about the best way to handle it. You may not have to give away your company's back 40 to entice this guy to buy. The enticement can be as simple as providing a little extra TLC (that's right — tender loving care), such as sending him thank-you notes or making a few extra calls after the sale to let him know how important he is.

Buyer #3: Purchasing Polly

Purchasing Polly is a distant, matter-of-fact type who carries a high level of responsibility. (You'll find her in business-to-business sales situations.) As with many other purchasing agents, she may have little personal contact throughout the day besides the contact she gets from the salespeople who parade through her office. She can't risk liking you too much because she may have to replace you with the competition at any time.

When you're dealing with Purchasing Polly, give a no-fluff presentation. Don't try to become too familiar. Stick to the facts and figures. She'll be grading you every step of the way. By being low-key, you'll be different from the other all-too-typical salespeople she encounters — and she'll remember you for that. Let her know that you understand how important and challenging her position can be. Send her thank-you notes. Present all figures to Polly in the most professional manner possible. And do everything in writing; she needs the certainty of documentation in case she needs to present it or defend her purchase to upper management.

Buyer #4: Evasive Ed

Evasive Ed is your most challenging buyer. He refuses to return your phone calls, postpones appointments or reschedules at the last minute, likes to shop around and keep you waiting in the meantime, and tests your patience at every turn.

If you've found yourself up against an Evasive Ed, enlist the aid of his secretary or support staff. (If you have an Evasive Ed in a consumer sales situation, enlist the aid of his spouse or another family member who knows him well.) They may be able to tell you how to get and keep his business. If they tell you "that's just the way he is," you'll need to work on creating urgency in your presentations so he'll see the benefit of making a decision quickly and, just as important, what he'll lose if he doesn't make the decision. A good example of this would be a special reduced investment or closeout on a product where you can offer it only for a short period of time or on a first-come, first-served basis.

Buyer #5: Griping Greg

Griping Greg always has something to complain about or something negative to say. The most important thing you can do for the Gregs of the world is listen and be empathetic. (Maybe he can't afford a therapist, and you're the next best thing.) To limit your exposure to Greg's negativity, call him a few minutes before his normal lunch hour or just before the end of the day, so he won't want to talk long. If he calls you at other times and begins to cost you valuable selling time, find polite ways to get off the line.

If you're dealing with a Griping Greg, you have to decide whether the income his business generates for you is worth all the energy he'll steal from you. If his business is not one of your bread-and-butter accounts, you may want to consider finding other clients who don't take so much out of you. *Remember:* No client is worth risking your mental and physical health for.

Stay pleasant and helpful; after all, that's why Greg gives you his business. If Greg gets to be too much to handle, the easiest and least costly thing to do may be to refer him to someone else in your organization. The person receiving this new client may not be as strongly affected by Greg's personality and may be able to get along with him just fine.

Buyer #6: Analytical Anna

Analytical Anna knows exactly what she wants — and she wants it written in blood or at least carved in stone. She nitpicks everything and needs to feel as if she has complete control.

Disorder in any form shatters Anna's day, so don't be a source of disorder for Anna if you want to get and keep her business. When you're dealing with Analytical Anna, be *very* organized. She appreciates — nay, she craves — organization. Handle every detail in writing. Be punctual. Double-check everything — and let her see that you do. When she knows she can depend on you, she'll do just that. Confirm appointments and always reconfirm details of your meetings with her in writing. Fax or e-mail a recap to Anna of every meeting you have with her. Also, contact her ahead of every meeting to let her know what information you need for your next appointment. In other words, treat her as she treats others. We all want to be around people who are just like us.

Buyer #7: Domineering Donna

Donna is a strong-willed ball of fire who most likely has designs on a more powerful position in the company. She often hides her needs because she expects that you've already done your homework and you know her needs. Domineering Donnas also appear in consumer and retail sales (for example, as a spouse who wants to be sure you know she has a major say in the purchase).

In talking to Donna, perhaps the most important thing you can do is to compliment her on her importance and remind her of the value of her abilities to her company. She likely bowls others over with her ambition for power — and most people try to avoid working with people who dominate like this. But you don't have that option. Besides, Donna can become a *positive* force for you if you have challenges with billing or want to sell your product to another department or branch of her company. If Donna believes in you and your product, she'll be your best supporter.

Buyer #8: Controlling Carl

For Controlling Carl, it's his way or the highway. He's a self-proclaimed expert, even though his expertise may be limited to his own company. He's also poor at delegating authority. Carl wants everyone and everything to be reported to him. He also may be rude and interrupt your presentation while he takes calls or gives directions to his subordinates.

When dealing with a Controlling Carl, be extremely polite, prepared, and concise. By all means, don't make any assumptions. Let him know that you value his time. If the interruptions become too distracting, offer to reschedule your meeting off the premises (choose a neutral location) — for, say, a lunch appointment — so that you can have Carl's undivided attention. Or you can simply enlist the aid of Carl's secretary or assistant in keeping interruptions to a minimum during your appointment. Unless Carl has a rule carved in granite that he takes all calls and sees all visitors, you're likely to get the assistance you want just by making a polite request.

You may encounter Carl in a consumer setting as well. He's the guy who asks you a question and then takes a call on his cellphone before you can engage him in conversation. Be agreeable with him and say things like "This will only take a minute" or "Let me take you directly to that product." This strategy lets him know that you're cognizant of how valuable his time is but keeps you in control of the sale.

Buyer #9: Cynical Cindy

Cynical Cindy is the first to say, "But we've *always* done it this way." She fights change, is suspicious, and questions your every move. She's very likely part of the old guard where she works — a long-term employee. In consumer sales, Cynical Cindy may be an unwilling spouse or even a child. She has no interest in whatever the other party wants and will do her best to make your job more difficult.

Welcome Cindy's objections — even compliment her for being smart enough to bring them up. Impress Cindy by dropping the names of people and companies she trusts; in order for Cindy to bring down her wall of doubt, she needs to know who else uses your product or service. For you, though, Cindy's hesitancy can become the best thing about her. Why? Because if *you* have such a difficult time overcoming her objections, you'd better believe that your competition will get discouraged trying to win her over. It'll be hard for your competition to persuade her to change her loyalties when she sees the value of becoming *your* client. And loyalty like that is what you're after.

Buyer #10: Drifting Dan

Drifting Dan is typical of many potential clients. He has a lot on his mind. The purchase you're discussing is just one of many duties or tasks Dan needs to handle. If your presentation isn't designed to keep him both mentally and physically involved, you lose him. It will take you longer to close the sale and complete the agreement.

Be prepared to deliver your presentation in small bites and include several brief summaries of what you've already covered in order to bring his attention back to the matter at hand. For example, when you notice Dan's attention has drifted, simply pause in your presentation as if you've lost your train of thought. Dan will catch the silence and rejoin you mentally to determine what just happened. Say, "Let's see, we just covered how our product will bring you a speedy return on investment. Do you have any questions about that, Dan?" This gives him an opportunity to catch up on what he missed without embarrassing him.

If the problem isn't your presentation, but just that you've chosen a bad time for the selling discussion (unexpected things come up occasionally), reschedule the meeting for a better time.

Responding to client fears

The toughest part of any selling job is helping other people admit to and overcome their fears so you can earn the opportunity to do business with them. Fear builds the walls of resistance that salespeople so often run into. You need to know how to climb over or break through those walls if you're going to travel the road to sales success.

The following sections identify eight common fears that you need to help your prospects overcome. When you recognize these fears as barriers to your ability to serve your prospects with excellent service, you're ready to discover how to dismantle those walls, one brick at a time, thus gaining your prospect's confidence and trust.

Your goal is to get your prospects to like you, trust you, and want to listen to you. They do that when you serve them with warmth and empathy.

Fear of salespeople

At first, all prospects are afraid of you. Why? You're a salesperson, and you want something from them — a commitment, their time, or their money. Plus, what you want usually involves some kind of a change on the prospect's part, and most people are afraid of change, at least to some degree.

As a salesperson, when you meet with someone who, like most people, tries very hard to hang on to his hard-earned cash (or at least not to part with it too easily), you can safely assume a certain amount of fear is involved. Most people separate themselves from their money only for products and services they believe they need. Your job is to help them recognize the need and highlight your product's ability to serve that need to such a degree that their fear of buying becomes a fear of what happens if they *don't* allow you to help them.

Most people, when you first encounter them, show their fear in their body language. They may cross their arms, lean away from you, or, in retail settings, take a small step backward when you approach them on the sales floor. To help overcome this instinctive retreat, warmly invite them to stand or sit beside you while you show them all the good stuff your product does or has. This tactic results in the two of you looking at the product *together.* Then you can encourage them to put their hands on the product, push buttons, turn dials, make things light up, heat up, or move. When they get involved with the product, their fear of you lessens. After all, you're the one who introduced them to the product, and look what great fun they're having now!

Fear of failure

Your clients may have a fear of failure. Why? Because everyone has made mistakes and experienced regret. Whether that failure was in choosing the wrong hair color or purchasing a vehicle that wasn't right for them, this fear is often associated with a salesperson: the hairstylist who told them that they'd look great with green hair or the car salesman who convinced them that their five kids didn't have to ride with them all the time when he sold them a snazzy convertible with only two seats.

Having a bad past experience generates fear in the hearts of some potential customers. If they've used a product or service like yours before, find out what kind of experience they had with it. If they hesitate to tell you, assume that the past experience was bad and that you have to overcome a lot more fear than you would if they had never used a product or service like yours before.

Try offering the product or service on a sample or trial basis. Give the prospect the names of your satisfied customers who will give unbiased testimony as to the value of your offering. (Check with those customers first to make sure they don't mind if you have prospects contact them.)

No one wants to handle a transaction in which the customer may be dissatisfied with the result. The grief you get from a dissatisfied customer isn't worth the fee you'll earn on the sale. You must go into every presentation with a sharp interest in the who, what, when, where, and why of your client's needs. When you've satisfied yourself that owning your product or service is in your client's best interest, it's your obligation as the expert to convince her that this decision is truly good for her. Take the time to talk your prospect through every aspect of her decision, giving her the time she needs to make a choice she'll be comfortable with.

Fear of owing money

Prospects are tremendously afraid of owing too much money — to you, to your company, to a finance company. Your fee for service is almost always a point of contention with prospective customers, and not just because they're being stubborn; they're legitimately afraid of paying too much money.

Although most people won't attempt to negotiate with a company about its fees, they will often try to negotiate with you because they don't see you as an institution. You're not cold, forbidding concrete walls and walkways. Instead, you're a warm, flesh-and-blood fellow human. Depending on your clients' negotiation skills, they may put off making a decision, forcing you to draw them out; tell you point-blank that they're concerned about the cost, or voice their concerns in a roundabout way. (Book III, Chapter 4 has all sorts of advice to help you overcome client concerns, and all of Book IV is devoted to closing even the most difficult sales.)

If you run into a client who truly is concerned only with getting the lowest investment, and you can't provide it, you may have to bow out of the picture. Do so gracefully and stay in touch. Chances are, he'll get what he pays for and eventually see the wisdom in investing more for the quality product or service that you can provide.

Fear of being lied to

One common buyer fear is the fear of being lied to. As a general rule, clients who are afraid of being lied to doubt everything you're saying about how much they'll benefit from your product, service, or idea.

When you face a client with this fear, a strong past track record comes into play. Having a long list of happy clients can help you calm this fear. If you're new and you don't yet have an established track record, tell your prospect you made a point of choosing your company because it has a great track record. If you're doing something entirely new with a new company, new product or service, or new concept, you have to build on the personal integrity and credentials of those involved in the project, such as a technical advisor who could review technical details of the manufacture or installation of a product, the actual installer, and the after-market customer-service folks.

There is *never* any reason to lie to a customer. If you're honest with your customers and always share the truth with them, even if it's bad news, they'll respect you and give you the benefit of the doubt. Honesty and integrity in every selling situation will make you a winner each and every time.

Fear of embarrassment

Many people fear being embarrassed with anyone who could possibly know about the decision if it's a bad one. Bad decisions make you feel like a child again — insecure and powerless. Because many potential clients have this fear of being embarrassed by a bad decision, they put off making any decision at all. If you're selling to more than one decision maker (such as a married couple or business partners), odds are that neither person wants to risk being embarrassed in front of the other. They've likely disagreed about something in the past, and they don't want to have that uncomfortable situation arise again.

Knowing that fear of embarrassment can block your sale, your primary goal when working with clients who are afraid of being embarrassed should be to help them feel secure with you. Let them know that they're not relinquishing total power to you; you're merely acting on their behalf, providing a product or service for which they've expressed a need.

Fear of the unknown

Fear of the unknown is a common fear in buyers. A lack of understanding of your product or service or its value to the prospect's company or life is a reasonable cause for delaying any transaction. Always spend a little extra time on what your product actually does and the benefits it brings when you're working with a customer who is unaware of your offering — and afraid of the unknown.

National name recognition can dispel some of the fear of the unknown, but if you work for a local company, you need to join forces with the rest of your company's sales staff to earn a great local reputation as a competent business with great products. Over the years, a great reputation saves you a bundle of time in the selling business.

Fear generated by others

A prospect's fear also may come from third-party information. Someone he admires or respects may have told him something negative about your company, about your type of product, or even about another representative of your company.

In this case, the third party stands between you and your prospect until you can convince or persuade him that you can help him more than that third party can because *you* are the expert on your product or service. You have to work hard to earn the prospect's trust. Enlist the aid of some of your past happy clients as references, if necessary.

Interacting Successfully with Others

When you're conducting business, the general rules your parents gave you — mind your manners, treat people with respect, be honest, think before you speak, pay attention when others are talking, and so on — go a long way toward making your business meetings successful. The following sections provide a few business-specific pointers that you can follow, regardless of where your prospective customers are: down the street, across the country, or around the globe.

Cultural etiquette 101

If you're planning to do business with people from countries different from your own, you need to invest as much time in understanding their culture as you do in understanding their needs in terms of your products and services. Here are a few general pointers from Sherri Ferris, president and CEO of Protocol Professionals, Inc. (www.protocol professionals.com), that can help when you're working with clients outside the United States:

✔ **Be patient when building trust and establishing relationships.** People from countries other than the United States generally need more time to build trust. Observing a greater degree of formality when becoming acquainted is important.

✔ **Speak more slowly than you normally do, but don't raise your voice because you think the other person can't understand you.** Volume doesn't usually increase comprehension.

✔ **Avoid slang, buzzwords, idioms, jargon, and lingo.** These all can be easily misunderstood by those who may not speak your language as well as native speakers do.

✔ **If you're using an interpreter, make sure the interpreter meets ahead of time with the people for whom he is interpreting.** This enables the interpreter to learn the language patterns, special terminology, and numbers used by the people he's translating for, such as product identifiers or other codes specific to a company or industry. All these details can change the whole dimension of what's being said.

✔ **Pay attention to nonverbal interaction cues.** In Asian cultures, the word *yes* or an affirmative nod often means "Yes, I hear you," not "Yes, I agree."

To find out about another culture, some wonderful resources are available to steer you in the right direction and tell you everything you need to know. Spend some time browsing through your local library or bookstore to see what's out there. Or check out the following books, all of which are very helpful:

✔ *Cross-Cultural Selling For Dummies,* by Michael Soon Lee and Ralph R. Roberts (Wiley)

✔ *Multicultural Manners: Essential Rules of Etiquette for the 21st Century,* by Norine Dresser (Wiley)

✔ *International Business Etiquette Europe: What You Need to Know to Conduct Business Abroad with Charm and Savvy,* by Ann Marie Sabath (Career Press)

✔ *Kiss, Bow, or Shake Hands: How to Do Business in Sixty Countries,* by Terri Morrison, Wayne A. Conaway, and George A. Borden, PhD (Bob Adams, Inc.)

Some very informative websites also are great sources for tips, articles, newsletters, magazines, and even personal consultants who specialize in cultural etiquette. Here are just a few:

✔ **BusinessCulture.com** (www.businessculture.com) offers access to worldwide business reports on over 100 countries, pre-departure reports, and executive business reports. It provides a list of countries for which it does research (over 100 at last count, ranging from Algeria to Yemen), along with some expert advice about cross-cultural issues.

✔ **eDiplomat** (www.ediplomat.com) offers an overview of cultural etiquette by country. Entries include overviews of the people; how to meet and greet; body-language cues; corporate culture; and tips for dining, dress, and the proper presentation of gifts.

✔ **Protocol Advisors** (www.protocoladvisors.com) "provides customized training in etiquette and international protocol to Fortune 500 companies." This includes helping companies in cutting-edge fields to familiarize their executives, sales staff, and those who may be transferring to another country with what to expect.

✔ **Protocol Professionals, Inc.** (www.protocolprofessionals.com) is "an international relations consulting firm specializing in protocol and etiquette training." This organization has worked with very high-profile groups, including the Diplomatic Corps and U.S. ambassadors. If your involvement in another country is going to be with higher-ups, this site is a great resource.

If you're planning to sell to clients from cultures other than your own, check out any of these resources before you make your initial contact.

Getting names right

A person's name is the most important thing to him. When a client hears you use his name correctly, he knows that you put forth the effort to get it right — and that goes a long way toward earning his respect and trust. If you forget a client's name — or mispronounce it — you have to work that much harder to remedy the situation and earn the client's respect in the future (if he's even willing to give you a second chance).

When introduced to Mr. Robert Jones, call him Mr. Jones unless and until he tells you otherwise. When meeting a couple you know to be married, use Mr. and Mrs. — after all, you can't be expected to know when one spouse didn't take the other's name, and if the couple doesn't bring it up, you've done nothing wrong. However, don't assume that a man and a woman shopping together are married. When you need to know first and last names of clients, ask directly — but not bluntly — for each person's name. Never address anyone by his or her first name unless you've been given permission to do. Similarly, never abbreviate a name unless instructed to do so. Robert is Robert, not Rob, Bob, or any other version. Elizabeth is Elizabeth, not Liz or Beth.

If your potential client has an unusual name, it's fine to ask him or her to pronounce it more than once and to spell it for you. Repeat the name to ensure you have it right. This shows that you care enough to get the client's business right as well — something that works toward building clients' trust in you.

In some cultures, a person's *surname* (or last name) is given before his or her *proper name* (or first name). Take the time to find out which cultures place the surname first, or you may find yourself addressing Mr. Ling as Mr. Bob. For example, Hispanic names often include both the father's and mother's family names. The father's name comes first and should be used as the term of address. So, if you're dealing with someone by the name of Luis Mendoza Trujillo, *Luis* is his first name, *Mendoza* is his father's family name, and *Trujillo* is his mother's family name. You should address him as Señor Mendoza. In Germany, the preference is to be addressed by your job title as opposed to the German equivalent of Mr. or Ms., so addressing someone as Vice President Schmidt is considered appropriate. In Italy, including someone's profession when introducing or referring to him is considered more appropriate (for example, "our engineer, Mr. Puccini").

Arranging meetings

Getting together with people on neutral, or at least acceptable, territory can be the most difficult aspect of selling. Decide which environment would be most conducive to doing business with your prospective client. Although many businesspeople prefer formal, corporate, conference room settings, others prefer more relaxed locations (such as restaurants or clubs) for business discussions.

When you're selling to a client from a culture other than your own, determine the best way to approach him for a meeting. In India, for example, mail delivery can be unreliable, so convey important messages, such as requests for meetings, by fax, phone, or e-mail. Find out whether the country you'll be selling in requires any similar considerations. In the Chinese culture, the location's *feng shui* (an ancient Chinese system of aesthetics regarding favorable positioning in relation to *qi,* or life force) can play an important part in how the business goes. Paying attention to details such as those may be the key to your success with Chinese clients. (For information on the principles of feng shui, look into *Feng Shui For Dummies,* by David Daniel Kennedy [Wiley].)

When you have an appointment, confirm all the details and do your homework on what to wear, what to bring with you, and how to give your presentation. Always be punctual, but don't expect the other person to be. In many cultures, relationships are much more important than time clocks. Value the time your client gives you, but don't count the minutes.

Presenting your business card

Having some business cards made with your contact information is a good idea. Hand these out when you meet the potential client or customer. If you're given business cards in return, take the time to read each person's card before accepting another card. Also, don't set the cards aside quickly; doing so is akin to dismissing the person to move on to someone else. Putting the cards in a card case shows respect for the person who gave it to you; shoving it in your pocket or notebook does not.

If you're doing business in another country, have your business card printed in the language of the recipient. If your card is two-sided, have your language on one side and the other language on the other, and always present your card with the client's language facing up. Then allow the client a moment to read the card before talking or moving on to the next aspect of your presentation.

Be sure to find out what rules apply in the culture or country you'll be visiting; some countries have specific etiquette surrounding the use of business cards. For example, if you're going to Japan, take plenty of business cards and give one to every person you're introduced to. Also, academic degrees are important in Japanese culture, so if you have a master's degree, be sure to list that on your card. Only pull out one card at a time; holding a stack of business cards in your hand is considered bad manners in Japan.

Respecting personal space

All people, regardless of the country they live in, have a need for *personal space* (the distance between you and another person when you're talking to one another). Personal space is just that — personal. But in each culture, the amount of personal space people need is different from what you may be used to. For example, the British want more personal space than people from the United States. (Next time you see a photograph of the Queen of England, pay attention to the people standing next to her. The people most likely won't be standing hip to hip.) Russians and people in the Middle East, on the other hand, need less personal space than most Americans do.

If you want to be sure that people feel comfortable around you (a necessity in the world of selling), don't invade another person's space. If you're working with people from cultures where less personal space is required than you're used to, be sure not to back away when they step into your larger personal space. That can be construed as a sign that you're fearful or hesitant about the other person — not the message you want to convey when you're dealing with potential business clients.

Meeting and greeting new people

In any country, including the United States, people shake hands when meeting and departing, but in some countries embraces also are included. Determine in advance whether your potential client would be more likely to welcome an embrace or a handshake. Inquiring about the person's health is a positive gesture in Middle Eastern culture. Also, when the relationship becomes closer, don't be surprised if you're given a kiss on the cheek — even from one man to another.

Taking time to read up on the small details of how people meet and greet one another in the country you'll be visiting can make a huge difference in how the balance of your contact time goes with each potential client. For example, if you're meeting with a woman in a Middle Eastern country, don't extend your hand to shake hers unless she extends hers first.

Giving gifts

The decision makers at most companies understand the value of appropriate gift giving and usually will establish certain parameters for gift giving by their staff. If your company doesn't have specific guidelines for you to follow, ask what it prefers. Or, better yet, suggest some appropriate parameters based on the potential value of each client to the company. If you're the sales rep who is the main source of contact with the client, you'll want to ensure that the client thinks well of you when she receives the gift. So, don't be afraid to jump in there with some solid suggestions.

The stronger your relationship with your client, the more personalized your gift should be. You wouldn't send a long-standing client whose business represents 20 percent of your sales volume a vinyl datebook. If you've done business with the client for a while, you should know what she likes and select a gift that will provide her the highest level of enjoyment.

If your customer or client is flying, offer to mail the gift to her home or home office, especially if the gift is large or fragile.

Before you give a gift to a client, determine whether the recipient's company has a policy on receiving gifts. Many companies don't allow their employees to accept gifts; if you offer one, your client may be in the uncomfortable position of having to decline or return your gift. If the company doesn't allow the receiving of gifts, ask the person with whom you have the best relationship in the company what you can do. Maybe you can send a box of candy or a basket of fruit for the department to share, but not a pen-and-pencil set for the individual.

Some cultures find the giving and receiving of gifts a personal matter, not a business matter. For example, in France, business gifts aren't given. If you're invited to a French business associate's home, however, you can bring flowers, chocolates, or a bottle of high-quality spirits, such as vodka or scotch, but not wine. (The French are considered by many in the world, including themselves, to be wine experts. The host or hostess would have already chosen the proper wine for the meal.) In addition, gifts that are considered very appropriate at home may be considered highly offensive in another country. A client from India would not appreciate a gift made of leather, for example, because cows are considered sacred in that country, and in Germany, red roses are given only in personal relationships, never in business ones. So, be sure to read up on the country in which you'll be selling so that you can avoid offending your clients with some unfortunate faux pas.

Dressing appropriately

Because your appearance is the first cue others get about how you feel about yourself and your business, take extra care in dressing for business meetings and events. When in doubt, dress conservatively and more formally than you would normally. As a rule, it's generally better to be slightly overdressed than underdressed.

If you're doing business with individuals from other countries, find out what constitutes appropriate business attire in that location. In many countries, such as Malaysia and some Middle Eastern countries, for example, it is considered inappropriate for women to wear slacks or shorts. Dress inappropriately, and your potential business may be over before you even get close enough to shake the client's hand.

Dining out with ease

Many business meetings take place over meals. If you're arranging the meeting, follow this general advice:

✔ **Choose an appropriate venue.** Business dinners don't need to take place in 5-star restaurants, but the environment should be comfortable and conducive to business.

✔ **Take into account any dietary restrictions your client may have.** Make sure you understand your potential client's needs with regard to specific foods or preparation of such foods, and take her to a restaurant where the menu includes selections she can choose from.

✔ **Balance the social and business aspects of the meeting.** As a rule, business meetings are generally more relaxed than meetings that take place in boardrooms, but they're still business. Let your hair down too much or kick back too far, and you can unintentionally undermine the client's perception of you as a competent professional.

If you're meeting with clients outside the United States, be aware of cultural expectations that may differ from your own. Consider these points:

✔ Asians, on average, dedicate more hours to work-related activities than do people from the United States, which means that they include after-hours dinners as a normal part of their workday. So, if you're working with an Asian client, you may be expected to wine and dine with him as part of the meeting. If you're the one being wined and dined in his country, be prepared to reciprocate before you leave.

✔ In some cultures, slurping, burping, and even drinking from another person's glass during dinner are perfectly acceptable; in others, it's absolutely not. When you're visiting another country, you don't necessarily have to join in on behaviors you have trouble with, but you should at least be aware of them so you don't act inappropriately shocked if your guest does so. At the very least, know what's considered rude, and avoid those behaviors during your meals.

✔ Consider customs the client may have, whether cultural or religious, with regard to taking a meal. You may need to allow a few moments for prayer or indulge the client in eating very slowly and consuming many courses.

Choosing Your Words Wisely

When you're getting to know your clients, you need to think about the effective power of language. Every word paints a symbol or picture in your mind, and many of these associations have emotions attached to them. Because you don't know in advance which words about you, your product, and your company will generate positive feelings in your clients, you need to become extra-sensitive to the way you use words if you want to have a successful sales career.

In the following sections, we fill you in on the best selling-related words and phrases to use, ways to incorporate jargon to build customer confidence, and how to fine-tune your vocabulary to create positive mental pictures.

Using the best words and phrases

Many words common to sales and selling situations can generate fearful or negative images in your clients' minds. The experience of hundreds of thousands of salespeople confirms that replacing such words with more positive, pacifying words and phrases is crucial.

Language is a salesperson's *only* tool. The salesperson who uses language well, for the genuine benefit of other people, is a salesperson who sells, sells, sells. The words are the very center of your profession. So, make sure your words stress comfort, convenience, and ownership from your prospects' perspective. After all, satisfying your prospects' needs is what the business of selling is all about, and the words you use are the only way that you, and not your competition, can earn the opportunity to satisfy those needs.

Replacing sign

If you replace nothing else in your selling vocabulary, at the very least, promise yourself to never again ask a customer to *sign* an agreement, form, or paperwork. When people are asked to *sign* something, in most cases, a warning goes off in their heads, and they become hesitant and cautious because almost everyone has had drilled into them from early childhood that they should never *sign* anything without careful consideration. So, they'll want to take time to review what they're signing and peruse the page for the infamous fine print, anytime during which they may even head for the door. Instead of asking your clients to *sign,* ask them to *approve, authorize, endorse,* or *okay* your *paperwork, agreement,* or *form.* Any of those word pictures carries the positive associations that you want to inspire in your clients.

Replacing sell and sold

The first terms to remove from your vocabulary are *sell* and *sold.* These words remind people of high-pressure sales tactics and usually turn them off. They make the transaction sound one-sided, as if the customer really had little say in the matter. So, what can you use in place of these common words? Replace *sell* or *sold* with *helped them acquire* or *got them involved* — phrases that create softer images of a helpful salesperson and a receptive customer becoming involved together in the same process.

Replacing contract

A commonly used word in sales is *contract,* but this word evokes negative images. Contracts bring with them fine print, legalities, and being locked into something. Where do you go to get out of a contract? Court — not a pleasant image for most people. So, stop using the word *contract,* unless your particular line of business requires it. Instead, use *paperwork, agreement,* or *form,* which are a lot less threatening than *contract.* And that's exactly what you're going for.

Replacing cost and price

When most people hear the words *cost* and *price,* they probably see their hard-earned cash leaving their pockets. But when they hear the word *investment,* they envision the positive image of getting a return on their money. For products for which the word *investment* just doesn't fit, use the word *amount,* which has been proven to be less threatening to most consumers than *cost* or *price.*

Replacing down payment and monthly payment

Most people envision *down payments* as large deposits that lock them into many smaller *monthly payments* for, if not an eternity, at least a few years. They see themselves receiving bills and writing checks every month — not a pleasant image for most people. So, replace those phrases with these: *initial investment* and *initial amount* or *monthly investment* and *monthly amount.* In the selling business, those terms are called *money terms,* and anyone who wants to persuade someone to part with money needs to use these terms well.

Replacing buy

What about the word *buy?* When people hear the word *buy,* they see money leaving their pockets again. Use the term *own* instead. *Own* conjures images of what they'll get for their money, where they'll put the product in their home, showing it with pride to friends or relatives, and many other positive thoughts.

Replacing deal

One term overused by salespeople is *deal*. This word brings to mind something people have always wanted but never found. Images of used-car salesmen are only too closely associated with the word *deal*. Top salespeople never give their clients *deals*. They offer *opportunities* or get them involved in *transactions*.

Replacing objection, problem, and pitch

Customers don't raise *objections* about your products or services. Instead, they express *areas of concern*. You never have *problems* with your sales. Every now and then you may, however, face some *challenges* with your transactions. Never *pitch* your product or service to your customer. Instead, *present* or *demonstrate* your product or service — the way any self-respecting professional would.

Replacing commission

As an authority or expert on your product or service, you don't earn *commissions*. You do, however, receive *fees for service*. If a client ever asks you about your *commission* on a sale, stress that your company compensates you for the high level of service you provide to each and every client.

Replacing appointment

Consumers view an *appointment* as interfering with their regular schedule. Instead of equating meeting with you to an appointment with a doctor or dentist, use the softer term *visit*. Better yet, offer to "pop by and visit." This phrasing creates an image of your popping in and popping out; in other words, it conveys the idea that you'll only be there a short time. In the business world, a "pop by" can conjure the image of a brief handshake and exchange of information in the lobby with no sit-down, conference room involvement at all.

Using only the jargon your clients know

You need to strike a balance between speaking the language of your clients and educating them about the *jargon* (words and phrases particular to a given field of work) they'll need to know if they're going to use your product or service. If, for example, you sell medical supplies to doctors, you need to know the jargon medical professionals use and use it yourself liberally. But if you sell medical supplies to the general public, you need to keep your use of technical terms to the bare minimum until you can determine your client's level of knowledge about the product. You don't want to alienate or confound your customers by using acronyms or words they're not familiar with. After all, your goal is to make your customers feel important, and it's tough to feel important when you don't feel very smart.

Many people won't stop to ask you for explanations of unfamiliar terms because they're afraid of showing their lack of knowledge and being embarrassed in the process. Others may get the gist of what you're talking about but struggle to keep up and, in the process, miss the valuable points you're trying to relay to them. If your subject sounds more complicated than your customer can comprehend, you risk squelching his desire to ever own or use your product or service *and* you risk losing the sale.

Developing your selling vocabulary isn't about mastering the words you were tested on in school. It's about taking the time to make a list of powerful but easy-to-understand words and phrases that are specific to your product or service. Then test those words on a friend or relative — someone who is *not* a qualified prospect. If your test person doesn't have a clear understanding of the terms, prepare brief definitions of those terms in *lay language* (language your test person — and anyone else — can understand). The first time you use a term with a new or prospective client, be prepared to provide the definition in lay terms if it's something vital to the transaction or if the term will recur frequently in your discussions.

Pay particular attention to the terms used in your sales training and other company literature. These words — which are so familiar to you, your colleagues, and the others in your industry — often masquerade as "common" terms that will leave your customers scratching their heads.

Listening to Your Clients

The human body has two ears and one mouth. To be good at persuading or selling, you must find out how to use those natural devices in proportion: Listen twice as much as you talk, and you'll succeed in persuading others nearly every time.

Yet, even though most people don't think they talk too much, the sad truth is that most salespeople are guilty of talking more than they need to. To develop your ear to hear these Chatty Cathies and Carls — and avoid becoming one yourself — try these two simple exercises:

✔ **Listen to a salesperson selling others or trying to sell you.** Pay attention to what his words are doing. While you're listening, ask yourself these questions:

- Do his words paint positive or negative mental pictures?

- Do his words say anything that may raise a new objection to his product or service?

- Are all his words necessary?

- Does he ask questions and then carefully listen to the prospect's answers?

- Does he move forward with questions, or does he get off course by talking about features and benefits the customer hasn't expressed a need for?

✔ **Record yourself when you're talking with a customer.** You may be shocked at how much chatter you can cut out. To detect what you need to cut, ask yourself these questions:

- What is the quality of the questions I ask?

- Am I asking information-gathering questions to help myself move forward with my sale, or am I just asking questions to fill a sound void? (Questions don't mean much unless the answers are helping you get the information you need to serve your customer better and keep the sale moving forward.)

When you do most of the talking,

✔ You aren't finding out about your customer or your customer's needs, buying clues, or concerns.

✔ You're shifting your prospect's attention from your offering and taking center stage away from her.

✔ You may be raising concerns the prospect may not have had in the first place, and you're giving your prospect more opportunity to disagree with you, to distrust one of your statements, or both.

✔ You aren't able to think ahead or guide the conversation.

As you discover more about selling well, the words *putting your foot in your mouth* will gain new meaning for you. After all, you can't put your foot in your mouth if it's closed. So, close it, and listen more.

Chapter 3

Knowing Your Product

One of the best advantages of a career in selling is that good selling skills are portable; that is, after you master basic selling skills, you have the education you need to sell any product that interests you (after you master that product's information). Product knowledge is one of the three fundamental elements you need to sell successfully (the other two are selling tactics and strategies, covered in Books III and IV); your own enthusiasm, attitude, and goals are also key.

This chapter offers a fairly broad overview of the kinds of things you can do to develop your product knowledge and be prepared for questions that come your way when you're with potential clients. Investing time in product research upfront pays off when you're ready to put your selling strategies to work. For detailed information on learning about the product you're selling — a key component of preparing yourself to prospect for new clients and customers — head to Book II, Chapter 2.

You can't know too much about your product or service. Customers love to feel that you have the inside track on the latest and greatest products and services; they want to believe that you're the most competent person in your industry. Face it: No one wants to be represented by a dud!

What You Need to Know about Your Product

What must you absolutely, positively, truly *know* about your product in order to sell it? Always begin with the obvious:

✔ **What the product is called and how it's perceived:** Know the specific product name and model, as well as the product/part number so that, if your customers refer to it by a number, you'll know exactly what they're talking about.

You also need to have a clear understanding of how your product is perceived in the marketplace. That includes what it does, because you're bound to run into potential clients who will refer to it as "that type of vacuum that picks the lint off of fleas — at least I think that's what it said in the ad I saw." Potential clients may not recall the brand or name of your product, but they'll always remember what grabbed their attention in your advertising.

In most cases, your marketing folks will use the benefits of the product to capture interest and generate leads. So, you have to know both the features and how those features are perceived as benefits by the end-users — not just what it does, but what it does for the user.

✔ **Whether the product is the latest model or release:** Many potential clients will want the latest version of your product. Others will hope to find a discount on a discontinued model. Either way, you need to be prepared.

✔ **How the product improves on a previous model or version:** Be able to list the new features or options and the benefits — what those features or options can do for your customers. This information is especially beneficial when you talk with existing clients who may be interested in upgrading or taking advantage of a technical advancement.

✔ **How fast, powerful, or accurate the product is:** If your potential client tells you she's comparison-shopping, be able to offer a comparison of your product to its competition so that you can tell your customer how your product stacks up. It's better if the comparison was done by an independent study group. If it's just your word against that of the competition, you may not have much of a leg to stand on with doubters. If no independent study is available, at least have satisfied clients who are already using your product give you a testimonial that it's better than what they had before.

If you must create a comparison yourself, base it on something the competition provides so you can show your clients that you're very exacting in the information you provide — that your comparison is truly apples to apples.

✔ **How to operate the product during demonstrations:** Nothing is worse than trying to demonstrate a product to a prospective customer only to find out that you're not sure how to make it do what she's asked. Be able to operate the product as well as you operate the car you drive every day — by reflex.

✔ **What colors the product comes in:** Being able to tell your customers right away whether you have a specific color available will come in handy when they want to know whether it meets their needs. Companies often discontinue colors and release new ones to meet and match current fashion and decorating trends.

✔ **What your current inventory is for setting delivery dates:** Your client may have seen a review of your product in a magazine, even though it isn't due out for two more months. You need to know what he's talking about, be prepared to inform him of delivery delays or future release dates, and see whether he needs the benefits of the product sooner. If the product is currently in production but on back order, brag about its popularity and know the projected delivery dates. In this situation, focus on the new model being worth the wait.

✔ **How much of an investment the product would be:** Be sure to phrase the price of the product in terms of an *investment* as opposed to a *cost* (refer to Book I, Chapter 2 for vocabulary that gets you closer to your sales goal). Also, be prepared to reduce that amount to a monthly amount if your product is something that requires financing. Many purchasing agents consider how much something will add to monthly overhead and how soon they can recover their investment. Other clients want to know how quickly they'll receive a return on their investment. Be prepared to do that math with them as well, which can be as simple as calculating the cost of your product and dividing it by the annual, monthly, or weekly savings you project after your product is doing its job. The answer you get tells the client when you project she'll have earned her money back on the initial investment.

✔ **What terms and financing are available:** If your company offers financing, consider it another product and know how it works as well as you know the product itself. Don't risk losing a sale when you've gotten all the way through to the financing stage.

✔ **Whether distributors may offer the product for less (if you work for a manufacturer):** If distributors sell the product, know who these distributors are and what price they're selling the product for. Don't be caught shortsighted by a client who has done more research than you have.

Even companies with the most basic product training should cover these topics with new salespeople before sending them out to talk with customers. Unfortunately, some companies provide only the bare minimum of information, and you have to develop the rest on your own.

With all this preparation, you should be pretty well off. However, be prepared to encounter a potential client who will ask an odd question — something out of the ordinary that you can't discern the answer to with your current knowledge. Never make up an answer! Tell the person that you'd be happy to find out the answer to that question, and then do it — quickly — before she considers the competition's product over yours. In cases such as this, you may have to do a lot of additional information gathering in the course of researching the answers to your customers' questions. And that's okay because you build your product knowledge as needed.

If a potential client ever comes to you with valid information about your product or service that is a surprise to you, your credibility with that client will be on shaky ground. After all, you're supposed to be the expert clients come to for information or advice. If they know more than you do, why do they need *you?* Make a commitment to stay on top of your game!

How to Get the Product Information You Need

How can you be sure you're armed with the product knowledge you need before you head out to make a sale? Take advantage of as many different resources as you can. If your company offers training sessions on the product, attend. If you're given brochures and pamphlets, know them backward and forward. Talk with your existing customers about the product so that you know what questions or comments they have, discuss the product with your fellow salespeople to get suggestions, and tour the facility where your product is made (if possible). Also, be sure to know your competition's product so you can tell your customers how your product measures up. Each of these resources is covered in the following sections.

Product information doesn't just come from the technical booklet that comes with the product. It's everywhere the product has been. In seeking out as much information as possible, you'll earn and keep your expert status, and more people will want to take your advice.

Attending training sessions and reading product literature

Your company or the manufacturer of the products you represent may hold regularly scheduled training sessions about the product. If it does, then by all means go to these training sessions. They're your best opportunity for getting the scoop about your product from reliable sources. And *always* attend these sessions with a list of questions and a way of capturing the answers, whether in a notebook, on a voice recorder, or on a computer. If the speaker doesn't answer your questions during the presentation, find a way to ask your questions before this knowledgeable person gets away.

Average salespeople resist training after their initial orientation period with a new product; that's why they remain average. Keeping your eyes and ears open to new and better information or ways of selling your product is critical to achieving success in your selling career.

In between training sessions, watch for e-mail or online updates of product information from the company as well. Visit your own company's website every morning and watch for a product revision date, if those are posted. If something has changed in the past 24 hours, you need to read the updated information and be familiar with it as soon as possible. After all, your best new prospect may have read that information already, and you want to be able to show that your information is current.

If you get industry information from online news sites like CNN (www.cnn. com) or MSNBC (www.msnbc.com), take advantage of the customizing features on those sites. Many news sites let you tell them what industry or company you need the latest news for. When you visit your customized home page on the site, links to that information show up automatically.

Your company will probably inundate you with brochures and technical information on your product or service, even in the absence of specific product-training sessions. Set aside a specific amount of time in your schedule to sit and read such literature, but don't read through it the way a customer would. Study it. Read it every day for at least three weeks. By the end of that time, you'll have the information memorized and know exactly what your customers are referring to when they ask questions. Nothing is worse than having to look to a higher source when your customer asks a question that you should know the answer to.

Getting your hands on product samples

If you sell a tangible product, get your hands on a product sample right away. Be like a kid with a new toy: Play with it, experiment, read through suggested demonstrations, and try it out as if *you* were the customer. Make notes on things you find hard to understand. Chances are, at least one of your prospects will have the same questions or concerns that you come up with. Resolve those concerns now, and you'll be well prepared for your demonstrations.

Send the questions you come up with to your customer-support department online. See how long it takes to receive an answer and how detailed the answer is. What you receive is what a customer would likely receive when using that service after a sale. If the return time is unacceptable for the type of question you asked, see whether you can do anything within the company to help speed things up. Or if you know the response time is slow, you may recommend, during your presentation, that your clients contact you directly with questions. This strategy shows that you provide added services *and* that you're knowledgeable about the product.

Make sure that responding to customer-support questions and concerns doesn't take up so much of your time that it interferes with your selling time. After all, you're paid primarily to find and serve new customers for your business, in addition to keeping those you've already gained.

Talking with current clients

Get as much feedback as you can from the people who already use and benefit from what you sell. Ask what their experiences have been with your product. If feasible, gather this information in person; however, if you have a large client base, consider using a short survey. Your surveys can be printed pieces mailed to your clients or, for even better response, e-mail or online surveys they can quickly complete with a few clicks. If you prefer the personal touch and feel the time is valuable, handle those surveys in a personal phone call. By talking to people personally, you may be able to discover something new that will help you serve all your clients better.

Your current customers are an extremely valuable resource — *if* you keep in contact with them. We cover several strategies for keeping in touch in Book IV, Chapter 8.

Picking your colleagues' brains

Veteran and top salespeople have all kinds of information about products that they may never document. Talk with them as much as you can in order to put their knowledge to work for you.

Keep your meetings with other salespeople focused on product knowledge and information that can help you make sales; otherwise, your time won't be well spent. When two or more salespeople get together, getting off the subject at hand and descending into old war stories or other unrelated matters is all too easy. If you want product knowledge, focus the conversation there. Now is not the time for sharing gossip or reliving past glories.

Ask your sales manager for permission to do a ride-along with the top salesperson in your territory — this request is almost always approved because it shows your manager that you're sincere in wanting to become the best salesperson you can be. Watch how this salesperson handles everything: herself, the client, brochures, proposals, visual aids, and the product itself. Listen to the words she uses in describing the product and pay attention to the images her words elicit. Notice the mood she sets. After all, the *how* of handling products and information is as important as the *what* and *why*.

Have the veterans provide you with their research web addresses. If these pros are as good as you think, they'll have a tremendous database of sites they rely on to get their latest and best information about your product — and that of the competition.

Being a student of selling

When you're in a learning mode, you need to set the stage for learning. That may mean gathering pen and paper, brochures, and a demo piece of equipment and locking yourself in the company conference room to study. It may mean setting appointments and interviewing with a training director, company owner, or top salesperson. It may involve watching hours of product training videos or attending classes on the products. It may involve interviewing current customers.

It doesn't matter what the type of education is, you must begin every session with a clear respect for what's to come. Treat the sessions

like gold. Show up on time, if not early. Have plenty of paper for note taking. Bring a couple pens in different colors to highlight the most important information. And be courteous to those who are sharing their knowledge with you. What they're imparting will make you money — treat them and their messages with the utmost respect. The better you treat the people who are helping you, the more they'll relax. You'll be making them like you and trust you, which will lead them to offer you even more valuable information. Hmm, sounds a lot like selling, doesn't it?

Going directly to the source

If you sell a tangible product, try to create an opportunity to tour the facility where your product is designed and built. Better yet, try to visit with the originator of the idea. Find out what she was thinking when it all came together. Getting an opportunity to speak with those who work closely in the production of your product is always helpful in uncovering benefits such as quality issues as well.

This tactic may include attending a company meeting where the founder is present. If an opportunity for a question-and-answer period occurs, be prepared to ask questions and take great notes. If the idea for your product came from someone else on the company team, seek them out. At the very least, make a connection with someone in the headquarters of the company who can provide you with background information.

With most products, the original idea will have come from a need that wasn't being met. Some were stumbled upon while seeking the answer for a completely different need. Knowing your product's "story" comes in handy when selling to clients. If the story is particularly interesting (and not too long), consider weaving it into your presentations.

Keeping an eye on the competition

Most companies designate a person or department to gather information on the competition and to prepare analyses of that information for the sales staff. If your company has this situation under control, sing its praises and encourage the company to keep up the good work, because such research can be a voraciously time-consuming feat.

If your company *doesn't* provide this service, you need to take it on yourself. At least once a week, search online for information about the competition. Use keywords like your competitor's company name, product name, and so on. You're looking for the competition's latest news releases, as well as its products — good things to know, especially if the competition is in trouble with the government or involved in a lawsuit based on one of its products, for example.

Bookmark the websites you want to check regularly. Also, set up Google Alerts for the keywords you're searching on, to save yourself some time. Just go to www.google.com/alerts, enter a keyword, and set a few options. You can create up to 1,000 alerts and have them delivered once a week, once a day, or as it happens.

Don't rely solely on yourself to gather this information. If you're in business on your own, consider enlisting a family member to find juicy tidbits of information on competitors' products for you.

If you call on customers who've had past experiences with your competitors, ask whether they would mind sharing their thoughts on the product with you. If they answer in the affirmative, asking the following questions in a sincere, caring manner sends the message that you want to do better, be better, and help them have a better experience than ever before:

✔ What did they like about the product? Which particular features and benefits did they find especially beneficial?

✔ How were their contacts with customer service handled?

✔ What would they like to see improved upon?

When they tell their tales, take good notes and keep them handy for future reference. If a new customer has just switched from the competition to your product, find out exactly what the deciding factor was and work it into any presentations you make in the future where circumstances are similar.

Book II
Prospecting for Gold

The 5th Wave   By Rich Tennant

"I sell subscriptions to a heavy metal magazine, and believe me – it's not easy getting sales prospects in a mosh pit."

In this book . . .

1f you ask 100 sales professionals what their favorite aspect of selling is, chances are, 95 percent will not mention prospecting. Prospecting may never be your favorite part of selling, but with the information in this book, it will be a task you approach with confidence.

Chapter 1

An Introduction to Prospecting

In This Chapter

▶ Understanding prospecting

▶ Looking at a variety of ways to make contact

▶ Setting and meeting prospecting goals

*1*f you've been in the selling profession any length of time, you remember how challenging your first few weeks were. You found out more about your product or service than you ever dreamed possible. You may have had no idea how to sell, but you knew if you could talk with enough people who were interested in the product, sooner or later you'd bring back one of those papers with an order on it or move one of those products from your car, briefcase, or store into someone else's hand. And someone would pay you for doing so.

But finding just the right people isn't always easy. That's where the art of prospecting comes in. This chapter gives you a brief overview of sales prospecting; the remaining chapters in Book II go into the details that will make your prospecting efforts successful.

Prospecting Defined

When you *prospect,* you find the right buyer for your product or service. Prospecting involves two components:

✔ **Finding the people to sell:** That's what Book II of this All-in-One is all about.

✔ **Selling the people you find on their need for your product or service:** Book III of this All-in-One is devoted to this topic.

Sounds simple enough, doesn't it? But as simple as the concept is, prospecting isn't easy, nor is it something that you can take lightly. You have to get organized, plan, stay motivated, and, most of all, act.

There are almost as many different ways to prospect as there are types of prospects. But the methods break down into two general categories: cold calling and what you can think of as "warm prospecting." We cover both in the following sections.

Research your prospects as much as you can to prequalify them. Even if you're canvassing a neighborhood making cold calls, you still can take time to look at the city directory in the reference section of your library. A wealth of information is available. For example, you can find out whether the prospect rents or owns a home, his marital status, his place of employment, and often his job title. Then you can use all this information not only in evaluating the prospect but also in your sales presentation. Pay attention to ads and articles in the local newspaper that may tell you of changes in people's lives — changes such as getting a promotion or moving to another location mean opportunities. For more information on qualifying your prospects, head to Book III, Chapter 2.

Cold calling your way to prospecting success

Cold calling is contacting people you don't already know or have had some connection with. Depending upon the product you represent, cold calling could involve getting out the phone book or going to an online directory and, starting with Aaron Aanderson, calling people at their homes. Others count on the Yellow Pages — either print or online — for business leads. Still others put on their walking shoes and start knocking on homeowners' doors or entering lobbies at businesses to seek prospects. The key is to work as effectively and efficiently as possible to find the ideal candidates for your product. (**Note:** Be knowledgeable of and compliant with the National Do Not Call Registry. The later section "Using the telephone to prospect for clients" has the details.)

Cold calling can be an overwhelming endeavor, one that can easily dishearten you if it isn't done properly. That's why so many salespeople avoid it like the plague. It's a good part of the reason that the mere mention of the term *prospecting* elicits groans from salespeople the world over. But if you approach cold calling with a winning strategy, you can overcome any trepidation you may feel and make the contacts necessary to gain valuable clients. Here are some general tips:

✔ If the prospective client is unavailable when you initially make contact, try to gain information that will bring you one step closer to meeting him the next time around.

✔ Be polite. Whether you're leaving a voicemail message for the prospect or talking to her assistant, remember to acknowledge that you appreciate her for giving you a bit of her time.

✔ Briefly mention the benefit that your service or product offers.

Take a look at the following conversation, which demonstrates these three principles in action:

> YOU: Good morning. My name is Peter Smith. I'm in business in the community. Who in your company is responsible for the training of the fine sales staff you have there?
>
> RECEPTIONIST: That would be Jake Carlton.
>
> YOU: Is Mr. Carlton in?
>
> RECEPTIONIST: Yes, he is, but he's in a meeting.
>
> YOU: By the way, what is your name?
>
> RECEPTIONIST: Anne.
>
> YOU: Thank you for your help, Anne. May I ask when the best time is to reach Mr. Carlton?
>
> RECEPTIONIST: Probably first thing in the morning. He spends a lot of his day in meetings and training sessions.
>
> YOU: That's perfectly understandable and probably why he does such a great job. I'd like to leave my card, Anne. Would you please give it to Mr. Carlton with a message that I'll contact him early in the day tomorrow? I need only two minutes of his time. I have some information to share with him that could greatly enhance the training he is currently providing, with the end result being increased sales and a great amount of time saved in his current efforts. Again, I thank you for your assistance, Anne. You're doing a great job here!

**Book II:
Prospecting
for Gold**

Using cold calling, as in this scenario, you didn't get to meet Mr. Carlton because your timing wasn't convenient for him. You did, however, gain a bit of knowledge about him that will bring you one step closer to meeting him tomorrow — even if the meeting takes place over the telephone. You can bet that, when you call in and address Anne by name in the morning, she'll remember your courtesy toward her and try to continue to help you by getting you through to Mr. Carlton.

Cold calling may be the hard way of reaching your prospects, but if you currently have no other means of getting yourself in front of them, go for it!

Warming up to warm prospecting

Warm prospecting involves contacting people who you have good reason to believe will become clients and with whom you have some sort of connection. Your connection could be a referral from someone else, or you could already have met your warm prospect through a social or business situation. In these situations, do the following when you make contact:

> ✔ **If you met the contact through a social or business situation,** remind her of your initial contact. If this contact is the result of the referral, explain how you got her name.

> ✔ **If you're meeting the prospect through a referral,** briefly explain why you think she may be interested in your product or service, possibly by alluding to how useful the person who referred you to her finds the same product.

Here's an example of a contact with a warm prospect:

YOU: Hi, John. I'm Mary Doe with Worldwide Widgets. Sam Smith at Acme and I have been working on some projects involving our products, and he said that you're a lot like him: always on the lookout for ways to do things better.

PROSPECT: Yeah, Sam and I go way back. We've been known to browse a few trade shows together.

YOU: Well, we have a new widget that Sam is putting to use on their Alpha project, and he thought it would interest you. Is there some time next week I can stop by and show it to you?

PROSPECT: Hmm. If Sam's using it, it's probably something I'd want to know about. Sure, let's get together.

Warm prospecting brings about far better and faster results than cold calling does.

Getting the prospecting mindset

Although prospecting is a task that average salespeople who have a high fear of rejection would just rather not think about, top sales pros know that prospecting is the key that opens the door to success and plan doing it regularly. If you don't acquire the prospecting mindset — the one that accepts that *everyone* is a prospect — you're slamming those doors in your own face, bruising your nose, chipping a tooth, and developing a great big bump the size of an apple on your forehead, none of which is conducive to closing a sale. You must begin to look at the world differently, to develop a new attitude.

Take a look at a downtown street during the noon hour. All those people are your prospects. They need what you can provide. Get excited about that! Look at all those folks! Virtually every one of them has car keys in a pocket or a purse. They write with fountain pens, wear clothes, need insurance, want a pool, are saving for a trip, and are just waiting for your product or service. If, for some reason, some people don't need what you have at the moment, they will in the future, and they probably know someone else in need, too! Every time you see a crowd, a group of people, a club, a family, or even a single person, know in your heart that they really are your prospects. Make yourself look at life this way every chance you get. Make it a habit, a good one.

See the people: STP

The key to success with prospecting is to remember the acronym *STP*. In this case, it doesn't refer to oil additives. Instead, it stands for *see the people*. Dogs and cats aren't going to invest in your product or service, are they? Will vending machines invest with you? Nope. You sell products and services to people only. So, you must get yourself, your voice, your ad, your letter, whatever, in front of people in order to make sales.

You can even use this little acronym to set your sales goals — *see twenty people* or *see thirty people,* for example — depending on how many you need to meet to close the number of sales necessary to reach your monthly income goals.

After you develop the prospecting mindset, you've taken a giant step toward becoming a master prospector, a master salesperson — a champion.

Your Prospecting Options

You can approach people in many ways, but a combination of techniques works best: the telephone, direct mail, online involvement through social media or e-mail, and face-to-face meetings. A potentially very powerful prospecting option involves social-media sites, like LinkedIn and Facebook. The following sections provide the details.

REMEMBER

You may need to make several attempts before you determine the right approach for someone. Some may respond to mail; others may not respond until they hear from you three times. Each method reinforces the others.

Using the telephone to prospect for clients

You can make a lot of calls in a short period of time by using the telephone. The phone is also easy on the budget. You can find one virtually everywhere, and almost everybody has a phone.

Before you make any call, take a moment to clear your mind (and your environment, if necessary). Focus your attention on the matter at hand. With a telephone, you can easily become distracted by whatever is in front of you, be it a computer screen, papers on your desk, or general activity going on around you.

Ask yourself: "What is my intended result for this call? Is it to make an introduction? To get an opportunity to meet with someone in person? To get permission to send information via e-mail or snail mail?" Be sure that your purpose is clearly defined.

Also, have at hand any necessary reference material: a report, key product information, or a website. If your client asks a question you can't immediately answer, you want to be able to get the answer as quickly as possible.

The downside to using the phone is that saying "no" over the telephone is remarkably easy. In addition, interruptions — real or invented — can cut short your presentation. Your prospect on the other end of the line has complete control of the situation and can hang up on you.

Before making initial contact with prospective clients, make sure you understand the rules and regulations stipulated by the National Do Not Call Registry (www.donotcall.gov), which prohibits telemarketers from calling individuals who place their phone numbers in the Do Not Call Registry. Abiding by the law takes some attention and extra work. The registry is managed by the Federal Trade Commission (FTC) and enforced by the Federal Communications Commission (FCC), as well as state consumer protection agencies. For more information or to receive a copy of the Do Not Call Registry, go to http://telemarketing.donotcall.gov.

Making contact with direct mail

Direct mail is efficient and cost-effective because you send the information directly to the person you want to receive it. Still, prospects have an easier time tossing a piece of paper in the trash can than actually reading it.

As much as possible, customize your direct mail to your clients' needs. In some cases, for example, you can include a cover letter with your brochures or other printed information. With the capabilities of today's digital printing services, you can customize your brochures with client names and include photos specific to their industries or related to their locales. You can even highlight particular features of your product that would suit their unique needs.

When you create your direct-mail pieces, remember that you don't want too much "telling" instead of "selling." Engage readers with questions they should ask themselves as they consider owning whatever product you offer. If you get your readers to think about what their lives would be like if they owned your product, they'll be more likely to want to talk further with you after reading your direct-mail literature.

Getting a face-to-face meeting

A face-to-face meeting with a good potential client is ideal. It is simply the finest, most effective way to sell a product or service. It's difficult for someone to get rid of another human being (unlike a phone call or direct-mail piece). Increase the number of your face-to-face contacts, and you'll increase the number of presentations to people who need your product.

When you go door to door, make sure you knock on the right ones. If you say the right words and say them properly and pleasantly, you can meet people who want to learn about your product or service. Follow this two-step strategy:

Book II: Prospecting for Gold

1. **Mail a letter of introduction to your potential clients.**

   Say that your company has given you an assignment to conduct a brief survey to get feedback from people in the community. Thank them in advance for their help and note that you'll be calling soon. Make sure that the letter is brief, simple, and polite. Here's an example:

   > Good morning, Mr. and Mrs. Sanders.
   >
   > My name is Tom Hopkins. I help people gain greater control over their financial future with the services provided by Champion Financial. My firm has asked that I contact 20 people in the area with a brief two-question survey to help us determine what services we might need to add to our current ones. I will call you next Thursday afternoon to ask you those two quick questions. I thank you in advance for your help in this matter.
   >
   > Sincerely,
   >
   > Tom Hopkins

2. **When you call or plan to make a personal visit, use the letter as an icebreaker.**

   > Hi, I'm Tom Hopkins. Did you get my letter of introduction? I sent the letter because I didn't want to be like so many people in our business and just drop by unannounced.

This letter is an exceptional technique because it sets you apart from the crowd. The simple courtesy makes you different from all the other salespeople. It presents you in a positive light. Never forget that the number-one key to success in sales is getting people to like and trust you. You then ask permission to ask your survey questions, which will hopefully lead to a qualifying sequence, an opportunity to present, and then a sale.

Networking online

The Internet can be an incredible and powerful source of leads — when you know how to use it. If you do business with other businesses, as opposed to working with individual customers, you can visit that business's website to glean valuable information, such as the business background, its product line(s), and, often, the best person to contact.

As mentioned earlier, social networking is a wonderful way to connect or reconnect with people whose needs you might serve. Through these sites, you can share ideas, activities, events, and interests. To use these sites successfully, find commonalities among your clients and seek out groups, activities, or events within social networks where you can connect with your type of client.

Networking sites like Facebook, Twitter, and LinkedIn can be great tools for expanding your contact lists. But be cautious about how you use these sites for selling your product or service; many companies and individuals have suffered the backlash of "friends" and "colleagues" who don't appreciate receiving hard-sell communications on their social networks. Instead, focus your efforts on providing value to potential clients by blogging information and linking your blog posts to your Facebook, Twitter, and LinkedIn accounts. (Turn to Book VII, Chapter 7 for more on blogs and other online sales tools.)

Key Paths to Prospecting Success

Prospecting must be the foundation of your business. E-mail correspondence, support marketing pieces and brochures, or any other tool is the icing on the cake. Prospecting *is* the cake. Without a solid foundation, a house won't be safe, secure, or stand for decades into the future. Without the foundation of prospecting, a sales career won't hold up, either.

Being a good representative of the product

You've undoubtedly heard the phrase "Be a product of the product." This means that not only do you represent the product or service, but you use it yourself. Your statements regarding features and benefits gain tremendous credibility if your potential client knows that you speak from experience. You see, if you try to sell people a Ford truck but drive a classic Chevy, you lose credibility with your prospects — even if they also love classic cars. You sell yourself and your company as much as, if not more than, you sell your product or service.

Whatever your product and whatever your level of experience in selling it, you can develop a thorough product knowledge. By seeing things through your customers' eyes, you can turn your awareness of its many features into real benefits. Forget the "what's in it for me" attitude, and think about what's in it for the other guy. That's when you both start winning. Book II, Chapter 2 has more information.

Selling yourself

When you prospect, you need to make your potential clients want to be involved with you, too, not just want to buy the product or service you sell. After all, a relationship with you is part of the bargain with most product sales. You are, in essence, the agent for the product. Your personal integrity is as important to the sale as the history of the company and quality of the products. Products and services can't speak for themselves until after the client owns them and uses them.

**Book II:
Prospecting
for Gold**

How do you sell yourself? You begin by taking a sincere, serious look at yourself in a full-length mirror. Do you look like someone you would trust? Do you carry yourself with confidence? Do you dress appropriately for the industry you represent? When you can answer yes to these three questions, you can move on. It's wise to consult with a trusted friend or loved one after you do your own assessment. Encourage him to be candid. He may notice something you didn't. If you need to improve in any of these areas, get cracking. Head to Book III, Chapter 1 for pointers on the impact your body language and attire can have during initial meetings.

Your attitude sells you, too. Do you begin every contact — even those on the phone — with a warm smile? People can feel smiles over the phone. Are you enthusiastic about your product? Don't be afraid to let the world see that you're excited about what you do. Excitement builds curiosity, especially if your prospects don't have much excitement in their lives. Your attitude is more critical to your success than you probably think.

How's your level of confidence? If you're confident about what you do, your potential clients think that you know what you're doing. You're in control because you've done your homework. You've learned how to move from finding people to selling the people you find and then selling to the people they know by referral. You're a pro and it shows. You may want to flip to Book II, Chapter 5, which offers all sorts of information on how to approach prospects in a way that makes them want to work with you.

Networking for prospects

A network is simply a group of people helping each other get where each wants to go as quickly, as easily, and as efficiently as possible. In sales, a network is a powerful way to get to a qualified prospect in the least amount of time and with the least amount of difficulty.

A serious, fully functioning network offers many benefits to its members, such as:

- ✔ Increased access to products and services
- ✔ Moral support
- ✔ Introductions to new people
- ✔ Friendships
- ✔ The opportunity to be of service to others
- ✔ Help in reaching goals
- ✔ Knowledge
- ✔ Power
- ✔ Fun

 A real network is not a group of acquaintances who might be able to help you out someday. Instead, a network is an association of individuals who have a solid relationship with each other and a strong commitment to the success of everyone within that group. And you can start your network with the people you already know. To find out how to build and maintain a network that can, among other things, help you attain and nurture your professional sales goals, turn to Book II, Chapter 2.

Changing Your Mindset: Prospecting Can Be Fun!

Few salespeople are dying to prospect. *No one* gets up in the morning, leaps out of bed, and says, "I'm excited today — I get to make 200 cold calls!" But face it: Prospecting is the bedrock of sales success. And it can even be fun if you approach it with a can-do attitude and the right tools, outlined in the following sections. Honest.

Setting and achieving goals

When you're first starting out in sales — or in a new sales job — start with easily attainable goals as you build healthy prospecting habits. You don't run a marathon without having trained for weeks or months to increase your endurance. Nor would you set the goal of 100 contacts in a day of sales prospecting — that's marathon-level prospecting!

In setting daily and weekly prospecting goals, concentrate on following these three steps, which flow into each other and help you establish your goals:

1. **Establish a number of contacts.**

   The number of qualified prospects — decision makers who are able to purchase your product or service or can refer you to someone who could — that you decide to call must be based on your goals, sales cycle, and sales ratios.

   Sales numbers of any kind vary greatly, based on product or service, cost, sales cycle, presentation length, and any number of factors. But as a general rule, a safe minimum is 15 to 25 contacts a day. Seem low? *Remember:* A contact is two-way conversation with a potential prospect. It's not a voicemail message, a discussion with a gatekeeper, or a call to gather background information.

   It may take several weeks for you to build up to this number. After you find yourself comfortably achieving 15 to 25 contacts a day for three weeks straight without missing a single day, you're ready to ratchet up: 30, 35, 40 a day.

2. **Calculate the number of leads.**

   After you review the list of all those people you *contacted,* this list is the total number of contacts who demonstrated a motivation and desire to make an investment in your product or service. They said something that led you to believe that your product or service is a viable solution to their problem — and that they have the financial capacity to make the investment.

3. **Project a number of appointments.**

   From that list of leads, you must establish a list of follow-up, face-to-face, or phone meetings that you must schedule. During this appointment, you discuss in more detail their needs and wants, share more information about your service or product and how your company works, and build the foundation for a relationship. The more you can secure an exclusive relationship, the more control you can have in the sales process.

Book II: Prospecting for Gold

Building the four pillars of prospecting

You need a system of support for your foundation of prospecting. You can't just go at it without a little forethought and elbow grease. You need some specific guidelines for carrying out your plan in order to accomplish your sales goals. The following four pillars of prospecting are just the thing to stabilize your sales efforts and build long-range success.

Pillar #1: Find a set time and place for daily prospecting

Many salespeople make the commitment to prospect every day, but their mistake is trying to work it in around their day. That approach doesn't work long term. Instead of working your prospecting around your day, work your day around your prospecting. Schedule a segment of your day — same time every day — to prospect and have a set place for it.

If you're unable to reach the person you're calling, you need to vary your approach. You may want to periodically add additional prospecting sessions on differing days and at different times. You may be trying to catch someone who will never be available in your primary prospecting block.

When you identify a prospecting space, make sure it has these items:

- ✔ A computer
- ✔ A telephone with a good-quality headset (check for features such as sound quality, comfort, fit, and range)
- ✔ Prospecting and objection-handling scripts where you can see them

Having all your tools within reach or in sight ensures that you're ready for anything, without fumbling for a moment with a prospect.

 Standing up while prospecting is an amazing technique to pump up your passion and energy. Your body language accounts for 55 percent of your communication — even when you're on the phone. A headset frees up your hands so that you can use them to engage in the sales process more effectively. The combination of standing and freeing up your hands is guaranteed to raise the level of passion, conviction, and enthusiasm your prospect hears when talking to you.

Pillar #2: Fight off distractions

Distractions are a fact of sales life. And truth be told, average salespeople are *looking* for them: the inbound phone call, a difficult client, an e-mail, another salesperson who wants to talk, a problem sale, a broken fingernail. Any distraction will do; you can call it creative avoidance.

And don't think you're off the hook after you achieve telephone-sales success. Top salespeople have more potential for distraction because they have a greater volume of business. The sooner you accept the fact that distractions are a constant threat, the better prepared you'll be to fight them off.

So, what do you do when distractions hit? The best way to fend off distractions while you're prospecting is to not let them happen in the first place! Hold all calls and messages. Put up a do not disturb sign on your office door. Take whatever steps are necessary to divert distractions.

Ironically, your own effective prospecting efforts may be the biggest distraction-making culprit. Prospecting calls always generate production-supporting activities. Many prospects want more information, future contact, comparison data, and outside input. And, of course, each call may require a follow-up thank-you note or a recap of your discussion. But don't break your stride now. Take a moment to jot down a few notes about the tasks you need to do so you can remember them later and get back on the phone now. Be in the moment. Stay on your prospecting path — the quickest route to sales success.

Pillar #3: Follow the plan

Prospecting is effective only if it generates a truly qualified lead — someone who is interested in what you offer, needs the service you provide, and has the ability and authority to become a client of your business (or refers you to someone who could). A contact isn't a secretary, a voicemail, an assistant, the babysitter, a 10-year-old, or a teenager. Those salespeople who strike it rich at prospecting set their sights on the best opportunity for making sales. They don't waste their time calling iffy contacts who may not even be in the market for their product or service.

Success boils down to some very simple formulas. Following the right steps in the proper order is one of those formulas. In short, you need a plan. For best results, set up your daily prospecting plan at the end of the prior workday. Before you leave your office *today,* lay out your call schedule for *tomorrow.* Set everything you need on your desk so you're ready the minute you walk in the door in the morning.

Establishing a daily routine reinforces your commitment to the process and helps build good habits. It can be as simple as the following steps:

1. **Research prospects and set up your call list the day before.**

   Invest the time in determining who you're going to call tomorrow before you leave today. If you can invest time in researching before you leave, you'll be better prepared for tomorrow's calls.

2. **Set aside time to practice your script and rehearse responses just before you begin your calls.**

   You want to spend about 20 minutes practicing your scripts and dialogues before your pick up the phone for the day.

3. **Do a quick review of your list and daily goals.**

4. Repeat (out loud) your favorite affirmation statements.

Using affirmations is a great way to get your mind in a positive state before you make your prospecting calls. You can say your own, or try some of the following:

- "I am a great prospector."

- "I will generate _____ leads today."

- "I am going to make _____ sales today."

By following a similar routine, you can be warmed up and ready to give your task your best effort — just like any professional. The minute you pick up the phone, practice is over; the limelight's on you.

Adequate preparation and warm-up is important, but too much can be a sign of creative avoidance (see Pillar #2)! If you spend more than 30 minutes getting ready to call, you're spending too much time.

Pillar #4: Finish what you start

To win, you have to finish the race — the *whole* race. That means fulfilling your daily goals every day, down to the very last contact on your list. Don't accept anything less!

If your day has been particularly grueling, throwing in the towel and cutting your calling short is easy: "What's the point? One more call won't pull up my stats." If you've hit record numbers, justifying quitting before you're done is also easy. "Hey, I've exceeded my goal — I don't need to make any more calls today." Again, resist the tendency to seek any excuse to avoid fulfilling your prospecting goals. Don't settle; finish what you start.

Finishing what you start is more than just making it through your list. You also must follow through with the contacts you made. A great way to wrap things up most effectively with a contact is to compose a handwritten thank-you note and mail it in a small (*not* a standard business size) envelope. Unlike an e-mail or even a generic, preplanned regurgitated form letter, your personal note will get noticed. The typical consumer receives dozens of e-mails a day, selling everything from no-interest loans to Viagra. And the post office delivers stacks of junk mail. Although most of this ends up in the "circular file," a handwritten letter breaks through the clutter, which means it gets read — and keeps your relationship alive until you talk again.

Chapter 2
Prospecting Preliminaries

. . . .

. . . .

*P*rospecting. Brings to mind images of the Old West, doesn't it? History has made the determined prospector who spent every backbreaking day panning for gold in a churning river or swinging a pickax into hard rock mythological. However, lots of miners returned to their homes with nothing. Some were seduced by get-rich-quick schemes — card playing, stagecoach robbing, and so on. And plenty, after a brief taste of the demands of the work, realized that an easier way to make a living had to be out there somewhere. Only a handful of dedicated and persistent forty-niners withstood the harsh conditions and, day in and day out, continued the grueling task. To these folks came the fortunes of the Gold Rush.

Prospecting really isn't so different for sales professionals. They just mine for a different kind of reward: sales! Success requires rolling up your proverbial shirt sleeves and digging in — committing to the day-to-day work involved in finding customers who need your product. Any shortcut to bypass this effort leads only to fool's gold.

In this chapter, we fill you in on the first steps toward prospecting success: learning everything you can about the product you're selling, using your listening skills to glean key information from your prospects, and building a network you can rely on. This chapter also tells you how to enhance your reputation and build your business by following a code of ethics.

Finding Out Everything You Can about Your Product

You really can't talk to people and determine whether they're good prospects if you don't know your own product inside, outside, top to bottom. You don't have to work on the manufacturing line or pursue a degree in design and engineering, but you do have to know what you're selling so that you can relate it to your customers' needs. The following sections explain how you can get the information you need.

If your company is one that sends new salespeople out into the world with a handful of brochures and a "don't come back 'til you get a sale" — a strategy tellingly named *walking the plank* — you must make building a thorough knowledge of your product *your* responsibility, even if you have to do it on your own time.

Boning up on your product

You can't possibly know every little thing about your product, but you do need to know a lot about it. Start by making a basic list of key information you need to know, things like

✔ Product name and model number(s)

✔ Differences between models

✔ Product features

✔ Sizes and colors available

✔ Price range

✔ Financing and terms

✔ Warranty and service

That's a pretty basic list, but you may be surprised at the number of salespeople who charge into the marketplace without even this amount of information.

As you create your list of need-to-know information, put yourself in your customer's shoes. What's important to him should be important to you. If you're still wondering whether you've adequately covered all your bases (true professionals never assume anything; they always seek tidbits of information that may help them gain someone's interest in their product or service), then ask a friend or loved one this question: "If you were in the market for a brand-new Whatzit, what would you need to know about it? What would your concerns be?"

The following sections explain what resources may be available that you can tap into to get the information you need.

Signing up for training sessions

If you work for a truly effective organization, your management provides company training sessions for new employees, as well as ongoing training throughout the year. The manufacturer or distributor of the product you sell also may offer training sessions, at least on new products. Attend every training session you can, especially if you're new. In these settings, you receive information from someone who is highly knowledgeable and skilled when it comes to your product offering.

To get the most out of these sessions, follow these suggestions:

**Book II:
Prospecting
for Gold**

- ✔ **Compile a list of important questions to take with you and don't be shy about asking them.** If you have to, make a real effort to buttonhole the speaker before he gets out of the room. You don't want to waste the opportunity to mine a valuable resource for information that may help you. The question you don't ask could be the very one your prospect asks the next day. Saying, "I'll, uh, get back to you on that," has lost an awful lot of sales.

- ✔ **Ask the expert what types of businesses use the product or service.** This question helps you explore other potential sources of business than those you already know about. Questions like "What's the most unusual business you know of that uses our Jimjammer?" or "What group represents the largest client base for the Jimjammer IV?"

- ✔ **If the expert conducts in-house training for clients, ask him what questions clients frequently ask.** Ask about the biggest challenges with training client staff. What features do staff members have the most difficulty with?

The answers you get to these questions can help you anticipate the kinds of questions your own customers may have about the product.

Getting the most out of product literature

Most companies recognize the value of printed literature. One of the most common examples of product literature is the sales brochure. Sure, it probably has beauty shots of the product, but you shouldn't approach it as a customer flipping through the pretty pictures. Instead, you need to pick a time of day for serious study and read it as homework. Study this material every day for three weeks. Have someone in your family ask you questions from the material until you can pass the most rigorous test. You'll be amazed at what you can learn by reading the product literature your company produces.

Some clients read every detail of those brochures, so you'd better know what the material says. If the brochure lacks vital information, make sure you have that additional information at your fingertips before meeting with or talking to your prospect.

Many kinds of other materials can increase your knowledge:

- **Fact sheets:** Many companies prepare these, especially for news releases. They consist of simply stated facts about the product, the service, the manufacturer, or the company.

- **Video brochures:** Very popular, these are often highly professional presentations of important information. Most companies make them available on their websites either for the general public to see or in a password-protected area that salespeople can access during their time with clients.

- **Audio demos:** Many companies send out news-release-type information to top clients in professionally produced audio formats such as on CDs or in MP3 downloads. If the product you represent is sales training, for example, a condensed version of the program may be used in its promotion. Find out what the marketing department is promising that you'll bring to potential clients.

- **Video training sessions:** These sessions can contain a wealth of information about the workings of the equipment, construction techniques, installation methods, company history, and other facts of possible interest to a buyer. They are, in essence, infomercials for your product.

- **Recent newspaper or magazine articles, especially those from trade journals:** Favorable product reviews by trade publications are excellent sales materials. Scan the review or article and include it in e-mails to clients as a PDF. For example, if you market something to consumers, be sure you know what *Consumer Reports* thinks of it. If nothing else, quote some of their statistics to build credibility for your company or your product. You also can use trade journals to research your competition.

- **Technical data, such as the Material Safety Data Sheet (MSDS):** Technical data often is very dry reading and very, well, technical, but you may discover a few good bits of valuable information. Make it easily digestible for your clients. Be cautious about using industry or technical jargon with those not already familiar with your type of product.

Always treat your sales materials with respect, especially in front of potential or current clients. Brochures, videos, and fact sheets represent your product, your company, and all the people working there. If you trash your sales material, your prospect will begin to wonder, "If that's how he feels about his company, how the heck does he feel about me?"

Trying out the product yourself

If you represent a tangible product, play with it. Take it out for a drive. Boot up the system and run the software. Drink it, and see if it really offers the "zesty, tingly flavors of freshness" your marketing folks say it does. Try one on for size. Sit in it. Toss it to your kid. Get to know it inside and out — what it does, how it does it, and how it compares to the competition.

If you're selling a service instead of a product, you still can get important information about it. If you represent a bus line, take a trip or two. See whether you can get from here to there "on time with friendly service from people who know that you are number one." Talk to clients. How does the service make them feel? Listen especially for the adjectives they use to describe the service, and then use those adjectives with potential new clients.

Book II:
Prospecting
for Gold

While you're kicking all those tires and experiencing all those services, think about how the customer fits into the picture. A lot of good customer-service ideas come from people just looking around the company with a fresh viewpoint.

Connecting with co-workers

Top producers in the organization probably know an awful lot of information that you just can't get from standard product literature. Such information is extremely valuable. So, pick out the top salespeople in your company and ask them about the product.

Be polite and don't monopolize all their time. They're in business to sell, not to teach. Most people, however, are flattered by attention and are more than willing to show you the ropes. Besides, they know that at some point, in some way, you'll be in a position to return the favor. That's just good business.

If you have a chance to talk with a top producer in your company, keep the topic of conversation focused. Avoid general questions, like "What does the defrickler do?" — they imply that you didn't do your homework and are looking for an easy answer. Instead, say something like, "I'm working on a sale of the XRG Model, and my client has asked about its capability to defrickle. Do you have a client that uses that feature?" Such a focused question is more likely to get a helpful answer.

Companies sometimes partner a veteran with a new employee for a short training period. If your company doesn't do this, go ahead and ask for one anyway. Explain that you think having such a resource will help you know your product better and, thus, better serve your clients. When you go out with veterans, use this valuable time to really study. Observe how they prepare or gear up for presentations. Pay attention to their attitudes, body language, and manner of greeting and handling people. Learn how they create moods by using word pictures and how they work through the seven-step selling cycle (discussed in Book I, Chapter 1) one element at a time. Note how they address concerns; present visual aids; use trial or test closes to see if the prospects are ready to go ahead; and thank the new, happy clients for their orders.

Looking at client feedback

People who already use your company's products or services and are familiar with its pluses and minuses can be excellent resources of product knowledge. If possible, make a list of candidates, create a product survey, and give them a call. Ask their opinions of the product, how has it served them, what they like most and least about it, what they tell their friends about it, and so on.

In addition, making a friendly call and asking a few questions is an excellent way to keep you, their salesperson, in mind. We don't live in a static world. Other salespeople could be, and probably are, calling your customers.

Identifying what you're really selling

What do you *really* sell? Ask 100 professionals this question, and you'll probably get close to 100 different answers. You'll hear "financial services," "health and beauty products," "business opportunities," "computers," "real estate," "luxury automobiles," and so on. But these answers miss the point. The preferred answers? "Peace of mind with regard to financial matters," "enhanced self-esteem through effective self-care," "the freedom to make your own choices in a profitable business," "methods for saving time and money while enhancing your company's image," "places where memories are made," and "comfort and security on the road."

Can you see the difference? As a sales professional, you must realize first and foremost that you do not sell products or services. You sell what those products or services will *do* for the people you serve. Janitorial services, for example, don't sell office or home cleaning. They improve the image of businesses. They help families find more time to devote to leisure or other more important activities. If you begin to see your product in that light, your prospecting efforts will yield more positive results.

Marketing experts use words, phrases, and images that show their clients how their products do one or more of the following:

- ✔ Save money
- ✔ Save time
- ✔ Improve their status
- ✔ Improve their looks or health
- ✔ Are easy to use or comfortable
- ✔ Allow them to have better sex lives

Chances are, you don't know anyone who doesn't want at least two of these things. Take a moment to think about the product or service you represent. How do you tell people what you do? Think about how you can use these six ideas to make people more interested in what you sell.

How much knowledge is enough?

Can you ever have too much product knowledge? Absolutely.

Consider the cautionary tale of the brilliant engineer who was promoted to a plant manager position that required a lot of selling skills in certain areas, particularly community relations. He had a great idea: Create a short video on the facility to tell the plant story to the community. The program was to be targeted to the "chicken-and-peas circuit" — Rotary Club, Kiwanis Club, and similar organizations. He hired a professional video crew, an experienced writer, and a well-known narrator. And the program bombed. Totally.

The problem? The engineer/plant manager overloaded the video with information. He wanted every facet of the story told — how the equipment worked, the physics behind the

processes, the nature of the atom, and so on. He produced a beautiful, if highly technical, video that was 45 minutes long. Those of you in service clubs are already thinking, "Uh-oh."

Why? Because service clubs don't generally have 45 minutes. Most club members have time to meet and mingle, eat their chicken and peas, hear a 15- to 20-minute presentation, and get back to work. In short, no one wanted to see the video because no one had time to see it. The plant manager concentrated on the product rather than the needs of his prospects.

The amount of product knowledge you need depends on your product or service and the needs of your potential clients. Get enough valuable information to answer all their questions, but draw the line somewhere before you get to the nature of the atom.

Honing Your Prospecting Skills by Becoming a Better Listener

You may think that to learn what you need to know about your prospects, you need to ask the right questions. But the right question is only one part of the equation. The real key to learning is *listening*. This is true in everything, including prospecting.

By asking the right questions and then really listening to the answers, your prospect will, at some point, reveal how your product can benefit him. Prospects may make statements such as, "I'm looking for something that is comfortable but that gets really good mileage." Or they may ask, "Will it seat two adults and four children comfortably?" And they will almost surely express concern with something like, "I really don't think I can afford it."

Astute listeners gather this revealing information, turn it around, and tell prospects why they should buy from them.

Hearing what your prospect is saying

How do you learn to listen? By breaking down the process of listening into four basic steps:

1. **Hear with all your senses.**

   Concentrate all your senses on the other person. Pay strict attention to every word being said and more. Notice body language, pauses that indicate concern or interests, shifty eye movements that may signal nervousness, levels of vocal stress, sweating, head shaking, toe tapping, finger rapping, scratching behind the ear, and anything else that communicates information.

2. **Translate what prospects say.**

   Translation is the art of distinguishing between what is said and what is actually meant. Think of it as reading between the lines. No matter how many words prospects say or how long it takes them to say those words, they always express a core of truth. You usually can boil down the words to 25 words or fewer.

3. **Evaluate your translation.**

   Make sure you interpret your potential client's needs and wants into the benefits provided by your product. Evaluation is the connective tissue between what the prospect says between the lines and what you have to offer.

4. **Follow up with people by responding to them.**

   If you've practiced steps 1, 2, and 3, this response should be appropriate and should get you the desired results. Your goal may be to gather more information, cinch the individual as a client, or get referrals. You must be specific and focus on the potential clients' real concerns.

To be a successful prospector, you must practice all four of these steps every time you meet with anyone. Otherwise, you'll miss not only what people are really saying but opportunities, clients, and sales as well.

Showing your prospect that you're listening

To truly listen, you need to put your whole body, attitude, and mind into it. Not only will this show the prospect that you're really paying attention, but it will enhance your own listening skills. Here are some suggestions:

✔ **Be conscious of your body language.** Your body language says "I'm listening" when you make eye contact (without getting into a staring contest), lean slightly forward, nod in the affirmative, or even stroke your chin with your hand.

✔ **Take notes.** Doing so shows interest, especially if you break periodically to make eye contact. (Doodling a comic caricature of the client or the beer you plan to have after this meeting, however, doesn't count as note taking.)

✔ **Ask questions.** Something directly related to the heart of the matter under discussion is best.

✔ **Let the prospect finish.** People don't like to have the end of their sentences chopped off by someone overly eager to jump in with his own words of wisdom. Such amateurish rudeness builds massive walls between the salesperson and prospect.

✔ **Show interest with nods, uh-huhs, and go ons.** Sometimes all it takes for a client to tell you more is a simple nod. Hmms and uh-huhs work well, too. An occasional "I understand" or "I see" gets you great mileage as well.

✔ **Repeat key points back.** Never hesitate to use repetition in conversation. "Now, let me make sure I have this absolutely straight. . . ." Repeating shows you've been listening.

✔ **If you're easing the conversation in a different direction, make sure you note and respond to what your prospect has said.** Suddenly jumping into a separate topic may totally disrupt the flow of conversation and generate a bit of resentment or even hostility. Instead, segue into the change diplomatically.

✔ **Show respect and interest even if you don't feel it.** If the old boy is prattling along about trekking 10 miles in the blizzard of the century to get gas for his first vehicle, just remember that patience and good technique allow you to bring him around to the subject of your eight-cylinder, turbo-charged, special-bonus-from-the-sales-manager-if-it-sells-today, deluxe, luxury automobile. Eyes that continually glance out the window, a tapping toe, or comments that are just a tad off base show disrespect and will probably send your potential client to someone more appreciative of his precious memories.

Book II: Prospecting for Gold

Building a Working Network

A network is simply a group of people helping each other get where each wants to go as quickly, easily, and efficiently as possible. In sales, a network is a powerful way to get to a qualified lead in the least amount of time and with the least amount of difficulty. A serious, fully functioning network offers many benefits to its members, such as

- ✔ Increased access to products and services
- ✔ Moral support
- ✔ Introductions to new people
- ✔ Friendships
- ✔ The opportunity to be of service to others
- ✔ Help in reaching goals
- ✔ Knowledge
- ✔ Power
- ✔ Fun

Most people think of networking in terms of receiving something from others: leads, prospects, clients, guidance, hints, techniques, or moral support. But starting your networking by first considering what you can offer to others is important. So, take some time to carefully examine what you have to offer someone in your network. What capabilities, skills, information, talents, connections, and words of wisdom can you provide that can help build someone else's business or career? Here are some things you may come up with:

- ✔ Education
- ✔ Job experience
- ✔ Skills or talents
- ✔ People you know or those you're going to know
- ✔ Access to resources (books, videos, or audio presentations)
- ✔ Club and organization connections

Almost everything is useful to someone. For example, the fact that you're on a first-name basis with the owner of the local service station, flower shop, or antique mall may be a valuable asset at some point to someone in your network. Think!

A real network is not a group of acquaintances who may be able to help you out someday. Instead, a network is an association of individuals who have a solid relationship with each other and a strong commitment to the success of everyone within that group. And you can start your network with the people you already know.

Picturing your network

Take out a pencil and paper and try this exercise: Draw a circle in the middle of a sheet of paper, and write your name inside it. Then start drawing lines, like spokes of a wheel. Add circles, and place the names of people you know within them. Include the names of anyone and everyone who could possibly help you achieve your goals. Think about all the people you know at work, at church, your civic club, the chamber of commerce, or other organizations where you're active. Consider also the many people you see regularly and who may be of service to you or to someone within your network. Now draw more spokes from those wheels to the names of people they know who also may help develop your career.

Is this just an exercise in doodling? No. You've just drawn a picture of your network. After you complete this picture, you may be surprised at the depth of support available to you. You also may notice that although you're smack-dab in the center of your own network, you're also a spoke on someone else's network. Teamwork! That's how you keep the wheels of progress turning.

You can also extend this exercise to people you would like to meet, as well as those you already know. Thinking through centers of influence that may be gateways to a bigger network may be just the incentive you need to take action in meeting new people.

Starting your network

How do you start networking? Here are four methods:

✔ **Become a copycat.** Sincerely study and emulate a talented and skilled individual who is successful at networking. Observe how this person handles herself and then carry on the same way. If you're lucky — and if you pursue the matter properly — this individual may even take you under her wing and become a mentor. Imitation really is the sincerest form of flattery. And, the bonus is that if she likes you, her existing network is now accessible to you.

✔ **Get involved with organizations that provide opportunities to meet and interact with people.** This is especially important if you need encouragement in coming out of your fear-of-networking shell. One such organization is Toastmasters, which fosters self-confidence, public-speaking skills, and positive interaction among individuals. Find your local chapter at `www.toastmasters.org`.

✔ **Play the part.** Shakespeare wrote, "All the world's a stage, and all the men and women merely players." So, begin acting the role of a confident networker, and before you realize it, a transformation will take place and you *will* be a confident networker.

✔ **Become an interested introvert rather than an interesting extrovert.**
Become interested in other people. Ask questions about their interests,
their concerns, their ideas. They'll open up, and before you know it,
you'll have a group of new friends and acquaintances and a start on your
network. Develop a sense of what are comfortable questions for them.
Always start on light, noncontroversial topics and watch their body-
language responses to those topics.

Learn to recognize when your potential client seems resistant to answering
a question. This resistance could be an indication that you asked a nosy
question. An interested question may be, "Where did you get that lovely
coat?" A nosy question would be, "And how much did you pay for it?"

Finding people and making contact

Will Rogers used to say, "I never met a man I didn't like." That's a good way
to approach life and a great way to approach networking. Everyone is a prospect; everyone can become a member of your network.

Although a network is not a formal organization with a written charter,
bylaws, and weekend retreats in the islands, your network is a powerful tool
and an important part of your career. So, you want people who can help you
and — equally important — people you can help. How can you make contact
with them? Here are two categories you should think about:

✔ **The obvious choices:** Certainly, if the corporate head of marketing at
one of your city's largest companies asks you to golf, go. If you have the
opportunity to serve on a service-club committee with one of the prominent bankers in town, take it. Cultivate relationships with anyone who is
in a position to know others in the business community. If you want to
roll with the movers and the shakers, you have to be invited into their
club.

✔ **The not-so-obvious choices:** If you're a white-collar worker, don't limit
your network to other white-collar workers. You never know who may
be in a position to assist you. The auto mechanic may service the vehicle of someone you need to know or, better yet, he may be the good fellow's cousin. The receptionist or telephone operator can probably help
you more than all the vice presidents in that tall building downtown.

No matter how tempting or easy staying close to home is, network with at
least a few people outside your organization. Why? Getting important information from outside sources can be easier than getting that information
from within your own organization. Many companies have a very regimented
organizational chart that prohibits employee or manager A from talking to
co-worker G without first going through Mr. B, Mrs. C, Ms. D, and those two
guys, E and F, over in accounting. That's why your network is so valuable. If
you have news for someone in the group, you just pick up the phone and call

direct. Similarly, you can get "just the facts, ma'am," from your friendly neighborhood network.

Keeping your network up and running

A network is no good — no good to you and no good to anyone else in the group — unless you work it. Treat a network as you would an expensive, finely crafted instrument. Here are a few tips to help you make sure you and your associates are getting the most out of your association.

Stay in touch

Obviously, pass along any valuable information to the appropriate member(s). Such information can be a good lead, the fact that a new business is moving into or out of town, a warning about a shady member of the business community, encouragement about an upcoming presentation, or anything that falls into the "Hey, what you do is totally your business, but I thought you ought to know . . ." category.

To avoid members feeling neglected or fading away from the group, keep the lines of communication wide open and information flowing by looking for ways to keep in touch. Here are just a few idea starters:

- ✔ **Make a note of important dates, such as birthdays or business or personal anniversaries, and drop cards in the mail.** To easily handle this task and keep track of these events annually, consider the service SendOutCards. The company offers a free trial of its service by going to www.tomhopkins.com/SOCcontact/SOCcontact.html.

- ✔ **Keep an eye out for appearances in the newspaper or magazines.** If you see an item in the paper or a magazine that may be of interest to a member of the network, clip or copy it and drop it in the mail with a quick note.

- ✔ **When passing through a contact's town, see whether you can arrange a breakfast, lunch, or dinner, or at least make a call from the airport to let that person know you're thinking of him.** Come on, you don't think networks are limited to your hometown, do you?

- ✔ **Use e-mail to stay in touch and don't forget to pick up the phone periodically just to say "Hi."**

These contacts don't have to be lengthy or take on the appearance of an obligation; in fact, spontaneity often makes the contact more enjoyable. The main thing is to make contact and to keep on making contact.

Make a point of calling or visiting people you normally don't approach, especially a contact you haven't been keeping in touch with. Sometimes we're too shy or even embarrassed to contact the very people we need to contact the most. Go ahead. Pick up the phone or, better still, go pop by.

Ask for help

If you've kept the lines of communication open, don't hesitate a second to seek the support you need. You won't be considered a burden. Quite the contrary: People want to help other people. Asking for assistance helps you ease down the road of success and reinforces the fact that when the time comes, you'll be there to help the other party.

When you ask for help, keep two things in mind:

- **Say what you really mean.** Phrase your request in words that allow the other party to understand your needs. "We've just added a new line of whatchamacallits. Who do you know that may need one?" is a lot more effective than "Got any prospects for me?"

- **Be polite.** "I need you to help me get some prospects" borders on rudeness, even if you don't mean to be so impolite. "I'm in need of a little help here and was wondering if you could spare a few moments of your time" is a better, more sincere way of opening the conversation. And never forget to say "thanks" for any information passed down the pipeline. That one little word is the least-expensive, easiest-to-give, and most-neglected form of compensation on the entire planet.

Volunteer your help

Be aggressive about providing leads, information, and service to the members of your network. Don't just pass along information that happens to come your way. Go out of your way to find ways to support your network. Don't wait for someone to ask for your help. Make a point of contacting the members of your network to see whether you can be of service. Even if there's no particular need at the moment, they'll certainly appreciate the thought and you'll have further cemented a valuable relationship.

Provide excellent service

Because people talk and your career is most definitely influenced by word-of-mouth advertising, become known for the excellence of your service. When you get a referred lead, for example, act immediately. Return phone calls, provide requested information, be on time, and deliver on your promises.

When you get a reputation for excellent service, people will want to work with you and introduce you to others who need excellent service.

Maintain your focus

A network is a living entity. Once or twice a year, evaluate the effectiveness of the people in your network to see whether you need to add more support in a particular area. If you're all give and you're getting nothing back, you need to correct the situation or find a new network. But the opposite is also true — *you* may be all take and no give — so honestly evaluate your own effectiveness to the other group members.

When you evaluate your network, go through your list of members to make sure that all the information is up to date, that all addresses are current, and that important information is added. You can really be embarrassed and do great damage to your network by asking how little Abby is doing in grade school when she just graduated from college and is getting married next month. Ouch!

Make networking an integral part of your lifestyle

Don't think of networking as an activity to be scheduled. "Today I will network between noon and 5 p.m." A champion at prospecting realizes that virtually every waking moment can offer an opportunity to use, build, or assist the network.

Follow the 3-foot rule: Approach anyone within 3 feet of you. Never hesitate to start a friendly conversation. It can bring you a lead, a sale, or even a new and valuable member of the network.

By making your network more successful, you make yourself more successful. As the individuals within the network grow, succeed, and prosper, your range of contacts increases. Your connections with successful people connect you with an ever-growing circle of more successful people. The depth of your support group increases, as does your access to more and more powerful resources. All this leads directly to more and more prospects.

Professional Ethics for Prospectors

We all pay when someone in our business acts without ethics. Unethical salespeople not only do a disservice to their customers but also make life more difficult for all of us in sales. High standards of honesty and integrity should be as much a part of your career as education, training, ambition, and punctuality.

Because you can't count on everybody having such high standards, you, as a wise prospector, must be prepared to face prejudices that you had no hand in creating. To overcome these prejudices and to ensure that you don't contribute to their creation, follow the advice outlined in the following sections.

Book II: Prospecting for Gold

Helping people make decisions

Many salespeople, at one point or another, are concerned that they'll talk someone into buying something that she really doesn't want. But keep these points in mind:

- ✓ **If you take the time to properly qualify your potential client, then you know whether your product or service can benefit her.** When you know those needs, your duty is to make the benefits of that product or service available as quickly as possible. Part of that duty requires you to help the prospect make decisions.

- ✓ **A prospect won't spend valuable time with you without already having some legitimate interest in your product.** The world is just moving too quickly these days to waste a minute of the day on unnecessary purchases.

Despite the occasional stories about the sale of the Brooklyn Bridge or swampland in Florida, most people don't buy something they don't want, especially when you get into big-ticket items. Even if the prospect knows that she needs the product or service, even if she really wants it, you still face an uphill struggle to get her to make the decision to make the purchase.

- ✓ **Two key components of the superior service you provide your prospect are information and honesty.** You want to answer all her questions truthfully, and in doing so, you can help her get to the word *yes*. If you've put her interests before your potential income, then you're truly doing the right thing and there is no reason in the world to think yourself unfair or unethical. Think of it this way: If you know the needs of your prospect and know that your product can meet those needs, then not allowing her the benefits of your product or service would be unfair.

- ✓ **As a professional, you have a duty not only to your clients but also to the profession of selling.** As a sales professional, dedicate yourself to creating an honest, positive impression of people in the industry and providing genuine service to your clients.

- ✓ **Don't treat the competition as the enemy.** Running down a competitor is one of the fastest ways to run down yourself and a surefire way to turn off your prospect. Even if your competitor exhibits this poor behavior, don't get drawn into playing that game. It's a sucker bet, for sure.

The key to success in sales is to make people like and trust you, and doing that is surprisingly easy. If you ever have doubts about what you're doing, just ask yourself whether the action really puts your prospect first. The truthful answer tells you all you need to know.

Greed is a costly expense

An advertising/marketing firm was having trouble with one of its major accounts. Miscommunication, questions about billing procedures, and challenges with making deadlines were creating a major rift between client and agency. Not only was the account very profitable, but it was also one of those prestigious, high-visibility types. The agency president decided to save the situation. He invited the president of the account to lunch at an upscale restaurant to discuss and resolve the situation.

The presidents met at the appointed time. The agency owner brought the account executive and the art director to help emphasize the importance of the company's business to the agency. The executives resolved the problems amicably, and the meeting broke up with the agency head grabbing the check and heading back to the office.

At the end of the month, the client was shocked to see that the agency had billed him for the entire lunch. Worse, the agency had billed him for the hourly rate of the art director and the account executive on top of everything else!

The agency had saved a bad situation only to make it worse by letting greed rear its ugly head. The client fired the agency the next day.

Being honest in all your dealings

You can't become a champion unless you're honest. You can't lie, cheat, beat, or steal in any degree. Consider "little white lies," which tend to grow into big problems, part of that list, too. Take one dishonest step — even a small one — and, before you know it, you're walking on shaky ground.

Sometimes, even mistakes can be construed as dishonesty. To avoid that trap, follow this advice:

- ✓ **Thoroughly educate your prospects about your product or service before closing the sale.** Don't leave any surprises for them down the road. Surprises have a nasty tendency to turn into land mines that can blow a relationship to smithereens.

- ✓ **Be very careful about exaggerating your product's capabilities, and make sure that you know what you're talking about before opening your mouth.** Always make sure that any claims made about your product, service, or company are up-to-date and accurate. Be sure you can back up your claims with survey results, statistics, or other methods of proof.

The lack of honesty costs the salesperson his credibility. No matter what your product or service, if you don't have credibility, you don't have anything to sell.

Delivering what you promise

Every contact you make with a prospect involves some kind of promise: a call back, an appointment, delivery of information, and so on. Always deliver, no matter how small or how large the challenge. If you promise a call within two days, be sure you make it. If you promise to drop by the prospect's office with promotional literature, make sure you or someone pops in with the goods. If you say you'll call back at 2 p.m., don't leave a prospect sitting at a desk, drumming her fingers and looking at the clock.

The goal is to build a feeling of trust so that no matter what you promise, the customer knows you'll deliver. The client also begins to realize that, if you don't promise something, it probably can't be done.

Delivering on your promises builds long-lasting relationships and good reputations. People who make and always keep smaller promises have a much better track record in sales than those who promise the moon but don't always deliver. A prospect may never remember the fact that you've returned all his calls, but the one call not returned will live forever.

If you mistakenly state a falsehood or discover that you can't deliver on a promise, don't wait for your prospect to find out the hard way. Pick up the telephone or pop in and explain the situation as soon as possible. The more time that passes between your call and the time your prospect makes the discovery, the more it sticks in her memory. You also have to work longer to win back your credibility . . . if you can.

Being a standard-bearer

An ethical salesperson never violates his personal code of behavior, no matter what the temptation. In spite of what you may see in the movies, on television, or in tabloid headlines, most people respect a person of integrity and want to trade with that type of person. Even people who try to get you to compromise your standards will admire your strength of will and commitment. If, in those rare occurrences when you actually lose a temporary advantage, an appointment, or a sale, for example, compromising your standards would be far more costly to you in the long run. In a very real way, living up to your own high standards is delivering on a promise to yourself.

Protecting proprietary information

Salespeople often encounter valuable information about a company, how its product is made, how the service is performed, and plans for expansion. In-depth research is a natural and necessary part of how you provide the best service possible. In some cases, you may even need to sign a nondisclosure agreement to protect valuable company information. Even if you never sign such an agreement, always respect the confidentiality of your prospect or customer. The information you come across or that is shared with you is not meant to be shared with others, certainly not with any competitors you may also serve.

Protecting confidential information isn't as easy as you may think. A seemingly unimportant bit of news or information may have no significance to you, but in the wrong hands it can prove costly to your potential client and, eventually, you. People in business can generally discover the source of an information leak. Even if you made your disclosure casually without realizing the seriousness of your remarks, the damage is the same. Even if you were totally unaware of the significance of speaking out of turn, your prospect will know that you can't be trusted with important information. Talking about your prospect's business just isn't good business.

Chapter 3

Fishing for Prospects in the Likeliest — and Unlikeliest — Places

. . . .

In This Chapter

▶ Knowing where to look for potential customers

▶ Using direct mail and press releases to draw leads to you

▶ Growing your client list through referrals

. . . .

Think about all you need to be a successful fisherman. You need the proper equipment (poles, lures, and more) and knowledge (how to bait a hook, how to angle, for example), and you need the location (a freshwater lake or the local pond, for example).

Selling actually has quite a few things in common with fishing, except that your equipment includes your product, your knowledge about the product, and your selling skills and motivation. And your "fishing hole" is the market in which you're selling.

But even if you have all the things previously listed, success will elude you — whether you're a salesperson or a fisherman — unless you can find where the fish are biting.

This chapter tells you how you can increase the size of your potential client pool through people you come in contact with every day. You also can find information on how to use news media to catch the attention of strangers who can benefit from the product or service you're offering. And finally, it explains how to make the most of referrals.

Strategies to Grow Your Prospect List

Where should you go fishing? The following sections give you effective ways to find the people or organizations willing and able to pay for your product or services. Believe me, all the hard work pays off.

Talking with friends and relatives

To become a successful prospector, you don't have to begin by calling on the biggest, meanest hombre west of the Pecos. Start with people you know, people with whom you are at ease and who are at ease with you. In other words, start with your friends and relatives. Consider this group your *warm market* (or *natural market*) because you can work on your presentation before a receptive, friendly audience.

Friends and family members are in your corner. They already like and trust you and are much less likely to say no, especially if the product or service you sell can truly benefit them. Give them a call or stop by (at a time that's convenient for them), and tell them about your new business or career. Share your enthusiasm for this new opportunity.

Here's a key phrase that works extremely well in getting friends and family to allow you to present your new product or service: "Because I value your judgment, I was hoping you'd give me your opinion." Examine that beautifully crafted sentence. *Because I value your judgment* says to them, "You are an important, experienced, and wise individual." The phrase *I was hoping* shows concern for them and signals that you won't pressure them. The phrase *you'd give me your opinion* says, "You and your thoughts are important, and I believe I could learn from them." Understand that sentence. Use it and watch a willing world place itself in the palm of your hand.

Never, never forget that the first rule of prospecting is to never assume that someone can't help you build your business. What about dear old Aunt Gertrude? At 78 she may not be much of a candidate for the washboard abs video you're selling, but what about the young people she teaches at church or the joggers and speed-walkers she meets at the park or cousin Fred in Illinois who happens to call Aunt Gertrude every week! She knows people who need the product or service you provide. The question you should be asking yourself is this: Who do I know who knows the people I want to do business with?

Getting reacquainted with acquaintances

After going through your list of friends and family, you're ready to focus on acquaintances. Acquaintances include business and social associates, people with whom you do business, such as the dry cleaner or the cashier at the grocery store, and anyone you meet or with whom you strike up a conversation — even the guy next to you in line at the coffee shop.

Stop for a minute and think about all the people you meet (or could potentially meet) every day or week who may benefit from owning your product. If they can't benefit, they probably know someone who can, and you probably can at least get a referral.

Prospecting isn't selling. Just have a pleasant conversation and let people know what you do. If you use your day-to-day contacts and take advantage of the opportunities that appear to simply step up and say hello, you'll be amazed at the doors that will swing wide open for you.

How many people do you meet in a day?

You may be surprised by the number of potential client leads or referrals you can get just from casual conversation with the people you run into on a given day. Take a look at the following list of people you can meet while doing your daily business:

✔ **Getting the morning paper:** Neighbors, joggers, people walking pets

✔ **Taking the kids to school:** Teachers, coaches, other parents, crossing guards, office personnel

✔ **Getting a haircut:** Stylists, other customers, styling-product representatives

✔ **At your annual physical:** Doctors, nurses, people in the waiting room

✔ **At the civic group luncheon:** Businesspeople, guest speakers, and waiters and waitresses

✔ **During a trip to the bank:** Tellers, people in line, loan officers, the person you help with a flat tire in the parking lot

✔ **At the grocery store:** Checkout clerks, stock clerks, people demonstrating new products, more people in line

✔ **At a fast-food restaurant:** Clerks, neighbors from down the street, and everyone else in line

✔ **While picking up the baby-sitter:** The sitter's parents and, of course, the sitter

✔ **At a church meeting:** Pastors, deacons, church members

Get the picture?

Tapping into business contacts

Become an active member in one or more of the business clubs and organizations in your community. (See Chapter 7 for details on networking.) Join one of your local chamber of commerce committees that organizes semi-social events designed to help business people. Check out your own industry to see whether it has any trade associations. These groups can provide up-to-date information about business trends, valuable notices of who's who and who's doing what, classes and seminars, and a variety of opportunities for you to increase your networking efforts.

Many cities also have a number of networking clubs where people in noncompetitive businesses meet informally to exchange business cards and actively seek new business in a relaxed atmosphere. Usually, one member of the club makes a presentation about his or her business or service, and there's time to meet and greet other members.

Develop solid relationships with the people you meet in these organizations. You may even find it easier to get to the heart of the matter with these folks than with people you know socially. After all, they're in business to do business and expect to hear sales presentations.

Talking to salespeople who serve you

Who meets more people and who has more potential for acquiring leads than a salesperson? If you're a client of several salespeople and aren't in competitive businesses, why not get other salespeople on your team? Find an appropriate time to discuss sharing leads. Or ask them to keep you in mind the next time an opportunity to recommend your product or service comes along. Naturally, you offer to provide the same service in return. You can soon build a small army of allies by making and aggressively working these contacts.

Prospecting through other businesses

People in business love to be appreciated, to have their skills, abilities, and services praised by their satisfied clients. Smart businesspeople display letters of praise on bulletin boards, in frames on the walls, in portfolios that they show to their new potential clients, and even in their advertising and promotional materials. When you receive excellent service, draft a well-written letter to the owner or manager of that business, expressing your satisfaction. Other people will probably see that letter, take note of your professionalism and courteous attitude, and perhaps remember you when they require your services.

If nothing else, you'll have made a positive impression on someone doing business in your community, someone who will at some time be in a position to make an enthusiastic referral.

Helping those wanting to replace a product

One strategy devised by Tom Hopkins for working with past clients is called the *itch cycle*. Many people buy new products for reasons that have nothing whatsoever to do with having a real need for replacements. With some folks, for example, having the newest product is a matter of status. They don't want to just keep up with the Joneses; they want to run circles around the Joneses. Some people just want to be on the cutting edge. They have to have the latest and greatest gizmo or technology. How many people do you know who define themselves by logos, owning, wearing, and driving only the brand names that fit their conception of themselves.

People naturally want to improve the quality of their lives. By recognizing how they define quality, you can succeed by providing them with the latest and greatest of whatever they crave. Keep in mind, however, that your approach is critical. Don't call your client to say, "I've got something better than the whatchamacallit I sold you last year." This approach belittles your company and product and your clients' intelligence, and you run the risk of alienating good clients who may have been delighted with their (then) state-of-the-art purchases. You may not only lose Bob as a client; you may also lose any referrals he could have provided.

Try a smarter approach:

> YOU: Bob, this is Larry down at Stereo City. I'm calling to see if you're still enjoying that SuperBoom surround system you got last year.
>
> CLIENT: Hi, Larry. Oh, yeah. It's great. I have it on all the time.
>
> YOU: That's great. I know you invested a lot of your time and effort into researching the equipment at the time to find just the right one for you. Because I value your judgment, Bob, I'd like to get your opinion on something new we may be offering.
>
> CLIENT: What's that, Larry?
>
> You then describe the latest and greatest, getting Bob so excited that he can't wait to jump in his car and head down to Stereo City tonight.

Anything new — innovations, upgrades, new technologies — can trigger your clients' itches. Ring up good old Bob, and ring up that sale!

Book II:
Prospecting
for Gold

Touching base with old clients

When salespeople change jobs or divisions, or get promoted, some of their happy clients may fall through the cracks and never get called on for repeat business — a situation that happens far too often with turnover and as companies grow and change. Similarly, old clients are too often forgotten as time passes after a sale. Think about how many times *you've* purchased a product or service that you were satisfied and happy with but then made your replacement purchase from another company. Maybe that original company just wasn't on your mind, or a salesperson from another company called at the right time. Whatever the reason, the first company *allowed* a sale to go to a competitor. Fortunately for you, these situations present real opportunities because these "forgotten" clients are excellent sources of new business.

Any business in operation for any length of time should have a healthy satisfied client list. Ask your manager whether those people whose salesperson no longer works there have been assigned to another salesperson. If not, ask for permission to contact them yourself. This group generally is a receptive audience for your message. After all, the people on this list have bought from your company before, and they're familiar with the company's products, service, and employees. If your organization has lived up to its promises, these people will want to do business with a company or brand they trust again and again and again.

Reading the newspaper for client leads

Millions of people sit down every morning with cups of coffee and their newspapers (print or online), never realizing that they have at their fingertips one of the greatest prospecting tools in the world. Here are some of the great leads you can find in the newspaper:

- ✔ **Key promotions and personnel changes in businesses:** Someone just promoted to vice president of XYZ Company is probably looking for a new wardrobe, maybe a more upscale automobile, or an advanced course in budgeting software. Perhaps the new job will entail significant travel, and she'll need airline tickets, hotel reservations, and an exceptional travel agent like you.

- ✔ **New businesses opening the doors:** The entrepreneur who just opened that little shop downtown is probably going to need a computer, a copier, a delivery service, office supplies, and customers!

- ✔ **Birth announcements:** The new parents are surely going to need items for the nursery, a minivan to cart the stuff around, and maybe even a new and bigger house. What about insurance, a college fund, and in a few months, a quiet weekend away without Junior?

All you need to do is drop the clipping in the mail with this note: "I saw you in the news. I'm in business in the community and hope to meet you someday in person. I thought you might appreciate having an extra copy of your article to share with friends or relatives." Don't forget to include your business card. Then follow up in a week or two with a phone call.

Getting to know service and support people

Get to know the customer service and support people in your own company because they're most often on the front lines of customer challenges, which you may be in a position to turn into opportunities. The people in your service and support departments frequently spend extended periods of time with your clients, often in the clients' places of business or homes. They may know about personnel changes and business expansions and have a wealth of insights into your clients' businesses that you can use. If your company provides services to individuals, the service and support folks can tell you about challenges your clients are having that could lead to new opportunities for you. So, debrief service or support technicians after they visit any of your clients.

**Book II:
Prospecting
for Gold**

Striking up conversations with strangers

Smart salespeople automatically classify anyone coming within 3 feet of them as a potential client. That's right. Unqualified, unknown strangers can turn into fully qualified, satisfied clients with remarkably little effort. All you need is the willingness to say hello and the ability to be a pleasant conversationalist. For more information on the 3-foot rule, refer to Book II, Chapter 2.

Never be discouraged by the fact that the person next to you is a stranger. After all, the very fact that you know nothing about this person means it's impossible to write him or her off as a potential client. You just don't know, so find out. How do you do this? Simply start a friendly conversation. Look for something to compliment: "If you don't mind my saying, that is a beautiful tie/ lovely purse/interesting lapel pin." Then keep the conversation going. Soon the appropriate moment for exchanging names will arrive naturally. That's also the appropriate moment to politely mention your business, product, or service, as these examples show:

- ✔ Have you been to John Doe's new store downtown? (Of course, you're John Doe or his number-one salesperson.)

- ✔ Don't you wish you could get designer suits at an economical price? (Your new acquaintance can if he orders directly from the manufacturer through your online service.)

- ✔ Wouldn't it be great to spend a couple weeks on the beach/in the mountains/out of town? (Your travel agency would be delighted to make the arrangements.)

The answers to the right questions are almost always yes. Then you have an opportunity to describe how your product or service exactly meets that need. You may not close the sale, but you'll have planted a seed and made a potentially valuable contact. You may even receive a call from a friend of that person: "I heard from my neighbor that you can get me a real deal on designer suits."

Sure, your sales average may not be very high with this approach, but it will be zero if you don't try. If you have time, even only a brief moment, what do you have to lose? If you *don't* make contact, the answer is "a sale."

Finding Potential Clients via Direct Mail

Direct mail, when used properly, can be one of the most effective ways to prospect, reinforce, sell, and just stay in touch with people you meet. The medium offers many proven benefits.

Although direct mail may seem expensive on a cost-per-contact basis, if it's done correctly (that is, it comes from a known source or is personalized to the needs or potential desires of the recipient), you have little or no waste audience. Unlike mass media such as television, radio, and newspapers, which reach thousands of people who aren't your market, direct mail goes precisely to the individuals you want to contact. Because you know exactly who every piece went to, you can precisely measure the success of your mailing. Plus, studies show that, when people get a piece of direct mail, they're receptive to receiving more from the sending company. You can easily become a known and welcome entity.

You can customize the piece to narrow segments of your market. For example, if you're a boat dealer advertising on television, you'd better promote a broad range of products to attract the attention of the broad range of viewers. In direct mail, you can target your efforts to only those people likely to be interested in canoes, ski boats, yachts, or even accessories.

Here are some questions that can help you acquire a list that will deliver the goods:

✔ **Is the list vendor a reliable firm?** Ask for references — preferably from someone or some company in a similar industry or your same geographical area. As with any other industry, direct mail has its share of top-notch companies and people, its share of fly-by-night organizations, and its charlatans. If you can't get any references, there's probably a very good (perhaps a very bad) reason.

✔ **How much is the list?** The amounts companies charge for their lists of names and addresses vary. They can range typically from 10¢ up to $1 per name, depending upon the information you get with the name. Most companies can give you age ranges or geographic areas; sometimes they can break the list out by education level or income levels.

Investments for lists can vary company to company. Shopping around never hurts, but make sure all things really are equal. A lower investment means very little if the vendor has a poor delivery system and your list arrives the day after your sales event.

✔ **What is the minimum order?** You can always expect a minimum order, and that, too, varies. Some companies may send you a test list of, say, 100 names so you can do an early mailing and see what type of response you get. Some require a minimum purchase of 1,000 names.

✔ **How accurate is the list?** Accuracy is everything. All your time, energy, creativity, and budget get wasted if the direct-mail piece doesn't get delivered to the right person. If you want to do business with the presidents of banks in your area, find out if the list directs your materials to the individual by name, to "President," to the bank's address, or just to "Occupant." Some of the more accurate list companies ask for any returned mail you get as a result of poor addresses, and they even reimburse you for your lost postage. The companies use the returns to keep their lists up-to-date.

✔ **When was the last time the list was updated?** The importance of this question depends on the stability of movement of the potential clients within your target area — but, obviously, the more recently updated the list, the better.

✔ **How are the lists organized?** You can buy a list for just about anyone organized by zip code, municipality, state, business or industry, organizations, clubs, interests . . . well, you name it and there's probably a list for it. Just take the time to make sure that you find and purchase the list that corresponds exactly to your needs. Why buy the entire town, when you need only the west side?

✔ **Does the list company offer additional services?** Many list companies sell only lists, but other list providers offer handling and postage services, pickup and delivery, and even a print shop. Again, look around, but also evaluate the convenience of one-stop shopping.

✔ **What formats are available?** In general, you can get a list in all kinds of formats, including computer formats or peel-and-stick labels. Some companies actually direct-print the name and address on the envelopes or postcards you'll use. Note that printed mail pieces are more effective than those with labels because they're more personal. Consider your budget but also the impression you want to make.

Book II: Prospecting for Gold

You really don't buy a list; you rent it, usually for one mailing at a time. Never try to slip by a fast one and use a one-time purchase twice. Mailing lists are "salted" with the people representing the list vendor who are on the lookout for exactly that kind of activity.

Going Directly to the Inbox: E-mail Marketing

Most sales organizations complement their direct mail and other hard-copy materials with e-mail marketing. Indeed, some businesses have dropped hard-copy promotional materials entirely and rely solely on Internet-based marketing tactics — websites, social media (Facebook, Twitter, LinkedIn, and so on), and e-mail to generate interest, leads, and, ultimately, sales.

E-mail marketing can be a highly effective sales tool, but only if you use it properly. In the following sections, you find some tips to make the most of your e-mail outreach efforts without running afoul of either e-mail regulations or the sensibilities of your prospective clients.

Understanding how people read e-mail

Like direct mail, e-mail campaigns can target specific types of prospects. And, also like direct mail, the most effective e-mail campaigns provide relevant information and a strong call to action.

Unlike direct mail, however, your e-mail readers may not be looking at the same thing when they open your communication. According to various surveys, about two-thirds of decision makers read e-mail on their cellphones, which means many of them may be reading text-only versions of your e-mail. Although smartphones and tablet computers have enhanced graphics capabilities, users who read e-mail on their mobile devices tend to prefer text-only e-mail because it's usually faster to download and easier to skim through.

What does that mean for you? Simply that content is king when it comes to e-mail marketing. Images are nice, but your text has to make sense without the pretty pictures because those pictures and graphics won't always be displayed. You can always send e-mail newsletters as plain text and include a link to a web-based version of your newsletter with all the fancy graphics.

Brief is better when it comes to e-mail. Most people — especially those who use Microsoft Outlook for e-mail — decide whether to open an e-mail by previewing it first, without opening it, so you want to get your point across in the first couple lines of your e-mail.

Those who don't have a preview option decide whether to open an e-mail — or delete it without reading it — based on the "From" and "Subject" headings. E-mails from recognizable sources with plain-language subject lines stand a much better chance of being opened and read than e-mails from a robotic-like address such as EZ-maillist-July-11@sellabunch.com. And recipients are more likely to automatically delete (or report as spam) e-mails whose subject lines include the words *free* or *money,* or whose subject lines are typed in all caps.

Making your e-mail campaign relevant

One school of e-mail marketing thought holds that personalizing your e-mails to each recipient increases the odds that people will open, read, and respond favorably to your e-mail. In fact, putting the recipient's name in the subject line doesn't significantly change responses to an e-mail campaign.

What *does* affect your response rate is relevance. If I'm in the market for what you're selling, chances are, I'll open and read your e-mail. If I'm not ready to buy right now, but I'm thinking about buying in the next few weeks or months, I'll either open your e-mail or flag it so I can read it later. However, if you send me information that I don't need and can't use, regardless of the medium, I'm going to ignore it.

Relevant e-mail communications do the following:

- ✔ **Have an engaging, value-oriented subject line.** "Three Tips for Getting Fiscally Fit" is more intriguing — and has a greater perceived value — than "Call me to schedule your fiscal checkup." Your subject line should always be geared toward the prospect's needs, rather than your sales goals.

- ✔ **Provide clear, concise information.** Remember that many people decide whether to open an e-mail based only on the first few lines they can read in the preview pane, and those who read e-mails on mobile devices prefer short, text-only communications. Get to the point, give your call to action, and get out.

- ✔ **Give the recipient a reason to act.** E-mail campaigns can be incredibly effective in directing potential clients to your website, Facebook page, or blog (see Book VII, Chapter 7), but you have to give them a reason to go there. Your call to action should focus on serving the prospect, not yourself. "Like us on Facebook" doesn't serve the prospect. "Subscribe to our newsletter for special discounts" provides a benefit to the prospect, not just to you.

Respecting e-mail recipients' rights

Spammers have given e-mail marketing a bad rap, but surveys indicate that many people appreciate receiving relevant, useful e-mails from companies and individuals they trust. Recipients' biggest concerns are privacy and the ability to stop receiving e-mails they don't want.

As a salesperson, you have a responsibility to respect the rights of your e-mail recipients. Every e-mail marketing piece should contain a brief privacy policy statement (with a link to the full policy) and a way for recipients to opt out of your e-mail mailing list. The opt-out can be as simple as a link to an e-mail address where recipients can send an "unsubscribe" message.

The opt-out function isn't optional for e-mail marketers; the CAN-SPAM Act requires all commercial e-mails to provide recipients with an opt-out in every piece of e-mail.

Ideally, your e-mail campaigns should include an opt-in function, too. With a *single opt-in* function, recipients simply submit their e-mail address to your mailing list, and they automatically begin receiving your e-mails. With a *double opt-in,* recipients submit their e-mail address and then receive a confirmation e-mail from you, usually with a validation link that they have to click before they're added to your mailing list. Double opt-in is a longer process, but it helps prevent erroneous subscriptions and lowers the risk of your communications being labeled as spam.

Using News Media to Drum Up Prospects

How do you think all those notices get in the paper or on the TV or radio? News organizations can't cover all the events, pound every street, or attend even a fraction of the meetings that occur in any town. Smart people and organizations don't wait for reporters to come to them. They deliver the goods to the news media themselves. You can do the same thing, too — it's called public relations.

By making the job easier for reporters, editors, and producers, you stand a good chance of getting your story told. You don't have to have a degree in journalism, a friend on the paper or at the news station, or a big advertising budget, either. All you need is a respect for the medium, an understanding of how to get the information to them in a format that they can use, a willingness to promote yourself or your business, and a bit of information about how the system works.

Picking a medium for your message

The media can cover short notices such as promotions, transfers, expansions, and new product lines. They also may be good places for interesting articles about you, your product or service, or some fascinating fact related to your business. But to work with the media, you need to understand how each medium works.

Radio

Some stations are all news; others use large blocks of time, such as the noon hour, for expanded news coverage. Most stations provide only five minutes of news and weather and traffic once an hour. Much of that time has to be devoted to the big stories of the day. That leaves precious little time to tell the world that you've moved your location to serve your clients better. Getting free publicity through the radio can be tough unless you tie your company to a local charity or fundraising event (see the later section "Producing an eye-catching release" for info on how to inform a radio station about your involvement). Alternatively — and if your budget can support it — consider sponsoring opportunities.

Book II: Prospecting for Gold

Television

Television stations generally devote more time to news. Don't neglect the special programming opportunities such as public affairs shows or popular local events, even if this means you have to wake up with the chickens to be on the air. Your potential clients may be watching television at that time.

Send a press release that lets the station know you're fun and interesting and you have a great message to share with the community (not just that you're having a sale on gel pens.) Follow up your release with a phone call to the person responsible for the appropriate segment of the news. Establishing yourself as a credible, trustworthy, and flexible resource may get you on the news more than once.

Television is a visual medium, and the producers, editors, and reporters think about what makes for "good video." Why do you think fires receive such great coverage? Smoke and flames and scurrying firefighters in bright yellow suits make for interesting pictures, even if the blaze is in an old house abandoned in 1942. Therefore, when you take a news story to TV stations, you're more likely to find yourself flying through the airwaves toward your potential clients' living rooms if you deliver a visual hook. Good visual hooks include action — lots of it. Show your product in action: Show people (preferably happy ones) using it, include testimonials, show graphics of statistics. Talk as if this is the most exciting news of the day. Also, always smile while delivering your message — unless you're selling cemetery services. The smile carries over as enthusiasm in your voice.

Newspapers

Newspapers carry more news word for word than any other medium. In fact, the amount of news in the average half-hour TV news program doesn't fill up a single page in the average newspaper. If you want your story covered in a newspaper, keep these points in mind:

- ✔ **Contact the newspaper before pulling together your story.** Find out whether it has a particular format or preferred style for submissions. Some newspapers have forms you can fill out.

- ✔ **Always send your information in to the newspaper in advance of your event.** If the newspaper feels the story warrants more extended coverage, the lead time gives the newspaper time to prepare.

- ✔ **Include a current, professional photo of yourself (maybe in front of your place of business) and your product with the news item.** Don't rely on the newspaper to dig up a shot, or you may end up with an old high school photo! Clearly identify the names of the people in the photo and the name of the product, if you've included it.

Magazines

Many larger cities have local or regional publications devoted to the business community, the arts and entertainment, homes and gardens, and the general public. These publications often carry short notices such as promotions, transfers, expansions, and new product lines. They also may be good places for interesting articles about you, your product or service, or some fascinating fact related to your business.

Many magazines are monthly or quarterly publications, so timeliness isn't quite as important as in other media. In addition, many such publications use full-color photographs, which always will present you in a better light. Magazine editors also may be more selective in the information they print, which can give you an added bit of celebrity status just for getting in the issue — especially if you're in a feature article.

Attracting clients with press releases

After you've identified which media you want to pursue, you're ready to write and distribute a press release announcing a major product release, a new service, a change in management, or any other newsworthy item.

Producing an eye-catching release

The news that's "fit to print" is generally the news that reporters and editors can use with the least amount of hassle. That means you need to produce a ready-to-go fact sheet in the proper format, with correct spelling, and using the king's own English. It also should include the kinds of facts listed in Table 3-1.

Table 3-1	Checklist of Media Information
For the Individual Prospector	**For a Small Business**
Name	Name
Occupation/job title	Contact name and phone number
Number of years in sales	Location
Sales volume	Number of years in business/in the community
Type of industry represented	Number of people employed; annual payroll
Particular product represented	Sales volume
Family	Brief description of major product
Community involvement	Community involvement and/or impact
Accomplishments	Awards won
	Future growth plans

**Book II:
Prospecting
for Gold**

You can write this information like a story. If you choose to do so, keep the following bits of advice in mind:

- ✔ **Choose your title carefully.** The term *Important News Release* raises the hackles of any editor. Editors decide what is and isn't important. Use the term *For Immediate Release* instead. If the information should not be published until a certain date, simply write *For Release On [fill in the blank with the correct date]*. And use *News Release* instead of *Press Release*.

- ✔ **Include key information.** Here are some details to put at the top of your release:

  - • **City, state, and date:** Begin the first paragraph with this information. Location and time set the stage for the rest of what you have to say.

  - • **Contact information:** Always place the name of a contact person and a phone number at the top of your releases. That way, if the editor gets excited about the story and wants to expand it or follow up on it, he has the contact info at his fingertips.

- ✔ **Write your release in what is called the *inverted pyramid* style.** That means that you place the biggest, most important news at the top of the page and the least important news at the bottom. News editors often trim stories by starting at the bottom and moving up.

- ✔ **Limit your release to a single page.** You have very little time to make your point. Remember, your goal is to convince people who read the release to call you. The best press releases are 300 to 750 words long.

Leave out all the fluff. Flowery descriptions may please the subject of your release, but they won't please the editor who may delete them. Similarly, leave out information that isn't relevant to the story.

✔ **Don't advertise.** A press release is an announcement worthy of the news, not an advertisement for products or services.

✔ **Do not write "the end" at the end of the release.** Just center the word *end* at the bottom or use the journalist's symbol for the same thing (—30—) centered at the bottom.

After you've written and carefully edited your press release, you have to find some way to get it into the media channels. One option is to hand-deliver your release to the proper reporter or editor. Although old-school, this strategy may get you the attention you crave if you can actually spend a few minutes with the news decision maker. Other options involve filing story information according to instructions on the publication, television, or radio website. Alternatively, several companies offer such services, including PRWeb (www.prwebdirect.com), RISMedia (www.rismedia.com), and 24-7 Press Release (www.24-7pressrelease.com). You can search the web for "press release distribution" or other related words and phrases to find a hundred other such companies.

Following up after delivering your release

After you send off your most professionally prepared news release with appropriate and eye-catching photos, half your job is finished. Now you need to persistently and professionally follow up your submission to ensure that it lands in the right hands and is actually seen. Here's how:

✔ **Make a quick call to the intended recipient.** Say that you're just checking to see if the release was received and offering to be available to answer any questions that may arise.

✔ **Send a thank-you note after this contact.** Do so even if the contact was made by voicemail or e-mail.

✔ **Don't call daily, don't call the intended party's superior, and don't complain if your information isn't published.**

✔ **Update the information and send it again in about a month.**

Don't Forget — or Neglect — the Referrals!

A "sure thing" doesn't exist in this world of ours, but referral sales come pretty darn close. People in sales know referrals are significantly easier to meet with, talk to, follow up, and get an agreement from than any person contacted through a cold call. Many people don't realize just how much the math works in favor of referrals. Of course, working with referred leads doesn't mean your work is any easier, but you do get a considerably higher return for the same effort. It's like finding a couple extra workdays in every week.

Studies show that the closing rate with nonqualified prospects is only 10 percent. However, the closing rate with qualified referrals is 60 percent! As they say down at the track, "How's about *them* odds?"

Yet even experienced salespeople often shy away from asking for referrals. Some salespeople assume happy clients will simply volunteer referrals. Some feel that it's impolite to ask for anything further once a sale has been closed. Some fear that asking for referrals may offend clients. Some may even suffer from cowardice or laziness. But all the excuses, all the dissembling, all the "good" reasons for not getting referrals really boil down to just two:

✔ The request for referrals is inadequate.

✔ The request is never made.

Like sales, referrals are something you have to make happen. The following sections tell you how.

Don't trick yourself into thinking that selling to a referral is a sure thing. If you take referrals for granted and don't treat them with the respect with which you treat your other clients, you're displaying an unprofessional attitude and doing a real disservice to the people who make referrals by making them look bad for referring someone so ill prepared, out of touch, and overconfident.

Where to look for referrals

Where do you get referrals? Take off your Sherlock Holmes deerstalker cap, put away the oversized magnifying glass, and put the bloodhounds back in the kennel. There's no need to go looking for the trail of the referrals. They're all around you, everywhere, every day. Think not? Then take a look around:

✔ **Family and friends:** These people are probably the easiest, most accessible source of referrals you have, yet they may be the ones you resist asking the most. But if your product is good and you're personally dedicated to superior customer service, why should you deny those things to people who need them?

✔ **People you network with:** Most professional, business, and civic groups have regular meetings for handshaking, backslapping, and wolfing down chicken and peas. Smart salespeople use these meetings for networking to obtain referrals. Volunteer to work on committees and special projects that can put you in touch with a different group from your "regular crowd" and provide even more opportunities.

**Book II:
Prospecting
for Gold**

✔ **People you meet anywhere:** You can use any kind of gathering to interact with even more people: concerts, religious or school functions, recreation, sports, hobby clubs, and similar group meetings or get-togethers to interact with even more people. Even Saturday's game of golf, the fishing trip, and the annual Girl Scout planning session can provide you with a wealth of contacts and opportunities for referrals.

✔ **Satisfied customers:** What do most people want to do the moment they buy something? They want to talk about it. Can there ever be a better time to get referrals than when excited buyers show their new whatchamacallits to anyone and everyone within earshot? Your job on the day of the sale is to ask who he'll be showing off to right away and get those referred names now!

Satisfied customers can't give you solid-gold referrals unless you continue to provide them with solid-gold service. If you don't take care of your customers, or if you engage in unethical business practices, word spreads. Satisfied customers may tell only three people about their positive experiences with you. Dissatisfied customers go out of their way to tell 11 people about their unpleasant experiences!

✔ **Customers who *didn't* buy your product or service:** Sometimes things just don't work, and you don't make the sale. Her decision to not buy from you may have had nothing to do with you or your product. If, in the course of your interactions with this client, you provided exemplary service and built a friendly rapport, there's no reason why you can't ask whether she would be willing to give your business card to, say, three of her friends or acquaintances who may be interested in your product.

If you leave a client's place of business without referrals, you haven't done your job to the best of your abilities. It's a bit like having a great meal at a fine restaurant, but walking out before the dessert cart rolls by. You've had a good experience, but look at all the goodies you've let pass you by.

✔ **Other salespeople:** Don't subscribe to the theory that the competition is the enemy. Professional salespeople are always in a position to refer business to others, and they want to refer people to fellow professionals. They also know that those other professionals will someday, somehow, return the favor. That's how this game is played.

✔ **Attendees at engagements for which you're one of the speakers:** If you get a reputation as being very good at something, such as sales, people want to hear what you have to say. Business and civic clubs, seminars, and schools all are looking for experts to impart valuable knowledge. If you can handle yourself in front of a crowd, you can look at these speaking engagements as fine ways to bring in referrals. Anyone who becomes a speaker automatically becomes an expert.

Getting referrals in six steps

Getting a referral is like climbing a ladder. You step up to the top one rung at a time. The referral ladder has six rungs:

1. **Isolate the referrals' faces for your prospects.**

   If you ask outright for the names of referrals, your unfocused customers will probably draw blanks. You have to channel their thoughts into specifics — the people who they realize need your product or service. For example, instead of saying, "You don't know anybody else who needs cable-pulling equipment, do you?" say, "Is there anyone in your trade association who may be considering moving their overhead wires underground?"

   Also, have a pen and paper ready when you ask for a referral. This alone will prompt referral sources to think harder about who they might know.

2. **Write the referrals' names on cards or enter them into your contact list.**

   Make sure that you get the correct spellings and pronunciations of all names.

3. **Qualify the referrals.**

   You must get all the information you can about the needs of the referral so that you can provide real service rather than what you think the referral may need. For example, ask simple questions, such as, "What made Mr. Jackson of ABC Company come to your mind?" Your prospect may reply, "We talked at the last association meeting. I told him what we were considering, and he said it was a project on his list, too."

4. **Ask for referrals' contact information.**

   People usually refer others whom they know well enough to also know how to reach them. But if your clients don't know all the information, get as much as you can, such as the referrals' streets or neighborhoods — any kind of information that will help you locate them.

5. **Ask your clients to set up an appointment or introduction with referrals.**

   The purpose of having your existing, happy client set up the appointment is so that she can introduce you to the referral. Many people are much more welcoming with someone they know.

   You're probably thinking, "But I just can't ask somebody to make an appointment for me!" Yes, you can, and all you have to do is ask. Nothing can be more simple. If your clients don't mind doing that, proceed immediately. However, if they are the least bit hesitant, back off and relieve the pressure with Step 6.

TIP

Book II:
Prospecting
for Gold

6. Ask to use the happy clients' names when you call the referrals.

People may not be willing to make calls for a number of reasons. They may not know the other individuals very well. They may just be shy or even afraid of making a sales-related call. Asking for permission to use their names when you call referrals takes them off the hook, so to speak. Few people will be willing to call, but most will be more than willing to allow you to use their names.

This system will work for you, but you have to use it, and you have to use it every time you make contact with prospects and customers. Learn it, practice it, and have faith in it.

Chapter 4

Prospecting for Untapped and Under-Tapped Markets

*W*hen you run out of leads, you may be tempted to think that you've run out of market. You can discover additional opportunities, however, in untapped and under-tapped markets — opportunities you may not have considered yet.

In their early days, for example, cellphones were primarily used for business. They quickly made their way into the home markets, and now even kids are packing cellphones. Why? Because clever marketing people were able to convince families that a cellphone is an essential communication tool for every single family member. When these marketing folks discovered they were running out of road, they made more road.

Whatever you happen to sell, you usually can find untapped or under-tapped markets that could use your product but simply don't know about it. This chapter encourages you to explore other markets and provides several clues on where to begin looking for ideas.

Seeing Business Where It Isn't

Sales opportunities don't exactly slap you in the face. They're extremely difficult to notice because opportunities, by their very nature, are vacuums — they're invisible. You have to train your mind to look for the signs of a vacuum and, even better, envision something filling that open space. You have to train yourself to see business where it isn't.

To see business where it isn't, you need to look for markets that you and your competitors are not serving. Some people can naturally think of a thousand and one ways to market a product, but you don't have to be born with a gift for it. You can train your mind to look for business where it isn't and spot new opportunities. Here are some suggestions that can open you to new sales and marketing opportunities:

- **Look for trouble.** As a salesperson, you're selling solutions. Find a group of people with a problem that your product or service can solve, and you've discovered a new market. In the real-estate business, for example, you may see problem areas, like foreclosure, probate, and divorce, as opportunities to build up entirely new communities.

- **Network extensively.** People often talk about their problems because they hope that someone can solve them or simply want to vent some frustration. In either case, networking enables you to hear more problems and discover more opportunities for solving those problems. Networking also can open you up to partnerships that may lead to other markets. (For detailed information on the benefits of networking, as well as how to build and maintain a network, head to Book II, Chapter 2.)

- **Read extensively.** Reading articles, especially articles that seem to have nothing to do with what you're selling, often can make your mind more receptive to opportunities.

- **Juxtapose two or more ideas.** Sometimes, neither of two separate ideas or technologies can open any doors for you, but when you combine the two, something magical happens — sort of like combining chocolate and peanut butter.

Become a lifetime learner to continuously open yourself to new ideas, markets, and opportunities. Get out there and find out what's happening. Seek out the most recent trends and discover ways to tap into their momentum. Only by becoming a lifelong learner is this possible. Fill your mind, keep it active, and it will do the rest for you, intuitively making the connections that open the doors to new opportunities.

Considering a Different Demographic

Are you serving all markets, regardless of race, ethnicity, beliefs, or lifestyle choices? If you're not, then you're not tapping the full potential of your consumer base. You may be completely unaware that your marketing materials target a particular group of people at the expense of missing opportunities with different groups. By catering to these under-served customers, you often can win over a huge market segment that your competitors have neglected. The following sections explain how.

Targeting a generation

Salespeople often focus on people who are part of the same generation they are. Plastered all over their brochures, websites, and other marketing materials are people who look and dress just like them. After all, selling anything is easier when you're selling it to someone you have more in common with. When you're looking to boost sales, however, you may need to be more accommodating in both your marketing and sales. The following sections offer tips on how to bridge the generation gap.

Book II:
Prospecting
for Gold

Every generation has a set of common experiences, values, and way of doing things that distinguish it from past and future generations. By remaining sensitive to these differences, as discussed in the following sections, you can market and sell more effectively to people from different generations.

G.I. Generation, born 1901–1924

The G.I. Generation experienced the two Great Wars — World War I and World War II — and managed to survive the Great Depression. People in this generation tend to be frugal, respect traditional values, and generally own their homes, which they don't plan on selling any time soon.

When selling to the G.I. Generation, be prepared to focus on quality and value. Most of the customers in this category are likely to be living on fixed incomes and are very focused on making their money last.

Silent Generation, born 1925–1945

The so-called Silent Generation was born and raised between two great periods of global upheaval — the two World Wars and the Vietnam Era, complete with its Cold War. They may not have fought in the Great Wars, but they certainly suffered through them and, perhaps as a result, came to value family and security above all else. Because of this, the Silent Generation has been officially labeled the generation of the "withdrawn, cautious, unimaginative, indifferent, unadventurous, and silent."

When marketing and selling to people in the Silent Generation, keep the following information in mind:

✔ Risk assessment is likely to play a major role in the purchase decision.

✔ Work ethic is highly valued. Don't be late, and be prepared to work hard to gain your client's respect.

✔ Treat your clients with respect, addressing them as Mr., Mrs., or Miss, followed by their last names. These folks are likely to prefer being treated more formally.

✔ Be prepared to talk about costs. This generation grew up during tough times when food and other goods were rationed. They're generally very conscious of price and value.

✔ Speak and act conservatively.

✔ Focus on convenience, simplicity, ease of use, service, and support.

✔ Present your products and services with a "you earned it" message. Give them permission to spend their money.

✔ Don't waste their time.

✔ Face-to-face meetings are generally most productive.

✔ Although people of this generation may be fairly affluent retirees, they are living in a time when medical advances have greatly increased life expectancies, and many worry about outliving their savings. Depending on what you're selling, this could be good or bad, but you should be aware of it.

Don't assume that the Silent Generation is technologically illiterate. Many members of this generation are quite skilled on the computer and spend hours on the Internet, even using "hip" social media sites like Facebook, Twitter, and YouTube. And whatever you do, don't refer to them as "seniors."

Baby boomers, born 1946–1964

Baby boomers grew up during a time of unprecedented wealth and freedom that happened to collide with the perceived hypocrisy of the world around them. As a result, they collectively formed what's often referred to as the "Me Generation," relying on the guidance of their own inner visions and resources rather than what society was telling them. Baby boomers generally feel a sense of entitlement; they deserve the "good life" and believe that they have what it takes to ensure it.

When marketing and selling to baby boomers, take an approach that's more in line with their thinking and the way they perceive the world. Here are some suggestions:

✔ Appeal to the boomers' sense of independence and rebelliousness.

✔ Play up the convenience of products. Boomers are money rich and time hungry. They crave anything that will save them time and effort.

✔ To boomers, the Internet is a tool, not an end in itself. Although some boomers are geeks, most simply see technology as a necessity.

However, like most people, boomers like to socialize online and off, so build a strong presence via social media — blogging, Facebook, Twitter, YouTube, and so on. Book VII, Chapter 7 offers suggestions for how to tap into the power of social media.

✔ Keep it simple. Provide boomers with enough information to make a well-informed purchase decision without burying them in details. *Remember:* They don't have time for that.

✔ Don't quote "company policy" as a reason you *can't* do something your customer requests. Boomers don't trust organizations and think of rules and policies as a way of controlling them. Flexibility is key.

✔ External image is important to boomers. Even if they try to play it down, possessions, status, and appearances count.

✔ Boomers tend to be less trusting than other generations, so communicate honestly and openly and be prepared to answer questions. If the boomer senses that you're not genuine, you haven't got a chance.

✔ Word-of-mouth referrals carry a great deal of weight with this group, both in real and virtual communities like Facebook, so network effectively. See Book II, Chapter 2 for additional guidance on developing productive relationships.

Generation X, born 1965–1976

Generation X has been saddled with all the problems caused by the G.I. and Silent generations that the baby boomers have failed to fix. At least that's how they see it. In addition, they're facing a future of increased insecurity and decreased financial opportunities while having to deal with the media labeling them as slackers.

Xers have grown accustomed to a chronically unstable job market, protected neither by the government nor the unions. As a result of this and increased opportunities via the Internet, they've become much more entrepreneurial. Some estimates claim that Xers start 70 percent of the new businesses in the United States.

When marketing and selling to Gen Xers, keep the following information in mind:

✔ Most Xers shop online or at least do some portion of their product research online when making a purchase decision. Online buyers comparison-shop and value the convenience and time savings of shopping online. Consider all this when formulating an online sales strategy.

✔ Gen Xers are also very much engaged in social networking, and, whether they're buying online or off, they look to their online communities for advice and recommendations. Make sure you have a strong presence online, especially in social media and networking venues like Facebook, Twitter, and YouTube.

✔ Reassure Xers that they're making a savvy purchase or investment decision. Xers tend to feel insecure about their decisions.

✔ Give Xers more control. They tend not to be team players and may
cringe at long-term commitments. Forcing them to sign a multiyear commitment for service may scare them off.

✔ Offer time-saving solutions. Xers aren't slackers, but they will seize any
opportunity to perform a task in less time with less effort so they can go
back to having fun.

✔ Present information in snippets, avoiding any kind of lengthy discourse.

✔ Brutal honesty trumps any slick marketing and advertising. Xers
demand an honest, straightforward presentation that's fun and unique
without being pretentious.

Generation Y, born 1977–1994

Although the members of Generation Y were born later, they're a step ahead
of their Gen X parents and siblings in terms of technology and communications. When you're marketing and selling to members of Generation Y, the
Internet and newer communications technologies are even more important:

✔ Never underestimate a Yer's reliance on technology for massive
amounts of information.

✔ Yers are truly democratic. They don't rely on traditional establishments
to tell them what's safe to buy. They rely more on community, especially
online, virtual communities for referrals.

✔ Yers are open to all forms of communication, including face-to-face,
cellphones, text messaging, and instant messaging. The more communications media you can handle, the better able you are to accommodate
their needs.

✔ Maximize the use of multimedia marketing. Yers require a lot of sensory
stimulation to stay interested in whatever you're selling. Whatever you
do, don't bore them with a stodgy presentation.

✔ Be clear, to the point, and assertive in your presentations. Yers have
grown up in the high-velocity Internet/technology age and expect presentations and marketing messages to be clear and concise. Where
boomers will resist being told what to do, Yers like being told what you
think they should do — not leaving it up them to figure out — and then
they'll decide if they'll do it or not. Xers, on the other hand, will want to
ask someone else what she would do before taking action.

Yers grew up downloading music, video, podcasts, and a host of other media
and information from the Internet for free. Be prepared to deliver quality,
dynamic content to win their business. Any technology working in an inferior
manner loses Yers in a nanosecond. The Boomers will assume if technology

doesn't work, it's about their competency. Xers and Yers assume if it doesn't work, the technology is broken.

Generation Z, born 1995–20??

Those born from the mid-1990s to the present are considered members of Generation Z, which is sometimes referred to as Generation I (Generation Internet). In terms of marketing and sales, they're almost identical to Gen Yers, discussed in the previous section, but to a greater degree.

One unique characteristic of this generation is that it surfs the ever-changing wave of technology. During the writing of this book, the wave was driving a convergence of online and offline marketing and sales and a merging of communications media. For example, a client may find you online via the Internet and carry you along via cellphone or some other electronic communications device. Customers are now able to download coupons to their cellphones and have them scanned at the store or use electronic devices to engage in real-world games to win products and other incentives.

To appeal to Gen Zers, stay on top of the current technology and use it in creative ways to engage and incentivize customers and clients.

Book II: Prospecting for Gold

Selling to the disabled

When your competitors are busy avoiding the disabled, do yourself a favor and embrace them. This under-served market demands some attention and service, and you could be the one salesperson in your area who provides it for them. In addition to increasing sales, you receive a much more valuable benefit — the friendship of entire groups of people who have a very unique perspective and something to offer that you can't get anywhere else.

If you have a disability, you already know this, but for those who don't have the advantage of the insight that comes with the experience, keep in mind that most people who have a disability don't want to be treated any differently than anybody else. You may need to adapt in some way, however, so you can provide them with the same level of enthusiasm and service you offer your other clients. Consider using assistive technology — a teletype machine, for example, that can help you communicate with clients who can't hear. Also, remember that you can't change the situation these clients are in, so don't try, and don't pity them. Just adapt to their needs. Every time you do, you open yourself to a new and valuable relationship and a host of new opportunities.

Overcoming racial and ethnic barriers

Some salespeople actually let their prejudices get in the way of making money, even though green should be the only color they see when they're selling. If your goal is to maximize your profit, what difference does it make who buys it? If someone wants your product, offers you the right price for it, and is intent on closing the transaction, why on earth would you not grab that deal?

To seize your share of the multicultural market, adjust your practices to meet the unique needs of people who have come here from all over the globe: Hispanics, African Americans, Asians, Middle Easterners, and other groups. Collectively, these minorities in America buy nearly $2 trillion in goods and services every year. Following are some basic suggestions that can help you when you're meeting someone from a culture you're unfamiliar with:

- ✔ **When you greet people from outside your own culture, never assume anything.** Greet your customer verbally, let your customer make the first move (if you have to, hesitate a moment to see what the customer does), and then follow his lead. In the Unites States, we often assume that a firm handshake is universal, but that's a Western custom. The most common greeting in the world is the bow, not the handshake. Joining hands can actually be offensive to people who don't believe in touching people they don't know.

- ✔ **Pay attention to your customer's body language to detect clues about personal space.** You can't see it, but surrounding your body and extending out for anywhere from a few inches to several feet is an extension of your body commonly referred to as your *personal space*. Your body immediately identifies anyone crossing the border into that space as an intruder.

  In business situations in the United States, we stand about 2½ feet away from the other person. People from more formal countries in the same situation, including Japan, may stand about 4 feet away from each other. Conversely, people from the Middle East and Spanish-speaking countries tend to stand much closer than Americans are accustomed to — sometimes only 6 inches away.

  Instinctively, your body moves to constantly reestablish its comfort zone. Avoid this tendency when you work with customers from other cultures. Let them determine the personal space that's comfortable for them. If they step back after the greeting, get used to the distance and just speak a bit more loudly to bridge the gap. If they step toward you after your greeting, resist the temptation to back up — and be sure to have a breath mint handy.

- ✔ **Don't misinterpret the lack of eye contact as rudeness or lack of interest.** When a customer in the United States looks away, you're likely to think that the person isn't interested in what you have to say. That's because American culture teaches that establishing eye contact demonstrates interest and respect. Many groups, however, including the Vietnamese, Japanese, and Koreans, avoid direct eye contact as a way of showing respect. To them, looking someone in the eye is intrusive and rude. To honor the other party, they look down. In these situations, look down yourself and try to find something else your customer can look down at — the product itself, product brochures, rate charts, flyers, or other material.

Of course, not all cultures interpret eye contact or the lack of it the same way. Middle Easterners and Hispanics, for example, may crave even more direct eye contact than most Americans are used to. This can make the average salesperson in the United States feel as though the customer is being confrontational. Feeling challenged, you may become a little too aggressive or simply look away, and either move could jeopardize the sale. Simply adjust your eye contact accordingly. Mirror your customer.

- ✔ **Be aware that what's acceptable for a man is not always acceptable for a woman in other cultures.** Many traditional Middle Eastern, Indian, and Japanese women, for example, are distressed by touching any male who is not their husband, often because in their own country it's forbidden. So when you greet a woman from one of these cultures, avoid the natural urge to shake her hand; instead, nod respectfully in her direction to acknowledge her presence — unless, of course, she extends her hand to greet you.

- ✔ **If you have questions about your customer's culture, ask in a non-threatening way.** Chances are, your customer wants to talk about her culture to assist you in gaining understanding and acceptance, and perhaps even talk about something that's more interesting than the weather. You're likely to be very surprised at just how much you can discover about other cultures as well as how people from other cultures perceive your culture.

If you're going to ask one customer about her culture, ask all of them, including those who may not appear to be culturally different. You don't want to create the appearance of singling out anyone.

Going Global: Exploring International Markets

Today's global marketplace hasn't quite flattened the world, but it has made selling in foreign lands much easier. With the Internet and global shipping at your fingertips, you can create a web store from the comfort of your living room and sell and ship products to customers in Canada, Mexico, South America, Europe, Asia, and anywhere else.

You may not even have to ship the products yourself. By hooking up with a drop-ship supplier, you can sell the products, collect the money, and then have the supplier ship the products directly to your customers. With the world population at over six billion people, many of whom have Internet connections, just think of the potential boost in sales you would see if you could connect with even 1 percent of that market!

Before reaching out to the global market, I suggest you do the following:

✔ Research any laws that may govern the sale of your products in foreign lands.

✔ Consider establishing a partnership with foreign companies who sell the same or similar products or services.

✔ Address the language barrier. Although many people in other countries speak English, you may need to hire someone who speaks the native language to be most effective. Fortunately, in the United States, you usually can find someone who can fill the position.

If you're interested in marketing and selling products online, Wiley offers a small library that covers just about every aspect of Internet marketing and sales, including *Web Marketing All-in-One Desk Reference For Dummies* by John Arnold, Ian Lurie, Marty Dickinson, Elizabeth Marsten, and Michael Becker; *eBay For Dummies,* 6th Edition, by Marsha Collier; and *Buzz Marketing with Blogs For Dummies,* by Susannah Gardner (all published by Wiley).

Exploring Other Sales Channels

Customers want what they want, when they want it, and how they want to buy it — in a store, from a catalog, over the phone, online, at a shopping kiosk, or even from a handheld device. The way customers prefer to pay for their orders also varies. Some prefer to pay with cash or check, some buy everything with a credit or debit card, and online shoppers may enjoy the convenience of PayPal.

To appeal to the broadest selection of customers, accommodate a wider selection of preferences. If you sell goods primarily through a traditional bricks-and-mortar storefront, consider expanding to online sales. If you're selling online, you may be able to increase sales by opening a local store. Or if you're already selling online and through a local store, think about advertising in a magazine and having readers phone in their orders.

This is an age in which customers want to customize and personalize everything. Just look how popular ring tones have become. Just about everyone who owns a cellphone has it set up to play a different ring tone. This says a lot about customers — mainly, that people like options. By expanding your sales channels, you deliver goods however your customers want to order and pay for them.

Looking for Bundling Opportunities

Clever bundling of products and services often can make your products and services more appealing and seem more valuable. Here is some general guidance on how to select among different bundling options. The first step is to decide on the purpose of the bundle:

- **To attract new customers:** You often can use bundling to attract new customers by offering increased value or convenience or (as in the case of extended warranties) reducing the worry a customer has when making a major purchase.

- **To retain existing customers:** If your customer-retention rate is slipping, offering additional products and services at a reduced rate may boost revenue while increasing retention rates.

- **To bring ex-customers back to the fold:** Bundled products may be used to encourage ex-customers to try the service again, particularly if you've improved your products and services and prices have dropped since the time they left.

- **To introduce an unproven product to the market:** Bundling new, unproven products and services with highly successful ones is a common strategy for gaining market share.

Book II:
Prospecting
for Gold

The purpose of the bundle should drive your choice of which products and services to bundle and how to most effectively market the bundle. A bundle designed to introduce new products to the market is obviously going to differ from one that's designed to attract or retain customers.

The next step in introducing an appealing bundle is to select the products and services you want to bundle and then research the market to determine which bundling opportunity is likely to be most successful. Your market research should be designed to turn up information about the following:

- The market segments you want to target.

- The needs of those market segments.

- The product and service combinations that can best meet the needs of the targeted market segments. This may include checking out bundles that your competition is offering and determining how you can improve the bundle.

- The buying habits of the targeted market segments, so you have a clear idea of how to market and sell the bundle.

Partnering with other product or service providers

Bundling products doesn't always require that you have all the products and services available to piece together an attractive package. You may be able to partner with other businesses and salespeople who sell complementary offerings. A real-estate broker, for example, could partner with a mortgage broker to offer home buyers a one-stop solution to buying a home and securing the financing to pay for it. They could even bring a title company onboard to handle the closing or partner with builders to sell newly built homes.

Think creatively about what you're selling and what you can add without having to do any more work. And remain on the lookout for partnership opportunities. Whenever you notice that your customers tend to use certain goods and services that you don't offer, you have an opportunity to either add those products to your product line or team up with another business that offers those products and services. Just make sure you're not getting yourself into a conflict-of-interest situation and that the partnership offers your clients a real value-add.

Bundling doesn't mean giving away the store. You can bundle products and services and charge even more than if the customer purchased everything separately. The key is to put together a bundle that separates you from the competition and convinces your customer that your bundle has value that justifies (or more than justifies) the sticker price.

Chapter 5

Approaching Potential Clients without Scaring Them Away

In This Chapter

▶ Discovering how to keep potential customers open to you

▶ Communicating your message in a way that keeps the prospect engaged and interested

▶ Interacting with retail customers

Getting the ball rolling with a potential client is critical. Yet all salespeople know that the most challenging part of making a sale occurs when they approach people for the first time. What you say, how you say it, and how you handle your prospects' responses impact whether the initial meeting goes well and leads to further discussion or goes poorly and leads to a lost opportunity.

This chapter shows you ways to start a business conversation and keep your potential clients engaged and interested and gives advice on how to avoid common blunders that can lead to the prospect tuning you out.

Keeping Your Prospects Open — To You, That Is

Many people have an almost instinctive aversion to being approached by a salesperson. Think about it: No one particularly *likes* being sold something. The phrasing itself conjures images of being manipulated. So, the first thing you need to do is overcome the perception that you're out to sell anybody anything. Your goal is to make sure your prospective customers realize that what you really want to do is help them solve a problem or fulfill a need. The following sections explain how you can make your intentions clear and let the potential client know that you're a resource he can rely on.

Overcoming hurdles of your own making

To become a champion salesperson, you have two high, difficult hurdles to overcome: your ego and your desire to make money. To overcome these hurdles, follow these two suggestions:

> ✔ **Take yourself out of the picture every time you meet with a potential client.** Why you use your product or how you use your product means very little or nothing to anyone but you. Potential clients aren't looking for your personal endorsement. It's a given than you would endorse the product — after all, you want to sell it. They want the hard facts and figures on how your product can solve their challenges.

> ✔ **Always put your customers' needs ahead of your own natural desire for wealth.** In other words, get the dollar signs out of your eyes. Just as wild animals can smell fear, customers can smell greed. If they see even the slightest hint of selfishness in your eyes or sense even the tiniest amount of desperation in your voice, you've planted a seed of doubt in fertile soil. Any solid rapport you may have felt quickly fades away. The good relationship you've so carefully built soon begins to sour, and the genuine interest in your product turns into a series of rather obvious glances at wristwatches.

Most salespeople have trouble clearing these two hurdles because doing so requires that they change the way they think about their profession and their clients. But here's an exercise that can help: Put yourself in your prospect's shoes. First, make sure you know all you can about your prospect's company, its corporate history, its product line, possible plans for the future, and the personality of its management staff and your contact. Then imagine that the salesperson (you) has just made a presentation. Now ask the prospect (you, again) a series of questions, and answer as the prospect would:

> ✔ What will this product or service do to solve my immediate crisis?

> ✔ What will it do for the company in the long run? Will it increase profitability or enhance productivity?

> ✔ Are any downsides balanced by equal or better upsides?

> ✔ What's in it for me?

Sometimes you may work with an executive who must report to higher-ups for a final okay on making a purchase, and recommending your product could possibly put his job on the line, a concern that may outweigh all others. Even final decision makers have to report to management staffs, presidents, or boards of directors. That's why the "What's in it for me?" question is so important — it gets to the heart of the matter: What will the big guns think of me personally if I recommend or purchase this product or service?

If you have any doubt about your product's ability to do what the client needs, handle those doubts *before* the client recommends it to the higher-ups. If the decision makers okay the purchase of your product and it's a poor choice, the client could lose his job, and you lose your reputation with that client. And because an unhappy client will tell others about your poor performance, you could lose a lot of business overall. Don't take risks like that! If you can't answer all the questions to the potential client's benefit, go back and do some more homework.

Figuring out what your prospect wants

Numerous surveys have been conducted to find out what businesses really want from suppliers and representatives of their suppliers. Here, in no particular order, is a short list of what your prospects want from you:

- ✔ Being there when they need you
- ✔ Timely response and prompt return of phone calls
- ✔ Honesty and sincerity
- ✔ Product, industry, and market knowledge
- ✔ A commitment to long-term service
- ✔ Consistent performance
- ✔ Interest in their success with the product or service
- ✔ Quality products at a fair investment

Interestingly, price is often at or near the bottom of most such surveys. Also, notice that there's nothing on this list about your having to be a technical wizard or having to possess a sparkling personality. Not everyone can tell a good joke, and few of us can ever take apart a gizmo. Every one of us, however, can return a phone call or do any of the other things on that list.

Getting your prospect invested — and involved

Whether you meet potential clients in face-to-face encounters, over telephone calls, through the Internet, or by letters, you must get prospects involved. A key way to do that is to engage as many of the five senses as possible: sight, hearing, touch, smell, and taste. Doing so enriches your presentations and makes them memorable, for all the right reasons.

**Book II:
Prospecting
for Gold**

Of the five senses, seeing, hearing, and touching are generally considered the top three ways people experience the world. And although everybody uses all five senses in varying degrees, most people have one sense that dominates the others. People don't choose to be seers or hearers, however. They're born that way, and that's the way they respond to the world throughout their lives. That's also how they respond to you.

The more you discover about the relative order of importance of the five senses, particularly if you can discover prospects' dominant ones, the better you can communicate with your potential clients. Listen for the subtle clues about which sense dominates your prospect, and then talk in terms your prospect understands best and responds to. The following sections offer clues to help you recognize your client's dominant sense and tips on how to use that knowledge to make an even more effective presentation.

After you find and implement your prospects' dominant senses in your presentations, don't neglect the other four. If your prospect is visually oriented, paint beautiful word pictures throughout the meeting, but also sprinkle the conversation with sights and sounds, tastes and smells. Bring everything into play that you can, and use every powerful image you think appropriate.

Taking a look-see

If the potential client speaks in visual terms, saying things such as, "Let's take a look" or "Let's see what you've got," or if your prospect talks about color, clarity, brightness, or darkness, then you can pretty well assume that your prospect is focused visually.

People who respond to the world visually have great memories for the way things look. They can call up the image of a golden sunrise, the color of a field of flowers, or the shape of that spot of gravy on your suit coat. When working with these folks, be conscious that they judge you primarily in terms of how things look. A wrinkled suit, improper makeup, a gaudy presentation packet, or sloppy visual aids make a far greater impression than the golden, pear-shaped sounds of your presentation voice.

Because these people view the world in pictures, you should present your product or service in visual terms. The more effectively you can do this, the better your prospects can start building pleasant images within their own minds. The more vivid, eye-appealing word pictures you create, the easier it is to bring those buyers to the point where they decide they'd like to see your product serving their needs.

Hearing is believing

If your client describes things by stressing sound — the sound of the wind or birds chirping, the rustling of leaves, or the joyful laughter of a child — then you're dealing with a listener. Look for key words and phrases related to hearing, such as "I hear what you're saying," "That sounds about right," or "Please, tell me about. . . ."

For those who get their "view" of the world by listening, their decision making tends to rely more on what they hear than what they see. So bring sound into your presentation. If you sell swimming pools, describe the laughter of the kids and the splash of the water as they perform their best cannonball dives. Create a mental audio picture of the neighbors complimenting them on the new pool and all the fine days and evenings of pleasant, intelligent conversation they'll enjoy in the new environment.

Feels right to me

People who get their primary information about the world through touch make buying decisions based on how they feel, and those decisions often are made quickly. How they feel about you or a given situation is more important than how you look or how the presentation sounds.

In meetings, these people will most surely shake your hand, but they also may pat you on the shoulder, touch you on the arm to emphasize a point, or even tap their own chests with a finger or thumb. They aren't hesitant at all about reaching out and touching. You also can look for clues and cues in their speech patterns:

- ✔ "Why don't we touch base next week?"
- ✔ "I've got a good feeling about this."
- ✔ "I'm under a lot of pressure here."
- ✔ "We'll hit a home run with this one."
- ✔ "I'm having a hard time grasping your point."

If you're a "touchy-feely" type, note that physical contact in the workplace is a major source of litigation. One person's basic and innocent need for contact is another person's abuse of power or position. Be aware and be careful not to do anything that may create discomfort for your potential client. Legal action for harassment will not build the reputation you want.

Taste the smell of success

A much smaller percentage of the population makes a connection with the environment through taste or smell, but you certainly run into some of them during your prospecting efforts, so you'd better know how to sniff them out.

Look to your prospects for key words that indicate that they're dominated by their senses of taste:

- ✔ "I like a little spice in my life."
- ✔ "We can't go on an empty stomach."
- ✔ "I really relished the moment."

Body language that puts others at ease

Initial impressions, firm ones, are formed within the first ten seconds of a contact. Your goal is always to be a person others like and trust, and your body language is what usually gets this complex process moving, or grinding to a slow halt. Whenever you meet a prospective client, smile, make eye contact, and shake hands firmly. Beyond that, there are a few other points to keep in mind:

✔ **Consider your posture.** Your posture sends a message about your level of energy and enthusiasm for what you're doing. Carrying your shoulders properly indicates confidence, whereas a slouch, even a slight one, shows the lack of it.

✔ **Consider your stride.** If you walk purposefully, people get the feeling that you have purpose and determination in your life. Dragging your heels, walking too slowly, walking with your head down (as if you were watching every step), or taking large steps can make a negative impression on your prospect.

✔ **Consider your body size.** If you're tall, be sure to stand back slightly when you meet someone who is shorter than you. (Having to look up at someone much taller is uncomfortable and puts the shorter person in a subservient position.) If the size difference is extreme, or you sense that your client is uncomfortable with your height, try to minimize the height difference by sitting, if appropriate. If you're shorter than the people you're meeting, don't do things — slouch, avert your eyes, make mincing hand gestures — that could be interpreted as signs of a lack of confidence. Also, standing a bit farther from a taller person tends to neutralize the height difference.

People oriented toward smell give other clues:

✔ "The deal just didn't smell right to me."

✔ "We knew we'd caught the scent of a good thing."

✔ "Before committing, I thought I'd better nose around a little."

How do you sell a swimming pool with examples of taste? You can't very well rub your tummy and describe biting into a chlorine tablet. If you think about it, however, you can come up with a number of effective ways to bring taste or smell into your presentation: the taste and smell of the fat, juicy burgers they'll be grilling around the new pool, for example.

Sharing Your Message without Getting Shut Down

Informal networking at business and civic gatherings is a terrific way to prospect. In these settings, you have the opportunity to meet lots of new people and introduce them to your product or service. The key word, however, is *informal.* If you come on too strong, you can easily lose the interest of the very people you're trying to engage. By following the advice and guidelines in these sections, you discover how to be an approachable and engaging salesperson in any informal networking situation.

Working a room like a champion

Many people object to the typical "talking salesperson" trying to push his product or service to people who aren't that interested. Many potential sales have been scuttled by over-eager, pushy sales presentations given at the wrong moment. In informal settings, your goal isn't to wow listeners with your sales presentation; instead, it's to obtain enough information to determine whether a follow-up contact is appropriate and then to discover the best way to follow up with each individual.

The same guidelines apply to social gatherings as well. Although talking business at your niece's wedding may not be good form, many good potential clients for your business may be at the wedding. Don't let them slip away. Be casual about what you do. If you think someone may be a good prospect, ask someone else who knows him to introduce you. Be sure to chat about the lovely couple and fun group of people attending, and then ask the other person what he does for a living. It doesn't matter if you already know. By asking, you're obligating him to ask you the same question, thus opening that small window of opportunity you were hoping for.

Working a room can be broken down into six basic, very effective steps, explained in the following sections. By following each of these steps, you'll be pleasantly surprised (perhaps amazed) at how much real prospecting you can do in an informal setting.

Step 1: Prepare

You need to take an "M&M" approach — mental and material — when preparing to prospect. First, you need to have the right attitude. You must realize that you have a responsibility to create, maintain, and nurture a persuasive environment for you and your potential client. Whether on the telephone, door-to-door, or in an informal group, bring to the session all your energy, enthusiasm, curiosity, and interest. Be casual and nonthreatening in your appearance, manner, and language, but be genuinely interested in the other person. You have to create an environment that proves to prospects that they really are important and that you want to serve their needs.

Dale Carnegie's secret

Dale Carnegie was widely regarded as a great conversationalist. People raved about the pleasurable experience of talking with him. Carnegie's secret? He asked people questions and then shut up and listened. He made himself an interested introvert rather than an interesting extrovert.

Now's the time to disabuse yourself of the idea that salespeople should be bubbly fountains of interesting talk and dazzle their prospects with their knowledge, experience, and brilliant wit. In prospecting and sales, just the opposite is true. Smart salespeople never try to dominate conversations; rather, they try to draw out the people with whom they speak. When they're speaking, they're only covering content they already know. When sales pros get their potential clients talking, they're learning how they can serve those people's needs.

Remember: When you're prospecting, let your clients be the stars. Make them feel important — because they are. Become a quiet asker of questions. Draw out your prospects, and you (yes, even you shy folks) can become a great conversationalist. Carnegie's secret was to make the other person his main focus. People loved it because people love being the center of attention. They still do.

You also need a couple of simple props:

- **A handful of business cards:** This may seem to be a no-brainer, but how many times have you seen salespeople desperately fumbling through pockets, purses, and wallets only to produce coffee-stained, half-torn cards with out-of-date addresses or phone numbers? How many times have you been that person?

- **A method to capture any appointments you make:** Whether it's a simple notepad and pen or your BlackBerry or iPhone, you need a way to keep track of appointments.

Step 2: Mingle, mingle, mingle

Say hello and converse with people at informal meetings. Make sure to mingle with people you've never met. Don't be shy about introducing yourself to strangers. If a group is engaged in conversation, simply stand nearby and wait for an opportunity to enter. At some lull in the conversation, someone may make eye contact and acknowledge you. Step up and politely introduce yourself. You're not intruding; most people attend such gatherings specifically to meet other people.

Make sure that your initial forays are casual. Talk about nonthreatening subjects such as the reason for the meeting, the weather, or a subject of common, local interest (avoiding politics and religion). Have a list of ice-breakers or good opening questions, already prepared:

> ✔ Where are you from?
>
> ✔ How did you hear about this group or meeting?
>
> ✔ Who else do you know? Could you introduce me?

Of course, you can always improvise on the spot: "I couldn't help noticing your lapel pin. What organization does it represent?"

Don't forget to ask questions. People love to talk about themselves and the things they care about. Seek to draw them out, and rest assured that, at some point, they'll ask you questions about your profession. See the section "Asking effective questions," later in this chapter, for more hints on how to ask questions.

Book II: Prospecting for Gold

Step 3: Qualify for quality

Not everyone is a qualified potential client; actually, most people aren't. To find out whether someone is a good candidate for your product or service, wait for the right moment, and then informally ask a few, carefully phrased questions about the individual's specific needs as they relate to your product or service. Advertising/media salespeople can ask something like, "What type of response are you getting from your advertising and promotional efforts?" If you sell home security systems, you can ask, "What are your biggest concerns regarding the safety of your family?" Try to find out what people need and when they need it, their plans, and who can say yes to a purchase.

Step 4: Present your case

During the qualifying phase, the person you're talking to may mention a current situation relating to your product or service. You can present your product without seeming pushy by telling your prospect how you were able to help someone else in a similar situation. Illustrating how you helped someone else is not very threatening and may even lead to one of those "Well, do you think you could do something like that for us" responses.

Make sure you keep your questions in a conversational mode. If people appear somewhat skittish about the way the conversation is going, just back off and ask for their cards and permission to contact them later. Save your official prospecting with those people for a later time, which may be at a later date or just later in the evening. If people show legitimate interest, however, continue asking questions. After you determine that they have a need you can fulfill, pique their interest. If what you market requires a more formal sales presentation, try to get a commitment for a time and place to meet for that presentation to take place.

Take your business card seriously

Your business card is an advertisement for you, your company, and your company's products and services. Whenever someone receives a card, she immediately makes a conscious decision as to whether the card is worth keeping. If she doesn't find a reason, the card can get either lost or tossed. Lynella Grant, author of *The Business Card Book* (Off the Page Press), has some tips on creating cards that prospects will choose to keep.

Avoid these blunders:

✔ Standard, prepackaged selections

✔ Cheap stock; basic, tacky paper

✔ Too much information packed on the card

✔ Type that's too small to read and/or is in too many typefaces

✔ Grubby or marked-up cards

✔ Missing information (like e-mail address, website, direct phone number, and so on)

Add these for spice:

✔ Simple humor or a witty or inspirational thought

✔ Eye-catching visuals, such as puzzles, illusions, images that challenge

✔ Useful information, such as data, formulas, maps, conversion charts

✔ Tactile sense, such as unusual embossing or texture of paper

✔ A miniature of your product as your card, if appropriate

✔ Uniqueness — something that sets you apart in your industry

Your visual identity is a vital business asset. Develop one that attracts those you want to serve, and then display that identity with flair.

Step 5: Call for action

After making your informal presentation, don't waste a lot of time, but do offer one of your business cards. Trading cards is such a ritual these days that you probably don't even have to ask for your prospects' cards. If your prospects don't have cards with them, ask them to write their contact information on the back of one of your cards.

Don't allow the other person to say, "I'll get back in touch with you." You have to stay in the driver's seat. If people show real interest, volunteer to pull together some information or tell them that you'll call later to arrange to get them some interesting or valuable information. End the conversation by saying thank you and then move back into the crowd for some more serious mingling.

Step 6: Follow up

Send out thank-you notes to all your new potential clients no later than the end of the next day. Don't put off this little strategy. Your conversations may have generated some interest in your product or service, and you want to keep that interest alive.

Keep your note short and sweet, but make sure you include a thank you. Mention the event at which you met (because some people attend a lot of meetings). Also, refer specifically to the individual, the company, or the situation you discussed, and tell him that you'll call within the next week.

Words to use — and avoid

Words are the tools of the sales professional's trade. These tools may seem simple, but they have great power for promoting good or for presenting challenges. Your goal is to use words that not only sound positive but also engender positive feelings in your listeners. The problem is that some words that sound positive actually create negative pictures or feelings in listeners' minds. Most salespeople use such words every day, completely unaware of their negative effects on potential clients. Table 5-1 offers a handy, at-a-glance summary of these words. With this list in mind, carefully examine each word in your presentation, remove the negative ones, and replace them with positive words and phrases.

**Book II:
Prospecting
for Gold**

Table 5-1	Winning Words and Phrases	
Instead of . . .	*Say . . .*	*Comment*
Appointment	Visit	*Appointment* sounds like too much of a commitment, especially for a consumer or in-home sale.
Buy or pay	Own	*Buy* and *pay* just mean that prospects fork over some money, but *ownership* means that they actually acquire something of value.
Cheaper	More economical	*Cheaper* conveys lesser in quality. *More economical* conveys thrift.
Commission	Fee for service	Respond like this: "Fortunately, the company has built a *fee for service* into our transaction. However, the service you receive will far outweigh any fee, and that's what you really want, isn't it?"
Contract	Paperwork, agreement, or form	*Contract* conjures up images of being obligated for a long, long time and legal battles to get out of it.

(continued)

Table 5-1 *(continued)*

Instead of . . .	Say . . .	Comment
Cost or price	Investment or amount	When you say *price* and *cost,* people visualize their hard-earned money slipping through their fingers. An investment, however, is something that comes back to them.
Customer	Client or people you serve	Champion salespeople keep their attitude of servitude at the forefront of every client contact.
Deal	Opportunity	You want your prospects to envision your product or service as something positive.
Down payment	Initial investment or amount	This is not the first of a long string of payments. It's the initial move toward a major life goal.
Just looking	Research	Ask about the *research* they're doing in order to make a wise purchasing decision.
Monthly payment	Monthly investment	Prospects won't visualize themselves paying bills. They'll see themselves in a more positive light, making a regular commitment.
Objection	Area of concern to be addressed	When prospects object, they stop the forward movement of the sale. In reality, they're expressing concerns that need to be addressed in order to move forward.
Pitch	Presentation or demonstration	*Pitch* sounds like "I'm going to throw something at you." Contrast that with *demonstration,* which sounds like "I have something worthwhile to show you."
Problem	Challenge	A *problem* is negative. It gives you a headache, or stops you in your tracks. A *challenge* is something you can overcome.
Referral	Quality introduction	You don't want just the name of a warm body to talk with. You're asking for a personal introduction to someone with similar needs. They need to have confidence in you in order to want to do this.
Sell or sold	Help, acquire, or get involved	People don't want to be *sold* anything; use alternatives to make them feel like partners in the process.

Instead of . . .	Say . . .	Comment
Sign	Approve, endorse, okay, or authorize	The thought of signing on that dotted line raises all kinds of red flags, but authorizing or okaying something is merely a formality.
Store	Location or display area	A *store* is a place to buy things; a *display area* is a place to learn.

Every business or industry has its own terminology, words, symbols, and phrases, but don't try to use them to impress your potential client. Jargon is technical and intimidating to the uninitiated. Talking over someone's head just gets in the way. Some people will become frustrated and give up trying to follow you. Others will struggle along trying to keep up, missing a lot of valuable sales points along the way. You can't sell if you're not speaking the same language as your client.

Book II: Prospecting for Gold

Before launching into your presentation, determine your prospect's level of understanding of the jargon and adjust accordingly. Determine a good test question for your industry. If they know what RAM is, for example, you should also be able to talk about computer processor speeds and gigabytes of storage without having to explain all that. If you have any doubt about their level of understanding, define each industry term the first time you use it. If they get it, you'll see the light of understanding in their eyes. If their eyes glaze over or they look confused, backtrack to a more elementary level of conversation.

Asking effective questions

You can ask two basic types of questions: open-ended and closed. Consider the latter group dead-end questions because that's exactly where they lead. A dead-end question requires a simple, brief, and, sometimes, one-word answer. Closed questions don't encourage prospects to talk about themselves so you figure out how you can help them. Closed questions work against both you and your prospects.

Closed or dead-end questions usually begin with two words that guarantee a short answer. Try to avoid the following openings whenever you need important information:

- ✔ Do you . . .
- ✔ Will you . . .
- ✔ How many . . .
- ✔ Are you . . .

Although closed-ended questions are helpful in some situations — like when you need specific information about very specific areas or you want to rein in a conversation that's drifting the wrong way — be careful when you use these questions because they usually lead to dead ends in the conversation.

Instead, use as many open-ended questions as feasible to get important information from the potential client. These questions keep your prospects talking. Not only are open-ended questions the best way to get information directly, but they also make people feel important because they end up doing most of the talking. A few basic but powerful words are virtually open-ended questions by themselves. Journalists call these power openers *the five Ws* (and they always toss in an *H* for free):

✔ Who?

✔ What?

✔ Where?

✔ When?

✔ Why?

✔ How?

Most people find it very difficult to answer those questions (or questions built around them) with short or one-word answers. Even if you get a one-word answer, you can keep digging because it's practically impossible to answer every question with a short answer. Unless you run up against someone who shrugs and says, "I don't know" to everything you ask, you'll hear something important from potential buyers sooner or later. Here are a couple open-ended questions framed around these words:

> I'm curious — why do you prefer a 16-foot craft?

> How did you get involved in sailing?

> Where do you prefer to do most of your sailing?

You may be tempted to respond to some of these questions by jumping in immediately with a feature or benefit of your product or service. Resist this temptation. Except for those rare times when the opportunity presents itself, don't sell when prospecting. Instead, keep prospects talking by asking more open-ended questions.

As you use the five *W*s, try not to sound like you're conducting an interrogation; otherwise, you may find the other person backing away from you. Keep the conversation as casual as circumstances permit.

Approaching the Retail Customer

If you're in retail sales or have ever been a retail customer (which effectively includes all of us), you know that approaching a new customer can be a tricky business. It's your job to offer assistance and generate sales, but at the same time, you don't want to be overbearing or seen as a pest. So how do you accomplish both tasks? And how do you recognize when a customer who professed not to need your help earlier now could use and appreciate your assistance? The follow sections offer advice.

Asking the right question

The stock answer to the question "May I help you?" is often a simple "No, thanks — I'm just looking." This answer effectively shuts down the conversation — unless you want to run the risk of becoming a pest, which can kill any opportunity to make a sale.

Book II: Prospecting for Gold

"May I help you?" is a no-question. But by adding one little word to this sentence, you turn this dead-end question into one that requires a real answer. The magic word is *how*. "How may I help you?" requires a real answer — an answer with some thought behind it. The answer to the question "How may I help you?" brings real interaction to the initial contact.

You also can use other open-ended questions (refer to the section "Asking effective questions," earlier, for an explanation of open-ended questions) to initiate a conversation with your potential client. These kinds of questions are nonthreatening, and they keep the lines of communication open. Here are some examples:

- ✔ **What are you shopping for today?** The answer to this question gives you cause to lead the customer to the appropriate item, drumming up conversation along the way, and making the customer like and trust you.

- ✔ **When was the last time you were in our store?** If you've recently remodeled or reorganized, this answer could turn you into Mr. or Ms. Tour Guide, helping the buyer find items that have been moved or directing him to the new line of whatchamajigs.

- ✔ **Where else have you been shopping today?** If the customer has visited the competition, you know she's doing price comparisons, and you need to get your selling antenna up for decision-making time.

- ✔ **Why did you decide to come to our location today?** If you have a special sale going on, that's great. If not, the customer probably came in for a particular reason. Perhaps a friend just bought an item at your store and he's coming in to check it out for himself. In that case, he's practically sold already.

- ✔ **How did you find our business?** There's a difference between the person who wandered in because he was in the area and the person who drove 25 miles to get there because you carry a one-of-a-kind item.

Don't be a space invader

In retail, be careful of your approach. Too many salespeople charge in like rhinos when they set eyes on someone stepping into their location — a behavior that immediately intimidates most of the people you hope to serve. No one likes to be charged. Never walk directly toward a potential buyer who has just walked into your retail location.

Instead, approach respectfully. Make contact without causing fear or concern. Just let the customer know that you're available to assist when necessary and then back off. Easing away from a potential customer is a marvelous way to put him at ease. For one thing, it's the last thing in the world he expects to happen. The sheer relief drives away a lot of tension.

You don't want to circle around like a hungry shark, but you do want to keep an eye on your customer. Usually, he'll make a beeline for the object of his interest the moment you leave. By watching his actions, you soon can figure out the reason for the visit and begin formulating your plan of action to be of service. When he begins examining the article, that's the time to ease back in his direction. Again, don't come charging in — just make sure you're nearby to handle any questions about the purchase. A friendly nod or a brief smile of acknowledgment is okay, but don't stare — it makes you look hungry.

Respond to buying signals

If a potential buyer spends any time at all examining a particular item or set of items, it's a clear sign that he wants to move from being a prospect to becoming a client. That's the time to ease over and ask a service question. Start with an open-ended question, something that can't be answered with a conversation-slowing "yes" or "no." Open-ended questions also provide you with information to help you move the sales process along to the desired conclusion.

If you're selling automobiles, for example, you may ask if the purchase is to be used as a work vehicle or family vehicle. The answer to this question tells you that the individual is interested in making a purchase, involves the prospect, and gives you specific information to help you get even more information to better match the buyer with the right vehicle.

You can press on by asking how many people are in the family; how much travel will be involved; if the vehicle will be used primarily in town or on long trips; whether the prospect is more interested in safety, fuel efficiency, or power; and so on. All these questions, handled politely and respectfully, put and keep your prospect at ease while bringing you ever closer to the sale.

Book III

Turning Prospects into Customers and Clients

The 5th Wave   By Rich Tennant

"That was like taking candy from a baby."

In this book . . .

When you approach people with your product, service, or idea, you have to realize that they probably aren't looking for you, your product, or your idea. In fact, they may not know that you exist, or they may view you as trying to convince them to buy something they don't need or want.

So, you have quite a job in front of you. You have to show them that your goal isn't just to get the sale; it's to help them see that your product or service is the best one to meet their needs.

The chapters in this book tell you how to find the people who need what you have and how to schedule meetings with them. You also find out how to make sure your product is right for them and how to deliver a winning presentation. Finally, this book tells you how to address their concerns.

Remember: A prospect is not an enemy to be battered into submission. She's actually your partner in success.

Chapter 1

Getting a Meeting and Putting Your Clients at Ease

. . . .

In This Chapter

▶ Reaching out to your prospects via phone, mail, e-mail, and face-to-face interactions

▶ Figuring out how to get in touch with the difficult-to-reach decision maker

▶ Winning people over with a good first impression

▶ Standing out in a retail setting

▶ Building rapport with your prospective clients

. . . .

*I*n virtually every situation in which you can use selling skills, if you don't get face to face with the right person, all your hard work was for naught. (In telephone sales, being able to speak with someone directly counts the same.) If you aren't live and present to your clients, you'll never be able to discover their needs in order to figure out how you can satisfy them.

So, how do you get face to face with the people you want to persuade to own your product, start using your service, or consider your idea? First, you must sell them on scheduling time to meet with you or, at the very least, agreeing to allow you to pop by and visit. In this chapter, you find out exactly how to get an appointment (which, as a sales professional, you call a "visit" or a "meeting") with your prospective clients and advice on how you can put them at ease when you finally do come face to face. When they're comfortable, they'll listen to what you have to say.

The important thing to keep in mind when you've come up with a list of prospective clients is that not all those clients need your product or service. You may have to contact 20 people to find one who wants just what you have to offer. But every one of those other 19 calls brings you one call closer to the right person. So, you just need to stay focused on your ultimate goal; don't let a little bit of rejection send you scurrying to the nearest hidey-hole.

Knowing the Basics of Contacting Prospective Clients

How you contact a prospective client may differ depending on how you received the person's contact information:

- ✔ **If the prospective client contacted you by telephone:** In this case, the call is always the most courteous response. You get the full scoop on telephoning prospects later in the next section.

- ✔ **If you got the person's name from a referral:** If another client or business associate recommended that you get in contact with this particular person, ask the person giving the referral to introduce you to the new prospect. If that isn't possible, at the very least, call the lead and let him know that so-and-so asked you to contact him.

  In the latter scenario, you need to decide whether an introductory letter or phone meeting would be best. Which you choose usually depends on the formality of the situation. If you're selling luxury yachts, for example, dropping a note first is probably a better tactic than interrupting the prospect's life with a sales phone call.

- ✔ **If the person left his name and e-mail address on your website:** In this case, the potential client would probably prefer to be contacted first by e-mail. In their visitor registration areas, many websites ask how the clients prefer to be contacted. If your website doesn't already ask this question, see whether the site can be changed to include this question.

Your goal when you contact a prospective client (whether by phone, mail, or e-mail) is to get in direct, live contact with him, so you must approach the sale of the appointment very carefully. You first have to sell the prospect on the fact that he'd be better off speaking with you than not speaking with you. And that means you must offer benefits to him in your very first contact.

Keep the following pointers in mind when you're trying to get a potential client's attention via phone, mail, or e-mail:

- ✔ **Always be courteous.** Say "please" and "thank you." Refer to the person as Mr. or Ms. Last Name; don't be too quick to use first names. And don't ever assume a woman is a Mrs. or a Miss. Getting that wrong can truly start you off on the wrong foot.

- ✔ **Do anything to meet the potential client.** Even if you have to drive miles out of your way to be where he is and all you get is an introduction, those miles can turn into smiles when you later close the sale.

✔ **Hit the high notes early.** You must pique the potential client's interest right away. Ask about her areas of interest regarding your product. Then tell her about a benefit that she would be likely to enjoy — saving money, making money, and improving lifestyles are big ones for most people.

✔ **Confirm all the details about where and when you'll meet.** Verbal confirmation is a must. Written confirmation is even better because it provides documentation (be sure to copy yourself). Include any agreed-upon next steps or goals, and mention that you'll invest plenty of time in researching just the right information for the meeting to make it worth his while — a strategy that often prevents the person from canceling your meeting lightly.

If you do your best to be courteous, secure an appointment no matter how busy the prospect is, and confirm the details of when you'll meet, you're well on your way to a great meeting.

Reaching Your Potential Clients by Telephone First

Book III

Turning Prospects into Customers and Clients

When you're ready to approach prospective clients, you'll make an introductory phone call, send an introductory note or e-mail, or meet face to face. In this section, we cover the telephone approach; in the next section, we cover the other three.

To make sure you cover all the key details on the phone in a way that keeps the potential client's interest, you need a strategy. Here's a strategy that includes seven simple steps, all covered in more detail in the following sections:

1. **Offer a greeting.**

2. **Introduce yourself and your business.**

3. **Express your gratitude for the person's willingness to talk with you.**

4. **Tell the person the purpose of your call.**

5. **Get appointment commitment to talk with the person face to face.**

6. **Thank the person while you're on the phone.**

7. **Write a thank-you note and send it either by regular mail or e-mail.**

The rest, as they say, is selling.

When you're about to contact your prospective clients, keep three things at the forefront of your mind: your belief in what you're offering, the happiness of your current clients, and your desire to serve others. This advice applies whether you're selling yourself as an employee, your skills as a freelance writer, or a million-dollar computer system as a career sales representative for a Fortune 500 company.

Step 1: The greeting

When you call a prospective client for the first time, begin by using the most important thing for anyone to hear: her name. Using a formal approach, such as "Good morning, Ms. James" or "Good morning. I'm calling for Ms. James," is best because it conveys respect. (Take into account time zone differences. You don't want to look like a complete flake by bidding someone good morning when it's 1 p.m. wherever Ms. James is.)

Use "Good morning," "Good afternoon," and "Good evening" rather than plain, old "Hello." They sound more professional and can distinguish you from all those other people who call your prospective client.

Too often, people are tempted to use a person's first name over the phone. Some people don't mind strangers referring to them by their first names, but others find it disrespectful. Also, don't use nicknames (calling Mr. Robert Smith "Bob," for example). Many people perceive the use of nicknames as being too familiar. In both cases, wait until you're given permission — Mr. Robert Smith says to you, for example, "Call me Bob." Read more about how to address people in "Step 5: Offer your name for their names," later in this chapter.

Step 2: The introduction

After offering your greeting, introduce yourself and give your company name. If your company name doesn't explain what you do — as it would if your name were, say, Jensen Portrait Studios — then you must also mention briefly what type of business you're in. The key word here is *briefly*. Keep it short and sweet. Now is not the time to spend 45 minutes extolling the features and benefits of owning a magnetic resonance imaging scanner.

To keep your potential client on the line and awake, describe your business in terms of benefits to them. If you work for a carpet-cleaning business, for example, you know that clean carpets give a good impression, and dirty carpets harbor germs, but you would say something like this (notice that you don't mention carpets at all):

We're a local business that helps companies like yours enhance their image with customers and reduce employee sick time.

Is Ms. James ready to hang up? Probably not yet. Your description is creating all kinds of pictures in her mind because you haven't been so specific as to mention carpet cleaning. Your business could be anything from sneeze guards to high-tech air-cleaning systems. Because she probably doesn't have that clear a picture yet of what you're selling, she'll be curious to know more. After all, no one likes to end a conversation with all the blanks not yet filled in.

Paint a tantalizing picture with the words you use, but keep it simple. Keep in mind that this all happens in a matter of seconds. You're trying to get Ms. James to give you anything with which you can extend the conversation.

Step 3: Gratitude

After you introduce yourself and your business, you need to acknowledge that your prospect's time is valuable and thank her for taking your call. A statement like the following lets her know you consider her to be an important person:

> I appreciate you for giving me a moment of your valuable time this morning. I promise to be brief.

Step 4: The purpose

After expressing your gratitude, you need to get right to the heart of the matter by letting the prospective client know why you're calling. You should always express your purpose with a question. Something like this may be appropriate:

> If I could show you how to reduce employee sick time while improving the image your company presents to its customers, would you be interested?

What you do next, depends on the answer:

✔ **If she says "yes,"** ask permission to ask her a few brief questions. When you have her permission, start with your qualifying questions to determine what she has now and what she'd change if she were to make a new product purchase. (You can find a discussion of qualifying questions in Book III, Chapter 2.)

✔ **If she says "no,"** be prepared with one more question that may pique her interest, such as "Do you believe an improvement in the image of your business would have the effect of increasing sales?"

✔ **If she still says "no,"** you may want to be more direct. For example: "Most of the companies I work with clean their carpets once a month. What frequency have you found adequate for your standards of presentation while maintaining a healthy work environment for your employees?"

If she says yes at this point, you're ready to move on to the prequalifying questions (see Book III, Chapter 2), but if she says it's been only a week, you may just need to remain polite and ask how often they have the carpet-cleaning service performed. Then ask for permission to contact her when she needs the service again. Thank her for her time, put a note in your calendar to contact her a couple weeks before she needs the carpets cleaned again, and move on to your next potential client.

Assignment: Survey

Here's a strategy, called the *survey approach,* that may benefit you. The purpose of conducting this brief survey is to get the person on the other end of the line talking. Hopefully, what she tells you will give you the information you need to state benefits that build her curiosity enough to commit to that vital face-to-face visit.

To begin, have your manager or the business owner assign you the task of surveying your client base or a list of new potential clients (it's important that this be an actual assignment because you *never* lie to clients or potential clients). During your survey approach, when you get to the point in the call when you state your purpose, you say something like this:

> The company I represent has given me an assignment to conduct a quick two-question survey of just ten people. You're the sixth person I've contacted. We would greatly value your opinion. Would you help me by answering two brief questions?

When you ask for the potential client's help and show that you value her opinion, she's likely to comply. After all, who among us doesn't have an opinion? Plus, by informing her that your company is having you do this, you're likely to gain her empathy and cooperation. Be careful, however, that you don't just go from one question to the next without really listening to her answers. She'll know by how you phrase the next question whether her last answer was heard. If she thinks you're just waiting to pounce on her with a canned list of questions rather than sincerely trying to get valuable information, she'll quickly hang up and send you off into the dial-tone void.

To show that you're really listening to what the other person is saying, paraphrase her responses before moving on to the next question. When she hears that you cared enough to listen, she'll be more inclined to continue — and you escape your instant journey into the vortex.

Step 5: The actual meeting

If, after sharing with your potential client the purpose of your call and asking the questions you've prepared, the client seems inclined to set a time for a visit, be prepared to tell her just how long you'll need. Keep your initial contact as short as possible. Most people will balk at giving you an hour or even 30 minutes of their time. Twenty minutes or less seems to be an acceptable time commitment for most people. If you know your typical presentation runs longer, that's okay. State the situation this way:

> The length of time required to cover the details is flexible, Ms. James. Most of my clients find that 20 minutes is sufficient to get the gist of what we're offering. Anything longer than that will depend on you and the questions you may have.

When the client agrees to give you the 20 minutes you need, give her an option of when to meet, with an alternate-of-choice question — for example, "Would tomorrow at 10:20 a.m. be good for you, or is Wednesday at 2:40 p.m. better?" This question lets your prospect choose, but keeps you in control.

Notice that the example mentions off times: 10:20 rather than 10 a.m. or 2:40 rather than 2 p.m. Using off times differentiates you from all the other salespeople, showing that you must know the importance of punctuality if you can keep a schedule using those times. If your visit will last only 20 minutes, it also lets your prospect schedule other appointments around yours in the more standard time slots.

Book III

Turning Prospects into Customers and Clients

Step 6: The over-the-phone thank-you

When you've secured an appointment, you move on to thanking your potential client again, reiterating the time that has been agreed to and verifying the location of her office (or the place where you'll be meeting).

You never, ever want to take a chance that you'll be late for a first meeting because you don't know where you're going (nothing is worse than showing up late and presenting the excuse of getting lost) or because of circumstances beyond your control. If the location is difficult to get to, *now* is the time to ask for explicit directions. If this is The Big Sale you've dreamed about for years and you finally have the appointment, drive to the office the day before and get familiar with the area. Know at least one alternate route in case traffic presents a challenge or a road crew is scheduled to repair potholes that day. If possible (and the appointment is an important one), schedule any meetings you have during that part of the day in the potential client's part of town. That way, you're already in the area as the time for the meeting approaches.

When your meeting is at the client's place of business or home, your odds of the appointment actually occurring improve tremendously. When you set appointments for people to come to your place of business or to a meeting, you can expect anywhere between 20 percent and 50 percent of those who committed to actually show up. Between the time you contact the person to set up the appointment and the time the appointment arrives, any number of conflicts may occur. At the very least, they may decide to sleep in that day. An important call may come in. They may change their mind about the value of spending their time with you. They may be running late. Or they may just plain forget.

Step 7: The written thank-you

If your appointment is more than two days from when you call, immediately send your potential client a thank-you note (preferably by regular mail), confirming the details of when you spoke and what was agreed to. A professional-looking piece of correspondence can dispel any doubts the client may have about this commitment.

Keep in mind that if your prospect prefers contact by e-mail and has given you a home e-mail address as opposed to a work one, she may not check that e-mail account daily, which means that e-mail may not be the best method of reaching her. In most business situations, however, people communicate frequently by e-mail, so the recipient will be more likely to see your message right away.

Including your picture on your letterhead or on your business card and enclosing that with your thank-you note never hurts. Get a professional portrait taken if you choose to use a photo — sending something that looks like your driver's license headshot is bad news. Knowing what you look like increases the prospect's comfort level when you finally do meet in person.

Putting Mail, E-mail, and Face-to-Face Interactions to Work for You

You can contact your potential clients in four major ways: by phone, by mail, by e-mail, or face to face. We cover phone contact in the previous section; the other three methods we cover here. Most professional salespeople integrate all four methods into an effective prospecting strategy. For some, one method works better than others. Different situations call for different strategies, so be well versed in how to handle each. As you gain experience in prospecting, you'll figure out which methods work best for you and at which times.

Mailing it in

If you use mail as your primary method of prospecting, choose your mailing list carefully. Mailing is a great way to prospect, but mail sent to the wrong list of people is a tremendous waste of your time, money, and effort. Nothing is easier to get rid of than a piece of paper that arrives amidst a stack of other papers — especially if your prospecting piece of paper winds up in the mailbox of someone who wouldn't care about your product or service in a hundred years.

Instead of talking about your product or service in the mail you send, consider mailing a single-page introductory letter to the people most likely to want to get involved with what you're doing. In this letter, indicate that you'll call on a certain date and time and include your photograph on the letterhead or on a magnet or other enclosed novelty item.

Whatever you send in the mail, be absolutely certain that it includes your web address and e-mail address. As much as some people love talking on phones, they'll more likely visit your website first, to check you out and see whether your site includes anything that would make it worth their while to talk with you in person. If the purpose of the mailing is to generate sales, also let the recipients know whether online orders are possible. That way, they don't have to wait until they can catch a live sales representative on the phone — especially if they read their mail at 2 a.m.

Book III

Turning Prospects into Customers and Clients

E-mailing options

Your goal with e-mail is to make a personal connection, pique the recipient's interest, and tell him how to learn more. You can handle e-mail prospecting in two ways:

✔ **Purchase an opt-in e-mail list from a list broker.** *Opt-in e-mail lists* are lists of people who have agreed to have information about the things they're interested in sent to them via e-mail. Opt-in e-mail lists receive an open rate ranging from 5 percent to 15 percent — a huge increase over traditional direct-mail response rates. The *open rate* is the ratio between the number of people who are sent an e-mail and the number who actually open it. Curiosity-building subject lines are very important to open rates. And using opt-in e-mail lists can help you avoid making a negative impression by e-mailing unwanted information to people.

Check out www.postmasterdirect.com to find out more about how you can benefit from e-mail promotions.

✔ **Search out the e-mail address of a purchasing agent or appropriate contact at a business and then mail a very specific, customized e-mail to that person.** You can find e-mail addresses on many corporate websites. If you don't find e-mail addresses on a company website, call the office and ask for the name and e-mail address of the person who makes decisions about your product.

Getting consumer e-mail addresses is a bit more complicated, but some salespeople have had success in finding their clients via social-media sources such as LinkedIn and Facebook. With either of those services, you can send a direct message to the person.

In either case, you want to use your e-mail like the introductory letter mentioned in the preceding section. Introduce yourself and your company, and list the benefits your product would provide to the recipient. Then finish in one of the following ways:

✔ **For the opt-in list, you may wrap up your letter with a call to action:** "Reply to this e-mail within 24 hours, and we'll have a specific proposal to you by Friday of this week."

✔ **For the custom e-mail option, you may tell the recipient that you'll call within 48 hours to ask two quick questions:** This is the survey approach from the earlier sidebar, "Assignment: Survey."

Sending something that looks more like a letter or typical e-mail message is more effective that sending an e-mail that looks like an advertisement. Just keep it short.

Interacting face-to-face

Face-to-face prospecting is almost always the best method, but it's also the most time intensive. Walking from office to office or home to home trying to find decision makers is physically exhausting, which can be tough. But even worse is the sad fact that you may not get many leads out of all your legwork.

What you will get, though, is a load of information from neighbors and receptionists. Because they provide great prequalifying information, they can be powerhouses who help you either eliminate a family or company as prospects or increase your chances of obtaining an appointment that lets you make a presentation to the decision maker.

Receptionists, secretaries, and assistants hold the keys to opening the doors you want to get through; that's why they're called "gatekeepers." Too many salespeople interpret this moniker to mean their job is to keep you out. In reality, it's to let the right people in. You just need to figure out how to demonstrate that you *are* the right person. One way to demonstrate that is to treat receptionists or secretaries with the respect they deserve. If you try to rush past a receptionist or quickly ask to see the boss without first showing concern or interest in her, you may as well not have gone in at all. Introduce yourself, ask the receptionist's name, and then try to have a friendly dialogue with her before you ask to see the boss.

Getting to the Elusive Decision Maker

As you seek an appointment with a prospective client, what you really want is to get in with the *true final decision maker,* the person who has the ability to make decisions about the products and services purchased. In consumer sales, the decision maker is most often the head of the household (even though one spouse or partner may defer to the choices of the other). The decision maker isn't always easy to identify. In some situations, for example, the end-user — such as a child or parent of the person you believe to be the decision maker — is the actual decision maker, because he or she has the final word. In this case, the person you initially identify as the decision maker may have his hands on the purse strings but he's working to please someone else.

In the case of a purchasing agent or business owner, the decision maker may have an entire hierarchy of people around her whose role is to screen calls on her behalf — a situation that can lead you to wonder exactly where your prospective client is and what she's doing (jetting to exotic locations for meetings, perhaps?). But it doesn't matter what she's doing, as long as you can eventually get to her. The following sections provide pointers on how to get through to those elusive decision makers.

When you have trouble getting through to the decision maker, you may have to work harder and be a bit more creative before you finally succeed. People who are hardest to get to will be tough on your competition as well. If you stick it out and win their business, you'll be on the inside of that same protective wall, and those same support people will keep your *competition,* not you, at bay.

Going head-to-head with the receptionist

If you're having trouble getting through to a company's decision maker, begin with the receptionist who answers the phone when you call. If possible, get the name of the decision maker on your first contact. Tell the receptionist that you need his help and ask, "Who would be in charge of the decision-making process if your company were to consider getting involved in a [whatever your product or service is]?" The receptionist is the person who has to know what each employee's area of responsibility is in order to direct calls properly, so he should be a great help. Then, whenever you make follow-up calls, use the decision maker's name.

Book III

Turning Prospects into Customers and Clients

Be sure to ask for the correct pronunciation and spelling of any names the receptionist gives you. Never guess about names or take the chance of writing them down incorrectly; business practices like that are likely to haunt you later. It never hurts to get the receptionist's name as well.

If the receptionist is especially helpful — as receptionists tend to be — take a moment to send a thank-you note to him along with your business card. A little bit of recognition now can prove valuable later on. When you've built a solid relationship with the receptionist, he'll always look forward to hearing from you or seeing you, and future visits will be much warmer. He also may help guard your account against infiltration attempts by your competitors.

Working with the decision maker's assistant

If the decision maker has an assistant, the receptionist probably will put you through to that person first. The assistant can make or break your chances of ever getting an appointment, so the best thing to do is ask for the assistant's help as well. You can accomplish a great deal of research with the assistant's help — and you may even be able to prequalify the decision maker through her assistant (see Book III, Chapter 2 for more information on qualifying).

To get the assistant on your side, follow these two, easy steps:

1. **Tell the assistant the benefits the company stands to gain from your product or service.**

   These benefits may include that you have a way of increasing efficiency while decreasing the costs of a service the company is already using, for example. A statement like this provides the assistant with just enough information to either want to know more or want to help.

2. **Explain that you need his help and simply ask how to get an appointment to speak with Ms. Decision Maker.**

   Most businesses have an established procedure for setting up appointments with the head honchos. By asking what that procedure is, you show that you're not trying to beat the system; you just want to find out what the system is so you can work with it. When you show respect for the system that's in place, you move up a notch on the respect scale.

Unless the procedure for meeting the honchos is too complicated, or your offering has a stringent time deadline, try it their way first. If the system doesn't work, consider how much effort the company's business is worth. If it's a once-in-a-lifetime proposition, then you need to get creative. The following section has more information.

Getting creative in your efforts to meet with the decision maker

Whatever unusual method you choose for getting in touch with the decision maker, always consider how the decision maker will receive it. Your goal is to find an inoffensive method for getting people's attention, but your method has to be creative, too. You don't want to risk alienating anyone, but if she's important enough to contact, you need to find out what her hot buttons are and build your contact method around that. Again, this is where receptionists, secretaries, and assistants (along with even other family members) can come to your rescue.

One salesperson sent a loaf of bread and a bottle of wine in a basket to a hard-to-reach decision maker. She included a note that said, "I hate to w(h)ine, but I know I can save you a lot of dough if you'll just meet me for ten minutes." It broke through the barrier in a creative way, and she did get a confirmed appointment. (Of course, before you send alcohol to a prospective client, find out whether she drinks or abstains from alcohol. If she doesn't drink, this bit of creativity could make the wrong impression.)

A creative way to make a good impression on the decision maker is to ask her receptionist or assistant who the decision maker respects and listens to in her field. If you find out that your prospect is a member of the PTA or Rotary Club, think about who else you may know who's a member and try to network your way into a meeting that way.

If you're working your business correctly, you're bound to find some way that your circle of contacts connects with the prospect. The real skill in meeting people is turning those points of contact into strong links.

If the decision maker's schedule really is strict and all else fails, try to arrange for a telephone or online meeting instead of a face-to-face one. You'll have to adjust your presentation to give it just the right impact. But it may be a method worth trying.

Book III

Turning
Prospects
into
Customers
and Clients

Getting Your Potential Clients to Like and Trust You

When you meet people, your main goal is to help them relax with you. No one gets involved in a decision-making process when he's uptight. You want your prospective clients to like you and trust you because, if they don't, they won't do business with you. Always remember that your goal is to be a person whom other people like, trust, and want to listen to.

Your prospective clients make many decisions about you in the first ten seconds after they meet you for the very first time. That's right. Within *ten seconds,* you can be either chopped liver or Prince or Princess Charming. So how can you help your prospective clients like and trust you? Just follow the steps outlined in the following sections.

Step 1: Smile deep and wide

When you first come into contact with a prospective client, smile. (Yes, it's that simple!) A smile radiates warmth. If you're not smiling, if your smile appears fake, or if it looks like it hurts when you do it, your prospect will want to avoid you, and he'll put up a wall of doubt and fear in just a few seconds.

If you're contacting people over the telephone, smiling still counts. Believe it or not, people can hear a smile (or a lack of one) in your voice. Try this trick: Put a little mirror by the telephone so you can see yourself when you're talking with clients. If you see that you're not smiling, chances are good that the person on the other end of the phone can sense it, too, which certainly has a negative effect on the relationship.

Step 2: Make eye contact

When you meet a potential client, look in his eyes. This builds trust. People tend not to trust those who can't look them in the eye; after all, people usually glance away when they're lying to you. When you don't look your clients in the eye, they may doubt what you're saying.

Although looking your clients in the eyes is very important, be sure not to go to the extreme and lock onto their eyes. Getting into a staring contest is dangerous in any selling situation because it's perceived as aggressive or unreasonably intense. Give your prospect a couple seconds of solid eye contact while smiling, and he'll most likely be the first to glance away.

Step 3: Say "Hi" (or something like it)

Your greeting will be affected by the particular circumstance of how you're meeting each potential client. If you have any doubt at all about what kind of greeting is best, err on the side of formality. Depending on the situation, any one of the following greetings may be appropriate:

✔ "Hi."

✔ "Hello."

✔ "How do you do?"

✔ "How are you?"

✔ "Good morning" (or "Good afternoon" or "Good evening").

✔ "Thank you for coming in."

✔ "Thank you for seeing me."

If you already know your prospect's name, use it with your greeting (for example, "Good morning, Mr. Williams"). If you don't know your prospect's name, don't rush to get it. Pressing strangers for their names is fine in many parts of the world and in many situations, but it can be seen as pushy in other situations.

Step 4: Shake hands

The handshake is appropriate in most instances, but only if you do it properly. If you've ever shaken a hand that feels like a dead fish or been brought to your knees by a bone-crusher, you'll understand how important a good handshake can be.

To convey the highest level of trust, confidence, and competence, you need to grasp the whole hand of the other individual and give it a brief but solid squeeze — not too tight, but definitely not loosey-goosey either. Keep it brief. There's nothing more uncomfortable than to have someone keep holding your hand when you're ready to have it back.

Here are a couple other pointers:

✔ **Some people don't want to shake hands.** The reasons for this reluctance vary: Some people just don't like physical contact with strangers; others may avoid it for health reasons; still others may suffer from arthritis and find shaking hands painful. Whatever the reason, if someone appears uninterested in shaking hands, don't take it personally.

To avoid an awkward moment, keep your right arm slightly bent and held by your side. If you see the other person reach toward you, you're ready to extend your hand. If the other person doesn't reach toward you, you haven't committed the grand faux pas of reaching out too eagerly.

✔ **If you're meeting a couple, shaking the hands of both is appropriate.** In most selling situations, one person or the other will speak first. Reach out to that person to shake hands, and then shake hands with the other parties involved. If they have children with them, shaking the kids' hands is a nice gesture as well. After all, if the product you're selling involves the children, you want to earn their trust, too. If you can tell a child would be uncomfortable with having his hand shaken, simply give him a moment of eye contact as well. Or possibly ask them to "give you five" and gently slap hands. Don't do any cheek tweaking or hair tussling of the kids. Remember how you hated it when Aunt Minnie did it to you?

Step 5: Offer your name for their names

The handshake is the most natural time to exchange names. Depending on the situation, you may want to use the formal greeting of, "Good morning. My name is Robert Smith with Jones & Company." If the setting is more casual, you may want to give your name as Rob or Bob — whatever you want your prospects to call you. Make sure they get your name right, though. Nothing is more difficult than correcting a potential client who calls you Bob when your name is Rob. Besides, when you've won them over and they've begun sending you referral business, you don't want the referrals asking for the wrong person and letting someone else earn your sales.

After you square away what you want your clients to call you, how do you figure out what to call them? Following are some important guidelines. Although this approach may seem old-fashioned, it's what sells. People yearn for a time when they were treated with more respect and courtesy:

✔ If a woman says her name is Judith Carter, use Ms. Carter when you first address her. Don't jump to the familiar Judy. Why? Because that's what a typical salesperson does, and getting too familiar too fast is impolite and may cause Ms. Carter to raise her guard against you.

✔ Let your prospect decide when you may become more familiar, and let *her* give you the appropriate first name to use. Don't shorten someone's name (from Judith to Judy, for example) unless she tells you to. Some people prefer their given names to the more common nicknames.

✔ When you're involved more deeply in the qualification or presentation stages of selling (see Book III, Chapters 2 and 3) and you feel some warmth building, using first names often feels more comfortable. If your prospect hasn't given you permission to do so, politely ask for it. With Judith, just ask, "May I call you Judith?" If that's what everyone calls her and she has built some confidence in you, she'll probably say yes. Or she may say, "Call me Judy."

✔ If you're being introduced to a group of people, be careful to use the same level of formality with each member. Don't call one person Mr. Johnson and call Mr. Johnson's associate by his first name, Bob, just because you can't remember Bob's last name. That's more offensive than having to ask again what Bob's last name is.

Step 6: Establish rapport

Your clients feel comfortable around you when you know how to establish rapport with them, which is what selling situations are all about — establishing common ground. The following sections tell you how to establish this bond during the initial meeting. As things progress, you'll have other opportunities to reinforce this connection, as the later section, "Building Common Ground in Any Situation," explains.

Emphasizing similarities

People like to be around other people who are similar to them. Bringing out the similarities you share with your prospects proves that at least one salesperson is not an alien being from another solar system. You're not even from the dark side of the moon — you're just like them: You have a family, you have a job, you have similar values, and when you're seeking any product other than the one you represent, you work with salespeople, too, just like your prospects. You just happen to be more of an expert on the particular product line or service you represent than your prospects are, and you're happy to use your knowledge to their advantage.

If you sense that the other party is concerned that you're on the same page as they are, saying something like this helps you get across the point that you're just like your clients:

> Mr. Williams, when I'm not helping people get involved with my product, I'm a consumer, just like you, looking for quality products at the best price. What I hope for when I'm shopping is to find someone who can help me understand all the facts about the item I'm interested in so I can make a wise decision. Today, I'd like to earn your confidence in me as an expert on state-of-the-art stereo systems. So, feel free to ask any questions you may have.

Don't wince at the thought of using these words — they've been proven to work successfully in lowering barriers people put up when dealing with salespeople. Although no one likes hearing "canned" material, it's only canned if you let it sound that way. In sales, how you say it is as important as what you say. Always remember to speak with a sincere concern for your customers. If you're not truly concerned for them, you shouldn't be in this field.

Book III

Turning Prospects into Customers and Clients

Showing a sincere interest in your clients

To build rapport with your clients, you have to be truly interested in them. You need to be sincere in wanting to get to know them well enough so you can help them have more, do more, and be more. Even if you're selling to a loved one, he needs to feel that high level of personal concern as well. If your clients believe you're being real — speaking from your heart — they'll put their confidence in you much more quickly.

Approaching Potential Clients in a Retail Setting

Selling in a retail environment is really no different from selling in any other environment: You need to get each customer to like you and trust you enough to ask for help. Immediately pouncing on your customers with a reflexive "May I help you?" does exactly the opposite of what you want. It causes your customers to erect immediate barriers or to respond reflexively — like the children's game "hot potato." They'll toss an answer, most likely "No, thank you" back at you as quickly as you toss "May I help you?" their way.

As a customer, you may have heard variations of the "May I help you?" greeting, including something like this: "Hi, I'm Bob. What can I do for you today?" What kind of response does Bob hear 99.9 percent of the time he says those words? "Oh, nothing. I'm just looking." If something doesn't work 99.9 percent of the time, doesn't it make sense to try to come up with a better initial greeting?

If you work in retail sales, following these two important suggestions will increase your sales and the sales of anyone else in your company you share these suggestions with:

- ✔ When people enter your establishment, never walk directly toward them.
- ✔ When you do approach customers, don't rush.

Think about a time when you've been approached by a quick-moving, overzealous salesperson, and you had to step back away from him. You don't want your potential customers to have the same reaction to you. Approach your customers as if you're just walking around the store, not making a beeline to them. Smile. welcome them, and let them know you're there in case they have questions. Then get out of their way and let them look around.

Finding alternatives to "May I help you?"

So, what can you say instead of "May I help you?" Try saying,

> Hello, thanks for coming in. I work here. If you have any questions, please let me know.

> Hello, welcome to Standard Lighting of Arizona. I'm happy you had a chance to drop by today. Feel free to look around. My name is Karen, and I'll be right over here if you have any questions.

These greetings project warm welcomes rather than overbearing ones. You've just invited your customer to relax, and when people relax, they're more open to making decisions.

After you make your greeting, pause momentarily in case the customer does have questions, and then step away. Stepping away is vital to the success of this approach. Here's why:

- ✔ By stepping away from the customer instead of toward her, you distinguish yourself from all the typical salespeople she's ever encountered — and for most customers that's a very good thing.

- ✔ Left alone, customers walk toward what they want. By observing them from a discreet distance, you know exactly what they came in for.

If you work in a setting that's so large that people usually *do* need a guide (or at least a map) to find their way around — not an uncommon scenario for automobile dealerships or some furniture stores — you have to take your customers to the type of product they want. But, again, step away from them when you get them where they want to be, and let them relax. When they're ready to talk with you, they can still find you quickly, but you haven't invaded their space and taken control of their shopping experience.

When the customer finally stops in front of something for a moment, that's when you want to move closer to be ready to answer questions. Don't hang over them like a vulture, though. Just be where they can find you when they look around for help. The next section has more information on how to read customers' signals.

Recognizing the signals your buyers project

In any place of business where you have a display area or showroom, let your buyers look around before you approach them. Being laid back is much less threatening and far more professional than mowing down your fellow

Book III

Turning Prospects into Customers and Clients

associates and careening toward your potential customer like a runaway freight train the moment she walks in the door.

If a customer doesn't look around but remains by one item for a while, then you may walk up and ask a question. Use an involvement question right off the bat because she'll have to answer it with more than a *yes* or a *no*. Plus, you'll discover something that will help you keep the conversation going.

For example, if the customer is looking at a piece of furniture, ask, "Will this chair replace an old one, or is it going to be an addition to your furnishings?" When she answers, you'll know why she's interested, and you can then begin guiding her to a good decision. (For more on how to ask questions that get your customers talking, refer to Book II, Chapter 5.)

In a large retail environment, potential customers may have a challenge locating exactly what they're looking for. In that type of situation, try this:

> Welcome to Furniture Oasis. What brought you in to our store today?
>
> Welcome to Valley of the Sun Furniture. What may I direct you to today?

If they're looking for children's furniture and it's in the back of the store, you'll want to walk with them to that area. Letting these folks wander on their own, potentially getting lost along the way, does them a disservice.

Building Common Ground in Any Situation

After the introductions have been made and you're out of those first ten seconds of a meeting with a prospect, you need to smoothly transition into establishing common ground. How do you do that? By being observant. The power of observation is incredibly important to develop as you work on your overall selling skills.

The following sections provide guidelines to reach common ground with potential new clients. (These suggestions also work when you're meeting with existing customers with whom you may not yet feel entirely comfortable.)

Keep the conversation light, but move ahead

By allowing your prospect to first see the human side of you rather than the sales professional side, you'll help him break through the natural wall of fear that encloses him when typical salespeople walk through his door. Here are some suggestions:

- ✔ **Comment on things you see in the client's office or home.** If you just walked into Mr. Johnson's office, and you noticed that he has family photos all over the place, ask about his family. You don't need to know details now. Just say, "Great looking family," and let him decide how much to tell you. If you see trophies, comment on them. If you can see that he's a fisherman and you're a fisherman, too, bring up the subject of fishing.

- ✔ **Mention mutual acquaintances.** If Mr. Johnson was referred to you by someone else, mention the mutual acquaintance; that's usually a great starting point. "Good old Jim" may have an excellent talent, great family, or wonderful sense of humor. Those are all nice, noncontroversial topics to cover.

- ✔ **Offer a sincere compliment.** *Sincere* is the key word here. Sincerity takes you everywhere; blatant, insincere flattery gets you nowhere. A stale line like "Gee, Mr. Gargoyle, I'll bet everybody tells you that you look just like Brad Pitt" does not qualify as sincere.

   If you give a lot of in-home presentations, and the people you're presenting to have a nice home, you can say something like this: "I want to tell you that I spend a lot of time in other people's homes, and you should be proud of what you've done here. Your home is lovely." You also can look for signs of hobbies or crafts that you can comment on. If a woman is an artist and has her paintings on display, you can say, "You did that? What a great talent to have." That way you're not lying if you think the painting is really poor. Painting *is* a great talent — whether or not your prospect has any is in the eye of the beholder. If your prospect has any hobby he's obviously proud of, give him a sincere compliment about it. People always enjoy hearing compliments.

- ✔ **If all else fails, bring up something in the local news.** Just make sure it's a noncontroversial subject. Try your best not to bring up the weather — if you start off talking about how hot or cold it is today, your prospect will know you're struggling for something to talk about or that you're nervous, and that will make him nervous or hesitant to do business with you.

To keep the conversation moving forward, try an approach called *piggybacking*. In this technique, you simply ask a question, and when your prospect gives you an answer, acknowledge it with a nod or an "I see," and then ask another question based on the potential client's response. For example, if you meet someone at his office, the piggybacking may go like this:

Book III

Turning Prospects into Customers and Clients

> YOU: Good afternoon, Mr. Johnson. I appreciate your time. Nice-looking family you have there.
>
> PROSPECT: Thank you.
>
> YOU: What grades are your children in?
>
> PROSPECT: The oldest is a freshman in college. The middle one is a junior in high school. And the youngest is a freshman in high school.
>
> YOU: You must be very proud of them. What's your oldest studying in college?
>
> PROSPECT: Business. She wants to work for me when she graduates. I told her I would hire her only if she had straight As. A degree is a degree, but grades will tell me how much someone really learned.

What you've also just learned from that conversation is that Mr. Johnson, will expect you to be the best at what you do as well.

Here's another example:

> YOU: Good afternoon, Ms. Thompson. I appreciate your time. I was wondering how long the company has been in this location. I know I've seen your sign on the building for many years.
>
> PROSPECT: We've been here 25 years.
>
> YOU: That's great. And how long have you been with the company?
>
> PROSPECT: I started ten years ago in the area of inventory control. For the past five years, I've handled all the purchasing.

When you piggyback, don't make a hog out of yourself by asking too many questions unless you think that the other person is agreeable to answering more. The purpose is just to get the conversation going and make him feel comfortable with you. You're not conducting an interrogation.

Avoid controversy

Be cautious that the prospect doesn't tempt you into a conversation about a controversial subject. Some people do that just to test you. Specifically, avoid discussing politics and religion at all costs. Here's how to get around any topic that may lead you down the wrong path:

> I'm so busy serving clients, I haven't had time to stay current on that topic. What do you think?

By tossing the ball back at the prospect, you've dodged what may have been a fatal bullet, plus you got in a plug for your professional abilities. If the prospect comes back at you with a very strong opinion, you'll know to avoid that subject in future meetings. Or you may feel the need to brush up on it if he's deeply involved, so you'll have a better understanding of this person before you build a long-term working relationship with him.

In any business contact, be certain to never, *ever* use any profanity or slang. It doesn't matter if such language is widely used on today's most popular television programs; it has no place in the business world. You never know the values of the person you're talking with when you first meet him and you don't want to risk offending him. The same goes for off-color, political, ethnic, or sexist jokes. Be sensitive to the values, beliefs, and morals of the person sitting or standing across from you.

Keep pace with your prospect

Taking time to become aware of your normal speed of talking is extremely valuable. And notice the rate of talking of everyone else you encounter. Once you're aware of your speaking rate, you need to know what to do about it. If the person you're trying to persuade talks faster than you do, you need to increase your rate of talking in order to keep her attention. If she speaks much more slowly than you do, you should slow down or pause more often in your side of the conversation.

Any distortion in your rate of speaking can be deadly. You may lose her if you talk at the rate of a professional auctioneer, or her mind may wander if you're too slow. Try to time your rate of talking to your prospect's rate of talking. *Remember:* A potential client must be comfortable with you before he'll consider getting comfortable with your product or service.

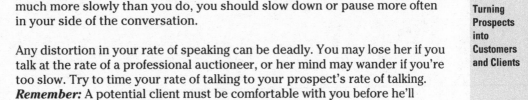

Book III

Turning Prospects into Customers and Clients

Chapter 2

Qualifying Your Way to Success

In This Chapter

▶ Thinking like a top detective

▶ Using five quick questions to discover whether you should move into a presentation

▶ Asking the right questions to guide potential clients toward your product or service

At the qualification stage in the selling cycle, you've found your potential client, made an initial contact, and received a commitment to meet either in person or via the telephone. The prospect has shown a certain level of interest in your product or service. Now you need to determine not only whether your prospect has a real need for what you're offering but also whether he has the authority and resources to make the decision to buy. All those factors must be present for you to consider this person a *qualified buyer*. If you discover that he isn't a qualified buyer, you'll need to politely withdraw and move on to another potential client. If you pursue presenting to and trying to close an unqualified buyer, all you're doing is wasting his time, getting in a little practice with your presentation, and allowing your confidence to take a hit. That type of situation is part of what has given sales a bad name in the past. Don't go there!

Qualifying your prospective clients properly is the single greatest factor separating those who win most often in their selling presentations from those who don't. Statistics from surveys of more than 250,000 sales professionals show that the biggest gap between six-figure income earners and those averaging around $25,000 per year is their skill in qualifying. That statistic alone should make you want to master this area of selling. And all it takes is asking the right questions. This chapter explains what you need to know about qualifying.

Qualifying Basics, or How to Think Like a Detective

You need to know your prospect's circumstances *before* you go into a full-fledged presentation and try to convince him to go ahead. Qualifying is particularly important in situations in which you don't have a close enough relationship with your potential buyer to know whether he needs your product or service. Qualifying is also important when the person needs to make a financial commitment or a personal commitment in order to go ahead.

If buying your product or using your service requires a financial commitment, your prospective client has to have the money or some credit to draw upon. If a personal commitment is required, he may need to check with someone else, like a spouse, before going ahead. In some situations, as with insurance, the person may need to qualify in terms of his health.

When salespeople try to convince or persuade others, one of the biggest mistakes they make is going into a full-blown presentation before they know whether the listener is a qualified decision maker or needs what they have to sell. Nothing is worse for either you or your prospective client than getting caught up in a presentation that ends up being a total waste of valuable time for both of you. So, for goodness' sake, when you see the word *receptionist* on a desk, don't give the person behind the sign your whole presentation.

So, how do you get started in qualifying people? You need to ask the right questions. In some cases, you wait and watch for the perfect opportunity to ask. Other times, you have to create the opportunity to ask. Think of yourself as an investigator, a gatherer of information to solve the mystery of your potential client's buying needs. If all you had to do was come up with a couple of questions that would always be answered completely and honestly, your life would be simple. But it isn't always that easy. Being able to discover your prospect's needs and concerns, as well as successfully incorporate such information into the opening of your presentation, takes a lot of time and practice before you ever meet them.

This information-gathering aspect of selling isn't unlike what you may have seen on the popular television programs about crime scene investigators (CSIs). These professionals are trained to ask questions in several different ways. If potential suspects come up with a different answer to a rephrased question, they know that they're not telling the truth or that they know more than they're letting on. Such information is valuable for them in continuing to seek out answers.

The following sections highlight key strategies you can use during the qualification step to get information from your potential new clients.

Keep out of the limelight

CSI detectives never presume to know the answers to the crimes they're investigating. They approach each scene with all their senses on high alert. They have the tools they need to gather evidence. They let the crime scene speak to them so they can deduce the right answer — the solution to the crime. When talking with suspects, the detectives ask questions that their observations have already provided the answers to. They're trying to match up what science tells them with what the humans have to say.

Likewise, your job isn't to enter your potential clients' lives and push anything on them. You're a wise observer seeking clues to what they need before asking questions. Your prospect believes you know more about the subject than he does, or he wouldn't invest his time with you. The prospect needs to share certain information about himself for you to know how to help him. Your goal in qualifying, then, is to involve the prospect in an educational experience where he participates in finding the solution through the use of questions. Each of your questions builds on his answers to the previous ones. You're seeking agreement that your observations are correct.

It's important that you get your points across in an educational style rather than a know-it-all style. A know-it-all may say something like, "Our product is the best in the industry." An educator would use facts to get the same point across like this, "*Car and Driver* magazine has ranked this model number one for reliability three years in a row." When you enter the classroom of a great teacher, is the teacher the star? No, she's not. The education — the learning — is the star. The teacher is just the facilitator.

Use nonthreatening language and a sympathetic tone

When CSIs are talking one-on-one with people involved in the crime, they often include the phrase *I understand how you feel . . .* and let the suspect in on something personal in their lives that shows they truly do understand. The goal of this line of questioning is to get the suspect to relate to the officer, let down her guard, and be upfront about her feelings or information she has about the crime.

Book III

Turning Prospects into Customers and Clients

You can adopt this same strategy. Consider using the Similar Situation Closing strategy even though you're not ready to close. Think of another client who was in the same or similar situation as this potential new client and tell their story:

> I understand how you feel, Bill. Just last week, another client was thinking about trading in his single-cab truck for an extended cab. After talking about his family and the way they use their vehicle, he decided the dual cab would make more sense. Tell me more about how you might use your truck on a day-to-day basis and how often your family joins you.

Then you would cover a brief summary of the benefits that helped the other client consider something that would serve his needs better than what he originally planned on buying.

Meeting potential clients on their home turf makes them more comfortable. Many business negotiators will tell you that you need to meet on your turf to hold the power — the home-court advantage, so to speak. In sales, you're not in a win-or-lose situation. The goal is to reach a win-win agreement. Making people feel comfortable with you is the first step you take in coming together to determine what the best solution will be.

Always take notes

Taking notes is vital, but CSIs don't rush to get every word of vital information. Instead, they jot things down casually. Their notepads aren't large and threatening. They're small enough to fit in a pocket and rather nondescript. And they refer back to the information gathered again and again during their investigations. The information they turn up helps direct future efforts with each suspect.

If your type of selling is via telephone or the web, it may be more effective for you to enter your notes into your computer. Just let your potential client know that's what you're doing. Otherwise, when she hears the clicking of keys in the background, she may think you're not giving her your full attention.

Taking notes is just as important for you. Of course, in selling, you don't have suspects, you have *prospects* or, more optimistically, *future clients*. Here are some pointers:

✔ **Jot down key information.** What's key information? Your prospective client's responses during the qualification sequence. This may include the size, make, or model of their current product. You should note the feature or benefit they most like about the product and what they dislike. You want to know who will be using the product or service and how much use it will get. Also, jot down any dates or events they mention where the product may be needed or used.

✔ **Make sure that the device you use to take notes isn't threatening.** If your company provides a standard form that has 100 blanks, your potential client will probably feel that you must fill in each empty space with information about him — which is a somewhat daunting and threatening prospect. At the very least, you should have a guide list of questions you know you need answered in order to determine if you can serve the potential client's needs.

✔ **Refer back to your notes.** When you state a fact back to the prospect, glance or point to where you have it in your notes. This shows that you have the correct information and that you're on top of the details. Referring to your notes also reminds you what questions you already asked and what the client said his needs were.

Notes also save you from needlessly repeating questions. Inadvertently asking the same question twice (or more) doesn't inspire confidence in the customer about you or your product. Not only do written notes help you during the presentation, but they also help you to remember what you've already covered when you follow up with the prospect after he's become a regular, happy client. In fact, that's part of how you keep him happy.

Ask permission to take notes before you start taking them. Getting permission to take notes is easy. All you need to say is this:

> Over the years, I've found it very beneficial to make notes during meetings with potential clients. Doing so enables me to do a better job. I wouldn't want to forget anything that might save you money or time as we move forward. So I hope you won't be offended if, while we chat, I make a few notes.

Putting it that way gives you an opportunity to admit that you're human and that you're also smart enough to have learned how to do your job well. These little sentences help put your clients at ease and build their confidence in you.

Some people get nervous when you start writing down what they tell you. For all you know, they may visualize themselves being grilled in a court of law on what they say to you. If you think you're with someone like that, give her a pad or piece of paper and a pen (preferably with your company name on it) so that she can take notes, too. Being prepared for this situation helps you avoid, or at least to handle, uncomfortable situations.

Book III

Turning Prospects into Customers and Clients

Make the people you're questioning feel important

CSIs always remind their suspects how accommodating they are to let them impose on their busy schedules. They thank the suspects profusely for their time and the vital information they provide. No matter how small the tidbit of information, they make those involved feel as if it's the single most important key to solving the case.

In addition to thanking your prospective clients for taking the time to see you, you can do the following to reinforce their importance:

- Make comments on the facts and figures the people provide you with. (These things should be in your notes; refer to the preceding section.)

- Compliment them on being on top of things enough to know these details without looking them up. And if they *did* look up some of the figures, compliment them on their dedication to accuracy by not calling out details from memory.

Ask standard and innocent questions

CSIs rarely come out and ask a suspect "Did you do it?" Instead, they ask what sounds like typical police-type questions about times, people, and places to gather background information and disarm the suspect, such as "Where were you when this happened?" or "What were you doing when the crime occurred?" Basically, these questions address the key point in a way that doesn't cause the person being questioned to immediately put up defenses.

In sales, the most uncomfortable topic for most people is money, but sooner or later, you need to talk about it. So, instead of just asking "How much have you got?," you need to be more discreet: "Mike, if we were fortunate to find just the right widget for you today, how much did you plan to invest to own one?"

Pay attention to both verbal and nonverbal responses

CSIs notice *how* people tell them what they have to say. They pay attention not just to the words being said but also to the body language of the speaker. They know and evaluate not only people's postures, but also what they're wearing, the surroundings they spend their time in, and even the cars they drive.

Noticing these same types of things can give you some important information about the potential client. If a woman lives in a $500,000 home and drives the latest Mercedes, for example, it's likely she'll be interested in owning the top-of-the-line model of your product as well. In other cases, if a person is looking at the top-of-the-line model but then steps away when you approach her, her behavior may be indicating that she's hesitant about whether she can afford it.

Build on the answers you get

Rarely do suspects realize they *are* suspects until they've let their guard down a bit and said something that doesn't fit with a previous answer. They often find themselves uncomfortable having to explain the difference in the two answers. They try to give credence to their errors and still keep their innocent attitudes.

You also can look for discrepancies — not to create a "gotcha!" moment, but to glean important information that hasn't been explicitly stated. Suppose, for example, that someone tells you that he invested $40,000 in his last series of widgets. An important qualifying question to ask would be, "And is that your current budget for a new purchase?" Never assume that this customer would be comfortable investing in that price range again. If, when you get to your presentation, your bottom line is that same amount and this customer says he can't afford it, you know that something was missing in the information you were provided.

Don't call the client out on the detail — as important as it is — just ask more questions: "Mike, I thought you told me you invested this much the last time. Was I wrong in my understanding that it was an acceptable amount?" This gives Mike an opportunity to explain further without your coming out and saying, "Hey, you gave me bad information!" It could be that Mike did pay that much and was reprimanded by company higher-ups for going over budget.

If a potential client initially says she has to have a car that seats six, but then, due to the higher investment, backs off to wanting a model that seats only five, she's potentially embarrassing herself with that discrepancy and may be uncomfortable if you bring it up. A six-seater may be her dream, but she didn't realize that it was out of her investment range and she only *really* needs to seat five. Just go with the flow of her needs and find her the right vehicle, even if it's not the one you originally thought would meet her needs.

Relieve any tension your questions create

Another famous CSI team tactic is to have one of its detectives return to ask just one more question . . . just as the suspect is breathing a sigh of relief and letting her guard down. This usually catches the suspect off-guard, and she trips herself up by revealing important information that is critical to solving the case.

Some people just don't handle decision making well. They're worried that they're going to be lied to or ripped off. So, they protect themselves by not giving you all the information you need to help them with their decision. Their thinking is that you can't force them into buying something that way. In reality, they're keeping themselves from becoming fully educated about your product. That strategy only hurts them. But fear of being taken advantage of is a natural part of selling on the buyer's side of the situation. So, you need to be ready to relieve any tension you may feel arise in your clients. You're not the bad guy who steered them wrong in the past (or that mom and dad warned them about). You may have to reiterate what your job is all about — helping people make decisions that are good for *them* based on the information you gather about their needs.

Let them know you'll be in touch

Any good salesperson who doesn't make a sale on the first contact will do whatever she can to leave the door open for further discussion with a potential client:

> Mr. Scales, I know you haven't agreed to do business with my company, but may I have your permission to stay in touch with you regarding our latest developments in case something in the future would be of benefit to you or your company?

Of course with CSI, letting the suspect know that a CSI agent will be in touch is plenty to think about in its own right.

Satisfying NEADS: The Nuts and Bolts of Qualifying Prospects

Good qualifying is a basic of selling that you can't overlook or slough off. Don't set yourself up for failure. Work on your style and questions, and then watch your income and your base of happy customers begin to grow.

The average salesperson today either lets the consumer totally make the decision as to what he wants or tries to steer the person to what that salesperson likes best. Both of these approaches are wrong. You will recognize steering if you hear (or say) any of the following phrases, especially prior to qualifying:

> I know just what you're looking for.
>
> This is my favorite.
>
> I have the best thing for you.
>
> We have the best products.
>
> This one looks so good in red.

To help you stay focused on what matters most when it comes to qualifying your prospective clients, remember this acronym: NEADS. The following sections cover the five parts of the NEADS equation, but the acronym itself is what's most important. Granted, the spelling is a little creative, but that spelling will help remind you of how you can determine the *needs* of your customers. Each letter stands for a question you should ask your prospective clients in an effort to discover their needs.

The success ratio for your entire company would rise if you could get all the salespeople to say to themselves when they meet a customer, "I am concerned about my customer's NEADS. I will discover my customer's true needs and lead my customers to the right product or service for them." Satisfying NEADS helps you accomplish more in your business.

WII-FM: What's in it for me?

An old sales-training lesson goes like this: What's everyone's favorite radio station? The answer is always WII-FM. The call letters in this case stand for "What's in it for me?"

People have a WII-FM mentality, whether they admit it to themselves or not. Human beings are selfish creatures whose natural propensity is to make themselves as comfortable as possible. Be painfully honest: When was the last time you did something for someone else with absolutely *no* expectations of getting anything in return? Now before you start congratulating yourself on what a self-sacrificing person you really are, think about that answer for a second. Remember a time when you did something for someone else without expecting *anything* in return for what you did — no thank-you, no undying loyalty, no promises that the object of your benefactions would someday return the favor, nothing . . . zip, zero, zilch, nada, *nienti*, goose egg.

If you're like most people, you'll have difficulty thinking of such a time. Most people are motivated to do for others only if they themselves expect to receive compensation that they value in return. The compensation may not always be monetary, but people *always* want something, anything, even a crust of bread in exchange for their efforts. Even if the sought rewards are intangible and emotional — compliments, hugs, kisses, pats on the head, a warm smile — a reward is a reward is a reward.

And that's the same philosophy your customer holds every time you contact her. She needs to quickly realize the benefit to her for taking your call or setting up a meeting with you. Help her see you as someone who can eliminate a discomfort from her life. To her, you must be someone who can give more than he receives, which is what she expects when she thinks of customer *service*. You contact your customer for one reason: to serve her needs, whether you do it by providing information, a service, or a product. You always answer her question of "What's in it for me?"

N is for "now"

The *N* in NEADS stands for "now" — as in, "What does the customer have now?" Why should you ask this? Because average consumers don't make drastic changes in their buying habits. If you know what your prospect has now, you have a good idea of the type of person he is — and you have a good idea of what he'll want to have in the future.

If past experiences often dictate future decisions — as they undoubtedly do — then you need to explore your customer's past experiences. You need to know what he has now so that, in your mind's eye, you can see the type of buying decisions he'll make in the future.

Show an experienced salesperson your current vehicle, home, style of dress, or style of jewelry, and she can probably tell you what your next version of each of those products will look like. This experienced salesperson isn't prejudging you. She's simply aware that most people are creatures of habit. People usually don't make drastic changes in their lives unless they've recently won the lottery or received a large inheritance or windfall.

E is for "enjoy"

E, the second letter in NEADS stands for "enjoy." You need to know what your customer enjoys most about what he has now. What was his major motivation for getting involved with his existing product or service?

To discover what your customer enjoys, you need to structure your questions so you can discover the customer's past. There's a good chance that what he *enjoyed* about the product or service in the past, or what he *enjoys* about what he already has, is exactly what he'll want again. That's usually true — unless you can demonstrate a benefit in *your* product or service that is even better than the one he enjoyed when he purchased his present product or service.

A is for "alter"

The *A* in NEADS stands for "alter," as in, "What would the customer like to alter or improve about what he has now?"

Because it's constant, change is a potent force in business. In some ways, everyone is looking for change — more benefit, more satisfaction, more comfort. Your customer's normal urge to improve his present condition is why you want to develop questions to find out what he would like to change. What would he like to be different? When you know your customer's answer to that question, you can structure your presentation to show him how your company can provide the changes he wants in his present product or service.

D is for "decision"

The *D* in NEADS stands for "decision." Specifically, you need to know who will be making the final decision on the sale.

Many times salespeople meet a customer who is looking for a car, a home entertainment system, maybe some furniture, and they meet only that one person. Is it wise for the salesperson to assume that the person she's met will be the decision maker? No. Never assume anything about your potential clients. The customer may be scouting or researching, planning to bring a spouse or parent in later, when it's time to make the final decision.

So, you need to ask qualifying questions to discover whether the person you're talking with is the final decision maker. Here are some examples:

Will you be the only person driving the car?

Who, other than yourself, will be involved in making the final decision?

Are you the type of person who likes to consult with others when making decisions like this?

You never want to imply that the people you're qualifying aren't capable of making decisions on their own. You are simply clarifying that they have the final say in the decision.

You've probably heard the standard response to a decision-qualifying question: "I'll have to talk it over with my husband/wife/parents/best friend from college." Many times the salesperson who hasn't properly qualified the prospect will go too far in the presentation before finding out that the real decision maker is not present. You do nothing more than practice your presentation when you present to non–decision makers. That doesn't mean, however, that the non–decision maker isn't important. You need to be equally enthusiastic to everyone you meet. Even though the person isn't the decision maker, he can be an influencer or a champion of your cause.

If the product you're offering is something to be used by a family or a couple, it's wise to at least attempt to present to both parties. One or the other may tell you he's the final decision maker, but in most relationships and for many types of purchases, such decisions require at least input from both parties. If it's impossible to get both spouses together for a presentation, at least suggest you get the other party on the phone so you can answer any questions they have directly.

S is for "solutions"

As a salesperson, you're in the business of creating solutions. And, coincidentally, that's exactly what the *S* in NEADS stands for. You're in the solution business. You find out what your prospects need, and then you come up with a solution. With properly qualified prospects, the solution is that they take ownership of the benefits of your products or services.

Here's an effective introduction to the qualifying process that you'll want to adapt to your product or service:

> As a representative of [name of your company], it's my job to analyze your needs and do my best to come up with a solution to satisfy those needs so you can enjoy the benefits you're looking for.

You serve customers by finding out what they need and then creating the right solutions. When you do this, you create win-win relationships where people want to do business with your company and they get the products or services they need. They give you business; in turn, you both grow and prosper.

Questioning Your Way to Qualifying Success

Part of qualifying your potential clients includes knowing the right questions to ask. Your goal in qualifying is to get the information you need to have before narrowing down the best solution for your client. The best solution is what you'll present in the next step of the selling cycle. The preceding section covered the NEADS questions as an easy qualifying strategy to remember and use. However, true professionals in selling invest their time wisely in developing questions that go even deeper into finding out exactly what the client expects the product to do for him.

You can use questions to acknowledge or confirm a statement your prospect made that is important to getting her final commitment — the decision you want your listener to make. For example, if your prospect tells you that gasoline mileage is very important to her in buying a new car, before you would present the vehicle you think is best for her, you would include a question like this:

Didn't you say that fuel economy was your primary concern?

Such a question starts the *yes* momentum you need to excite her about the product you're planning to present. The *yes* momentum is what every persuader strives for. After you get your prospect agreeing to things, if you simply keep asking the right questions — kind of like following a flow chart — she'll follow where you guide her. Plus, she'll have enough information at the end of your presentation to make a wise decision, which you hope is that she can't live without your product or service.

Questions also create emotional involvement. If you're marketing home security devices, you can ask:

Wouldn't you feel more confident about entering your home in the evening knowing you would be warned beforehand if there were any danger?

What does that question do? It raises a prickle of alarm on the back of your prospect's neck about the unknown possibilities of walking into an unprotected home. You don't want to frighten anyone into purchasing your product, but you do want to get him picturing himself owning its benefits. That's emotional involvement — and it's a requirement in any selling situation. *Remember:* Think of at least two ways to build emotion, through the use of questions, into every presentation you make.

The following sections provide the details you need on how to use questions to confirm a prospect's statements and make an emotional connection.

Before you ask any question, remember this: To sell or persuade, you need to make the other person feel important (refer to the earlier section "Make the people you're questioning feel important"). Your prospect needs to feel smart, too. So never, ever ask a question that your listener can't answer. For example, if you ask someone what the available memory is on his computer and he doesn't know, you've just made him feel uncomfortable. Avoid that result at all costs. If he hasn't brought up the subject of available memory, you should ask whether he has the information available on his current computer. Chances are, he does. If you tell him specifically the information you need, he can get it. But if you assume that he knows it, and he doesn't know it, you've just embarrassed him. And he may find someone else to buy from who is a little more sensitive and able to make him feel important. And where does that leave you? Without the sale.

Book III

Turning
Prospects
into
Customers
and Clients

Tying down the details

One of the most popular questioning techniques is called the *tie-down*. A tie-down does not involve tying clients into their chairs until they say yes. Instead, tie-downs involve making a statement and then asking for agreement by adding a question to the end of it. Here are some effective tie-downs:

- **Isn't it?** For example, "It's a great day for golf, isn't it?" When your caller agrees, you set a tee time.

- **Doesn't it?** For example, "Jet-skiing at the lake this weekend sounds like fun, doesn't it?" When your client agrees, pull out the rental agreement — pronto.

- **Hasn't he?** For example, "The previous homeowner has done a great job with the landscaping, hasn't he?" When the prospective new homeowner agrees that he likes the landscaping, he's just moved one step closer to liking the whole package — house included.

- **Haven't they?** For example, "The manufacturers have included every detail about the questions you asked in this proposal, haven't they?" Having all the details covered and having the buyer agree she's covered helps reduce the possibility of stalling when it's time to close.

- **Don't you?** For example, "Cleaning up the lot where your employees park is important, don't you agree?" When the person agrees, sign him up for your cleanup service and have him choose a date he wants it done.

- **Didn't you?** For example, "You had a great time the last time you went hiking, didn't you?" Then pull out the latest style of boot while your client is in a positive frame of mind about the last trip.

- **Shouldn't you?** For example, "With so many choices that you enjoy on the menu, you should come here for dinner more often, shouldn't you?" If it was an enjoyable meal, suggest a date for a return visit and book the reservation.

- **Couldn't you?** For example, "You could let your spouse have a whole day just to relax and rejuvenate, couldn't you?" Get a commitment to a spa package!

The goal of using tie-downs is to get your prospect thinking in the affirmative about the subject you've just tied down. While he's agreeing with you, you can confidently bring up whatever it is you're trying to get a commitment on.

Professional salespeople often use tie-down statements such as this:

A reputation for prompt, professional service is important, isn't it?

Who can say no to that? The salesperson who asks such a question has begun a cycle of agreement with the prospect who, hopefully, will continue to agree all the way through the selling sequence.

Giving an alternate

You've certainly seen or heard the *alternate-of-choice* questioning technique used before, but you probably didn't recognize it as a sales strategy. This strategy involves giving your prospect two *acceptable* suggestions to choose from. It's most often used for calendar events such as appointments, delivery dates, and so on. Here are some simple examples:

- ✔ **"I can arrange my schedule so we can visit on Thursday at 3 p.m. Or would Friday at 11 a.m. be better?"** Either answer confirms that you have an appointment.

- ✔ **"This product comes in 55-gallon containers or 35-gallon containers. Which would you prefer?"** No matter which container your prospect chooses, he's still chosen to take one of them.

- ✔ **"We'll have our delivery truck at your home on Monday at 9 a.m. sharp. Or would 2 p.m. be more convenient?"** Whichever option your prospect chooses, you've nailed down the delivery.

You also can use the alternate-of-choice technique when you want to focus on or limit the conversation to certain points. For example, if you're selling playground equipment to a school or homeowners association (HOA), you don't want to open up a debate about placement of the equipment when you're preparing a proposal. You just need to know the specifications required for the materials and equipment desired. In that case, you can ask, "Which do you think would be a better surface under the equipment, wood chips or sand?" It helps you get right to the point of the matter and gives only the two solutions you need addressed.

Alternate-of-choice questions are particularly effective in surveys. The market researchers are seeking particular information, not general answers, so they build the questions in such a way that the prospect is limited in his responses.

Book III

Turning Prospects into Customers and Clients

Getting prospects involved

Another questioning technique is the involvement question, in which you use questions to help your listeners envision themselves *after* they've made a decision to agree with you. If you're marketing office equipment, you can involve your prospect with a question like this:

Who will be the key contact for us to train on the use of the equipment?

Now you've got her thinking about implementing training *after* she owns the product, not about *whether* she'll own it.

Similarly, if you want to involve someone in business with you, use a question like this:

What will you and Janet do with the extra income that our business plan says we'll generate in the next year?

Is your listener thinking about whether to get into business with you? Nope. He's just envisioning spending the money he'll earn *after* he goes into business with you. If what he plans to spend the money on is something he wants badly enough, there's a good chance that he'll find himself *having* to go into business with you to satisfy a need he's been feeling without knowing how to fulfill it. Aren't you the good little helper for bringing him just the right business opportunity?

Chapter 3

Winning Presentations

. . . .

In This Chapter

▶ Ensuring a good first impression

▶ Following the basic rules of presentations

▶ Making sure the product is in the spotlight

▶ Using visual aids and demonstrations to your advantage

▶ Holding your clients' interest during presentations of intangible goods

▶ Avoiding Murphy's Law in the world of presenting

. . . .

The presentation stage of the selling process is the show, your chance to get your prospective client's senses involved. Major companies prepare for the presentation stage by investing hundreds of thousands of dollars and a great deal of time in creating graphics, models, and samples. Some even invest millions in building entire presentations using video or Flash animation with hopes of picking up new clients online that salespeople may not be reaching.

A presentation can be as simple as giving out a brochure with a quick explanation or as complex as what you may see at a trade show — complete with bells, whistles, food, clowns, and fireworks. How you present your show depends on what product or service you represent, your company's directives, and the potential investment of the prospect.

This chapter steers you through the possibly frightening territory of the sales presentation (frightening at least until you're trained) — everything from discovering the power players in the room to giving a presentation over the Internet. It also gives you some great tips for avoiding common presentation pitfalls. So, before you give a presentation, read on.

You must have your presentation well rehearsed. Memorize anything that you may be required to say. Practice until you can deliver your presentation smoothly and without sounding like you're delivering rote information. How long this takes will depend on your product and your own dedication to getting the job done. Because your presentation engages the clients, you have to be prepared to handle potential breaks in your presentation due to client questions and get smoothly back on track to complete the task.

Getting More Than a Foot in the Door

When you've earned the right to give a prospective client a presentation of your idea, concept, product, or service, you're nowhere near done. The decision maker has chosen you — probably from several other contestants — and given you the opportunity to prove that your offering is as dazzling as you've been saying. But having an appointment to give a presentation doesn't automatically grant you favored status or guarantee you a warm welcome. It doesn't mean that you'll become the buyer's favorite supplier. What many prospects are saying when they let you in the door is, "Okay, wonderboy, impress me!" or "Okay, wondergirl, back up your claims." No pressure here, is there?

Every day, salespeople bombard your prospect with overtures for their business. Your contact person may be a real decision maker or someone designated to narrow the field to two or three potential suppliers for the real decision maker to talk with. Many times when a large purchase is required, a purchasing agent will bring in several competing companies to give presentations to a committee. If you've done your homework well, you'll know exactly who will be present and why each one of them is there.

It's absolutely vital that you identify who you'll be presenting to and what's in it for each of the people present. (Understanding the perspective of your contact person is vital, a point that is covered in detail in Book I, Chapter 2.) With this information, you'll know who will need more persuading and how to go about doing just that.

The following sections provide pointers on how to start your presentation off on the right foot.

Find the power players

When you begin an in-person presentation, thank and acknowledge the person who invited you, make eye contact with each person in the room, and see if you can tell which member of your audience is the power player. There's one in every group (including families), and she may or may not be the person you've already been talking with. Just by watching how the other members of the group treat each other should clue you in.

Workplace behavior isn't much different from what you see in a documentary about the social habits of wolves. Just as in wolf packs, in most workplaces the subordinates usually defer to the power players when important issues arise. Another hint for identifying the top dogs in a workplace: They often take the best seat in the house during presentations. The best seat is usually at the head of the table or at the 12 o'clock position at a round table, with you at the 6 o'clock position. Or the power player may sit closest to the door in anticipation of an interruption for a vital call or message. You won't be able to make a perfect call every time, but as you hone your skills at the people game, you'll start picking out the power players in minutes.

Some power players don't play the game the way you'd expect and may sit unobtrusively in the back of the room. By watching everyone else's body language, though, you should still be able to recognize that person.

Be quick or be sorry

In today's world of the ten-second TV commercial, few people bother anymore to develop their ability to concentrate. In fact, the average person has a short, downright gnat-like attention span, which means that you must compress the heart of your presentation down to a matter of only a few minutes. After those few minutes, spend the rest of your time involving your prospects directly in the presentation through questions, visual aids, or a hands-on demonstration. (You can find discussions of these topics in more detail later in this chapter.)

To help your prospect focus on your presentation and to help yourself stay on track, state your objectives prior to beginning your presentation. Limit your objectives to three. For example, you might say the following:

> Mr. and Mrs. Bradshaw, today I would like to cover three things. First, I would like to better understand your business. Second, if what you tell me about your business makes sense, I would like to demonstrate a product I think you will find beneficial to your company. And finally, if you see the value in what I am presenting to you today, I would like to discuss the action steps required to help you benefit from it as soon as possible.

Practice, drill, and rehearse your presentations to get through the nitty-gritty in just under 17 minutes. Go past 17 minutes, and your prospect's mind wanders and her eyelids droop. Besides helping to keep your prospect awake, brevity and conciseness demonstrate concern for her valuable time. She may not consciously realize that she appreciates your concern for her time, but on some level she will appreciate it — and that concern will make a difference.

Book III

Turning Prospects into Customers and Clients

This 17-minute time constraint may challenge you if your product is, say, a complicated mechanical system. If that's the case, you may want to plan for a short break or a summary or question-and-answer period after the first 17 minutes are up. Letting your prospect stretch her legs or be actively engaged will increase the level of concentration she gives you. When the blood stops circulating in your extremities, paying attention is difficult. The mind can only absorb as long as the body can endure.

The magic 17 minutes do not begin the moment you enter the room or while you're building rapport. The 17-minute period begins when you get down to the business at hand and cover the finer points of your product's benefits and value to your client. It also does not include the time you invest in answering client questions, overcoming their concerns, or closing. It's just the amount of time you should target for the actual product benefit presentation. You need more time with complex products, but even then you should refine your presentation to only the most critical elements in order to develop the interest of your clients.

Break well, and prosper

If you choose to schedule a break, or even if an unplanned break occurs, here's a vital piece of advice you must take to heart: Always do a brief recap before starting back into your presentation. A *brief recap* is just a restatement of the major points that you've covered so far, a quick way to bring everyone back to where you were before the break.

Any break in the action allows your listener's mind to wander. She starts looking at her watch, she thinks about lunch or her next appointment, or she wonders what the rest of the office is doing. She may even leave the room to make a call. If she does leave, her mind focuses on the matter dealt with during the break, not on your presentation. And you'd better believe that the emotional level your prospect was at when the break began will not be the same when she comes back. Before you can move on with your presentation, you must take a moment or two to bring her back to where she was.

Knowing the ABCs of Presenting

The general guidelines for giving effective presentations are simple. They're the same ones you learned in English class for writing a good story: Tell them what you're going to tell them, tell them, and finish by telling them what you've told them.

This method serves the same purpose in oral presentations as it does in written ones. It helps the person on the receiving end understand and remember the story you've told him. And when you're selling, you want your presentation to be a memorable occasion for the decision maker. Master the four basics of presentations — talking on your customer's level, pacing your speech, using the right words to create ownership, and interpreting body language — and you're on your way to earning favored status in the mind of every prospect who hears your presentation. (These tips work even if you have to give a presentation on the phone or online.)

Being multilingual (even if you're not)

Know enough about your prospect — going into the presentation — that you can talk with him on his level. What does it mean to talk on someone else's level? Consider this example.

Suppose you're in your 30s, and you're trying to sell a refrigerator to an older couple who want to replace a 20-year-old appliance. What do you say to them? Well, with these prospects, you'd probably talk about dependability and the new features that your product has over their older model. You'd also point out the benefits that would accrue to the couple if they owned those features. The benefits would be lower utility bills with increased efficiency of new appliances, longer food storage time (which means less waste and greater convenience of getting at things), whether it has an outside drink door, and so on.

Now cut to a different scene: You're trying to sell the same refrigerator to a newly married couple for their first home. Do you talk to them the same way you did to the older couple who were replacing an old appliance? No, with the younger couple you would accent the features and benefits that apply to their situation and satisfy their present needs. The features are the same, but the benefits are seen in a different light when viewed from their perspective. They may want something less expensive because that's all they can afford. But if you can show them the overall savings of getting a bigger or better fridge now, as opposed to the replacement costs once they start a family, you'll be farther ahead because they'll be more comfortable making the investment when the decision is rationalized for them.

Consider this versatility of message as being *multilingual*. You speak senior citizen. You speak yuppie. You speak single parent. You speak high end. You speak economy. Being able to converse with someone at his level — whatever that level is — pays big. If you want to test this theory, try talking at your normal business level to a 5-year-old and see how long you keep her attention.

Book III

Turning Prospects into Customers and Clients

Then talk with her on her level and watch the animation in her face as she realizes that you've just entered her world.

To become multilingual when you sell a product or service to different businesses, pick up industry magazines, visit websites, or use some other equally respected source to familiarize yourself with their language — their world. If you're trying to sell insurance to an architect, why not visit the architect's website? If you can speak with the architect about something of interest to him, he'll like you. *Like* builds to *trust* and *trust* helps to develop *commitment.* The same applies to whatever industry your potential client is in. If you can at least ask intelligent questions about her industry, she'll be more likely to open up to what you have to say about yours.

Also, within a committee or family, you may have decision makers with different interests. For example, in a business situation where you're presenting to a committee, you may have a finance person, a technical person, and an executive in the room. They all have different "languages" they use in evaluating products or services from their perspectives. Know who is in the room and be prepared to "speak" to each. (For help in identifying generational differences and communicating with each generation effectively, refer to Book II, Chapter 5.)

Recognizing the posted speed limit

When you give a presentation to a prospect, you need to be sensitive enough to recognize the proper demeanor to have with each client. This part of your presentation is kind of like what stage actors and actresses do: They play off of the attitude and enthusiasm of the audience. If you're too energetic for your audience and speak at too fast a rate, they'll be turned off. Then again, if you're too mild mannered for them and speak too slowly, you may lose them as well.

The ideal approach is to pay attention to the rate and pitch of your prospect's speech and then closely match it. When this happens, on some subconscious level, your prospect gets the message that you're like he is. Plus, he'll understand you better.

Forcing yourself to slow down to another person's level can have an adverse effect on your entire presentation. If his pacing is very slow, you can speak at a level slightly above his. With a little practice, you'll develop a good sense for what's right. Similarly, if the other person has an accent different from yours, be very careful not to adopt it (a tendency that, believe it or not, is pretty natural). If you adopt his accent, he'll think you're mocking him or that you're insincere.

Using words that assume your client will buy from you

Speak as though your prospect already owns what it is you're selling. Don't say, "If you join our neighborhood safety awareness group. . . ." Instead, say, "When we meet, you'll enjoy the value of participating in our neighborhood safety awareness group." Or talk about what life is like *after* your prospect owns your product, as in "After the system is installed, you'll enter your home after work every day knowing that you saved energy without having to turn the thermostat up or down." Giving your prospect the ownership of your idea, product, or service helps to move him closer to making a decision. This is called *assumptive selling*.

Assumptive selling is not the same as *suggestive selling* — when you order nothing more than a chocolate shake but your friendly McDonald's server oh-so-sweetly asks if she can get you an apple turnover today. With suggestive selling you're being offered something you haven't yet asked for or about. Assumptive selling is operating as if the buyer has made the decision to own a product or service he has expressed an interest in.

Deciphering the human body's grammar, syntax, and vocabulary

The study of body language has been around for a long time. In fact, most people are aware of body language, but they don't consciously read it and benefit from it. Here are just a few examples of the kinds of messages body language communicates (and how to read them):

- ✔ **Leaning forward:** If you lean forward when you're talking to someone, you're showing that you're interested and paying attention. When you recognize that positive sign in other people, you should keep moving forward. In fact, you may be able to pick up the pace of your presentation a bit if your entire audience is leaning forward.

- ✔ **Leaning back or glancing away:** When you lean back or glance away from someone who's talking, that means you're losing interest in what he's saying or that you're uncomfortable with what was just said. What do you do if you recognize this body language in your audience? Pause if you're in the middle of a long monologue, summarize the last couple of points, and ask your client a question. Or, if it's a group presentation and you see several of your clients displaying this body language, suggest a short break or a question-and-answer period.

✔ **Crossed arms:** If you cross your arms when you're listening to someone, this indicates that you doubt what the other person is saying or that you're not truly interested in hearing what she has to say. When you receive this sign from your audience, move to a point-proving demonstration, chart, graph, or diagram. Or, ask a question such as "On a scale of 1 to 5 with 5 being very important, how valuable is this point to you?" If it's not valuable, skip ahead in your presentation to the next topic.

Just as important as knowing how to read the language is knowing how to speak it. When you understand positive body language cues, you should practice them as a part of your presentation. They can be as critical as the words you say. If you want to successfully persuade your prospects, you need to be able to give positive, warm, honesty-projecting gestures, such as the following:

✔ **Sit beside the person you're trying to persuade instead of opposite him.** You're not on an opposing side. You're on your prospect's side.

✔ **Use a pen or pointer to draw attention, at the appropriate times, to your visual aids.** Some people hesitate when they use a pen or pointer, and that hesitation says that they are uncomfortable. (You always want to avoid any suggestion of discomfort during demonstrations.) This is something you should practice as part of your rehearsal for presentations.

✔ **Use open-hand gestures and eye contact.** Open-hand gestures (such as exposing your palms or pointing with your whole hand rather than an index finger) and lots of eye contact say that you have nothing to hide.

These are just a few of the basics of body language, but the whole field of study on body language can help you so much more. When you begin paying attention, you'll find that many other body language cues will become obvious to you. (Check out *Body Language For Dummies,* by Elizabeth Kuhnke [Wiley], for more on body language.)

Delivering on long-distance presentations

When you can't possibly meet in person with your prospective client and you have to conduct business over the telephone or online, you need to be aware of certain strategies to apply.

Phone presentations

Because you can't see your clients when you're on the phone, you may have trouble knowing whether they're being distracted or interrupted. Even though you can't read body language over the phone, you can definitely listen to their voice inflections (just as they'll be listening to yours). You can tell fairly easily whether someone is paying attention by counting the length of pauses between their comments and the number of *uh-huh*s or *hmm*s you hear. Also, pay attention to any background noise on the other end of the line. If you hear barking dogs, doorbells ringing, or small children, chances are good that you won't have this person's full attention.

If you're in doubt as to whether your prospects are on the same page with you, ask a question of them. Don't, of course, ask if they're paying attention. Instead, ask how something you just covered relates to their business or what they think of it. Restate that point or benefit clearly so they're not embarrassed if they really weren't paying attention.

Another strategy to use when you're giving phone presentations is the *pregnant pause.* If you briefly pause during your presentation, the pause will make your prospects wonder what happened and draw their attention to what you'll say next, thus drawing them back to the point at hand.

The product needs to be the star of the presentation — especially if you're not meeting in person. If at all possible, be sure to send a sample product or, at the very least, an attractive visual of it to the client so she'll be seeing what you want her to see during your presentation. Alternatively, have them log on to your company's website and direct them where to look, what to click, and so on.

Video or web presentations

If you're asked by a prospective client to join him for a presentation via videoconference or through an online service but you're not savvy to these types of communication tools, you'll need to find someone who is and take a quick lesson. They're not too difficult to work with, but the logistics of setting the stage just right can be tricky. For example, when videoconferencing, you'll probably use an "eyeball" sort of camera attached to your computer or the one built in to your laptop. You may even be doing this from home.

When you participate in videoconferencing, you need to

- ✔ **Make sure you're centered in the frame.** Place your camera and rehearse your presentation while recording a short clip of yourself moving naturally as you do while at your computer. See if you lean out of frame when you reach for something. Do you make any repetitive gestures that may be distracting? Take note of how your local newscasters appear and act on camera. Their head and shoulders are in the frame, but not much else. Newscasters also make great eye contact with the camera — they smile into it, smiling with their eyes.

- ✔ **Be aware of what else is in the picture with you.** Make sure you have an attractive background even if you have to borrow something to put up behind you. And check your camera to be sure that it doesn't allow your next potential major client to see a torn poster hanging on the wall behind you or a neglected plant. These kinds of objects can harm your credibility. Also, make sure that nothing behind you is at the level of and near your head. In this position, the object will look like it's sprouting from your cranium.

If your presentation online requires you to show slides or other visuals, maintain as much control of the flow as you can. For example, you can control a PowerPoint presentation from your computer while it's being viewed online from someone else's computer. In PowerPoint, you can save your work as *ready-to-view HTML* documents. Clients and co-workers can then launch the presentation in a web browser, even in full-screen mode. They can view slides in any order or repeat important slides at their convenience. *Presentation on demand* is another feature within PowerPoint that allows people to rerun your presentation at any time that's convenient for them. Visit `www.microsoft.com/office/powerpoint` for a tour of the latest features you may benefit from.

Letting the Product Be the Star

One key in presenting or demonstrating anything — a new hobby, a multimillion-dollar piece of high-tech equipment for a Fortune 500 company, or anything in between — is really pretty simple: Let the product shine; let it be the star. You're just the host who introduces the key players (your product and your prospect) to each other and then fades into the background to let them get acquainted.

Even though one of the players may be an inanimate object, even an intangible one, you need to think of that object in terms of the future primary relationship between the product and its new owner. And you need to let the possibilities for that relationship develop (with your encouragement, of course) while keeping the entire process under control.

Getting out of the picture

As a salesperson, you aren't unlike the matchmakers of old. You may help someone find a mate, but after they've met, you step out of the picture and let the relationship develop. Of course, you may occasionally monitor the progress of the relationship, but you won't be coming to live with them.

Even though the product must be the star, never forget that your prospective client needs to always remain the focus of your presentation. Never give so much attention to the product and what it can do that you ignore what it will do *for* the person sitting there with you — your prospective client. If you start putting your hands on the product or turning your eyes, back, or chair more toward the product than the people, you risk losing their attention. It's better to allow the client to get their hands on the product even if it means they turn their backs on you. You remain the director of the presentation, assisting them in their experience with the product.

Staying in control

Don't let your potential clients see what you want them to see until you're ready for them to see it. The product has to be the star, but you need to be the guide — or the bodyguard — letting them close only when it's appropriate.

If your demonstration involves the use of a piece of equipment, don't let your prospective client come in and begin punching buttons or demanding answers to a lot of questions — taking control of the presentation away from you. Just tell the prospect that he has great questions and that you'll cover most of them in your presentation. Then ask that he hold his questions until after the demonstration. When he recognizes that you've planned something special for him, he'll probably settle down and let you do your thing.

 Keeping control can become a challenge when you have several things to display. If your demonstration falls into this category, you bring something (like a cloth) to cover your display items, uncovering only those items you're prepared to discuss. Or, if you can, simply leave anything not pertinent to the moment out of their line of sight. If you're using a video or computer screen, be sure to have an attractive screensaver or a blank screen that you can go to when you need your prospect's attention focused back on your planned presentation. Otherwise, your prospect will probably try to read ahead on the screen instead of listening to what you're saying.

Mastering the Art of Visuals

You've heard the phrase *seeing is believing*. That phrase comes from the desire of most people to be shown the proof that what they're being told is real, or at least that it can come true. Take a moment to see the difference between *telling* someone about a new product and letting her *see* it, either in picture form or through a product demonstration. Obviously, letting the prospect see it will involve more of her senses. And that's where visual aids come into play.

Visual aids should show three things to new clients:

- ✔ **Who you (and your company) are:** Visual aids should identify your company and the industry to which it belongs. The story of your company builds credibility.

- ✔ **What you've done:** If the latest hot app uses software developed by your company, brag about it in this portion of your visual aids. This is also where you mention or show your company's rating from an independent source.

✔ **What you do for your clients:** This is the part your prospective client is most interested in. Whether she asks it directly or not, what she really wants to know is "What's in it for me?"

The best visual aids include all three of these key points. If they don't, be sure to try to verbally incorporate these points into your presentation. The following sections describe two types of visuals and how to use them: the kind supplied by your company and the kind that you make yourself.

Using the visuals your company supplies

If you represent a company's products or services, you've probably been exposed to their visual aids. These are usually slick, high-quality sheets or slides with graphs, charts, diagrams, and photos. Such visual aids often contain quotes from various well-thought-of authorities about your product or service or, at the very least, testimonials from satisfied clients. For organizing and storing printed visual aids, many companies provide you a great-looking binder that also stands up like a miniature easel.

You may work for a company that's more high-tech than this. For example:

✔ You may get computer-generated graphics that appear on a projection screen and include music and professional announcers, such as those created using PowerPoint, video, or Flash animation. For computer presentations, you'll most likely have a laptop computer and multimedia projector.

When you prepare for one of these high-tech presentations, be sure that your prospective client has a whiteboard or screen for you to project your images onto. Presenting your product professionally is tough when all you have to work with for a background is wood paneling or flowered wallpaper.

✔ You also may work with videos for your presentations. Videos often include recorded testimonials from actual happy customers your potential buyer can relate to. When your prospect sees someone just like herself who is benefiting from your product or service, the relationship between the prospect and your product grows a little stronger.

Whatever your specific visual aids depict, the important thing to remember is this: Your company invested in the creation of your visual aids for a reason. And that reason was not to make your life more complicated by having to carry all this stuff around and keep it updated. Instead, your company did it because many, many years' experience has proven that visual aids are very effective when they are used properly.

So, what's the best way to use visual aids provided by your company? Most likely, it's the way your company recommends. Few companies succeed in business by putting out garbage as visual aids and then leaving their salespeople to figure out how to use them. Typically, companies rely on a task force of some sort that includes top salespeople, manufacturing people, and marketing people. All their suggestions usually have to be approved by a director or manager of the marketing department — someone who will ultimately be held accountable if the brochures, videos, or sample products do the job of moving product into the hands of consumers (or if they don't).

If for some reason you don't like or have trouble using the company's visual aids, talk with the people who trained you on how to use them. If their suggestions don't satisfy you, talk with a top salesperson — someone who does use them effectively. You may even want to go on a customer call with that salesperson to watch how she handles things. After you master her suggestions for using the visual aids as well as possible, if you still think you have room for improvement, ask to meet with the people who put them together. They'll probably be glad to offer you constructive suggestions and, hopefully, listen to yours.

Developing your own visual aids

If you have no visual aids to work with, put some thought into what you can develop on your own. Involvement of the senses in attempting to persuade others is critical. Book II, Chapter 5 has more information on how to involve the five senses.

Say, for example, that you want to sell your family on vacationing in the woods when you know they'd rather go to the beach. You can involve their senses by showing a video highlighting nature in general — flowing waterfalls, gentle breezes blowing in the trees — and the outdoor adventures available in the woods: canoeing, hiking, horseback riding (whatever appeals to your audience). Such a video would involve two senses: sight and hearing. If possible, you may even want to have a little campfire going in the yard while the family watches your video (smell). Or prepare some hot dogs and s'mores ahead of time so that they get their sense of taste tied in to the joy of that vacation in the woods. Invest in hiking boots, lightweight backpacks, or canteens filled with spring water in order to get the sense of touch involved.

All these things (the video, the campfire, the food, the equipment) are sensory aids that are vital to your presentation if you're serious about persuading your family to go on this type of vacation. When they accept ownership of all these feelings, it'll be an easy sale (unless you have a family member with a very strong phobia of bugs or wide-open spaces).

Book III

Turning Prospects into Customers and Clients

The same strategy applies to formal business sales presentations: The more senses you can involve, the better. Start with developing aids that focus on sight and hearing — charts, graphs, computer graphics, videos, and the like. To strengthen the impact of the visual aids, find ways to get additional sensory involvement. You can involve your prospects' sense of touch just by handing them things. Smell and taste are a little tougher, especially if you're selling an intangible object like a service.

With intangibles, you may want to paint visual pictures that bring those senses into play. For example, if you sell a cleaning service to a working mother, you may not necessarily want to have her smell the cleaning agents you use — but you can talk about how fresh the home will be after your professional crew has completed its duties. You can find a discussion of product demonstrations and how to talk about intangible goods later in this chapter.

Demonstrating Products to Prospective Clients

When you demonstrate a tangible product, you have to be like a game show host. You want a lot of excited contestants, and the way people get excited is through involvement. ***Remember:*** Selling is not a *spectator* sport; it's an *involvement* sport.

One of the greatest fears all clients have in selling situations is that they'll trust what the salesperson tells them, buy the product or service that's for sale, and then, after they own the product or service, find out that it doesn't meet their expectations or meet their needs. The best demonstrations give people the opportunity to prove to themselves that what the salesperson is telling them is true. Here are some pointers:

✔ **Let the customers push the buttons!** The best computer salespeople stand or sit at their client's shoulder, giving him instructions on how he can do whatever it is he just asked about. They make sure the client's hands are on that keyboard and mouse. That way, the client has a positive experience with the product and builds his confidence in the capabilities of the machine. He may even be overcoming a fear of computers altogether. And if he overcomes that fear and gets comfortable using the product, you can bet he'll be much more likely to want to own it.

Suppose you sell copiers. During your presentation, you shouldn't be the one pushing the buttons, making double-sided copies, changing the paper, and opening and closing the machine. Let your prospective clients perform the functions, and they'll feel involved.

✔ **Stay focused on the capabilities that matter most to your customer; don't go overboard on the most complicated features.** It won't matter to the office manager that you've won all the time trials at your office for making the most complicated copying challenges come out perfect. Instead, what matters is how simple it is for everyone on your prospect's staff to meet those challenges — and you should build into your demonstration the proof that they can do so. During your demonstration, your prospect and her staff members should be able to make normal copies simply and to find out something about a new feature that's going to make their job easier. Your key contact person should see exactly what all the warning lights are on the machine and what to do about each one. (Don't go overboard here, though. They may begin to wonder about the quality of the machine if there are so many warnings. Just assure them that if anything is amiss, the machine can diagnose itself. Then she just needs to follow the instructions for whatever button lights up.)

✔ **Gear your presentation to take the least amount of your potential client's time as possible.** How long this takes depends on the product you're offering. A kitchen knife can be demonstrated in seconds. A software application may require longer. Only go longer if the client is really interested, wants to see it again, asks questions, and so on.

✔ **Be prepared for malfunctions or things going haywire.** If you have a challenge with your demonstration, you should be prepared to take another approach to demonstrating it. After you master the initial presentation of your product, start asking other salespeople about how they handled situations where things just didn't go right; then build those strategies into your preparation. Analyze your presentation with questions that begin with "What do I do if . . ." and do your best to cover all the bases as you prepare.

Book III

Turning Prospects into Customers and Clients

Presenting Intangible Goods

If the item you're selling is intangible — insurance, financial services, banking services, wireless phone service, education, and so on — your presentation will differ from that of salespeople offering tangible items. When a potential client can't see, touch, hear, taste, or smell what you're selling, you need to develop ways of keeping his attention during your presentation.

Fortunately, many companies employ software that can provide immediate analyses of individual needs. For example, if you sell financial services, you may be able to plug Jim and Sally's number of years to retirement and existing savings into a calculator of sorts that will project what their incomes will be at retirement age. Playing with the numbers in various scenarios can be fun for them and will definitely keep them involved.

If you don't have anything other than paper (brochures, flyers, proposals, and so on) to work with, there are specific strategies to consider:

✔ **Don't hand your prospects anything to read until you want them to read it.** Their attention will be on the printed piece, not on what you're saying about its contents. If your printed piece contains several points that you want to address separately, hold the brochure so your clients can see it and point to each area with your pen as you discuss them. When you're ready to move away from the brochure, you can fold it back up and set it aside, telling them you'll gladly leave it behind with them to review again. This way, you keep control of it instead of having them pick it up again and get distracted from what you're saying.

✔ **If a comparison chart showing how your products or services stack up against the competition isn't available, create one.** Be sure that any information your client gathers is perceived correctly (as in comparing apples to apples). Let them know you created the comparison chart, but list your sources in a footnote at the bottom so they can see that you didn't just make up the information.

When talking about intangible services, you have to work at creating mental pictures in the minds of your potential clients. You don't have anything physical to show them, but you can create images in their minds of how much better their lives will be after they own what you're offering. For example, they'll have greater health if starting a new exercise program or joining a gym. Get them thinking about feeling better, stronger, and more energized. Help them *feel* the satisfaction of having their clothes fit better and *hear* the compliments they'll receive from others. If you're selling insurance, focus on the peace of mind they'll have knowing they're properly protected. If you're selling retirement programs, help them *envision* what their future lifestyle can be like through the commitment they're making now. Constantly take what the intangible *is* and help them see what they can *be, do,* or *have* when they own it.

Avoiding the Crash-and-Burn Scenario of Presentations

If you've been in the business long enough, you've either heard a presentation horror story or experienced one first hand. The unfortunate thing is that many of the problems at the crux of these catastrophes could have been avoided if a few simple precautions had been taken. The following list covers the things that should become a vital part of your preparatory checklist when you're getting ready to make a presentation.

✔ **Find the electrical outlets and know how to reach them.** If your demonstration requires the use of electrical power, find out in advance exactly where the available electrical outlets are and how you can plug in to them. If you're running the show on your computer battery, check and double-check that it's fully charged prior to your presentation — and bring a spare, fully charged battery with you, just in case.

✔ **Be sure your visual aids are in order.** Food stains and bent corners on your presentation materials give the impression that you don't care about details. And if your materials are confiscated by a roving band of evil, invisible little gremlins who mischievously rearrange your slides into a state of utter chaos, your audience will be less than thrilled. So, before your presentation, be sure to review each and every piece of equipment or presentation material that your audience will see. You'll sleep better knowing things are in order.

Never use your materials immediately after someone else has been through them. Misplacement of contents is rarely intentional, but it does happen.

✔ **Test everything ahead of time.** You may have a very dependable demonstration model of your computer software. In fact, it could be one you've used for several weeks or months without any challenges. But on the day of your big presentation, Murphy's Law may strike. So, always arrive early enough to test your equipment on-site. And test it early enough that, if you find something isn't working, you can adjust for it.

✔ **Customize as much as you can.** No one loves a generic presentation (the ones that have been given, word-for-word, to at least 40 other audiences before). By making the extra effort to customize your materials, you'll appear competent and knowledgeable about your customer's specific needs. And that's just the kind of person she's looking for.

✔ **Bring a protective pad.** If you're scheduled to make a presentation in someone else's office, don't take a chance that any of your equipment will mar his furniture. To prevent damages, always check the bottom of your equipment before placing anything on a potential customer's furniture and have protective padding on hand. Rough edges can easily leave scratch marks.

Book III

Turning Prospects into Customers and Clients

Chapter 4

Addressing Client Concerns

. . . .

. . . .

*U*nless you sell balloons at a parade, few customers will contact you, make an impulse purchase, and go away happy. What really happens is that potential clients — anyone who has any interest at all in what you're offering — will always have questions. Some of those questions can include the following:

✔ Will the product or service do what you say it will?

✔ Will you really be able to make their required delivery date?

✔ Have they negotiated the best investment?

✔ Are they making a good decision?

✔ Is it something they need right now, or should they wait?

All these little doubts and fears creep up on potential clients when they feel the urge to invest in your product or service or to commit to your idea. In some cases, a desire for a clearer understanding, and not fear, is at the root of the concerns; these customers want to be sure about what your product will do for them.

Although the concerns that arise when a potential client feels moved to make any commitment involving his time or money are completely natural, most people new to persuading think that a "No" or a sign of hesitation means "Good-bye, Charlie." The seasoned persuader, however, knows that, if interpreted correctly and handled properly, a question or objection is another opportunity that can lead to "Yes!"

Until you come to expect client concerns, you won't know how to handle them. And until you know how to handle client concerns, you won't come close to reaching your highest earning potential in sales. So, go into every presentation anticipating concerns, and you'll come out ahead. This chapter gives you the help you need in addressing client concerns.

Reading Your Clients' Signals

Clients can have good reasons to hesitate. The best reason of all is that the client feels himself leaning toward "Yes," in which case the hesitation can simply be a sign that he wants to slow down the selling process in order to absorb all the information you're giving him. Or hesitation can mean that the client needs *more* information before he feels comfortable making a decision. When a potential client hesitates or gives you a stall, just think, "He is asking for more information."

Prospective clients give you three important pieces of information when they voice objections or raise concerns during your presentation:

✔ **They're interested, but they don't want to be thought of as an easy sale.** If you've properly qualified the prospect (see Book III, Chapter 2 for more information), you know what he has now, what he enjoys most about it, what he would alter, and that he is the decision maker. Armed with that knowledge, if you're confident that the prospect would benefit from your offering, chances are he's interested, but he just doesn't want you to think of him as an easy sale. In that case, you want to slow down the pace, encourage questions, and generally get him relaxed and chatting before you ask him to make a decision.

✔ **They may be interested, but they aren't 100 percent clear about what's in it for them.** If your prospect is already asking lots of questions and looks somewhat perplexed or doubtful, he's interested, but he just doesn't have a clear enough picture of what's in it for him. This situation is especially common when the prospect doesn't have previous experience with a similar product and you're educating him from ground zero. To respond to this kind of prospect, you have to cover the features and benefits in a bit more detail — asking questions along the way that will help you create the right word pictures in your presentation. (See Book III, Chapter 3 for more information about winning presentations.)

✔ **They may not be interested, but they can be if you educate them properly.** If you face this kind of questioning client, you must first earn his trust so he'll give you the time you need to educate him on your product. You also have to build the prospect's curiosity about the product, service, or idea so he wants to know more.

All three situations tell you one thing: The prospect needs more information. By backing up and clarifying exactly what it is the prospect is objecting to, you find out just which direction to take for your next step.

Most persuaders find it hard to influence people who voice no objections and raise no questions. In negotiation situations, you carry the presentation forward by directing and redirecting your course of questions and information based on the feedback your prospect gives you. If she tells you nothing, the communication often stalls. When that happens, you have to guess which direction to follow next — and guessing is very bad because when you guess, you're no longer in control. Guessing is like casting your line with no bait on it. The people who don't get verbally or physically involved in your presentation likely have no intention of going ahead with your proposition. Those who *do* bring up challenges for you to address are, at the very least, interested. If they're really tough to convince, they'll probably become your best customers when you finally do convince them. So, the next time you hear an objection, be glad. Getting objections and getting past them are necessary steps in the selling cycle.

Adopting Simple Strategies to Address Your Clients' Concerns

Objections from potential clients are just part of the business of selling. What's important is that you know how to handle them. Fortunately, you can use some key strategies to address your prospects' objections so that they come away with more information *and* more respect for you and your product. This section shows you how.

If you get nervous or afraid when you hear an objection and start beating a hasty retreat for the door, you're leaving empty-handed. So why not experiment with ways to address your client's concerns or handle his objections? If he doesn't like the way you handle it, you're going to be heading for the door anyway, so you haven't lost anything. The worst that can happen is that you won't get what you want and you'll be free to move on to the next likely candidate. The best that can happen is that your client sees how competently you handled his concern and that his concern wasn't strong enough to keep him from going ahead with your offering.

Bypassing the concerns completely

If you know your prospect wants and needs the product or service you're offering, but she feels a natural inclination to object, you often can bypass the objection altogether. Simply say, "That's a good point, Ms. Smith. I believe it will be addressed to your satisfaction by the end of my presentation. May I make a note of it and come back to it later?" If she gives you permission, she'll be paying attention to the rest of your presentation for a satisfactory answer. Or she may see enough benefit during the balance of the presentation that the value outweighs her concern and it becomes a moot point.

Book III

Turning Prospects into Customers and Clients

If you're new to persuading, don't ignore any objection without testing the waters to see how big a concern it truly is. Sometimes just acknowledging the concern is enough. Your prospect will be satisfied that you're really listening, and then she'll move ahead. Also, keep in mind that, when your prospect raises a concern, it doesn't necessarily mean "No way." It may simply be a way for the prospect to say, "Not *this* way." If that's the case, you just need to adjust what you're saying and take another path to the same destination.

Helping clients see that they're trading up

If your prospective client has money, credit, or both, but he just doesn't want to part with it now, you haven't convinced him that he'd be better off with the product than he would be with his money. In this situation, you need to work on building the value of the benefits of your product or service.

If an investment you're offering requires the person's time, "No time" is not a valid condition (see the later section "Distinguishing conditions from objections"). It's an objection. Everyone has the same 86,400 seconds in every day. How people use them is their choice. If you want someone to invest his time with you, you have to show him enough benefits for him to *want* to spend his time on your offering instead of on what he's already planned.

Beating your clients to their own concerns

If you know that your prospect is likely to voice a particular concern, beat her to it. By being in control and bringing up the issue when you want it brought up, rather than when your prospect thinks the time is right, you can brag about it and turn it into an advantage.

For example, if you know your product costs more than others on the market, you can be fairly certain that your prospect will be concerned about that cost. But you can beat the prospect to that objection by explaining upfront that your product requires a higher investment because it contains only the highest-quality ingredients. And those high-quality ingredients make people feel better, last longer, or perform in a superior manner. Those benefits are worth bragging about *before* your prospect gets busy laying bricks for that wall of defense against the investment.

The following sections describe specific tactics you can use to beat your clients to their own concerns.

Addressing specific concerns about money

When the concern is specific to the cost of your product, you can use one of the following strategies. Your choice between the two methods is going to be a judgment call. When the customer raises the concern, if you think that he has developed a certain belief in you — in your competency — then you may prefer to use the second approach.

✔ **Strategy 1: Stress what they're getting for their money.** Here's an example:

CLIENT: Tom, I'm sure I can find this product, or one just like it, for a lot less money.

TOM: Well, Jim, I understand your concern. You know, I've learned something over the years. People look for three things when they spend money: the finest quality, the best service, and of course, the lowest price. I've also found that no company can offer all three. They can't offer the finest quality and the best service for the lowest price. And, I'm curious, for your long-term happiness, which of the three would you be most willing to give up? Fine quality? Excellent service? Or low price?

This client is going to have a tough time coming back at you and saying, "Well, poor quality and crappy service are okay as long as they're cheap."

✔ **Strategy 2: Link your reputation and credibility with the quality of your company and its products.** Here's an example of this strategy in action.

CLIENT: Tom, I'm sure I can find this product, or one just like it, for a lot less money.

TOM: Jim, I could have chosen to work for any company in the area in my particular industry. After careful research, I chose my company because I wanted to be able to sit with my clients, look them in the eye and say, "You are doing business with the highest-quality company in the industry." I know you appreciate quality and, because of that, those few extra pennies you'll invest per day to enjoy the finest quality will benefit you in the long-term scheme of things, don't you agree?

With this approach, you enhance the credibility you've already established. In effect, you're telling your client that you're not an amateur. You have a concern for your own reputation, as well as your clients' satisfaction, and you plan to be around in the business a while.

Bringing up and bragging about concerns

Instead of waiting until a prospective client brings up a concern, bring it up first, but instead of being apologetic about it, turn it into a benefit. Say, for example, that you market copy machines to small businesses, and your machines are so popular (and you're so good at selling them) that your company sometimes has trouble keeping enough inventory in stock to keep up with all the sales orders. Instead of waiting for your client to ask about the delivery date, you bring it up early in your presentation, in a way that accounts for much of the uncommon sales volume. You can say something like this:

The lady doth protest too much

If prospects bombard you with objections, you may want to ask a few questions to get them to express their *real* objection. If people protest too much, they're either not interested and don't have the guts to tell you so or they're hiding the real reason they aren't going ahead. For some people, liking your offering but being unable to afford it is hard to admit. So, instead of admitting that they're strapped, they come up with a hundred other reasons why your product, service, or idea isn't right for them. Eventually, you may need to say something like this:

Mrs. Johnson, obviously you have quite a few concerns about our product. May I ask, what will you base your final decision on: the overall benefits to your family or the financial aspects of this transaction?

This way you're asking, as is your right, for the real objection to your product or service while still being nice, warm, and friendly.

Remember: You can't move beyond this step in the selling cycle until you identify and handle that real final objection.

Jim, I'm confident that at the end of my presentation you'll want to own this copier, as so many of my happiest clients have done. I must say that we're excited about that. You see, if you had decided to get a copier from one of our competitors, they probably would have it available immediately. Maybe that's because there's less demand for their machines — I don't know. If you decide on our machine, I'm going to have to ask you to be patient because we're currently in an oversell situation — everyone seems to want this particular machine. Its popularity speaks for itself, doesn't it?

Having product that's back-ordered can be a serious challenge if you let it. But bringing it up and bragging about how popular the product is puts back-ordering in a different light — a light that many customers will accept.

Take advantage of this tactic with concerns that you know are most often heard about your product or service. If people object to the cost, have a testimonial on hand from a happy client who had the same concern and now feels her return on investment was well worth it.

Many companies post testimonials on their websites. You can easily impress your prospect by calling up the website on your laptop right then and there to address the prospect's concern. Let him read it instead of telling him about it. In fact, asking your prospective client to take a look at your company's website prior to your presentation is always a good idea. Send the prospect an e-mail with your web address and a few suggestions of areas within your site that he may find helpful.

This method of beating prospects to their concerns — by bringing it up, bragging about it, and then elaborating on it — has proven successful for many salespeople. If you tend to see common challenges as stumbling blocks, change your thinking: They're actually springboards to success.

Distinguishing conditions from objections

If your customer's objection is "I'm totally broke," and you're selling a luxury item, chances are you've just heard a condition, not an objection. And there's a big difference between the two.

A *condition* is not an excuse or a stall. It's a valid reason that the prospect can't agree to what you're proposing. If you're trying to exchange your offering for your potential customer's money, and the customer has no money and has no credit, just thank him for his time, get permission to stay in touch should things change in the future, and move on. With so many potential clients out there who have no conditions, you have no good reason to beat your head against the wall with those who *do* have valid conditions.

Always leave people who voice valid conditions on a positive note, though. You never know how that person's situation may change down the road. He may win the lottery tomorrow. Old Aunt Thelma may leave him an inheritance. He may borrow money from his rich grandpa. Or, better yet, he may convince Gramps that your offering would make a great birthday or Christmas gift for him.

If he wants what you have to offer badly enough, he'll call you. And you can rest assured that his calls won't go to someone else with whom he doesn't have a positive relationship. After all, why would he call a stranger when he can rely on a salesperson who he knows to be knowledgeable, competent, and considerate?

Book III

Turning Prospects into Customers and Clients

Understanding the Do's and Don'ts of Addressing Concerns

Before you get too deep into dealing with your prospect's concerns, you need to be aware of some basic do's and don'ts of this important step in selling. The advice in this section can guide you through any selling situation.

Do acknowledge the legitimacy of the concern

Dismissing your prospect's concerns as unimportant can cause those objections to get completely blown out of proportion. In many cases a simple "I see" or "I understand" is acknowledgment enough. In other cases, you may do well to say, "Let me make a note of that so we can discuss it in depth after we cover the benefits you've indicated you need most," and then jot it down. Jotting down the concern validates the concern and shows professionalism on your part. Your presentation may cover the concerns the client had or create so much value that those concerns become nonissues.

If you do need to circle back around to the questions or concerns that you set aside during your presentation, state them back to the client in his own words. "Now, John, you mentioned that you were concerned about taking your people out of the field to train on this new software." If John is now really excited about the benefits of the software, his concern about this may no longer be an issue.

You don't have to go back and answer every concern. In some cases, you just need to bring it up. The client may already have an answer for it with the information you presented after he expressed it.

Do get the clients to answer their own concerns

The most important "do" of addressing concerns is to get the other person to answer his own objection. That advice may sound tricky to follow, but here's why it's so important. Because you're trying to persuade your prospect, he'll automatically have reservations about anything you do or say. Why? Because anything you say must be good for you, too. Until the prospect realizes that you're acting in his best interest, he'll doubt you.

Here's something to help you remember that last point: When *you* say it, they tend to doubt it. When *they* say it, they believe it to be true. And *that's* why you want to get your prospect to answer his own objections — because he's much more likely to believe *himself* than he is to believe *you.* All you need to do is provide the information that answers his concern and let him draw his own conclusions. You let him persuade himself.

You may need to nudge him a little by asking a question to get him to state the desired answer: "How do you see that feature impacting your company's level of efficiency, Jim?" It's much more powerful when he answers than if you just say, "That feature will increase your company's efficiency by 20 percent." See the difference? Take advantage of the strategy, and you'll close more sales because your clients will be convincing themselves.

This technique often works well when you're persuading a married couple (children, take note). When one partner objects to something, don't respond immediately. *Average* persuaders are quick to defend their offering. But there's a better way: Learn to sit tight. Many times, one spouse jumps in with the next comment, and you have a 50/50 chance that the originally silent spouse will answer the objection for you. If the second spouse agrees with his partner's objection, then you know you'll have to work a little harder to overcome it. The point is that these two people already have a positive relationship (you hope) and trust each other's judgment. Being quiet while they think it through can cause the objection to evaporate into thin air right before your eyes.

When something important to you is hanging in the balance, being patient is difficult. During such moments, seconds feel like hours, and you can quickly become very uncomfortable. To keep yourself from jumping in too soon, try this trick. Silently count to 20 or 30 (to avoid going too fast, use the old "one-thousand-one, one-thousand-two, one-thousand-three, . . ." tactic). Some salespeople recite a short poem to themselves to kill that time — just don't let your mind wander off from the matter at hand. Whatever method you choose, be careful not to let them see your lips move.

What you never want to do when you're waiting for a response is look at your watch or at a clock in the room. Even a slight glance at a timepiece can distract the prospects because they're already looking at you, waiting for your next move. Practice this step until you're comfortable with it.

Don't argue with your client

Although not arguing with your client may seem obvious, when you're negotiating with someone, emotions can take over and things can get out of hand. Arguing or fighting an objection or concern raises a barrier between you and the person you're trying to persuade. You're trying to persuade her to something, not go ten rounds with her. If you keep the perspective that objections are simply requests for further information, you shouldn't have much of a challenge with this advice.

Don't minimize a concern

To the person you're persuading, every point he raises is valid. Remember to put yourself in his shoes. How would you react to someone who acts as though your concerns are stupid or unimportant?

Never ignore a concern that's raised during a presentation. Asking to reserve the answer for later (as mentioned previously) demonstrates that you take the customer's concern seriously. Also, never respond to a concern by saying anything like "That isn't really an issue" or "None of our other clients has been concerned about that." These phrases imply that because no one else has been worried about that particular item, he shouldn't be either. Keep in mind that he may not give a darn about what other people think about this area of concern. It's *his* concern and needs to be addressed to *his* satisfaction.

If you dismiss your potential customers' thoughts or feelings about something, they'll very likely want to dismiss you as their salesperson.

Handling Concerns in Six Easy Steps

In the following sections, I give you six steps for handling objections or addressing concerns that almost always work in your favor. If you practice and apply the following steps properly, they'll take you a long way toward achieving your goal of selling to others, even when they raise objections or concerns. (They also work pretty well in diffusing unusually tense situations, so heed them well.)

Before you begin the six-step process, take note of the following general pointers on objections:

✔ **Sometimes you'll hear more than one objection or concern from a potential client.** If you start running through all six steps with each objection you hear, you can spend a lifetime trying to persuade them. Experience helps you tell which concerns you need to address and which you may be able to bypass (see the section "Bypassing the concerns completely" earlier in this chapter).

✔ **If a concern or objection is raised during a group presentation and you have to do a bit of research and get back to them, be certain you have the contact information (specifically, an e-mail address) for each person in the group.** Never rely on one person to relay vital information in the manner that you know to be best for moving the selling process forward. Send the exact same e-mail message to each person, and let them all see that they're part of the group e-mail. If each person receives it individually, they could all wonder what else you may have shared with the others.

✔ **Include the link to your company's website for each member of the group to peruse.** Often in a committee decision-making situation, only one or two members get the whole package of information. They then break it down for the balance of the decision makers. This may be the way the *company* wants the process handled, but what *you* want is to get as much information as possible equally distributed.

Step 1: Hear them out

When someone trusts you enough to tell you what's bothering him, do him the courtesy of listening. Don't be quick to address every phrase he utters. Give him time; encourage him to tell you the whole story behind his concern. If you don't get the whole story, you won't know what to do or say to change his feelings. Don't interrupt, either — you may jump in and answer the wrong concern.

Step 2: Feed it back

By rephrasing your client's concerns, you're in effect asking for even more information: "So, what I'm hearing you say, Jim, is that you aren't 100 percent sure this new system will resolve the challenges for every department. Is that right?" You want to be certain that he's aired it all so that no other concerns crop up after you've handled this one. You're saying to him, "Go ahead. Lay it all on me. Get it off your chest." In doing this, you're asking him to trust you.

Step 3: Question it

This step is where subtlety and tact come into play. If a potential client objects to the amount of space your product will take up, don't say, "What's wrong with it?" Instead, gently ask, "Would you feel more comfortable with a smaller model?" or "Is that the only thing that's holding you back?" If it is, he'll tell you why. Maybe he's concerned about appearing ostentatious. If so, you have to further build his confidence by stressing the benefits the product provides.

Step 4: Answer it

When you're confident that you have the whole story behind your client's concern, you can answer that concern with confidence. If the prospect's concern is cost, you can engage in the following dialog:

> YOU: I can certainly appreciate your feelings. But I think we ought to keep that $1,000 in the proper perspective. Over the years, most of my happiest clients received true enjoyment/value from this product for at least five years. This fact really makes that $1,000 only $200 per year, doesn't it?

> PROSPECT: Yes, it does.

> YOU: If you're like most people, you'll receive the benefits of this product for 52 weeks per year, which means that $1,000 breaks down to about $3.85 per week. Then, of course — and this may sound ridiculous — it finally boils down to about 55¢ per day. Do you think you should avoid enjoying all the benefits we've discussed for 55¢ per day?

> PROSPECT: Well, when you put it that way, it does sound a little silly.

And you've just gotten the prospect to answer his own concern.

Book III

Turning Prospects into Customers and Clients

Step 5: Confirm your answer

When you've answered the objection, confirming that your prospect heard and accepted your answer is important. If you don't complete this step, the prospect very likely will raise that concern again.

You can confirm your answers simply by completing your answer with a statement such as, "That answers your concern, doesn't it, Bob?" If Bob agrees with you that your comment answered his concern, then you're one step closer to persuading him. If he isn't satisfied with your answer, now is the time to know — not later, when you try to get his final decision to go ahead.

Step 6: By the way . . .

By the way are three of the most useful words in any attempt to persuade or convince another person. Use the phrase to change gears or move on to the next topic. Don't just keep talking. Take a conscious, purposeful step back into your presentation. If it's appropriate, turn the page in your presentation binder or booklet. Point to something other than whatever generated the objection. Take some sort of action that signals to the other person that you're forging ahead.

> By the way, what delivery date works best for you?
>
> By the way, how would you like to receive your monthly statements — via e-mail or at your postal address?

Book IV

Closing Like a Champ and Getting Referrals

The 5th Wave   By Rich Tennant

"They've been that way for over ten minutes. Larry's either having a staring contest with the customer, or he's afraid to ask for the sale again."

In this book . . .

To be a championship salesperson, you need to know as many closes as you possibly can, because you'll encounter every possible type of decision maker and situation in your sales career. In fact, a change in the selling climate can occur within one single transaction. Statistics have shown that the average closed sale requires five closing attempts, which means that the average salesperson needs to know at least five closes. You'll quickly fall to less-than-average status if you know only two or three closes. And less-than-average status means you earn a less-than-average income — and who wants that?

Mastering the multiple closes outlined in this book is the best way to keep yourself fresh, to keep your options open, and to keep closing more sales.

Chapter 1

The Anatomy of a Close

natomy is the study of separating parts in order to ascertain their relation to each other — that's *Merriam-Webster*'s definition, anyway. Although this chapter doesn't cover traditional anatomy, it does dissect the "anatomy" of a close — and in the process, answers the questions that most often come up about closing: When do I close? Where is the best place to close? How do I close?

When you make the decision to ask the closing question, you do so based on the information and feedback your client has provided you, the buying signs you've noticed, the body language you've observed, and so on. This chapter dissects closing into four sections: when to close, where to close, how to try a test close, and how to skillfully move into the final close.

The discussions about closing the sale that you find here assume that, up to the final close, you've done everything else right: Your potential clients like you, trust you, and feel good in your presence; you've discovered your clients' needs; and you've demonstrated to them that you have just the right product or service to meet those needs. In other words, you're prepared to get the final agreement.

Recognizing When to Close

So, when do you close? Here's the answer: Clients display telltale clues when they realize that they want the benefits of your product or service. These clues are buying signs. When you see them, you're ready to initiate the close.

A *buying sign* is an indication from your potential clients that lets you know they're prepared to go further. Always be on the lookout for two types of buying signs: verbal and visual.

Verbal buying signs

Verbal buying signs let you know that your clients are interested in owning your product or service. They start when your clients make positive comments about your product or service, ask pointed questions, ask you to repeat something, or speed up the buying pace.

Recognizing verbal buying signs is often a matter of listening well, but how do you know if you listen well? Here's a test: At any given moment with a customer, you should be able to do the following:

- ✔ Clarify your customer's needs.

- ✔ Offer feedback on the areas the customer questions, is unclear on, or is not yet educated on regarding the product or service.

- ✔ Reinforce the benefits of your product or service that are specific to the customer's needs.

- ✔ Evaluate the depth of your customer's commitment to making a decision today. (You do this with test or trial closes, outlined in the later section "Mastering the Test Close.")

- ✔ Assess the customer's ability to own. Does your customer have the money? This is part of the qualification step of the selling cycle, done mainly by asking questions. (Refer to Book III, Chapter 2 for more on qualifying customers.)

When you've listened this well while conversing with your customers, you know that you're tuned in to their verbal buying signs.

Asking technical questions

One particular type of question — a technical question — lets you know that they're interested in owning the product. A *technical question* is any question that your clients don't need to know the answer to unless they own the product. Here are some examples:

✔ If you sell computer equipment, your clients may ask, "How much memory does this computer come with?"

✔ If you sell copy machines, your clients may ask, "How will it handle runs of 500 copies?" or "How long does the toner last?"

✔ If you sell real estate, potential home buyers may ask, "How much are the property taxes?" or "What does the electric bill run each month?"

✔ If you sell cars, potential buyers may ask, "What type of gas mileage can I expect to get?" or "What type of warranty does the car come with?"

Pay particular attention to technical questions. Few people ask these technical questions unless they're seriously thinking about owning the product or service — a clue that it may be time to close.

Asking for info to be repeated

Another verbal buying sign occurs when clients ask you to repeat information. Whenever a buyer says, "Could you go over that again?," you should be saying to yourself, "Hot dog! Clients never ask me to repeat information unless they're serious about going ahead."

With this type of verbal buying sign, the clients are slowing down the buying pace a bit, but they're still giving you an indication that they're getting ready to close.

Some clients, on the other hand, may speed up the buying pace — and clue you in with verbal buying signs — when they're ready to close. These clients take it slow when doing their research, but as soon as they make a decision, they're ready to get the details behind them, make the purchase, and move on to their next project. In this type of case, the clients may give you a synopsis of all the benefits, conduct a quick review of the financial aspects, ask if their interpretation of the information is correct, and look for a pen to approve the paperwork — or reach for their wallets.

Visual buying signs

Visual buying signs are more subtle than verbal signs and involve an understanding of *body language* (the visual cues we all give to others, consciously or unconsciously, with our posture, facial expressions, and hand gestures).

REMEMBER

While you're observing your clients, keep in mind that they'll be observing you, too. You always want to look your best and be on your best behavior. Determine the judgments you want your clients to make when they meet you by controlling the image you convey through your appearance and business demeanor.

Reading body language for buying signs

Body language plays a tremendous role in any communication process. The nonverbal communications in Table 1-1 are just a few of the signs you'll notice if you pay attention. (For a more detailed discussion on body language, refer to Book III, Chapter 3.)

Table 1-1	Interpreting Body Language
Body Language	**Interpretation**
Crossing arms in front of chest	Not open to new ideas, not listening
Tapping pen, fingers, or shoes	Bored, aggravated, impatient
Leaning back in chair; pressing fingers together	Confident, in control
Taking glasses off; putting stem in mouth	Interested, but needs a slower pace
Looking at watch or clock	Bored, ready to go
Wrinkled brow, opened mouth	Surprised

Here are a few other visual buying signs that indicate a customer is ready to close:

✔ Clients lean closer to you.

✔ Previously nervous or unfriendly customers warm up to you.

✔ Buyers start to smile.

✔ Clients intently read some paperwork you've given them.

✔ Clients view the product again.

✔ Clients touch the product again, reread a brochure, taste another sample, and so on.

Observing your clients' surroundings

Visually observing your prospective clients means looking at everything that surrounds them as well as the signals they give you. For example, if you get a chance to see a client's office, take a look at the office furniture, wall decorations, desk pictures, and organizational habits. Look at the predominant colors of the office, the seating arrangement, and the place your customer decides to position himself or herself. If you meet on neutral ground and it's your customer's choice, pay attention to the chosen meeting place — it may be his or her favorite restaurant or favorite hotel lobby. Or you may even meet at the client's home. Everything you see at the meeting place should add to the overall impression you develop about your client.

Floating a test question before jumping to the close

You may encounter a wide variety of buying signs over the course of your career. Some clients may be ready to close after they give one buying sign. Other clients may have to give you five or six buying signs before they're ready to close. Nothing beats personal experience. The more situations you have to learn from, the better you will be at judging when the time is right. Until then, if you see a couple of buying signs, ask a test closing question such as:

How do you feel so far about everything we've discussed?

If the customer gushes that everything's wonderful, go for the close. If she shows any hesitation, keep talking about her needs and the benefits that your product or service provides. For more on how to read the client's feelings about what you've discussed so far, head to the later section "Mastering the Test Close."

As an expert closer, you can turn these observations into an opportunity to close. Here's an example:

> I can tell by the fine quality of furnishings in your office that you're concerned about giving the proper impression about your business. We at XYZ Cleaning understand how it can hurt that impression if your offices aren't kept "white glove" clean. In our Service Excellence Decree, which each member of our staff commits to, we promise that if at any time you're not satisfied, one phone call will bring us — the person responsible to meet your cleaning needs, his or her direct supervisor, and me — here within the hour to correct anything you may be dissatisfied with. This is the quality of service that you and your company deserve, isn't it?

Choosing Where to Close

The quick answer to "Where should I close?" is "Anywhere!" You close wherever the client is standing or sitting when you recognize his or her buying signs.

✔ If you sell farm equipment and you're in the middle of a field talking with a busy but interested, farmer, you should close right there in the field! Let the farmer authorize the paperwork on your back if you have to. Mastering that ability can make you outstanding in your field. (Pun intended!)

✔ If you sell health products and you're in the locker room of a gym when someone shows interest, close right there in your underwear if you must.

Book IV

Closing Like a Champ and Getting Referrals

✔ If you represent a cleaning service or security system for which you need to walk through an entire home, carry a clipboard or notepad with your paperwork readily available so that you can close in the hallway if the timing is right.

✔ If you have a pool-cleaning service or landscaping service, be prepared to close in the yard or on the patio or the hood of your truck if need be.

✔ In a retail setting, closing may occur in the aisle or in a fitting room, as well as at the cash register.

The following sections offer pointers about different closing locations and advice on the location you should choose if you're the one who gets to do the choosing.

Finding a neutral location

When deciding where to close, your best bet is to find a *neutral location* — not on your turf or your client's. Here are some examples of natural locations:

✔ A restaurant

✔ A golf course

✔ A coffee or bagel shop

✔ The office or location of a mutual acquaintance

Many times, a client has too many distractions in her office — be aware that these distractions can be a power play that she purposely uses to make you uncomfortable, giving her the upper hand. If neither her place of business nor yours is conducive to making business decisions, go ahead and suggest another place to get serious.

Closing at your client's office

Some clients go out of their way to capitalize on the home-court advantage in their offices. You may know the strategies: The clients have their backs to a window so that the blazing sun will blind you from your paperwork; they allow you two feet of space between your chair and the wall so that you're barely able to move; and somehow they make you — with your picayune purchase order or expenditure — feel as though you're interrupting a major world leader during a crisis.

Here's what you do: Begin by smiling and showing empathy for your client and then offer an alternative. Here's an example of how to make this suggestion:

> I can see that you're extremely busy today, and I believe that you have a strong desire to make a wise decision regarding my product and its benefits to your company. To allow you the opportunity to consider the benefits we have to offer without other matters weighing on your mind, how about if you let me take you to a nice restaurant for a business lunch where we can cover the details uninterrupted?

What have you just done? You acknowledged your client's importance and her dedication to making wise decisions, and you subtly indicated that the interruptions are detrimental to the decision-making process. However, you also offered a solution — one of many that you hope to offer this company. And you offered the client a free lunch, which most people would have a hard time turning down.

If it's an afternoon meeting and your client has already had lunch, try the following:

- ✔ Suggest rescheduling the appointment for a better time.

- ✔ Recommend meeting for lunch the next day.

- ✔ If a conference room is available, suggest that you move in there, away from office distractions.

- ✔ If a snack bar is close, recommend taking a break from the office or taking a short walk to help the client think clearly. Getting up and physically moving around is good for clearing the brain.

Not all clients put you in unfavorable positions on purpose. Many of them operate in these surroundings day in and day out without ever realizing the negative impact the mental stress has on their abilities to make wise decisions and work well with others. Your consideration of their personal needs, as well as their business needs, may put you above your competition.

Closing at your client's home

When you visit clients in their homes, try to give your presentation at a kitchen or dining room table. This setup allows you to orchestrate your presentation for maximum impact. The kitchen or dining room table provides an excellent location for authorizing paperwork, which, when tried on a coffee table, can make your clients feel cramped and vulnerable, like zebras at the watering hole — not a good position for making confident decisions.

Try to avoid giving presentations in the living room or family room unless you absolutely have to, because these rooms are where people get comfy, chat, and relax. Many people go into a living room because they want to be entertained — mostly to watch television — which means that your customers don't have to participate in your discussion.

Using a closing room

In some businesses, the company wants you to move from a showroom floor to an area called a *closing room*. This room is usually just a little bit larger than a walk-in closet and contains either a small desk or table and some so-so chairs. It may or may not have a phone, artwork or posters on the wall, or a window — the decor definitely wouldn't win Martha Stewart's approval. But that's okay, because the closing room's sole purpose is for reviewing details and getting a final agreement.

Never, never, never refer to that location as a closing room within earshot of anyone who could ever possibly be a customer! The term *closing room* creates fear, destroys the rapport you've built to this point, and probably even raises the hairs on the backs of your customers' necks — not a good thing when your goal is to set your customer at ease. (See Book II, Chapter 5 for more on words and phrases to avoid.)

If your company requires that you take your customers to a closing room, take it in stride and learn to guide your potential clients to the room smoothly, perhaps offering them a soda or glass of water or suggesting a place for them to relax while you serve their needs.

Mastering the Test Close

A *test close* is a question you ask to get a reading on how the client feels (so far) about everything you've been discussing. A test close helps you draw out and overcome objections, create urgency, and obtain clues about your customer's desire to actually close the sale.

Think of a test close as dipping your toe into the water to test the temperature before jumping in. You're getting your feet wet, but you're still close enough to shore to be safe. The test close leads you toward closing, but if the response from the client is negative, you haven't caused any discomfort by attempting to close.

A great test close is this:

> How are you two feeling so far about the financial program we've been discussing?

If the customers agree that it sounds great, go for the close. If they hesitate, draw them out about the concerns they may have. If they give you a specific concern or objection, handle it. Then test again, with this:

> Are there any other concerns you may have that would keep you from owning this product tonight?

Test closes are softer and gentler than just asking for the sale. A pro never bluntly asks the buyer to buy the product. You'd never hear a professional salesperson say, "Okay, you want to buy this thing or not?" No, no, no, that's too blunt. Instead, the pros use a test close.

Addressing concerns

This phase of the sales process is called either *addressing concerns* or *handling objections.* Either term applies, but the first term presents more of an attitude of helpfulness than the impression you're protesting or opposing something they said. (Refer to Book II, Chapter 5 for other terms that help present you in a better light.)

Average salespeople tend to cringe internally upon hearing a customer express a concern about their product or service. The pros, however, get excited. If they object, they're interested. Think about it. Would you waste your time objecting to something that you have no interest in owning?

Champion salespeople sometimes flush out objections with test closes — questions that determine how ready people are to make buying decisions, covered — recognizing that they need to uncover some unidentified objections. Usually, concerns are about money, but in some cases, concerns will be the time frame or time required to change over to the wonderful new gizmo that you're selling.

The initial way that customers express concern is that they can't commit to a product or service. When your clients say they're "not sure" about a product, you know that it's time to fish for the details they aren't sure about and answer their questions. Be sincerely concerned and ask your customers to help you understand by trying either of the following:

> Please help me understand your concerns.

> Would you mind elaborating on your feelings of uncertainty for me?

Ask your uncertain clients the five *W* questions: who, what, when, where, and why. As a sales detective, your goal is to determine what's really bothering them — why they have a concern. After you find out the concern, you can develop a solution. Here's an example of the five *W* questions you'd ask a customer who was at a computer system:

Book IV

Closing Like a Champ and Getting Referrals

✔ Who, other than yourself, will be involved in making the final decision on your new computer system?

✔ What are your primary concerns regarding the upgrade of this system?

✔ When would you like to have the new system up and running?

✔ Where would you like us to conduct the training? On site? Or at our training facility downtown?

✔ Why have you decided to make the change at this particular time?

Potential clients may ask other questions that indicate concern. Pros learn to ask questions during the qualification stage of the selling process that ferret out many of these concerns (see Book III, Chapter 2 for more on qualification). However, you may encounter customers who are very good at hiding or denying these concerns until it's time for a decision to be made. Table 1-2 shows some questions from customers and strategies that you can use to address their concerns.

Table 1-2	Overcoming Objections
When the Client Says . . .	*You Need To . . .*
"Well, we need more time to decide."	Take a look at the overcoming-procrastination closes in Book IV, Chapter 5.
"I don't think I can afford it."	Be prepared to increase the value that the potential client sees in the product or service to the point where she'll benefit more by having the product than by keeping her money.
"It won't fit in our garage."	Help them discover other places to put the new speedboat, such as a covered area alongside the house, their very own slip at the marina, a storage yard, or a relative's house.

Creating a state of urgency

Sometimes clients think that they're not at all ready to own at this time, but as soon as you establish an urgency, they feel the sense of urgency, too, and decide they really do want the product. The next thing you know, they own it! The following list shows some examples of how you can create a sense of urgency:

✔ If you sell real estate, create urgency by letting your buyer know that the seller is highly motivated and will likely take the first offer that's presented — or let her know that interest rates may rise and change the amount of house she can afford.

- ✔ If a product is in great demand, the potential of dwindling inventory could spur someone on to making a decision to own the latest color laser printer today, instead of delaying the decision and then finding that the product is back-ordered with no definite delivery date.

- ✔ If you sell financial services, remind clients that the sooner they begin investing, the sooner their money starts earning more money! Create urgency by showing charts on how much more clients will need to put aside each month at a later date rather than how little they need to start now.

- ✔ If you own a boat dealership, remind clients that boats are in high demand just before the Fourth of July, so a May purchase is wise.

- ✔ As a contractor, help clients see the logic in remodeling in time for a major holiday, such as Thanksgiving or Christmas.

Suggesting to customers that they place their orders today in order to guarantee their needs are met in a timely manner creates urgency and knocks some customers off the "indecision fence."

Moving into the Final Close

A final close happens when you decide to ask the buyer to make a decision. The moment is right when you believe that you've presented the product or service in a manner that demonstrates that it meets the customer's needs, answered all her questions, and covered the financial aspects of the transaction. After you ask the final closing question, you wrap up the sale in one of two ways: with a signature on your paperwork or with an exchange of money.

Practice the following closing techniques so that you close with confidence:

- ✔ Use everyday language.
- ✔ Use comfortable mannerisms.
- ✔ Stand or sit with a dignified posture.
- ✔ Convey complete competence.

You want your future clients to be sure that you're able to provide your service or deliver your product better than your competitors.

Shifting to paperwork

Suppose your business requires you to fill out paperwork as the final stage in a close. The close begins by moving to the paperwork after your test close receives a favorable response. How, though, do you move to your paperwork without an obvious shifting of gears?

The least obvious way to shift to paperwork is to have paperwork in front of your clients *during the sales process*. Get permission from your clients to take notes early in the sale, which gets them comfortable with the paperwork.

If you haven't taken notes throughout the sale, though, you can still move to the paperwork in a variety of ways.

While you fill out your paperwork, always chitchat with your clients. You can't remain silent. In order to keep talking, though, you must know your paperwork by rote. So, make sure that any piece of paper you fill out is as familiar as your best friend. Memorize it before you ever begin a sales call.

The "Let me make a note of that" approach

Suppose that, in response to your test close, your clients ask how soon they can receive a product. (This is called a porcupine question, which is covered in Book IV, Chapter 2.) If, in response, you ask them when they'd like the product, and they give you a date ("We're having guests over on the holiday weekend — I'd sure like to have it by then"), you say, "Let me make a note of that," and you're into your paperwork.

The "Let's draft up our feelings" approach

Some people may react negatively if you say you're going to "put the whole thing together" and then let them take a look at it. You may be moving too fast for some clients; they may think you're being pushy. You're better off to calmly and sincerely ask a test question to determine where they are in the decision process. If the response is positive, then move — again gently — to your paperwork. You can ask, "How are you feeling about all this so far?" or ask a question that they're likely to answer in the positive:

> YOU: Do you see why we're so excited about this product/service?
>
> CLIENT: It sounds great.
>
> YOU: Well, then let's just draft up our feelings about the product on paper to see if it even makes sense.

What an excellent way to move on to your paperwork!

The "You can take the facts with you" approach

Clients who are a little nervous during your presentation may become even more nervous when you turn to paperwork. To help them relax, offer to draft the paperwork as a way to determine whether the sale makes sense.

If you sense hesitation from your clients, that's okay. Simply exude confidence that, after all the information is on paper, it'll make more sense to them. You also may want to reinforce that your paperwork doesn't entail any kind of commitment at this time.

The "Let's outline the details" approach

When you begin any paperwork, your clients may start getting cold feet and stop you. This type of reaction is normal. Expect it. Plan for it. When your clients say they want you to wait because they're not sure, affirm their feelings ("I understand how you feel") and explain that you're only outlining the details of the transaction so that you and they can carefully analyze the best course of action to take.

The "correct spelling" or "correct mailing address" approach

Another way to begin paperwork is called the *order blank close,* when you ask a test close question such as "What is the correct spelling of your last name?" (Only use this technique, of course, if your client has an unusual name; don't try this approach if the client's last name is Jones or Brown.) Another order blank close is "What is your correct mailing address here?" You're on your way to the paperwork.

The "Do you know the date?" approach

Ask any cashier in the grocery store and he or she will probably tell you that at least one in ten customers who write checks for purchases ask for the date as they begin writing their checks. This statistic shouldn't come as a surprise, though — we're all busy people and keeping the calendar fresh in our minds isn't always one of life's major details. In some fields of sales, you may give four presentations, field a dozen calls, talk to eight prospective buyers, and put out three fires — all before noon!

This craziness presents another method for moving on to your paperwork: Simply verify the date with your clients. You won't look incompetent; if you've acted professionally and sincerely up to that point, your clients won't give this question a second thought. They'll answer it by reflex. In fact, they may have to glance at a wall calendar or their watch to verify it for themselves, unless today's date has special meaning to them (besides being the day they invest in your product!).

When they answer your question, say, "Let me jot that down." Chances are, they won't object to seeing you begin writing on your paperwork.

The "I'll need your approval" approach

This approach is the most uncomplicated way of getting to a final agreement. You may have customers who are willing to go ahead — there's been little hesitation and few objections. Everyone in the room agrees that it's in their best interests to invest in your product. At this point, don't fuss or get fancy. Simply put all the details down on paper. Review those details for accuracy, and then turn the paper around in front of your clients. As you hand over a pen, say one of the following:

> In analyzing all considerations, I sincerely feel this decision makes good sense. With your approval right here, we'll arrange delivery and begin giving you the finest service possible.

> I'll just need your approval to set up everything.

After that conversation, just point to the line, put your pen on top of your paperwork, sit back, and let your clients make the decision. This may seem a bit simplified, but simplicity is a good thing when you're asking someone to make a decision. You can read more about this strategy in Book IV, Chapter 3.

Closing the retail sale

When you work in a retail setting such as a clothing store, most customers simply bring their purchases to a cash register when they're ready to close the sale. However, as a retail salesperson, you need to walk the floor of the store, tend to the fitting rooms, move about the aisles helping customers find what they want, and make suggestions — rather than simply standing behind a cash register, waiting for customers.

In retail sales, the entire selling cycle may take less than ten minutes, which is not very long for you to sell and close the sale.

The "Let me reserve a fitting room for you" approach

In retail sales, placing an item in your customer's hands is the best way to start closing a sale. Physical involvement creates emotional involvement — and people buy emotionally. You have a variety of options to get your product into (or onto) your customers' laps, mouths, backs, feet, and so on!

- ✔ Grocery stores offer free samples.
- ✔ Upscale cosmetics companies offer personal makeovers.
- ✔ Athletic shoe stores let you walk or run around the store before you buy.
- ✔ Car dealers promote test drives.
- ✔ Furniture stores let you try an item in your home before you buy.
- ✔ Home improvement stores showcase expensive cabinets in kitchen-like settings.
- ✔ Magazines offer free trial subscriptions.

The bottom line is that customers need to physically touch your product.

The "Will this be cash, check, or charge?" approach

As soon as a customer indicates a desire to own your product, take the product from her and say something like, "This blouse is a good color for your skin tone. I'll be happy to take this up to the register for you. Will this be cash, check, or charge?"

If you have the product in your hands that the customers have indicated they want and you start to walk away, the clients are going to follow you or stop you to possibly add on to their purchase. Either way, you're winning.

Chapter 2

Questioning and Listening Strategies of Champion Closers

In This Chapter

▶ Understanding the four types of questions

▶ Discovering useful questioning principles

▶ Figuring out how to be a better listener

As a young person, did you ever have this experience? You're talking with an adult — say, at Thanksgiving — and you're catching up with old Uncle Joe and he says, "Hey, Sally, you know, you're quite the talker. You should go into sales. You'd be great at it." Well, Uncle Joe has a stereotypical view of what salespeople are all about — talking their way into closed sales. You may have taken old Uncle Joe's advice to heart and chosen a career in selling, but you still aren't talking your way into enough sales.

The average salesperson may be all babble, but you're not striving to be average. Champion salespeople know that the best way to a successful close is to ask questions and to listen.

This chapter is about the talk — namely, the questions — champions use to close sales, and just as important, the listening tactics of champion closers. After you ask the question, you have to listen to the answer. Ask the right questions and your potential clients will tell you exactly what they'll say "yes" to.

Questioning Your Clients

Asking questions is key to closing a sale, but you don't want your potential customers to feel like they're being interrogated. In this section, we fill you in on the four types of questions no salesperson should be without. Then we give you pointers on how to ask questions that bring you to the close.

The four types of questions

To get the information you need in any particular selling situation, you have to ask the right kind of question. As a professional salesperson, you should be familiar with and understand the function of these four commonly used question types:

- ✔ Discovery questions
- ✔ Leading questions
- ✔ Closing questions
- ✔ Involvement questions

The following sections are devoted to these questioning strategies — what they are, when they're used, and how they affect your ability to come to a successful close.

When you get really good with your questioning strategies, you're able to combine several types of questions into one. For example, you can ask a leading question that enables you to discover a lot of information in the process. When you begin to ask questions in this manner, you save a lot of time and become very targeted in the information you glean from your potential clients.

Discovery questions

Discovery questions are ones that help you find out more about your client and his or her needs with regard to your product or service. Discovery questions tend to be pretty automatic with most salespeople. Wanting to find out all the information possible about your prospective customers is only natural. You need to keep in mind a few rules when asking these types of questions, though.

When forming your discovery questions, remember that you're trying to gather information, so ask questions that require thought and discussion. Typically, these questions begin with *who, what, when, where, why,* and *how*. They encourage the potential client to provide details. Yes-or-no responses are not what you want to use during discovery. In fact, there's really no room in the discovery process to ask a question that can be answered with a no. In fact, during the discovery process, you should never ask a "say-no" question.

Here are some examples of questions to use to get the information you need to discover:

What product and/or service do you own now?

What would you change about the product and/or service you currently own?

When will you be looking to own your new product and/or service?

What is the one feature you find most attractive about the new model?

Often, the best discovery questions don't end with a question mark, but instead come out like statements. For example, "I understand you use a great deal of PVC piping" isn't really a question. By posing the question like this, the potential clients are encouraged to talk to you more about the topic. In fact, statements are a much more controlled and targeted technique of discovery.

Using discovery questions can take a while because you're asking the customers for information they have to explain, so be patient.

Leading questions

Leading questions are questions that help you steer the conversation to the information that helps you determine whether your product is right for your client.

These questions *guide and convince.* Many salespeople are tempted to tell their prospective customers what to believe instead of asking questions that allow the customers to come up with their own belief statements. The difference is subtle, but important. If you say it, they can doubt it; if they say it, they believe it's true!

Here are some examples of leading questions:

What was it that brought you to our location today?

What are your fitness goals?

What type of decor do you have in mind for your new home?

How are you currently handling your financial planning needs?

Salespeople who are unfamiliar with asking leading questions crowd the conversation with facts, feature functions, warranty information, and delivery possibilities, during which the prospective customers' eyes glaze over and their attention is drawn further and further away. Instead of the potential clients being led toward a successful close, they're being pushed back against the wall. When this happens, one of two things will occur: Either the customer will build a wall of sales resistance or he'll melt into the woodwork and find a reason to get away from you quickly. No matter which of the two types of behavior they display, at that point you've killed the possibility of a close.

Instead of pushing information on a customer, gently lead and guide her toward your way of thinking by making statements regarding your product or service, and then tying her down with contractions like "isn't it," "don't you agree," and "wouldn't you" to get her to agree with you. (More on tie-downs in the following section.) Here are some examples:

Book IV

Closing Like a Champ and Getting Referrals

The particular shade of blue in this blouse sets off the blue of your eyes, don't you think?

The latest safety features are vital when considering the safety of your daughter in her first new car, aren't they?

Having a solid financial plan is a wise move when you have a family to think of, don't you agree?

Be sure you know what the answers are that you're seeking before you ask the questions, and be sure your potential clients know the answers as well. Nobody likes to be asked questions that make him feel stupid, and that certainly won't lead the customer toward a close — unless it's to close the door in your face as he leaves the building!

Understanding tie-downs

Tie-downs are questions that you put at the end of statements that call for agreement from the client. Most tie-downs are forms of leading questions, which get the clients to either agree or disagree with your statements. Their answers help you to know what direction to take next. One thing to remember, though, is to mix up the different ways of wording tie-downs so the prospective customer doesn't suspect that you're using a technique on him.

The following phrases are some common tie-downs you'll find useful (see the following section, "Placing tie-downs in a sentence," for where and how to use them):

Aren't they?	Haven't they?
Don't we?	Won't they?
Isn't it?	Couldn't it?
Didn't it?	Hasn't he?
Aren't you?	Hasn't she?
Shouldn't it?	Won't you?
Isn't that right?	Doesn't it?
Wasn't it?	Don't you agree?
Can't you?	Can't you just imagine?
Wouldn't it?	

Customize the tie-down to each situation. ***Remember:*** The more creative you can be, the more effectively you'll lead the people to closed sales.

Placing tie-downs in a sentence

You can sneak tie-downs into just about any sentence:

✔ **Standard tie-down:** Placed at the end of the sentence.

> A company's reputation is important when choosing a firm to do business with, isn't it?

> Your children will be pretty excited about all the fun times they'll have on this new boat, won't they?

> You'll sleep better at night knowing that your property is protected by a top-notch security system, won't you?

✔ **Inverted tie-downs:** Used at the beginning of a sentence. The inverted tie-down can make your questions sound a little warmer.

> Can't you just picture yourself sitting by the fireplace on a cold winter's night?

> Isn't it about time you treated your family to the vacation of a lifetime?

> Shouldn't you be offered the highest return by placing your securities in ABC Bank?

✔ **Internal tie-downs:** Placed in the middle of a sentence. Internal tie-downs are actually the smoothest way to hide the fact that you're using a technique and make it sound like you're asking a matter-of-fact, I-just-thought-of-this question.

> This new computer game is fun, isn't it, once you get it set up?

> Because you're planning on delivery by the middle of June, don't you think that ordering now would be a good idea?

> Now that we've eliminated that concern, don't you agree that we can move forward in the building process?

✔ **Tag-on tie-downs:** Add-on sentences. Tag-on tie-downs are used when your prospective customer makes a positive statement that you want to reinforce.

> CUSTOMER: The Copier 2000 can certainly crank out the copies fast.

> YOU: Can't it, though?

> CUSTOMER: This Corvette is incredibly beautiful!

> YOU: Isn't it?

> CUSTOMER: I'll be so glad to never have to wash another dish by hand!

> YOU: Can't you just imagine it?

The key with tag-on tie-downs is that they must be used only after the prospective customer has made a positive statement about your offering. Be patient. Wait for those positive statements to pop up, and then tie them down with a tag-on tie-down.

Book IV

Closing Like a Champ and Getting Referrals

Closing questions

A closing question is one that calls for a decision on the purchase. When non-customers are asked why they didn't purchase a product, most of those who liked the product said they didn't purchase it because they were never asked! Hard to believe, isn't it? Salespeople would never want to admit that they don't ask closing questions, but some salespeople are uncomfortable asking people for their money and will dance around the issue, never asking a customer, point blank, if he wants to own the product.

Some salespeople may say things like, "So what do you think?" or "It's a good product, isn't it?" Even though the clients may agree with them, they never actually ask for the money, the credit card, or the approval on the paperwork. Closing questions sound more like this: "How would you like to cover the investment for your new window coverings?" or "With your approval right here (indicating signature line of paperwork), we'll get a delivery date set so you can begin enjoying your new entertainment system." In retail sales, the most common close is this: "Will this be cash, check, or charge?" Is the client asked to buy the product? You bet. After you have confirmation from a closing question, do what the professionals do: Close.

The following sections examine a few closing questions and show how and when to use them.

The alternate advance

The *alternate advance* gives the prospective clients a choice of a positive answer or a "yes" answer. The idea behind this is that, either way, the customers indicate their intentions to own. These types of questions are never merely yes-or-no questions; instead, they require a choice.

Here's how the alternate advance question works. Instead of asking the customer if you can come by to show him your product, use the following:

> Would Tuesday morning be a good time for me to drop by, or is Wednesday more convenient for you?

See the difference? The customer can much more easily say no to you when you just ask if you can stop by. But by asking what time is best for you to drop by, you force the customer away from a simple "no" answer.

If you're asking a question that requires an investment from your potential client, word it like this:

> The people we serve have found it a good idea to reserve their vacation spot by placing a deposit; would you prefer 5 percent or 10 percent as an initial investment?

If you ask a question that can be answered by either a yes or a no response, you may well get a "no" — and a boot to the door. Alternate advance questions simply allow you to avoid getting that "no" answer.

The porcupine technique

The *porcupine technique* is one of the strongest forms of closing questions, but like tie-downs, customers will grow suspicious if you overuse it. You use this technique when customers ask you a question and you need to establish where they stand on the issue, so you counter their question with one of your own.

The reason this type of closing question is called the porcupine technique is because no one wants to hold a porcupine for very long. Throw the porcupine (question) back immediately, before you get stabbed by a flying quill you hadn't counted on.

The following scenario is one in which you'd use the porcupine technique:

> CUSTOMER: Is there a park nearby?
>
> YOU: Is it important to you to have a park near your home?

Don't assume you know the customer's likes and dislikes. Instead, use the porcupine technique to feel out the customer. Consider this example. Suppose the same question (Is there a park nearby?) has been asked. Instead of using the porcupine technique to see where the customer stood before answering, you could immediately come back with a response like this:

> You'll love the park that's two houses down. It's a great place for the kids to play, and you can keep an eye on them.

Seems like a reasonable response, right? Not necessarily. What if the customer has no children and doesn't want the noise and traffic that a park would add to the neighborhood? By immediately assuming that the customer would *like* the park, you just killed your chances for a successful close.

Involvement questions

An *involvement question* is any positive question about the benefits of your product or service that buyers would ask themselves after they own it. Involvement questions let you know exactly where your prospective customers stand on the idea of owning your product.

Here are several examples of involvement questions:

> If you were to go ahead, where in the office would you put the soda machine? (The soda machine would have to be conveniently located for his employees, so the customer pictures the flow of traffic in the office and sees people using the machine.)

Book IV

Closing Like a Champ and Getting Referrals

How do you think your furniture would fit in this room? (By asking this, you cause the customer to visualize the furniture in his home.)

How often do you think you'll be entertaining after having the patio improvements made? (Here the customer starts picturing a party and how he'd set it all up.)

Involvement questions are usually a combination of leading, discovery, and closing questions all wrapped into one. Involvement questions require a bit more finesse and planning in order to achieve the positive results you're looking for, but practice makes perfect.

Pointers for successful questioning

In this section, we give you some pointers on questioning strategies. If you apply them diligently, they'll almost always move you to a successful close.

Ask how you can help

When you first meet potential new clients, you need to ask questions to determine just what you can do for them. The single best question for this strategy is simply, "How can I help you?"

You're not asking *whether* you can help the customers — you know you can help them. You want to know *how* you can help them. With this question, you're figuring out specifically how you can serve the customers' needs. In order to serve, they must tell you their needs — and this is a good question to get the ball rolling.

The answer to this question may tell you that you can't help them today. For example, if you sell playground equipment, people may stop by your location just to see what kinds of fun things you have, but their only child may be just 3 months old, so you probably can't be of service to them today. You want to determine that rather quickly, make them feel good about your products, and then let them browse and leave with brochures. Then you can make yourself available to the next group that pulls in with four children under the age of 8.

Determine specific benefits

In qualifying and presenting, use this strategy to narrow your offering from the many options you have to give the prospective client. Determining specific features and benefits is helpful in the information-gathering stage of the sale; however, you also can use it to close the sale.

Here are some examples that show how you can narrow the options to those your prospective customers are most interested in:

> Did you want the bay window on the north side of the living room or on the east?

> That set comes in a choice of colors. Would the Bluejay Blue go better on your patio or the Grassyknoll Green?

> We can provide your company with several solutions. Let me ask you which is more important to you in providing a new healthcare plan: a wide range of benefits to meet the myriad needs your people have or a more narrow range available at a lower investment?

As part of your closing summary, reiterate all the things that your customer told you he wanted up to this point. This shows you were paying attention, that you can keep track of details, and that you're covering all his needs effectively. After he agrees to this review, you ask your closing question.

Acknowledge the facts

You can do more with questions than just ask about the client's needs. You can state a fact as a question and get his agreement. If your product involves a warranty, ask early on whether having a warranty is important to the client. If it isn't, don't bring it up again. However, if it *is* important, bring it up in the form of a question to get your client in the agreement mode as you prepare to close the sale. For example:

> You said that the ten-year extended warranty was important to you, wasn't it?

When your client agrees with you on this point, you can confirm that he's going ahead. After all, he wouldn't agree to wanting the warranty if he wasn't serious about getting the product or service, right?

Then proceed to the next step in the selling sequence, which is to review all the financial details. If the client is agreeable to all that, ask for his approval on the paperwork or whatever form of investment he's using.

Test their level of commitment

If you're not sure how strong the customers' desire is to go ahead after you've given them all the details about the product or service, ask!

REMEMBER

You test their level of interest or desire to go ahead with *trial* or *test closes,* which are covered in greater depth in Book IV, Chapter 1. Test closes are simply a matter of testing how the potential clients feel at this moment about everything you've covered — kind of like taking the temperature of the sale.

Book IV

Closing Like a Champ and Getting Referrals

A test question like "How are you feeling about everything we've discussed so far?" gets your clients to let you know whether they're for, against, or indifferent to what they've discovered about your product and how it suits their needs:

- ✔ **If they're for owning the product,** proceed with your benefit summary, review of the financial details, and close.

- ✔ **If they're against it,** ask them to elaborate on how they're feeling so that you can find out what's holding them back.

- ✔ **If they're indifferent,** you need to ask more questions about their needs. Use tie-downs to review the points they've agreed to and confirm that they want those benefits. Ask whether anything else is keeping them from making a decision. When they're indifferent, something is missing. You have to find out what's missing and get it covered — you do that by asking questions.

Arouse emotions

Arousing and directing emotions can be tricky. You want to be certain that you're arousing the right emotions for the situation.

For example, if you're selling home-security products, you can ask, "Won't you sleep better on the road next week, knowing that your wife, children, and pets are protected by our security team?" With this question, you help the potential client picture his family and pets sleeping peacefully and protected — which conjures a positive emotion. He'll also feel less guilty about being gone overnight.

Don't try to raise emotions when discussing the money aspects of the sale. Most people conjure up negative images about money leaving their hands for good. For example, don't say, "Won't you feel great knowing this $200 per month is going toward little Johnnie's college education?" The client may picture little Johnnie needing new shoes because he's growing so fast and how expensive shoes really are and begin to feel overwhelmed about his responsibility as a parent and so on. When you're talking about money, stick to the facts and figures unless money is the final objection. If it is, then you may want to tie it to something emotional that the client may miss out on by not going ahead today (like little Johnnie's college graduation ceremony).

You can find out how to overcome money objections in Book IV, Chapter 4.

Get the minor yeses flowing

Getting minor yeses means getting your clients to agree on minor points. Minor agreements accumulate into major ones, and that's where you want to end up — with a major agreement! Here's a great question for getting a minor yes:

This brand of furniture has an excellent reputation for quality, and quality is important when making a purchase of this sort, isn't it?

Are they going to disagree with that? Nope. You've just gotten a minor agreement. You know that name-brand furniture is what they want. Most clients know that name brand means quality, and that quality means a higher financial investment. This minor yes gives you a foundation for knowing how much they may be willing to invest in the furniture they're discussing with you. From this point, narrow their specific needs to pieces, styles, finishes — all the details. After they choose what they want, you can cover the money.

Involve your customers in ownership

This strategy is to get your prospective clients picturing themselves owning your product or service.

If your product is something tangible, such as a car, you can ask questions about placement of it after ownership. Where will it reside? Do they have garage space for it? Will it be parked on the street? If so, would they be interested in having a security alarm as an added-on feature? Ask who will be using the car. If it's a spouse with small children, discuss safety with them. If it's a teen, perhaps the cost of insurance is foremost on their minds — if the safety features of a particular model lend to receiving better insurance rates, you may want to bring that up. Get the picture? Ask how the customers think it will look, feel, and work. Ask how the car will benefit them and their loved ones.

If your product is intangible, you have to help customers picture themselves owning the benefits of it. If your product is a cleaning service, help them see themselves relaxing instead of cleaning — walking into a clean home at the end of a busy day. If your product is insurance, help them see themselves covered in an unfortunate instance.

The more you help customers feel ownership of your product or service, the less closing you have to do later.

Isolate areas of concern

Say your clients have been going over a new insurance plan with you. They've brought up a few points along the way that could be considered objections. (Try to think of — and refer to — objections as *concerns*. The word *objection* is too harsh.) You need to isolate their areas of concern before you can move to the close.

Concerns are simply points that need to be addressed or readdressed to make your client comfortable enough to make a buying decision. Customer concerns generally fall into three categories:

Book IV

Closing Like a Champ and Getting Referrals

✔ Will your product or service really do what you say it will?

✔ Is this truly the best product for them and their particular situation?

✔ Do they really want to spend the money on this?

The third point — the money — is the final area of concern that you have to address in 90 percent of closing situations. However, you can't ignore the other 10 percent unless you want to be only 90 percent of a champion or meet 90 percent of your quota or earn 90 percent of what you could potentially earn.

The concerns that make up the other 10 percent relate to whether the product will perform as expected and whether it's simply the best choice for them. If they're being held back by a concern that your product will perform, you need to pull out testimonials from happy clients or give them a list of clients they can contact as references for the product. To show that this is the best product for them, you have to rely on your expertise regarding the products your competition offers.

To isolate the customer's primary concern, simply ask this question at the end of your presentation:

> So your primary concern seems to be the financial aspect of this plan. Am I correct in my understanding of that?

If something besides the money needs to be addressed, you want to know about it before you start going for the close on the money.

Make sure concerns are settled

After you address a concern and you believe the customers are satisfied with the information you've given them, you need to get confirmation so the same concern doesn't come up again when it's time to close. This strategy is simple, yet powerful. After you've addressed the customers' concern and they seem comfortable, say:

> Now that settles that, doesn't it?

If they truly are comfortable, they'll agree and you can move on. If the issue isn't settled, you want to find out while you're still on the topic of their concern and get it settled once and for all.

Stay in control

If you feel you're not in control of the selling situation, ask a question to bring the conversation back to the task at hand. If you sell backyard play equipment and your prospects start talking about anything and everything having to do with their kids rather than talking about your product, take control with a question:

> It's wonderful that your children are so active. Now, let me ask you what the specific current motor development skills are of each of your children so we can talk about customizing your equipment for their particular needs.

Bring them back to the task at hand — choosing a product — by showing how that information they've just relayed about little Susie and her soccer team or Billy and his karate relates to benefits they'll receive from your product.

For intangibles, listen for something important to them in the side story and apply it to a need your product will meet. For example, if they're concerned about Grandma being alone, your senior monitoring service fills that void, doesn't it?

Rationalize decisions for your clients

People buy products and services emotionally and then defend the purchases logically. If you doubt this, take a look at this progression of emotion:

1. **Judy is a working mom.**
2. **She hates spending her evenings and weekends cleaning house and doing laundry.**
3. **The kids are growing up quickly and she wants them to have fun memories — and she wants to be a part of those memories.**
4. **She decides, based on these emotions, to hire someone to clean house and do laundry for her for $75 per week.**

As soon as the emotional decision is made, guilt and fear make their attack, telling Judy that $75 is a lot of money to commit to spending every week. She could take the kids on some great outings with that money. So, Judy starts second-guessing herself. She needs logic to defend her decision.

Book IV

Closing
Like a
Champ and
Getting
Referrals

How would a champion salesperson close this sale? By asking questions and rationalizing the decision for the client.

> YOU: I can see that you're hesitant to make this financial commitment. Let's think this through for a moment. How much time do you think you spend on these chores?
>
> CLIENT: I probably spend at least 10 to 12 hours per week cleaning and keeping up with the laundry.
>
> YOU: Okay, let's go with 12 hours per week. Based on the amount of time you say you put into taking care of these chores, the $75 per week investment boils down to $6.25 per hour, which is less than minimum wage. I don't know what you earn in the working world, but don't you think your time is worth more than $6.25 per hour?

The spending of money has been rationalized. The cleaning service is hired, and the guilt disappears in a sprinkle of rationalized dust. The customer is more relaxed, and she feels she has more of herself to give to her family. Plus, she's having more fun. All this for only $75 a week!

Ask for the close

There are right and wrong ways to ask closing questions. You (obviously) don't flat out ask, "Do you want it or not?" You do, however, ask for the clients' approval, okay, endorsement, or authorization on the paperwork so you can immediately begin serving their needs.

Always ask in a professional, nonthreatening manner, but do ask! Never, ever, ever let yourself leave the presence of a client without asking for the sale! Chapters 3 through 7 of Book IV cover specific closing situations and the phrasing for closing the sale with each.

Listening While You Work

For most salespeople, listening just isn't the natural way to spend most of their time. Too bad, because the more you listen, the more you earn! If you doubt this, consider that many psychologists earn $100 or more per hour to listen to the challenges people face. Of course, they're providing solutions as well, but aren't you supposed to do that, too?

Here are some interesting statistics that should greatly influence your desire to become a good listener:

✔ Good communicators spend at least 40 percent of their time listening.

✔ Approximately 35 percent of a good communicator's time is spent talking.

As a sales professional, you should spend about 30 percent of your time talking and 30 percent prospecting, doing research, and preparing presentations. To help you remember and stick to this advice, think about the proportion of ears to mouth in the human being: We have twice as many ears as mouths, right? Use them in that proportion if you want to succeed.

Become aware of the level of listener you are and realize what pitfalls may await you unless you change your ways. The great thing about changing your listening habits is that you can begin immediately and practice every day without people ever knowing what you're doing. Becoming a good listener is definitely a learned process. Read on for more information on how to become a better listener.

Looking at the three types of listeners

The following are the three major types of listeners. Take a look and see which one fits you. Evaluate what listening type you are, to what degree you fit in that particular category, and as you continue reading this chapter, think about what you can do to improve your listening skills.

✔ **Poor listeners:** These are the people who catch themselves zoning in and out of conversations that they're supposed to be a part of, realizing that they weren't focused on the other speaker. They may wonder what details, if any, they missed during their "timeout," but they're too embarrassed to ask the speaker to repeat himself.

✔ **Average listeners:** These listeners hear the words, but may not be watching the body language of the speaker or catching where the speaker puts the most emphasis, which is vital to interpreting messages that the speaker doesn't send verbally.

✔ **Empathetic listeners:** These listeners pay total attention to the subject at hand. They are not only good listeners but observant as well. When the atmosphere contains many distractions, the empathetic listener is able to block them out and concentrate on what's important.

What kind of listener are you? To find out, think about your most recent conversation (it doesn't have to have been with a client — it could have been with a co-worker or significant other) and answer yes or no to the following questions, tallying your results:

Book IV

Closing Like a Champ and Getting Referrals

✔ Did you listen intently to what the other person was saying?

✔ Did you make eye contact several times during the conversation?

✔ Did you repeat important points back to the other party to ensure that you understood him correctly?

✔ Could you now accurately repeat the details of the conversation to another person?

✔ Do you recall the bodily movements of the speakers? How was he standing? Or was he sitting? Were his arms crossed or open? What was his level of eye contact with you?

✔ Did he repeat a point in several ways for emphasis? If so, did you catch the importance of that point?

If you answered no to any of these questions, you have room for improvement in your listening skills. You may want to jot down these questions on a 3 x 5 card and carry the card with you. Review the questions prior to your next conversation, and then see how you do afterward.

Your listening skills can vary by many degrees. You may even discover that your listening habits vary with whatever it is you're focused on learning. If you're interested in what is being discussed, your focus will be greater and your attentiveness will be, too. Naturally, if you're indifferent to the topic, retaining what you hear won't be of major importance to you. In addition, distractions, fatigue, stress, or physical ailments can interfere with our ability to listen, learn, and retain.

Getting your client's attention

When the table is turned and you're the person who wants to be listened to, what can you do to improve the habits of a poor listener? Here are ways to attract and maintain the attention of your listener, the customer:

✔ **Make sure the room is comfortable and free of distractions.**

✔ **Ask questions to get the customer to communicate or relax.** To get your customers to relax, ask about a subject they're comfortable discussing to establish rapport — and keep their attention. For example:

> I see by your cap that you're a Phoenix Suns fan. Do you go to the games?

✔ **Maintain eye contact with the customer when speaking.**

✔ **If you see signs of the customer's attention drifting, use the customer's name in a sentence.**

✔ **Avoid being critical or judgmental.**

✔ **Watch the customer's body language.** If you're losing him, suggest a break or do a brief recap where you summarize what's been discussed or agreed to up to this point. (The purpose of summarizing is to bring everyone up to the same level of understanding.) Remember to do a recap after taking a break.

✔ **Don't let any visual aids you use in your presentation distract your listener.** Visual aids should complement the message, not confuse it. After you finish with a particular visual aid, put it out of sight and move on.

✔ **Ask questions about what the customer has said that's relevant to your product and/or service.**

Chapter 3

The No-Frills Close

*E*very now and then, a sale closes so smoothly and quickly that it may surprise you. You just never know which potential future client will realize that you're just the right person with exactly the product he's been looking for — and he's as excited to own your product as you are to sell it. This chapter covers those easy situations in which you need do little more than be professional and ask politely for your client's signature on paperwork or for his cash, check, or credit card.

These easy closes can happen even with very large purchases. Heck, it happened with a home Tom Hopkins once showed. The people just knew it was their dream home the moment they pulled up to the curb. They practically ran through the house and then insisted that Tom call the seller right away with an offer so that no one else could get the home before they did.

If an easy close falls into your lap, don't act surprised in front of the clients. If they see your surprise, they may think they missed something in the details about the product or the financing and start second-guessing themselves, unclosing the sale just as quickly as it closed.

The Basic Oral Verbal Close

The basic oral close is nothing more than a question you ask that calls for a commitment to go ahead. The basic oral close is by far the simplest, easiest, and best close to master. When this close works, you're in hog heaven. If it doesn't, you've committed no fouls, and you can attempt to close another way.

The following sections offer examples of these types of closes and give you tips on how to phrase the question and react to whatever response you get.

Asking for a purchase order number

If you work in industrial, commercial, and governmental sales, you know how important it is to get the purchase order number. This number makes the sale concrete. For that reason, this type of basic oral close is often used in these industries.

You can phrase your questions like this:

> By the way, what purchase order number will be assigned to this requisition?

If the customer says he doesn't know, ask:

> How do we find out?

Some companies have a check-and-balance system where each purchase order has two lines for approval signatures. So, after you have the purchase order number, it's always wise to ask whether anyone else needs to approve the purchase order. Be sure to look at any purchase order you're given to be sure that you have the correct approval(s) before going ahead with arranging delivery. Some companies have tiny lines for initials where the next manager up the line needs to put her okay. For some large purchases, the chief financial officer needs to put a seal of approval on the purchase order. Just be aware of the possibilities and never hesitate to ask for clarification on the company's internal systems for making purchases.

Without doing this little check, you run the risk of seeing one of your orders canceled because the decision maker needed to get a second approval on the paperwork and you just didn't know about it.

Cash, check, or charge? Asking how payment will be made

Asking whether the customer will pay with cash, check, or charge is the simplest form of a close, especially in a retail setting. The words for the basic oral close may go like this:

> Will this be a credit card, check, or cash purchase?

With this basic oral close, if the client hesitates, you're still okay. You haven't hurt the relationship. You haven't raised additional concerns. You've just set the stage for further closing to take place. For example, your customer may not have everything she came in for, so this gives you an opportunity to increase the amount of her order. Or the customer may not have decided for sure on the purchase. If that's the case, ask what her concerns are, try to address them, and then close again.

The Basic Written Close

The basic written close has also been called the "let me make a note of that" close. You typically use this close when your paperwork requires a lot of details like measurements, choice of finishes, colors, or unusual delivery or billing requirements.

Here are some of the details you may need to get on your paperwork. You can ask questions and "make a note of that" to get your entire agreement filled out, with the customer's permission:

- ✔ Names, with correct spelling
- ✔ Shipping address
- ✔ Billing address, if different
- ✔ Vital statistics such as date of birth
- ✔ Social Security number
- ✔ Phone and fax numbers
- ✔ Required delivery date
- ✔ Product or service specifications (size, color, shape, texture, fabric, and so on)

You usually can justify asking for any information that needs to be on your form by saying that you want the form to do its job when it leaves your hands. After all, unless you're also the one performing the service or packing the shipment, you need to relay all this vital information to the person who fills the order so the client gets exactly what he wants and needs.

You can find a detailed discussion about asking for permission and other key elements of this type of close in the following sections.

WARNING!

Don't ask rapid-fire questions as if you're interrogating the customer for the crime of the century. Simply make sure you work all the required details into your conversation during the presentation and preparation for the close.

Obtaining permission

The key to the basic written close is getting permission to take notes early in your presentation so you don't miss any pertinent details. Obtaining permission means asking potential clients for their permission to take notes, which is a strategic move. By giving you permission to take notes, the customers are saying that they're okay with seeing you write things down. Ask for this permission upfront to avoid a knee-jerk, "Whoa, wait a minute" reaction when you start writing on the paperwork — as there may be if you never write a thing until it's time to get serious.

Be prepared! Make sure you have something to take notes with. A nice pen and a portfolio that holds a legal pad of paper and your agreement — or whatever paperwork is necessary to complete the transaction — are fine. For some products, all the information is entered directly into the company order-processing software from your laptop. Whatever method your type of product requires, know it well and be prepared.

Follow these steps to obtain permission from your client and have a smooth written close.

1. **Ask the customer for permission to take notes.**

   Here's an example of the kind of phrasing you can use. Notice how this kind of approach is nonthreatening:

   > Would you mind if, while we chat, I jot down a few notes?

2. **When you come to any concrete detail that needs to be included on your paperwork, simply say, "Let me make a note of that."**

3. **Write the pertinent details on your agreement or, if the customer seems uncomfortable with that, on one of your blank note pages.**

If the client shows any discomfort with your taking notes, simply remind her of the value of taking notes with something like this:

> I organize my thoughts to keep everything in the proper perspective. I do that on the paperwork so I don't forget anything — particularly anything that could cost you time or money.

What is a potential client going to say to this? That she doesn't care about losing time or money? Of course not. After all, you haven't asked her to sign anything. (Asking for her signature is the last thing you do.) Demonstrating that you're a detail-oriented professional only shows your level of competence.

Double-checking and getting a signature

After you have all the details covered, take a moment to review the paperwork.

- ✔ Is the paperwork legible? Writing legibly is very important. You can't expect anyone to authorize illegible paperwork when making a purchase.
- ✔ Are any details missing that may cause a delay in the processing of the order?
- ✔ Is the information correct according to instructions from the buyer?

After you've checked everything, turn the paperwork around toward the client and hand her a pen. Ask her to review the details to be sure you have everything correct. Then say something like the following:

> With your approval right here (point to signature line), I'll welcome you to our family of satisfied clients and get started on serving your needs.

Now you shut up. Give the clients an opportunity to review the paperwork and approve it. Waiting may be tense, but resist the urge to speak. Just let the decision-making opportunity hang.

The Assumptive Close

If you've done everything properly and you know in your heart of hearts that your product or service is truly good for this person, group, or company, but you sense hesitation, use an *assumptive close*. In this kind of close, you act and speak as if the client is going ahead with the purchase.

Here's an example of an assumptive close:

> After you complete this beauty regimen for a week, you'll see wonderful results. Your skin will be softer, and your loved ones will ask what you've been doing differently to take care of yourself. You'll look better and feel better about yourself, too. By the way, did you want the basic cleansing kit or the enhanced beauty system?

The assumptive close has also been called the *secondary question close*. If the customer agrees to the secondary question (in this case, asking for the prospect's preference between basic kit or enhanced system), the first part (ownership of your product) is automatic. In this example, for instance, you're not giving the customer a choice of whether she wants to buy the beauty products. She just needs to decide which package she'll walk out the door with.

Following are a few tips to help you master the assumptive close:

✔ State the major or primary decision in terms of benefit to the client.

✔ Avoid pausing between the benefit statement and your secondary question.

✔ State the secondary question in the form of an *alternate advance question* (a question with two answers, either of which moves you closer toward the decision to go ahead; see Book IV, Chapter 2).

✔ Keep your attitude casual.

Bridging between Closes

Say you tried to close and the clients still came up with something to keep them from making an immediate decision. That's okay. No harm, no foul. If they haven't ended the conversation or walked out the door, you're still in the game. You just need to address their concern and bridge to another close. The following sections have the details.

Building closing bridges doesn't require a degree in engineering, but it does require you to delve deeply into your courtesy skills and then go back to your professional selling skills.

Apologize and address their concerns

Whether you've done something that requires an apology doesn't matter. What *does* matter is that your potential client may have been feeling a little or a lot of pressure when you asked your first closing question. As with any apology, the faster and simpler it is, the better. Here's an example:

I'm sorry. I thought you were ready to go ahead with the purchase. I didn't mean to rush you. What other concerns do you have that we haven't addressed?

Then address the concerns they bring up and/or answer their questions.

Summarize with questions

After you feel you've covered everything (again), begin a summary review of everything the customers have agreed to thus far, including the new points just covered.

Don't rush this part. Your goal is just to get them agreeing on the minor points with tie-downs and statements so you can move on to the major point of ownership. *Tie-downs* are simple questions that are added to statements of fact, which call for an agreement from the client. (See Book IV, Chapter 2 for the lowdown on tie-downs.) Here are a few examples of tie-downs:

> This model has a little more capacity than you need, so it can handle your growing needs, correct?

> The product will fit fine in the space you've allotted for it, right?

> We've agreed that you're comfortable with the financing arrangements, haven't we?

Beware of using too many tie-down questions in a row because it becomes redundant. Yes, you need tie-downs for summarizing, but hopefully, after you get them started, the customers will start listing things they've agreed to along with you, and you can simply nod in agreement.

If your customers disagree after your summary review, ask them to clarify what's missing from your summary. Perhaps they've thought of something else that you didn't cover but that needs to be addressed.

Ask a lead-in question

After you've completed your summary review, get the clients to agree that you've covered everything they can think of with these words:

> Those are all the things we've discussed so far, and we've agreed on all of them, correct?

When they say yes, go for the close again. You may be able to use the same closing phrase as before:

> With your approval right here, I'll schedule your order for delivery and immediately begin serving all your needs.

Asking for their approval tells the customers that you're back to decision time again. However, if you feel you must approach the close differently, try one of the other methods recommended in this chapter and in Chapters 4, 5, and 6 of Book IV.

The single most important advice we can give you on closing — whether it's using a simple close like those in this chapter or the more complicated closes that Chapters 4 through 6 discuss — is just ask. The number one reason customers don't buy is because they feel they were never asked. Never, never, never leave your potential clients without clearly and succinctly asking for the sale.

Chapter 4

Closes That Overcome Fear

Fear is such a powerful entity in any decision-making process that you should think of fear as another person involved in the situation — a very negative, devil's advocate type of person who is definitely not sitting on your side of the table. Your mission is to dissolve the worries and doubts that old Mr. Fear brings into play so your client can make a buying decision with confidence.

Fear causes people to stall in making decisions. So, be aware that any time the potential client stalls, there's a fear that needs to be addressed. Many of the fears you'll encounter have been encountered by other salespeople in the past. This chapter covers those fears so you'll be able to recognize them — and in some cases, avoid them entirely. This chapter also includes information on how to handle the fears you can't avoid.

Covering the Basics: Fear Fundamentals

When you work with people's fears, you need to understand certain fundamentals, including the following:

✔ Every potential client experiences some sort of fear in the decision-making process.

✔ Fear can be a direct response to something the salesperson has said or done.

- ✔ Fear can be from something outside the realm of this particular selling experience.

- ✔ Occasionally, fear wins and everybody loses.

- ✔ The more you understand fear in selling situations, the more you'll be able to control and even overcome it.

Experienced selling professionals — those who've had a certain degree of success — have probably earned the equivalent of a degree in psychology, just through their personal experiences. In this business, you have to gain a good understanding of how the majority of people react in pressure situations, which is what often occurs when people have to make decisions.

Potential clients aren't the only ones who experience fear. Salespeople do, too. Instead of doing all the things that help customers set aside their fears, many salespeople are unable to face their own fears of rejection, so they avoid dealing with the fear factor altogether. After all, they're trying to persuade people they've never met before to part with their hard-earned money for their product or service. Salespeople have no idea going in what the customers' personality types are, what their financial situations are, or what their hopes and expectations are for the product. These fearful salespeople have no idea how the customers will react, so they decide to ignore the customers' fears, hoping that they'll just go away. Well, they won't. You have to address customers' fears. No customer is going to make a buying decision when he's afraid the decision may turn out to be a bad one.

Identifying the Source of a Buyer's Fear

Dealing with customer fears takes time. Unfortunately, some salespeople become so impatient with potential clients who can't make decisions that instead of putting them at ease, they give up the sale and let the customer know they're ready to move on by saying something like, "Well, let me know if I can be of any more assistance" or "Call me when you're ready to make a decision." Then they rush off before the buyers can actually ask for more advice or answers.

What's sad for these salespeople is that instead of closing potentially long-term clients, they give up trying to help them make a buying decision and write them off as a "no sale" — maybe just about the time the customers were ready to say yes. So, what happens? The customers go elsewhere. And when the customers enter the next selling situation, many of their questions have been answered and their minds are made up. Because of you, the new salesperson is able to close them in a flash. You don't even get a thank-you for the warm-up!

This section covers several things that commonly create fear in customers. By figuring out how to recognize each fear and how to respond, you can have better control over your opportunities to close sales.

Your buyer fears you

You are a typical salesperson in the buyers' eyes — until you show them differently, customers may fear you. They believe you have the single-minded goal of selling them your product or service. You know it. They know it. They raise the drawbridge and start boiling the kettles of oil the moment they agree to talk with you. Barriers will easily go up simply because of who and what you are — a salesperson. Your job is to make sales. You're going to try to move them to a decision, and initially they aren't sure your product or service is their answer. Understanding this, your number-one goal when you meet new potential clients is to help them see you as an industry expert they can rely on for sound advice.

Building rapport to overcome fear

Your primary goal is to establish rapport with your buyers and let them see that you are a sales professional, not a sales stereotype. You're there to serve their needs. Of course, if making a sale serves their needs — whoopee! But if your product or service doesn't meet their needs, you have to show them that you won't try to persuade them to buy it. In other words, you have to let your high standards of professional ethics show. Book III, Chapter 1 offers detailed steps for establishing rapport with potential clients.

Over the past few years, many salespeople and many companies have tried to work around this common initial fear by using different titles for their profession, such as *marketing executives, investment counselors, consultants,* and on and on. If a change of title helps relax the fear barrier, go ahead and use it.

Don't let these alternative titles make you stop believing that you truly are a salesperson. If you do, you may end up leaving many potential clients for the competition. Don't let a new title lead you to behave more like an order taker than an expert advisor and sales professional whose goal is to help clients make decisions that are good for them. So, remember, no matter what title you use, you're a salesperson at heart.

Book IV

Closing Like a Champ and Getting Referrals

Overcoming bad experiences with other salespeople

Prospective customers vividly remember what happened to them in past selling situations — the bad ones, in particular. If they had a bad experience with someone selling copiers and you're there to show them the new and improved model to replace their malfunctioning one, chances are, they won't see *you* when you first walk in — they'll see that other salesperson who sold them a machine that couldn't hold up.

When the negative past experience was with a salesperson from your company, you're going to have to work twice as hard. In this situation, the customer not only doubts the product, they doubt your company. Here's a strategy that works really well in such a situation. Consider it the old "put the shoe on their foot" strategy: Simply ask the client how he'd handle the situation if he were the person in charge:

> I can understand your concern. Would you, for just a moment, pretend that you're the president of XYZ Company and you've just found out that a representative of yours made a poor recommendation to a valued client? What would you do?

Chances are, you're going to hear something like, "I'd have the jerk fired or at least put him back through product training so he didn't make the same mistake again. Then, I'd send my best person out to try to make amends with the client." At this point, you smile warmly and say:

> That's probably just what happened because I've been sent here to you today to help you resolve this situation. We at XYZ Company want you to have the finest-quality products and service that will meet your needs not only today, but as your business grows in the future. Please tell me more about your current needs and any expectations for expansion.

If the client's bad past experience was with another company, you won't have to work as hard to become the hero. You will, however, find yourself under a good bit of scrutiny as the client does his best to avoid another bad experience. (Take a look at the section "The make it better close" in this chapter for more on how to handle the customer with a negative past.)

To differentiate yourself and your product from the negative experiences of the past, try this technique used by one of Tom Hopkins's students. Walk in with a whiteboard and markers and list the previous challenges and concerns that the client had and then, after discussing how much better your company handles each of those areas of concern, get the prospective new client's permission to erase each challenge on the list. At the end, what do you have? A clean slate — literally.

Your buyer fears making a mistake — again

Face it: We've all made bad decisions at one time or another in our lives. Do you think the customer you're working with has ever made a bad decision? Probably. Was he or she called on the carpet for it? Maybe. Was it a pleasant experience? Of course not. Do you think there will be a certain amount of fear about making a mistake again? Yep. The same applies to consumers. Who hasn't made a buying decision he later regretted for one reason or another?

Old Mr. Fear will be happily reminding your buyers of all their bad past decisions at the same time that you're trying to show them why your product or service is just right for their current needs. If you sense a lot of hesitation in your buyers, you may want to point-blank ask them this question:

> I sense some hesitation here about making this decision. Please help me to understand what you're thinking so I can best serve your needs. Can you elaborate on what your hesitation is about?

Or if your potential client makes a negative comment about your product, service, or company, it could be due to something that happened in the past. You need to get to the bottom of it. Try saying,

> You obviously have a reason for saying that. Would you mind elaborating on it for me?

This response shows that you care enough to hear him out. The buyer is probably referring to a bad past experience that had nothing to do with you. After he's finished explaining, help him to see the difference between then and now. Then move back to the topic at hand: how your product or service will make his life better. Use testimonials or proof letters from existing clients to enhance the credibility of your company and your product.

If the customer made a decision about a similar product that he has since regretted, keep him talking about it until you find out all the details. Then demonstrate how your product and the current situation are different, building his confidence in making the right decision this time.

Your buyer fears being lied to

Some customers believe that a salesperson would lie to make a sale. Unfortunately, this stereotypical image of the money-grubbing salesperson has been perpetuated by Hollywood over the years. Until you build your customer's confidence in your desire and abilities to serve his needs, this fear is likely to nag at him.

Reduce this fear of being lied to by being your highly professional self. If a question comes up that you don't know the answer to, tell the potential client you don't know the answer but that you'll find out for him as soon as the meeting is over — sooner, if it's critical. This action shows him that you're not too slick. You don't make things up off the cuff. You don't lie to make the sale.

Your buyer fears incurring debt

Having a good credit rating is important to any consumer or business. In order to have a good credit rating, customers have to have used some form of credit somewhere along the line. Sadly, many people have learned the hard way the perils of misusing credit. It's oh-so-easy to get into debt! Getting out of debt is another story — millions of people have gotten in over their heads and either filed bankruptcy or severely restricted their styles of living until they could pay down their debts. In cases such as these, it's normal for people to have a certain reluctance about incurring new debt.

If your product is large enough that most people finance its purchase, you'll face this fear on a daily basis. Your job is to build the value of your product or service to the degree where not having the product is more uncomfortable than not having the money. With the example of a vehicle, the cost of repairing and maintaining an older model will likely be outweighed by the reassurance of owning something newer, even though debt will be incurred to get it. Having a vehicle that starts every morning and has a bumper-to-bumper warranty makes the investment so much more worthwhile than keeping the old clunker and never knowing where it might break down.

Your buyer fears losing face

Losing face with industry peers can be suicidal to a career. Purchasing agents are responsible for many millions of dollars' worth of purchases each year. A few bad decisions and their credibility — and probably much of their authority — goes out the window. A bad decision may even lead to their having to find a new career. Even if they remain as purchasing agents, tales of their big embarrassment are bound to resurface every now and again. No one wants to be in this type of situation.

In consumer sales, not too many individuals are solely responsible for millions of dollars; however, everyone wants to know that the money he lays out is spent wisely. No one wants to be the butt of family jokes about his supposed great deal way back in '98 (or whenever). Those stories go on forever and are handed down through the generations — it's not what anyone wants to be remembered for. Your customers don't want to lose face with their peers or their relatives.

If your product is new or on the forefront of what is predicted to be a trend, anyone who gets involved will be taking a certain amount of risk. The risk may or may not be financial; it may be a risk of credibility. In these potentially high-risk situations, you need to work extra hard to develop the customer's confidence in you and your product.

Your buyer fears the unknown

Fear of the unknown makes a lot of sense. Unless — and until — you have a good understanding of something, self-protecting fears instinctively arise in you at the thought of the unknown. So, if this is the first time your prospective client has considered a purchase of your type of product, be ready to address his fear of the unknown. You'll have to gently and enthusiastically educate him about your offering. Include statistics, testimonials, and as much hands-on experience as possible. You're the teacher, so be creative with your "classroom" technique.

After your potential clients are educated or experienced with regard to a product or service, they can relax — their fear of the unknown will begin to dissipate. You should be able to observe this transition quite easily as your potential clients start asking questions to clarify their understanding of what your product or service can do for them.

Your buyer's fear is based on prejudice

Prejudice about a product and/or service (or even toward a company or salesperson) is usually based on lack of knowledge.

If you represent any brand of merchandise, you're bound to encounter someone who is prejudiced against your brand. Overcoming this kind of fear requires you not only to prove yourself, but also to provide proof that you, your company, and your product or service will do what you say you will. Then you have to do the hard part: Deliver!

On the upside of prejudice, you'll also encounter people who won't consider owning any other brand than the one you represent because it's what they grew up with. Your product is what their whole family uses, and a competitor would be hard-pressed to get these customers to consider making a change.

Your buyer's fear is based on third-party information

Many times your prospective clients may be consulting a third party for advice, and this third party can't seem to bring himself to a decision. Depending upon the type of client you sell to, your third party could be a spouse, parent, business partner, committee, boss, or manager. Even when this third party does come to a decision, it may not be in your favor. In this case, Mr. Fear has brought in reinforcements.

Book IV

Closing Like a Champ and Getting Referrals

Are you aware that a third party almost always says no when the decision maker presents the information on the product he wants to buy? For example, say the decision makers are a young couple, and they consult with their parents. Inevitably, after consulting with parents, they'll come back to you with a negative response. Why? People are always going to be safe by saying no. If the third party encourages you to own and then things go wrong, who do you think will feel responsible for your loss? Yep, the third party — the people who gave you the go-ahead. The suggestions of friends or family members that you shouldn't make a purchase is human nature. They don't want to hurt you, so they figure no action is better than taking action on advice that ends up being wrong.

Figuring Out and Overcoming Buyers' Fears

Fear can be debilitating, stopping people from making good decisions and moving forward, even when doing so is in their best interest. If you're working with a buyer whose fear is getting in the way of her making a buying decision, you must work to allay the buyer's fear so you can move closer to the sale. Of course, one of the first hurdles is figuring out what the buyer actually fears. After you know that, you can employ a number of strategies to help her overcome those fears.

Uncovering the client's fears

Identifying the buyer's fear isn't always easy. When figuring out exactly what the potential client is afraid of is as easy as pulling an elephant through a keyhole, you have to take several steps to get the customer to voice his fears.

Follow this easy, three-step process:

1. **Put yourself in the customer's place.**

   Ask yourself what you would want a salesperson to do with you (with you as the client) in the same situation.

   Don't empathize yourself out of a sale. You don't have to become the customer and experience all his problems; you just have to understand how the customer feels and then help him turn those fearful emotions into buying emotions.

2. **Act on whatever comes to mind and continue to do this throughout the close because it will help you address the buyer's fears and concerns.**

   If you would be feeling a certain way in the same situation, chances are that the customer is feeling it right now.

3. **Empower the potential client by putting him in control of the questioning process by saying, "What questions do you have regarding this product and how it meets your needs?"**

   Before you ask the potential buyer any question that can possibly create fear, reveal something about yourself that helps the customer relate to you. People are empowered when they believe they're not alone in a situation. Be the good guy — be on their side.

   > You know, when I'm not here at work, I'm a consumer just like you. What I hope to find when I have a buying decision to make is someone with excellent product knowledge who can answer all my questions. My job here, today, is to be the expert you rely on for information. So, please share with me your questions and concerns regarding this product, and let's see how I can help you.

The following sections give you other advice on strategies you can use to overcome existing customer fears and avoid creating new ones.

Replacing rejection words with go-ahead terms

What you say creates pictures in the minds of your buyers. Think about it. When you hear the word *dog,* do you see the word *dog* in your mind? Probably not. Most people visualize a dog, not the word. With the visual image, they experience a positive or negative reaction depending on whether they like dogs.

Now think about the words you use when you're attempting to close the sale. If you use any words that can possibly create negative images in the minds of your buyers, you have to work harder to close the sale. Create a strong enough negative image and there'll be no way you can make the sale.

These negative, fear-producing words are what we call *rejection words.* Rejection words scare your prospects so much that most of them will reject you and your product or service. Before you even realize what's happened, the possibilities of a successful close shrivel up and die right in front of you. Figuring out how to replace rejection words with words that build positive images will help you close more sales.

Book IV

Closing Like a Champ and Getting Referrals

Each of the following sections lists a word or phrase that you need to immediately drop from your selling vocabulary if you want to be a master closer and lists more positive words and phrases you can use instead. For even more information on choosing your words wisely, head to Book I, Chapter 2.

"Objection" versus "concern"

Objection is yesterday's word. An objection is like throwing down the gauntlet. It presents an image of injustice or opposition. Think about it: When you hear or use the word *objection,* you likely hear in your mind an attorney in a courtroom drama shouting out, "Your honor, I object!"

Instead of *objections,* use *concerns* or *areas of concern.* The term *concern* is softer. It's something for everyone to consider, not just the judge. A concern may sidetrack the main theme of conversation for a bit, but it doesn't halt progress. The client is concerned, so you're concerned and you commit to addressing that concern.

> I understand your concern about that point; with your permission, I'd like to make a note of it, and we'll cover it at the end of my presentation.

"Cheaper" versus "economical"

Talk about stirring up emotions. Never let potential clients hear the word *cheaper.* Not many people really want cheap goods or services in the context of *cheap* meaning *less than.*

If you say something like "Our product is so much cheaper than that of any of our competitors," the next thing that could pop into your customer's mind is the question, "Why? Is it of lesser quality? Do you have an overstock because no one wants them? Why? Why? Why?"

Referring to your product or service as *more economical* lends itself to more of a positive impression because being economical is a wise thing to do.

> Not only is our product of the highest quality, but it's much more economical than most brand-name models.

"Closing room" versus "conference room"

You'd think professional salespeople would have graduated beyond using the phrase *closing room.* Just imagine the picture those words create in the mind of the prospective client: The customers will feel like you're taking them into a cell for holding until they cough up the cash. Use the term *presentation room* or *conference room* instead:

> Our conference room is much more comfortable and private. Follow me, won't you?

See how much better that sounds than "Let's finish up right over here in the closing room."

"Customer" versus "someone you're serving"

Customer is a difficult word to stop using when you're with your clients. After all, *customer* is a word you commonly use in private conversations with fellow salespeople. Yet, the word *customers* creates an impersonal categorization of people. Why risk having a potential new client feel that he'll become just one of hundreds of others in a statistic?

Serving others is really what selling is all about. The best way to stop using the word *customer* is to think of the customer as someone you are *serving*:

> The people we serve in the Phoenix area truly enjoy the benefits of our product.

"Lookers" versus "researchers"

Your clients are never just *lookers;* they are *researchers.* For example, if a young couple came into a furniture store, a professional salesperson would approach them as if the couple were researching what living room set would look best in their new home — not as if they were there to just look around.

> Thanks for coming in today. Let me ask you, are you candidates for new furniture today, or are you just researching your options?

If you assume or even risk asking if people are "just looking," you're allowing them to have that mindset. Your goal should be to have them develop an ownership mentality. They have a need to be fulfilled and are conducting research to find the right person or company to serve them.

"Have to" versus "happy to"

As a salesperson, never make your customers feel as though you are there because you *have* to be. They'll feel better (and less pressured) knowing that you are *happy* to be there serving them.

This sentence:

> I'll be happy to check our inventory on that item for you. Please give me just a moment.

sounds much better than this sentence:

> I'll have to go see if we have any in stock. Hang on while I call the warehouse.

Book IV

Closing Like a Champ and Getting Referrals

"Prospects" versus "future clients"

Although the word *prospects* has been a favorite for a long time, today it's more appropriate to refer to prospects as *future clients*. Referring to the prospects as future clients is a form of assumptive closing that, when used properly (and with sincerity), demonstrates your confidence in your ability to meet the clients' needs and become their new supplier.

> It's always a pleasure to meet with potential future clients like you and ask a few questions so I can determine exactly what you require in this product.

Understanding the decision-making process

Decisions are made emotionally. Not only are purchasing decisions made when buyers are in an emotional state, but the decision also is linked emotionally to feelings about the salesperson and the product or service. This is where you, the salesperson, need to show up as the white knight on your valiant steed to defeat wily Mr. Fear. When you accomplish this feat, you empower the buyer by making him feel confident in his wise decision to own, and the customer links good feelings about himself with you and your product.

If during the decision-making process something negative happens, your customers may link negativity to you and your product. For instance, say they decided to own your product, but then they overhear a conversation between another representative and an unhappy customer. What do you think they will picture when they think of you? Dissatisfied customers. This is a bad link — perhaps an inaccurate link — but a link all the same. If you know this has happened, explain to the future client how you would personally handle that situation.

You may need to focus on yourself rather than your product. If the potential clients are comparing products that are very similar and they cannot distinguish the difference, focus on the level of service that you and your company provide. Reinforce and boost the level of confidence they feel in you personally. Show them how you'll serve their needs better than the other guy or gal. Then make sure you live up to the belief they put in your ability to serve them.

Adapting to the emotional environment

The more you study human emotions, the more you realize how we all communicate our feelings quite differently. To handle the differing ways people express themselves, you have to be a chameleon. A chameleon has the ability to change to the environment, to blend. Emotionally, this is what you have to do as a professional salesperson — you need to blend with each situation.

As a master closer, not only do you need to be emotionally flexible to change, but you also have to form a comfortable fit in communicating with your buyers to put them at ease. You must be willing to adapt, to relate to them. Being able to blend like this will take work. You have to stop talking and expressing values, be willing to ask questions, listen, and then respond to potential clients in a way to which they are most able to relate. If all you're aiming for is average sales with average ability to close, you can continue your current practices. To be a master, however, you have to be versatile.

Closes That Overcome Fear

Refuse to accept fear as a reason your buyers decide not to own your product or service. Remove fear from the equation by creating comfort in place of fear. How? Get active when you see fear creep in. Distract the customers from their fears. Make them remember instances when they said yes and everything turned out great. Identify the source of the fear and do what you can to bring it out into the open. Fear is always much more powerful when lurking just below the surface, stalking the customers who are ready to own. Help the customers face their fear and diminish its power.

So, how do you do all this? You keep asking questions. The deeper the fear, the more questions you must ask to uncover it. When you've done a great job at getting rid of the fear, go for the final close. Use the following closes to turn the tables on Mr. Fear. Each close is designed to overcome fear and bring you and your customers to a successful end.

Book IV

Closing
Like a
Champ and
Getting
Referrals

The "If you say yes . . ." close

In this close, you begin the closing statement with "If you say yes . . ." and complete the statement with something that gives the customer incredible benefits. For example:

If you say yes to what I'm proposing here today, you'll have financial freedom for the rest of your life.

If you say yes, you'll have the satisfaction of knowing your son will have the financial resources to complete his college education and walk across the stage on graduation day.

By using the "If you say yes . . ." close, you definitely turn the tables on Mr. Fear. If fear tells the potential client to say no, the client is forced to think of what *won't* happen if he says no. So, the fear becomes that there will be no financial freedom or that the son won't be able to graduate from college. This strategy makes the client reevaluate the situation — and he's more apt to say yes to you.

The negative economy close

During your sales career, you're bound to encounter at least one negative economy situation that requires the negative economy close. And even if the economy isn't really all that bad, you'll meet up with a Joe and Jenny Negative who firmly believe that the economy is bad in their little section of the world. When you encounter Mr. Fear in these situations, here's what you say:

Years ago I learned a truth: Successful people buy when everyone else is selling and sell when everyone else is buying. There are many people talking about the bad economy these days, and I've decided not to let it bother me. Do you know why? Because many of today's fortunes were built during poor economic times. The people who built these fortunes saw the long-term opportunity rather than the short-term challenges. They made buying decisions and became successful. Of course, they had to be willing to make positive decisions. You have the same opportunity to make the same kind of decision today.

The facts presented in this sample dialogue are true. If you studied the major companies of today, you would see that most of them began when everyone else was immobilized — they took advantage of the opportunity. The negative economy close is a very true, beautiful close. The beauty of it is that after hearing this, the customers realize that going with Mr. Fear may hold them back from growing their business, achieving greatness, and beating the competition.

The big bargain close

Everyone is always looking for a bargain. However, the bargain is in the eye of the beholder. If your client has expressed a concern regarding rising prices, you're working with someone who fears inflation. If your product is truly a bargain, it's your job to help the client view your offering as such.

> During inflation, everything is a bargain. Do you know why? During inflation, knowledgeable people exchange money for things. During a deflation, they exchange things for money. So, following this reasoning, whatever you acquire today will be more expensive tomorrow. This (name your product or service) is a bargain today because inflation may hit pricing tomorrow, and you do want a bargain, don't you?

The big bargain close doesn't work with high-tech equipment. The equipment is quickly outdated, and the new releases can be more and more economical. With high-tech products, you have to sell the strong value of having immediate benefits and stress that those benefits will save them time or money in the long run. Get the customers to understand how much productivity they can lose (in dollars, if you must) if they decide to wait for prices to come down. Remember to modify the big bargain close when dealing with high-tech products.

The money or nothing close

The money or nothing close works great for long-term purchases like homes, furniture, a special vacation, and so on. You also can use it with educational products like a seminar on selling skills. The point of the close is to increase the value of the products that you're offering above the value of holding onto money.

> You know, everything depreciates — cars, homes, retirement plans, products, even money itself. These days, we all have to make the same decisions. Do we want to retain all our spendable income and watch it depreciate? Or do we want to invest some of it in things we really want, things that will provide enjoyment for our families and ourselves? By the way, I wouldn't want you to make this decision if I wasn't so sure, but from what you've told me, you would receive the benefits from my product for years to come.

Book IV

Closing Like a Champ and Getting Referrals

Again, sincerity is critical here. You must truly believe (and express this belief) in the joy, additional income, or satisfaction your product will provide the client.

The increased productivity close

Often when marketing to clients of a corporation, they aren't aware of how much an increase in morale can add to the productivity of the entire company because morale can't be measured and tracked in a spreadsheet. Their fear of spending the company's money for something that cannot be measured needs to be rationalized. The business productivity close brings that point home, so you're not only educating your clients on the power of employee morale, but you're also giving them something to prove it with. This close pours on value for the benefits of your product.

> What I'm offering is not just a good health insurance program; it's a boost in employee morale. Have you ever noticed how anything new increases job interest and excitement? Excitement increases morale. Morale increases the desire to be more productive, and what is increased productivity worth?

Increased productivity is worth a heck of a lot to any company. Point out to your clients that increased productivity can generate enough increased income to more than make up for the increased investment. On top of that, point out to the clients how investing in your product also can increase loyalty and reduce turnover, thus saving them even more money on advertising for new hires. Wow, all that from a four-sentence close!

The competitive edge close

Everyone wants to be the best. They want market share and are afraid of losing it to the competition. Companies need ways to increase their competitive edge. The competitive edge close appeals to the desire in the buyer to get ahead of the competition.

> Keep in mind that many of your competitors are facing the same challenges you are. Isn't it interesting that when an entire industry is fighting the same forces, some companies do a better job of meeting those challenges than others? My entire objective here today has been to provide you with a method of getting a competitive edge. And gaining edges, large or small, is how you can make your company one of those few companies in your industry that is doing a better job.

Fear would have kept the client's company from doing a better job — it would have kept them from implementing what you have to offer, which gives them that leg up on the competition. With this close, you've greatly diminished the power of fear by instilling a fear of what will happen if they *don't* go ahead.

The law of ten close

The law of ten close operates under the assumption that everyone has had at least one experience in their lives for which they have to admit that they're ten times better off because of the experience. This close works exceptionally well with things that build memories, like cameras, vacations, and holiday events. This close also works for computers, time-saving devices, and security devices. After all, one instance of a smoke alarm saving someone's life or a prized possession makes the investment appear minuscule, doesn't it?

> I've found over the years that a good test of the value of something is to determine whether it will stand the test of ten times. For example, you may have invested in a home, car, clothes, jewelry, or something that gave you great pleasure. But after you owned the item for a while, how would you answer this question: "Am I willing now to pay ten times more for this product than I originally did?"

> In other words, has the product given you that much pleasure? If you paid for some advice that greatly improved your health, it was worth more than you paid for it. If you received some information that allowed you to have a life-changing experience or increase your income or self-image, it was worth more than you paid for it. There are a lot of things in our lives that I think we would have paid ten times more for them, considering what they've done for us.

> Now, step with me into the future. Ten years from now, will today's investment be worth more or less to you than what you're investing in it today?

If your product or service fits the category just described, this is a great close, because it takes the client away from the immediate financial decision and helps him to focus on the overall benefits and future rewards. The law of ten close is excellent for diffusing money concerns.

The make it better close

You can use the make it better close when customers tell you that they've done business with salespeople in the past who didn't call back and didn't

Book IV

Closing
Like a
Champ and
Getting
Referrals

give them good service, and they're afraid the same thing will happen with you. An important thing to remember is that you never knock your competition — knocking others makes you look small and petty.

> First of all, even though it wasn't my company, I apologize for times other companies have sold you products and then let you down with the follow-up and service. Let me assure you, our company will always be available to you and will contact you on a scheduled basis to make sure of your satisfaction. In fact, that's one of the reasons I chose to work with this company. We're always here for our customers. Your ongoing business is important to us, and I won't do anything to jeopardize the relationship we're establishing here today.

For the times when the poor salesperson is from your company, take a look at this chapter's section "Overcoming bad experiences with other salespeople" for how to handle the situation.

The buyer's remorse close

You're probably already familiar with *buyer's remorse,* the second thoughts a client has about the decision he's made to purchase your product that lead him to cancel the transaction. Buyer's remorse is a favorite of Mr. Fear's. Buyer's remorse raises doubts about the decision. It builds regret. And it's a master of instigating second-guessing. Use the buyer's remorse close to take some of the wind out of Mr. Fear's sails — or is it sales? (Sorry, the pun was too good to pass up.)

> I feel good about the decision you've made to get involved in this insurance program. I can tell that you're both excited and somewhat relieved. From time to time, I've had people just like you who were positive about the decision they'd made until they shared it with a friend or relative. Well-meaning friends or relatives, not understanding all the facts and maybe even a little envious, discouraged them from their decision for one reason or another. Please don't let this happen to you. In fact, if you think you may change your mind, please tell me now.

By asking the buyers to tell you now if they're a little dubious, you can take the opportunity to resell value and recap the benefits of owning your product. Use this close and you'll reduce the number of lost sales caused by buyer's remorse.

The economic truth close

When your product is of higher quality and a little less economical than the competition's, use the economic truth close to instill doubt about the other product and value in yours:

> Guiding your buying decision by price alone is not always wise. Investing too much is never recommended; however, investing too little has its drawbacks as well. By spending too much, you lose a little money, but that's all. By spending too little, you risk more because the item you've purchased may not give you the satisfaction you were expecting. That it's seldom possible to get the most by spending the least is an economic truth.
>
> In considering business with the least expensive supplier, it may be wise to add a little to your investment to cover the risk you're taking in purchasing a lesser product. If you agree with me on this point and are willing and able to invest a little more, why not get a superior product? After all, the inconveniences of an inferior product are difficult to forget. When you receive the benefits and satisfaction from the superior product, its price, no matter how much, will soon be forgotten, don't you agree?

Now you're making Mr. Fear work with you. Fear may have initially made the customer not want to spend too much. But with this close, the customer will begin to fear making a bad decision and losing face by buying an inferior product. Your argument for investing a little more may first cause confusion on the part of the customer, but then the answer becomes perfectly clear: Buy your superior product and avoid any risks of an inferior one.

The time trap close

The time trap close is kind of long, but it's extremely valuable for certain products like insurance and investments because it demonstrates how quickly things can pass us by. If we don't pay attention and take care of things now, we may have regrets later. The logic behind this close is incredible, and it builds emotionally as you go through it.

Book IV

Closing Like a Champ and Getting Referrals

YOU: More than 90 percent of the people in the United States won't have the kind of money they need to retire comfortably during their golden years. The biggest reason for this, I feel, is what I call the time trap. To illustrate this point, I'm going to ask you a question. What do you feel you'll be doing 25 years from now?

THEM: Well, that's so far in the future, but hopefully we'll be retired and enjoying ourselves.

YOU: Yes, I hope you will be, too, but it will take more than hope. We need to turn that hope into reality. Try to imagine life 25 years from now. What will the world be like? I know it seems incredibly far away, but is it really that far in the future? Let's look at 25 years in a different light. What were you doing 25 years ago?

THEM: Let's see, uh, we were in high school.

YOU: When you look back at high school, can you remember your senior prom and some of the things you were doing in high school?

THEM: Yes.

YOU: Does it look very far away?

THEM: No, it seems like just yesterday.

YOU: That yesterday was 25 years ago. Isn't it amazing? If you were sitting in high school discussing what you would be doing now, 25 years later, it would have seemed really far away, but when you look back at it, high school seems like just yesterday. Time passing too quickly is the situation millions of older Americans are finding themselves in now. Back 25 years ago, when you were in high school, these older folks were 40 years old but still thought that today was too far away and wasn't worth considering. Now, 25 years later, they're working two part-time jobs just to make their Social Security checks stretch far enough to eat and keep a roof over their heads. Time has a way of looking like a wide expanse into the future, yet it compresses as we look back into the past. I want to make sure that 25 years from now, you're not looking back and wondering where the time went with no time left to enjoy your golden years. I'm here to help you avoid the terrible ramifications of this time trap that's trapping over 90 percent of the people in this country. Now, let's see what we can do about securing your financial future.

You've taken your clients from the care-free days of high school to the potentially care-burdened days of retirement in a matter of minutes. No one wants to picture himself flipping burgers at 65 like he did at 16. Back then, it may have been fun. Now it may not be.

Be sure you know the personality type of the client before attempting this close. The thought of flipping burgers at 65 may make Mr. Smith feel like a kid again, and he may want something like this to occupy his time.

The gaining versus losing close

You'll come across some clients who are more afraid of not having the benefits of the new product (a negative motivation), than they are excited about having them (a positive motivation). For example, this fear may occur with a piece of manufacturing equipment that will put the client on the cutting edge and ahead of the competition. The fear that the competition will outpace the client may be the biggest motivation to own.

You also may find this type of fear in families where there's a lot of competition and they're always trying to outdo each other by having the smallest cellphone, the biggest flat-screen TV, or the newest model of car or computer. In those cases, you need to build the emotional appeal and commitment to the product or service based on those facts. If you hear any hesitancy, you can subtly remind them that this is the latest and greatest item on earth and that they'll be the first in the neighborhood, maybe even in town, to have one — but only if that's the truth. Nobody likes to miss out on the good things in life, so make customers feel like they'll be missing out on all kinds of things if they decide not to own.

Without asking the customer some questions, you won't be able to tell which is her strongest motivator — the negative or the positive. You have to discover some important information. For example:

- ✔ **How long has she been looking for your product or service?** If it's been a long time and she still hasn't been closed, she's probably not very motivated by the pain of not owning your offering.

- ✔ **How has she been getting along without owning a product like the one you offer?** If she tells you how miserable it has been and complains about the discomfort of not owning, you can probably rest assured that she's motivated by the pain of not owning your product.

- ✔ **How will owning your product will make her feel?** If your product is a brand-new car, and she starts talking about her excitement of driving across country in her new car and showing it off to her relatives, you can assume she's motivated by the fun and excitement of ownership instead of the pain of not owning.

After you discover what motivates the customers, close them accordingly.

Book IV

Closing Like a Champ and Getting Referrals

Chapter 5

Closes That Put an End to Buyers' Procrastination

· ·

In This Chapter

▶ Figuring out why people procrastinate

▶ Understanding behaviors customers use to procrastinate

▶ Exploring closes that end procrastination

· ·

Procrastination can wreak more havoc on lives than Godzilla in Tokyo. Procrastination is easy to identify when it's a flagrant disregard for getting things done and making decisions. But not all procrastination is of this variety; some procrastination takes more subtle forms. In other cases, the procrastinators make it look like they're getting a lot accomplished when they're really just treading water. This scenario also makes procrastination hard to recognize. For this reason, this chapter helps you understand why people procrastinate and what to look for to determine whether you're dealing with a procrastinator.

Of course, being able to recognize procrastination is one thing; doing something about it is another. When you're dealing with a procrastinating potential client, it's up to you to either stop and wait for him to make decisions or figure out a way to get the buyer moving toward owning your product or service. You can find many strategies for moving things along in this chapter, as well as how to become more effective when dealing with procrastination so you can close the sale successfully.

Why Do Buyers Procrastinate?

People procrastinate for any number of reasons. In order to choose the best method for helping potential clients get over their current bout of procrastination, you have to find out what their particular reason is. The most common reasons are listed in the following sections.

Whatever fear is holding the customers back, realize that it's not your fault. Unless you were the salesperson who helped him acquire something he later regretted, you're not the bad guy. So don't take his hesitation personally. You do, however, get to be the hero in helping the customer overcome his procrastination and move on to enjoying the benefits of your product or service.

Procrastinators refuse to make a decision because they need more information, but they're so busy making themselves *look* busy that they never actually get around to making a decision. So, when the time comes and the decision must be made, the procrastinator tends to drown in a sea of panic. The trick for you, the sales professional who's trying to close a procrastinator, is to invite him into your lifeboat and save his skin in a hurry.

They fear making decisions

A common fear of potential clients is making a bad decision. Maybe the buyer made a poor decision in the past on a similar purchase and is afraid it will happen again.

If your client is fearful of making decisions, you need to be patient and ask a lot of questions. Get her talking about why she's hesitant and listen for something solid you can grab hold of and help her with. Then clearly show the buyer that this is an entirely different situation with different products and (hopefully) even more benefits than the past situation held for her.

For more information on overcoming a buyer's fear, take a look at Book IV, Chapter 4.

They lack trust in you

Maybe the potential client has been told over and over again to never trust a salesperson. Millions of people out there think like this, and unfortunately, a number of untrustworthy salespeople in the world perpetuate all the stereotypes that lend support to the belief that salespeople can't be trusted.

You, however, are different. You are a sales *professional.* You can be trusted to help your clients meet their needs and make decisions that are truly good for them. You just need to help them see this so they'll go ahead and listen to your recommendations. Prove this by doing the following:

- ✓ **Pay attention.**
- ✓ **Be courteous.** Hold doors open for clients. Say "please," "thank you," and "you're welcome."

> ✔ **Lead them to the product of interest while asking about *their* needs.**
>
> ✔ **Respect their time.** If you know your product demonstration takes only 10 minutes, promise clients that you won't take more than 12 minutes of their time. Some salespeople even put their watches or a stopwatch in plain sight of the client and are certain to wrap up their demonstration in less than the promised time. They make a point of showing the client they value the client's time by not running over.
>
> ✔ **Fulfill your promises and deliver on time.**

They want your attention

Ever consider that maybe the buyers enjoy your attention and don't want the process to end? Hey, you're a nice person to be around, right? If you sense that your easy rapport with your customers is part of what they're buying (as it should be), take a few moments to let them know that they're not just investing in a product or service; they're establishing a long-term relationship with you and your company. Use their enjoyment of your attention as part of your strategy to close the sale.

Now's the time to tell the buyers about your follow-up program. If you give some sort of recognition for referred leads who also become clients, tell them about that program as well. Make your potential clients feel like they're not just getting a product; they're joining the family of happy clients your company serves. Affiliating buyers with your "family" may be just the ticket for getting them to make their decision now.

They're seeking education

A buyer may balk and say that he doesn't know enough about the product to make a decision. If you feel you've done a good job of getting the information across and the buyer still hesitates, do a brief summary of all the points you've covered. Ask what you may have missed. You should be able to do this quickly from the extensive notes you've taken during your time with the buyer. Better yet, you should have a summary page in your proposal that provides just that information.

Here is one case of procrastination that may be your fault. You may not have been thorough enough in your presentation, leaving the client feeling that he doesn't know enough to make an educated decision. Strive to cover every aspect of your product in an effort to make the buyer comfortable. You can't call yourself a sales professional if you don't have the skills to discover the most important needs of each client and educate him on the features and benefits of the product you represent.

Book IV

Closing Like a Champ and Getting Referrals

They want to compare apples to oranges

If your product is being compared to that of the competition, you need to ask a lot of questions about how the competition presented their information. You need to be certain that both products are considered on the same basis. Although it may seem indiscreet to ask what the competition is offering (when, for example, the client is asking you to bid against a competitor), it's never inappropriate to ask how the information is presented. Do it this way:

> Your complete and total satisfaction is our goal. I want you to have the best product for your specific needs and would never recommend something if I didn't truly believe it was in your best interest. I'm certain you're taking great pains in analyzing our product against that of the competition. I'm curious, though, about the analysis itself. Are you comfortable that the information I'm providing you allows you to accurately compare the benefits and value of our product with those provided by other companies you're researching, or is there something more I can provide you with to make your comparison easier?

If the customer reveals that the competitor's information is formatted a bit differently, so she has to convert some of the figures to get to the same bottom line, do the following:

- ✔ **Ask for the details.** When you know that finding the same bottom line is a bit of a challenge in the decision-making process, you can dig a little deeper into the information format the competition has used.

- ✔ **Step in to help.** If you need to, change the format of your presentation so the buyer can more easily make her comparison. But don't let her do the conversions herself. Get on your computer and revise your format so you can deliver the figures in the same way the competition did. Your extra efforts will show your determination to do well in serving their needs and may also help the buyer make his decision much more quickly — hopefully, in your favor.

Why should you never let the clients do the conversions themselves? Because one minor math error on their part can mean an end to the biggest sale of your career. *Always* revise your data to meet their needs.

They lack interest in the product

Sometimes your potential clients may not seem to care too much about your product or service, so they procrastinate making a decision either way. When this happens, you need to be prepared to build value. Show the buyers what's in it for them. As an example, say you're talking to a parent about the latest video game. They may never play it, so they have rather lukewarm feelings about it. To make a close, you're going to have to build the value of the child's appreciation into your sale of the game. Using this approach will be more effective than talking about how you can blast 500 aliens into smithereens in three minutes.

> Just picture the delight and excitement on your son's face when he opens this gift on Christmas morning. He'll know you cared enough to get him just what he wanted.

If they've made any disparaging remarks about little Johnny during your time with them, you can add:

> Plus, he'll run off to the den to play it for several hours, giving you some time to relax.

The benefit of the product is in the eye of the buyer. Your job is to determine which approach to use and then deliver accordingly.

Signs of a Procrastination in Progress

Certain traits are common among procrastinators. If you're beginning to suspect that your buyer is a procrastinator, here are some things to watch for. If you see any of the following signs, your suspicions are probably correct.

Changing the subject

Procrastinators will talk to you about almost anything except the situation at hand, which — in this case — is making a buying decision. You'll know more about their kids, their golf game, their last vacation, their hobbies, even the personality conflicts in their offices than you will about their buying preferences.

If you encounter buyers like this, be patient. Learn to listen well. Watch for an opportunity to redirect the conversation back to the purchase. Ask them a question that brings them back to the subject at hand. The buyers may counter by asking you questions about yourself, your kids, the car you drive, and so on. Everything they counter with is a stall.

Your mission is to keep dragging them back to the selling situation with questions regarding their needs. You may have to pointedly ask what exactly is going on if the chitchat drags on too long or the buyers change the subject every time you take control:

> YOU: I sense that you're not really ready to make a decision on this product today.
>
> BUYER: Well, I really haven't made up my mind yet on what I'm going to do.

Book IV

Closing
Like a
Champ and
Getting
Referrals

YOU: That's no problem. Can you tell me what your thoughts are so far so I can tell if there may be some information I've left out of my presentation?

Let the potential clients summarize their thinking. Take note of not just what they say, but how they say it. Try to discern the area of discomfort and then review the details.

If the meeting gets a bit drawn out and you don't feel there's anything you can do to make the sale today, reschedule.

I can tell you're not really ready to go ahead and that you may just need a bit more time to consider this purchase. Why don't we schedule another meeting for Thursday morning when we're both fresh and you can give the matter your full attention?

Rescheduling is a last resort. If you're in the game against the competition, it may be to your advantage to risk going for the close today rather than having the competition spend more time with the client. However, if you truly feel you're getting nowhere, move on to other clients and reschedule your time with this one.

Body language clues

People tend to make several body language moves when they want to slow things down. By watching their body language, you can generally target a procrastinator right off the bat. The following lists several moves procrastinators tend to make:

- ✔ Taking off their glasses to clean the lenses and/or chewing on the ear piece
- ✔ Pushing backward in a chair
- ✔ Tapping a pen or playing with a paper clip
- ✔ Glancing out the window
- ✔ Shuffling papers or flipping the pages of your proposal

Any of these signs tell you that the buyers aren't really ready to go ahead with a decision. Now your job is to find out why:

- ✔ **Did you just say something prior to one of these moves that may have raised a concern?** If so, restate that point and ask if it's something you need to clarify.

✔ **Did the buyers just think of a detail that had been left out of previous conversations?** If so, they may be a bit embarrassed to bring it up now. You can solve this by asking how they're feeling about things so far and whether you've covered all the details that concerned them.

✔ **Do the customers simply feel you're moving too fast?** If that's the case, ask whether the potential client has any questions at this point.

✔ **Maybe the buyers see no further reason to hold off making the purchase but are allowing themselves time to second-guess.** In that case, ask them to elaborate on the reasons why they may not go ahead with this decision.

If you're truly serious about your career in selling, being able to read a person through body language can save you a lot of time and grief and, most important, can help you serve your clients better than the average sales professional. (For more on reading body language, see Book IV, Chapter 1.)

Allowing interruptions

Say you're dealing with Joe Buyer. Joe is handling the negotiations of a purchase of computer equipment for a new branch office his company is opening. Obviously, you can expect things to be hectic. Joe agrees to meet with you, and when you arrive, you notice that he doesn't close his office door when you enter. Uh-oh. An open door is an open invitation for interruptions. Then Joe sits behind his desk with several stacks of papers between the two of you — another potential source of distraction — and a literal wall of sales resistance. The phone rings and Joe makes a face as if to say "This will just take a minute." He then takes the call, handling a matter totally unrelated to your computer equipment. Is Joe serious about making a decision, or is he procrastinating? More than likely, he's procrastinating. However, he may not even be fully aware of what he's doing.

With the Joe Buyers of the world, you need to subtly take control. Here's how to address the obstacles Joe Buyer has placed in the way of a meeting without distractions:

✔ **The open door:** Upon entering the room, simply close the door. Chances are, the potential client won't even immediately register the fact that the door is closed. If your closing of the door appears to concern the customer, say:

> Do you mind if I close this? I'd hate to have anything distract us from something so critical to the productivity of your employees.

If you're a male selling to a woman, you may want to offer to keep the door open just a crack. This will still deter interruptions but not risk putting the woman on the defensive because she's in a closed room with a strange man.

✔ **The cluttered desk:** Suggest you sit at a conference table if the customer has one. If not, say something like the following:

> I have a few things to show you and will need a bit of space. Would you prefer that I help you clear some space on your desk or is there a conference room that would be more appropriate for our meeting?

✔ **The phone interruptions:** Say either of the following.

> Just one more thing. Do you have a secretary or assistant who can screen your calls for our brief time together?"

> Do you have a Do Not Disturb feature on your phone that we could take advantage of? I understand how valuable your time is, and I don't want to take up any more of it than necessary today, so the fewer interruptions the better, don't you agree?

By eliminating the distractions, you diminish the chances of procrastination taking over your closing sequence. Being proactive is critical when it comes to facing down procrastination.

Canceling visits

You're bound to encounter procrastinators who put off seeing you the way they put off a visit to the dentist for a root canal. That's one of the reasons the selling business is rife with canceled appointments. Buyers sometimes cancel visits ten minutes after you confirm them. They cancel the night before via voicemail so they don't risk talking with you in person. They cancel by calling you on your cellphone as you're driving to their office. Sometimes, they even have the receptionist tell you they've canceled after you've arrived on time, fully prepared and ready to close.

Here's how to handle someone you sense will put off your next scheduled visit:

✔ **As soon as the appointment is scheduled, put a confirmation in writing and send it either by e-mail or snail mail, whichever is appropriate for your industry or type of client.**

✔ **Call to confirm your meeting at the end of the preceding day if you're scheduled to visit in the morning.** If you have an afternoon appointment, confirm the morning of the same day. Say something like this:

> Hi, this is (your name here). I'm really looking forward to our time together at (confirm again the time, date, and location). I really put some work into the presentation and pulled together some exciting information that I believe you'll be surprised to hear. I've worked hard to be well prepared so as not to waste any of your time. I'll see you then.

Now, if you deliver these lines with sincerity and enthusiasm, how can the buyer cancel on you? You've worked so hard for him! Also, you've built his curiosity about the "exciting information" you have in store for him.

By the way, top salespeople — especially those who work with consumers — refer to appointments as *visits,* a kinder, gentler term that doesn't raise barriers of fear.

Certainly, there will be times when something truly important comes up and the reason for the cancellation is legitimate. In most of these cases, the client is happy to reschedule with you — and will go out of his way to be prepared the next time. If you've demonstrated a high degree of professionalism to this point, he's going to want to learn more from you.

Not returning calls

Procrastinators are excellent at shuffling messages, losing messages, misplacing phone numbers, and letting time slip away from them — so they just *couldn't* get back to you.

If you know you're working with a procrastinator who uses this method, try not to leave the ball in his court. Leave assumptive messages like:

> Based on our conversations to this point, it appears you're most interested in testing the Triple A model. If I don't hear from you otherwise, I'll contact our scheduling department to find out how quickly we can have that model delivered to you for a trial.

Now, if the client isn't interested in that model, chances are pretty good that you'll hear from him. Plus, having a demo model show up and having other staff people *ooh* and *ahh* over it only to have to return the product makes the buyer look a bit incompetent.

Book IV

Closing Like a Champ and Getting Referrals

A little understanding goes a long way. You may have a client who is quite simply overwhelmed with his current workload, and returning calls to salespeople gets shoved to the bottom of his to-do list. In cases like this, just be persistent and sympathetic. Give him a call for action and a deadline for re-contacting you about a critical point in the process. A deadline may be what gets you moved up on the to-do list.

Offering an alternate suggestion for communication is also a good idea. Some people respond better to e-mail than to voicemail because they can do it on their own time, not during set business hours.

Wanting to do lunch — a long lunch

Some potential clients will take advantage of you by dangling their business out there in front of you and then subtly (or not so subtly) suggesting that you discuss your proposal with them over lunch, at an NBA or NFL game, on the golf course, and so on.

A lot of business is conducted outside the confines of homes and offices, and that's okay. You just need to be aware of who's serious about doing business with you and who's taking advantage. Polly Purchasing Agent, who can't seem to schedule you in for an appointment but suggests meeting over lunch instead, may just be looking for a free lunch and not your products.

You have to make a judgment call as to what you feel is best for each situation. If you do take Polly to lunch before she becomes a client, take her to a nice restaurant, but don't take her to the best restaurant in town; that would be inviting her to take advantage of you. If Polly dawdles over lunch and skirts around the business at hand, she's very likely a procrastinator and is using your lunch as a screen to cover for time she should be spending doing something else.

Handling Procrastinators with Ease

Procrastinators are comfortable just the way they are, and they don't handle change well. The only way to get procrastinators to make a move is to create so much desire for the outcome that they become uncomfortable staying the same and have to make the change to achieve a new level of comfort. The following sections discuss several ways to do just that.

Creating a sense of urgency

To get procrastinators off the fence, nothing works better than creating a sense of urgency. If you know there's a price increase for your product next month, use that knowledge to help your clients make decisions now that will save them money in the long run. Everyone wants to save money.

Another way to create a sense of urgency is with delivery dates. If you know that in order to make a January shipping date, for example, you need to have the order by the end of the week, tell your buyers that.

Working the responsibility angle

For some procrastinators, the need to meet their responsibilities is what gets them moving. If they're uncomfortable about the current situation but lack confidence in their own decision-making abilities, try discussing their responsibility regarding the decision.

Only use the responsibility angle when you know for certain that your product or service is truly good for them and that they can afford it. Never use it to push your buyers into something.

For example, something most people — not just procrastinators — put off is saving for their children's educations or protecting themselves with enough insurance to have their families cared for if something should happen to them. No one is in a hurry to admit that before he knows it, his children will be grown. No one wants to face the fact that he may not be around to see it happen. If you help procrastinating clients imagine a real-life situation in which their own children are at risk, they'll most likely make an immediate move to become more comfortable regarding that situation. The way they get more comfortable is to increase their insurance coverage or start that mutual fund. Get them comfortable with the new sense of security this provides; then close the sale.

Showing customers how to be a hero

When your client is a decision maker — say a purchasing agent, a business owner, or the head of a household — he may make decisions about products or services that he'll never personally use. In those cases, the decision maker may not be as motivated to make a decision (unless his staff or family is especially good at nagging). He isn't personally being restricted by not having cable television or the latest mailing equipment, so he doesn't feel the immediate reward, either.

In this case, you need to help that decision maker see himself as the hero who makes wise decisions that bring benefits to all those he cares about. Receiving gratitude or recognition for doing something good can be quite a motivator.

Book IV

Closing Like a Champ and Getting Referrals

Assuming the close

Some people just don't want to make a decision because they've gotten used to bantering with you. They may not have other projects of interest to move on to. Or they may just not know how to wrap something up. When you're confident that you've covered all the bases and that not a single reason exists for the customers not to go ahead, you may have to become very assumptive and call for their approval on your paperwork:

> Because you have no further questions or concerns, I can assume that my company suits your needs. With your approval right here, I'll get your account established, and we'll begin serving your needs immediately.

Having an agenda — in writing

Having an agenda works well with clients you find yourself spending way too much time with. If you're with a new client, this strategy shows your dedication to staying on task and valuing their time. Simply go into your presentation with a brief agenda or checklist of the important items to cover. Then say the following:

> I so appreciate your time today. I know how busy you are. To keep us on track and keep our meeting as brief as possible, I've prepared a brief agenda of topics we'll need to cover.

Hand the agenda to the customer. Including check boxes on the agenda is helpful with some procrastinators because they can check off an item when you complete a topic. An agenda is a tool that enables you to keep the customers focused and your presentation moving forward.

 Don't put "Ask for the sale" on your list. Instead, you may want to word it this way: "Confirm that our product meets your needs." Also, structure the agenda to call for the close as the second-to-last item. The last item should be to thank the customer for his business.

Recognizing the buyer's stress

When buyers procrastinate, they create a situation of constant worry. But isn't it better just to do what needs to be done when it needs to be done and with a clear head? Worry caused by procrastination can be a constant distraction; it can interrupt your days to the point that you're unproductive at everything. Help your clients get on with their other tasks by getting this decision made today.

I understand that you're hesitant to make a decision today about my product. You probably have a lot on your mind. I learned a saying from a speaker once that makes a lot of sense when it comes to handling business matters. The saying goes like this: "I must do the most productive thing possible at every given moment." Makes sense, doesn't it? Now let me ask you, what's the most productive thing you could be doing right now?

If the customer says something that has little to do with the buying decision, say this:

> Then, let's get this decision out of the way so you can get on to something more productive.

If the customer says the buying decision is the most productive thing he could be doing right now, say this:

> Good. Then we're handling just what you want to do right now, which is to make a decision about my product. With your approval right here, we'll be in business.

Using the scale approach

The scale approach is a decision-making tool that has been used for hundreds of years. This particular approach has been refined and updated for today's selling situations. In this strategy, you use a scale to weigh the facts regarding the benefits of a product or service against the concerns that a client has about purchasing. You don't need an actual scale. Instead you can draw one (see Figure 5-1).

Figure 5-1:
Draw a scale like this for your clients.

Book IV

Closing Like a Champ and Getting Referrals

When the client expresses hesitation or says that he wants to weigh it out in his mind, you, ever so kindly, do the following:

1. **Offer to help by using the scale approach to help weigh the fact before making a decision; then draw a scale.**

2. **On the left side of the scale, pile up — just like small weights — the reasons the customer feels it makes good sense to go ahead with the purchase; on the right side of the scale, pile up the reasons the customer feels are against the purchase.**

Work with the customer to come up with reasons. Two tips when using this method: Go for a minimum of six reasons for the decision, and don't help on the right side!

Relating to a similar situation

Relating a story of someone else who was in a situation similar to the buyer's is always effective because the buyer will identify with that person. Tell the potential client about someone who procrastinated and wished he hadn't, or conversely, tell him about someone who *didn't* procrastinate and received tremendous benefit from making an immediate buying decision.

Thinking it over

You're guaranteed to hear a variation of the phrase "I want to think it over" from one out of every five potential new clients. Some of the variations you'll hear may be:

- ✔ "I want to sleep on it."
- ✔ "I'll get back to you."
- ✔ "We'll review all the facts and then make a decision."
- ✔ "We never make a decision on the first visit."

The exact words you use don't matter much; what really matters is that you recognize the stall and are ready with an acknowledgment that indicates the buyer must be seriously interested in your product, asks that she give it careful consideration, and clarifies what, exactly, she needs to think over:

Just to clarify my thinking, what phase of this opportunity is it that you want to think over? Is it the quality of the service I'll render? Is it something I've forgotten to cover? Is it the return on your investment? Is it any of the financial aspects? Seriously, please level with me.

A tip when using this strategy: Don't pause after the word *over*. If you do, a client is likely to answer "Everything" or "The whole idea of going ahead," and you're dead in the water.

Your goal here is to review what the customer has already agreed to. In other words, you're weeding out all the other concerns and narrowing it to the most common final objection, which is the money. Handle the money objection — see Book III, Chapter 4 for some pointers and Book IV, Chapter 6 for dealing with tough customers — and begin re-closing.

Keeping track of inflation

The U.S. has a supply-and-demand economy, and the economy goes through cycles of both *inflation* (a general increase in the price of goods and services over a period of time) and *deflation* (a general decrease in the price of goods and services over time). During an inflation cycle, as people watch prices go up and the purchasing power of their money go down, they tend to focus on how expensive things are and cut spending — which can present challenges when you're trying to close a sale. But you can actually use what happens during an inflationary cycle to explain to your prospective customer why buying now is actually a sound financial decision.

Use the following close when a person is dubious about the investment and wants to wait for things, such as interest rates, to come down:

> The most critical decisions we have to make today are money decisions. We no longer have the luxury of deciding between three factors: save, spend, or invest. Today, because of inflation, we can no longer afford to just save our money, and I'm sure you know why: Every time Washington decides to keep rolling those money presses, every dollar we have saved is worth less than it was when we earned it. Today, we must make whatever money we have left after meeting our basic expenses do something positive for us. We really have only two choices: We can find an investment that will actually show a return greater than the inflation rate or we can improve our standard of living. Now, we have found what you really want. What you really deserve is a reward for all your hard work. Tell me, are you or are you not entitled to a reward for all the work you've done?

Showing that you get what you pay for

No doubt, you've heard a customer say, "I can get it cheaper somewhere else." Often, this is a defense mechanism the customer uses when what she really wants is time to shop around. Using this closing technique helps the customer rationalize the decision and go ahead with your product today:

> You may well be able to find this product for less elsewhere, and in today's economy, we all want the most for our money. A truth that I've learned over the years is that the cheapest price is not always what we really want. Most people look for three things in making an investment: (1) the finest quality, (2) the best service, and (3) the lowest price. I have never found a company that can offer all three — the finest quality and the best service at the lowest price. I'm curious. For your long-term happiness, which of the three are you willing to give up? Quality, service, or low price?

Here's why this close works:

- Very few people are going to choose a low-quality product. And very few salespeople are going to want to represent one.

- If the item being purchased requires a good bit of after-the-sale service such as computer equipment or cars, service won't be their choice. After all, who wants so-so service when you're without a car or your computer is down?

- The majority of people will choose to do without low price because, after all, everyone knows the old cliché "You get what you pay for."

Fitting your product into the client's budget

You often come across people who use their budget as a way to keep from committing to a purchase. Use this close to remind them of the true purpose of a budget and who's actually in control.

> I understand your need to stick to your budget, which is why I contacted you in the first place. I'm fully aware of the fact that every well-managed business controls the flow of its money with a carefully planned budget. The budget is a necessary tool for every company to give direction to its goal. However, the tool itself doesn't dictate how the company is run. The budget must be flexible. You, as the controller of that budget, retain for yourself the right to flex that budget in the best interest of the company's financial present and competitive future, don't you? What we've been examining here today is a system that will allow your company an immediate and continuing competitive edge. Tell me, under these conditions, will your budget flex or will it dictate your actions?

It's important to speak these words with the proper tone. You're not throwing the control of the budget in her face — you're reminding her that she's the one in charge of how money is used to benefit her company.

You can tweak this script for a personal sale, too, if people rely on their household budgets as the final stall. What they're really saying is that they don't see enough value to take the money from something else they've budgeted for and put it toward your product.

> I understand your need to stick to your budget. I'm fully aware of the need for people today to have a good handle on where their money goes. Would you agree with me that your budget is an excellent tool for helping you achieve the things you want with the money you earn? However, you are the one using the tool; the tool itself doesn't dictate how the money is spent. Your budget has to be flexible for emergencies and changing needs, right? You, as the controller of that budget, retain for yourself the right to flex that budget in your own best interest, don't you? What we've been examining here today is a product that will allow you (or your family) an immediate and continuing benefit. Tell me, under these conditions, will your budget flex or will it dictate your actions?

Reaching a compromise

Use this tactic when you have two or more decision makers who can't seem to agree. They both want the product, and they're qualified for it, but they've come to an impasse and need a little nudge. They both know there are enough reasons why they should go ahead and make the decision today; you just need to help them along:

> When two people are required to make one decision, it's often impossible to find one solution that satisfies both of them. So, life again becomes a matter of compromise. Now, the measurement of each decision is through the use of this question: Does the product satisfy most of the wants of each of the parties?

Incorporating a third party

In essence, the purpose of this close is to get permission to talk with a subordinate or third party when a decision maker is procrastinating. By giving authority to another person, the decision maker is getting out of making the decision altogether, and that's what some procrastinators want — not to be accountable.

> My experience in the past has proven that people in your position operate under terrific time constraints. I understand the value of your time. In many cases, my clients and I have found it helpful if I do most of my groundwork, while working with someone you choose to provide the information. I can then use that information to prepare a proposal for your fine company. Who is it that I should speak with?

When the buyer gives you the name, respond with this:

> Thank you. Will you please let him know that I'll be calling this afternoon?

When the times comes to end the third-party relationship, be sure to tell the third-party person how appreciative you are.

Always review the information given by the designated third party with the decision maker before presenting your recommended solution. Review the information by asking questions like this:

> According to your assistant, the company is looking for. . . . Am I correct in my understanding of this?

Going over the information beforehand leaves you an out if you've assumed something incorrectly or if the third party has given you inaccurate information.

Putting yourself in your buyer's shoes

Put yourself on the same level as the buyer by describing yourself as a consumer and telling what you go through when making decisions. When the buyers realize that you also face the same kind of decisions, they'll be more open to your recommendations.

> I recently made a purchase myself. I began by gathering information and looking at various models. To be honest with you, the more I looked, the more confused I became. Finally, I decided to just go with my gut feeling and get the decision-making process over with. You know, the time we spend considering decisions is valuable, but in most cases, we usually end up going with our instincts. So, I've found that the quicker the decision is made, the sooner we can concentrate on other things. Is that about the way you feel, too?

If you've been working with this buyer for quite some time, that little speech can knock him off the fence and get him to agree that he should just get on with it. However, if it's a major decision, this may not work. If the buyer disagrees with you and just loves pondering decisions, you'll have to resort to another one of the tactics or strategies this chapter covers.

A decision that your client attempts to put off is better than a decision that's a flat refusal!

Chapter 6

Closing the Tough Customer

Chances are, you'll come up against prospective clients who give you a very tough time, and when you do, you'll feel as if a gauntlet has been thrown down. These buyers challenge you to come up with a better reason for them to do business with you than they can come up with to take their business elsewhere. They may not say it directly, but you'll definitely get the message from their behavior and demeanor: "Okay, Mr./Ms. Sales Expert, I dare you to try to close me."

It's important to understand they're acting this way because they're very cautious with their money or that they just like to negotiate. You're a professional. You have your clients' best interests in mind. You rise to the challenge with your usual composure and win them over with your skills.

These tough shoppers are looking for a challenge as much as they are for a bargain, and in doing so, they present all sorts of opposition that can stymie an average salesperson — but you're not average. You're a pro. You'll probably close fewer sales with these folks. Nevertheless, you can employ a few strategies to increase your chances of success. This chapter has the details.

Recognizing a Tough Customer

Being able to recognize early that you're dealing with a tough customer is crucial. You probably won't be able to spot him just by looking at him, but you can look for the following:

- ✔ He may carry a small notebook full of detailed information from multiple sources. This tells you he's been shopping for a while — and has not yet made a decision.

- ✔ He may hold an ad from one of your competitors and ask you for the same item in your store.

Without these obvious signs, though, you won't be able to tell he's a tough customer until you begin talking with him. Most tough customers won't hesitate to let you know they're looking for "the best deal" or that they're "just looking around." And some of your toughest buyers don't start out looking like they'd be tough. They're nice enough, give you a couple of common objections, but when it comes time to get their approval on the paperwork, they dig in their heels all of a sudden and bring the sales process to a screeching halt with demands.

After you identify the buyer as this type of potential client, you need to adopt a what-have-I-got-to-lose attitude (don't confuse this with a devil-may-care attitude), and you need to be very shrewd in determining what he really wants to gain from the transaction.

Using the Triplicate of Choice for Money Strategy

The triplicate of choice for money strategy works equally well with tangibles and intangibles. In this technique, you get buyers to agree, before closing, on an amount of money they'd be willing to invest should they decide to go ahead and own the product or service. Having the customers agree on an amount ahead of time really helps avoid the most common money stalls: saying that your product or service costs too much, that she can get the product cheaper somewhere else, or that that she wants to think it over.

The strategy? You have to offer three different levels of investment for the buyer. Why three? Because it's a proven fact that if you give people three choices of something, they usually choose the one in the middle. Don't ask why it works — it just does. The following sections provide specific, proven phraseology for you to use in each of these situations and tips for using it successfully.

Following simple steps to success

You know that most people are going to object to the cost. So, why not head this objection off at the pass by using the triplicate of choice for money closing strategy during your qualification sequence? Doing so lets you eliminate the money issue and close even sooner.

Here's how you employ the triplicate of choice for money strategy:

1. **During the qualification phase, ask questions about the potential client's likes, dislikes, and general needs.**

   The questioning should follow a linear pattern: Base your next questions on the answers to the previous questions, gently leading the buyers toward the solution that you're determining is best for them.

2. **When you're ready to ask the money question, the one that will give you the final determination of how much they're prepared to spend, set up a scenario in which you present three amounts, and then ask the buyer which category she fits in most comfortably.**

   Say the something like this:

   > Most people interested in acquiring a brand-new washer/dryer set with all the features you've indicated you need are prepared to invest $1,350. A fortunate few can investment between $1,700 and $2,000. And then there are those on a limited or fixed budget who — with the high cost of everything today — can't go higher than $1,100. May I ask, which of these categories do you fit into most comfortably?

   Most people want to be status quo, so your customers will typically choose the middle figure, $1,350.

3. **Base your response on what the customer says.**

   - *If your customer chooses the middle figure* (which she most likely will), point out that the actual amount for the item you feel will meet her needs is substantially less than what she said she was prepared to invest. Say, "Then I'm excited to tell you that the set that meets your requirements requires an investment of only $1,100 — substantially less than you say you were prepared to invest."

Book IV

Closing Like a Champ and Getting Referrals

What can she say? She's already said she'd invest the higher amount, so she can't come back with the objection that the product costs too much.

- *If the buyer picks the lowest amount,* remind her when it's time to close that this was exactly what she planned to spend, again eliminating the money concern.

- *If the customer chooses the highest amount,* you may have misjudged her needs or she may be open to add-on options or services that you hadn't thought she'd go for. As with any client contact, you have to be ready and willing to change your course midstream in order to give her what she expects and what will best suit her needs.

4. **Move to close the sale.**

With the triplicate of choice for money strategy, you're benefiting from the psychological makeup in most people that hesitates to admit they're on a tight budget. Even if she is on a tight budget and has to admit that, you've still got her agreeing to making an investment.

Figuring out the math

To use this strategy to your best advantage, you have to know your math, and you have to know the investments for your various products very well. Here's the formula for developing the triplicate of choice strategy for money (with practice, you'll be able to do this quickly in your head):

✔ **The middle figure:** This figure is 20 percent to 25 percent above the investment you think your customer should make. State this figure first (refer to Step 2 of the preceding section). Starting with a higher amount sets up the customer for thinking that that's how much she'll have to invest to get the product she wants.

✔ **The high figure:** Give a range from 50 percent to 100 percent above the amount you think the customer should invest. This amount ($1,700 to $2,000 in the preceding example) is way above what you think your customer will want to invest. You mention this number second so that when you offer the last (and lowest) amount, the actual amount of the product the customer will be happiest with, that number will come as somewhat of a relief.

✔ **The lowest figure:** This is the actual amount for the product you think best meets the buyer's needs. Give this as the last figure.

More Ways to Close the Tough Guys and Gals

All too often, when salespeople encounter a tough buyer — especially the stealth kind, who doesn't reveal himself until you're already at the close — they start discounting the product or throwing in freebies, anything to get this person to own. They may end up giving more than they get as they give away items equal to or greater in value to the fee they would earn on the transaction. Instead of letting a client take control of the sale in this way, try the tactics outlined in the following sections.

When considering whether and what to discount or what request to accede to, think about the request in terms of its relative proportion to the overall sale. If you're selling million-dollar aircraft and your client wants a larger TV included, that's not much of a request (unless it requires rebuilding the cabinetry that holds it), and one you may justifiably decide to agree to. However, if he wants the entire interior upgraded to leather and mahogany at no extra charge, that's another story. Of course, when negotiating something like this, you would work within parameters set by your company.

Build value

Your first duty when you're faced with someone who's holding out for more than you've offered is to build the value of what she's already getting. You do this by summarizing the benefits she's already agreed to and talking about the emotional and financial value of those benefits.

Here are some ideas about the kinds of things you can mention (the examples throughout involve an intangible health club membership):

- **Any points that make the current investment a particular value:** If you're selling a health club membership, for example, you could say something like the following:

  > Let me reiterate the benefits you're gaining by joining our fitness center today. With the plan that you've indicated works best for you, you're getting 18 months of additional membership for an upfront investment of only two years' service.

- **Any value-added items she receives above and beyond the membership she's paid for:** Be sure to state the value of the thing she's getting for free:

Book IV

Closing Like a Champ and Getting Referrals

You're receiving three private sessions with a personal trainer, which is something you indicated would be especially beneficial in getting you started. Our trainers are certified, and on their own time could demand up to $75 per hour for these services.

With your initial membership, we'll include three ten-day passes for friends or relatives of yours to join you at the club so you'll have workout buddies right away. And we offer over 40 classes each week, again with certified instructors, in the areas of aerobic training, Pilates, yoga, and various dance-based exercises, as well as self-defense, so you should be able to fit those classes you're interested in into your schedule and change up your fitness options.

✔ **Things that make doing business with you better:** With a health club, for example, you may decide to talk about cleanliness and the quality and availability of the equipment:

The cleanliness of a health facility is very important to our reputation. Our fitness centers are required to surpass the standards deemed necessary by the health department, but our own standards are even higher. In fact, we have an 80-point checklist that our service people must review on the cleanliness of the sink areas alone. That checklist is completed and filed every 48 hours.

All our equipment is state of the art, and we evaluate the usage of each piece of equipment on a monthly basis. If something is in high demand, we'll replace another machine that's not used as often with a duplicate of the more popular one, so you should rarely, if ever, have to wait to use a piece of equipment.

After a summary that reiterates the value your customer is getting, holding out for a free water bottle or T-shirt will seem silly. If she insists on something extra, however, go with whatever your manager allows.

Empower your buyers

One of the biggest complaints buyers have is that they feel out of control in the buying process, which makes the process an unpleasant experience for them. The more expensive the product or service, the more important it is to empower your buyers. After you've identified the decision maker, give that person the power to make the decision to own your product or service. Be the expert advisor, the decision counselor — not the controller.

If the potential client wants to shop around, let him know that you think that's a good idea and help him do so. With your knowledge of not only your product but that of the competition, you could assist him with making comparisons right there in your store or showroom. No matter how you choose to handle it, always agree that it's wise to become educated before making a final decision. Encourage potential clients to trust their own decisions.

Praise their negotiating skills

Tough buyers enjoy participating in the negotiations. Getting the best price isn't really good enough. They may not want to be given anything; they just want to earn the best investment. Making the buyers players in the negotiations process empowers them: They believe that it was because of their efforts — and that they were smart enough and clever enough — that they got such a wonderful investment for your product or service. They'll feel great if they think they got the best of you. Too many potential clients feel like the salesperson is out to take their money, so help them to feel like they have the upper hand without being patronizing. To really make the buyers feel good, ask for double the number of referrals and say it's because you need them to make up for the beating you took at their hands. Do this and watch them puff up! The best part is that they *will* send you double the referrals because they feel wonderful about your product and their abilities as a negotiator.

Follow Up Even If the Buyers Don't Buy

Expect success when closing, but should success elude you for a short while, practice great follow-up (Book II, Chapter 5 offers specific advice). If you're not following up now on resistant buyers, you should be. Whatever the reason for resistance to the close, there's usually a solution to that challenge — if you're a persistent salesperson.

What are some of the ways you can follow up with potential clients who resist your attempts? Make a phone call. Don't assume they've purchased from your competitor. Resistant buyers are just as difficult for your competition to handle as they are for you. If your buyer is a corporate account, you may want to try an e-mail message or even a fax. Add a little urgency to your message. If your product or service is a limited offering, you may want to reinforce this and encourage the potential client to get in touch with you immediately. (Check out Book IV, Chapter 8 for more on following up.)

Book IV

Closing Like a Champ and Getting Referrals

Following up after an attempted close is probably one of the most difficult things for less-experienced salespeople. If you think of yourself as a failure because the buyers didn't come back after using a creative close, look at things with a different perspective. Not every selling opportunity ends in a sale. Nor does every selling situation end with the first "no," either. Almost every "no" or "maybe" can be changed to a "yes" with the right motivation and strategies. So develop strong follow-up skills and practice them consistently. The only way to become a good closer is to close.

Chapter 7

Remote Closing

. . . .

In This Chapter

▶ Phoning your way to success

▶ Getting documents to clients quickly

▶ Closing online

. . . .

*I*n the past, many companies divided territories by geographical area to minimize the amount of time salespeople spent traveling. Today, many salespeople specialize in particular products or services and concentrate on clients who have needs that match the product — no matter where they are. So companies are more likely to claim as your territory any client who has a need for your specialty. That means your client base may quite literally be anywhere in the world. If that's the case with you, you'll do very little face-to-face selling and a whole lot of remote closing.

What do you do when you're not closing face-to-face? Well, when you close from a distance, you call upon your skills as a closer and rely on the wonders of technology like computers, phones, fax machines, the Internet, e-mail, and express or overnight delivery services.

Ensuring a Successful Close by Phone

Imagine you've presented to International, Inc., in Los Angeles. Your presentation was precisely detailed. You established great rapport with the three committee members, they told you they had to make a decision by today, and you followed up with thank-you notes to each individual before you left L.A. Now you're back in the home office in Boise.

Telephone closing checklist

Copy and hang this checklist close to your phone and review it before your next sales call.

✔ Smile.

✔ Amplify your voice.

✔ Speak clearly.

✔ Don't rush (especially when leaving voice-mail messages).

✔ Stand.

✔ Dress professionally.

✔ Vary your tone and inflection.

✔ Use picture-drawing words.

✔ Conference in a third party.

What are your chances of getting the agreement? Very good if you take every one of the steps outlined in this section.

Check in with the client before he makes his final decision

If your client has given you a date by which you can expect a decision, call him one or two days prior to the "decision day" to check and see whether he has any remaining questions about the ability of your product to satisfy his needs.

Even if the potential client dismisses you with an "I'll get back with you," that doesn't mean you sit and stay like a good little puppy until he calls. You're a professional. Be proactive. Calling a day or two before the decision to see whether anything new has come up doesn't make you a pest. This call is a courtesy — a professional courtesy — and a way to protect your interest in the client. You can bet the competition is trying to lobby for their products, so why shouldn't you?

Arrange a specific time for the call

If during your courtesy call, your client says he'll get back to you, immediately use your closing abilities to arrange a specific time to visit with him by phone. Say something like the following:

I know how important this investment is to International, Inc., and how valuable your time is. To ensure that I'm available to you, and in case there are any details we need to discuss further, shall we arrange a telephone call at 11 o'clock on Thursday, or would 11:15 be better?

If you don't set up a specific time and urgency for the call, you risk the result of this huge opportunity (for you) being shuffled off to the realm of voicemail. Establishing a specific time also keeps you from wasting a day staying off the phone in case the client calls. Finally, initiating the call lets you prepare and be at your best. If the client can't give you a certain time for a call, you've at least shown your determination to serve by trying to make these arrangements.

Following are a few other suggestions:

- ✔ The arranged time must best suit your client's needs. If he's in Singapore, that could mean you need to make the call at a pretty odd hour in Boise.

- ✔ If the client prefers to make the call, never risk having a closing call go to voicemail. A client can much more easily say no over voicemail than in person. If the client has to give you his answer in person — in this case, meaning voice-to-voice — he has to at least allow you the courtesy of asking a few questions regarding the decision, which may open that window of opportunity right back up.

Thoroughly review the account details before the call

Make sure you're intimately familiar with the details of the account before the call. Reread the entire file on this account so that all the details are fresh in your mind.

Also, fill out your brief summary review (your list of everything your client agreed that he liked about your product), making sure to include emotional involvement phrases — ones that help your client know what he'll feel *after* he takes ownership of the product — and have that on hand for the call.

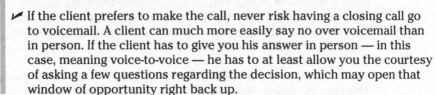
Book IV

Closing Like a Champ and Getting Referrals

Ease into the close

Never, never, *never* begin a closing telephone conversation with, "I'm calling for your decision." Mistakes like this are selling suicide. Instead, always try to have a new or interesting tidbit of information at the ready when you make the closing call. A tidbit is especially powerful when it relates to something the clients mentioned in a previous conversation. For example,

> I'm excited about something new I have to share with you regarding our X-Pro voicemail system. I know you had some concerns about how easily your staff can access their messages on those days when they're off-site. I spoke with our technical services department, and they've come up with a way to modify that feature on the system to reduce it from a three-step process to only two steps for your people to retrieve their messages from any location. Isn't that great?

Such a statement shows you've already gone the extra mile for this client even before he decided whether to own your product or service. The hinges on that door he thought about closing are beginning to creak, thanks to your preparedness and professionalism.

Now you can proceed to your closing question — the one that asks for a firm commitment today. Make sure you've prepared and rehearsed this question before you make the call. (For information on closing questions, refer to Book IV, Chapter 2.)

Hold the buyer's attention

When you're closing over the phone, you have to work a little harder to get your message across and keep the buyer attentive. How many times have you been simultaneously on a call and checking your e-mail? We're all tempted to do more than one thing — especially when the other party isn't in the room with us. But you can employ a few strategies to keep your client focused on you and the matter at hand.

Engage the client in a hands-on way

Because the ears and only one small part of the brain are focused on listening, you must plan for your phone conversation to make the experience as hands-on as possible, including as many of the five senses as you can. Doing so lets you better hold the customer's attention.

For example, you can engage your client visually by sending material before your call and referring to it throughout the call. Be sure he receives it in plenty of time to review it before the call. For example, you could e-mail a list of benefits the buyer will enjoy after he owns your product or service. Then, during the conversation, you can involve him visually by referring to the e-mailed benefit list. Or you can engage him tactilely by asking him to use a calculator to figure the savings he'll enjoy with your product.

If you can't engage your potential client physically, describe things in a way that engages his senses. Book II, Chapter 5 has all sorts of suggestions.

One of the most effective remote-closing strategies is to tie in a third party through a conference call. The third party can be a technical specialist who can address technical concerns or a satisfied customer who can add valuable information. Or the third party may be an existing satisfied client who will provide a nice testimonial and answer questions about how she's using the product. Another use of a third party would be to have someone higher up in the company on the call to demonstrate how important the potential client's business is to the firm and to answer any questions that may be aimed at a higher level than "salesperson." Just make sure the prospect knows that the third party will be joining the call.

Draw a pretty picture

When closing by telephone, use language that creates a picture to keep the customer's mind engaged. For example, use fun and interesting adjectives. Here are some examples of adjectives that evoke pleasant images:

- **Stylish:** "As you can see in the catalog, our new CS5000 printer has a sleek, *stylish* design that takes up less of your valuable desktop space."

- **Airy:** "Because they understand that size is an important consideration for retirees, our condominium designers have added ceiling height, sky-lights, and plenty of windows to make even the smaller model homes have an *airy,* open feeling."

- **Time-saving:** "With the latest version of this software, we've added many *time-saving* features. Never again will your staff have to reformat the fields of your mailing lists to match the word-processing feature. The software will automatically read over 100 standard formats."

- **Spacious:** "All our hotel suites have *spacious* living areas, which include desks or large tables with Internet access."

- **Cost-effective:** "Can you see how the larger print run of these brochures will be more *cost-effective,* especially if you see yourself using these pieces for the entire year?"

Book IV

Closing Like a Champ and Getting Referrals

✔ *Efficient:* "The upgrade of your mailing equipment will streamline the process, thus making your staff more *efficient* in handling your larger marketing mailers."

✔ *Morale-boosting:* "An increase of this sort in the amount of coverage you place on each member of your staff will have a tremendous *morale-boosting* effect. And most of our clients find a tremendous increase in productivity after implementing such a change."

✔ *Fabulous:* "The implementation of this new training program has brought about *fabulous* increases in bottom-line revenues for the last six clients I've worked with."

✔ *Excellent:* "Our customer service department has consistently received an *excellent* rating from our existing clients in the customer satisfaction surveys that we conduct every quarter."

✔ *Powerful:* "The new chip in our Compu-Plus computers makes them the fastest, most *powerful* units available today. And added power means it will run your software more efficiently."

Notice how each of the preceding includes a benefit statement that is either specific to the current client or that expresses how past clients benefited. Be sure to include these kinds of statements in your own descriptions to link the advantage of owning your product with the client's particular need.

Use analogies that resonate with the client

Use analogies and examples from satisfied clients. If your potential client is a sports fan, this should be easy. If he hates all sports but has kids, use the kid angle. No kids? How about pets? Interest in movies? Everyone has an interest that can be used in an analogy or related example if you just keep searching for it. Here are some examples:

✔ Compare the business to the local winning team, no matter the sport. If the client is a fan of a particular team, use that team in your analogy as to how they plan, strategize, and practice to become winners.

✔ If your product involves future positive results and your clients have kids, talk about how fast those kids grow and how one small change made today can have a powerful impact on their futures.

✔ Watch for and make notes of satisfied clients and be ready to tell their success stories to each new client.

Every top professional in the field of selling is a collector of stories, facts, and figures from actual clients. This collection is often the salesperson's most valuable tool in getting new clients onboard.

Keep your tone interesting

Speaking to someone over the phone tends to diminish your message — and your voice. You have to project your voice, your enthusiasm, and your upbeat personality. The loudness, tone, and inflection of your voice need to be amplified a bit for your voice to carry at the optimum level. Here are a couple tips:

- ✔ **Be extra enthusiastic and, above all,** *smile.* The person on the other end won't be able to *see* your smile, but they can definitely hear it in your voice. People can tell when you're happy to be talking with them and that makes them feel good — and that's what you want when you're closing. Even if you're having a tough day, don't let that affect your communication with the customer on the other end of the line. Pros have mastered how to put aside any other challenges when talking with clients.

- ✔ **Vary your tone.** Phone conversations can bore your customer if you mumble or speak in a monotone, so add inflection to your voice. Think about how gifted storytellers or narrators use their voices to keep the attention of their audiences, and try to do the same.

Many professional salespeople who market their products or services over the phone find it helpful to stand when talking to clients. Standing gives them more physical energy, which is reflected in their voices. Standing straight also eliminates the tendency to slouch. Having good posture is good for your voice transmission.

- ✔ **Don't shout your message.** Shouting is reserved for rooftops. Speaking too loudly into the telephone is irritating to listeners, and you can damage both your image in their eyes and the drums in their ears.

- ✔ **Speak up and speak clearly.** When leaving a voicemail, speak clearly and at a slow enough pace that the person listening to the message will not have to replay your message in order to return your call. Luckily, the technology is in place for the recipient to replay messages easily, but you don't want to do anything to cause frustration, especially when you're near to closing time. It's also wise to leave your telephone number twice — once at the beginning and again at the end of your message.

For more advice on how to make the best impression possible over the phone, head to Book VIII, Chapter 5.

Book IV

**Closing
Like a
Champ and
Getting
Referrals**

For network marketers

Network marketing — when you're involved with a company as a distributor of its products or service — also has been called *multilevel marketing* or *direct selling.* In network marketing, you can build an organization of which you're the leader without having to come up with your own product or even your own marketing strategy. The product and marketing materials are already in place for you, and the companies are simply seeking representatives to bring their products to market.

You may have heard of some of the larger direct-selling companies such as Amway, Nu Skin, and Primerica. Their network marketers build distributorships, nationally and internationally. Some of the top people in these companies have huge organizations around the world — with very few distributors in their local areas. Some companies have literally thousands of people in their organizations whom they have never met face-to-face. Your involvement entitles you to offer your same opportunity to others,

and you can earn an income from their sales as well as from your own.

The general closing strategies explained throughout this book work beautifully in network marketing. But by using remote-closing techniques, you can help potential recruits understand — emotionally and otherwise — how they'll benefit from your network marketing opportunity. The use of conference calling (or three-way calling) can be especially effective.

Here's a good closing question for network marketers:

Who are the first three people you're going to present the product and opportunity to?

The reason this question is so effective is that, when the potential recruit starts thinking about his list of potential clients or recruits rather than his previous concerns, he's closer to being closed on the opportunity.

Sending Documents for Remote Closes

If you've closed over the phone — or you're just about to close — but your client needs to review some paperwork, chances are, you'll be using a fax machine or sending the documents via e-mail for your remote close. You may need to send the final agreement so the client has a hard copy for signatures. Your client may want to clarify some of the legal aspects of the agreement if it's a large sale and, of course, this all needs to be in writing.

In the following sections, you can find a few guidelines for getting these documents to their intended recipients quickly and efficiently.

Just the fax, ma'am

To ensure that your faxed document gets to the right person, always send the fax with a cover sheet, with the name of the person whom the fax is for, the number of pages that the fax includes, and a sentence that identifies the information in the fax. Also, include a single summary page with any fax of more than three pages. The summary page should be in large print and list explicitly what the recipient has and what he needs to do with it. If time is of the essence, print that in bold on the fax cover sheet, perhaps with the date by which the paperwork must be completed and returned.

Follow up every fax with a quick phone call to ensure that the recipient really did receive the information, that it transmitted clearly, and that all the pages are there. Your follow-up call shows your concern for details and also gives you an opportunity to move right into the close. For example:

> And by the way, while I've got you on the phone, I'd be happy to review this with you now, while we both have the facts and figures right in front of us.

E-mailing your closing document

E-mail is fast, efficient, and easy to use. Plus, it offers a comprehensive transfer of information and time-saving efficiency over trying to connect by phone or hoping the business owner receives and reads his faxes in a timely manner. (E-mail can give you a better chance of connecting with clients who dread meeting a salesperson face-to-face or whose schedules are so busy that they automatically say no to any sales call.)

The main challenge with e-mail, however, is that people tend to write sloppily or in a sort of shorthand — neither of which is appropriate for a business communication, especially when you're closing a transaction with a client.

Therefore, you need to prepare your e-mail with the same care you'd use if you were drafting a formal letter or proposal. Use bullet points, summaries, and a bit of *white space* (blanks between salient points to make your e-mail as eye appealing as possible). Here are some suggestions:

✔ **Avoid long, dense paragraphs of text.** Break up information into chunks and add extra spacing between sections or important points for appearance's sake or for emphasis.

✔ **Differentiate your section headings from the body of the document.** Doing so helps your client navigate through the e-mail message and find relevant information. You can use all caps for section headlines, for example, or underlining.

✔ **Be especially careful about the wording you use.** In person, the client picks up on your tone, inflection, and body language as part of your message. E-mail depersonalizes communication to a great extent, so if you decide to include verbiage that reflects your personality, make sure it's appropriate. If in doubt, run it by your manager or supervisor or another third party who will give you honest feedback.

✔ **Proofread the e-mail before clicking Send!** Use the spell-check feature of your e-mail software. Also, consider printing out a copy of the document for yourself and have it proofread — preferably by someone else with a really good eye — before you send it. As with anything you write, you may be so close to the material, knowing what you want it to say, that you believe you've covered everything, but have minor typographical errors in the writing. You may have all the words spelled correctly but have an incorrect word in your document (for example, *you're* instead of *your*). Most important, have someone else double-check any figures you put into a document. Showing poor math to clients will put a huge dent in your credibility.

Send the closing document as an attachment rather than in the body of the e-mail. Doing so lets you create a professional-looking document in your word-processing program and use all the standard editing and proofreading tools available. This gives you the best of both worlds.

Internet Closing

Many people today are finding shopping on the Internet to be ideal. They can find what they want, "window-shop" for new ideas, place orders, and never leave their desk or have to talk with a salesperson. The Internet is the next generation after catalog shopping — with one of the biggest advantages being that there's nothing to recycle.

Of course, if you sell your products over the Internet, you're closing over the Internet, too.

Making sure your website lets customers close easily

The possibilities are practically endless when it comes to closing on the Internet. Seeing the innovative ideas people are coming up with on their websites is always interesting and goes to show that the sky is the limit.

As with any marketing tool, the Internet should not be left to stand alone; it needs support. Here are some simple rules to follow when developing your site:

- **Advertise your website.** You can use traditional advertising methods (radio, TV, and print media) or print your web address on all your business materials, and alert folks through social media platforms like Facebook and Twitter. For information on tapping into the power of the web and social media for sales, head to Book VII, Chapter 7.

- **Make your website attractive, interesting, and easy to navigate.** The site should entice the viewer into wanting your product or service. Make sure it includes the following info in prominent places:

  - Product information.

    If you're using your site as an online catalog, you can do one better than print by showing your products in a three-dimensional mode. If your product includes audio or video, you can demo it through the computer.

  - Call(s) to action for customers to place their orders.

  - Contact information (e-mail, toll-free phone numbers, and so on) so that your customers can reach you easily.

  - Order forms that are easy to fill out.

  - Chat. Many companies include a chat feature on their sites during hours when a live customer-service representative is available. (*Note:* That might be you!)

- **Make sure your transactions are secure.** This means that if customers are sending you a credit card number or other financial data over the Internet, you've taken steps to prevent others from gaining access to it. And let your potential clients know how secure this process is. With the proper procedures for credit card processing, shopping online is much safer than handing your card to a waitperson in a 5-star restaurant.

- **Have a system in place to acknowledge orders.** Some companies manually send a brief reply to anyone placing an order. Others have a capability built in to their sites that sends acknowledgments as soon as the transmission is complete and sends a confirmation letter with order details via e-mail.

Using the Internet's unique capabilities to close a sale

Because of the interactive, information-laden, dynamic nature of the Internet, you can do things on your website that would be impossible or cost-prohibitive in any other type of media.

Providing an online demo

Providing a demo is a strategy called the *puppy-dog close* in sales training. (How do you find new homes for cute little puppies? You send them home with the children.) In this type of close, you let your clients actually use the product or service before they agree to own it. The idea behind the strategy is that, after using a product, people will wonder how they ever did without it and then will agree to the purchase.

Several businesses make their products — software, reference materials, and more — available for free for a limited time over the Internet. Signing up is easy, and making the buying decision is almost pain-free, requiring little more than a couple clicks and entering billing information. If your business sells a product that lends itself to a demo, you may want to consider offering this opportunity on your website.

Then when the time comes to close the sale, send out a pre-close e-mail to open the door for the final close. In addition to thanking the potential client for trying your product and mentioning some of its virtues, also include a question like "If you had the opportunity to tailor this product specifically to your business, what would you change or add to the service?" Here's an example:

> Mr. Smith,
>
> Thank you for taking the opportunity to try our new Checkpoint research service. We're extremely excited to offer the latest breaking *<insert topic>* news to your desktop the moment it happens.
>
> As you know, this technology is relatively new, and Checkpoint is an evolutionary product for us. We're always looking to the people we serve for ways to make our research products meet their individual and changing needs. I'll contact you in a few days, and I'd be interested in hearing your feedback and comments on the following questions:
>
> - What did you enjoy most about the demo/service?
>
> - What would make you want to continue benefiting from it?
>
> I look forward to speaking with you.

The purpose of this correspondence is to get the customer to identify his hot button or major area of concern, which you'll want to hear about during the promised future call. Most of the time, the hot button — that is, a benefit your customer has already indicated he wants to own — is something the service already does, but the customer hasn't discovered that yet, which gives the representative the opportunity to turn the customer's reply into a close by demonstrating that particular feature.

Putting your entire presentation online

If it's appropriate for your particular product, think about putting your entire presentation online. Of course, you can customize an in-person presentation, but having your fine-tuned presentation available for potential new clients to view online can lead to some pretty easy closes when you finally make direct contact with them.

The best way to determine if your product is appropriate for online sales is to see how many of your competitors are using the Internet as a sales tool and try to determine how well they're doing with it. This can be as easy as calling or e-mailing one of their salespeople, telling her that you're doing research on the Internet (no lie, because you are), and ask questions about their product such as how clients are liking it, what special features seem to appeal to users, and so on. If no one else with your particular product is online, it may not be the best avenue for your particular product or service.

Another consideration would be to consult with a company that creates web pages and get some preliminary suggestions on how they see you succeeding on the Internet with your product or service. Of course, if you decide to go ahead with them, you'll pay a fee for building your site and managing it, but if they're really experts, they'll know ways to make it work for you. Always ask for multiple references from existing clients. Call those folks and ask a few pointed questions about what they like about the provider and what they would change if they were starting over.

Presenting remotely with a webcam

In today's digital marketplace, true sales professionals need to know how to effectively present via streaming audio and video presentations. This includes using webinars, webcams, and services such as Skype. These services give you the opportunity to be eyeball-to-eyeball with clients, even when you can't be across the table or desk from them.

Wendy Lipton-Dibner, creator of the Move People to Action System for sales professionals and entrepreneurs (www.movepeopletoaction.com), has this to say about the potential benefit of embracing the interactivity potential of the web:

> Market share will go to the sales professionals who learn to look directly into the camera lens and help prospective clients feel as if they're engaged in a live conversation with a human being who speaks their language, connects, aligns, and ultimately builds a lasting relationship. Through a proven process called community giveback, sales professionals will serve online visitors with a steady stream of free information that ultimately builds trust and establishes the sales professionals as the go-to resource for all their potential clients' needs.

Book IV

Closing Like a Champ and Getting Referrals

Chapter 8

Getting Referrals from Your Present Clients

For many seasoned salespeople, referrals are a major source of new business. Clients who come to you from an existing client's recommendation are usually more inclined than cold-call clients to want to listen to what you have to say. Why? Because they already have positive feelings about you and your offering — and the source of their positive feelings is someone they already know and trust. This is what is referred to as a *prequalified lead*. Prequalified leads are often slam-dunk sales: They've already been sold on you because the person who referred you to them thinks you're a true pro. With referrals, you enjoy tremendous credibility right from the start.

When it comes to qualified referrals, studies show an average 60 percent closing rate. Compare that impressive figure to a typical closing rate of 10 percent with non-referred leads, and you can see just how much harder you have to work on cold calls. When you can learn how to be successful at getting referral business right here, leaving all those choice clients for your competitors to pick up just doesn't make sense.

This chapter is all about effective ways to benefit from referral business. Here you find a proven, highly effective referral system that can help you produce a much greater number of referred, qualified leads. The system may not work 100 percent of the time, but even if it works only 50 percent of the time, it will generate many more selling situations with clients who look forward to finding out about you and your offering than what you're getting now.

Understanding Where, How, and When Referrals Arise

With qualified referrals providing you a closing ratio of a whopping 60 percent on average, you can't afford not to know how to identify and obtain such a substantial increase in your sales potential. That's why it's surprising so many people take part in referral-building activities without recognizing — and taking advantage of — the opportunities. If only they had read a good overview that would help them recognize referrals when they see them — an overview just like the one you're on the verge of reading right now.

What if getting referrals isn't all that important to your particular selling situation? Instead of seeking them out for yourself, consider garnering leads for your clients or other members of your team — if you have one. Becoming a source of referrals for others increases your value to all those you work with and eventually results in sales that translate into increased income. One way or the other, whether as a source of potential clients for your own business or as general goodwill for your clients, referrals play a key part in your success in sales.

Figuring out where to get referrals

Referrals are like flies: They're always buzzing around you. But unless they land in your soup, you don't always notice them. The key to success in getting referrals is to become like flypaper and catch all the referrals that fly by. The following sections describe several great sources of referrals.

From family and friends

Perhaps the easiest and most accessible referrals are those that your family and friends can give you. Why not keep Grandma in the loop about what you're doing? She may not be an ideal candidate for your product, but she may know others who are. Besides, Grandma is likely to keep her loving grandchild in mind as she goes about her daily routine. If you're lucky, she'll become a downright excellent qualified lead collector. Spread the word to other family members, close friends, and acquaintances (as described in Book II, Chapter 2), and you'll be racking up referral business in no time.

If you're of the mindset that you don't want to "burden" those close to you by asking for their help, you'd better rethink just what it is you're selling. After all, if you really believe in your product, service, or idea, don't you want the people close to you to enjoy its benefits, too? By assuming that your offering will burden others, you may be cheating them out of all the enjoyment that it can give them.

Through informal networking

Networking at business conferences, clubs, professional organizations, and religious gatherings is a way to increase your number of referrals (see Book II, Chapter 2 for details). But the gatherings don't have to be formal affairs. Getting referrals can be as simple as mentioning to others what you do or something exciting that has happened during your busy week of selling.

When you're excited, other people will be, too. People are attracted to energetic conversation and happy dispositions, so be a people magnet. If you're having a particularly great week, share it with the world. Let them enjoy the positive vibe created by your success! Don't brag. Just allow yourself to be exuberant about your accomplishments. Exuberance is contagious.

If, on the other hand, your week has been particularly trying or difficult, consider asking for the advice of the people you respect. Most people are generally kind and helpful. In order for them to help you, you'll have to have the opportunity to tell them your story. Of course, your story involves your product offering. You can use this as a way of getting others interested in what you're selling, too. The next time they see you, they'll want to hear your appreciation of the positive effects their advice had for you.

So, what have you done? Through your willingness to share your concerns and victories, you've involved others in your career. Other people now have a vested interest in your future success.

From happy customers

Satisfied clients tell at least three people about their experience with you. Take advantage of this fact! Knowing this, you may want to broach the subject of referrals by saying, "I can see how happy you are about your decision to own this new vehicle. Who will you show it to first? Your neighbors? Family members?" When they tell you who they'll share the good news with, ask if those folks may also be in need of one.

If you leave your client's office with a sale but no referrals, you have unfinished business to attend to — kind of like having a great dinner, but leaving before dessert. It's never too late to get referrals, but when you leave empty-handed, you also deprive your clients of an opportunity to do good or to brag. It's true! What's the first thing you want to do when you shop

Book IV

Closing Like a Champ and Getting Referrals

nonstop for days and then eventually, finally, find a great bargain? You want to tell people about it! What's the first thing you want to do when you own a beautiful new car? Show people! What's the first thing you want to do when someone comments on what a terrific new whatchamacallit you have? Let him know where he can get one just like it for a great price! Don't cheat your happy clients out of all their fun by not giving them the referral tools they need to help others benefit from your excellent product and service.

Good referral business comes from clients with whom you have good relationships. This doesn't necessarily mean that they own your offering. For example, you may have built a good relationship with a past or potential client who for some reason is unable to own your product at this time. If you've kept in close contact and done a good job in building rapport with the customer, though, he more than likely would be willing to steer you toward a business associate who can benefit from your product or service.

To garner the referrals you're seeking, you must make sure that your product and service are beyond reproach, because negative news spreads like wildfire through dried country meadows. Slip up just once, even just a little bit, and where visiting your clients and their associates was once comfortable, it becomes awkward — maybe so much so that you avoid old clients altogether. For example, avoid promising the moon and the stars within a two-day delivery period unless you also can wave Harry Potter's magic wand and make it happen. It's so easy to get carried away and tell your client what he wants to hear even when you know your information is inaccurate. In the long run, not only will you lose the disillusioned client, but you can also kiss goodbye all the wonderful referral opportunities he could have steered your way.

Dissatisfied clients tell at least 11 people. Negative stories generate more sympathy than positive stories do. So, don't allow the flames of discontent to spread far when a challenge arises. If a poor reputation precedes you, you'll have to work harder to get the first sale (if you even get a real opportunity to do so) and prove your value before asking for referrals. Honesty and integrity must be first and foremost in your mind if you intend to succeed in business and in life.

From other salespeople in your field

Thinking of other salespeople in the same or related fields as your enemies is neither necessary nor productive. Believe it or not, thinking of them as a possible source for referral business is much more profitable. For instance, if you're in the healthcare field and you meet a sales rep who's extremely successful selling surgical supply equipment and you're selling diagnostic testing equipment, that salesperson may be able to provide referrals or at least be willing to swap referrals with you.

If your relationship with other salespeople is based on mutual respect, you'll find other salespeople sending clients your way whether you have a formal arrangement to do so or not. Perhaps another salesperson's company is smaller than yours and unequipped to handle clients of a certain magnitude. Bingo! He sends the Big Clients to you. Or maybe a contact insists on having a feature that your competitor's product doesn't have — and another prospective client gets headed right your way.

Of course, returning the favor is only common courtesy. It isn't unusual for salespeople at car dealerships or insurance agencies to recommend another salesperson who is better suited to meet a particular buyer's needs. Professionals who have the needs of the client at heart and know they would do the client a disservice by handling those needs ineffectively work this way. They also know the value of giving good "customer" service to their fellow salespeople.

Through public-speaking engagements and teaching opportunities

Public-speaking engagements and teaching opportunities are great for referral business, especially if you're the professional chosen to give the presentation or to teach. (You may find this type of opportunity through a homeowners' association, retirement community, or other groups that bring outsiders in to speak at their meetings.) When this happens, you're automatically considered the expert in your field. But to earn the reputation you've been awarded, you'd better be prepared and handle your presentation well. Compare it to giving your best sales presentation to an audience of 50 or more potential clients all at once. Pretty important, isn't it?

Participate in these situations only if you can carry it off effectively. Too many people get carried away with the moment of stardom and forget that they're there to build their business, not to audition as a replacement for David Letterman. (For advice on creating a winning presentation, head to Book III, Chapter 3.)

Tom Hopkins once went to a conference where the speaker provided cards on which participants wrote their names and the names of others to contact who would also benefit from attending the conference. Each referral was put on a different card along with comments on why the participants believed that their referrals would enjoy and learn from the conference. The speaker encouraged participants to fill out as many cards as they liked. Then they put the cards into a large barrel. Each day of the conference, a member of the speaker's entourage pulled a card from the barrel to see who would win weekend getaways, free admission to advanced seminars, audio or video recordings, or books that were being sold at the conference. At the end of the conference, the speaker had the makings of another conference. What a system!

Unlocking the key to getting referrals: Ask!

Getting referrals is simple! You get referrals by asking for them. It's as simple as that. Of course, how you ask makes a difference. You don't want to just plunge in and say, "Do you know anyone else who may want my whatchama-callit?" If you ask that way, your client probably won't be able to come up with a name. You have to *prepare* her in the art of giving good referrals. This important topic is covered in the upcoming section "Getting Referrals in Six Easy Steps."

You'd be surprised how many salespeople feel awkward asking for referrals. How do such salespeople "solve" the problem of their awkwardness? They avoid the referral part of the selling situation altogether — and in the process cost themselves and their companies big bucks. Or some salespeople try to get referrals without the necessary prep work to help their clients identify possible referrals and end up with a "Sorry, I can't think of anybody." Such a salesperson concludes that asking for referral business didn't really work for him, and so he abandons the attempt altogether. However, by setting aside such self-defeating strategies, anyone can get referrals.

Salespeople universally agree that referrals are easier to persuade than non-referrals. But some salespeople think that getting referral business is next to impossible, so they refuse to give referral methods much attention. These salespeople take the attitude that attaining referrals is just a haphazard, sometimes-it-happens-and-sometimes-it-doesn't way to prospect. Don't buy into such thinking for a second. Professional salespeople consistently benefit from referral business — so consistently, in fact, that they shoot holes in this theory every day. In fact, by implementing the referral system outlined in the following sections, you can produce a much greater number of referred, qualified leads.

Figuring out when to get referrals

So, specifically, when *do* you get referrals? You prepare to get referrals the moment you make contact with someone. From the first words your potential clients utter, you should look for areas in which you can help them isolate names and faces that they can give you later (the names, that is, not the faces). Always listen carefully, not just to what will help the present client, but also to what will help the present client's referrals — your future clients — who also may need your services.

Beyond that, there is one specific time when your chances of getting referrals are better than most: just after you have successfully closed a sale and the satisfied client is excited about owning your offering. At that moment, the client is usually more than happy to give you referrals — names of other people who need what the client now owns. Just after the sale is a time when enthusiasm is high and resistance is low.

Be cautious about asking for referrals before you've closed the sale with your present potential client. Asking before you have their autograph on your paperwork or their credit card approved is like putting the cart before the horse. It appears that you're no longer interested in them, just in what they can do for you. And that's not a part of professional selling.

Getting Referrals in Six Easy Steps

This section's easy, six-step process to obtaining referrals will give you so much more success in developing your referral business that you'll make it an automatic part of every selling situation. Begin by setting a goal for how many referrals you want from each contact. Start with a goal of just one referral and work your way up to a place where you know the steps so well and they flow so naturally that you'll get at least three referrals with every contact you make. You may even be able to get as many as five or ten referrals from every client by implementing this simple strategy (you can find details for each of the following steps in the next sections):

1. **Help your client think of specific people he knows.**

2. **Write the referrals' names on cards.**

3. **Ask qualifying questions about the referrals.**

4. **Ask for the referrals' contact information.**

5. **Ask the client to call and set up your meeting with the referrals.**

6. **If the client shows nervousness or refuses to call, ask if you can use the client's name when you contact the referral.**

Memorize these six steps to getting referrals. The better you know them, the better you'll mine the rich lode of referrals that's just waiting for you in your current clientele.

Book IV

**Closing
Like a
Champ and
Getting
Referrals**

Step 1: Help your client think of specific people he knows

When you ask for referrals, you can't give your client the whole world to think about. Instead, use the information you've gathered about him, such as friends and family or other business associations he has. Help your client focus on a particular group of faces. Centering on one or two faces is impossible when his thoughts are bouncing off the wall with his new offering — which means your job is to get him focused again.

Refocus your clients by using a method like the one shown in the following hypothetical situation:

> YOU: Bill, I can see you're excited with your new car, aren't you?
>
> CLIENT: Oh, it's sweet. I can't wait to drive it off the lot!
>
> YOU: You were a tough negotiator, Bill. I guess it feels good to know that you received significant savings on the car, too, doesn't it?
>
> CLIENT: Yeah! I didn't expect to be able to afford a car this nice!
>
> YOU: So, tell me, Bill: Where do you plan to drive your new car this first week?
>
> CLIENT: Well, I'll be going back and forth to work, of course. And I play baseball in a city league every Thursday night. I can't wait to drive up in my new car.
>
> YOU: I wish I could be there to see your face, as well as the faces of your co-workers and teammates. Bill, is there anyone at your workplace or on your baseball team who may be in the market for a new car?

By mentioning work and baseball, the client focuses in on those people he is closest to and with whom he'll be in contact that very week — while his excitement over his car is still fresh. And the salesperson has helped him do that.

Step 2: Write the referrals' names on cards

After your client has thought of specific people he knows, take out a few 3-x-5 index cards or a small notepad and write down the names of those referrals. (Be sure to ask how to spell the names of the referrals.) Keep the cards out so you can jot down the information your client gives you. Plus, you'll need those notes to qualify the referrals (see the following section).

Step 3: Ask qualifying questions

While your client is busy answering questions about the referrals, you should jot down notes to help you remember specific things about them. Here's some information you may want to know when you contact the referrals from the example provided in the preceding section (Bill and his new car):

- ✔ **What made the client think of this particular referral?** In the example with Bill and his new car, imagine that Bill mentions Sally. Ask him, "What brought Sally to mind when I asked who you know that may be interested in getting a new car?"

- ✔ **What does the referral use in place of your product now?** For example, you'd ask Bill, "What kind of car does Sally drive now?"

- ✔ **How would the referral use the product?** For example, "Do you know if Sally would be the primary driver of the car?" and "How many people are in Sally's family?" (You want to learn the first step in our NEADS qualification sequence, What does she have now? For more on NEADS, head to Book III, Chapter 2.)

- ✔ **How did the referral react to the news that the client was shopping for your product?** For example, "What did she say when you told her you were looking for a new car?"

When you get in touch with the referral, you'll be able to begin a conversation based on information you got from your client. When you've taken a few good notes, move on to the next step.

Never assume that what your client tells you is 100 percent true about the referral's needs. He may not know all the answers to your questions and guess at some of them. And never tell the referral that your client told you all of this information about her. Just have your notes handy to use as you qualify her further during your contact.

Step 4: Ask for contact information

Asking for the contact information of the referrals is more difficult because your client may not know this information offhand. But don't let that deter you. You can't just settle for the name because he may not be listed in the phonebook or may have a common name that makes tracking him down difficult. And knowing how to contact the referral is critical to successfully selling him. At the very least, try to get the full name and a phone number or e-mail address.

When asking for referrals, have your client go to her contact list either on her computer or in her cellphone. As she scrolls through looking for the person she mentioned, it's likely she'll come across someone else she hadn't thought of who also may need what you offer.

Step 5: Ask your happy client to call the referral and set up the meeting

This step is where most novice salespeople balk. They won't even try it. But keep in mind that this question is simply setting the stage for the final step.

Few clients will be comfortable calling to set up a meeting for you. But they'll be so relieved that you offer to do it yourself (see Step 6) that they'll jump on it. If you go directly from Step 4 to Step 6, you may not get the same response.

When you ask your client to call the referral, say something like this:

> Thanks so much for the referrals, Bill. You know, since I won't get to see your excitement when you show off your new car, would you mind calling Sally and sharing your good news with her? Then we can work on arranging a time for me to meet with her.

If your customer is fine with acting as the liaison, then good: Start dialing. But if he hesitates and acts uncomfortable — and chances are, he will — take the pressure off *immediately* by moving on to the next step.

Step 6: Ask to use the client's name when you contact the referral

Your client may not know the referral all that well, or he may feel uncomfortable making the call. If this is the case, let him know you understand his hesitation, but ask if you can bother him for one more favor. Ask for his permission to use his name when you contact the people he referred you to. He'll probably be relieved to be let off the hook and be more than happy to give you permission to use his name.

Setting Up Meetings with Referrals

When you call someone and you already have an "in" with that person's close personal friend or respected business associate, you have common ground. You also have the benefit of knowing some pertinent information that may be relevant to arranging a meeting with them.

Qualifying the referral

Before you call such a referral, review the information you wrote in your notes (see the previous section) and decide how you'll set the stage for this selling situation. If you properly qualified the referral, you know enough about her to ask just a few additional questions to get her interested in your offering and want to meet with you.

Through testimonials from your mutual business associate or friend, you can tell the referred lead what your client (and their friend) thought was most attractive or appealing about your offering. Chances are, your referral will be just as interested in those same special features as her friend or associate was. If she's not interested, keep asking questions until you discover what about your offering does interest her. Here's an example:

SALESPERSON: Hello, Sally, my name is Allen, and I work at B & B Motors. I just helped Bill Robinson get his dream car. He mentioned that you may be in need of a new vehicle yourself, and I promised him I would call you and let you know about the special offerings we're having on our vehicles this week. He just bought a beauty and told me you two had been talking about your needing a new car as well. Tell me, Sally, what are you looking for in a new car?

REFERRAL: Well, I'm not really ready to buy yet. I've just been looking around.

SALESPERSON: What have you seen so far that you like the best?

REFERRAL: Well, what I like and what I can afford are two different things.

SALESPERSON: I hear you. Bill said the same thing. That's why he wanted me to call you and let you know about our special promotion that's going on now. You know, you aren't too far from our dealership. I work late tonight, so I'm available around 6 o'clock this evening. I know Bill said you shared his love for sports cars. Is that right?

REFERRAL: Yes. But the ones I've seen are so expensive. I think I'm just going to wait a while.

SALESPERSON: I'll tell you what. Why don't you come on over after work? Tell me your situation and let me share with you what we're doing. There's no obligation. I just wouldn't want you to miss out on an opportunity that might be just right for you. Because of the success of the promotion, our dealership is serving munchies in our lobby. So, don't eat first — you can munch out here while we talk. Is 6 o'clock good for you, or would 6:30 be more convenient?

REFERRAL: Actually, 6 o'clock is better for me.

SALESPERSON: Great, I'll see you then. Just come to the front desk and ask for Allen Brice.

Not only did this salesperson use the qualifying questions from his referral notes, but he further qualified Sally by asking more questions. He was more likely to get the appointment because Sally knew that Bill had purchased a similar car and perhaps had similar financial concerns — and she knew that the salesperson was able to work out a way for Bill to own his dream car. The salesperson's ability to help Sally's friend Bill encouraged Sally to find out whether the same would be possible for her.

What do you think the chances were of getting the potential buyer to come in if the salesperson had been making a random cold call? You're right — they fall in the slim-to-none category.

Here are some things to remember about contacting referrals:

✔ **Getting a meeting with a referral may require some time and persistent follow-up.** People who are referred to you don't have a relationship with you. So, you need to build that relationship by keeping your face and name in their minds and in front of their faces all the time. The next section gives you more information about following up with referrals.

✔ **Even if you don't get a referral meeting, you should always try to get referrals.** Now may not be the right time for that potential client, but that doesn't mean that she doesn't know anyone else who may be ripe for getting involved with the product, service, or idea you represent. Always ask, "Is there someone else among your loved ones or circle of friends who might have a need?"

You may not get a meeting with every referral. But then you don't need to in order for referrals to become a highly productive way for you to find new business. Selling is a numbers game. Everyone you meet is likely to know someone else who may benefit from your product or service.

Keeping your energy and effort high

Never take a referral for granted. As with any other sales technique, method is not the only factor to consider when you try to get referrals. Salespeople must show referrals the same positive attitude, the same high energy level, the same respectful manner, and the same quality presentation that they show to cold calls. Referrals are only *partially* sold on you or your product. The important thing is that they're willing to give you the chance to convince them of how they'll benefit from your offering.

If you're successful at convincing them, referrals will just keep on coming. Before you know it, you'll create an endless chain of happily involved clients who are more than willing to contribute to your success. Happy clients love to think that they're partially responsible for your success, and encouraging their continued participation and interest in promoting your career certainly doesn't hurt.

When you make a referred client happy, you've impressed two people — the referral and the person who did the referring. All this happiness converts to even more leads for you because you did the job right.

Following Up with Your Referrals

Often, the ability to get the referral appointment depends on the success of your follow-up program — if, of course, you use one at all. It's disheartening to go through all the work to get referrals, only to lose them because you lack an organized follow-up system.

When you follow up on those who offered the referrals, they're happy to refer you again when the situation arises. When you follow up on the referrals themselves, you give yourself greater opportunities to increase your profitability. How? By improving your closing rates through cultivating an effective referral business. Remember that 60 percent closing rate mentioned at the beginning of this chapter?

The following sections offer suggestions and strategies that will help you maximize the results from your follow-ups.

Book IV

Closing Like a Champ and Getting Referrals

Imposing order

Follow-up sounds so simple when somebody advises you to send a letter or to just pick up the phone and make a call, but establishing an effective follow-up system involves much more than that. For your follow-up to be effective, and because follow-up is a constant in the selling process, you must organize your follow-up time and program to ensure that your business stays productive.

You can set up your follow-up system in several different ways — choose the method that works best for you. For example:

✔ You can use something as simple as 3-x-5 index cards to keep track of your follow-ups, such as when you contacted the person and the basic details of what information was covered. Or you may want or need to use a more sophisticated customer relationship software.

✔ If you have a lot of people to keep track of, using a sales force automation software program designed to store the maximum amount of information in the minimum amount of space may be the most efficient system of all. By setting up a database specially designed for follow-up, you can save time and energy that you can then devote to face-to-face selling. Some of the most popular software programs include Sage ACT! (www.act.com) and GoldMine (www.frontrange.com/software/crm/goldmine). Other methods are Internet-driven services, such as www.salesforce.com.

If you already use one, invest some time in learning how to maximize the "tickler" or "reminder" features. If you don't have one, be sure these features are easy to manage in any program you decide to use.

Whichever way you choose to organize your time and the follow-up information you collect, your method should enable you to systematically and periodically keep in touch with all your contacts.

As you schedule your follow-up time, keep your existing clients informed of the best times to contact you by sharing with them your work schedule (as much as possible). And then make sure you're accessible at the times you tell them to contact you. They'll appreciate being able to reach you when you say you'll be available, and you eliminate telephone tag or the nagging fear that the contact you've waited for all week will come when you're out on an appointment.

Gauging your nuisance quotient

Whether you receive a *yes* or a *no* from people to whom you present your product or service, you should include them all in your follow-up program. Why?

✔ With those who become clients, service is key, and you can't serve them if they don't make a connection with you. Surprise, surprise — not many of them will reach out to make that connection. The job is up to you.

✔ For those people who choose to purchase from someone else or to not make any purchase at all, you need to get their permission to stay in touch with new developments that may apply to their situation.

In the following sections, you discover when and how often to contact people in your follow-up program and what actions to take when someone still says no to your product or service after follow-up.

Knowing when and how often to make contact

With your clients, you want to stay in touch fairly often, depending upon the product or service they acquired. If they're purchasing office supplies from you, you may need to be in touch weekly. If the purchase was a Lear Jet, you may only need to be in touch once every other month or so.

Your clients may need a comfort scratch every now and then to feel you're really there for them. Your non-clients, on the other hand, may feel you're scratching your nails on their blackboard if you call too often. You'll develop an instinct for this with time and experience.

If you're a beginner, ask each person how often he would like to hear from you. Don't say, "How often shall I contact you?" though. He may answer with, "Don't call us. We'll call you." Instead, suggest it this way, "With your permission, I'd like to follow up with you in about 30 days just to see how well the product is meeting your needs and find out if you have any questions. Would that be all right with you?" He may suggest you call sooner or that he'll have a better idea of how things are working out in 45 days. You can gauge your nuisance factor based on his response.

One of the most important tidbits of sales wisdom is this: Avoid harassing your customer. Sometimes knowing when keeping in touch with your client has crossed the line to downright bothering him is difficult. But you defeat the entire purpose of follow-up if you fail to recognize the signs of annoyance a customer may be sending your way. If a customer hangs up on you, that's a pretty good sign that you've failed to recognize his annoyance. How many hang-ups do you get on a given day? Other signs of annoyance are more subtle; long pauses, distractedness during conversations, and so on can be other signs that your calls are no longer welcome.

Book IV

Closing
Like a
Champ and
Getting
Referrals

Be sensitive to your clients' needs. Don't call on a Friday before a holiday and try to get them involved with your new offering over the phone. This kind of call is not follow-up; it's irritation. Similarly, don't call at lunchtime or at the very end of the day and expect a long, drawn-out conversation with your client's undivided attention. Her mind is set on beating a path to the door, not on listening to your offering.

Keep your follow-up short and sweet, and do it at times most convenient for your potential clients' schedules. Interruptions are sometimes unavoidable, but when too many interruptions occur, give your customers the opportunity to get back with you at a time better suited to their busy schedules.

Treading carefully with someone who says no after follow-up

If, after all the follow-up, you still get a *no* from a client, leave the contact or meeting on a positive note. If you know that his answer was not based on your poor performance, you may still be able to get a referral from him or do future business with him when his situation changes.

Be polite! Find out when he expects his situation to change and ask his permission to call back again. He may be receptive to hearing what you have to say a few short months down the road when he is ready to own your offering. If you leave him with a positive feeling and continue to build rapport through constant and persistent follow-up, the only thing stopping him from owning your offering is time — and that, too, shall pass.

If your customer admits that he has bought from your competitor, don't you think you need to discover why he chose your competitor over you? If this situation arises, don't get angry with your prospective client. Instead, make him feel important by asking him if you can take up just a few more moments of his time to get his advice on how you can improve your sales skills or your product offering.

If you've invested a lot of time with a buyer who has decided not to take you up on your offering and has instead gone with someone else, he may even feel obligated to meet with you. These meetings can be the best learning experiences you have. Not only will you find out what you may need to improve, but you may gain new insight into what your competitor says about you and your company. He also might clue you in on something the competition is offering that you didn't know about. Think of these times as invaluable opportunities to become a better salesperson. And don't forget to take this opportunity to follow up with a thank-you note to the customer for his advice.

If you're diligent in following up with buyers who choose not to own your offering, you may just sneak them away from your competitor the next time they get the itch to own. By keeping in touch with them even better than the salesperson with whom they chose to do business, you'll make the customer wish that he had done business with you. Let him see your organization and care for his well-being through your effective follow-up — and when he needs a new-and-improved version of what he now owns, he'll probably think of you first.

Being disappointed and letting your clients know you're sorry not to have the opportunity to do business with them is okay. Let them know that you're not giving up and that you still hope to win their trust. And for the clients you obtained because of your effective follow-up, remain just as consistent and persistent in the service you provide. Make sure they know that you're concerned about continuing to meet their needs.

Keeping track of your successes

Keep thorough notes on all your follow-ups and the success you have with your current follow-up methods. When you do something great that gets an excellent response, write it down in a *success journal* (a place where you can keep track of everything that has worked for you, follow-up or otherwise). Be specific and detailed, and describe the selling situation in which you implemented the successful follow-up method. The more information you record, the more likely you are to repeat the experience in the future.

When customers tell you what you need to work on, put those comments into your success journals, too. If you take all this time to write down what you do well, in addition to what you need to improve on, you should take the time to review your journal periodically and evaluate whatever changes you make.

You may need to solicit the help of another professional salesperson in your office to hold you accountable for making the changes you know you need to make and to help you implement such changes. When your colleague sees you kicking back and relaxing, she should have your permission to give you a gentle wake-up call, a reminder of what you said you wanted to do to improve your sales results.

Sticking with the follow-up program

How well your prospects respond to your follow-up depends entirely on the effectiveness and efficiency of the method of follow-up you use. If you follow up quickly and regularly (and with a bit of flair), you can expect higher percentages of response from your potential clients. Of course, the response you get will also depend on whether you're working with buyers who can truly benefit from owning your product or service.

Don't get discouraged if some people don't respond at all. Sometimes, no matter how good your follow-up, you get zip, zero, zilch for your efforts. If you take the goose egg more times than not, you may benefit from evaluating your methods of follow-up and putting another kind of zip into your messages.

Knowing which methods work best for you and which types of clients respond to one method of follow-up as opposed to another can take time. So be patient. Don't give up if, after your first few attempts at follow-up you get disappointing results. Instead, keep seeking ways to improve your follow-up program. Contact other professional salespeople who are willing to listen, look at your follow-up program, and offer advice. Good follow-up techniques can sometimes take as long to master as good selling techniques. It doesn't happen overnight.

Book V

Negotiating Skills Every Salesperson Should Have

The 5th Wave   By Rich Tennant

"Or, we could just agree to disagree."

In this book . . .

Anegotiation is any communication in which you're attempting to achieve the approval, acquiescence, or action of someone else. The skills you need to be a successful negotiator in your everyday life are the same skills required for major international and industrial negotiation.

Sure, you can refine these skills with additional techniques and strategies, and you enhance them with your own personal style and personality. But only these six skills are essential:

- ✔ Preparing thoroughly
- ✔ Setting limits and goals
- ✔ Maintaining emotional distance
- ✔ Listening well
- ✔ Communicating clearly
- ✔ Knowing how to close a deal

The chapters in this book cover these topics.

Chapter 1

Preparing for Negotiating Success

Good preparation forms a solid negotiating foundation, giving you the confidence you need to negotiate successfully. If you prepare adequately, you approach the negotiation from a position of strength. Armed with facts and background information, you can correct any perceptions that you're weak.

The act of preparing continues throughout a negotiation. If you listen well during a negotiation, you uncover additional information that may not have been available from any other source. What's more, if you confront the same subject matter in future business transactions, the benefits of this preparation can continue long after that particular negotiation is over.

Most people take the path of least resistance, and preparation is one of the first places that busy people cut corners. You can give yourself an enormous advantage just by taking the time and expending the effort to prepare properly for a negotiation.

The One with the Most Knowledge Wins

Some people think that power comes from size, gruffness, or clout, but the easiest and most effective thing you can do to increase your power is to prepare. You may be facing the greatest negotiator in the world, but if you're prepared and the greatest negotiator isn't, you have the upper hand.

Yet people routinely shortchange themselves when it comes to preparation. Even experienced negotiators often sacrifice solid preparation on the altar of self-confidence or a crushing time schedule. Some negotiators don't fully appreciate the value of spending the extra time and effort on thorough preparation. To others, preparing just feels like drudgework.

Preparation doesn't have to be dull. Preparing for a negotiation can trigger the same type of excitement experienced when preparing for a military scouting mission. Your palms may not sweat, but the rush is similar. You're about to head into the unknown. The outcome is uncertain. Pulling together data is like girding your loins, checking your ammo, becoming secure, and getting ready. Prepare as though you're going into battle.

Playing Detective

You should know about all aspects of a negotiation before you begin. Why? Because the negotiator with the most information wins! So, identify the items that are most important for your next negotiation and get to work. The task breaks down into three major categories:

- ✔ **The issue under negotiation:** When you begin the actual dialogue, try to make sure that you know more about the subject matter than does the person with whom you're negotiating. Obviously, when you're negotiating over the sale of your own product or service, you must know everything there is to know about that product (a topic you can find out about in Book II, Chapter 2), but just being able to explain the features or cost isn't enough. You also need to know what turns on other buyers so that you can use that information in your sales pitch: "Everybody loves this feature." "Everyone was asking for this so we made it standard on all models." The herd mentality rules.

- ✔ **The competition:** Bone up on the competition. "Nobody else offers this." "The ProVac is better than the Room Whiz because. . . ." Do the shopping for your customers to keep them from going elsewhere. For information on how to research your own and your competition's products, head to Book II, Chapter 2.

- ✔ **The person with whom you're negotiating:** Find out as much as possible about your counterpart and what that individual wants out of the negotiation. Leave no unanswered questions about your counterpart or your counterpart's client.

Pop quiz: How prepared are you?

Here's a little quiz to find out how well you tend to prepare for a negotiation:

- In preparing for a negotiation, do you often consult an outside source for information?

- List five resources, other than your personal knowledge and intuition (books, people, or periodicals), that you used during the last year in preparing for a negotiation — any negotiation.

- Name the five most widely recognized sources of authoritative information in your profession. Of these five sources, how

many are in your personal library or your office library?

- Think of your last negotiation. Try to recall five pieces of information that you learned during the course of the discussion. Could you have obtained that information before the negotiation ever started?

As you answer these questions, you can decide for yourself how prepared you've been in the past. No matter how good you are at preparing, you can become better. Time spent on preparation pays off in handsome dividends.

Some people just seem to know instinctively how to prepare. They're born researchers: They look up anything and everything they want to know about because they're not content to let any question or quandary go unsolved. Every family seems to have such a person — he or she is the one who, when planning a vacation, prices out every hotel, gathers information on every restaurant, compiles a list of all local attractions and activities, and more. These folks enjoy making all those calls and being the repository for all there is to know about the area being visited. If preparation know-how doesn't come naturally to you, you can still uncover the information you need by following the suggestions outlined in the next sections.

Solving the mystery of value

If you're entering a negotiation to sell a product or service, you need to solve the mystery of value. What is the product or service worth? Forget about the asking price — what is it really worth?

In determining the real value of an item, begin with these two important points:

- **Value is always in the eye of the beholder.** Whichever side of the table you're on, only you can conclude the ultimate value a service or product holds for you. You're the one who will be spending (or receiving) your money. You must decide. Similarly, having a sense of what your competition values can help your negotiating strategy.

Firsthand knowledge is best

Consider the negotiator who learned early on in his consulting career not to assume that he knew what specific problems managers were encountering unless he visited the worksite himself. The person who taught him this lesson was a production manager on the F-18 assembly line. As the negotiator waxed eloquent about management theory based on praising employees to maintain good performance, the line manager interrupted him with, "Hey, you ever bucked a rivet?" The negotiator's response: "No, what's a rivet?" The six other male managers in the class laughed, and immediately, the negotiator realized what the real question was: Did he know what he was up against in that particular situation?

The plant manager explained what "bucking a rivet" meant. The process involves using a very heavy piece of hydraulic machinery, like an electric screwdriver, to drive a small screw-like piece of steel into the fuselage of a jet fighter. Hundreds of these things are riveted into each piece of steel. The riveter makes a horrible sound (many workers wear earplugs) and is extremely heavy. The negotiator said,

"Well, I've never bucked a rivet, but I probably should." All the others chuckled, and one said, "Be at my station tomorrow at 6 a.m. in pants and soft-soled shoes. We'll issue you a hard hat and safety glasses."

The negotiator recognized that this suggestion was a dare. Despite his small stature — 5 feet tall and not much over a hundred pounds — he took the issue up two levels to the vice president of human resources to get the go-ahead. The next morning, wearing the requisite gear, he learned a great deal about the people this man supervised. Before the experience, he never would have dreamed of the things that motivated the employees, information that he absolutely needed to know to negotiate effectively in this environment. After bucking rivets for a morning, he knew that a short 15-minute break meant a great deal, as well as strong coffee and the availability of a certain kind of jelly-filled donut. Since then, he tries never to teach about an environment he hasn't physically seen, about people he has never spoken to directly. In business, this principle is called *needs analysis*.

✔ **All sorts of resources assessing value are at (or near) your fingertips, if you know where to look.** From diamonds to dime stores, experts compile price surveys and put out a report on the item's value; these publications are how insiders know what's going on in the world. Whether you're selling a hotel or a holiday in a hotel, you can find insider information on the value that others are putting on such a purchase. Make sure you read these publications so that you can see what information your buyer has access to (yes, assume that your buyer has done this research). The following sections explain the kinds of resources that publish this kind of information.

Values change over time. One important thing your customers must decide is how long they're going to keep the item they're thinking about buying. The longer they plan to keep the purchase, the longer it needs to hold its value. Information about normal depreciation is as available as information on current value — usually in the same place. Knowing the rate of depreciation for an item is certainly just as important as knowing its current value.

Consult Consumer Reports

Consumer Reports (www.consumerreports.org) is an old standby. It has tested, rated, valued, and devalued a wide range of products and services. Why reinvent the wheel?

You can now view specific articles from *Consumer Reports* through its website. You no longer have to rummage through back issues of the magazines — just visit ConsumerReports.org and use the Search bar located at the top of the page to search for a particular report. It's a very efficient way of viewing any reports that you may need, without ever talking to a human being.

Browse online services

The Internet is a giant warehouse of information on any topic you can imagine. Browse the web for information about your product before you begin any critical negotiation. You also can buy a directory of Internet locations, similar to a telephone book.

A great deal of the information on the web is glorified advertising put up by companies trying to sell something. Don't assume that the material you find is objective just because it's on your computer. Dig deep into the pages to see whether the material is created by an objective resource or someone with a financial interest.

Visit the library

What a concept! The library is one of the most underused negotiating resources in your community. Reintroducing yourself to this great institution can be a blast. The library has all sorts of resources you can use to find the value of various goods or services.

When you go to the library, don't be afraid to ask for help. Most city libraries designate a staff person to assist in research. In our experience, we've found librarians to be among the most helpful people in the world.

Shop the competition

Don't hesitate to do your own research. Rather than read about value, pound the pavement for the information. A firsthand look can be a real eye-opener. Suppose that you're planning to purchase an apartment building. You may want to play the role of a prospective renter before ever offering to become an owner of the entire building. The same is true if you're on the other side of the deal. If you own a building and want to reset some rents, the same exercise works for you. Walk through the neighborhood, visiting other apartment buildings. In an hour, you can become the world's leading expert on the price and availability of apartments in that block or two. That approach always produces more reliable information than reading some generalized report or statistics that cover the entire county instead of your immediate neighborhood.

Whether you're buying or selling, a shopping trip is one of the best ways to educate yourself about price, availability, and quality considerations. Of course, you're not going to buy, you're going to gather information. During this expedition, make notes. You'll be gathering a great deal of new information, most of which you may remember, but without good notes you won't remember where you *got* the different pieces of information.

Ask questions

Even after a negotiation gets under way, you can continue your preparation by asking your counterpart questions. Some people are reluctant to ask questions because they're afraid of appearing dumb. This is false pride at its most expensive. You're flying blind without accurate information. You can't worsen your position by requesting information from your counterpart. Your job is to get a good outcome, not to impress the seller. If you have unanswered questions, ask.

Keep in mind that the answer you receive during a negotiation may or may not be accurate. Always accept it with respect . . . and then check it out for yourself. You have an obligation to be sure that any information you're relying on is, indeed, reliable.

What if you're out of your element? Don't try to hide your lack of expertise. If you're dealing with someone who is really knowledgeable in a field, and you aren't so experienced, honesty — once again — is the best policy. Reveal your inexperience yourself; then you can ask all the questions necessary and request additional time to research the topic.

You don't have to make a deal until you're ready. Closing a deal is a voluntary act. Get your information from anyone you can — including the opposition. The more your counterpart wants to reach an agreement, the more quickly you'll receive the data you need to make your decision.

Read insider reports

Take time to find out what the people in the business pay for the goods or services you want to buy or sell. This strategy can save you a fortune over the course of your career. Don't rely solely on what colleagues tell you, although they may provide good hints and direction. Go to the people who tell the merchants what to charge. Go to the source the insiders use.

No matter what the subject, someone has devoted a lifetime of work to evaluating and commenting on it. This is just a fact of modern life. Nothing is too arcane to study, dissect, catalog, and chronicle, as the following list shows:

- For automobile dealers, the bible is called the *Kelley Blue Book*.

- Prices of gold and other basic metals are printed in the Sunday paper.

- The cost of money for almost anything (home mortgages and interest paid on savings accounts or car loans) is printed regularly in *The Wall Street Journal*.

Stay informed

Prepare yourself on an ongoing basis for the most common negotiations in your life. If you sell boats for a living, you should know more about the kind of boats you sell than anybody else in the world. Attend boat shows open to the general public as well as seminars for the professional salesperson. Seek out the designers and manufacturers of your boats for detailed information. Talk with your co-workers over the watercooler. Take advantage of all these varied resources.

The quality of the advice and information you receive varies widely. Decide what to keep in your treasure box of information and what to reject, but keep exposing yourself to anything and everything that can increase your stockpile of information. You never know when some bit of trivia can become your secret weapon in a negotiation.

Researching your opponent

Even experienced negotiators who focus on preparation as a separate step almost always shortchange themselves in one area: They fail to gather enough information about the individual with whom they are negotiating. This person may be a spouse, a valued employee, or a vendor. There really isn't one word to describe that person; *opponent* isn't appropriate for many situations. Whatever you call this person, find out all you can about that individual.

Knowing the other party is important in every transaction, even in transactions that involve tangible things (houses, cars, paintings, lawn mowers, and so on) that can be inspected by an expert. Knowing why the seller wants to unload the article is key to making the best deal possible. The importance of knowing about your counterpart becomes absolutely crucial, however, if the issue under negotiation is intangible. Services or intangibles such as the right to do something (cross land, publish a book, distribute a movie) require complete knowledge about the reliability, honesty, and ability of the other party. In order to work, long-term contracts and intangibles rely heavily on the other party. You simply must gather as much information as possible about your counterpart.

Don't buy or sell a house (or anything else) from strangers

Regardless of what is being bought or sold, each party in a negotiation has particular requirements they want met before they're ready to seal the deal. Take real estate, for example. Whether you plan to buy or sell a house, you probably have a lot of data about sales prices in the neighborhood and such. You still need to find out about the other party. The other party's situation is an important ingredient in an accurate assessment of the marketplace. Make a conscious effort to find out what financial and other pressures the other party is under. For example, is a divorce involved? Is a change of job or city involved? When must the other party move? Has the other party already bought another house or sold their current home?

So, how do you uncover this important information?

You can best glean most of the answers through casual chatting with the other party, any agent representing them, or even outside sources. To obtain this information, begin by putting people at ease. Don't start with direct questioning like a prosecutor. That approach can turn people off. Lean against the fence and have a friendly, get-to-know-you kind of conversation. This information is like money in the bank.

Today, a lot of information on the other party resides right on the Internet. Type in the other party's name and city, and you may be surprised what you learn. Follow up with the same kind of research about anyone or any organization or business that shows up in the first pages you open, and you'll soon have a composite picture of the person on the other side of the table.

Don't undervalue information

Is all this gathering of information really necessary? If you're intent on collecting enough information, you're bound to gather some unnecessary scraps. However, having too much information is better than not enough.

What do you do with all that data? You use the relevant information to build a model of what the upcoming negotiation is going to look like. Figure 1-1 shows why information is critical and how the entire negotiation is shaped by your perception of your own position and the other party's.

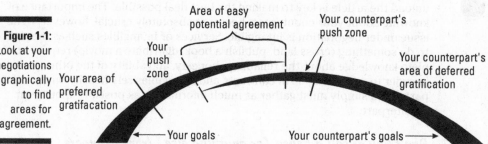

Figure 1-1: Look at your negotiations graphically to find areas for agreement.

Area of easy potential agreement

Your counterpart's push zone

Your push zone

Your counterpart's area of deferred gratification

Your area of preferred gratifacation

Your goals

Your counterpart's goals

Note the large center portion of Figure 1-1 in which the agreement will most likely occur. This area represents the terms with the most potential for resolution; the parties can probably reach an easy compromise on these issues.

The areas to the upper left and upper right represent points of contention that require you or your counterpart to compromise more than is desirable in order to reach an agreement. Consider these areas the *push zones*.

The area on the lower left represents goals that you may not be able to achieve during this negotiation. The area on the lower right indicates the goals that your counterpart may not be able to attain during the current negotiation. You and your counterpart may have to defer demands for these terms to future negotiations.

Identifying the Right Person

You can't very well research the person with whom you'll be negotiating if you don't know who that person is. Finding out exactly which individual you're going to be negotiating with is critical to proper preparation. Sometimes you can choose the person, and sometimes you can't.

Often, you're approaching an organization from the outside. Research the organization and make your initial contact as high up the organizational ladder as possible. It never hurts to have the boss's boss send a memo down the line asking for someone to give you an audience. The person you deal with won't know that you got the letter from cold calling and should treat you with the respect due someone who came in through the boss.

Working with what you get

Many times, you don't get to designate the person with whom you negotiate. More often than not, you end up negotiating with an assigned person.

Some people try to negotiate with someone higher up the corporate ladder than their assigned negotiator. That tactic usually backfires, because it violates the corporate culture within which the deal is being made. Besides, sometimes negotiating with a higher authority is downright impossible. You can't very well say, "Send me a sales rep I know" or "Hire a different Realtor if you want to sell me your house."

Be sure that the designated negotiator is enthusiastic about the final agreement and believes that the deal is good for his company or client. Turn that person into an ambassador for the agreement by negotiating hard, but in a friendly manner. Never lose your cool. After you reach an agreement, the person you're negotiating with has to sell the final result to his company or client. That person must feel positive about the outcome.

Choosing the person you negotiate with

In some situations, you really do have some control over which person you negotiate with. For example, if you're going to negotiate strenuously for a particular item in a small shop, you want to negotiate with the shop owner, not a summer clerk. (Of course, you should state this request gently so that you don't insult the summer help.)

If you don't know whether you're talking to the best person for the negotiation at hand, start with a friendly conversation. In the course of finding out how long the person has been on the job and what that person's previous experience was, you can make a pretty good assessment of how much authority — and flexibility — the person has. People who are new to an organization tend to have less authority and less flexibility than people who have been with an organization longer. If someone has been repeatedly passed over for promotions, you know that you're dealing with a person who may have frustrations and a lack of loyalty to the company.

How do you get to the head honcho? Follow the Six Degrees principle, which states that you know or can effectively contact someone who is the first person in a six-person chain that leads directly to the person you want to contact. It comes from the theory that only six people separate you from anybody else on Earth. Say you want to talk to the minister of commerce for Germany. Perhaps the closest person in the six-degrees-away-chain is your old college roommate (6) whose uncle (5) plays tennis with a business associate (4) whose wife (3) translates manuscripts for a renowned German economist (2) who occasionally advises Germany's Minister of Commerce (1). Make contact with the first person, and you're on your way!

So, how do you find the person six degrees away from the person you want to talk to? You find out all you can about the person you want to meet. In the example, that would be the German minister of commerce (1). Find out who is around that person. You'll come up with a number of people including the renowned German economist (2). Googling her, you would learn that some of her books are in English, which leads to the translator (3) who is the wife (4) of your uncle's (5) tennis partner (6). It's a lot of hard work with ever-expanding concentric circles of contacts, but it's true that there are only six degrees of separation between everyone in the world.

Watch John Guare's play (or the wonderful movie it was made into, starring Stockard Channing and Will Smith) called *Six Degrees of Separation*. It's based on the true story of a street hustler who successfully convinced several members of the upper crust of New York City that he was both a school friend of one of their children and the son of Sidney Poitier. He obtained money, meals, housing, clothing, and enough information to move on to the next high-rise and repeat the scam. The victims were too embarrassed to report the matter until one couple went up to Sidney Poitier in an airport to tell him how much they enjoyed having his son at their home. They learned that Poitier has no son!

Preparing for someone you know

When it comes to gathering information about the other party, every day is different. Don't assume that you can commence any negotiation without special preparation, no matter how well you know the person. When a seasoned purchasing agent sees a regular salesperson, the purchasing agent often opens the conversation by saying, "What's going on with you these days?"

Pleasantry or preparation?

A neighbor who's about to ask you to stop parking in front of her house begins by saying, "Hi. How is the family doing today?"

Pleasantry or preparation?

After the January 1994 earthquake in Los Angeles, even the least skilled negotiator first asked how the person on the other side had fared in the tumbler. No one pressed for resolution of matters until housing and offices returned to some normalcy.

Even if such questions have been a pleasantry for you in the past, start making them part of your preparation and treating the person according to the answer. You may even decide to put off a negotiation if the person sounds stressed out.

Looking below the Surface: Hidden Agendas and Secondary Motivations

As you prepare for a negotiation, be alert to the fact that everything is not always as it seems. Maybe, besides buying what you have to sell, the buyer wants to establish a relationship with your company. Maybe the buyer wants to know how your business runs in order to enter the field as well. Maybe the buyer wants to teach another supplier a lesson. In the world of negotiating, these ulterior motives are called *hidden agendas*. A cousin to the hidden agenda is the secondary reason for being in the negotiation. Seldom does anyone have only one reason to be in a negotiation. If you pay attention, you often can discover what this secondary reason is. By being aware of hidden agendas and secondary motivations, you can maneuver through the negotiation more successfully.

For life's everyday negotiations, gathering information about your counterparts is key. To get what you need and want, you must learn their hot buttons — what turns them on and what turns them off. People won't be motivated to give you what you want unless something's in it for them. A key part of preparation is to find out what matters to your counterparts and how they can benefit from a negotiation.

Uncovering hidden agendas

Hidden agendas are difficult to ferret out; that's why they're called hidden agendas! Without introducing paranoia into the process, be mindful of the possibility of hidden agendas. You rarely uncover them early in the process — or by asking directly. As part of your ongoing preparation, gather all the information you can about motive. The more you know about the other person's motives, the more you can create possibilities for yourself. Sometimes, you may even decide to walk away from a deal.

At work, the hidden agenda is sometimes hard to spot. On the surface, everyone should be working toward the same goal. The goals of the company are the goals of the individual: better production, higher sales, or faster turnaround. But individuals within the company have personal goals in addition to company goals. They want to get ahead within the company, or they need peer approval, or they desire neatness in the workspace. Their personal, secondary agenda is rarely stated. If it is, it's couched in the general statements about company goals. For example, someone wanting to get ahead in the company may volunteer to work overtime to get an important project done. Someone who needs to be liked may help a co-worker attain a desired goal. These strategies aren't good or bad — just reality. The trick is to recognize these hidden agendas as early as possible so they can be considered for what they are.

Recognizing the secondary reason behind the negotiation

Most people have more than one reason to be in a negotiation. Consider, for example, the person trying to sell his car because he wants to drive a different (better or newer) car. This primary reason for being in the negotiation is apparent: He wants to get rid of his old car so that he can buy a new one. But the seller also wants to get the most money for his old car that he can. This — maximizing the amount of money made — is another, separate reason to sell the car. By making a good deal on the old car, the seller may be able to purchase the new car on desirable terms.

Finding out what's on the test

Remember being in fifth grade, sitting at a little desk, listening to the teacher drone on and on, boring you to sleep? Invariably, some kid in the back row would yell out, "Hey, teacher. Is this gonna be on the test?"

You may have thought the kid was obnoxious for asking that question, but you listened very carefully to the answer. If the answer was no, your reaction was probably to go back to daydreaming and counting minutes until the class ended. But if the teacher said, "Yes, this will be a very important part of the test," you straightened up, borrowed a pencil, and took notes.

The point? People do only what they perceive to be on the test. They do only that which promotes or satisfies their interests in some way. In school, the motivation was grades. Teachers got students to pay attention to what they were saying by putting it on the test. In adult life, the goal is money, happiness, or freedom from hassle.

Find out what motivates the person with whom you are negotiating. Then, during the negotiation, be sure that the other party understands how you can satisfy those needs. Put your priority on your counterpart's test.

The more you know about what is driving the deal from the other person's point of view, the more likely you are to come up with a solution that enables the deal to close to your benefit.

No hard-and-fast rules apply to every negotiation, except this principle:

> Keep your antenna out for all the information you can possibly gather about the people you negotiate with — their motives, their hopes, and their needs.

It's ironic but true — you get more of what you want by being more attuned to what the other party wants.

Putting It in Writing: The Information Checklist

Make a mental checklist before commencing a negotiation. An even better idea is to write down the checklist. Here's some of the information you should assemble about the person you plan to negotiate with:

✔ What is your relationship to this negotiator?

✔ How long has the negotiator been with the organization?

✔ What are the negotiator's future plans with the company?

- If the negotiator is planning to leave, when and to what sort of situation?
- How qualified is this person for this negotiation?
- What company policies exist with regard to this type of negotiation?
- How is the negotiator compensated? Is there an incentive program if money is saved on this negotiation?
- Is the compensation based on commission or straight salary?
- What time constraints exist for the other side?
- What other pressures originate from the negotiator's place of work?
- Who else must this person consult before a final decision can be rendered?
- Is there a cutoff to the negotiator's authority? That is, is there a point under which the negotiator is authorized to close the deal and over which higher authority is needed? If so, what is that point?
- How is the negotiator for the other side perceived by superiors?
- What is the negotiator's attitude toward you? Your company? Your subject?
- Who has made similar deals with this person in the past? How can you contact that person? What does that individual have to say about this negotiator?
- What is your overall assessment of this negotiator?

How elaborate or detailed your checklist is may change with the complexity of the negotiation, but the wisdom of writing it down does not. Even for a simple and straightforward negotiation, writing down the essential facts before you start negotiating is very helpful.

For example, if you're selling a used car, write down the price of the car you want to sell (see the section "Solving the mystery of value" earlier in this chapter for a discussion of where to find this value). Also, write down any time constraints and some data on the buyer's situation, if you know it.

Even more important than writing down the information you gather about the subject of the negotiation is making notes each time you find out something about your counterpart. Lack of knowledge about the person with whom you are negotiating is the most common failure in preparation. The best way to avoid that pitfall is to retain whatever information you do have about the other party. Write it down. Save it. Add to it. This information is golden.

These days, you can let your computer do the remembering for you. Computers are great at remembering birthdays, the names of spouses and kids, and other information about the people involved in the negotiation. None of this information is irrelevant.

Why bother writing down the information you gather? Here are just a couple of good reasons:

- ✔ **Research indicates that the very act of writing something down improves your chances of remembering the information, even if you throw the note away immediately!**

- ✔ **Writing down information gives you an easy retrieval system.** If passion causes the seller to fudge the facts a bit, you don't need to challenge reality. You can merely say, "Let's check our notes." Read the original statements back. That approach is much less insulting than saying, "But you said. . . ." The latter frequently starts an argument that no one can win. The former generally settles or avoids an argument all together. Remember these words: "Gee, my notes reflect . . . but you said. . . ."

Preparing to Negotiate across the Globe

If you're involved in an international negotiation, you have to prepare for a whole host of issues. Most people have some advance notice if their business is heading in the direction of an international negotiation. If you have an inkling that international negotiations are in your future, start early to gather as much information about the culture, laws, and business practices of the nationality of the person with whom you're negotiating.

The people who negotiate best in a culture other than their own have usually had the good fortune to live in that culture for a part of their lives. If they're really lucky, they were young at the time and could absorb the culture without judgment. If you weren't fortunate enough to have lived in the same culture as the person with whom you're negotiating, you have some extra prep work to do.

It's one thing to read a briefing paper about a culture that is different from your own. It's quite another thing to absorb that culture so that you can move comfortably with its rhythm and its rules. Step one is to respect a culture. When you respect the culture and truly understand its people's roots, you advance a long way toward effectively dealing with the individuals within that group.

How to speak like a native when you aren't

International negotiations require special preparation, but the tools are out there. Read books about the history, geography, customs, and religion of the people with whom you plan to negotiate. Such specialized knowledge makes your international negotiations much less frustrating and more fulfilling. If your negotiations take place on your counterpart's turf, the knowledge you gain in preparing for the negotiation adds immensely to your enjoyment of any free time you have on the trip.

The sources for your preparation are wide ranging. Here are just a few:

- ✔ Talk to your friends and business associates who have experienced the culture.
- ✔ Read the many books that are available and watch travel videos as well as movies that take place in that culture.
- ✔ The Internet can provide an electronic gateway to other cultures. You can chat with computer junkies from other countries or just visit international web pages.
- ✔ Many large cities have cultural centers sponsored by the foreign government or expatriates from the country you want to visit.
- ✔ Ethnic restaurants can be another fun resource. Chat with the owners. You often find out a wealth of information about your counterpart's country while learning firsthand about that country's food.

Spend time acquainting yourself with the nature of foreign-government involvement in your transaction. Corporate executives in the United States complain a great deal about business regulation. Many Americans think that their own federal, state, and local governments are too involved in supervising businesses. Americans often have a tough time with the even greater involvement of some foreign governments in individual business deals. Americans are surprised when they see an official — often a high-level member of a foreign government — right at the negotiating table on many deals that would be considered purely private in the United States.

The more you know about the level of government involvement, the less troublesome that involvement will be. You never help your cause by being judgmental about such things. Life is different in every country in the world. There is no abstract right or wrong — just different ways of doing things. Research these variations before you leave so that you can return home with more of what you want.

How to research the right culture, subculture, or individual

Before you dive into your cultural research, you must first be sure to identify exactly what culture you're dealing with. You're not negotiating in Asia, for example. All of Asia is not a single culture — the differences among Japan, China, and Korea are enormous. You can't lump them together if you're going to prepare effectively.

Within cultures exist subcultures. The Muslims and Christians who live side-by-side in Malaysia have very different values, even though they have a great deal in common by virtue of being Malaysian. Of course, the code of cab drivers seems to be the same all around the world. Rickshaw drivers in the Orient, jitney drivers in Manila, or taxi drivers anywhere all have a penchant for driving the stranger along the strangest (and longest) route and charging whatever the traffic will bear. If that happens to you, you're just paying the price for not preparing.

As you gather specifics about the culture of the person with whom you plan to negotiate, don't forget that you must also prepare information about the individual with whom you'll be negotiating. Although a vender at a roadside stand may know only her own culture's traditions, you can expect a highly experienced international negotiator to know your style and play to it.

What to Do When You're Not Ready

Never begin negotiations until you're ready — until after you prepare. This is not just a rule; it's a fact of life. Neither side should start negotiating prematurely. You can stumble around on an impromptu basis, but you cannot negotiate effectively unless you prepare.

Still, the other party may want to begin a negotiation at a time when you aren't ready. In that situation, follow these steps:

- ✔ **Just say, "I'm not ready to discuss this yet."** If you're called upon to respond, merely admit that you aren't ready to negotiate and set a time to return with a response.

- ✔ **Listen.** Effective listening, especially at the commencement of a negotiation, is often merely an extension of preparation. If you listen when the other person talks, you can't lose. You also may ask whether the other person wants to tell you anything else so that you don't lose an opportunity to gather more data.

  Listening is a good way to pick up needed information *and* turn an ambush negotiation into a roaring success.

- ✔ **Ask for the precise data you're missing from your preparation.**

  One way you know that you are asking for an essential piece of information is the intensity with which the other party refuses your request. If the response to one of your questions is, "Oh, I can't tell you that," you know that you've asked for an essential piece of information. Keep digging. Get the answer either from that person or from someone else but be assured that the answer is important to you if the other side is trying to keep it from you.

This technique is one you can use to comfortably stall when you're negotiating on behalf of a client or company. The other party knows that you have to get instructions from your principals, that you're part of a team, and that you can't go off on your own tangent.

When you're negotiating on your own behalf, you sometimes get a derisive response to an avoidance technique: "What do you mean, you don't know what you want to pay?" or "How long will it take you to do the job?" The implication is that the right person would know this information. This situation calls for the absolute truth, calmly stated: "Oh, I could give you a quick answer right now, but I'm not going to. I want to be sure that I give you a number I can live with, and I want to check with my associate." State exactly what preparation is needed and how long you think it will take.

Being specific reassures the other side that you aren't just playing some silly negotiating game. You must treat your need to prepare with dignity and respect in order to have the other side adopt the same attitude.

When the other party fully understands and agrees with your need for a little more time, you can say, "However, if you have a figure in mind, I'd like to hear it." If you rush this important question, your refusal will just look like a reluctance to put the first offer down. If they don't want to make such an offer, try to find out why. This information can give you an interesting insight into the other party. For example, you may learn that company policy prevents the other side from making an opening offer or that they aren't ready to enter into discussion either. You may decide that the whole thing is a bluff, that they really want to do business with someone else so they don't dare make a firm offer to you. The reasons for their reluctance can be as informative as the information itself.

Chapter 2

Choreographing the Negotiation

In This Chapter

▶ Setting the stage for productive negotiation

▶ Deciding who should attend

▶ Making an agenda

▶ Making a great first impression

*W*hatever the subject of your negotiation, you face some common issues in preparing for that first session. Even if you're prepared for the issue at hand (refer to Book V, Chapter 1), you still need to decide where and when to set the meeting, what to wear, and what to do if you're having a bad hair day. Stage fright sometimes sets in no matter how well prepared you are. This chapter helps you prepare for that first meeting so that you can walk through the door with confidence.

Controlling Your Environment

People often spend very little time considering the best environment for negotiating, and they rely on rules that make arranging a time and place difficult. When both sides consider it mandatory that the negotiations occur in their own office, getting things started is impossible.

If your position is low on the food chain and you feel you have no control over the details of the negotiating environment, giving this issue some consideration is even more important because there are ways you can make even the least inhospitable negotiating environment more receptive.

Finding a place for the negotiations

Your own office often provides a powerful advantage because it's your home turf. You have all the data handy. You have supplemental staff, should you need their expertise. It is, after all, your operational base. Your comfort level will be at its highest in that environment.

But you may not be able to negotiate on your home turf. As a salesperson, you often have to go to your client's office or your customer's home to negotiate a deal. Keep the following points in mind about either of these locations:

- **Your client's office:** Sometimes, meeting in the other party's office is actually better for you. If your opponent in a negotiation always claims to be missing some document back at the office, meeting in said office could help you avoid that particular evasion. And if bulky, hard-to-transport documents are critical to a negotiation, the best site for negotiation is wherever those documents happen to be.

- **Your customer's home:** This environment presents opportunities and challenges galore. On the one hand, you can learn a lot about people by visiting them in their homes — their home, hobbies, and health issues are all on display — and you can use this knowledge to better present or finesse your approach. On the other hand, no place provides a greater opportunity for kibitzers, kids, and general craziness than the home environment. Assess an invitation to "drop by the house to discuss this" with great care. Try to agree to a time when the homeowners will have the fewest distractions and when all key parties will be present.

When deciding where to negotiate, be sure that both sides can listen to everything that's said. If your negotiating environment includes constant interruptions or overwhelming noise, listening may not be possible, no matter how hard you try to do so. And if you can't concentrate on what the other person is saying, you can't negotiate. It's a physical impossibility.

What about negotiating in a restaurant? After all, people often choose a lunch meeting to discuss important matters. In our culture, meals are inherently social. That makes lunch meetings good for developing relationships, bringing people together, and getting to know one another. However, meals are generally not a good time to negotiate anything of any importance, at least not the nitty-gritty details. First, many a trendy restaurant is synonymous with noise. Second, restaurants are rife with distractions, not the least of which is the wait staff constantly inquiring about your desires, the quality of service, and whether you'd like more water. Meeting in a restaurant isn't a good idea unless you have a place you know very well (and they know you) and a private area is available.

Chickening out

Here's a cautionary tale about how the wrong location can undermine even the most positive beginnings. The scenario: The largest chicken ranch in California was for sale. A deal had almost been struck between the seller and the enthusiastic buyer, and only a final meeting was left. For the final negotiating session, the seller invited the buyer to the ranch to close the deal.

As scheduled, the negotiating teams arrived at the ranch, which was situated away from freeways, flyways, and functioning industrialism to encourage the chickens to maximize production. It was a place of perfect, rural solitude. Yet despite having a pleasant office large enough to accommodate the entire group, the seller thought that a nonstop walking session around the ranch was the best venue for settling the deal. On the contrary, with the dust, the disorganized clumps of people traipsing around the property, and tens of thousands of chickens complaining nonstop about their cramped quarters, all he accomplished was to thoroughly confuse and wear out a previously receptive group of people.

Because time to close the deal had almost run out, another day of negotiating was organized. The suggestion: a dinner, hosted by the buyer's lead negotiator, to be located in a quiet place where the two groups could talk. The seller, charged with selecting a restaurant, chose what was to him the perfect place: the neighborhood watering hole where everybody he knew from miles around congregated. Because of the interruptions, the negotiating teams were never able to discuss the deal. The deal didn't close, and the buyer and seller parted ways.

Seating with purpose

Seating arrangements are the subject of many jokes, and sometimes the importance of seating can be overemphasized — but not often. Definitely don't leave seating to chance. Of course, how much control you have over the seating arrangements depends on the scenario. Team negotiations in a conference room are very different from one-on-one negotiations in your client's office, which in turn is very different from negotiating with a couple in their home. The following sections provide suggestions for how you can project an air of confidence and power in each of these situations.

The following sections outline three distinct scenarios, but you may find yourself in a situation that doesn't exactly replicate any single one. The general concepts, however, are applicable in any situation, so feel free to adapt these strategies to meet your needs in any particular negotiation.

Advantageous seating arrangements in a conference room

The seating arrangements around a conference table send many subtle and not-so-subtle messages and can impact the balance of power and influence. Here are some seating tips that can help you ensure that you or members of your negotiating team aren't at a disadvantage:

✔ **Sit next to the person with whom you need to consult quickly and privately.**

✔ **Sit opposite the person with whom you have the most conflict.** For example, if you're the leader of a negotiating team, sit opposite the leader of the other negotiating team. If you want to soften the confrontational effect, you can be off-center by a chair or two. Sometimes the shape of the table or room gives you the opportunity to be on adjacent sides with your opponent, rather than dead opposite.

✔ **Consider who should be closest to the door and who should be closest to the phone.** If you expect to use the phone or to have people huddling outside the negotiating room, these positions can be positions of power. The person nearest the phone generally controls its use. The person nearest the door can control physical access to the room.

✔ **Windows and the angle of the sun are important considerations, especially if the situation generates heat or glare.** Your handling of this issue often reflects your style. Some negotiators want everyone to be comfortable and able to listen, so they reduce the adverse impact on everyone to the extent possible. Others relish in taking the "power" position — with their own back to the glare and the customer facing the glare. To each his own. Be aware, however, that such decisions impact the tenor of the negotiation, so make sure your decisions foster the negotiation environment most conducive to your goals.

✔ **Be sure that you can clearly see everyone on the other negotiating team.** You need to be able to pick up on facial expressions and body language.

When you're one-on-one in your customer's office

If you have to meet in your customer's or client's office, take a seat that keeps the balance of power between the two of you as equal as possible. If your client's office has a conversation area, for example, try to move there for the discussion. Sofas or round tables are the great equalizers.

If your client is firmly planted behind the desk, stay standing for the beginning of your presentation so that you're meeting at eye level. Then when you need to sit, make sure you move the chair, even if only a few inches. People who anchor themselves behind a desk may not have any other choices in their office. More typically, they're consciously or unconsciously trying to maintain a power position. It's difficult to completely reverse the situation, but a minor adjustment in the chair's position helps.

Of course, wherever you end up sitting in relationship to the client, be sure that you sit tall but relaxed, and in a position that allows you to keep good eye contact. If you'll need some papers or a computer during the meeting, say so upfront so that you have a convenient place for these items.

Negotiating in your customer's home

This requires a rapid survey of the situation. Buy some time with a comment such as "What a beautiful home you have." This gives time — and an excuse — to look around a bit and see if you can find a place that is quieter, is less prone to interruption, has proper space to spread out (if necessary), or is away from other potential interruptions.

Identifying a suitable location in your customer's home requires a bit of agility on your part. You'll have to make a snap judgment and then try to enforce it pleasantly with the reason for your request: "Oh, maybe the dining room table will work better for you to see the nifty little pop-up book I brought." Don't automatically plop down wherever you're invited to do so. Stay in charge at this point, and you're more likely to stay in charge during the course of the sales call.

Checking the Guest List

Who does or does not attend any given negotiation session can be the subject of some intense negotiations itself. For all the moaning about "one more meeting," some people get very bent out of shape if they aren't included.

When you arrange a negotiating session, don't invite one more person than is necessary. (*Necessary,* in a negotiating session, means that the person has something essential to add to the dialogue that cannot be contributed by someone else.) Each person in attendance adds exponentially to the problem of control in communications. The chance of words being uttered when silence is needed rises sharply with each additional person.

Two types of people in particular often want to join, even though the negotiating team is complete without them:

- ✓ **The marketing team:** They've worked hard to land the deal and they may be worried that the negotiating team will come down too hard and blow it.

- ✓ **The boss:** The boss is best left out of the room because you may need to have a reason to "check in with the boss." You can't do that if the boss is in the room.

Compensate for not being able to invite someone by sending that person a memo. (Paper is cheap; extra voices at a negotiation session can be very expensive.) That same memo should go to anyone who is part of the negotiating team but can't attend a session.

Sometimes you want to include a person with special expertise — an accountant, for example — in a single negotiating session, even though that person is not a part of the other sessions. Don't hesitate to bring in an expert to make a presentation and answer questions. However, it's most effective to have that person leave after all the information you want to share is on the table.

When you're negotiating with a couple, the plot thickens in ways you may not even be aware of. You think you sold the husband, for example, and find out later that the unseen wife nixed the deal. To avoid scenarios like this, follow these suggestions:

✓ **Assess the relative power of the couple.** This task is very tricky but important. Although these are not hard-and-fast identifiers, some clues can help you assess who the "final" decision maker is:

- Who asks or answers the most questions?

- Does one tend to defer to the other, either verbally ("Mona, what do you think?") or more subtly (looking to the other partner to answer a question you ask)?

✓ **Get both partners in the room at the same time.** If you can't get them both in the room at the same time, be sure to inquire explicitly about the how the missing spouse may feel. Beware of "Oh, don't worry about her" or "I'll take care of her." Both suggest that the reception may not be all that warm and may require some selling by the customer in front of you. Ask what the objections may be and see what you can leave behind to help with the hidden presentation.

✓ **Pitch to both parties.** Don't leave either one out. Sit where you can see both equally. Don't sit between them because you could be noticing one nodding approval and miss that the other one is sawing the air in front of his or her neck with a stiffened, blade-like hand.

When you're negotiating with people from another country, the presence of a culture divide is more obvious and more accentuated, so get the help of an expert. Most big-city governments and every state have protocol officers that can give you some tips. In addition, because practices vary all over the world, read culture-specific books. In different countries, the role of women ranges from purely secretarial to fully participating members. In some Asian countries, women participate fully during the business portion of the meeting, and then the men go out by themselves. If you aren't sure, you can defer to the lead negotiator from that culture. In fact, deferring to the lead negotiator in such matters can help you build rapport.

Setting an Agenda

Agendas are wonderful control devices. An agenda makes it more difficult for the other side to avoid addressing an uncomfortable issue. Creating the agenda is an advantage to you even if you aren't in charge of the meeting. If you don't want to, or aren't ready to, discuss a certain topic, leave it off the agenda. Alternatively, you can include a related topic.

The written word has real power in our society. A written agenda in front of all the participants in a meeting has a power and an authority all its own. A plan also brings clarity to a meeting. By providing what amounts to an outline for the meeting, a written agenda inspires people to take notes on what's happening.

If you're meeting with individual customers, an agenda can still be helpful. You may want to take the time to prepare one, if for no other reason than to help you clarify the key points to be addressed and goals to be achieved. An agenda also can be helpful even in relatively straightforward situations. When selling a paint job for a house, for example, you want to find out right away about potential schedule conflicts and assess whether you can deliver on time. Plus, if you decide to share the agenda with your customers, you've indicated in a powerful way just how serious you are about doing your job well and thoroughly.

Share the agenda with the other side before the negotiating session; ask whether they'd like to add or subtract anything from the agenda.

Creating the written agenda can be an art form unto itself. Here are some guidelines:

1. **Scrawl out all the things you want to talk about and everything you want to find out that you don't already know.**

2. **Check off the items you want to include on the written agenda.**

   Information you want to extract from the other side goes into your private notes, not on the written agenda that goes to everyone involved in the negotiation.

3. **When you know what you want to talk about, determine the order.**

   Start a session with things that fall in one of the following categories:

- Items that are more factual and less subject to negotiation. For example, the couple is going on vacation and wants the work done in their absence.

- Items that are less emotional and easier to reach a consensus on.

- "Threshold" items, those on which you must reach agreement in order for a deal to be made at all. If, for example, the item must be manufactured in the United States but all your factories are in Peru, you help your customer find the right manufacturer; or your customer needs financing to buy the car, so you help them get pre-approval on a loan.

An agenda *suggests* the order in which issues will be discussed but does not dictate the order. If controversy arises on a particular point, an agenda enables you to easily move past the point and come back to the dispute later. An agenda also prevents such sensitive points from being permanently swept under the rug. Don't be upset if someone else reorganizes your perfect order, especially if you aren't in charge of the meeting.

4. **Make enough copies of the agenda for everyone at the meeting.**

Make extra copies for people who wanted to attend but could not or were not included. Make additional copies for note taking and filing.

Leave a lot of white space on the agenda. It encourages note taking.

The psychology of meeting planning could span volumes. The easiest shortcut is to set your agenda intuitively. Then close your eyes. Picture the table. Envision the faces. See the meeting start. Play it through in your mind. Create a comfortable rhythm to the meeting.

Leaving Enough Time

How much time to allocate for a negotiation session or for the entire negotiation is always a tricky matter because you aren't in control of the other side. If you want to have the negotiation over by a certain time, say so upfront. If a good reason exists for your desire, state that also. Leaving more time than you actually need for a negotiating session is always better than allocating too little time. You can always use the extra time for something else if you've overestimated the time that a negotiating session will take. Leaving enough time in a sales scenario is particularly important. Often, the close is accomplished by sitting quietly until the customer says, "I do."

Negotiating across cultures

Today, very few salespeople get through a month without at least one sales session with someone from another culture. Generally, an international deal takes longer to complete than the very same domestic deal. Be prepared to spend twice as long to complete such a deal. Several factors create a need for this extra time.

✔ **There are cultural differences related to time.** Latinos, for example, have a more casual attitude toward time than the stop-watch Brits.

✔ **Both sides proceed more cautiously as they assess the cultural differences between the parties.**

✔ **Language differences take time, even if both parties are speaking the same language but with different accents.**

✔ **Fatigue sometimes sets in when a host pushes a special event each evening — as is common when entertaining visitors from abroad.**

Remember: Don't forget to take into account the different attitudes toward time around the world. Be sensitive to the differences, celebrate the diversity, and never lose a deal by misreading a cultural cue.

Preparing Yourself

You're the most important element in this negotiation. Even if you're the assistant to the assistant to the assistant, your performance at the negotiation is more important to you and your future than any room, agenda, or seating arrangement. Don't shortchange yourself. Take some time out of checking on all the arrangements to check on yourself. This concern for self is an important investment that pays off handsomely.

Being alert

To negotiate at your best, you must be well rested and alert. Here's why:

✔ You're more likely to be quick witted and able to respond to questions or attacks.

✔ Your concentration and ability to listen are improved.

✔ You won't be rushing to tie things up so that you can get home or get to bed.

Traveling smart

Don't be penny-wise and pound-foolish when it comes to long-distance travel for negotiations. Here are some suggestions:

✔ If you're taking the red-eye, try not to set your first negotiation session for a 7:30 a.m. breakfast. Give yourself some time to go to your hotel, shower and freshen up, and gather your thoughts for a 9 a.m. meeting.

✔ If you can't get enough rest on an airplane to function well the next day, travel the day before.

✔ When going overseas to negotiate, if you can, give yourself one and preferably two days to get over jet lag.

✔ If possible, never change planes on a business trip.

If your company makes all travel arrangements or has cost-saving measures in place that limit your travel options, you still need to do everything you can to be fresh upon arrival. It's your commission that's at stake, not the bean-counters' back at the home office. Adjust your watch to the new time zone as early as possible and eat light. On a cross-country trip, never sleep going east. Take a sleep aid at your new destination to get your body in the right time zone. When you fly internationally, look into the various jet-lag-fighting aids that are available today, and take advantage of them!

Your performance at any negotiation is aided by a good night's sleep. Sometimes, getting that sleep is easier said than done. If you find yourself thinking about a negotiation just when you want to go to sleep, try this trick: Pull out a pad and jot down your thoughts. Keep going until you've cleaned out your mind. Often, this exercise enables you to doze off and secure some much-needed rest.

Dressing for success

The rules, when it comes to dressing for a negotiation, are really very simple:

✔ **Don't dress to distract.** You're not there to show off your personal style, wow them with your funky jewelry, or draw their eye to your well-toned body. You're in a negotiation. You want people to listen, and you need their eyes as well as their ears. Women pull the listener's eyes away from their faces if they wear dangling earrings or expose any cleavage. Men never improve a business environment with gold chains or a sport shirt open to reveal that remarkable chest. Although this attire may get you attention elsewhere, it doesn't contribute one bit to your negotiating position.

If a particular type of outfit works for you on vacation or at a party, more power to you. But don't confuse those casual social environments with the negotiating environment of the business world.

✔ **Dress to build rapport.** In business negotiations, you want the other parties to consider you to be a person they can connect with, someone who understands, someone who is simpatico. Part of appearing simpatico is dressing like the client dresses. If you're negotiating in a conservative industry and your clients wear dark suits, wear the same type of attire. If you're negotiating with an artsy, architectural firm in its beachfront, converted-garage office, a business suit may not be the best choice because it could separate — and possibly alienate — you from the client. In that case, go for a little flair: a pantsuit with artsy jewelry or a suit jacket rather than a traditional pinstriped suit. Sometimes, a power suit is jeans and a sweater, if that's what your counterpart is wearing.

Sometimes outside circumstances get in the way of these good ideas. Maybe the only time you can see a client is en route to a black-tie affair. In this case, merely explain the monkey suit or evening gown as the first order of business. This kind of opening explanation can actually enhance the deal making because the client will appreciate the extra effort you made to take care of his matter in spite of the other demands on your time.

Mirroring your environment

As you prepare yourself for your first negotiating session, try to mirror your environment: Respectfully absorb what's around you. Sink into the surroundings. Become a part of them. Some negotiators even adapt to the pace of the speech. In New York, where people tend to talk fast, good negotiators speed up their pace a bit; in the South, where people tend to talk slowly, good negotiators slow it down a few notches. (Don't go so far as trying to take on the local accent unless you happen to be Meryl Streep.) Above all, know that good manners are different from place to place. When in Rome, do as the Romans do — out of respect for the Romans, not to one-up them.

If the negotiation involves a meal, it's not enough to just mind your manners, because manners differ from household to household and country to country. You may have to learn new manners, especially if the meal is on foreign turf. It never hurts, in such circumstances, to wait a beat while the host leads the way and then follow that lead.

Taking Control from the Moment You Walk through the Door

No matter how sleep deprived, harried, or down in the dumps you may be, always enter the negotiating room perky and assertive. Establish confidence and control from the opening moment. That moment sets the tone for the entire meeting. This fact is true even if you aren't officially in charge of the meeting. These guidelines can vault the most junior person at a meeting to MVP status almost immediately.

Never forget the pleasantries. If the last negotiating session ended on a bad note, clear that away first. Otherwise, you run the risk that unrelated matters may ignite the controversy all over again. If you can resolve the situation upfront, you can move forward unfettered. Ignoring such a situation just leaves the ill will hovering over the negotiating table. The bad feelings creep into and influence every conversation. The negativity taints all the proceedings until it has been cleared away.

Here are some guidelines for opening a meeting effectively:

- ✔ Make sure that all participants are present and ready to listen.
- ✔ State your purpose for having the meeting.
- ✔ State the items on the agenda and their time allotments.
- ✔ Make a clear request for agreement on the agenda and procedure.
- ✔ Acknowledge the participants' attitudes and feelings as they relate to your purpose.
- ✔ Summarize your desired outcome and begin according to the agenda.

Chapter 3

Keeping Your Emotions in Check

▶ Taking time out during high-tension situations

▶ Dealing with strong emotions that can undermine your composure

▶ Finding ways to take control of stress

All master negotiators possess a certain skill that intimidates, inspires awe, or just plain leaves others in the dust. This essential negotiating skill is hard to discern as you sit with a master negotiator, but you know it's there. So, what differentiates master negotiators from very good (or merely lucky) negotiators? The ability to maintain emotional distance from whatever is being discussed.

The best way to maintain emotional distance in a negotiation is through a technique called *pushing the pause button.* Knowing when and how to push the pause button not only endows you with an aura of composure and confidence but also gives you control over all the critical points of the negotiation. This chapter gives you the details on how to use the pause button effectively. It also discusses the emotions that commonly arise in any negotiation and suggests ways to handle them in yourself and others.

Pushing the Magic Pause Button

Pushing your pause button is just a method of keeping some emotional distance during high-stress situations — at home, at work, anywhere you need a little space. Basically, the concept at the core of this technique is that waiting is good, that doing nothing is sometimes the right action. The idea is encapsulated in this maxim: "If you're getting stressed out, don't just do something . . . sit there."

The purpose of the pause

Pushing the pause button just means putting the negotiations on hold for a moment or an hour or an evening while you sort things out. Everyone owns a pause button, so to speak, and everyone pushes it in a different way.

When you push the pause button, you freeze-frame the negotiation — much as you freeze-frame a DVD with your remote control. You step away, physically or psychologically, to review the work you've done up to that point and check over your plan for the rest of the negotiation. You take a break. This break may be purely mental and imperceptible to the other side, but you give yourself whatever time you need to review matters before you continue.

This focused review is a separate activity from the other basic elements of negotiation. It gives you an opportunity to regroup, catch your breath, and be sure that you aren't missing anything. The pause button gives you that little bit of emotional distance that allows you to make the decisions you want to make in your business and your life.

Pushing the pause button gives you the opportunity to review the entire process of negotiating and to make sure that you aren't overlooking anything. It allows you to avoid getting boxed into a corner. By pushing the pause button, you keep your emotions from ruling (and ruining) the negotiation.

Knowing how to use your pause button is so important that you may want to make a pause button that you can carry with you. One side can contain nothing other than the word *pause* or the capital letter *P*. Whenever negotiations get heated, having this card with you should serve as a reminder to press your internal pause button. On the back of this card, write down the six basic skills of negotiation: preparing, setting limits and goals, listening, pushing the pause button, communicating clearly, and closing. After you press pause is a good time to review these skills as they relate to the negotiation at hand.

Telling the other person that you need a pause

Everyone has a different way of pushing the pause button. Sometimes, how you push pause depends on the situation:

- ✔ **Ask for a night to think the negotiation over.** Most people will respect your request to "sleep on it."

- ✔ **Excuse yourself to the restroom.** Who's going to refuse *that* request?

✔ **For a short break, just lean back in your chair and say, "Wait a minute, I have to take that in."** For a dramatic touch, try closing your eyes or rubbing your chin.

✔ **In a business situation, having someone with whom you have to consult before giving a final answer is a convenient excuse for pressing pause.** Simply say, "I'll have to run this by my partner (or consultants or whatever) and get back to you tomorrow morning."

Admitting early in the negotiation that you don't have final authority is often beneficial. Make it clear that someone above you must approve the decision. That way, the other party won't get angry with you. Working this information into the beginning of your negotiating institutionalizes the pause button and sets the tone for a thoughtful, considered negotiation.

Taking notes is helpful at many points in a negotiation. One of the best times to pull out your pen is when you need to pause. Writing down statements that are confusing or upsetting is an excellent way to push the pause button. Instead of blurting out an inappropriate or angry response, tell the speaker to hold on while you write down the statement. Asking the other party to check what you've written to be sure that you got it right can be enormously effective if the words upset you because they indicate a bias against you or your company. The process of putting those words to paper almost always causes the other party to backtrack, amend, or, better yet, erase the words altogether. You'll find that most people don't want their biases on paper for all the world to see.

Knowing when to pause

Your first practical opportunity to use the pause button arrives before you participate in the first session of a negotiation. Ask yourself whether you're as prepared as you need to be. Then, when the first sentence is uttered, you're ready to listen because you've pushed that pause button. When you speak your first words, you're more clear for having taken that break.

Use the pause button at each critical moment to review the negotiation or to decide when to close a deal. Definitely use the pause button whenever you're feeling pressured or under stress.

Parties can get caught up in the emotions of a negotiation. They're afraid to lose face. They become angry or distrustful of the other party. They fall in love with the deal and ignore facts that are important to decision making — especially if the decision ought to be to walk away. They let their own moods, or the moods of the other party, rule the negotiating sessions, causing the negotiations to wander off course. These problems disappear when you use a pause button.

Don't be an animal — remember your pause button

The pause button is one thing that separates people from animals. A cat, for example, doesn't have a pause button. When it hears the sound of the electric can opener, it may go nuts, meowing, jumping, clawing at your legs. The cat is unable to push the pause button and think, "Before I expend all this energy, is that my tuna fish or yours?"

Of course, sometimes even we humans forget that we have pause buttons — especially when someone else is pushing our buttons. For example, you ask a co-worker to do something, and she responds, "That's not my job." Feeling your blood pressure rise, you may be tempted to blurt out, "Well, it's not mine either, blockhead!"

This response may come to your mind, but it doesn't have to come out of your mouth. You have a pause button. When you push it, your realize that, if you utter your first response, you won't get the job done and you may alienate the co-worker. (**Remember:** Friends come and go; enemies accumulate.) So instead you say, "I understand."

And you do: The person feels overworked and underpaid — who doesn't? Then you may say, "I know that you're swamped, but this thing has to get done to meet the deadline. Can you give it any time at all?" And the negotiation begins. Now you have a chance of getting what you want.

The moral of this story: Every cat ought to have a paws button.

If you want to watch a negotiator with his hand firmly on the pause button, rent the HBO movie *Barbarians at the Gate*. This film stars James Garner as the president of Nabisco and depicts his efforts to buy the company. Unfortunately for him, another buyer — played by Jonathan Pryce — is better prepared and carries a pause button with him everywhere. Watch him make millions of dollars by delaying a deal one hour. The main things that separate the winner and the loser are preparation and the effective use of the pause button.

Pausing before a concession

Every request for a concession calls for pushing the pause button. Your moment of reflection gives the concession some significance. You must treat the concession as significant, or you aren't perceived as having made a concession; the other party doesn't realize they've gained anything. No concession is unimportant. By emphasizing each concession in your own mind, you haven't given ground for naught.

Pausing prior to a concession is not just an act. A pause, no matter how slight, before making a concession gives the concession some importance. Of course, you want to be sure that you always have something to give up in order to hold on to what is important to you.

The obvious and easiest example is conceding a price too quickly. Too often, a quick concession robs the other party of the good feelings that they rightfully deserve after making a good bargain. It leaves the other party feeling that they priced the article too low and that they could have gotten more if they'd been smarter. Although that may be true, what advantage is it to you that they feel that way? None. Worse, now they're out to prevent that mistake from occurring the next time you negotiate, or they compensate by taking a hard line on another aspect of the deal.

Pausing under pressure

Some negotiators use pressure to get what they want from you. Don't give in to these pressures. Tell whoever is bullying you into reaching a decision that, if you're not allowed to use your pause button, you're not going to negotiate with him at all. Sometimes, the pause button is your only defense against being pressured into making a decision based on someone else's deadline.

Decisions made under artificial pressures — especially time pressures imposed by the other side in a negotiation — are often flawed, simply because the decision maker doesn't have sufficient time to consult that most personal of counselors, the inner voice.

Unfortunately, many people still allow themselves to be pressured into making a decision before they're ready to do so. You don't have to answer every question the moment it's asked. You have the right to take the time you need. Anyone trying to keep you from using the pause button is, in effect, trying to interfere with your decision making. If you find yourself in such a situation, give yourself permission to pause. Don't say, "I can't decide." Say, "I'm going to think over everything you've said and get back to you tomorrow."

If you're feeling pressure to reach a decision immediately, you can even push the pause button to assess whether you need to push the pause button. Take a few moments to consider whether the pressure for a speedy response is reasonable. Certain external circumstances do require immediate decisions — but they are few and far between.

What to do when you pause

Of course, the pause you take is only as valuable as what you do during it. Ask yourself specific questions during these brief respites. Circumstances differ for every negotiation. Usually, you need to ponder a specific point. You also may want to use the time to check over the other essential skills in a negotiation:

- ✔ **Prepare.** Do you need any additional pieces of information?

- ✔ **Set limits.** Are the limits you previously set still viable considering the additional information you have acquired during the negotiation?

- ✔ **Listen.** Did you hear everything the other person said? Did it match up with the body language and everything else that occurred during the negotiation?

✔ **Be clear.** Is there anything that you wish you had expressed more clearly or directly?

✔ **Know when to close.** Have you had plenty of time to live with the final proposal before accepting it?

When you become conscious of pushing the pause button and what to do during the pause, such a quick review as the preceding one is almost automatic. Sometimes, you're just giving your mind a break. Sometimes, you're pushing the pause button for everybody involved in the negotiation, especially if things have gotten a little heated.

When you're not the only one to pause

Your awareness of the pause button sets you apart from other negotiators. But don't worry if the other side is also aware of this technique. Don't think of the pause button as a top-secret weapon, because when your negotiating counterparts have their own pause buttons, the negotiations proceed even more smoothly and come to a more satisfactory resolution. Allowing the other party to push the pause button, or pushing your own pause button, makes the negotiating process more focused, effective, and pleasant for everyone involved.

Sometimes, you have the strong sense that the other person needs to push the pause button. Never say so in so many words. Instead, be very explicit about your need to take a break. Mince no words: "I need a break" or "You know, things are getting a little heated in here — can I take five?" or "Let's call it quits for a while — can we get together tomorrow morning to pick this back up?"

When someone else asks for a break, be very cautious before you resist it. If a person needs thinking time or needs a moment to regroup, allow it. In fact, take a break yourself. But be alert. If you conclude, after one or two breaks, that the other party is unfocused or isn't paying attention, you may decide to try to extend a session. You have to distinguish between the other party using a pause button and the other party just being restless or tired.

Handling Hot-Button Issues

Everybody experiences emotions and responses. Just because you're involved in a negotiation doesn't mean that you'll remain cool, calm, and collected throughout. In fact, the more important the negotiation is to you on a personal level, the more likely it is to stir up your emotional responses.

The ability to respond emotionally is a part of every healthy human being. When you feel emotions welling up inside you, having control means that you choose to use these emotions to your advantage, instead of allowing them to send you to the locker room in defeat or cause you to blow up.

To negotiate masterfully, you must stay in control of your emotions. This means having the confidence to take control in the first place and the skill to channel your emotions effectively as the negotiation progresses. You can usually do this — with one exception: when people or situations push your hot buttons. *Hot buttons* are stimuli that trigger a response of resistance and cause you to be tempted to go out of control.

Negotiators (and, in fact, humans in general) deal with many different emotions all the time. The following sections discuss the most common hot buttons that come up during (and often get in the way of) negotiating.

Pushing the pause button on anger

Negotiations naturally involve a risk of being upset. When people don't get what they want, one natural response is to get angry. Everyone knows what it feels like: the pressure literally builds inside the body. You feel like exploding — and sometimes you do. However, you have the ability to express anger calmly, but firmly. Anger is often useful in helping determine your limits. (Truth be told, you usually get angry because you allowed someone to cross your limits.)

When you're genuinely angry at something that happened in a negotiation, letting the other side know is usually best. This advice doesn't mean that you go ballistic. If you don't consciously and calmly express your anger, it will slip out anyway, in a more destructive way. Here is what you do: Use *I* statements. For example, say, "I feel really angry because. . . ." Avoid *you* statements such as, "You are wrong because. . . ." *You* statements invariably escalate the emotional charge in the situation.

A prime factor in effective negotiation is the honest communication between the parties. If you're truly angry about something that has happened, you need to tell the other side. People are not mind readers. They don't know when they have stepped over the line unless you tell them. Let some time go by, but don't let the point go, especially if your relationship with the other party is one that matters to you.

Using anger to reset limits

Not too long ago, a negotiator was negotiating the details of a major stage presentation scheduled to appear at one of the leading theaters in Los Angeles, which he represented. The producer and the negotiator for the theater had a two-page agreement covering all the big stuff — dates, ticket prices, and such. But they were having a devil of a time with the details.

The theater owner was talking directly with the producer over some technical points when tempers flared. With a rising voice and a "we'll teach you a lesson" tone, the producer told the theater owner that the production would just bypass Los Angeles altogether. Such a rescheduling actually would've been more convenient for the producer than sticking to the promise to come to Los Angeles on the agreed dates.

After a couple weeks, things had settled down. The theater owner didn't want to "make a stink about it," but the negotiator convinced him that the constructive comment was useful. The next time the negotiator talked to the producer's lawyer, he told her how wrong he thought her client's approach was. He calmly said that threats to break the written agreement really made him angry, that his client was angry as well, and that threats had no place in the relationship.

Her initial reaction was the same as the theater owner's: "Oh, that has all blown over. We didn't really mean it." The negotiator reiterated his position clearly and firmly. When she tried to minimize it, he told her he wasn't looking for an apology, but he felt he had to stick with the point until he was sure that she understood. By minimizing the situation, she gave the impression that she didn't understand that all the discussions had to take place on the premise that each side would live up to its commitments in the written (and signed) short-form agreement. She paused, and then finally said, "I understand."

The negotiator and theater owner never heard such a threat again, and they've negotiated more shows with the same company and expect to continue to work with them for years to come.

Note that the first outburst (in which the other party threatened to bypass Los Angeles) nearly blew the entire negotiation and damaged the relationship. The negotiator's statement (noting that both he and his client were angry about the way they'd been treated) went a long way to clear the air. Although no one apologized, the two parties reached an understanding and — to date, at least — no more threats were made.

Expressing enthusiasm

During negotiations, you'll feel very enthusiastic about things you want, and this feeling will bubble to the surface when you're offered that thing you're so excited about. The question is: Should you express your enthusiasm?

In a word, yes. Don't be afraid to show that you really want something, that you like it, that you think it's terrific, that you would do anything to own it, and so on. (This is especially true when you're buying a home, although most real-estate agents will tell you otherwise; very few people are interested in selling their homes to someone who doesn't appreciate it.)

But keep this caveat in mind: Always resist the temptation to gloat or make an outburst when you think that you've won a point. Gloating is expressing excessive satisfaction and tends to tell your counterpart that you defeated him. Gloating suggests to the other side that he shouldn't have made the deal. It's better to stay humble (not arrogant) even when you won every point. You don't want your counterparts to feel exploited. Just tell them how much you enjoyed working with them.

Many people are afraid that if they reveal how much they want a negotiation to end in their favor, they'll be taken advantage of. But as long as you properly prepare (refer to Book V, Chapter 1) and know how far you're willing to go, you can't be exploited. In fact, letting others know how much you want what they're selling can give you a great advantage. You can even get the seller to become sympathetic to your position when you reveal how much you want the item in question.

Acting assertively

Do you find expressing what you want and need difficult? Are you unable to respond at times when you think you should? Are you frustrated by a feeling of powerlessness in some day-to-day negotiations? You don't need to change your basic communication style to make your needs known. You can be direct softly and appropriately.

The art of being *assertive* is a crucial skill, involving the ability to confidently and comfortably express your wants and needs without hurting or being hurt. Many people didn't learn the art of being assertive as children. In fact, many people had their assertiveness deprogrammed. As a result, they're ill prepared to meet the challenges of the workplace, where people need to get results through other people. Priorities compete for attention, and the squeaky wheel often gets the grease, especially in ego-driven environments.

Life is all about confronting challenges, standing your ground, and, most of all, having the courage to state clearly what you need and want.

In your life, you face the same choices over and over again — you must choose between telling the truth to someone who needs to hear it or keeping the truth tucked away unsaid. You must choose between being comfortable and safe or risking discomfort and even the loss of some of your perceived popularity in order to set your limits and get what you want. The payoff for taking the risk is better relationships built on trust and honesty.

Book V

Negotiating Skills Every Salesperson Should Have

Passion pays off

Expressing enthusiasm is important when a broadcaster wants to acquire a piece of programming. Oprah Winfrey launched OWN network in January 2011. She went to Sundance that year in a quest for "the best documentaries" available. She fell in love with *Miss Representation,* a documentary about how the media misrepresents women. The filmmaker was Jennifer Newsome, the wife of the lieutenant governor of California, both of whom were powerful advocates for women's rights. OWN was a startup operation and couldn't offer as much money as Jen was hoping to obtain. The entire OWN team expressed their enthusiasm and Oprah's personal enthusiasm for the film.

They talked about the type of the promotion they could do and the support they could provide to the education initiatives that Jen wanted to launch.

This approach works.

Not only did OWN acquire the television rights to *Miss Representation,* but it also acquired rights to a slew of other films that were screening at Sundance. Nobody is better than Oprah Winfrey at convincing folks of her genuine, heartfelt enthusiasm for a subject. She wears her passions on her sleeve — and it has paid off in every area of her life.

A lot of people confuse being assertive with being loud or rude or insulting or some mix of those things. Such boorish behavior may be obnoxious, but it often hides fear, lack of preparation, or a serious personality deficiency. After the explosion passes, you often discover someone who needs some education about the deal before them and the options on the table. So hit the ALT button:

✓ **Ask questions** to find out what is really bothering the other person.

✓ **Listen carefully** to be sure you understand the other party's position

✓ **Take a break** to gather your thoughts and your cool.

Dealing with discouragement

In a protracted negotiation, you must be prepared to face frustration again and again. Anything worth doing has the potential for triggering a great deal of frustration. Nothing of value is handed to you on a silver platter. As a salesperson, you know this better than anyone. Selling, even when it's done well, involves a great deal of rejection and failure, which can lead to feelings of frustration and discouragement.

So, how can you deal with the frustration that inevitably comes? By following these suggestions:

- ✔ **View failure as a learning experience.** Investigate the reasons for the failure. When you discover what went wrong, you can prevent those pitfalls from happening again.

- ✔ **Think of failure as the feedback you need to change direction.** Negative feedback (also known as rejection) is really just the information you need to get on course again. When a client tells you what she doesn't like, you have a place to start selling the benefits they should want to own.

If you take negatives personally, you'll undermine your own ability to respond in an effective way, and others around you will be hurt by your untimely explosions.

- ✔ **See failure as an opportunity to develop your sense of humor.** Can you remember having an absolutely disastrous negotiation? At the time, you probably wanted to crawl in a hole and never see daylight again. But what did you find yourself doing about two weeks down the road? Sure enough, after a little time to heal, you told the story to your peers, embellishing it to provide special effects, and everyone — including you — got a good laugh.

  When you're facing failure, you have to learn to laugh sooner rather than later. Laughter is a powerful tool in healing hurt feelings and wounded pride. As a matter of fact, when you share your humorous stories with other salespeople, you find out that similar things have happened to them. Misery loves company, you know!

- ✔ **Look at failure as a chance to practice techniques and perfect your performance.** When you do everything you were supposed to do and the client *still* doesn't decide to own your offering, you may think you got nothing for all your hard work. In reality, you got an opportunity to practice and perfect your skills. In those cases, look at the experience as an opportunity to practice.

- ✔ **View failure as the game you must play to win.** Selling is a percentages game — a game of numbers. The person who sees more people and faces more rejection also makes more money. So, even if you haven't gambled before, you begin to do just that when you get into the game of sales. With every "no" you hear, you're one step closer to hearing a "yes."

- ✔ **Remember LOA.** It's a little acronym that that can see you through slammed doors (even metaphorical ones) and dirty looks. LOA stands for the *Law Of Averages,* which dictates a certain number of successes for every group of attempts. Knock on enough doors, in other words, and you'll get the sales you desire.

Not failures — steps before success

Before he finally succeeded, Thomas Edison tried 2,386 different times to sustain light, using electricity. "Wasn't that discouraging?" he was often asked. "No," was his constant response. "Each time something did not work, I knew I was one step closer to success."

No one could use this new invention until Edison invented a distribution system, meters to measure the use of electricity, and devices to be sure that customers got the same strength of electricity no matter how far they were from the source. Edison experienced failure far more often than success — unless you consider each so-called failure to be a step toward the successful end.

Edison was able to do this because he kept the ultimate goal in mind. With the light bulb, his purpose was to find that elusive combination of filament and containers that would sustain light. He didn't care what the specific combination turned out to be, so he kept going when any particular combination failed to work. He knew that he would eventually find the answer. You can handle your own small setbacks when you stay focused on the larger objectives.

Handling Stressful Situations

There you are, in the same negotiation . . . again. A few people are stubbornly saying the same things they said last week, and you can't see any progress. "I hate being here," you begin to think. You start to worry about being late to your next appointment. Your face feels hot, and your temple starts to throb. Just then, someone says something about the computers being down (again) and that's why the new figures aren't ready yet. On top of it all, the room is terribly warm and, remember, you're never supposed to let them see you sweat. "These people don't know how to control the temperature," you think, glaring at strangers across the table. You feel your neck and shoulders tighten, and the throb in your right temple intensifies and spreads across your forehead. "My day is ruined," your internal voice declares. And it may be.

Stress is an internal response to an external event. All the people and situations in a negotiation make up the *external event,* and all your mental and physical reactions (including stress) are *internal responses.* Because the external events seldom are under your complete control, how can you change your internal response? Pretend to be happy when you're miserable or to like the people you can't stand? Not likely.

At war with yourself

Stress is caused by resisting what's going on around you. When you resist a stalled negotiation, a rude person, or an uncomfortable situation, you respond with three emotions: worry, anger, and resentment.

Notice that the first letters of these three words describe the stress response perfectly: WAR — that is, the war within you. If you look at a stressful event, you find that the worry, anger, and resentment are not a part of the event itself; the event is merely the trigger that sets off these three emotions *inside* you. Reread the example at the beginning of this section about meeting stress and try to distinguish the emotions from the events:

- ✔ **Worry:** You worry about being late. Are you going to a beloved, joy-filled place or to a place you'd rather not go, where you feel anxiety and pressure to perform? What's the worry really about — fear of reprisal or punishment? Is it perceived lack of choice on your part?

- ✔ **Anger:** You're angry at people you suspect aren't hearing you. Is the suspicion familiar? Do you often mistrust people — and yourself? Or is your anger related to the notion that you do more than most people and aren't properly recognized for your effort? Do you feel the duties you have in life are fairly distributed, or do you feel you do more than your share? Many external events can bring this anger to the surface.

- ✔ **Resentment:** You feel resentment at these people who don't know how to control the temperature in their own office! Are you often impatient with people who don't do things exactly as you do?

These emotions are human and normal. You gain control when you're aware of your emotions. When you ignore the WAR, the stress and tension builds up inside you. Awareness puts you in charge of your reactions.

Stop, look, and listen . . . before you have a cow

Are you someone who always seems to be stressed out? For example, do you resent strangers in the supermarket who always seem to be standing in a faster-moving line? How can you stop fuming and seething in the supermarket line and become the person pleasantly chatting with the customer ahead of you?

Take a look at your first reaction: resistance. Consider the opposite of this reaction — acceptance. Learn to accept. This doesn't mean you need to think, "Oh goody, a stalled negotiation!" It just means recognizing what's going on and your feelings to it; for example, "Ah — a stalled negotiation. That's one of the things that drives me crazy, and now I must deal with it." Use humor to accept your circumstances. Only when you accept a situation can you effectively act upon it. If you're busy resisting it, you're paralyzed.

Acceptance involves three steps: stop, look, and listen:

✔ **Stop.** Push the pause button. You can use it to gain control over an automatic emotional response.

✔ **Look.** Recognize that you're now experiencing one of your stress triggers. Then recognize that you have a choice about whether to get upset. *Look* also means to look at what you really want and ask, "Is being emotional going to help me get it?" Usually, the answer is no.

✔ **Listen.** Pay attention to what your inner self is telling you to do. Generally, if you don't like the deal you're being handed in a negotiation, you have three alternatives:

- Adapt yourself to the situation. Listen to what the person is saying. You may have unrealistic expectations about the time it takes some people to reach a resolution, and you may have to adapt to a delay.

- Alter the situation. Find alternative routes to your goal; prepare better before the negotiation starts.

- Avoid the situation. You usually can eliminate this option right away. Unless you avoid negotiations altogether, you can't avoid people and situations that may cause you to be overly emotional.

Your inner voice will tell you whether to adapt, alter, or avoid. Follow its advice and you'll no longer feel stress.

The best tool to handle emotional people is the empathetic statement. A sincerely empathetic statement shows that you're listening and defuses emotional people because, often, such people are being emotional to make their points heard. The empathetic statement is calming, comforting, positive, and specific. A good one takes only six seconds: "I understand how frustrating it is not to get the information when you want it." Six seconds. "I understand how easy it is to get impatient with that machine." Six seconds. "It sounds like you're very upset. It looks like you need our full cooperation." Six seconds. Not only do you defuse the other person, but you now have time to think of a response to achieve your goal while staying within your limits

Chapter 4

Telling It Like It Is

Raw power flows from the simple ability to be clear and accurate in every step of a negotiation, and the ability to communicate clearly is one of the six basic negotiating skills. Unfortunately, no one is born knowing how to express ideas clearly or even how to recognize that communications are veering off course. With practice, however, not only can you improve your communication skills, but you also can see how communication skills impact a negotiation and tell when your negotiation is faltering because of weak communication. This chapter is actually a short course in communication skills, showing you how to speak, write, and conduct yourself clearly at every stage of a negotiation.

Developing any skill takes practice. If you want to be the best at anything — whether it's improving your free throw or becoming a better negotiator — you need to practice the skills necessary to excel. To help you improve your ability to communicate clearly, this chapter contains activities you can perform.

Communicating Clearly

In many ways, clear communication is the other side of effective listening. Just as you can't listen *too* well, there is no such thing as being *too* clear. You can be too blunt, too fast, and too slow. You can't be too clear.

Being clear doesn't mean that you reveal your position at the earliest opportunity or that you lay out your limits as an opening salvo. Being clear simply means that when you speak, write, or otherwise communicate, your listener understands your intended message. Sounds simple enough. So, why aren't more people successful at it?

Most people communicate from the point of view of "What do *I* want to tell my listener?," which isn't effective. Instead, you should communicate by thinking, "What do I want my listener to do, think, or feel as a result of my communication?"

First, you must be clear with yourself about what your goals are. Then you must have information about who the listener is, what filters are in place, and how to get through those filters so that you can be understood. (See Book V, Chapter 1 for more on preparation.) Then you must present your information in a way that the other person can understand. The following sections offer strategies for making sure your message is crystal clear and advice on how to enhance understanding.

Presenting your ideas in a way the other person can understand

Present your ideas in an order that the listener can understand. You want the listener to be nodding in agreement with you as you speak. You don't want the listener to feel lost or unsure about where you're going. Be careful to lead the listener from point A to point B.

If this concept is new to you, try one of the simple techniques outlined in the following sections.

Using the P.R.E.P approach

P.R.E.P. stands for *point, reason, example, point.* Using this approach helps you organize your thoughts and communicate logically. This approach is great because you can use it in an impromptu fashion. Here's an example:

- ✔ **My point is:** My gizmo will save you money.

- ✔ **The reason is:** The power unit uses a lot less energy.

- ✔ **My example is:** Assuming electricity rates remain constant over the next five years and that your usage of gizmos remains constant over that same period, you'll save $6,822 by buying my gizmo instead of Joe's gizmo, and my gizmo is only $1,200 more.

- ✔ **So, my point is:** My gizmo will save you money.

Book V

Negotiating
Skills Every
Salesperson
Should
Have

This formula works with any presentation, from a 5-minute informal chat to a 30-minute formal speech using many examples. The P.R.E.P. approach is a great way to get organized and be clear.

Listing and numbering your points

Another strategy is to list and number your points. The following is an example:

> When you think about buying a new gizmo, consider
>
> 1. The cost over the life of the gizmo
>
> 2. Ease of use by your employees
>
> 3. Compatibility with all your other equipment

Numbering points in this way both focuses and organizes the discussion and lets your listener know exactly what to expect so that he can follow along easily.

If you use this technique, make sure you discuss the points in the given sequence. Veering away from the order you've so clearly delineated makes you look even less organized.

Checking your clarity

Most people consider themselves to be crystal clear in their communication with others. But if you truly want to know how understandable you are, you should consider taking a *clarity inventory*. This activity is one of the best ways to find out which areas you need to improve to be easily understood.

To take a clarity inventory, ask for feedback on how clear you really are from two sources: the members of your immediate family and your personal assistant or co-worker. Usually, these members of your inner circle are the most likely people in the world to understand what you're trying to say.

You need to take a clarity inventory only if you seriously want to improve your negotiating skills. If you aren't serious, just skip on. This topic is too sensitive and carries too much of a risk for hurt feelings to bother with unless you are serious in your desire to become a top-notch negotiator.

If, indeed, you want to build a real edge into your negotiations, sit down quietly with someone you trust. Tell that person that you're trying to improve your ability to communicate clearly. Ask for suggestions. Then listen. Don't correct, defend yourself, or explain.

Clear and to the point

Harry Truman was so clear with the American people that he became known as "Give 'em hell, Harry." Truman used simple language that everyone could understand.

Truman was equally clear with the Russians. In April 1945, preparing for the Potsdam Conference, he had his first personal exchange with Vyacheslav M. Molotov, the Soviet foreign minister, in Washington. The president used words of one syllable to convey his view that Poland had to be free and independent.

"I have never been talked to that way in my life," Molotov is reported to have said.

"Carry out your agreements, and you won't get talked to that way again" was Truman's retort.

Truman's blunt style created great successes in international negotiations.

Your goal is not to instruct the other person on how to understand you better. Your goal is to find out how to communicate better with this individual and with the other people in your life. Even if you believe that the entire communication problem is with the other person, don't let on.

Take notes when people give you feedback. The effort flatters them and gives you something to do rather than tell them they are wrong. Hearing how unclear you are is difficult. It hurts. You learn you fail far more often than you ever dreamed.

Knowing your purpose or goals

When you know exactly what you want to say, communicating clearly is much easier. In the past, you may have had the urge to say, "So, what's your point?" — usually with an exasperated tone. More often than not, a person who is asked that question looks surprised and fumbles for a good, one-sentence answer. When the speaker doesn't know the point, the listener is hopelessly lost.

In any communication, you should know the point and be keenly aware of the overall purpose or goal. Simply saying, "Oh, I just like to talk" is okay for recreational situations. But if you're in a negotiation, you need to have your short- and long-range goals in mind.

Book V

Negotiating
Skills Every
Salesperson
Should
Have

Cut the mumbo-jumbo

Some concepts are, by nature, just plain difficult to grasp. Sometimes, being clear requires creativity. Here are some suggestions that help you make listening easy and enjoyable for the other party:

✔ If you have many numbers to present, try putting them in graphs — bar, pie, or line charts. Keep the lists of numbers as a backup.

✔ Oversimplify technical points at first. You can explain fully later in the conversation, after you have your listeners hooked.

✔ Define jargon and spell out acronyms. Don't use "LAX," for example, if your audience isn't likely to know that LAX is the Los Angeles airport.

✔ Avoid references that may alienate your listener. In written materials, footnotes and appendixes serve the purpose of clarity. See the later section "Being clear in your written communication" for more information on how to convey your message clearly in writing.

Keeping your commitments

Being clear includes being consistent in the words you say and the deeds that follow. If you say one thing and do another, it's confusing. Your inconsistent conduct turns an otherwise clear communication into a real puzzlement. Keep each and every commitment that you make during a negotiation.

Keeping your commitments is the acid test of clarity; it's also the bedrock of trust. If you tell the other party that you'll call back at 9 a.m. tomorrow, be sure to call at that time. Breaking your promise calls your integrity into question and creates confusion about what you meant when you promised to call back at 9 a.m. Failing to keep your word is also upsetting for the other party. Such inattention may be considered, debated, and evaluated by the other side. Their loss of trust may call into question side issues and create tensions counterproductive to a negotiation.

If you're negotiating with someone on behalf of a client or company, failure to keep commitments is harmful to you and the party you're representing. This neglect can damage your relationship with your client or your standing within the company. Word often gets back about your unprofessional behavior. Sometimes when a person hasn't responded in a timely fashion, he'll falsely blame the professional negotiators on the other side for not returning calls or not providing documentation in a timely fashion. Don't provide grist for that mill.

Being clear in your written communication

The written word is often more useful than the spoken word when you want to communicate clearly. When you have something to say, write it down, look at it, edit it, and make it right. When the words are your own, you don't have to release them until they're as near to perfect as possible.

Many people believe they can't or don't know how to write as clearly as they speak, but this is rarely true. When you write instead of speaking the words, you can see more easily whether your message is unclear. You can see in black and white that the words are ambiguous or your thoughts are incomplete. Also, the written word doesn't allow for such conversational crutches as "ya know what I mean?" When used as a rhetorical question, this phrase doesn't clarify the issues. It moves the conversation deeper into confusion.

The process of putting your thoughts into writing brings you face-to-face with your failure to communicate clearly when you speak. Very few people are clearer when using the spoken word than the written word. Rather than bemoan your lack of writing skills, open your eyes and say honestly — maybe for the first time in your life — "Wow, I didn't realize how poorly I've been communicating my ideas."

The following sections offer advice that can ensure your written communications clearly convey your message.

Ensuring clarity by following basic rules

Here are some basic tips to get you on the road to clear written communication:

- ✔ Use short sentences.
- ✔ Use short words.
- ✔ Avoid jargon and abbreviations — even when you're writing to another professional in your field — unless the other person uses these terms exactly the way that you do.
- ✔ Complete your sentences.
- ✔ Stick to one idea per paragraph.
- ✔ Have a beginning, middle, and end to the overall communication.
- ✔ Be accurate.

Don't be afraid to number paragraphs to cover different points, but don't delude yourself into thinking that numbering paragraphs brings order to a document that otherwise lacks coherence or good sense.

Communicating like a journalist

When you think of clear writing, the most common reference point is your daily newspaper. From coast to coast, there is a consistency in stories written for the newspaper that seems to cross regional lines, ownership, and size of the newspaper. You may find it odd that so many journalists write in the same style with the same degree of clarity.

Actually, every school of journalism in the country teaches students about the "five horsemen" of journalism: *who, what, where, when,* and *why.* The journalist is supposed to answer these five questions in the first paragraph of a story. Each of the next five paragraphs should expand on the answer to one of the questions. The least important information appears at the end of the story. That way, if the story is too long for the available space in the newspaper, editors can just delete the end of the story, and no important information is lost.

To get the hang of how to draw out key points, look at a copy of one of the nation's leading newspapers such as *The New York Times* or *The Wall Street Journal.* Pick any story that interests you in the first section. (Why the first section? Because that section follows the traditional structure of news stories. Reporters depart from the structure in some of the special interest sections, such as the sports or entertainment sections.) Read the first paragraph and notice how the reporter explains:

- ✔ Who the story is about
- ✔ What the person did to land in the news
- ✔ Where the event happened
- ✔ When the event took place
- ✔ Why the event occurred

Read the last paragraph of the article and notice how trivial that information is compared to the first few paragraphs. Notice how the first few paragraphs after the lead paragraph are packed with important material compared with the information later in the story.

Use the same technique in your own communication, and you can't go wrong. ***Remember:*** You're providing the information your listener needs to know to achieve *your* goal. Organize the facts like a newspaper story.

Play Whisper

You may remember this game from your youth. Sometimes called Telephone or Rumor, this game is great for practicing listening and clarity skills. It also illustrates the dangers of believing a story handed to you through a number of different speakers.

First, come up with a one- or two-sentence story (you can pick a sentence right out of the newspaper). Whisper the story into the ear of the person on your left. That person repeats the story exactly to the next person, who then repeats it to the next person, and so on. The last person in the chain repeats the story aloud. Each additional person in the chain seems to add an individual twist to the story. Everyone has a good laugh when comparing the final story to the original. You can make the game more difficult by adding time pressure and distractions to the repetition process.

This game can produce a lot of laughs in a classroom, at a party, or at a dinner table. But at the negotiating table, miscommunication is no laughing matter.

Overcoming Barriers to Clarity

The biggest barriers to clarity are your own fears, lack of concentration, and certain phrases that immediately muddy the waters as soon as you utter them. For example, you fear that if you make yourself clearly understood, an adverse reaction will follow — some vague, unspoken, definitely unwanted reaction. Maybe you neglect to ensure your meeting will be free of interruptions, or you inadvertently use a phrase that undermines the rapport you're trying to build. By identifying the fears, distractions, and phrases that work against you, you can stop them from undermining the message you do want to communicate.

Fear of rejection

Fear is one of the biggest barriers to clarity. Everyone has a built-in fear factor. You may be afraid that if you present your ideas clearly, the listener will reject you or your conclusions. The natural inclination is to avoid rejection by blurring lines, being unclear, and failing to state your case accurately.

Instead, you postpone the inevitable. After all, when the listener eventually understands you, he rejects the concept with the added energy that comes from frustration. "Why didn't you say so?" he asks. "Why did you waste my time?" he demands. These are tough questions to answer.

If it's true that an accurate statement of intent would cause the deal to fall apart, being clear is even more important. When you close a deal without being clear, the parties have different understandings and expectations. You're finalizing a bad deal. In fact, you're closing a deal that can't possibly work.

Fear of hurting someone else

Often, people avoid hurting the feelings of others not out of compassion, but out of self-protection. Everyone wants to be liked; no one wants to be shunned. Toward that legitimate social end, you've probably learned to obfuscate with a vengeance.

Being clear and being confrontational are two different things. If you have bad news to deliver, do so with dignity and respect for the feelings of the person you're speaking to. Even if you feel, in every fiber of your being, that the person is overreacting to your news, don't say so. Let the feelings run their course. But don't flinch or amend your statement. Just wait. This, too, shall pass. Being clear in such situations takes strength and confidence. Never sacrifice clarity to avoid confrontation. Your desire to do so generally masks the real motive — which is to spare yourself the discomfort or trauma of delivering bad news.

Head to the later section "When You Have to Say No" for information on how to deliver a message that your listener doesn't want to hear.

General distractions

Other barriers to clarity can be fatigue, laziness in preparation, or the clutter of distracting interruptions.

- ✔ **Fatigue:** You may be just plain tired and unable to focus. Pay attention to your body's signals. Sometimes, a brisk walk outdoors revives you. Good nutrition and adequate rest are requirements for a master negotiator. If you eat right and get plenty of sleep, you can eliminate the need for cup after cup of coffee to stay alert. But, in a pinch, an occasional dose of caffeine works, too.

- ✔ **Laziness:** You may not have prepared well enough, and you're dreading being clear on some facts that are unsubstantiated. If this strikes a familiar chord, do your homework.

- ✔ **Interruptions:** Your listener may be doodling or not making eye contact. The room temperature may be extreme. Noise levels may be too high for you to be heard clearly. Hopefully, you're assertive enough to appropriately address or request changing these things.

If the conversation or negotiation is important, be sure that you're well rested, prepared, and in an environment where clear communications can be heard.

Inappropriate comments and phrases

Certain phrases go "clunk" against the ear every time you hear them. The sections that follow discuss phrases that have little place in life, let alone a negotiation.

When you hear these phrases, a yellow caution light should start flashing in your head. These phrases often indicate a situation that needs to be addressed. And if you hear one or more of these utterances come out of your mouth, stop immediately. Laugh about the slip or apologize, but don't assume that the listener doesn't have the same set of yellow caution lights that you do. Maybe the listener doesn't, but you can't take that risk.

"Trust me"

This overused phrase is now the hallmark phrase uttered in motion pictures by any character who is not to be trusted. People who say "trust me" are often the very people who don't deserve to be trusted.

When someone says "trust me" as a substitute for providing the specific details you requested, be very cautious. Ask again for a commitment. If the person balks, explain that it's not a question of trust, but an acknowledgment of the fact that circumstances change. Explain that the agreement must be enforceable, even if the current negotiators are no longer accessible. You want an agreement so clear that you don't have to trust the other person.

"I'm going to be honest with you"

So has this person been dishonest all along? This cliché is the cousin to the phrase, "I'm not going to lie to you." It makes you wonder, "Oh? Would you lie to someone else?"

William Shakespeare's great line delivered by Queen Gertrude in *Hamlet* is "The lady doth protest too much, methinks." Shakespeare knew a great deal about human nature. When people loudly declare their innocence, they almost always lose credibility, and those who are always reassuring you about their honesty probably aren't being very honest with you.

"Take it or leave it"

Even when you're making your final offer, presenting the deal as a "take it or leave it" proposition is a mistake. Even if the other side accepts the offer, the deal leaves them feeling bad about the decision. Yet some negotiators put this unpleasant tag on an offer that was otherwise okay. This label makes the offer sound bad even if the terms are reasonable.

Book V

Negotiating Skills Every Salesperson Should Have

 Don't let a bad negotiating style confuse you. If you hear this phrase, evaluate the offer on the merits, not on the way it was delivered. Especially if you're a professional negotiator, figure out whether the offer is acceptable based on what you want out of the negotiation. If you're negotiating for yourself, and you must continue working with your counterpart in this deal, you may want to consider whether you can maintain an ongoing relationship with a person who's bullying you with "take it or leave it" statements.

 If you're making a final offer, say so without using the antagonistic "take it or leave it" phrase. If you're feeling frustrated and anticipating a refusal, push the pause button (refer to Book V, Chapter 3). Calmly explaining the reasons that this must be the final offer is difficult. You're likely to use the verboten phrase *take it or leave it* or something similar and equally as off-putting. That approach hurts you in the long run because you look like a bully. And you don't increase the chance of your proposal being accepted.

A slur of any kind

Negative comments about the race, gender, or national origin of another person are no longer widely tolerated. A concern with being "politically correct" preoccupies many people. Some people are offended by any inquiry that could even identify these traits, such as "What kind of a name is that?" Unless you know differently for sure, steer clear of the most innocent of references unless they're relevant.

If the information is irrelevant, you should even avoid neutral statements such as, "The person was a woman" or "The man was from China." You may receive an angry response, such as "Just what is that supposed to mean?" or "Why did you mention that?" Worse yet, the person you're speaking to may think those thoughts without verbalizing them. This situation raises a barrier to communication that you won't even know exists.

 Even if you're with a group that seems to be quite open about expressing whatever they happen to think or feel about another group, don't join in. Be discreet. You never know who may be suffering in silence — feeling outnumbered and helpless.

 The last thing you want in a tough negotiation is to let an offensive phrase slip out just when you want to close. You can lose the deal you're working on *and* the trust and confidence of your counterpart in the negotiation. Unwitting slurs can stop a negotiation in its tracks. You may be pegged forever as a bigot — and some people don't negotiate with bigots. If you have some bad habits in this area, work on cleaning up your language.

Other communications faux pas that can really garble your message

Very few people strive to be bad communicators or deliberately muddle their messages. Most people, in fact, try to avoid quagmires and confusion in their lives. But even those with the best intentions still tend to do things that undermine their desire for clarity. To foster open and clear communication, avoid the behavior outlined in the following sections.

Raising your voice

If you want to get your point across, don't shout or scold. Both responses prevent any further intelligent discourse. This rule is particularly important when a language barrier is preventing someone from understanding you. When someone doesn't understand your language, the last thing you want to do is talk louder. *Loud* communicates the same message to people all around the world. *Loud* is disrespectful. *Loud* characterizes someone you don't want to do business with.

Leaving out details

Details let the other person know exactly what you want or need. Details also take time. Although you may be tempted to shave valuable minutes off the average communication by leaving out the details, doing so ensures that your message says fuzzy and poorly communicated. Plus, you'll probably spend *hours* cleaning up the messes that such an omission can create.

Not checking to see whether you were understood

One of the themes of this chapter is that people are often unaware when they're not being clear. Another theme is that, by adopting certain strategies, anyone can learn to communicate with clarity. One obvious way to determine whether your listener gets your message is to either ask ("Do you have any questions?" for example) or give the other person a chance to say, "I didn't understand xyz." Doing so gives you an opportunity to clarify any confusing issues.

Walking away and talking at the same time

Consider this bit of advice stage direction. Don't toss your request, instruction, or demand over your shoulder as you walk away from your listener. Doing so destroys virtually any possibility of being understood. Instead, make eye contact and look at the other person during conversation.

Not permitting any objections or questions

Some speakers don't leave time for questions, objections, or responses. The reasons for cutting off discussion? Lack of adequate preparation, a belief that the best way to reach a conclusion is to rush others to the end, or a fear

Book V

Negotiating
Skills Every
Salesperson
Should
Have

that any objections will kill the deal are often the culprits. Instead, be receptive to comments and questions; even those that are uncomfortable give you an opportunity to address any confusion that, once clarified, can help the conversation — or the deal — move forward.

When You Have to Say No

Sometimes, you just need to say no. Here's how to do it without alienating the person making the request: Imagine that your colleague Tom knocks on top of your cubicle partition, leans in, and asks, "Got a minute?" Instead of glancing at your watch and saying okay with a martyred sigh, you look up and analyze the request. You see his lower lip trembling and his eyes filling with tears. You know he wants to talk about his divorce — again — and you have a report to finish. You recognize that this will not be a 60-second interruption, no matter what he claims. You resist the reflexive hot-button response, "In your dreams, pal," because you depend on Tom in your job. A rapport with him is a priority for you. Use the following three steps:

1. **Acknowledge.**

   Tell him that you understand how he feels and what he wants: "Tom, you look upset — it looks as though you need to talk." This statement, which takes only six seconds to say, calms him because now he doesn't have to work to make you understand his feelings. You've said, in essence, "I understand your priority — and it's important" (another sentence that takes six seconds to say).

2. **Advise.**

   Let him know *your* priority — calmly and confidently. Say, "Tom, here's the situation. I have a report to finish for the boss, and it's due in half an hour." You've understood his need, and now you're asking him to understand yours. Many people, when told of your priority, will back off. But not Tom. That's why there's a third step.

3. **Accept or alter.**

   Accept the interruption with time limits ("I can give you five minutes") or suggest an alternative option ("I'll come to your cubicle after I finish the report").

This is the best way to say no. Use it as a model. You won't always be able to achieve the ideal outcome described, but try to come as close as you can.

With peers, you can suggest an alternative option, but what about with your boss? Tom will actually thank you and go away happy. With the boss, your best option is almost always to accept. The boss's priorities *are* your priorities — it's in the job description. However, don't leave out the second step. Always advise the boss of your activities and priorities. Sometimes, the boss is grateful for the information and withdraws the request or removes some of your existing obligations. Other times, you're expected to do all the work anyway. Advising puts the burden on the boss to say which task is to be done first. Never skip that step. Head to the later section "Too busy to be clear" for step-by-step instructions on how to get clarity from a superior.

Steering Others to Clarity

When the other party is not being clear, your job is to steer that person toward concise communication. Don't just toss him this book (although it may make a nice gift). Coax from your counterpart a clear statement of intentions, wants, and needs. Your technique for acquiring this information depends on the type of person you're dealing with. The following sections contain some tips for accomplishing this important task. Each section is devoted to a personality type you may encounter.

Tangent people

Some people are not clear because they ramble; that is, they go off on a tangent. In this situation, do the follow:

- ✔ **Listen up to a point.** You're listening especially for a good break point. You're listening for a point when you sense that the message has been completed. Granted, this type of person can go on and on and on, and you'll hear many false endings. Grab the second or third one you hear (you have to let this type ramble a little bit, so don't stop on the first). Although extreme cases do exist (you can read about those shortly), most ramblers will tell their story.

    In extreme cases, you won't be able to find a point because the tangent talker goes too far afield. Just say, "I'm sorry. I'm lost. I'm having a hard time relating all of this to [whatever is being negotiated]."

- ✔ **Be assertive when you interrupt.** Jump in with a purpose and with a positive statement. Here are some useful ones:

    Let me summarize back to you to be sure that I understand.

    So, if I understand what you're saying, you want me to. . . .

    If I'm hearing you correctly, you're deeply concerned about. . . .

    When you get an affirmation that you've correctly untangled the message, you can give your response — and give it quickly, before the rambler

Book V

Negotiating
Skills Every
Salesperson
Should
Have

starts at it again. If that happens, just say "Wait, Wait, I need to address your last point."

✔ **Your first statement should be a validation.** "Yes, you're right. Now, as to the purpose. . . ." That's how you get people with this type of communication pattern back on track.

Sometimes clients try to tell their stories too fast and use _he_ and _she_ and _them_ and _those_ frequently and without identifying who _he, she, them,_ and _those_ are. This makes it impossible for you (or anyone else, for that matter) to keep the players straight. In that situation, try this: "Wow. Too many pronouns. I can't follow who did what to whom. Let's back up and try to help me out by naming the players." Deliver that with a great big smile, so it isn't offensive. Or, for a softer (and safer) approach, try this: "I'm sorry — I believe I lost track of who you were referring to in your story. Let me see if I have this right. . . ."

Interrupters

These people even interrupt themselves. They lose their train of thought while they're speaking. With an interrupter, use these techniques:

✔ Take careful notes while an interrupter is talking.

✔ Concentrate and stay focused.

✔ Keep reminding him of the most recent statement before the interruption. Don't leave until you get a specific answer.

✔ Be appropriate, but keep pressing with your own specific questions.

Unprepared people

Some people may have difficulty getting fully prepared for negotiations. To ensure that you can get the information you need, your recourses are to

✔ **Postpone the meeting.** If the other party isn't prepared enough to provide the information you need, holding the meeting anyway is just a waste of everyone's time. Postponing the meeting gives her more time to prepare.

✔ **Conduct the meeting at the unprepared party's office.** Tactfully invite your counterpart's support people who may know more about the subject.

Too busy to be clear

These important people don't think they can take the time to be clear. They save minutes, but others may spend hours trying to figure out what they want and need. If you encounter this type of person, these strategies may help:

- ✔ **Schedule meetings at the beginning of the day.** Doing so avoids distractions and ensures everyone's full attention.

- ✔ **Guard against interruptions.** You can request that he hold his calls for ten minutes, for example, in order to get information.

- ✔ **Be efficient in meetings.** Have a written agenda even for a two-person meeting. The agenda shows others how much you value their time.

- ✔ **Show you're taking notes and recording comments.** Any inconsistencies will show up right away, and you can say "My notes don't make sense." And then point out the reason why. Or you can say, "I need some help here. I thought I heard you say X, but I just wrote down Y. Where did I go wrong?" Never blame the other person. You can blame your pesky note taking.

- ✔ **Be appropriate, but keep pressing for the details you need.** Apologies really help here. "I'm sorry, I really need to know how long it will take to survey the property. That will be the first thing my boss will ask me, and if I don't know, you and I will just have to start over." There is always someone up the chain of command you can blame for your need to know.

Sometimes, you need to steer your boss to clarity. The next time the boss slams papers on your desk and says, "We need this yesterday," do the following:

1. **Stifle the urge to answer "In your dreams."**

2. **Answer immediately.**

   Respond with a positive, "Yes, absolutely — will do." After all, this *is* the boss. And this reply will relax your employer because it's what any boss wants to hear.

3. **Ask for prioritization.**

   This step is essential: Because you're already *fully aware* of your priorities and the allotted time to accomplish them, answer, "Here's the situation, Boss. I've got these other two priorities you want by 3 p.m. today. Which of these can be put off until tomorrow?"

By following these steps, you've forced the boss to be clear. Your boss needs to prioritize — that's a boss's job. Sometimes, your boss will go away without making any further demands, realizing that you're already working on important projects.

Chapter 5

Win-Win Negotiating

*I*n the commonly used sense of the term, a *win-win negotiation* is a deal that satisfies both sides. In an ideal world, a win-win agreement is the only kind of deal that would ever close. Even in today's world, the vast majority of negotiations end in win-win situations.

Win-win negotiating does *not* mean that you must give up your goals or worry about the other person getting what he wants in a negotiation. You have your hands full looking out for your own interests. Let others bear the primary responsibility for achieving their goals. So, up to the point when a deal is about to close, look out for yourself. With style, respect, and intelligence, passionately pursue your goals. Hopefully, your opponent is doing the same thing. Nobody can figure out what is best for you better than you can. Nobody can figure out what is best for the other party better than the other party can. Before you close the deal, however, step back to be sure that you have a win-win solution.

Sometimes, you feel that you've done everything right in a negotiation, and the deal still won't close. The other side isn't interested, or gets angry, or goes off on tangents, or isn't available, or is making unreasonable or unrealistic demands, or, or, or. . . . This chapter looks at mishaps that occur in a negotiation to keep a deal from closing.

Creating Win-Win Negotiating

Some negotiations are pretty straightforward in terms of the interests of each party. When you're buying a car from someone who wants to sell a car, the negotiation is win-win if you find a price that works for each of you. In more complicated negotiations, the answers aren't always so easy to find. Sometimes, some head scratching and imagination are required.

Because creative thought is often necessary to arrive at win-win solutions, the best negotiators in a tight spot are generally people who enjoy games or riddles — people who enjoy figuring things out. This isn't to say that the only good negotiators are those with a Rubik's Cube lying around the house somewhere. But it does help if you enjoy the challenge of figuring out what serves both sides because the solutions aren't always easy.

To ensure a win-win resolution to your negotiations, heed the advice in the following sections.

If you're going to close the deal, be sure that the deal is positive for both parties. If you're thinking about walking away from the negotiation, double check that you aren't overlooking some way to achieve a mutually satisfying outcome. This may be one of the more valuable moments in the entire negotiation.

Know the difference between good and bad deals

Finding a win-win solution is difficult if you don't even know when your own team is winning. You may be surprised how many people can't tell the difference between a good deal and a bad deal. That situation should never be the case if you keep these definitions in mind:

- ✔ **A *good deal* is one that is fair under all circumstances at the time the agreement is made.** It provides for various contingencies before problems arise. A good deal is workable in the real world.

- ✔ **A *bad deal* is not fair under all the circumstances.** It allows foreseeable events to create problems in the relationship after the deal is struck. Some aspect of the agreement looks great on paper but simply doesn't work out in the real world — for reasons that were predictable during the deal-making process.

What is and isn't fair is very subjective. The parties must decide for themselves whether an agreement is fair based on their own criteria. Make sure that everyone is in agreement. Draw the other side out on this basic point before closing the deal. You don't want to sign a deal with someone who is harboring resentments over some aspect of the agreement. Be sure that the other side agrees that the deal is a good one.

When you work in a culture other than your own, being sure that you have a win-win solution takes a little extra effort. During a cross-cultural negotiation, be thorough in your investigation of what is and isn't acceptable. In Japan, for example, people are accustomed to the team approach used in the workplace.

Concern for the company's good overrides individual interests. In Japan, you're less likely to hear, "That's not my job." Sometimes, however, the cross-cultural aspect of a negotiation makes a solution harder to find.

Ask yourself some key questions

To be sure that you have a good deal and a win-win situation, take a break just before closing (push the Pause button — see Book V, Chapter 3). Ask yourself the following questions:

- ✔ Does this agreement further your personal long-range goals? Does the outcome of the negotiation fit into your own vision statement?

- ✔ Does this agreement fall comfortably within the goals and the limits you set for this particular negotiation?

- ✔ Can you perform your side of the agreement to the fullest?

- ✔ Do you intend to meet your commitment?

- ✔ Based on all the information, can the other side perform the agreement to your expectations?

- ✔ Based on what you know, does the other side intend to carry out the terms of the agreement?

In the ideal situation, the answer to all these questions is a resounding *yes*. If you aren't sure about any of them, take some extra time. Review the entire situation. Assess how the agreement could be changed in order to create a *yes* answer to each question. Try your best to make the change needed to get a firm *yes* to each question.

When you have a yes response to each of the questions, close the deal. Don't go for any more changes or risk the deal by bringing up a new point, no matter how inconsequential. Even if you think that the other person wouldn't mind, you never know!

If you can't alter the deal so that you can answer yes to each question, be very thoughtful before closing. If you decide to go forward, write down exactly why you're closing the deal anyway. For example, you may have a project or piece of property that no one wants except the person you're talking to right now. Your choice is to wait or accept less favorable terms. Your choice. Just write down why you're making the choice so that you don't become part of that army of people with tales of exploitation. This exercise is particularly helpful to your state of mind if the results don't work out — you have a record as to why you took the deal. You won't be so hard on yourself.

What win-win negotiating doesn't mean

Some people use the term *win-win* to justify caring too much and too early about a counterpart's feelings and sacrificing their own needs and goals on the altar of conciliation.

No book or informed advocate promotes giving up or subordinating your goals in the name of taking care of the other person. Always assume that there are two equal adults in the negotiation — unless, of course, you're negotiating with a child. Then you really want to hang on to your objectives. Let the child set the agenda, and you lose before you ever begin.

If you're someone who tends to be too concerned about the other party's welfare in a negotiation, be aware that sometimes, your own goals can be smothered in the process. In a negotiation, you must allow other people to take care of themselves. You don't have to make things "nice" for everyone. That's not a negotiator's job. Your job is to get what you want. Remaining true to that objective may involve upsetting someone. Part of negotiating well is having the strength to take that risk.

Getting Past the Glitches

Many circumstances and events can send the best of negotiations skidding off track. Glitches happen. You can't ignore them or be overly frustrated by them. You can't avoid them. They're part of the life of any negotiator. Heck, they're part of *life*. If you're prepared for them, you actually derive a certain pleasure from dealing with glitches when they come up in a negotiation.

The secret to successfully negotiating through any glitch is the same: Keep your ultimate goal in mind. You're trying to reach an agreement — don't get sidetracked by glitches.

The following sections provide both general guidelines and some easy steps for getting past the glitches.

Personality types that block closing

Certain types of people always seem to get what they want and leave a destructive wake of bad feelings behind them. When you negotiate with such people, you feel that the only thing that would get through to them is a sharp jab to the chin. Before you spend one more moment of thought deciding how to beat these people at their own game, understand one thing: You possess the tools to deal with difficult people. Unfortunately, in the heat of the moment, forgetting that fact is easy.

The following are some helpful tips for dealing with different personality types.

The bully

Bullies come in all sizes, shapes, and colors. They use a variety of techniques, such as making take-it-or-leave-it offers, screaming, needling, and making their counterparts the butt of a joke.

No matter what you do, negotiating with a bully is not going to be a pleasant experience. Whatever you do, don't try to outbully a bully. Instead, rely on the following basic skills (covered throughout this book):

✓ **Prepare.** Be sure that you know everything you need to know about your counterpart before you begin the negotiation. To be forewarned is to be forearmed. Knowing ahead of time that you're dealing with a bully somehow takes much of the sting out of the bullying remarks.

✓ **Set limits.** Be sure that you're very clear about the limits you've set. Never accept from a bully a deal that you wouldn't accept otherwise.

✓ **Maintain emotional distance.** Keep your finger close to your Pause button. Responding in kind is easy when someone is trying to bully you. Take a few minutes to cool off, if necessary.

✓ **Listen.** You must work hard to listen to a bully. First, bullies mask their message in language that is hurtful in some way or another. Second, your own animosity is building, so empathetic listening is virtually impossible. Finally, if the bully's purpose is to achieve a desired outcome by using intimidation instead of sharing information and reaching a common solution, the bully may never give you the information you need.

✓ **Communicate clearly.** This is very important. Don't speak often — but when you do speak, make it count. With as little emotion as possible, let the other party and everyone else in the room know exactly what you're after. Even if you don't persuade the bully, someone else may later intercede with the bully on your behalf.

✓ **Close.** Try to close the deal at every opportunity. After all, if the negotiation isn't fun, you don't want it to last any longer than it has to. After the deal is done, you're done. Fight the impulse to spread the word about the new Biggest Jerk in Your Life.

If you've followed these steps and closure still seems unachievable, try telling your counterpart that you're feeling bullied. Sometimes a bit of candor can defuse a situation. Yelling back at a bully does no good, but telling the bully that the behavior is having the intended result may just change that behavior. It's crazy but true: Even bullies don't want to be known as bullies. Your simple, unemotional assessment of the situation will go a long way toward turning things around — especially if other people are around when you make your statement. Use nonaccusatory words and *I* phrases, such as "I really feel beaten up when you talk like that."

Inside every bully is a real wimp that can't bear the thought of anyone finding out about that weakness. So, the more bluster you hear, the more frightened and scared the bully probably is. Although not all that comforting when you're being yelled at, this knowledge does make it easier to recognize when to push your Pause button, figure out your next move, and then present it calmly. Sometimes, talking about the other person's fears at the beginning of the next negotiating session can be very helpful. The other person generally denies any fear but often settles down because you've made fearful feelings acceptable. After that mask is removed, you can get on to the substance of the conversation.

The screamer

The screamer is anybody who does a great deal of yelling or screaming. This personality type is a variation on the bully, and three distinct types of screamers exist. Each type requires a very different response:

- **Screamers who are truly angry, upset, or scared:** This is the subspecies that this section is about.

- **Screamers who are habitual:** Like Old Faithful in Yellowstone Park, these people just pop off every now and again. These types are annoying but harmless; if you know you're dealing with such a person, just don't respond.

- **Screamers who are bullies:** If the person is just trying to bully you, read the preceding section.

The worst thing you can do is sink to the level of someone else's negative behavior pattern. If you aren't normally a screamer, don't start just because the person sitting across from you starts screaming.

A chilly "Are you through?" works well in the movies but is probably little more than an unimaginative insult in most real-life situations. A better, if more difficult, approach is to be sympathetic. Empathizing with someone who is yelling at you runs against every instinct in your body, but it may be the best way to take the fire out of an angry screamer. The next time someone is yelling at you, try one of these phrases:

> I hear from your voice that you're upset.
>
> Let me be sure that I understand you. . . .
>
> Tell me more about that.

All these phrases are surprisingly calming. It's not that you're agreeing with the screamer, but you're using empathy, telling your counterpart that you want to understand what he's saying and feeling. Let others know that you aren't upset by their hysterics and deal with the behavior independently of the substance of the conversation.

The emotional blast and the content are two different things. If you can draw a distinction between the two in your mind, the other person may also be able to establish the distinction. If the blast is more than a style — if it's born out of true emotional outrage — take a break. A situation is seldom so urgent that you can't take a breather and come back at a later time. Even a short break is helpful to clear the air after an outburst.

The star or the boss

Everybody is awestruck by someone. Negotiating with anybody in whose presence you feel helplessly speechless is difficult at best. You can't negotiate effectively if you can't even get the cotton out of your mouth to speak.

How do you handle these situations when you have business to transact?

- ✔ **Prepare yourself.** Make sure that you know well what you want, why you want it, and what the justification is for your request.

- ✔ **Find out about the human being under the image.** Inside every famous, powerful, or wealthy person is a person. Find out about the individual. Is he or she married or single? Are there children? What hobbies interest the person?

The best way to defuse the situation is gather information.

The biased buyer

Even though, as a society, we're in the 21st century, some negotiators still occasionally suspect that they're about to lose a deal simply because they belong to a particular group. Not fair. Not right. But it happens. And dealing with this phenomenon is particularly difficult because this subtle discrimination is never verbalized.

If you have substantive evidence that bias exists against you, facing it head on is best, in a matter-of-fact manner, calmly and with dignity. A well-rehearsed phrase, delivered without accusation or emotion, is very helpful. "Are you open to granting this contract to a woman?," " . . . to an African-American man?," " . . . to an Asian paraplegic?"

You almost always receive a torrent of assurances. After all, in this day and age, basing decisions on anything but merit is not politically correct. Today, being politically correct is very important, especially in the business community.

Accepting that assurance is in your best interest, regardless of whether the sentiments are true. The mere fact that the assurance was offered benefits your position, even if it doesn't change societal behavior in general. But after you acknowledge and accept the assurance, don't drop the matter too quickly. Ask this important follow-up question: "Exactly what is your criteria for making a decision about the terms of this deal?"

If the answer is price, press on. "What price must be beaten?"

If you're told the price level, ask whether your price will be *shopped*. Shopping means that one of the good old boys retains the contract by matching or minimally beating your price. This is important data to obtain in any event. The information is absolutely essential if you suspect bias. The earlier you obtain the detailed, specific data upon which the decision will be made and the more thorough you are, the less room the other side has to manufacture objective data later. Keep good notes.

Could it be you?

It's hard to admit and hard to face, but consider the possibility that the difficult personality in the room may be your own. No one likes to think this, but if two different people got upset with you in two of your last three negotiations, chances are, the fault lies with you. If your negotiations seem unnecessarily contentious, consider what *you* can do to change that pattern.

No matter how strong a case you can make that the situation wasn't your fault, it probably was. Your version of the facts isn't relevant. The only important fact is that people frequently get upset with you. Try to figure out what element of your style of presentation makes dealing with you frustrating, upsetting, or annoying. Ask someone who loves you point blank. Don't defend yourself. Sit quietly and listen to the whole awful truth. Then try to fix whatever is wrong.

One difficulty is *position negotiating.* If you get stuck on one position, you aren't well prepared. You don't have adequate information to understand where other safe areas for agreement may exist. You haven't identified your own goals and limits sufficiently enough to define your range of movement. If you've done your homework, you can have the flexibility to reach agreements. In your next negotiation, push your Pause button (see Book V, Chapter 3) and listen twice as much as you usually listen. These two simple changes give you an opportunity to observe yourself. If you really want to become a first-class negotiator, you have to take a hard look at yourself.

Tactics that torment

Most glitches in a negotiation are something the other person says or does. If you make a mistake, the error is easy enough to correct. The frustrations — the glitches — arise from something the *other* party does. Taking care of your own goofs is easy enough. Figuring out your counterpart's goofs and how to get around them takes special talent. Some of the more common, maddening moments in a negotiation are listed in this section.

Chapter 5: Win-Win Negotiating *403*

Book V

Negotiating
Skills Every
Salesperson
Should Have

A constant change of position

Any negotiation involves concessions. Each side makes these concessions based on the information the two sides exchange about the factual matters and the priorities of the parties. But, barring unusual circumstances, priorities should not change. Keep a consistent position about those items that are important to you and what your goals are.

If the other side changes its position concerning what is and what is not important, stop everything until you find out what happened:

- ✔ **Maybe the other party experienced a significant change of circumstances.** Get the new situation firmly in mind. Then revisit the point on which you thought there was agreement. Maybe the new situation calls for a new solution.

- ✔ **Maybe the other side is not as prepared as they should be.** If that is the case, take a break. Your negotiation will go better for both sides if both sides have prepared. Just say, "Maybe we should take this up tomorrow. That will give you time to meet and sort out any last-minute items. No rush. We want you to be ready for this."

- ✔ **Maybe the other side is trying to pull a fast one.** Follow-up memos are always helpful, but in this situation they're crucial. In crafting any such memo, be absolutely scrupulous. Never try to conquer a "fast one" with yet another fast one delivered by you. Do your best to accurately reflect the other person's position no matter how strongly you disagree with it. Write with respect. No editorializing. The same goes when stating your position. Always close on a hopeful note that is specific — for example: "I'm looking forward to speaking again tomorrow afternoon on the phone to be sure I have everything right in this memo and to set our next meeting."

Written memos are useful tools in this situation, but a caveat is in order: If a constant change of position is part of a person's negotiating style, expect the person to repeatedly lose your documentation, not have time to read it, misplace it, or simply ignore it. If you suspect that your counterpart may conveniently lose your written documentation, be sure to use firm and clear language in your memo: "If you disagree with any portion of this memo, please advise by such-and-such a date." This helps more than "as soon as possible" or "immediately," which mean different time frames to different people. Even more helpful is to distribute your memos to everyone the negotiator wants to impress. This way, the negotiator's peers, superiors, and colleagues can monitor the progress of the proceedings.

Good cop, bad cop

A less obvious but equally dangerous glitch is the good-cop/bad-cop ploy. This label grows out of the police interrogation technique of having one officer question a suspect harshly and another, gentler cop be the relief questioner. The gentler cop — the *good cop* — pretends to befriend the suspect. The theory is that the suspect will spill the beans to the good cop.

Don't fall in love with the good cop. The good cop, more often than the bad cop, does you in. If you doubt that, remember that the good cop is the knowing partner of the bad cop. One does not exist without the other. They don't wander unknowingly down different paths. They do what they do deliberately. The good cop is usually the more pleasant personality of the two, but in a negotiating context, they're in cahoots.

What's the solution? Use their little game against them. Go ahead and confide in the good cop. Confide to the good cop that the bad cop has just about blown the deal. Confide about your other opportunities. But never drop your guard. Set deadlines. Be clear. Don't lose focus. Your discussion with the good cop is an extension of your discussion with the bad cop. Don't forget that for one minute.

The invisible partner

One of the more frustrating glitches you can run into in a negotiation is to discover — usually late in the game — that the other side can't agree to anything without consulting some invisible or unavailable partner or boss. Overcoming this glitch can be like shadowboxing.

If you run into the invisible-partner glitch, you may not have gathered enough information about the other party (see Book V, Chapter 1). You should have determined the decision-making authority of your counterpart early in the negotiation. To a large extent, good preparation avoids the problem of the invisible partner.

Here are some strategies that can help:

✔ **If you sense a silent-partner excuse coming, ask for the opportunity to pay your respects to that silent partner — no negotiating.** You just want to introduce yourself and pay a courtesy call. Then keep your word: Don't use the first meeting to negotiate if you promised not to pursue a business discussion. After you've made a courtesy contact, however, you always have the option of making direct contact for the purpose of breaking a logjam.

Frequently, these folks in the wings work behind the scenes because they are really softies and have a hard time saying no themselves. You can use this vulnerability to your advantage.

✔ **Upon meeting Ivan the Invisible, express your gratitude for having the opportunity to meet him; then assure him that you're delighted to be working with the designated negotiator.** After the small talk, innocently ask Ivan whether they've had sufficient time to discuss the negotiating parameters. Can you close a deal with the designated negotiator? Does Ivan need to be alone with the designated negotiator to talk out any more limitations before you and he go further?

✔ **If you aren't successful in meeting Ivan the Invisible, try insisting that the invisible partner be in a nearby room or available by telephone during the next negotiation session.** Then if a question arises that requires his approval, the other side can't use the absence as an excuse for prolonging the negotiation. You need to prevent delays during the negotiation when you reach the point of conclusion.

You may not be negotiating, but the more you can do to close off this frustrating technique of an invisible authority figure doing you in at every turn, the happier you are and the more smoothly the negotiation goes.

The double message

Make sure your words and your actions are consistent. Nothing is a bigger barrier to communication than the double message. Here are some common double messages you may have received in your negotiating experience:

✔ **The threat to break off a negotiation, but the negotiation continues uninterrupted:** This behavior baffles the listener and throws into question every future statement the person makes.

✔ **Not mentioning an issue at all during the first negotiating sessions and then making it the most important item on the table:** The better practice is to get all the issues on the table as early as possible.

"Let's split the difference and be done"

The concept of splitting the difference is one of the most seductive negotiating ploys, but if someone suggests it to you, measure the result. Sometimes, people begin a negotiation with a number that is unrealistically high just to impress a counterpart with the size of the subsequent discounts as the bargaining proceeds. If you've been more than fair in your approach, splitting the difference isn't necessarily equitable. If the result is unsatisfactory, you need to say so. Don't be afraid of being called a spoiler by the other side.

So, when someone suggests spitting the difference, take time to evaluate the proposed compromise based on all the other basics, and, if it doesn't seem fair, explain why this approach doesn't work.

If you're in a situation where splitting the difference seems fair, suggest doing so and explain why it's fair. If you just say, "Let's split the difference" and nothing more, you invite the other side to come back with another split between the compromise you offered and their original position. This process can keep going until you're far away from where you want to be.

A bad environment

A whole cluster of problems that aren't caused by a counterpart can throw a negotiation off track. More often than not, these environmental glitches are as frustrating to the opposing party as they are to you. Often, you can engage the other side in the solution, unless the problem is bigger than both of you. Here are some examples of these types of glitches:

- **Too much paper:** So many completed forms are necessary that your buyer turns off. Too many demands for duplicate information may irritate the person to the point where she gets frustrated and wants to deal with someone else.

  Solution: Fill out as much of the paperwork as possible before you arrive. Have the paperwork well organized. Carry a clipboard so that signing is as convenient as possible. Don't solve the problem by having someone sign a blank form.

- **Poorly designed tools and resources:** If you reach for the contract to close the negotiation and the document isn't there, the delay may halt the negotiation. If you do have the contract but it is full of typographical errors or is outdated, the situation spells unprofessional, and the negotiation is a no-go.

  Solution: Check over all the materials you plan to use in your presentation in advance. Make sure that they're the best they can be, even if you have to reach into your own pocket to improve them. Your commission or the advancement of your career is at stake. If the document is a form that the company supplies, make the necessary corrections before you start your negotiating session.

The ultimate glitch — someone walks away

No glitch presents quite the challenge that arises when someone walks away from the negotiation. This ultimate glitch has the potential to be final. The sensitive situation also raises questions about how to get things going again. Obviously, the negotiation won't close if the parties don't start talking again.

If the other party walks away

If you believe that the other party is walking away impetuously or for effect, don't be afraid to make a lunge and pull them back. Shopkeepers have held onto marginal sales for centuries by grabbing the arm of a departing customer.

If your counterpart abruptly severs all contact with you by making a hasty exit from the office, slamming down the telephone receiver, or refusing to answer telephone calls, you may be unable to reestablish communications immediately. If the person you're negotiating with gets out of range, use the time to your advantage. Consider the limits you set, go over all the new information gathered since the start of the negotiation, and if, upon reflection, you believe that reopening the negotiation makes sense, do so. Don't stand on pride.

The breakdown of a negotiation is no time for emotion; it's a time for enlightened self-interest. Keep a steely eye on what you want in life. And never be too proud to pick up the phone and get things back on track, if that's what it takes to achieve your personal goals.

If one of your competitors walks away

If one of your competitors for a project walks away from the negotiation, move swiftly to close your own deal. Usually, the party on the other side of the negotiation is a bit vulnerable at this time, so you have a good opportunity to obtain a favorable result.

Try to find out all you can about the recent events. Usually the opposing party is your best source. "What the heck happened?" usually brings out more information than you need. Listen. Be sympathetic, even if the person speaking acted a bit unreasonably.

In the course of listening, try to find out exactly what your counterpart needed that your competitor didn't provide. Find out what both parties had on the table when things blew up. Be sure that the party you're courting is willing to deal with you and won't just use your offer as a club to close the other deal. All these things are better learned by sympathetic listening as opposed to direct questions. Direct questions can feel too much like cross-examination.

Speed is often as important as thorough preparation in this situation. Move quickly to establish communications. Try to listen lots and speak little until you're ready. You already know what you're willing to do in the situation. If you can do so comfortably, make an offer within the range that the other side wants. Close your deal as quickly as possible.

If you're the one walking away

If you decide (based on your solid preparation and honest judgment) to terminate a negotiation, don't send a conflicting message. State clearly the conditions under which negotiations can resume. Then walk. Don't look back or otherwise communicate hesitation.

Looking back is not natural. The human body doesn't work that way. Your feet and your face should point in the same direction. Besides, looking back is confusing — to you and to your counterpart.

Never terminate a negotiation when you're angry. We know that when you're angry is just the time you want to storm out of the room or slam down the phone. Fight the instinct. Before you walk away, give yourself some breathing room. If, after some thought, you want to terminate the negotiations, end the discussion in a way that doesn't damage your own reputation as a professional. What you absolutely don't want to do is burn any bridges.

If the other party comes crawling back

If the other party calls, be open to finding new ground. If the other person comes back to you, be sure to respect the opening comment, whatever it is. Even if the other party doesn't come as far as you want, be sure to acknowledge the willingness to make a first step. Under such circumstances, the smallest step may involve a major effort — and may be the key to a final settlement.

When negotiations begin again in earnest, don't dwell on the fact that you went to extremes to enable it to happen. This is not a time for hard feelings or for self-congratulations. Just go forward with the business at hand. Be glad you managed your way through the rough waters.

Book VI

Selling in Specialized and Growing Fields

The 5th Wave

By Rich Tennant

©RICHTENNANT

"I can show you this one. It's got a pool in the backyard. Then I got a six bedroom with a fountain out front, but nothing right now with a moat."

In this book . . .

Selling is selling, right? Well, for the most part. Certainly all the information and suggestions presented throughout this All-in-One are applicable in any sales environment and for any product or service. However, some industries — whether because of regulatory mandates, being targeted to very specific populations, potential ethical and legal challenges they may generate, and so on — present special challenges and deserve targeted discussion.

In this book, you find advice relevant to several of these specialized and growing fields.

Chapter 1

Selling Real Estate

Each real-estate agent defines success slightly differently. Some agents set their goals in dollars, some are attracted to the opportunity to be their own bosses and build their own businesses, and some want the personal control and freedom that a real-estate career allows. Achieving success, however, requires the same basic fundamentals regardless of what motivates your move into real estate. Agents who build successful businesses share four common attributes:

✔ **They're consistent.** They perform success-producing activities day in and day out. Instead of working in spurts — making 50 prospecting calls in two days and then walking away from the phone for two weeks — they proceed methodically and steadily, day after day, to achieve their goals.

✔ **They believe in the law of accumulation.** This law says that everything in life, whether positive or negative, compounds itself over time. No agent becomes an overnight success, but with consistency, success-oriented activities accumulate momentum and power and lead to success every time.

✔ **They're lifelong learners.** The most successful agents never quit improving. Their passion for improvement is acute, and they commit the time, resources, and energy it takes to constantly enhance their skills and performance.

✔ **They're self-disciplined.** They have the ability to motivate themselves to do the activities that must be done. A successful agent shows up daily for work and puts in a full day of work on highly productive actions such as prospecting and lead follow-up. They make themselves do things that they don't want to do so they can have things in life that they truly want.

You're already on the road to real-estate success, demonstrated by the fact that you've picked up this book to discover what it takes to become a great salesperson. This chapter sets you on your way to success by providing an overview of the key skills that successful real-estate agents pursue and possess. By applying the information contained in this chapter consistently and with the right attitude, your success in real-estate sales is guaranteed.

How the Business of Selling Real Estate Works

The real-estate business is really comprised of two core areas:

✔ **Acquiring sellers who have properties to list with you:** A *listing* is a property that you represent for a specific period of time in an attempt to procure a buyer for the property. You're responsible for

- Marketing

- Negotiating the contract

- All documents

- Having the property inspected

- Orchestrating all efforts to close the transaction

- Transferring the ownership to the buyer

✔ **Working with buyers to acquire the properties that have been listed and are available for sale:** Most people are more familiar with this part of the real-estate business because they see real-estate agents as people who put buyers in their cars and drive them around and find them homes.

As you read the rest of this chapter, keep these two core areas in mind.

Types of Real-Estate Sales: Residential versus Commercial

You may think that the best way to reach your financial goals as a real-estate agent is to focus solely on commercial real estate. And there definitely is the allure of wearing nice suits, driving fancy cars, and meeting over power lunches with those who make the business world turn. But, in fact, working in residential sales is the easier way to achieve your financial goals.

Comparing commercial real estate to residential real estate is like comparing apples to oranges. Both fall under the heading "real-estate sales," but that's where the similarities end. The selling process for commercial real estate hinges on numbers and return-on-investment (ROI) calculations. Residential real estate is nowhere near so cut-and-dried because it's more of an emotional purchase — many buyers make decisions based on the fact that the house just feels right to them. In commercial real estate, however, feelings and emotions account for little in the purchase; the key factor is the return on investment.

Book VI

Selling in Specialized and Growing Fields

Looking at commercial real estate

Commercial real estate is business focused. It involves property that is sold, leased, or used to achieve a predetermined business objective. It's used as an investment to achieve an anticipated rate of return on the funds invested.

Commercial real-estate agents are usually familiar with many of the commercial real-estate areas, but they generally specialize in one of the following areas or disciplines:

- ✔ Representing tenants or lessees by finding, selecting, and negotiating new space for client businesses

- ✔ Representing building owners or lessors by working to lease out building space for the highest possible price and with the most favorable terms

- ✔ Representing investors who want to buy and sell commercial property by finding opportunities that offer the lowest risk to the client, the best return on investment, and the best *capitalization rate* (the net operating income of the property divided by the sales price or value of the property)

Looking at residential sales

Residential real estate revolves around the wants and needs of a homeowner and his family. It involves property purchased for individual use, most often to provide housing for families. For the most part, residential agents represent the buyers or sellers of single-family, primary homes. Within the residential real-estate arena, agents also engage in the following specialties:

✔ Selling secondary homes to people seeking a "home away from home" to get away from it all.

✔ Working exclusively for a builder of new homes, usually by serving as the on-site salesperson for a new home community.

   In this role, the agent sells only the builder's homes. If buyers need to sell an existing home outside that community, usually another agent handles that sale.

✔ Representing residential real-estate investors who are looking to increase wealth through the ownership of homes, duplexes, triplexes, and fourplexes. Small-scale multiplexes are handled by residential rather than commercial agents for two reasons:

   • The purchaser often lives in one segment of the multiplex, creating a residence as well as an investment property.

   • A purchaser usually can buy up to a fourplex with a conventional mortgage.

Residential agents rarely represent buyers or sellers of multiplexes with more than four dwelling units. Purchasers of larger complexes must qualify for and secure commercial real-estate loans — which involve a more restrictive set of conditions, including higher interest rates, shorter amortization schedules, and considerably higher down payments.

Researching and Understanding Your Marketplace

Here's a fact: Most real-estate agents know too little about the markets in which they operate. You can give yourself an edge over other agents and establish yourself as a regional real-estate expert simply by doing your homework, researching your market area, and gaining a good understanding of the realities and trends that affect the real-estate decisions of your buyers and sellers.

Whether you're in a major metro market or a small town and regardless of the country, the economy, or even the day and age in which you're doing business, when you're in the field of real estate, three core rules apply to your business:

✔ **Real estate is governed by the law of supply and demand.** This rule is absolute and without exception. The appreciation of a market, the expectations of buyers and sellers, and the velocity of market sales are all dictated by the supply of — and the demand for — real estate for sale.

✔ **Real estate is governed by the law of cause and effect.** Put differently, positive situations cause positive outcomes and vice versa. For example, a vibrant economic growth leads to a vibrant real-estate market and strong appreciation of homes, while loss of jobs and a languishing economy produce exactly the opposite effect.

✔ **History repeats itself.** In any marketplace, you have cycles. Periods of rapid real-estate appreciation are followed by stagnant periods where values stabilize or even decrease. By acquiring marketplace knowledge, you can foresee trends both for your own benefit and for the benefit of your clients.

Book VI

Selling in Specialized and Growing Fields

Sources of market information

By knowing your market and watching regional statistics, you're prepared and proactive. The better you know every inch of that playing field, the more you can exploit it to your advantage.

The most challenging aspect of gaining market knowledge is determining what facts to collect and where to find the information you need. Fortunately, a number of readily accessible resources are available to real-estate agents. All you have to do is contact the right people and ask the right questions. The following sections help you on your data quest.

✔ **Your local real-estate board:** Most professional agents belong to associations that compile and make available a wealth of statistical information. The facts you can obtain from your local board include the number of agents working in your marketplace, the production of the average agent in terms of units and volume sold, and experience levels of agents in your field — information that helps you understand your competitive arena and to track whether your competition has expanded or receded over recent years.

✔ **Your local multiple listing service:** The *multiple listing service,* commonly called the MLS, keeps statistics of all the listings and sales in your area that are processed through the MLS. The MLS can give you key market statistics, including average number of days on the market, listing price–to–sale price ratios, listings taken–to–listings sold ratios, and geographically active markets inside your service area.

The MLS doesn't cover every sale due to the fact that some sales (new constructions builders, for example) bypass the system. However, the MLS in most markets covers more than 95 percent of all marketplace sales, and it represents the surest indicator of real-estate activity in your region.

✔ **The National Association of Realtors (NAR,** www.realtor.org**):** This organization produces some wonderful studies, reports, and market statistics; conducts annual surveys and studies of home sellers and homebuyers; and issues reports on second home markets, investment properties, financing options, and many other topics.

The NAR's monthly web-based publication, *Real Estate Insights,* provides a national view of real-estate sales: what's happened in terms of sales and days on the market, what people are purchasing, what financing they're using, emerging trends, and predictions for the future. *Real Estate Insights* is a powerful tool in the hands of a successful agent. If you aren't currently reading it, put it into your information arsenal immediately.

✔ **Other sources of marketplace information:** Consult your broker about company-compiled statistics on regional trends and also on your firm's market share and market penetration. Especially if you work for a regional or national real-estate company or franchise, your organization has likely commissioned studies that can be useful to your fact-gathering efforts. Also, if you live in a state where sellers provide title insurance to buyers, the title companies often conduct market trend reports that allow agents to better understand the marketplace they work in.

Analyzing market facts and figures

When you have access to solid facts and figures, take the time to interpret your findings in order to arrive at conclusions that can steer your business in the right direction, as the following sections explain.

Studying population migration patterns

To quantify population migration trends that affect the buyer and seller pool in your market area, determine the answers to these questions:

✔ Is your marketplace growing in population or are people migrating into your area (possibly due to births, migration, or immigration)? Conversely, is your marketplace losing population?

✔ Where are new residents coming from geographically and where are current residents going when they move away?

✔ At what rate are people arriving or leaving your area?

✔ What economic factors are driving population changes (such as jobs, unemployment, and business growth) in your marketplace?

If your answers lead you to believe that a population boom is pending, prepare yourself and your clients to take advantage of a seller's market and the positive effects of a high-demand, low-supply market situation. If your answers lead you to believe that a population exodus is beginning to take place, you can steer buyer and seller decisions with that knowledge in mind.

Real estate in your market area is affected by influences outside your own region. To determine how neighboring regional markets are affecting your market area, study migratory patterns and then research the reasons behind the population movements you discover.

Identifying market trends

To understand your marketplace and its economic condition, compare current market activity with correlating statistics from the previous year:

✔ **Compare number of sales and total sales volume, both on a year-to-year and on a year-to-date basis.** This comparison helps you understand and forecast trends in your marketplace and answer questions like whether the number and volume of sales is going up or down and whether the marketplace is ahead of or behind the pace of sales from the previous year.

✔ **Compare the number of listings taken.** The available inventory in a marketplace is the supply half of the supply-and-demand equation. Ask yourself these questions:

• Is the number of listings up or down? Fewer listings indicates a sellers' market; many listings indicates a buyers' market. Do you see more or less competition for buyers than in previous years?

• Is the selection better for buyers than last year at this time?

• Is the inventory of homes for sale growing or shrinking as compared to this time a year ago?

In general, a low inventory of homes leads to increased appreciation and more competition for high-demand properties (homes that are in superior condition and in superior locations). When inventory levels are high, the competition for buyers slows appreciation. It also extends days on the market and can even drop sales prices due to a lack of purchaser urgency to "buy now."

✔ **Compare last year's average sale price to this year's average sale price.** This info helps you determine whether the average sale price is going up or down (in a healthy marketplace, the average sale price increases), whether the marketplace is appreciating or depreciating in value, and how well the inventory of homes aligned with demand. In an appreciating marketplace, the inventory probably is lower than the demand for homes. In a flat or depreciating marketplace, the inventory or supply probably exceeds demand at this time.

Make sure to view the average sale price on at least a quarterly basis. A one-month change in this particular statistic doesn't indicate a sustainable trend, especially in small market areas.

Book VI

Selling in Specialized and Growing Fields

✔ **Compare the percentage of appreciation of average sales price this year versus last year and year to date.** You want to determine whether the appreciation percentage is increasing or decreasing compared to this time last year and whether the marketplace is gaining strength in appreciation or losing its power.

Prospecting Your Way to Listings and Sales

The purpose of prospecting is to develop prospective clients for your business. Real-estate agents seek two categories of clients: sellers, who become listing clients, and buyers, who become real-estate purchasers. The following sections provide tips for how to prospect for clients in each group.

Prospecting for listings

Listing leads come from past clients, those in your sphere of influence, expired listings, for sale by owner (FSBO) conversions, open houses, lead cultivation, and door knocking. To generate listing leads, you have to do some pretty active prospecting work, such as the following:

✔ **Use your networking skills.** Specifically ask those within your sphere of influence, your circle of past clients, or your referral groups to share the names of people who need or want to sell real estate.

✔ **Gather up expired and FSBO listings.** To achieve a greater listing inventory and develop a specialty as a listing agent, cultivate listing prospects by working with expired and FSBO listings (flip to the later section "Winning business from expired and FSBO listings" for details on how to excel in this area).

✔ **Prioritize your efforts.** You must prioritize your investment of time based on the probability of your success. Prioritizing must be done based on activity as well as the prospect. Some prospects warrant a larger investment of time and resources because of their short time frame, their higher level of commitment to you, or the amount of commission you will receive from them.

Prospecting for buyers

Prospecting for buyers is easier than prospecting for listings because referrals arrive more naturally and because open houses attract prospective buyers and provide you with a great prospecting platform.

The type of houses you choose to show determines the kinds of prospects you generate. Obviously, higher-priced and more exclusive properties draw more discerning buyer prospects, while lower-priced properties attract less affluent prospects.

To build your business quickly, work to generate leads from more first-time home buyers by planning more open houses in the low range of your marketplace. First-time buyer prospects benefit your business because they

✔ **Can be sold into homes quickly,** because they aren't burdened with the need to sell homes in order to make purchases possible.

✔ **Lack experience with other real-estate agents.** They don't have current agent affiliations, and they don't approach a new agent relationship with the baggage acquired from a less-than-stellar past experience.

✔ **Acquire strong loyalty when good service is rendered.** This allows you to establish a long-term relationship that may span 10 to 15 years with multiple home sales and purchases over that period.

✔ **Provide you with an opportunity to establish relationships** with their friends who may also be considering first-time purchases.

Book VI

Selling in Specialized and Growing Fields

Prospecting through open houses

Well-documented research shows that fewer than 5 percent of all buyers purchased a home they visited during an open house. This finding proves the open house to be, at best, a pretty ineffective sales approach. Despite this research, open houses are an important tool in an agent's business arsenal for a very good reason: Open houses are a great means for prospecting. They let you show your audience what a great agent you are, ultimately providing a terrific opportunity to generate prospects. And all savvy agents know that prospects are the lifeblood of real-estate business success.

So how many open houses should you host? Unfortunately, there's no pat answer. But here are a few good guidelines to follow:

✔ **If you're a new agent** trying to build a clientele and get your business off the ground, host open houses weekly, or at least regularly and frequently. Volunteer to hold open houses for the listings of other agents in your company.

✔ **If you're an established agent** working to increase your business and win market share, add up how many open houses you've hosted over recent months, and aim to increase that figure at least proportionately to the amount you're working to increase your business.

✔ **If open houses are fundamental to your lead-generation strategy,** you should hold an event at least several times each month.

Qualifying your prospects

The success of a listing presentation is largely determined by what you do before you even walk through the door. Many agents enter the meeting flying blind, ill-prepared, and oblivious to the needs, wants, desires, and expectations of the prospect.

In real estate, you want to focus your qualifying questions around the following topics:

✔ **Motivation and time frame:** Ask questions that allow you to gauge how excited the prospect is to buy or sell, and in what time frame they're hoping for.

✔ **Pricing:** These questions help you gauge the prospect's motivation. They'll also help you determine whether the prospect is realistic about current real-estate values and whether he is ready to sell or is just fishing for a price.

✔ **Service expectations:** Learning what your prospect expects from a real-estate agent is absolutely essential to establishing a good working relationship.

For general qualifying information, refer to Book III, Chapter 2.

Fundamentals for Presenting Listings

A quality listing presentation involves considerable planning, careful research and analysis, and highly developed presentation and sales skills. By taking these measures, you derive maximum impact from the little time you have to present yourself and your recommendations, close the deal, and obtain signatures on a listing agreement.

Including key points in your presentation

You can find general information about making winning presentations in Book III, Chapter 3. The following items provide real-estate specific guidelines that can help you win your prospects' confidence so that you can secure their listing.

Know the purpose of your presentation

The objective of a listing presentation is to secure a signed listing agreement before the meeting ends. It's not to pave the way for a *be-back listing,* where you plan to return at a later date to handle paperwork and secure final prospect approval.

If you let even a few days or weeks slip by, your prospects will have a difficult time separating your presentation from those of the other agents they met in the meantime. And the moment they lose sight of your distinguishing attributes they'll revert to a commodity mindset, focusing on price and selecting an agent based on who offered the lowest commission or the highest list price.

Share market knowledge

Become a student of the local marketplace and share meaningful statistics. Also, track trends in the national marketplace, both to enlighten your prospects and to distinguish yourself as a well-read, well-connected, and well-informed agent. Refer to the earlier section "Researching and Understanding Your Marketplace" for details.

Stay in control of your agenda

Developing an agenda for your meeting is vital. Your agenda might look like this:

1. **Review agenda for the meeting.**
2. **Visually inspect the property.**
3. **Discuss the client's goals, needs, and expectations of me.**
4. **Discuss my professional credentials.**
5. **Determine listing price.**
6. **Complete the paperwork so I can begin serving the client.**

Don't allow the seller's agenda to take over the discussion. The seller's agenda is simple: He wants to know what his home is worth, what you do to sell it, and what you charge for your service. And for sure he wants to know what he'll put in his pockets when the deal is done. If you allow the seller to take control and force you to orient your presentation to the order of his interests, you won't walk out with the listing.

If you talk about the price of the home and your fee structure before you've built trust, credibility, and value for your service, you'll lose every time. If the seller brings up a point that would cause you to abandon your presentation plan, pick up the agenda sheet and ask: "Would it be all right to discuss that when we get to this point in the presentation?"

Indicate what benefits you have to offer

You can set yourself apart by sharing a success story that shows the benefits you have to offer and how your success story translates to client benefits. For example, if one of your strengths is that you're able to convert leads at 16 percent as opposed to the 2 percent average, your clients have a higher probability of selling their homes. You can then tell your clients that your track record resulted in higher probability of sale, higher sales prices, and less hassle for the seller working with you. For help in identifying your strengths, head to the later section "Staking your competitive position."

As a newer agent, you may not be able to show your own strong numbers, but you can present your company's instead. For instance, you may focus on the fact that your company sells more units than its competitors, that your company has more agents to create more exposure, and that your company has high market share, which leads to increased ad and sales calls.

Discuss pricing information honestly

When you share your findings regarding the value of their property, tell the prospect the truth about the value of his home and make your recommendations clear.

The best pricing strategy is to price a home at market value. A home that's listed at market value stands out from the competition. Compared to all the overpriced options, it strikes buyers as a rare value and leads to traffic and a high number of showings by other agents.

Give the prospect a single price instead of providing a range. If you're a little unsure, you can give him a range, but make sure it's a very tight range — less than a $50,000 variance. Why shouldn't you give a range? Because invariably the seller will select the price in the highest part of the range or even above it, and you risk having a property that is overpriced because you weren't strong enough to tell the seller the truth.

Avoid overpricing just to please the buyer. Hope isn't a successful pricing strategy, and the please-the-client mindset is a difficult one to abandon. Agents who achieve listings with unrealistic prices find it difficult to later counsel their clients honestly. The pitfalls of a please-the-client approach are many and significant. By overpricing, you can practically count on a reduction in your productivity, profitability, and *salability* (your sales and success track) because

✔ **An unsold, overpriced listing costs you time and money to service while it delivers no revenue to your business.** The situation only gets worse the longer the listing languishes on the market. You'll end up deducting the expenses of this in-limbo listing from the proceeds generated by any revenue-producing deals you manage to close in the meantime, reducing your net profit and business success.

✔ **Unsold homes that linger on the market seriously diminish your salability.** Your salability is based on such key statistics as your average ratio of listing price compared to sale price and the average number of days your listings are on the market. Obviously, these statistics, which prospects rely on when choosing one agent over another, can be crushed if you want to get listings at any cost; they're also harmed by the tactic of starting high and reducing the price later. You also can develop the reputation of being an agent who only pounds for sale signs into yards. People notice when you haven't posted any sold signs.

No matter whether you're selling real estate or any other offering, pricing must reflect what the market will bear, not what the seller needs to net. If you allow yourself to be swayed by a seller's need to start higher than the property should be priced, you set yourself up for a costly error.

Get agreement from the client about pricing

After presenting your price recommendation and your case for its value, ask the prospect if he understands why his home is worth the amount you've recommended. Asking this question is the surest way to discover whether your prospects agree with your number. An alternate tactic is to prepare a full net-proceeds sheet, which shows the list price minus all closing costs. Walk him through each cost of closing based on the price you suggest. Then when you get to the bottom line — the estimate of how many dollars will go into his pocket — ask, "Is this enough to get you where you want to go?" If he agrees, the gate is open for you to go for the close and get his signature on the listing agreement.

If you don't gain agreement on price, you have nothing more to talk about during the listing appointment. There's no point in going further unless you can arrive at a meeting of minds on price.

Going for the close

After you prove that you and your company are the best, convince the seller of her home's value, understand her expectations of service and results, and guarantee that you'll meet and exceed them, you're ready to close the contract. Closing is the natural ending to a great presentation.

You may be thinking, "When do I tell the seller about the marketing plan?" You don't. It's immaterial to the discussion. The listing presentation is about the results that you achieve, not how you achieve them. If your key statistics and the distinguishing benefits of doing business with you aren't strong enough, no marketing plan will fill the gap.

Before you leave the meeting, recap what steps will happen next and what you'll be doing for your clients in the next 24 to 48 hours. Then reassure them that they made a great decision. Tell them that you look forward to serving them and working with them, that the goals they set will be achieved, and that they selected the right agent for the job. Then send a handwritten thank-you note the next day (at the very latest).

Other Ways to Maximize Your Real-Estate Sales Success

Real-estate sales is the greatest business in the world. In any marketplace, a real-estate agent has the opportunity to create hundreds of thousands of dollars in income. An agent's income is especially significant when viewed against the capital investment required by the business. Most agents need as little as $2,000 to start up their practices. Compare that to any other business, and you'll find that most involve sizeable investments and burdensome loans to buy equipment, lease space, create marketing pieces, develop business strategies, and hire employees — all to achieve what is usually a smaller net profit than what a real-estate agent can achieve in the first few years. It's almost too good to be true!

The preceding sections of this chapter are devoted to key fundamentals of real-estate success. This section offers a few other pointers to help you to achieve even more.

Putting the focus on winning customers

If you were asked to identify the function that makes or breaks a real-estate agent's success, chances are, you'd answer customer service (that's the answer that more than 95 percent of new agents give). Only a rare few see customer creation as the golden approach that it is. True, you have to be excellent at customer development *and* customer service; however, in terms of priority, you have to focus on customer development.

The way to do that is through developing exemplary sales ability. Sales ability is based on how effective you are in generating prospects, following up on those prospects to secure appointments, qualifying those appointments, conducting the appointments to secure an exclusive agency contract, and then providing service to that recently created client.

High-earning agents realize that sales skills are vital to success, and they continuously seek excellence in this area. To follow the high-earning agent's example, make it your priority to develop and constantly improve your sales skills in the following areas:

✔ **Securing appointments:** Refer to the earlier section "Prospecting Your Way to Listings and Sales" for key pointers on winning leads and appointments through prospecting and follow-up activities.

✔ **Persuading expired and FSBO listings to move their properties to your business:** The later section "Winning business from expired and FSBO listings" is full of secrets and tips to follow as you pursue this lucrative and largely untouched field.

✔ **Making persuasive presentations that result in positive buying decisions:** The earlier section "Fundamentals for Presenting Listings" helps you plan your presentation. It's packed with tips on what to include and how to reach a successful close.

Of course, people also base your ability on how quickly you can accomplish all these tasks!

In robust market conditions, leads are abundant and relatively easy to attract, especially buyer leads. But in slow markets, real-estate success becomes less automatic. Only great sales skills guarantee that you — instead of some other agent — will win clients no matter the market conditions. The best agents make more money in a challenging market than they do in a robust market. The way to build immunity to shifting market conditions is to arm yourself with skills in prospecting, lead follow-up, presentations, and so on.

Book VI

Selling in Specialized and Growing Fields

Staking your competitive position

In one sentence, your *competitive position* defines how your real-estate practice is better than all others in some unique and meaningful way. You may be dominant when it comes to selling ranch-style homes, or you may excel in high-end or low-end properties or properties in a certain neighborhood or design category. In all cases, your competitive position must be real, defensible, and definable, which means it must be based on statistics, and that's what the following sections of this chapter explain.

The best agents — the most powerful, experienced, high-volume agents — share a single advantage: They know the statistics of their market, the statistics of their own performance, and their statistical position in the overall marketplace or in a particular niche market area.

If you're a newer agent, you probably don't yet have the stats to stake your competitive position. However, if you selected your real-estate company well, your company likely does. Work with your broker to find out how your company excels in the marketplace and present your company's advantage while you build your own success story.

Three key statistics reflect real-estate sales success better than any other indicators. These statistics are

✔ **Average list price to sales price:** The average list price–to–sales price ratio quantifies your skill and success in achieving the result you and your client expected when you priced and placed a home on the market. By presenting a strong list price–to–sales price ratio, you clearly illustrate your effectiveness for your sellers.

✔ **Average days on the market:** Your ability to sell a home, on average, in fewer than 30 days clearly conveys to potential sellers your skill and success level. It further indicates your knowledge of competitive pricing. The 30-day mark is a good benchmark to shoot for, provided that your marketplace is either a neutral marketplace or a seller's marketplace. If you're in a buyer's marketplace, you may see that number push up a little higher. An agent with a strong track record for quickly selling homes presents a clear competitive advantage to sellers.

By showing that your listings spend a lower-than-average number of days on the market, you'll present proof that prospective sellers gain a significant competitive edge and financial advantage when they choose to work with you.

✔ **Average listings taken versus listings sold:** The average listings taken versus listings sold statistic is a competitive number that demonstrates to the world how well you do your job of selling homes. When you can say to a seller that you sell more than 98 percent of all the homes that sellers list with you, you present strong evidence to your clients that they can assume a greatly lowered risk when working with you.

One of the greatest fears a seller experiences stems from this concern: "What if I pick the wrong agent?" By presenting your track record in the form of a high percentage of listings sold versus listings taken, you quickly erase that concern and provide comfort and relief to prospects.

Sellers want to know their odds of success. Use your stats to show them the proven competitive advantage you bring to the table. In a neutral marketplace with good sale activity, the average listings taken versus listings sold ratio historically hovers around 65 percent. Your list-to-sale ratio goal should be at least 95 percent.

The following sections look at the value and power of each calculation.

Become a listing agent to be really successful

To create long-term success, a high quality of life, and a strong real-estate business, set as your goal to eventually join the elite group — comprised of fewer than 10 percent of all agents — who are listing agents. The advantages are many:

✔ **Multiple streams of income:** Listings generate interest and trigger additional transactions. Almost the minute you announce your listing by putting a sign in the ground, you'll start receiving calls from neighbors, drive-by traffic, and people wanting to live in the area. These calls represent current and future business opportunities that arise only when you have a listing with your name on it.

✔ **Promotional opportunity:** A listing gives you a reason to advertise and draw the attention of prospects that you can convert to clients or future prospects. And when your listing sells, you can spread the word of your success with another round of communication to those in the neighborhood and throughout your sphere of influence.

✔ **A business multiplier:** One listing equals more than one sale because every listing you take can result in additional business generated by ad calls, sign calls, and the fact that the listing seller generally wants to buy another home. The multipliers vary by agent, but they always result in a pretty impressive return on investment.

✔ **A free team of agents working for you:** The moment you post your listing, all the other agents in your area will go to work on your behalf. And the best part is, they don't require payment until they deliver a buyer, and then they'll be paid not by you but by your seller through the commission structure.

Book VI

Selling in Specialized and Growing Fields

Winning business from expired and FSBO listings

If you've been in the real-estate business for any time at all, you've probably already sensed that many agents have a preconceived negative impression of expired listings and FSBO listings. But you can reap great success by converting expired and FSBO listings to new listings for your business.

Any new agent with aspirations to climb all the way to the top tier of success in residential real estate should consider working expired and FSBO listings for the following reasons:

✔ **They exist in any kind of market condition.** If you're skilled at converting expired and FSBO listings, market conditions will have little bearing on your income and overall success. Here's why: In a market that's experiencing sluggish sales, buyers are in control and listings move slowly, if at all. As a result, a large number of listings expire each day, week, month, and year, providing you with a near-endless supply of conversion opportunities. On the flip side, when the marketplace is robust and listings are moving briskly, sellers enjoy quick sales, high list-to-sold ratios, and multiple offers. In this environment, an abundance of FSBOs sprout up. You can make your business bulletproof simply by shifting your listing emphasis to fit market trends — focusing on expired listings in sluggish markets and on FSBOs in brisk markets.

✓ **They're high-probability leads.** Working probable leads is much more efficient for a real-estate agent, and it's difficult to find a more probable lead than the owner of a home with an expired listing or one who has tried — and failed — to sell his home on his own. The owner has demonstrated the desire or need to sell and shows the existence of a problem — the home didn't sell — that you can help solve.

✓ **Securing these listings is pretty simple.** To win an expired listing, all you have to do is make a phone call or series of phone calls or use a phone and mail combination. With a FSBO, the owners sometimes have an agent in the wings just in case they don't have success on their own, so the best approach is to dial back your sales pitch and enhance your emphasis on service. Focus on helping the owners in their effort. Always encourage them and wish them success, but don't give away all your valuable services without a signed contract.

✓ **They're easy to find.** One of the most difficult steps in the sales process is locating prospects in need of your service. With both FSBOs and expired listings, you know who your prospects are and you know how to get in touch with them. To find expired listings, read the daily MLS hot sheet, where each day most MLS systems post newly expired listings under the category "expired listings." FSBOs are even easier to find because FSBO sellers *want* to be found. You just have to check the newspaper (print media is still the primary advertising avenues for FSBOs) and online sources; drive around and enlist the help of family and friends.

Consider subscribing to The Red X (www.theredx.com), a company that compiles information from FSBO newspaper ads, FSBO websites, and other real-estate sources to provide you with a complete list of FSBO opportunities in your area. For a low monthly fee, The Red X delivers daily e-mail lists of the most recent FSBOs right to your inbox. With a subscription, you also get full access to a searchable six-month FSBO history.

Even though both expired listings and FSBOs are great sources for generating listings, they can't be the only revenue streams you spend your time generating. You must have at least three areas from which you create leads, revenue, and listing opportunities.

Generating top-notch referrals

Generating referrals is among the easiest, most cost-effective ways to gain new business leads, but success doesn't happen overnight. Even your best referral sources need to be constantly contacted and reminded to send business in your direction. The following sections share tips on how to get the best referrals and make the most of them.

Categorizing your referrals

You can't afford to treat all referral sources with equal attention. Unless you establish priorities, you won't have the time or energy to devote to those sources who will benefit your business the most. For that reason, if you want to mine your resources effectively, you have to put most of your effort toward contacts with the highest referral potential:

✔ **First-tier contacts (the platinum group):** This category includes clients who were a delight to work with, people who are in key strategic positions, and friends and associates who are strongly likely to refer business your way. The people in this group deserve personal attention and personal interaction from you on a regular schedule. You may want to contact this group by phone on a monthly or bimonthly basis. The secret is personal contact by phone or in person.

✔ **Second-tier contacts (the gold group):** This group includes influential people who are likely to refer but only if you meet a few conditions. To develop this group, take time to establish your credentials and competitive position. By proving that you save clients more money, sell quicker, and handle smoother and better transactions, in time, you'll develop advocates that send you referrals for years to come. You may want to contact this group once a quarter by phone or in person.

✔ **Third-tier contacts (the silver group):** This group will include contacts who *may* refer someday, but the jury is still out regarding when and if. Still, because you know them and they know you, they deserve your attention and follow-up. Phone these silver-level clients at least once or twice a year to maintain the personal contact with them.

✔ **Fourth-tier contacts (the bronze group):** Consider creating a bronze category just to keep remote possibilities in your contact circle. Especially when your overall database is small, you want to wring potential out of every hope. Inexpensive, regular contacts are a step in the right direction toward engaging the interest of these contacts and converting them into future referral sources.

Whenever you receive a referral, note whether the source is listed in your platinum, gold, silver, or bronze categories. This will help you track whether those in each category are performing at the projected levels. If they're not, you'll know to enhance communications and general referral efforts accordingly.

Getting the type of referrals you seek

Before you launch a referral-generating effort, you need to know what you're looking for. After you know what you're looking for, you have to let others know as well. In a sentence, you need to be able to tell your referral sources exactly what your ideal real-estate prospect looks like. Include the following information:

- **Moments when people become great prospects:** Help your referral sources notice the signs that indicate that their friends are in the "thinking about moving" stage, because your goal is to enter the game before the transaction is already under way. Universal signs to watch for include pregnancy, recent adoption, promotion, transfer, trouble with aging parents, a recent empty nest, or trouble in a marriage or relationship.

    Left to their own good intentions, many people will call to tip you off about people they've just heard are in the process of buying or selling. By the time a mutual friend hears that someone is actively looking to buy or is in the midst of selling, it's too late. By then, the prospects probably already have an agent.

- **Your interest in helping people sell their homes:** Buyers are great clients and important sources of revenue, but the best agents build their businesses through listings. By cultivating referrals for those clients thinking about selling their homes, you'll put your business on a faster track to growth.

- **Your real-estate niche:** If you're particularly effective at serving a specific niche of real-estate clients, such as investors, seniors, and so on, let your referral sources know. Likewise, if you want to gain more of a certain kind of buyer or seller, inform your sources about your expertise in the desired segment and what prospects in that category look like.

The point of all this guidance isn't to get your referral sources to screen leads for you. Instead, the goal is to educate your sources. Make sure they know that you still want them to recommend the names of anyone who has interest in buying or selling property. In this case, less is not more.

Approaching your referral sources

Marketing for referrals with mailers, calendars, recipe cards, and other outreach and appreciation efforts is nowhere near as effective as prospecting for referrals by making personal calls and requests. When approaching referral sources, keep a few important rules in mind:

- **Don't ask for referrals by simply adding a throwaway line onto the end of another conversation.** For example, don't say, "Oh, by the way" before you ask for a business referral, which minimizes the importance of the referral instead of raising it to the high level of honor and respect it deserves. Instead, precede your referral request with the statement, "I have an important question to ask you."

✔ **Ask permission.** When asking for permission, use a script like this one:

> I'm delighted that I've been able to serve you. I was wondering about others you might know who would also benefit from my service. Could we explore for a few moments who else I might be able to serve?

The final question in the script is an important one. Too many agents ask for referrals and then leave the burden of thinking up names on the shoulders of their clients. The truth is that your referral sources don't want to work that hard. They'll work that hard *with* you, but they won't do it alone.

✔ **Get specific.** Don't just make a general request for referrals and leave it at that (for example, "Do you know anyone you may like to refer to my business?"). Instead, lead clients into areas or niches in their lives where they have day-to-day relationships. Ask clients about potential referrals among the families at their church or workplace, people they know through their children's soccer team, and so on.

Book VI

Selling in Specialized and Growing Fields

Handling the referrals you receive

When handling referrals, take these steps:

1. **Qualify the lead and determine the odds that your investment of time and resources will result in a commission check.**

   For more on qualifying leads, refer to Book III, Chapter 2.

2. **Develop only qualified referrals into client prospects.**

3. **Thank and reward your referral sources for every single lead they provide, whether the referrals work out or not.**

   Too many agents reward referral sources only when the leads they provide produce a return in the form of a commission check. This is a huge mistake. If you train friends and associates to think that you only value referrals that result in closed deals, you run the risk of them prescreening leads and passing along only the ones they think will result in sales.

4. **Keep your referral sources informed of the lead's progress.**

   Especially if you're faced with the need to drop a prospect, let your referral source know what's happening. Explain that although this time the match didn't work out, you sincerely appreciate the recommendation and are honored by the referral. Try to avoid the gory details as you walk the tightrope, sparing yourself wasted time while preserving the strength of your established referral relationship.

Chapter 2

Selling Insurance

- -

In This Chapter

▶ Building relationships before the sale

▶ Getting yourself known in your market

▶ Exploring education and licensing requirements

▶ Discovering additional resources

- -

You can buy insurance for practically anything these days. Professional singers insure their voices; models insure their faces, teeth, hands, and even hair; antique and art collectors often have separate coverage (called a *rider*) for their valuable pieces. But as a general rule, insurance covers three things: people, property, and liability. Policies for life insurance, disability insurance, and health insurance cover people. Homeowner's, renter's, and auto insurance cover property. Liability insurance covers legal claims against you for harm to people and property.

Some agents specialize in providing *commercial insurance,* which covers business operations. Again, commercial insurance covers people, property, and liability. Businesses often purchase health, life, disability, and worker's compensation insurance to cover their employees. Fire and casualty insurance covers physical losses at the business location. Liability insurance covers medical claims for customers who get hurt on the property or from the business's products, as well as malpractice, often called *errors and omissions insurance.* (Check out *Insurance For Dummies,* 2nd Edition, by Jack Hungelmann [Wiley], for a full discussion of the different types of insurance.)

In this chapter, you discover how insurance agents work, and get tips and techniques for finding new customers. We tell you how to use your expertise to build a reputation as a trusted advisor, and parlay that reputation into increased sales. Finally, you read about education and licensing requirements for insurance sales and look at additional resources to improve your understanding and your bottom line.

Exploring Your Role as an Insurance Agent

Insurance agents (often called *producers*) are either affiliated with a specific company (in which case they're called *direct writers* or *captive agents*) or *independent agents,* who can write policies from a variety of insurers.

As an independent agent, you can shop around to find your clients the best price on policies, and you have lots of insurance providers to choose from. On the other hand, if your clients choose their auto coverage from one company and their homeowner's policy from a different one, they lose out on multiple-policy discounts. And, if they have policies from many different companies, it can be harder for both you and them to identify gaps in their coverage.

As a captive agent, you can offer your clients the convenience of one-stop shopping for all or most of their insurance needs. It's also easier to make sure your clients' coverage limits are consistent across their various policies and to identify places where their coverage needs to be adjusted. Most insurance companies also provide discounts when people have multiple policies with them, which adds value for your clients.

Some agents choose to specialize in the kinds of insurance products they represent. But the trend these days is for agents to offer as broad a menu of products as possible. The more products you sell, the more licenses you'll need from the states in which you do business (see the section "Getting Licensed to Sell Insurance," later in this chapter).

Connecting with Potential Clients

Once upon a time, selling insurance was basically a numbers game: If you made enough cold calls, you'd get enough appointments to meet your quotas and goals. This method worked so well that many seminars and even company training sessions still emphasize cold calling.

But the world today is much different than it was when cold calling was king. Two-income households and caller ID mean you may not even get anyone to answer the phone. If someone does answer, you're just as likely (maybe more likely) to get a request to put the number on your do-not-call list as you are to get an appointment with a prospect. And if the number you dialed is on the National Do Not Call Registry, you could even get yourself and your agency in trouble.

Truth is, cold-calling for insurance is just too hard these days. As with many sales fields, successfully selling insurance is more about cultivating relationships than about how many phone calls you can make in a day. Networking is king now — but only if you do it right.

Effective networking is more than just exchanging business cards at the monthly chamber of commerce mixer. To build your client base, you need to start by positioning yourself as a trusted, knowledgeable adviser, which means providing value to potential clients *before* you close the sale. The more value people perceive in their interactions with you, the less likely they are to view you as just another pushy salesperson and the more likely they are to call you when they're ready to buy.

Most people who are looking for an insurance agent rely on referrals from friends and family members. Some people use the phone book or an online version of the phone book, but that's a crapshoot from your perspective as an agent. And people can't refer others to you if they don't know you exist. The following sections take you through some steps — less conventional than cold calling, but much more effective — to get yourself known, meet potential clients, and build relationships that lead to sales.

Book VI

Selling in Specialized and Growing Fields

Getting your information out there

The most effective marketing techniques often don't have anything to do with advertising or *tchotchkes* (calendars, magnets, pens, and so on) emblazoned with your name and contact info. New prospects *may* call you because they saw your name in the Yellow Pages or on a stack of sticky notes. But they're more likely to remember you if you provide them with something they can really use: information about insurance products in clear, everyday language.

As in any sales job, the more value you can provide to clients and prospects, the more likely those people are to view you as a trusted adviser — and, thus, the more likely they are to both buy from you and to refer their friends to you. Insurance provides countless opportunities to provide this added value in the form of "how does this affect me" information. For example, consider adding a blog to your website that explains changes in healthcare laws or gives advice on how to determine how much (and the type of) life insurance you need based on different circumstances or stages of life.

You have several options for disseminating this kind of information, and most of them are inexpensive to develop and deliver. Look through the following sections for ideas.

Creating a newsletter

Many agents deliver e-mail newsletters to their existing clients, full of information about their products, tips for choosing products and coverage, and so on. You can use this same vehicle to help position yourself as the go-to person when people are ready to discuss their insurance needs.

Research indicates that people spend an average of 51 seconds perusing newsletters, whether they're digital or hard copies. Effective newsletters, therefore, are short (no more than four pages for a hard copy) and get to the point right away. Fill yours with information that's useful to the reader, and forget trying to hard-sell your products in your copy. If one of your articles is, for example, "Five Things to Look For in a Life Insurance Policy," end the piece with a call to action (such as, "Linda Agent offers a full line of XYZ life insurance policies — call today to discuss your life insurance needs"), but don't write an ode to your products.

So, you've got a newsletter. Now what do you do with it? Here are some ideas:

✔ **Give or send copies to new contacts.** When you get someone's business card at a networking event, hand him a hard copy or ask if you can e-mail him your newsletter. If you've written about a topic you discussed with this person, even better. Say, "I covered that in my newsletter last month. I'll send it to you when I get back to the office."

Always get permission before you e-mail your newsletter to a new contact. Then, in your e-mail, invite the contact to join your mailing list. You never know — six months from now, that person may be ready to buy from you.

Make sure to give recipients a way to unsubscribe from your e-mail list, and abide by their requests. Consider sending your e-mail newsletter through a company like MailChimp (www.mailchimp.com) or Constant Contact (www.constantcontact.com); they'll make managing your list easier.

✔ **Hand out copies at personal appearances.** Whenever you give a speech, a seminar, or a workshop, or appear at trade and business shows (see the following section), have a stack of your most recent newsletter for people to take and read at their leisure.

✔ **Leave your newsletter as a door-hanger at people's homes.** Pick a neighborhood and leave copies of your newsletter at each residence. This tactic works because you're not intruding on people's busy schedules; you're simply leaving information for them to consider at their convenience. And the more useful your information is to them, the more likely they are to contact you.

Never leave any materials in mailboxes; doing so is a violation of federal law and can land you in trouble. Always check to make sure you aren't breaking any homeowner's association rules before leaving materials, too.

Writing articles for others

As an insurance agent, you're in a unique position to explain technical details about various insurance products to a lay audience. If you can explain how small businesses can navigate healthcare reform, for example, in plain language, write an article on that topic and submit it to your local newspaper, supermarket shopper, business publication, or any other media outlet. Even if your article isn't published, keep copies to hand out to prospects just as you do with your newsletter (see the preceding section).

Most people find insurance as a whole incredibly confusing, and changes in the laws (like healthcare reform) just exacerbate that confusion. If you can put these concepts into simple, easy-to-follow prose, you provide a genuine, needed service that will translate into business down the road.

Becoming the local expert

Getting yourself known as your community's go-to expert on insurance matters is a great way to raise your profile and connect with prospective clients. Focus on your main product area (life, health, commercial, or what have you) and who you want to reach with your information, then do your homework and figure out what your target audience wants to know and how you can reach them.

Fortunately, nearly every community provides lots of opportunities for you to exploit your expertise; read the following sections to determine which ones best suit your style and situation.

All the ideas listed here involve public speaking to some extent. If you want to hone your public speaking and presentation skills, or if you just want to practice in front of a live, friendly audience, look for a Toastmasters International group in your area (check out www.toastmasters.org to find local clubs). Membership dues are small — usually less than $50 a year — and these clubs are another networking opportunity for you.

Hosting seminars and workshops

Lots of insurance agents host free dinners at a nice restaurant or banquet hall to attract potential clients. The idea is that people are willing to come hear your information in exchange for free food.

The downside of this tactic is the expense. You can spend thousands of dollars mailing out invitations and providing the dinner, without necessarily getting any return on your investment.

However, you can minimize your cash outlay and maximize the value of these events in several ways:

✔ **Offer a Saturday morning session instead of a weekday evening dinner.** Providing coffee, juice, and pastries is much cheaper than feeding people a formal dinner. And instead of mailing out invitations, you can publicize the session through free or inexpensive advertising venues, such as your own website and newsletter, the calendar of events on your local media websites, and brief news releases to local media. If your target audience is businesspeople, you can do this on a weekday morning before the usual workday starts.

✔ **Give a free presentation at your local library or community center.** Your food and beverage costs with this option are minimal, and you may even get the meeting place for free or for a very low fee.

✔ **Present sessions at local trade and association shows.** Offer to lead a break-out educational session on a specific insurance-related topic. Your audience in these venues will be highly motivated, and you may even get paid for making your presentation. (Just make sure to pitch a topic that will be of interest to attendees.)

The goal of all these activities is to raise your profile and educate your audience. Don't expect to make sales at these events; instead, aim to provide valuable information and earn the trust of your audience.

Speaking to business and civic groups

Rotary clubs, chambers of commerce, Kiwanis, Elks, Lions, and other groups are always looking for speakers to present interesting, engaging, and useful information to their members. You may even receive an honorarium for speaking to these groups. But the real advantage to you in signing up for these engagements lies in building your image as a trusted expert.

Your appearance at these groups typically will involve giving a short presentation — say, 20 minutes or so — followed by a question-and-answer session. These time limits mean you have to keep your presentation focused on a single topic or aspect of insurance. For example, give your audience information about different kinds of annuities, how they work, their pros and cons, but don't try to explain all the minutiae — that would bore your audience anyway.

Your audience at civic clubs like the Rotary likely will include some of your direct competitors, so you must take pains to ensure that your presentation isn't viewed as "poaching." Focus on providing information rather than pitching your products or service, and prepare a useful (that is, informational instead of promotional) handout or "take-away" for your audience. The only strictly promotional material you should leave behind for these groups is your business card. And, because the competition for speaking slots is fierce in these groups, the more unique and educational your presentation is, the better your chances of getting the speaking gig.

Some people worry about being asked a question they can't answer, and they drive themselves nuts trying to prepare for every possible question. Be well prepared, but don't be afraid to say you don't know the answer. Make a note of the question and get the contact info of the person who asked it; then follow up with an e-mail or note the next day.

Build relationships with local media

Seek out opportunities to appear on local radio and television shows as an expert on a specific aspect of insurance. For example, you could present a New Year's "financial fitness" segment on your local radio talk show or television news program. Or you could offer insights into how changes in laws or regulations will affect the average worker or homeowner.

The key to becoming an expert that your local media outlets rely on is to offer information that's timely and relevant to their audiences. Follow developments and trends in your industry, and offer to help local reporters, talk-show hosts, and producers explain these developments and trends to their readers, listeners, and viewers.

People respond far more favorably to advisors than they do to sales reps. The techniques outlined in this section often are more effective than any amount of cold calling because they take you out of the salesperson's role and recast you as an expert who provides needed services. Spend your marketing energy and resources building this kind of reputation, and sales will ultimately follow.

Gaining Trust Before the Sale

Let's face it: Nothing about insurance is sexy. People aren't going to beat down your door and beg you to sell them insurance, and they aren't going to start forming lines at 4 a.m., waiting for your office to open so they can get their hands on the hottest new insurance product. Insurance is important, and most people should have at least three kinds of policies (auto, homeowner's or renter's, and health), but, at the same time, most people can find all kinds of things they'd rather do than discuss their insurance needs with you.

Many people find insurance confusing and intimidating. According to an Ipsos/ING Survey, Americans are more comfortable figuring out how to use electronic devices like DVD players than they are at thinking about life insurance. And most people would choose activities like bungee jumping, taking out a mortgage, or having a performance review at work over talking to a life insurance agent.

So, how do you overcome your potential clients' intimidation and confusion? The answer is also in the results of the Ipsos/ING Survey. Although respondents were asked specifically about life insurance, certain qualities are essential for all insurance salespeople, no matter what products you're pitching: trustworthiness and responsiveness.

If you read much about selling insurance, you'll find that many people advocate using fear tactics to close the deal. These advisors point out, rightly, that people decide to buy with their emotions and then justify their decisions with logic, so they recommend emphasizing what prospects could lose (life, health, belongings, financial security) and then presenting your insurance products as protection. This technique certainly may be effective, but it also can backfire on you; you can easily come across as pushy and manipulative. The fact is, most people know why insurance is important and most people know what kind of insurance they should have. Much of their sales resistance arises from a sense of bewilderment about the technicalities of insurance, not from a stubborn refusal to face reality.

Many prospective clients also hesitate to purchase insurance because they're unconvinced that their risk is high enough to justify the cost of buying insurance. This disbelief in risk is one reason fear-tactic selling is so popular; many agents feel that they can only convince prospects to buy if they emphasize worst-case scenarios. But the use of fear tactics is also one factor in prospects' hesitation about buying — or, in some cases, even talking about — insurance.

So, how do you overcome the confusion, distaste, and hesitation so often associated with insurance? Position yourself as a friendly, knowledgeable expert (see "Connecting with Potential Clients," earlier in this chapter). By doing so, you automatically increase the value you provide to prospects, as well as their comfort level in talking with you. (Such positioning also can help you compete with online insurance products, because many people would rather discuss normally intimidating topics with a friendly "live" person than navigate a website to find what they're looking for.)

Of course, as the Ipsos/ING Survey highlighted, trustworthiness and responsiveness are key to insurance sales success, too. Read the following sections to find out more about how to incorporate trust and responsiveness into your day-to-day business.

Being trustworthy

One of the reasons people don't like to think about insurance is that, too often, agents are focused more on making the sale than on serving the client. Prospects want to feel that you're working with them to solve a problem and fill a need.

You may need to educate your prospects about differences in price and value for various products. For example, although your commission likely is much higher for a whole life policy, the client sitting in front of you may get a much better bang for her buck from a term life policy. And you're more likely to get referrals and repeat business from people who perceive that you serve *their* needs.

Techniques for building trust include the following:

✔ **Asking questions:** The more you explore the prospect's circumstances, the better equipped you are to suggest options that truly meet his needs.

✔ **Answering questions:** Chances are, most of your prospects don't know much about insurance and are confused about what they do know. Use clear and simple language to explain features, benefits, and pricing, and answer questions as directly and completely as possible.

✔ **Providing value to the client:** Too often, salespeople in any field focus on their needs (commissions, quotas, and so on) and put the client's needs in second, third, or fourth place. In the long run, though, you damage your reputation and your career when you sell a prospect something he doesn't want or need. On the other hand, if you can help a prospect identify his real needs and provide an option that fills that need at a reasonable (to the prospect) price, you make the sale — and very likely will get referrals from this new client.

You can put risk in its proper perspective without abusing fear tactics. For example, most states require car owners to have a minimum level of liability insurance. So, how do you convince a client to purchase more coverage than the law requires? Here are some possible talking points and questions to get your client to think realistically about her needs:

Even if you're an excellent driver, you share the road with a lot of not-so-excellent drivers. Your coverage should be sufficient to protect you against the actions of other drivers.

If someone runs a red light and totals your car, would you have enough money available to replace it?

I recommend choosing a deductible amount that you know you'll always have available. If you don't consistently have $1,000 in your emergency fund, you probably should choose a $250 or $500 deductible, even though the premium is higher.

Regardless of what kind of insurance you sell, your questions and talking points should always focus on the prospect's individual needs and realistic risks. If you take this approach with every prospective client and use it consistently with your existing clients, you build both trust and respect — and trust and respect go a long way toward overcoming the distaste and confusion many people feel toward insurance. The more adept you are at partnering with your prospects to find solutions for them, the more sales you'll eventually make.

Being responsive

Nothing says "I don't care about you" to a client or prospect more loudly than failing to return a phone call or an e-mail in a timely fashion (or even at all) — but, unbelievably, some insurance agents are just lousy at returning messages. In this highly competitive field, you simply can't afford to ignore communications from clients and prospects.

Existing clients call because they need something from you — they have to file a claim, or they have questions about their policy, or they need to make changes to their coverage. If you don't respond promptly, you may lose their business; even worse, you lose their potential referrals to you.

Similarly, prospects don't contact you unless they're in the market for what you're selling. If you don't pay attention to them when you're trying to win their business, you're telling them that you won't pay attention to them after you get the sale.

Building responsiveness into your daily routine takes some planning, but that planning pays off in better customer service (thus, improving your chances at getting referral business). Try these approaches to ensure that you don't inadvertently leave clients or prospects waiting by the phone or computer:

✔ **Check e-mail at regular times throughout the day.** You can easily get caught up in dealing with e-mail at the expense of other tasks you need to complete, so set up regular times for this task. Give yourself half an hour at the beginning of your day, at midday, and at the end of the day to read and respond to e-mails. Set up an auto-reply to tell people when they can expect to hear back from you. A simple "Thank you for contacting our office. We reply to most e-mails within four hours during regular business hours" suffices for an auto-reply — *as long as you follow through with an actual reply within the time frame you promise.*

✔ **Check voicemail at regular times throughout the day.** You may not want to leave your cellphone on when you're visiting with clients, hosting an event (see "Connecting with Potential Clients," earlier in this chapter), or what have you. However, you should be able to check voicemail every 60 to 90 minutes throughout the day. As with your e-mail, record an outgoing message that lets callers know when they can expect to hear back from you, and then make sure you follow through. Even if you have to set up another time to talk to the client or prospect, returning the call to set up that other time puts you leagues ahead of many of your competitors.

If you're on vacation or otherwise unavailable to help clients and prospects, make sure your e-mail and voicemail messages give them options for finding what they need right away. Give them the option of leaving a message for you, and refer them to a colleague (with contact info) or corporate contacts for anything that can't wait until you get back. Then follow up on all messages from your absence to make sure the client's or prospect's needs were met. (If they weren't, you have an opportunity to shine by taking care of their needs now.)

Getting Licensed to Sell Insurance

Insurance agents have to be licensed by the state in which they operate, and they can't sell insurance if the actual risk — the person, property, or liability you're covering — is located in a state where you aren't licensed. For example, if you're licensed in Montana and a client wants to insure his vacation home in Florida, you can't write that policy unless you're also licensed in Florida.

You may need several licenses, depending on which types of insurance products you want to sell and the regulations of the states where you want to operate. Before you can get any license, though, you have to complete prelicensing training. In the following sections, we look at the different kinds of licenses insurance agents can get and typical training and education requirements you have to fulfill before you can get a license.

Looking at types of licenses

Although regulations and license types vary from state to state, most insurance licenses fall into one of the following categories:

✔ **Life, Accident, and Health:** This license allows you to sell life, disability, health, long-term care, accidental death, and bodily injury insurance. Some states separate life insurance from accident and health and require agents to get two separate licenses if they want to sell all these products.

✔ **Fire and Casualty:** As its name implies, a Fire and Casualty license permits you to sell insurance products that protect property, such as auto, motorcycle, boat, and RV policies; homeowner's and renter's insurance; liability coverage related to real estate and personal property; and special policies like flood or earthquake insurance. In some states, this license also allows you to sell a limited line of personal insurance products, such as disability and long-term care policies.

✔ **Limited Lines Automobile:** This type of license, offered by several states, limits you to selling auto and motorcycle policies.

✔ **Personal Lines:** Some states offer a Personal Lines license, which allows you to sell many of the same types of insurance as a Fire and Casualty license. Generally, Personal Lines licenses exclude you from offering commercial insurance products; you can sell only individual policies.

Most insurance agents — especially those just entering the field — choose to get either the Life, Accident, and Health license, or the Fire and Casualty license. Many new agents choose to get both so they can offer a broader range of products to their clients.

If, like many agents, you also want to offer financial services, you'll need a securities license in addition to your insurance license. Agents who offer a full financial planning package typically are licensed to sell mutual funds, variable annuities, and other kinds of securities. (See Book VI, Chapter 3, for more on selling financial services.)

Considering training and education requirements

Although pre-licensing education and training requirements vary from state to state, every state requires new insurance agents to fulfill a minimum number of classroom hours before they're eligible to take the licensing exam. In addition, each state has its own mandatory continuing education requirements for licensed agents.

Procedures and requirements for obtaining an insurance agent's license vary from state to state. The National Association of Insurance Commissioners has a states and jurisdiction map on its website (`www.naic.org/state_web_map.htm`) that provides links to every state's insurance regulatory agency. From there, you can find out about each state's requirements for training, testing, and licensing insurance agents.

In general, states require aspiring agents to take:

- ✔ 20 to 40 hours (sometimes more) of general insurance courses
- ✔ At least 6 hours of ethics courses
- ✔ Practice exams and quizzes as part of their coursework

After you've finished your pre-licensing coursework, you can take the state exam for the type(s) of license you want to receive. State licensing exams typically cover general insurance knowledge on the products covered by the license, as well as the state's specific insurance laws and regulations.

Insurance licenses are issued by state governments, not by the schools that provide pre-licensing or continuing education courses. Your school will provide you with a certificate of completion, which you must present in order to take the state exam.

Many new agents take their pre-licensing coursework online, which allows them to complete their studies at their own pace and as their schedules permit. Insurance Workforce has a list of accredited online insurance education programs on its website (`www.insuranceworkforce.com/education.html`).

If you also want to sell financial services like retirement planning, mutual funds, and so on, you'll need to get a securities license. All securities professionals, from salespeople to officers and managers, have to register with the Financial Industry Regulatory Authority (FINRA) and must pass exams to demonstrate competence in the areas in which they provide services. Exams typically cover general markets knowledge as well as understanding of the securities industry and regulatory structure. Check out FINRA's website (`www.finra.org`) for detailed information.

Checking Out Additional Resources

There's no shortage of resources for insurance professionals, and that's a good thing, because insurance professionals have to stay on top of changing laws and regulations, trends in the industry, sales techniques, and even economic news if they want to grow their businesses.

Here, in no particular order, are some resources that you may find helpful as you plot your insurance sales career:

- **The Agent's Sales Journal** (www.asjonline.com): This trade magazine offers how-to content on marketing and prospecting, information on products, and research on the industry.

- **The American Insurance Association** (www.aiadc.org): The only insurance trade group with representatives in every state, AIA focuses on issues of regulation and public policy at the state and federal levels. AIA represents both property and casualty insurers.

- **Health Insurance Association of America** (www.hiaa.org): HIAA conducts research and advocacy activities as part of its involvement in state and federal public policy debates on health insurance laws and regulations.

- **The Risk Management Society** (www.rims.org): RIMS provides daily news on risk, insurance, and benefits topics. The website also includes legislative updates, information on professional advancement, and searchable databases on a variety of topics.

There are literally hundreds (perhaps thousands) of smaller insurance trade groups and associations; every state has at least one such group. Tapco Underwriters, Inc., has a fairly comprehensive list (with links) of trade groups and associations on its website (www.gotapco.com/ News_AssociationLinks.aspx).

Chapter 3

Selling Financial Services

In This Chapter

▶ Exploring the field of financial services

▶ Understanding the types of products to sell

▶ Choosing the specialty area you'll enjoy selling

▶ Looking at selling skills that demonstrate professionalism

*B*etween the effects of the Great Recession and the Baby Boomers reaching retirement age, the financial services industry is growing rapidly. Add to that the fact that younger workers, in general, don't seem to have a lot of confidence that the Social Security system as we know it will survive into their retirement years. Those factors have all combined to create an explosion in the financial services industry — and by all facts and appearances, the industry will continue to flourish for quite some time.

According to the U.S. Census Bureau, there is a need for 2.2 million people to work in the financial services industry by the year 2016. Not only is there a huge availability of work in this field, but when managed properly, a career in financial services can be extremely lucrative.

If you think about it, you have to agree that it's wise to have a reliable resource for recommendations of how to protect your loved ones, your possessions, and your financial future. Most people pay other people for their knowledge of how to do this — and they pay them well. If you have any interest in this field, why not learn how to provide those services in the most effective manner and grow your own nest egg while helping others grow theirs?

Defining the Industry

The financial services industry encompasses a broad range of organizations that all exist to manage money. Among these organizations are the following:

- ✔ **Banks:** Banks accept deposits from those who have accounts and use those funds to provide credit either by lending or investing the money. Some banks operate locally; others are recognized internationally. Some of the latter include Bank of America, U.S. Bank, Chase, and Wells Fargo. Banking practices in the United States are regulated by the federal government.

- ✔ **Credit unions:** Credit unions are nonprofit institutions owned and controlled by their members and operated for the purpose of promoting thrift, providing credit at competitive rates, and providing other financial services. They differ from banks in that the members who have accounts are the owners. Only members may deposit or borrow money from a credit union. Initially, credit unions were started to assist the poor laborers who were denied standard banking services. In some cases, credit unions limit themselves to certain members such as the Teachers Credit Union, the Navy Federal Credit Union, and the Federal Employees Credit Union.

- ✔ **Credit card companies:** Credit card companies issue cards that are used as a system of payment for goods and services based on the cardholder's promise to repay the funds. For amounts not paid in full each payment period, the credit card companies charge a fee called *interest* on the balance.

- ✔ **Insurance companies:** Insurance companies assist people with risk management. In exchange for payment, an insurance company will agree to assist you with certain risks, such as property damage, illness, disability, death, and other hazards that could negatively impact a person's financial situation.

- ✔ **Consumer finance companies:** Consumer finance companies are referred to as alternative financial services (AFS) and are provided outside the traditional banking institutions mentioned earlier in this list. In most cases, low-income people depend upon consumer finance companies for cashing checks and making loans. In some areas, these places are known as check-cashing or payday loan businesses. Some such companies also offer debt consolidation and credit counseling because their clients may have been refused credit by traditional banks or credit unions.

- ✔ **Stock brokerages:** Stock brokerages assist people with buying and selling stocks to generate additional income on the money they invest. In some cases, they only carry out the client's instructions, acting as an agent and charging a fee for that service. Other brokerages act in advisory positions, making suggestions to clients but leaving the final decisions to the investors.

- ✔ **Investment fund firms:** Investment fund firms gather a group of clients together to pay the firms fees to manage investments on their behalf. Working with a firm like this allows people to split the cost of making investments with the group and to diversify their investments beyond what they could possibly do as solo investors.

Other industries also are associated with the more traditional financial services businesses:

- **Credit counseling:** Credit counseling is a process of offering education to consumers about how to avoid incurring unhealthy debt. Typically, this includes helping people establish budgets and develop plans for reducing their debts.

- **Credit card processing:** Credit card processing companies assist with the movement of funds from a merchant who accepts credit cards into the merchant's bank account. The processing service typically charges a fee that's a percentage of the value of the purchase in order to provide this service.

- **Leasing:** Leasing companies provide financing on things such as cars and equipment that the people using them may not want to own at the end of a period of time. The lease allows them to make a lower monthly investment for the use of the product. If they choose to own the item at the end of the term of the lease, there is a remainder amount that has to be paid. If they don't choose to own it, the item is turned back over to the business for resale.

You rely on the financial services industry if you do anything with money other than stuffing it in a mattress or tossing coins in a jar. Here are just a few of the daily doings in most people's lives that involve some aspect of the financial services industry:

- **Earning money:** If you receive a paycheck, you use some type of financial institution to either cash that check or hold that check's funds for you in a checking or savings account until you need to exchange it for goods and services.

- **Carrying money:** Where did you get that last $20 from that's currently resting in the folds of your wallet? From a bank teller? From an ATM? As cash back from a purchase transaction? All cash comes from sources that use a financial system to provide it.

- **Spending money:** Debit and credit card transactions are all part of the financial services industry. They allow you to exchange your money for other things that are of more value to you than money, such as housing, electricity, food, clothing, and, of course, the more fun things in life such as entertainment, vacations and luxuries. They allow you to do this without cash. By using your debit or credit card, you're authorizing the vendor to get money from your account at a banking institution or agreeing to pay a credit card company for lending you the money for the transaction.

- **Insuring anything:** Lives are insured in the event of loss. Loved ones who are left behind who may have been dependent upon the deceased for financial support receive money upon that person's death. Health is insured so an accident or major illness doesn't wipe out your finances; health insurance covers medical expenses. Disability insurance provides continued income if you're unable to work to earn a living. Possessions — such as homes, vehicles, boats, trailers, jewelry, collectibles, tools, and furnishings — are insured against damage or loss.

✔ **Planning for retirement:** Retirement accounts are those in which you save a little every day, week, or month when you're younger so you'll have money to spend in your later years when you no longer have to, want to, or can work to earn a daily wage.

To borrow a line from one of the songs in the movie *Cabaret,* "Money makes the world go around." Either you learn how to manage it for yourself or you'll end up paying someone else to help manage it for you. If you don't do either of those things, you're not likely to have much money in your life. And your world won't go very far around. Because nearly everyone on the planet is a potential client for some aspect of the financial services industry, there are plenty of career opportunities for you to sell them those necessary services.

Offering the Basics and More

You must believe in a product or service before you can ever hope to do well selling it. People buy from you based more on your conviction and belief in your product than on your knowledge and selling skills. Knowledge and selling skills are definitely critical to success, but if you don't believe in what you're selling, it'll show in your eyes, your body language, or some other subconscious way. Whatever it is, your potential clients will pick up on it. They'll become hesitant. They'll build a wall of resistance between you and them. Then they'll seek out someone else to buy from who really does believe in the product.

In this section, we review the basic categories of products you could consider selling if you choose the lucrative financial services industry as a career.

Banking services

At the most basic level, most people need savings and checking accounts. In today's world, those accounts typically come with debit cards to allow users to make electronic transactions instead of writing checks or paying with cash. An electronic transaction allows people to direct money from their account with a bank or credit union to their creditors such as a mortgage company, the company that provided them with a loan for their car, an insurance provider, a utility company, or a credit card company. Electronic transactions can be set up where the person authorizes your creditors to automatically withdraw funds from the account. Or it can be set up where the bank sends money to the vendor on behalf of the account holder. With the ability of most of the world to be on the go with mobile devices such as phones and computers, banking businesses also provide their services in mobile- or computer-friendly form.

In the category of savings, most banks also offer interest-earning money market accounts and certificates of deposit, also known as CDs. Some even offer programs where they help people move money from their checking to savings accounts automatically, so they barely notice it's been done — until they see how quickly their saving accounts are growing.

When customers are established with a bank, often the job of those in the business shifts from not only serving checking and savings needs, but to persuading clients to expand their use of services with that institution. In other words, selling banking services. Most banks and credit unions offer loan programs for things such as homes, vehicles, education, and other large purchases. Some offer financial advice, investment opportunities, and their own credit cards that they expect their employees to recommend to existing banking clients.

Insurance

Most adults have responsibilities. Those responsibilities include providing financial support to family members while they're alive and working. Wise adults invest in insurance to protect their health in case they have a major illness. They purchase disability insurance should they be unable to work for an extended period of time. They carry life insurance that will go to their loved ones to assist them financially when they die.

As an insurance agent for a particular company, such as State Farm, Aflac, Nationwide, American Family, and so on, you're expected to sell all the services offered by that company to qualified clients. Of course, not every client you have for one line of insurance will be qualified for another, but you're expected to seek out qualified buyers and sell the wide variety of products available from the company.

If you work as an independent insurance broker, you may represent several companies' lines of products. You'll be encouraged (and incentivized) to sell one company's product over another, but the final decision of what to offer will be up to you, after you know the real needs of your client. You'll always work in the best interest of the client.

You can insure practically anything. Famous actors and artists have been known to insure the various body parts with which they generate their incomes, such as the legs of dancers, the hands of artists, the voices of singers, and so on. Lloyd's of London is one world-renowned insurer of such things — everything from Bruce Springsteen's vocal chords to America Ferrera's smile.

Pending changes on the healthcare front

In 2010, the United States passed the Affordable Care Act, giving Americans new rights and benefits, helping more children get healthcare, allowing adult children under the age of 26 to stay on their parents' health insurance. and giving patients access to recommended preventive services without cost. If you're interested in selling health insurance, read up on the changes occurring in this aspect of the industry. The new law is making a direct and specific impact on the types of health insurance to be sold and the requirements of insurance agencies in providing health insurance. A good starting point is to read the Patient's Bill of Rights and other information about the law at (www. healthcare.gov).

College funds

The cost of education is constantly on the rise. The value of education is priceless. So, many parents (and grandparents) set up accounts that they contribute to for a number of years, dedicated to covering expenses related to educating children whose futures they care about. In the United States, there are several types of accounts that have various benefits to both the person setting them up and the young adult who will receive them.

These plans include 529 prepaid tuition plans, in which the investor locks in tuition rates for an in-state college; Uniform Gift to Minors Act (UGMA) and Uniform Transfer to Minors Act (UTMA) accounts; and good old U.S. savings bonds. Most of these plans are available through traditional banks. Some financial services companies, such as Fidelity and New York Life Insurance, offer the accounts but not savings bonds.

Retirement programs

The most common retirement programs involve investing money in stocks, bonds, insurance, and annuities. Some of the stock and bond programs include individual retirement accounts (IRAs), 401(k) programs, and other accounts with letters and numbers too numerous to detail here. They're available through banking institutions and through many insurance companies via brokers or financial planners. The goal with these accounts is to have money invested such that it works as another entity earning income on your behalf. Upon retirement, you withdraw amounts of money from retirement accounts to cover your living expenses or other needs a little at a time over time. The goal of selling this type of program is to help people set aside enough so they don't outlive their money and end up with nothing to cover their basic expenses. This field is growing due to the worldwide aging of the baby boomers — and it will continue to grow as their children (another large generation) mature and plan for retirement.

Qualifying Yourself

A full-time career in the financial services industry requires a certain level of commitment to education, training, and growth. The products offered can be very simple or very complex. No matter which area you find most compelling, you'll need to understand the products in great depth before you can sell them to others. Then you'll need to develop the people skills covered in the rest of this book in order to educate potential clients properly about the benefits of the products as they relate to their specific situations. Depending upon your particular market demographic, you may need to develop skills specific to the cultures of your potential clients. And you may need to make a commitment to higher education (including getting licenses to market them) and continued education to maintain those licenses.

Computer skills

Nearly every position in the financial services arena will involve some sort of computer work. At the very least, you need some basic computer skills. Our society is computer dependent, and with even the simplest banking services now available online, you better know your keyboard and understand the hows and whys of using passwords to access critical information.

More than one language

If you plan to work in an area where there may be folks who speak another language from yours as their primary language (for example, Spanish in communities near the Mexican border or various Asian dialects if you live in an area with a large Asian community), knowing that second language can be extremely helpful in getting your career off the ground.

Formal education

Entering the financial services field is not difficult. In most areas, you can begin as a basic bank teller with a high school diploma or equivalent and no experience. All you need is the ability to count and follow instructions. On-the-job training is readily available. As you can imagine, with such minimal requirements to enter the field, the income potential is quite minimal as well. However, it's a great way to gain basic knowledge of commonly used practices and procedures within the financial industry.

If you choose to stay in the banking arena, there are many opportunities for growth. With a few years of experience, you can quickly move to a level of more responsibility within a bank or credit union. However, some positions do require additional formal education. For example, to become involved in helping people with loans from financial institutions, most banks, credit unions, or loan companies require a bachelor's degree and a few years of experience in the industry.

To determine where to begin with such education, ask at your local community college or university or go online to job posting sites. Along with the job description, you'll usually find the level of education required — and sometimes the type of education preferred. Some institutions offer programs where they reimburse you for your educational expenses if you achieve a certain grade. Consider that when applying for a position.

In the insurance field, you could find an entry-level job as a claims coordinator with an associate's degree and some experience in the field or in a related area.

Licensing

As you grow in your career, you may need to take various courses to advance your knowledge and to acquire (and keep) licenses required by the government in order to sell specific products such as mortgages, insurance, mutual funds, and securities. As an example, to become a Chartered Financial Analyst (CFA), you need a bachelor's degree and 48 months of qualified work experience, in addition to passing a series of three six-hour exams. Most licenses require continued education to keep them current, so you'll need to make a commitment to attending additional courses as well.

If your interests lie in the more dynamic industry of stocks, becoming a stock broker requires a bachelor's degree and experience in the field or in a related area. In the United States, you also must meet state licensing requirements and become a registered representative with the National Association of Securities Dealers (NASD). Another requirement is that you pass the Series 7 exam (called the General Securities Registered Representative Examination).

To become an agent, you must be licensed to sell the various types of insurance. For example, you may need to take a licensing exam just for selling property and casualty insurance, another for selling life insurance, and so on.

Some companies have programs where you can join the company and start earning income quickly while going on calls with licensed agents as long as you're in the process of going through your own licensing training. Many of these companies have excellent and frequent training opportunities. The leaders of the companies are usually very helpful in getting others launched in their own careers, providing excellent guidance and mentorship.

It's important to research the requirements for the specific line of products you're most interested in and follow industry guidelines regarding education and licensing. If you want to get started immediately, consider taking a job at the lowest entry level your current education will allow. Then talk to someone who's ahead of you on your chosen career path for advice on courses to take that will help you get ahead as quickly as possible.

Identifying the Selling Skills You Need for Financial Services

People can be funny about their money. The type of "funny" we're referring to is not a laughing matter. Information about money is often considered something quite private and personal — not unlike personal medical information. Money also can be a very emotional topic for some folks.

In many cultures, how much money you have can be tied to how secure you feel. Some folks have been raised to believe that information about their level of wealth is something to be kept private — it's not good to talk about your money. In some cultures, this is because people aren't supposed to flaunt their wealth or make others who have less feel poorly. Or it may be because someone is poor and feels ashamed to admit it.

In my experience, very few people don't have strong feelings one way or another about money. For that reason, it's critical that you understand, learn, and use specific strategies when trying to help people with their financial needs through your products and services.

Be a product of the product

When starting out in any field of sales, be sure to buy your product first. For example, you wouldn't get a job as a teller at Main Street Bank, but do your own banking at Downtown Bank. If you're young and married and you have small children, you wouldn't try to sell life insurance to another young, married couple with small children unless you had your own policy in place. You want to be able to speak from personal experience about the benefits of the product you're selling. If you try to sell something you don't have personal experience with, it will negatively impact your credibility more in the financial services industry than in many others.

Obviously, if you're just starting out and you don't have dependents or own any property, you probably don't need a life insurance policy, so getting one would be poor judgment on your part. First and foremost, in any industry, but especially with something as important as people's financial futures, the decision to own your product or service must truly be good for the people buying them. And your purchase of or investment in those same products must be truly good for you, too.

Expect rejection

Money makes the world go around, so practically everyone on the planet is a potential client for financial services of some sort or another. You can talk to nearly anyone you meet anywhere you go, and they'll require knowledge, expertise, and products in the financial arena. The sad truth is that too few of the people you talk with will want to work with you . . . and may even reject the possibility of talking with you until you master the powerfully effective selling skills we cover here. But before we get into the skills to help you find, qualify, and get business, you need to be mentally prepared for the tasks ahead.

Even if you've chosen to become a bank teller, not every person who walks or drives up to your window will want any services from you (or your bank) other than to make a deposit, cash a check, or make a withdrawal. But you don't know which people are interested in other services and which aren't until you start asking. So, when you follow the protocol set forth by your employer, you may be asked to say to each and every client, "What other banking needs may we serve today?" Or, "How else may I assist you today?" Or even, "Were you aware that our current auto loan rates are the lowest in the area? How may we assist you in taking advantage of that?" No matter how wide you smile and how friendly you are with clients, most of them will reply to questions like those with, "No, thanks." That doesn't mean you stop asking! It also means that you don't take their rejection personally. You can't let it bother you that the first 10, 25, or 100 people you ask those questions of aren't interested. It has nothing to do with you — they just don't need any other services right now. However, should a need arise in the near future, they're likely to remember that you mentioned providing additional services and come back for more information.

In the areas of selling insurance and retirement plans, begin by reaching out to your own family members, loved ones, friends, and acquaintances when offering your services. This is called your *warm market*. These people already know you and have a certain level of trust with you. Even so, they may say, "No, thanks." Again, that's okay — it's all part of the job. The advantage you have with your warm market, though, is that most people will likely be willing to act as scouts or ambassadors for you, sending you other people who do have immediate needs for your products and services. So, never fear rejection, just look for another path to the prize.

Open the door of communication

Approaching people by telling them what you do is not going to get you very far very fast. As discussed elsewhere in this book, you must learn how to ask the right questions in just the right way in order to start a conversation. Then you build more questions on the answers from the first ones, to steer the conversation in the direction of financial services. When you're on the topic, don't push with facts, statements, or features. Instead, lead with questions and benefits.

For example, say you're standing in line at your favorite coffee shop at 7 a.m. and you decide to see if someone near you has a need for your services. You wouldn't walk up and down the line handing out business cards and saying, "Nothing happens by chance, my friends. I'm a certified financial planner. Everyone needs my services, including you. You and I are together in this place and time because we're supposed to meet. Here's my card. Give me a call so I can get your business." This kind of interaction is too abrupt, not to mention unprofessional and one-sided.

A better approach may be to simply smile at the person in line behind you. (Don't try to talk with the person in front unless he makes eye contact with you — leaning over someone's shoulder could cause him to have a bit of fear, and that's the last thing you want.) After you smile at the person behind you, make a general question/comment such as, "Nice day, don't you think?" If he replies in kind — with a smile and a nod or "yes" — he's given you an opening to speak with him again. You may say, "Do you live or work in the area?" This question isn't threatening. As far as he knows, you're a stranger to the area and may need directions or a recommendation of some sort. Follow his answer with, "What type of business are you in?" Then make a positive comment about his business. Now that the conversation is beginning to flow, you can say, "I love my work. I help individuals and families achieve their dreams with regard to financial independence." He'll likely reply, "How do you do that?" Now, you're getting somewhere.

No one will want to talk about his money situation standing in line in a public place — and that's okay. You don't want to sell him anything here anyway. You just want to earn the right to give him your card and, hopefully, get permission to send him some information. With that permission, you gain his contact information. During your follow-up, you'll get the commitment to meet privately to discuss his needs, hopes, and dreams, and the paths required to get there.

Prepare them so you can do your job right

When you finally get a potential client to agree to meet with you, it's time to kick into prep mode. You never want the potential client to feel unprepared or dumb for not having necessary information at the ready during your time together. So as not to frighten her away, say something like this:

> Mary, in order to do the best job of analyzing your particular situation, it would be helpful if you could have a few pieces of information available when we meet.

That statement tells Mary several nonthreatening things:

✔ You want to do the "best job" for her.

✔ You're treating her "particular" or unique situation.

✔ You're asking for "a few" pieces of information.

Most people aren't all that organized when it comes to their financial paper-work. That's why the financial services industry is booming. By giving your potential clients the opportunity ahead of time to dig up some essential infor-mation, you'll make them feel competent to a certain degree. If they simply don't know where the information is, you want to know that before you meet with them.

Depending upon the types of products you're offering, some of the informa-tion you may need includes the following:

✔ A recent bank statement for her checking and savings account

✔ A list of current investments

✔ A current statement from her investment provider (if she already has one who may not be doing a good job)

✔ Information on sources of income

✔ Information on debts

✔ Any written financial plans or goals

✔ Projected windfalls such as an inheritance or upcoming sale of a home

✔ Current insurance policies

✔ Known future expenses such as college expenses for a child or grand-child

Don't expect anyone to lay her hands on this information immediately. Most people will take a day or two to locate it. Say something to make the potential client realize that she's perfectly normal if she isn't sure about pulling all that information out: "It's quite normal, Mary, not to have that sort of information right at your fingertips. Just do your best and as we talk, other things may come to mind." This goes a long way toward putting potential clients at ease after they've agreed to let you look at their personal, private financial infor-mation and before they think about cancelling on you.

Always end your call with a new potential client (after she commits to meeting with you and before the actual meeting) by saying something like the following:

Mary, I so look forward to our time together. Between now and then I, too, will be preparing to provide you with the best and most current information as we analyze your situation and see about getting you on the track you really want to be on.

This tells her that you're always learning, always gathering new information. It also tells her that you're a competent professional without coming right out and saying it.

It will also make her think twice about cancelling on you last minute when she knows you'll be doing work on her behalf. It's the old reciprocal strategy: When you do something nice for her, she feels somewhat obligated to do something nice for you. It increases the number of people who actually do keep their commitments and meet with you.

Take control of the seating

Take control of the meeting as quickly as possible. If you're meeting in your office, try not to do it across a desk — doing so puts you and your potential client on opposing sides. Instead, sit at a table where you can be in a position of being next to her or perpendicular to her. This is important if you need to point out information on her paperwork (or yours) in such a manner that both of you have your eyes in the same spot.

If you're working with a couple, it's okay to have them sit across from you, but never allow them to sit on either side of you. Allowing them to have eye contact that you can't see is the death of selling. You need to be able to watch all nonverbal communication between potential clients.

Taking control is as easy as saying, "Mary, for ease of communication in reviewing the paperwork you have ready here, please sit here . . ." and point or gesture to where you want Mary to be. Then say, ". . . and I'll sit here." Don't sit so close that Mary feels her personal space is being invaded, but sit close enough to be appropriate for business.

The same sentence and gestures would work with a couple coming into your office. However, if you're meeting with them in their home (which does happen quite a bit with insurance and retirement product sales), you want to get them to the kitchen or dining room table. If you have a choice, go with the kitchen because it's more of a personal space and people are more likely to relax. You get them there by saying, "Bob and Sally, in order to properly show you the information I prepared, it would be best if we were sitting at a table together. You don't mind if we move into the kitchen, do you?" Again, gesture in that direction if it's obvious from where you're standing and direct them to seats next to each other but opposite you.

Calm potential clients' fears

When you finally do get the opportunity to sit down with potential clients, expect them to be nervous. Just by talking with you, they're admitting to their belief that they aren't doing everything they could or should do with their money.

Your first goal is to get them to like you, trust you, and want to listen to you. How do you do that? Be your good old likeable self. By that we mean the following:

- ✔ Be courteous and polite.

- ✔ Smile and make them feel comfortable in your presence.

- ✔ Show an interest in them personally — not just in what's going on with their money.

- ✔ Assure them that you have helped tens, hundreds, or thousands of people who had questions just like theirs.

Never say anything that makes them think you're treating them just like everyone else. As a professional, you'll look at each potential client with fresh eyes. Each person has unique, individual needs — at least in his eyes. You must address them in a way that tells them you're looking at their particular situation.

It's completely normal for people to be guarded with you initially. You are, after all, coming into their space. You're entering their world literally, if you meet in their home. In a way, you can be seen as invading their privacy just by the nature of the information you need from them. That's not to say that they'll be hostile — if they felt that way, they never would have set up the meeting in the first place. But they may be leery of everything you say and do until you earn their trust.

How do you earn trust? By saying you'll do something and then doing it. You can begin simply by saying upon meeting them, "I so appreciate the time we'll share today. Our meeting was scheduled for 4 p.m., and it's just that time right now." This not only demonstrates respect for their time but proves you keep promises. See how easy it can be?

Let them know what to expect. Don't launch immediately into the questions you need answered — that would be too abrupt. Instead, establish rapport and then introduce an agenda. It doesn't need to be in writing — it may be just a simple explanation of how your meeting will proceed, like the following:

> Bob and Sally, first I'd like to explain to you a little about the process involved in analyzing your specific situation. Then I'll share a little about our company so you'll feel comfortable with our reputation and the variety of products we offer. Then I'll ask you a few questions about your current needs and situation, as well as a few about your future plans and goals. Then we'll review the material you've gathered and see where you stand today versus where you want to be in the future. Rest assured that I don't believe in high-pressure sales tactics. My goal is just to help you see how what you've done already falls into your ideal plan. Then we can

discuss any area where there may be gaps or things we can do to help you get to where you want to be. Does that sound good?

At this point, they should visibly relax. They know what to expect and won't be on guard against surprises as they would have been if you hadn't begun your meeting this way.

Ask the necessary questions

When it's time to start asking personal questions, never jump right in. Take a moment to let them know the personal stuff is coming up:

> Mike and Susan, not to be personal, but in order for me to do a better job for you, I need to ask you for some confidential information.

If you've paved the way by asking them to have that information at the ready, they'll know it's time to bring it out.

As you review each piece of information they provide, ask questions appropriate to the product you're offering, such as the following:

- ✔ Who has been helping you with _____?

- ✔ What are your long-term financial goals? Are you happy with the progress you're currently making toward them?

- ✔ What short-term needs do you have?

- ✔ Are you satisfied with your current level of protection/investment/ growth? If not, what would you like to change?

- ✔ What factors motivated you to talk with me at this time?

- ✔ What would you change about your current situation if you could?

Depending upon the products you choose to represent, these questions may vary or you may have a much longer list. You'll learn this information from your employer during your training — and if you didn't learn it, ask.

Clarify answers

Before moving from one area of questioning to another, restate the answers provided by your potential clients. You'll want to use phrases such as *If I understand you correctly* and *So, your biggest concern seems to be.* When you restate their answers to your previous questions, they'll either agree or give you a better or more detailed answer. Either way, you're gaining the information you need to do your job.

If you feel they're holding something back or if they haven't answered a question fully, simply say, "I see. Would you mind clarifying that for me?" Or, "Would you mind elaborating on that point for me?" Or, "Please help me understand your thoughts on this a little better." You're very nicely asking for added information and keeping them talking. The more they talk, the more you learn about their feelings, expectations, dreams, and goals. And you need those answers before you can do a good job of analyzing their situation.

If you receive conflicting information such as, "We expect the kids to work and save money for college" and "We value education and plan to see that the kids get through college," you need to help them decide how much help they can realistically provide and how they feel about the amount of help they give.

Most companies that offer financial services have their analyses done on computer. So, at this point, you'll likely enter their information into your software to have it generate the report. When you present their individualized analysis, take the time to explain what it shows and how that answer is based on what they told you. The analysis isn't something general that is spit out for everyone at their income level.

Depending upon how well they've acted upon their financial needs on their own, the report could be a relief to them, or it could make them very uncomfortable. It's your job to make them as comfortable as possible. So, if you're reporting not-so-great news, frame it with, "When we see results such as this, we have solutions for you to consider to get you on that path you desire." The name of the game at this stage is reassure, reassure, reassure.

After you've given your potential clients their overview analysis, it's time to start making recommendations for getting them the most basic product that will move them in the direction of their dreams. This is where your product knowledge comes into play, followed by the closing strategies covered in Book IV, Chapter 4.

Chapter 4

Selling in the Medical Field

The medical field is ever changing as research and technology continue to produce advancements by leaps and bounds. Hundreds of billions of dollars are invested in medical research of one type or another each year around the planet. It's a huge field with wide-ranging employment opportunities. According to the U.S. Bureau of Labor Statistics, healthcare will generate 3.2 million new wage and salary jobs by the year 2018 in response to the rapid growth in the elderly population.

As long as we humans have the desire to live longer, healthier lives (and want our pets to do the same), there will be jobs in research. More important for you, as you consider a career in medical sales, is that whatever those genius researchers discover or develop will need to be sold.

Medical sales representatives are often the primary catalyst for persuading medical professionals to use new products and even new procedures. Medical sales reps deliver details of innovative products to healthcare professionals through demonstrations and training. It's a great job that can be very rewarding. Your success in this arena can make a powerful, positive difference in a patient's life and in the lives of those who provide treatment and care.

What Makes This Field Different

What makes the medical field different from many others is that your clients are not often the end-users of your product. Your clients are those who prescribe the drugs you represent, recommend the product you distribute, or will benefit financially from the return on investment from the equipment you sell.

Another difference is that you'll most likely be required to go to those potential clients. Medical sales is not a job where you can sit in an office or store and conduct business over the phone and in front of a computer. The doctors, boards of directors, purchasing agents, lab technicians, and retail vendors who use your products have their clients come to them in order to serve as many people as possible during a limited number of hours in each day. They can't easily pop out of their places of business to visit with you. So, you have to go to them. This makes travel an essential aspect of several areas of business within the medical field, whether it's traveling in a national territory or to several offices in a single large medical complex.

Depending on what type of medical product you sell, one of the perks of the field is that many positions include a company vehicle (or an allowance for one) with an additional stipend for gasoline, vehicle maintenance, and repairs. With the high volume of dollars you'll generate in sales, your employer won't want to risk your breaking down and missing appointments.

Another perk of the industry is that you may be required to attend medical conventions or educational events that are held in exotic locations around the world and at beautiful resorts. You attend these events to stay abreast of the latest developments in the industry, but the phenomenal locations where the events are held can make them enjoyable on many other levels as well. Just so you don't think that jobs in medical sales are all glamour, keep in mind that you'll inevitably have to attend some conferences at less-than-five-star hotels.

A plus point with some medical products, such as pharmaceuticals, if you call on doctors' offices, is that your company may grant you a budget for providing food for the doctors' office staffs. You bring lunch, and you have a captive audience, munching away while you present the benefits of your products. A medical assistant Tom Hopkins knows always comments about the great food brought into the office daily so the doctors and staff can relax while the representatives educate them about the latest developments from their research departments.

One of the advantages of working with products in the medical field over some others is in the area of prospecting. Most sales professionals in the medical arena have assigned territories and the potential to earn higher-than-average incomes. They don't have to wonder where their next point of business will be. The clients are listed in directories of all kinds and often have their own websites that tell you what they do, where they are, their hours of operation, and how to contact them. That alone makes the prospecting aspect of selling medical products much easier than selling some other products where you need to do extensive research to find potential clients.

One of the best aspects of a job in medical sales is the knowledge that what you're doing makes a difference in the lives of others. When you hear stories from doctors about patients with chronic illnesses who are experiencing greater comfort from your product or you get the rare opportunity to see a war veteran amputee walk again, you'll truly be touched and inspired to do your job of bringing solutions to those in need with an excited commitment and determination.

Defining the Industry

Loosely defined, if something could possibly impact the health and health-related comfort of a living creature, it will likely fall into some realm of medicine. This involves both the *preventive* side of things (where we're working toward growing better, healthier foods, and deciphering genetic codes to avoid or improve chronic health conditions) and the *therapeutic* side (where healthcare professionals try to help us fix what went wrong due to the ways we have maintained, or failed to maintain, our bodies and minds).

Determining the products you like

Having a firm belief in what you do is critical to your success in selling any product. You have to believe in what the product can do for the end-user and for the providers (doctors, hospitals, and clinics) you persuade to adopt, carry, or recommend it.

Beware of the emotional aspect to selling in the medical field. You may feel drawn to this field because of some personal experience you've had. For example, if you have a friend or relative who has had a particular disease or medical issue and you're aware of how he was helped by a product, you may feel compelled to help even more people by selling it. And that's wonderful! Your belief and conviction about the product will be strong and that's important in selling — but that product may not work as well for everyone else as it did for the person you know. Or you may have lost someone you deeply cared about due to an incurable illness and you want to devote your life to selling products that extend life or ease the pain of others facing the same disease. If either of those situations is the basis from which you're considering the medical field, be aware that there's a potential emotional toll that comes with that territory. For some in the field of medical sales, there's a high rate of burnout when industry knowledge allows them to learn about new medicines or practices being developed that may not arrive in time to assist today's patients, or when the product that they know helped one person simply doesn't do the job for another.

According to Chuck Vivian, Principal Consultant with the Cogency Group, sales opportunities in the medical field include six vertical markets:

- ✔ Pharmaceuticals
- ✔ Devices or implants
- ✔ Capital equipment
- ✔ Service
- ✔ Lab or diagnostics
- ✔ Distribution

In the following sections, we cover each of these markets in greater detail.

Pharmaceuticals

Can you think of anyone who doesn't have or has never had a prescription for something? We are a pharmaceutical-dependent society. Everyone relies on the medical profession to recommend and prescribe pharmaceuticals for everything from pain medications, to sleeping aids, to blood pressure and cholesterol medicines, to antidepressants. Even for those folks who lean more toward alternative medicine, the naturopathic doctors need suppliers of their "drugs" as well.

Alternative medicine is defined as systems of diagnosis, treatment, and prevention based on philosophies and techniques other than those used in conventional Western medicine. In some cases, these practices are used *in place of* Western medicine. In others, they are used *in addition to* Western medical practices.

Pharmaceutical sales (referred to as "pharma" inside the industry) is the biggest market inside the medical field. It employs approximately 80,000 representatives in the United States alone. The responsibilities of these sales reps revolve primarily around keeping their product top of mind for the prescribing physician and other healthcare professionals, such as pharmacists and nurses.

On average, pharma reps make about eight sales calls per day to answer any questions about their product and provide their assigned customers with updates. Most pharmaceutical reps call on doctors' offices; others call on hospitals to visit pharmacists, hospital-based doctors, and administrative personnel. If you enjoy those environments and working with professionals of that bent, this may be a good field for you to consider. You can be the superhero with the rolling product case of the latest and greatest samples. (You may need superhero strength to haul those samples through miles of hallways.)

In the United States, pharmaceuticals are regulated by the Food and Drug Administration (FDA) and must meet very exacting standards. Many pharmaceuticals are considered controlled substances, and their distribution is rigidly monitored. Your company will train you on the stringent rules the government has in place.

The exchange between a pharmaceutical sales rep and a customer is a very controlled conversation. As with all medical product sales reps, pharma sales reps cannot discuss *off-label applications* (using a drug for anything other than its intended purpose) or any other questions that are outside of FDA-approved guidelines. Again, your company will provide the necessary information and training, including information on what diseases are impacted by the drugs and how, as well as common side effects that have been documented.

Generally, pharma reps have an assigned number of specific customers they call on, and they can't operate outside that territory. As you may suspect, although prospecting skills are not as important in pharma sales, presentation skills are critical. Pharmaceutical reps typically have a very small window of opportunity to be with busy doctors to deliver very important messages.

Implants and devices

Implants and devices include heart pacemakers; knee, hip, shoulder, and elbow joint replacements; surgical staplers; and vascular implants such as heart valves and stents. If a patient is getting a total knee replacement, it's done with a knee implant from an orthopedic company. When a patient is getting a pacemaker, the pacemaker is manufactured and sold by a medical device company that specializes in pacemakers.

Somebody has to sell those knee implants and pacemakers to the healthcare professionals who use them, and that somebody could be you. Sales reps in this market call on physician specialists who use the products, nurses and other healthcare professionals, and people who work in materials management or purchasing at hospitals or surgicenters.

This is a very competitive vertical market, and sales reps have to undergo extensive training in order to provide technical support to end-users. As you may have guessed, when a new product is introduced, doctors don't all drop what they're doing and head back to medical school to learn how to use it. Sales reps provide training and technical support for doctors, nurses, and any other healthcare professional involved with the use of the product. You'll have to learn the language and the technical aspects of procedures where your products are used.

Healthcare professionals are very special people and very demanding. This is especially true when it comes to learning about new products from field sales reps. Your employer will train you well, so don't be afraid to pursue sales positions in this area. But keep in mind that you'll likely be required to provide technical support during actual procedures, so this vertical market is not for those who are uncomfortable at the sight of surgery or blood.

Capital equipment

Capital equipment is anything that is paid for from a hospital or clinic capital budget. This equipment can be as diverse as surgical robotic systems, diagnostic equipment such as magnetic resonance imaging (MRI) scanners that can cost millions of dollars, and high-tech equipment that can guide tiny devices through a patient's body. On the other hand, this category also includes hospital beds, operating room tables and lights, and sophisticated X-ray equipment.

Selling capital equipment sounds prestigious, but the sales cycles are typically very long. For this reason, sales reps in this market must be tenacious and focused. When a potential opportunity is identified, you can count on fierce competition. Like sharks to blood in the water, competitors are drawn to hospitals and clinics that are approaching a new budget year or have received generous donations from philanthropists. Hospitals just don't buy operating room tables or multi-million-dollar MRI machines every day. In fact, most capital equipment sales are based on a three-to-seven-year cycle before obsolescence or inter-hospital competition demands an upgrade. (Yes, hospitals compete for business. Think about it, if you required surgery, would you want to go to a hospital with outdated equipment or use the services of a doctor who does?)

Because of relatively fewer opportunities, a territory can be geographically extensive, requiring lengthy travel in order to engage potential clients. Unlike your pharma counterparts, if you choose to pursue an opportunity with a company that sells capital equipment, you're very likely to travel great distances. It may also involve more people and be more complex. You call on specialists who are your primary users, as well as hospital and clinic materials and purchasing executives and even hospital chief financial officers.

Some companies offer complete packages of capital equipment, ranging from design and layout of doctor and dentist offices, including cabinets, front and back office workspaces, dental chairs, examining tables, and soap dispensers. Others sell solely individual pieces of large equipment.

When large equipment purchases are considered by hospitals, clinics, and doctor's offices, there is often a committee involved in making final decisions. You would have to enjoy giving detailed presentations that include all aspects of the product benefits, including how the doctors will perform better for their patients, what the return on investment will be for the facility, and what the typical maintenance for the day-to-day workers involves. This information would be provided by the company you represent as you do the required preparation for your presentations (or at least you'll be given the information to use in preparing).

Nearly everyone who will have any type of interaction with the equipment may have a say in which product is purchased. You need to speak many languages. You'll speak from the high level of the board of directors who makes the final budget decisions. You'll speak anatomy and medical terminology with the doctors, nurses, and staff who will use the equipment. And you'll speak the language of the people who will be tasked with maintaining the equipment.

Typically, large equipment would be shipped to a facility, but you may be required to participate in or supervise the installation of it. After the equipment is installed properly, it may also be your job to inspect the equipment and then demonstrate its proper usage and maintenance to the users before a patient ever lays eyes on it or is placed in or upon it. As a follow-up service on large equipment, you may be required to revisit those facilities on a regular basis and continually check the equipment for anything that could cause a malfunction or risk to either the user or the patient. Your knowledge will come from intensive training sessions held by your company, and you'll work very specifically from "the book" — the owners' manual for the equipment. In some cases, your company is required by its liability attorneys to certify that you've completed a course of instruction at a specific level of understanding.

You'll never be directly involved with a patient or touch a patient in any way, even though you may be asked to join the surgical staff in the operating room the first few times your equipment is used in that environment to provide advice as to its best use.

Needless to say, this category of medical sales will call on all your sales skills, including prospecting, probing to uncover needs, presenting, objection handling, and closing.

Distribution

Distribution companies are logistical masters. These folks move billions of dollars of medical supplies from warehouses strategically located throughout the country to the point of use at the lowest possible cost and the highest level of reliability. Medical supplies are mostly consumable items. These are items that would be ordered on a regular and consistent basis as opposed to surgical lighting or tables that may be purchased only by a facility a couple times during your entire career. Medical supplies would include items that are consumed either by ingestion or injection or used and discarded.

This derivative of the field of medical sales could take you just about anywhere, from a large hospital to a dentist's or doctor's office to the first aid box on a construction job site. It may also involve working with facilities that are considered "retail" in the medical arena; these would be suppliers of home care products such as oxygen, tubing, bandaging, wheel chairs, braces, orthopedics, and such.

You could work with decision makers ranging from well-educated medical professionals to retail clerks who handle purchasing. In some instances, you carry samples of your products but don't fulfill the orders directly. Large orders are shipped to the facility or even to the ultimate end-user — the consumer.

Some medical products require customized fittings for the users, as is the case with braces and prosthetic devices. Part of your job may be to train the "retail" staff on how to properly measure people for your devices. However, with some products, you'll be responsible for transporting and delivering products, placing them in the facility, and toting out the empty boxes or other containers. So, there could be more of a physical aspect to this type of sales than there is in other markets.

Medical products distribution companies don't typically call on healthcare professionals. They call on materials management executives and staff. To lower overall cost while maintaining reliability and efficiency, distribution reps provide very sophisticated stock replenishment systems, just-in-time inventory support, as well as coordination between hospitals and manufacturer's representatives of the products that they distribute when confronted with a product issue.

Distribution companies are very important in the medical products supply chain because of the sheer number of manufacturers that are required to supply a hospital or clinic with the products that they need to operate on a daily basis. Everything from cotton swabs, bandages, syringes, patient welcome kits, and bedpans are delivered daily on a distributor's truck.

Competition is intense among distributors, but it is challenging for hospitals to oust one distributor for another without careful planning and coordination. Hospitals typically have one primary distributor supplying over 90 percent of their daily usage products and supplies. So, once you capture a client, they'll be yours for a very long time — as long as you provide the level of service they require.

Lab and diagnostics

Lab and diagnostics sales reps call on lab personnel and pathologists. You'll be selling reagents that are used in diagnostic tests as well as some of the capital equipment required to do the tests. Products in this vertical market are increasingly sophisticated, and competition is based on accuracy, efficiency, dependability, and cost. Companies in this vertical market provide tests for the flu, hepatitis, tuberculosis, malaria, HIV, and just about any test for which a blood, urine, or saliva sample is taken. As with the other verticals, this is a very specialized sales job that requires focus on a particular end-user.

Reps typically call on the following:

- ✔ Pathologists and lab technicians at lab facilities in hospital systems and clinics
- ✔ Nurses and technicians who actually do the tests
- ✔ Corporate medical facilities for general drug testing
- ✔ State-operated open clinics that provide medical diagnostics to indigent patients
- ✔ State correctional facilities

Service sales

Service sales is less defined as an independent vertical market. It's somewhat of a catchall including certain outsourced services. For example, most people think that when an X-ray or MRI is done, it's sent to radiology in another part of the building for analysis, but that isn't always the case. With advanced high-definition systems and reliable high-speed data lines, a great number of radiology "reads" are sent to points all over the globe for analysis, and the results are almost immediately reported back to the local doctor for diagnosis and treatment considerations. There are providers who handle this service for those healthcare professionals. Another example is the multi-million-dollar reprocessing business, in which high-quality disposable products are reprocessed, repackaged, resterilized, and resold back to hospitals at about half the original investment.

Reps in this market call on

- ✔ Individuals and departments who directly benefit from their services
- ✔ Hospital executives who understand the "big picture" and benefits of the service

Qualifying yourself

With some types of medical sales, you'll be required to have a bachelor's degree in pharmacy, medicine, bioscience, physiology, or some other health-related discipline. Some of those degrees have their own requirements for continued certification. You may need to complete continuing education courses on an ongoing basis to remain up to current standards required for the job. At the very least, you may need to have a solid understanding of medical terminology and an understanding of the laws and ethics governing medical practices. In other areas of the general medical sales field, you may need only a high school diploma and a winning personality.

In this field, you're likely to have to make many stops during your typical day. You'll probably be assigned a specific geographical territory or a "type" of medical provider to work with. Your days may be largely unsupervised, although there will undoubtedly be reporting required. You'll probably be required to set your own appointments.

If you're asked to work in a large metropolitan area (where most hospitals can be found), would driving in heavy traffic be a challenge for you? You may be expected to meet with as many as ten different doctors or health professionals on any given day of the week. In some cases, several of those people may be in the same building or office complex. In other cases, they could be across town.

If you live, as Tom Hopkins does, in the summer heat of Phoenix, Arizona, would you be happy doing whatever it takes to stay fresh when going from your car into a facility and back to your super-hot car again several times each day? If you end up working in a place where there's a lot of snow in the winter or rain year-round, the same question should be considered. Would having to be out in the weather have a negative impact on your desire to do the job as it should be done?

Are you prepared to learn new information on a regular basis? As stated at the beginning of the chapter, there are new developments in the medical field all the time. In order to work effectively within it, you need to invest time in study, reading. and research of your own, as well as with the materials provided by the company in order to pass the proper information along to your clients. This may involve having subscriptions to and reading medical journals, attending classes or seminars on new developments, or just reading up on the new information your company provides. At the very least, you'll want to tune in to some type of industry resource just to learn about new developments on the horizon and be the first to bring them to the attention of your clients. This will help you demonstrate competence to them and build their dependence on you as a reliable resource.

Are you detail oriented? With pharmaceuticals, each drug has its identifying marks — brands, if you will. This may involve the shape or color of the drug or a code stamped on it. The bottles are required to be clearly marked with the drug name, strength, and other warnings. You have to be absolutely certain you're delivering what has been ordered. If you're the provider of pharmaceuticals to the local drugstore and you fail to complete your order properly and deliver a critical product, it could impact someone's life drastically. In a large equipment sales situation, the purchase may require detailed specifications and measurements. Or the order may require multiple documents and signatures — miss one and the sale isn't closed.

Medical professionals must operate under strict guidelines in treating patients. In some cases, there is no margin for error and what you do or say could literally become a matter of life and death for someone. Your depth of product knowledge, especially if you become a pharmaceutical representative, needs to be strong. If you sell surgical tables, a strong understanding of human anatomy and surgical practices may be required. In some cases, you'll be the one initially educating doctors and other medical professionals on what your drug or equipment can and cannot do and the possible risks involved. For that reason, your verbal skills must also be very strong.

Are you physically prepared to handle the specific products you're interested in representing? In some fields, there can be a lot of information or samples to carry around with you to your appointments. Just the process of loading and unloading products and samples from your vehicle or toting lunch from a restaurant into a doctor's office could leave you feeling like you've done a two-hour exercise workout. If you're meeting with people in a large hospital environment or multi-building complex, there could be a lot of walking involved.

Book VI

Selling in Specialized and Growing Fields

Are you computer literate? You'll likely need a laptop or tablet computer as well. Everything in the medical field is trending away from paperwork and toward digital records. Some of your record-keeping will need to be done via computer software with reports uploaded to the company you work for on a daily or weekly basis.

Selling Skills for Medical Products

As with every type of selling, there's a process you must go through, starting with finding and meeting your potential clients, qualifying their needs, presenting your product, answering concerns, and closing the sale. You're bound to run up against competitors who are going after the same dollars or, as in the case with presenting to doctors, the same time frame you are. The primary keys to success in this industry are your attention to detail and your selling skills.

Your company will provide you with information that you need to impart to the doctors or end-users of the drugs or equipment. This will include both the benefits and the potential risks or known challenges. The responsibility about the proper use of what you sell lies with the medical professionals. All drugs come with contraindications clearly spelled out. It's up to the doctor to know whether each patient would be a qualified candidate for a drug or if they could take it in conjunction with another prescribed medicine.

All equipment comes with an instruction manual. If you're required by your company to inspect equipment on-site, the company is required to train you on what to look for and how to address typical situations that may arise. The liability rests with the company, not with you personally — unless you're truly negligent in performing your duties.

The selling skills you need to use are questioning strategies to assist you in closing for appointments, communication skills to impart the knowledge your clients need in order to make decisions about using your products, the knowledge to address their concerns, and the ability to ask directly and specifically for the order.

Expect stalls

There's a rather famous cartoon that pops up every now and then in the sales world. It shows a medieval-era leader of a large military battle — men fighting with bows and arrows — telling an underling, "I don't have time to meet with a salesman. I have a battle to win." And there, behind his tent is a salesman with something that looks like a machine gun. Even though medical professionals are deemed to be knowledgeable and on the cutting edge of advancements in their fields, the truth is that the day-to-day needs of their patients, their places of business, and their personal lives can get in the way of their continuing education — except in the areas required in order to keep their licenses.

You'll have to learn to expect meetings to be cancelled: "Dr. Crandall was called back to the hospital for an emergency." Expect delays: "The doctor is running about an hour behind. Can you wait until 2 p.m., or should we just reschedule?" If you have another appointment at 2 p.m., which you probably will, you'll have to reschedule and it may be weeks before you can get in to see that doctor again. A practice with several doctors on staff may require several members of the team to be involved in making a decision, and this may be the week that Dr. Critical-to-the-Decision has gone skiing.

When selling in a hospital or clinic environment, there could be a committee of anywhere from three to a dozen (or even more) people involved in voting on major expenditures. They may meet only once a month and their last meeting may have been yesterday. Before you even present to the committee, you may need to have preliminary meetings with the end-users, such as operating room nurses, maintenance staff, surgeons, and budget directors. In other words, everyone except the patients may need to be consulted on a major purchase. Just because they're on the committee doesn't mean they get to devote all their time to this. It may just be one more thing on their list of things to do. You need the skills and personality to win them over to investing the required time in their part of the process when and how you need it.

Just because a product sale is the most important thing in your life at that moment in time, it's probably not the most important thing to the person you're trying to persuade or gain information from. You can and should expect the people you need to talk with to put you off until their feet are to the fire with the committee to know how they fulfilled their action items from the last meeting, just like the way kids write book reports — they know about the due date for weeks but don't bother working on it until the day before it has to be turned in.

Determine the decision makers and influencers

Even though you may be told that Martha in purchasing handles the decisions about carrying your type of product, she may not be acting alone. She may, in fact, just be the point person on the decision. This is where my NEADS qualification sequence of questions in Book III, Chapter 2 comes in handy. The key question for the letter *D* is this:

> If you determine our product is a good choice for your needs who, other than yourself, would be involved in making a final decision?

Now, Martha might answer:

> I choose the products, but our office manager, Roberta, has to approve the purchase orders.

Now you know you have to close not just Martha on the value of your product, but you may need to persuade Roberta as well.

When your potential clients have more than one source to consider for equipment, supplies, or pharmaceuticals, there are bound to be people with their own opinions about what to purchase. And some of those people may exert great influence with the final decision makers. For example, a manager of a retail location that sells medical supplies may choose your competition's product over yours because a member of their staff felt snubbed by you when you came in to give your presentation. It may sound silly, but it has been known to happen.

You are *always* selling and selling everyone you meet. You sell yourself first, your company second, and your product third.

Treat literally everyone you encounter in the course of your day with the same courteous, professional manner you offer to the person you know is the final decision maker for the purchase of your product. You never know what type of influence the person you hold the elevator for has with your decision maker. If the decision maker is weighing you against the competition, something that you may consider insignificant can make the difference on the final decision. After all, they're not just purchasing your product, they're establishing a relationship with you that they, and you, should expect to last a very long time. For that reason, not only must your *product* perform, but they have to believe that *you* will, too.

There's a story about how to treat people that goes something like this: A professor handed out the final exam to his class, and it had only one question on it: "What's the name of the janitor you pass in the hallway outside this classroom every day?" The lesson was that everyone is important, and you'll never know how important they are to you (or you to them) unless you engage with them. Never assume you can't provide your service to someone. Never assume they don't have influence over something that will happen in your life. We're all connected.

Let's say, for example, that you're selling surgical tables to hospitals and clinics. People who may be involved could include the surgeons who will use the tables (and believe us when we say that their comfort level with your product is critical); the operating room coordinator, director, or supervisor who will have to know what types of surgeries are best performed on the table so they can handle their job of scheduling properly; the purchasing manager; the operations manager, whose job it is to handle any maintenance or supply issues related to the product; the budget director, who may have one of the most complicated juggling jobs in the world; and the top hospital administrator, who puts the final stamp of approval — or not — on the paperwork that completes your sale. Do you really need to know all of them? Yes. Will you speak with them all the same? No. They each have different perspectives for considering your product, and you need to be prepared to address each in their own way.

Open the door of communication

Always approach potential new clients with an attitude of servitude. You need to project an air of confidence about you, but tempered with humility and gratitude. When you talk with prospective buyers or influencers, they're giving you a piece of their day. You need to demonstrate great respect for that opportunity. If you don't, they're not likely to be as helpful in providing the information you need to do your job properly.

When you first meet someone and don't know yet if she's a decision maker or influencer, simply smile and say, "Could you help me, please?" or "Could you please answer a quick question for me?" People love to help others — especially those who are drawn to work in a medical-related field. In fact, that's usually the primary reason why they chose it. If and when they pause to see what you need, use the *W, W, W, W, W,* and *H* questioning strategy. Begin every question with one of the following words: *who, what, when, where, why,* and *how.* It's that simple. Questions that begin with those words are known as *open questions.* They require more than a yes or no answer. In some cases, the answers may be a single word, but that word will be a bit of information that takes you to the next step in your sales process or to the next person you need to speak with. For example:

Who is in charge of purchasing the medical supplies for your office?

What is the procedure for making purchasing decisions?

When are decisions made about major expenditures?

Where are the administrative offices located?

Why is it that you're scheduling (name your type) surgical patients six weeks out?

How do you handle inventory of pharmaceutical samples?

Book VI

Selling in Specialized and Growing Fields

You only need to ask one question to get started in the right direction. Don't worry about using all of them, but practice several to expand your repertoire. This is for two reasons:

- ✔ You won't become known as "that guy who always asks *x.*"
- ✔ You won't become bored with saying the same thing over and over again.

The answer to any open question should lead you to the next question you need to ask in order to move forward with getting to the decision maker, learning who and how many people are on a committee, finding out the procedures you must follow in order to make presentations, and so on.

Educate with benefits

The single best phrase you can add into your presentations is this: *and what this means to you is.* You can babble on all day about the features of your products — "it does this," "it does that," "it saves time here," "it generates profit for you there." But what really gets the attention of the people you're presenting to is discussing the benefit your product provides to them or, as is the case with most medical products, the benefit to the end-user (their patient or client).

Let's use the example of prosthetic devices. The end-users (patients) seek the highest quality of life possible after losing a limb. Their doctors want the same for them. If you represent a product that allows for more stability and flexibility, that feature is a win for both the doctor and the patient. But what it does for the patient is allow her to walk more naturally on uneven ground or up and down stairs. Many such patients don't want to call attention to their prosthetic, so if yours looks more natural or allows for a variety of needs such as women's shoes of varying heel heights, those features are excellent selling points. However, what the doctors and patients really base their decisions on are what you say after "and what this does for you is. . . ."

If you represent pharmaceuticals, what a new drug does isn't all that matters. The side effects that patients may have to endure are critical. If you have a new blood pressure pill that has fewer side effects than the current top brand, it's critical that you tell the doctor that her patients will no longer have to suffer those side effects or take another pill to counter those side effects. That can be as important as the value of what the new pill actually does for the patient.

It's also important to educate doctors about how this new drug works with other drugs. Few patients have just one health issue. You have to know not only your product but how your product interacts with other commonly prescribed substances. If your product is multifaceted and eliminates the need for another pill, that will lower patients' prescription medicine costs, and that's something you'll want to be sure to mention to the doctor.

Chapter 5

Selling Biotechnology

• •

In This Chapter

▶ Discovering the broad spectrum of biotech products and applications

▶ Understanding concerns (and sales resistance) about biotech

▶ Determining the best way to sell your biotech product

▶ Exploring regulatory and ethical considerations

▶ Taking a look at helpful resources

• •

The term *biotechnology* has a definite 21st-century feel to it, evoking images of white-coated scientists slicing genes and mutating bacteria to generate heaven knows what kind of new drug, food, or fuel. Indeed, pharmaceutical, agriculture, and energy businesses are some of the most prolific developers and users of biotechnology products and processes.

For salespeople, keeping up with the latest advances in biotechnology is only one challenge. Sales reps also may have to overcome considerable sales resistance from potential buyers, who have to deal not only with economic pressures but often with social and political controversies surrounding biotech materials and processes. In addition, many aspects of biotech sales are highly regulated, so salespeople have to be sure they don't overstep legal or ethical boundaries.

In this chapter, we explore a plethora of biotech products and processes, from many common, everyday uses to cutting-edge advancements. We discuss the challenges involved in finding and influencing potential buyers and some of the regulatory issues associated with biotech sales. And we provide some resources for you to further your understanding of this exciting sales field.

Exploring Biotech Products and Other Applications

Although the biotech industry officially launched in the 1970s with the development of *recombinant DNA* (a method of copying and combining genetic material to create proteins and other materials in the lab), humans have been using biotechnology since shortly after the dawn of civilization. People began domesticating crops and livestock about 10,000 years ago, using selective breeding and cross-pollination to cultivate the traits they wanted. The ancient Sumerians, Chinese, and Egyptians used yeast to leaven bread and ferment beer, and the Babylonians controlled their date palm crops by using pollen only from specific male plants to pollinate female date palms.

Today, of course, plant and animal breeding techniques are far more precise and complex. And biotech products are by no means limited to agriculture. In fact, many biotech products or processes are part of most people's daily lives:

✔ **In textiles:** *Enzymes* (substances, mostly proteins, produced by living cells) have largely replaced harsh chemicals in the production and preparation of fabrics, especially cotton and leather. The textile industry uses enzymes to reduce impurities in cotton fiber and to make it easier to weave; in leather, enzymes help prevent rotting and make the tanning process easier and more eco-friendly.

✔ **In detergents:** Enzymes in detergents help break down the proteins that cause stains, such as those in grass, mud, and red wine. Other types of enzymes called *lipases* are effective against fat and grease. And detergent manufacturers are looking for enzymes that work especially well in very hot or very cold temperatures.

✔ **In food and drink:** Wine, cheese, beer, and bread have used basic biotechnological processes for thousands of years. Today, food and beverage manufacturers routinely use enzymes and other biotech processes and products to enhance flavor, regulate sugar and alcohol content, and improve quality control measures.

✔ **In healthcare:** After Stanley Cohen and Herbert Boyer published details of a new technique for generating recombinant DNA in 1973, healthcare biotech really took off. Recombinant DNA allows drug companies to manufacture insulin for diabetics (see "Understanding concerns about cloning technologies," later in this chapter). Other biotech processes use microorganisms, including bacteria, to make antibiotics, vaccines, birth control drugs, and vitamins.

Industry regularly uses biotech products and processes for many different purposes. Agribusiness leaders like Monsanto (www.monsanto.com) and Pioneer (www.pioneer.com), for example, use biotechnology to create crops that are resistant to certain pests or diseases, able to withstand harsh environments, and produce higher yields for farmers. By 2005, more than 1 billion acres of farmland had been planted with biotech seeds. (Of course, biotech seeds aren't without their downsides; see the next section.)

Manufacturers use biotech to reduce waste and even to clean up environmental messes. In 1989, cleanup crews fertilized large swaths of the Prince William Sound shoreline in Alaska to counter the effects of the Exxon *Valdez* oil spill; applications of phosphorus and nitrogen encouraged growth of oil-eating microbes that use the carbon found in oil. The loss of the carbon breaks the oil's molecular bonds, so the oil dissolves.

Perhaps the best-known application of biotech processes is in healthcare and medical research. Hundreds of diagnostic tests, including those that screen donated blood for *human immunodeficiency virus* (HIV, the virus that causes AIDS), those that test for cancer and other diseases, and even the home pregnancy tests you can buy at your local pharmacy, were developed through biotech research. At this writing, clinical trials are under way to test more than 400 biotech drugs and vaccines targeting some 200 diseases, including Alzheimer's, diabetes, heart disease, and several forms of cancer.

Considering Biotech Controversies

Although biotech holds enormous promise for healthcare, food production, fuel, and environmental conservation and remediation, the field also has generated a fair share of controversy — some of which may affect your role as a biotech sales rep.

Your employer likely will provide continuing education and training to help you understand and overcome specific ethical, social, and political objections that you may encounter in the field. In the following sections, we discuss some common concerns that have generated headlines — and sometimes even new laws or regulations — that you should be aware of.

Understanding concerns about cloning technologies

Cloning simply means copying. Researchers routinely make copies of certain cells, genes, proteins, and other matter both for basic research — that is, to figure out how certain cells behave, how diseases develop, and so on — and to develop drugs or other therapies to treat diseases. Human insulin is manufactured by cloning lots of the human genes that make insulin, combining those cloned genes with specific bacteria, and using the mixture to make the insulin pills or injections that diabetics take to regulate their blood sugar levels. This technique, called *therapeutic cloning,* represents a huge step forward in creating safe, effective medicines and vaccines for many common human ailments.

However, the term *cloning* also raises the specter of sci-fi movies like *Invasion of the Body Snatchers.* Some people worry that the cloning techniques scientists use today may lead to *reproductive cloning* (manipulating human cells to create a genetic copy of a human being). Such fears are periodically inflamed by individuals or groups who claim to have produced a cloned human being, but, to date, none of these claims has been verified.

The scientific community, as well as the major biotech trade groups, are virtually united in their opposition to human reproductive cloning. In the first place, the technology is far too uncertain at this point to be judged safe for human cloning; nearly all cloned animals have some kind of genetic abnormality. In addition, cloning human beings raises serious ethical and social issues that most people — including scientists — find problematic.

Therapeutic cloning is an important weapon in the arsenal against human disease and suffering. As a sales rep, you may have to educate prospective buyers about the difference between therapeutic and reproductive cloning, pointing out the benefits of the former while assuaging their concerns about the latter.

Looking at genetically modified foods

Historically, humans have been creating genetically modified foods since they began cultivating crops. By cross-pollinating certain strains of specific crops, ancient farmers developed food plants that grew well in their environment and displayed some natural resistance to weeds, pests, and disease.

Since the mid-1990s, though, genetically modified (GM) crops have been developed in laboratories. According to the National Research Council, an arm of the National Academies (www.nationalacademies.org), more than 80 percent of the corn, cotton, and soybeans grown in the United States are now GM crops, and farmers see significant benefits from these versions, including

✔ Lower production costs

✔ Better yields

✔ Fewer pest problems

✔ Reduced use of chemical pesticides

However, the very prevalence of GM crops has given rise to some concerns about environmental impacts, sustainability, and long-term safety. For example, GM crops that are herbicide-resistant (Hr) can thrive even as herbicides (like Monsanto's Roundup) control weeds around the crops. But continual use of the active ingredient in Roundup, glyphosate, has led some weed species to develop resistance to the chemical, forcing farmers to use more and stronger herbicides — or other weed-control techniques that can reduce or erase any savings in production costs.

Many crops also are genetically engineered to produce *Bacillus thuringiensis* (Bt), a toxin that's deadly to certain pest insects. Bt crops significantly reduce the need for chemical pesticides, which is good for farmers, farm workers, and the environment. But no one knows yet whether pest insects may eventually develop a resistance to Bt from repeated exposure in the same way that some weed species have become resistant to glyphosate.

Farmers and seed companies like Monsanto and Pioneer have benefited from GM crops, but consumers have seen fewer benefits and raised more concerns about reliance on genetically engineered plants. GM foods aren't cheaper than traditional foods at the retail level; they have no added nutritional value; and they don't taste any better. Given the dearth of tangible consumer benefits, it's not surprising that many consumers and activist groups around the globe have voiced worries about the potential risks that GM foods pose. Those possible risks include the following:

✔ **Threats to biodiversity:** As GM seeds become more common, ensuring that they don't cross-breed with wild plants becomes a bigger concern. Organic farmers face this issue, too: If GM seeds mingle with conventional seeds, organic farmers lose a lucrative selling point for their products, as many consumers now consciously seek out — and are willing to pay a premium for — organic, non-GM foods. In addition, beneficial insects and non-target insect populations, such as the monarch butterfly, may suffer from the toxins produced by Bt plants.

✔ **Toxicity and allergenicity:** Some foods, such as peanuts, wheat, and milk, cause allergic reactions in significant numbers of people. Food regulators in the United States and abroad generally discourage using genes from known allergenic foods in GM foods; if genes from these foods are used, the producer has to demonstrate that the materials created by the genes don't cause allergic reactions. Likewise, researchers and GM food producers have to ensure that their products aren't toxic to humans (or to animals that may be fed GM foods and subsequently consumed by people).

✔ **Gene transfer:** If you eat a GM tomato, can the genetic changes in the tomato be transferred to the bacteria in your digestive tract or to the cells in your body? The probability of gene transfer from consuming GM foods seems to be low. But the possibility raises concerns for human health, especially where GM foods include genes that increase resistance to antibiotics. The World Health Organization and the United Nations both have gone on record to encourage GM technologies *without* antibiotic resistance genes so as to lower the risk of harmful gene transfers to humans.

The European Union and several other national governments heavily regulate the production, use, and labeling of GM foods. In 1993, the U.S. Food and Drug Administration (FDA) declared that GM foods are "not inherently dangerous" and don't require special FDA regulation. However, the U.S. Department of Agriculture and the Environmental Protection Agency do regulate some aspects of GM crop and livestock production.

Exploring the costs and benefits of biofuels

Technically, a *biofuel* is any fuel that uses living matter to produce energy. The wood you use to build a campfire is a biofuel, for example. Petroleum isn't a biofuel because it isn't composed of living matter.

In the context of biotechnology, biofuels typically combine nonliving, nonrenewable resources like petroleum with living, renewable sources like corn. The ethanol gasoline you pump into your car, for example, is a mixture of gas and specially treated corn starches. Ethanol gas typically burns more cleanly than straight gasoline and produces fewer particulates and greenhouse gas emissions from vehicles and machinery.

However, making ethanol is far from an environmentally friendly process. Growing, harvesting, and shipping crops for ethanol, not to mention the manufacturing process, require huge amounts of nonrenewable energy sources and produce plenty of greenhouse gases themselves. In addition, using food crops to produce fuel is controversial; rising wholesale prices and fewer acres devoted to food production can create unintended pressures on an already-strained global food supply.

Researchers are exploring other possibilities for creating biofuels, including using nonfood plants like bamboo and other types of grasses. But, at the moment, corn is the most common — and so far the most efficient — biofuel component, so the issues of environmental protection and food versus fuel remain unresolved.

Connecting with Biotech Customers

As a biotech sales rep, you may sell actual biotech products, such as drugs, textiles, biodegradable plastics, or other items that are designed for consumer use. Or you may sell biotech tools and processes that help your clients achieve their business goals, such as improved diagnostic tests or equipment for hospitals or "green" commercial solvents that allow a manufacturer to save time and money while mitigating its environmental impact.

Selling different products in the pharma/biotech field often requires different qualifications and personality traits. (See the nearby sidebar, "Pharma selling versus biotech selling," for a view of how these jobs can differ.) But, no matter what you sell, you need to follow the usual good practices for getting your product into buyers' hands. In the following sections, we explore three common ways pharma and biotech companies market their products.

Pharma selling versus biotech selling

Although biotech is a big part of the pharmaceutical industry, many experts distinguish between selling pharmaceuticals and selling biotech. The key difference is really in the kind of company you work for and how your job is structured.

Big pharma companies have long-established processes for their sales reps that include extensive training, established territories, and sales-call quotas. Pharma sales reps have to know what information they're allowed to share with doctors under FDA regulations, as well as where their products fit in health insurers' lists of approved drugs.

Biotech reps typically are expected to chart their own paths to sales success with much less formal guidance than big pharma companies provide. And, whereas pharma reps may deal almost exclusively with doctors, biotech reps are more likely to deal with a range of hospital executives, lab directors, and other high-level buyers.

Biotech firms often require their salespeople to have more relevant technical backgrounds than pharma companies do. In general, pharma sales requires a four-year college degree,

which may be in business, science, or even liberal arts. Biotech sales reps usually have a strong science background — some even have master's degrees in science — because the job requires you to have a full understanding of genetic engineering methods and technologies.

Selling medical devices typically requires even more technical expertise, because these sales reps often work side by side with surgeons in the operating room and conduct simulations in using the device. Medical device salespeople often have engineering or doctorate degrees because they need to understand virtually everything about how their product works.

Incomes are comparable for both pharma and biotech sales reps, although pay structures in biotech firms often include alternative compensation such as stock options. Some consider the biotech field to be riskier because of the lack of structure, but that view depends as much on your personality as anything else. If you prefer well-defined goals and the security of a vast sales support network, pharma may be the best choice. On the other hand, biotech tends to offer more scope if you long to have a strong and lasting impact on your company.

Selling to distributors

Biotech companies often are small firms that don't have the resources to deploy massive sales forces into the field. Healthcare biotech companies often partner with big pharma corporations to market their products. But sometimes biotech firms — both in healthcare and in other sectors — work with distributors to get their products to customers in the industry. The Open Directory Project (www.dmoz.org) provides links to biotech and pharmaceutical wholesalers and distributors, along with a brief description of each distributor's area of specialization.

When you're prospecting for distributors, you need to know the following:

✔ **Their market penetration:** If you don't know whether a distributor has good penetration in the industry you want to reach, ask. If they want to add your product to their list, they'll give you information to help you gauge their sales and influence in your targeted industry.

✔ **Their level of expertise with products like yours:** You wouldn't ask your hair stylist to install new plumbing in your house; likewise, you don't want a distributor that specializes in pediatric products to sell your Alzheimer's diagnostic test. Check the distributor's product portfolio to ensure that your product is a good fit.

✔ **How they sell products:** Check the distributor's balance of inside and outside sales, and weigh that against how your product is best sold. Size can make a difference, too: Would your product do better with a large distributor that has lots of products and lots of sales reps, or would it generate more end sales with a smaller distributor that can devote more attention to your product?

✔ **How your product would stand out:** If your product is similar to many other products in the distributor's portfolio, you may have a tough time convincing the distributor to represent your product. And, even if you make the sale to the distributor, sales to your targeted industry may suffer from a portfolio cluttered with similar products. Look for a portfolio mix that balances the distributor's expertise in your product line with fewer competing products.

If your target market is other pharma and biotech companies or research labs, be sure to establish and maintain good relationships with procurement agencies like VWR (www.vwrsp.com) and Fisher Scientific (www.fishersci.com). Universities, government agencies, and corporations use these services to streamline their purchasing processes and cut costs. It may not be easy to break into these behemoth distributors, but getting onto their preferred product lists can increase your sales significantly.

Selling directly to customers

Selling pharma and biotech products directly to the people who will use them presents some unique challenges for sales pros. For one thing, your customers are extremely busy, so just getting face time can be a challenge.

Pharma and biotech customers also face certain pressures that the average consumer doesn't usually have to deal with. Hospitals, clinics, and solo practitioners have to navigate complex regulatory and health insurance mazes; if your drug isn't on a health plan's *formulary* (list of preapproved medications), you're wasting both your and your prospect's time. If your diagnostic test doesn't save a lab time or money, or if your medical device breaks down, your customer is very likely to move on to cheaper, more reliable alternatives.

You can build stronger relationships with prospective customers — and eventually boost your sales figures — by using these strategies:

- **Be cheerful.** Healthcare providers spend most of their days dealing with people who are sick and often cranky. Lab directors have to contend with funding issues and political considerations. Farmers worry day to day, and sometimes hour to hour, about myriad factors that are outside their control, including the weather, commodities markets, and the price of fuel. A cheerful demeanor in a sales rep can be as refreshing as a day at the seaside for people who are continually confronted with problems and bad news.

- **Be honest.** You're dealing with highly educated, highly trained people who may well know more than you do about how your product fits into their business. Don't be afraid to say, "I don't know." And when you don't know the answer, be conscientious about getting the information the prospect requests.

- **Be helpful.** Sales isn't as much about a specific product's benefits and features as it is about solving problems. Be generous with information, even if it isn't directly related to your product. The more value you provide to a prospect before a sale, the more likely you are to eventually win a loyal customer.

- **Be respectful.** Your customers are extremely busy people, and many of them won't have patience for a lot of small talk before you get to the point of your sales call. In many cases, your best strategy may be to treat the initial contact as an informational call rather than a sales call. Give the prospect a clear, concise pitch; leave informational material for the prospect to review; then follow up with the actual sales call, where you can invite the prospect to ask questions and discuss the nuts and bolts of the deal. Very few prospects object to cold calls when sales reps respect their time constraints and provide worthwhile information.

Book VI

Selling in Specialized and Growing Fields

Taking advantage of digital media

Regardless of whether you're selling through a distributor or directly to the people who will use your product, you (and your company) should follow good customer relations management practices and make it easy for customers to find what they want or need from you. In the 21st century, good customer relations means having an online presence.

Websites and digital products like e-mail newsletters and blogs are especially popular when it comes to healthcare products and issues. According to one survey, almost nine in ten U.S. physicians use the Internet and other digital resources to find information about new drugs, new tests and devices, and new procedures.

Convenience is one main advantage of online resources; doctors and other time-pressed customers (including consumers) can find the information they want without having to juggle their already-full schedules to squeeze in a face-to-face meeting. Customer service portals tailored specifically to healthcare providers, such as MDLinx (www.mdlinx.com), let medical professionals stay informed on the latest scientific literature and continuing education offerings in their specialties. Other companies like Physicians Interactive (www.physicians interactive.com) provide extensive digital marketing services to link pharma and biotech companies with healthcare providers.

Sticking to the Straight and Narrow: Legal and Ethical Considerations

In the United States, the biotech industry is regulated by the Food and Drug Administration, the Environmental Protection Agency, and the Department of Agriculture. Biotech and pharma companies typically provide training on the specific rules, regulations, and reporting requirements that their sales reps must follow in the field.

On a broader level, the trade group Pharmaceutical Research and Manufacturers of America (PhRMA, www.phrma.org) issues a voluntary Code on Interactions with Healthcare Professionals that aims to address concerns raised by consumers and medical practitioners about the way pharmaceuticals are marketed and sold. Although adherence to the PhRMA code is voluntary, more than 50 of the country's largest "big pharma" companies — including AstraZeneca, Bristol-Myers Squibb, Johnson & Johnson, and Merck — have formally signed on to abide by the code's provisions.

Among other things, the PhRMA code

✔ Prohibits drug companies from providing small gifts like pens, pill boxes, and notepads carrying the name of the company or of a specific drug.

✔ Bars sales reps from "wining and dining" healthcare professionals outside their offices. (Sales reps can still pay for occasional meals at the healthcare professional's office, as long as the meal is in conjunction with an informational presentation.)

✔ Requires companies to ensure that their sales reps are adequately trained on applicable laws and regulations, as well as industry best practices and ethical considerations.

✔ Places restrictions on consulting and speaking arrangements with healthcare professionals.

✔ Raises standards for ensuring that continuing medical education efforts remain suitably independent.

The full PhRMA code, including a list of signatory companies, is available on the organization's website. Just search for "code."

Exploring Additional Resources

Like any sales field, success in biotech sales depends on making and maintaining strong relationships with colleagues, clients, and potential buyers. Biotech salespeople also have to keep up with the latest technologies and discoveries in this explosive-growth sector.

Trade groups and associations provide excellent opportunities to meet decision makers, learn about new advancements, track trends, and swap sales tales and tricks with your fellow sales reps. Biotech and pharma both have several professional associations and trade groups that may be useful to you in your sales career. Some of the best-known groups include

✔ **Biotechnology Industry Organization (BIO,** www.bio.org**):** BIO's annual convention and exhibition is the largest biotech event in the world, but the association provides much value throughout the year with an industry calendar of conferences and events, blogs and podcasts on biotech news and issues, and a variety of research and reports on the biotech industry.

✔ **Council for Biotechnology Information (**www.whybiotech.com**):** The Council for Biotechnology Information focuses on agricultural biotech and serves as a clearinghouse for information on new products and technologies, as well as social and political issues such as GM food safety and sustainable development through biotech.

✔ **Medical Marketing Association (**www.medicalmarketing association.org**):** The Medical Marketing Association comprises marketing professionals in pharmaceuticals, devices, diagnostics, and marketing and advertising. For biotech/pharma direct sales reps, the Medical Marketing Association can provide insights into the pressures that solo practitioners and small clinics face.

✔ **Pharmaceutical Business Intelligence and Research Group (PBIRG;** www.pbirg.com**):** PBIRG promotes global healthcare market research and business intelligence with an emphasis on strategic planning for pharma/biotech businesses.

✔ **Pharmaceutical Research and Manufacturers of America (PhRMA;** www.phrma.org**):** PhRMA's website provides information about new drugs, clinical trials, and issues in the pharma/biotech field. The group also publishes the voluntary Code on Interactions with Healthcare Professionals (see the preceding section).

Book VII

Becoming a Power Seller

The 5th Wave   By Rich Tennant

So—what the heck are you selling?

In this book . . .

Those who achieve the pinnacle of sales success act more like entrepreneurial small-business owners. They market and advertise, engage in unrelenting shameless self-promotion, constantly expand their address books with new contacts, develop synergistic partnerships, investigate new markets, take risks, implement the latest technologies to boost productivity, hire assistants to grow their businesses, and much more.

In this book, you get a vast collection of strategies, techniques, and tips on how to become a revenue-generating machine.

Chapter 1

Becoming the Power Seller
You Want to Be

In This Chapter

▶ Drawing up and executing a sales plan

▶ Enhancing your sales potential by studying new sales techniques

▶ Overcoming roadblocks to reach an unlimited upside

Far too many salespeople resign themselves to what they consider is a painful reality — they can't sell, because they have no customers to sell to. Mediocre salespeople constantly tell themselves, "If someone would just bring me a customer, I could sell." They rely far too much on the company they work for to market the products and services.

Entrepreneurial salespeople, on the other hand, blame nothing — not the market, the product, the boss, or the company they work for. Instead, they drum up their own business. They make business happen. They become revenue-generating machines, no matter where they work or what they sell.

This chapter helps you lay the foundation for becoming a true power seller. Here, you discover how to create and implement a plan that strategically leads you to your sales goals, how to expose yourself to a variety of other sales strategies that can broaden your skills, and what you can do to overcome some obstacles that salespeople commonly face.

Charting Your Road Map to Sales Success

Success rarely happens by mistake. It requires planning, execution, and hard work. You set a goal, figure out how you're going to get there, pull together everything you need to execute your plan, and then work your plan the best you can with the confidence of boosting sales and profits.

In this section, you chart the course to your sales success, draw up a list of tools and resources required, and formulate a clear idea of how you're going to get from point A to point B. And if you happen to veer off course, this section shows you how to get back on track and perhaps even discover a couple of detours to shorten the journey.

Always be planning. Planning is always a necessity, whether you're just starting out, have achieved some level of success, or recently suffered a setback. Effective planning assists you in achieving success, avoiding failure, and recovering from disappointments.

Drawing up your sales plan

Stop thinking of yourself as a salesperson or an employee. Instead promote yourself to entrepreneur. Regardless of whether you own your own business, you *are* a business, a revenue-generating entity . . . You, Inc. As such, one of your primary responsibilities is to draw up a business plan — in this case, a sales plan. You're going to plot point A (current sales) and point B (your sale goal), and then chart the course that leads you from point A to point B.

Drawing up a sales plan is a seven-step process, explained in the following sections.

Your sales plan may not work out quite the way you expect it to, but the process of planning forces you to think about your goals and, more important, how you're going to achieve those goals. Even if your plan is only 50 percent effective, that's 50 percent better than having no plan.

Step 1: Determining where you are

You have to establish where you are in terms of sales and marketing efforts to figure out where you're going in terms of sales, revenue, and growth. To get a clear idea of where you stand, jot down the following:

✔ Current gross sales annually or, if you're just getting started in selling or you're in a new sales position, conservative goal for gross earnings.

✔ Amount of time you typically invest in your business annually.

✔ Sales-per-hour earnings: Divide your annual gross sales revenue by the number of hours you work per year.

✔ Annual sales expenses, including your personal outlay for marketing materials, equipment, supplies, and so on.

✔ Dollar investment per dollar of sales: Divide your annual sales expenses by your annual gross sales.

The most important numbers you jot down are your sales-per-hour earnings and dollar investment per dollar of sales. Think of these numbers as your *sales efficiency ratings*. They're sort of like golf scores — the lower the number, the fewer times you have to swing to score a sale. Track the numbers over time to measure your progress.

Step 2: Setting a goal

By their very nature, sales goals are production-based; as a salesperson, your goal is to sell more stuff. Determination, effort, and your engaging personality are certainly important, but unless they generate more revenue, they don't really show up on the balance sheet at the end of the year.

When setting a sales goal, focus on increasing revenue. Here are a few examples of sales goals:

✔ Increase gross sales by at least 20 percent.

✔ Increase the net profit on products and services by at least 5 percent.

✔ Line up 15 new customers.

✔ Increase existing customer orders by 10 percent.

Note that these goals simply state the desired end result. They say nothing about how you're going to achieve that goal or the amount of time you have to reach your goal. You can attend to these details later, as the following sections describe.

Don't share goals with non-goal-setters, like your buddy who defines success as drinking a six-pack of beer every Friday night, or anyone who you aren't sure will support your efforts to succeed. People who don't set goals tend to put down those who do. They can kill your dreams.

Beware of sales quotas

Imposing a strict sales quota on yourself or having one imposed on you is often counter-productive because quotas can lead to several negative consequences:

✔ **Derailing the sales process:** Increased pressure to meet quotas can tempt you to push a prospective buyer right out of deciding to buy a product. You need to set your pace in relation to your customer, not in service to some arbitrary sales quota.

✔ **Reducing the profit per sale:** Sales quotas are often attached to certain dates, such as end of month, end of quarter, and end of year. When buyers are aware of these quotas, they gain an upper hand in the negotiating process and can pressure you to accept a lower price simply to close the sale.

✔ **Crushing a salesperson's confidence:** Failure can shake anyone's confidence. Conditions outside your control can cause you to miss the quota even if you did quite well given the conditions you were facing.

A sales quota, in and of itself, is not necessarily a bad thing, but an obsession with meeting a quota can negatively impact sales and profits. Use a sales goal or quota only as a tool to motivate yourself and a milestone against which you measure your progress or a given strategy's effectiveness. Focus more on the objectives, strategies, and tasks you must accomplish to achieve your goal. In other words, focus on the process you're going to follow, and your productivity is almost guaranteed to rise as a result.

Step 3: Setting a time frame

Setting open-ended goals is an invitation to procrastinate, so every goal should have a deadline. Now, that doesn't mean you should become obsessed with the deadline or let it influence sales negotiations or the way you treat your clients. A deadline simply enables you to measure your progress and efficiency.

After you jot down your sales goal, specify a time frame for achieving that goal. If the goal seems unrealistic in terms of the time frame, consider breaking down the goal into incremental goals. If you have a goal to sell 500 cars a year, for example, consider setting a goal to sell 40 cars per month. If that still seems overwhelming, think of it as selling two cars a day (based on a five-day workweek). And if the goal still seems unrealistic, consider trimming it back a bit. Goals should stretch you, not break you.

Have you ever noticed that the less time you have to complete a task, the more you accomplish? If you're constantly missing deadlines, you may be tempted to extend your deadlines. Instead of taking that approach, try tightening your deadlines to see what happens. Many people find that the tighter the deadline, the more energy they funnel into completing the task, and the faster they get it accomplished.

Step 4: Identifying your objectives

Objectives answer the question "How am I going to achieve my goal?" without going into great detail. Here are some examples that pair up goals with objectives:

Goal: Increase gross sales by at least 20 percent.

Objective: Convert 20 percent more initial contacts into sales.

Goal: Increase existing customer orders by 10 percent.

Objective: Improve relationships with existing customers.

Although the goal is fairly concrete, the *objective,* or the way you plan on achieving that goal, can vary. If your goal is to increase sales by at least 20 percent, for example, you can achieve that goal in a number of ways, including the following:

- Convert 20 percent more initial contacts into sales.
- Ramp up prospecting efforts.
- Implement an Internet marketing program.
- Increase up-sell opportunities.

Step 5: Figuring out a strategy

At this point, you should know what you're going to do and have a general idea of how you're going to do it, but now you need to figure out how you're going to fulfill your objective. This is where strategy comes into play. Think of strategy as the bird's-eye view of how you're going to meet your objective and, hence, achieve your goal. The following examples pair up objectives with strategies:

Objective: Convert 20 percent more initial contacts into sales.

Strategy: Focus efforts on high-quality leads.

Objective: Ramp up prospecting efforts.

Strategy: Devote one day per week to prospecting.

Objective: Implement an Internet marketing program.

Strategy: Launch a corporate website and blog.

Objective: Increase up-sell opportunities.

Strategy: Add a product line.

If you're having a tough time distinguishing between goals, objectives, and strategies, you're not alone. The differences are subtle. Think of it this way: If your goal is to learn a foreign language (Spanish, for example), here's how your goal, objective, and strategy may look:

> **Goal:** Communicate with Spanish-speaking clients.
>
> **Objective:** Study Spanish.
>
> **Strategy:** Read *Spanish For Dummies* (Wiley).

Step 6: Identifying tasks

Think of tasks as your to-do list. If you accomplish everything on your list, you can't help but achieve your goal . . . theoretically, at least.

Suppose you have a goal to increase sales by 20 percent. Your objective is to maximize up-sell opportunities, and your strategy is to add a new product line. Your tasks are then the steps you must take to add the product line. You may come up with something like this:

1. **Poll customers to determine market demand for various products.**
2. **Research products for salability and profitability.**
3. **Identify suppliers.**
4. **Compare prices, quality, and service.**
5. **Select products to include in new product line.**
6. **Market products to new and existing customers.**

When jotting down tasks you must accomplish, forget about the order of the tasks. Do a brain dump. Jot down all the tasks, and if they need to be accomplished in order, like steps, then you can go back and rearrange your list. What's most important is that the list covers everything.

Step 7: Identifying resources

When you're drafting your road map to success, don't overlook the fact that you need to pack some supplies. In the case of planning to achieve a business-related goal, the supplies you need basically come down to time, money, equipment, and people (human resources). An effective plan identifies all the resources you need and ultimately functions as a grocery list, simplifying the process of procuring essential resources.

To identify the resources required to accomplish your goal, answer the following questions:

 ✔ How many total hours are required to complete all tasks?

 ✔ How much time can I commit to the project?

 ✔ What expertise is needed that I don't currently have?

 ✔ How much money is this going to cost?

 ✔ Do I need any special equipment, such as a computer?

 ✔ Are some resources already available?

When developing your resource list, don't limit yourself. Make it a wish list. Ideally, what would you need in order to accomplish all the required tasks as quickly and easily as possible? Be creative. After you have your wish list in place, you can edit it based on the amount of time, money, and existing resources you have at your disposal.

Prioritizing your tasks

When drawing up a sales plan, you may find yourself with dozens of tasks you must tend to. Your to-do list can become overwhelming, perhaps so overwhelming that it causes you to freeze up. Not knowing where to start, you can't get moving. If you find yourself in the deep freeze, take some time to prioritize your tasks.

Prioritizing tasks doesn't always mean that you tackle the most important tasks first. When arranging the items on your to-do list, you have several options:

 ✔ **Step-by-step:** If the tasks must be performed in a certain order, prioritizing is as easy as one, two, three. Arrange the tasks in the order you need to perform them and then follow the steps.

 ✔ **Order of importance:** Complete the tasks that are key to the success of a project first.

 ✔ **Most profitable first:** If you have several tasks and one particular task has the potential of making you some quick cash or increasing profits immediately, why wait? Do the money-making tasks first.

 ✔ **Hardest thing first:** A difficult task can function as a huge mental block that prevents you from moving forward. If one task is significantly more difficult than the others, consider tackling it first. Once it's out of the way, the rest of the process is smooth sailing.

Book VII

Becoming a Power Seller

- ✔ **Easiest thing first:** If confronting the most difficult challenge first is just too overwhelming, deal with something easier. Doing so can give you some momentum to move on to other, more difficult tasks.

- ✔ **Most obvious first:** A task may present itself as obviously something you must do immediately: Perhaps it's something you have to do, and you have all the resources you need to do it right now.

Your first priority at the beginning of every day is to prioritize the items on your to-do-list. Figure out which tasks you're going to do first, second, and so on. You may decide, for example, to tackle the most difficult tasks first — calling the people you don't want to talk to — and then focus on the most profit-able activities (think of them as the *dollar-productive activities*), and, if you have any time left over, end the day by dealing with the remaining items in their order of importance.

Putting your plan into action

As beautiful and inspiring as a well-crafted plan may be, it's nothing without implementation. The specifics of how to put a plan in action differs with the plan. So, instead of giving you objective- or task-specific advice on how to execute your plan, this section focuses on giving you a system that enables you to effectively implement *any* plan for success.

The acronym for this system is Strebor (which, you may notice, is Roberts spelled backward), and it includes these components:

S: Sticktoitism (my version of *stick-to-itiveness*) is the dogged determina-tion required to ensure that you follow through on your plan.

T: Training provides you with the know-how and skills to properly exe-cute your plan.

R: Results are what you build on as you attain higher and higher levels of success.

E: Enthusiasm provides you with the ambition and energy required to follow through.

B: Benefits give you the motivation to succeed.

O: Optimism is the confidence that enables you to overcome obstacles.

R: Reach is your commitment to taking risks and seizing opportunities that make you grow professionally and personally.

Tracking progress and correcting course

Some people do a great job in the planning stage and may even succeed in executing their plans to perfection, but they drop the ball when it comes to tracking progress. As a result, they don't know whether they're making any headway. Put a system in place for tracking your progress. Following are some suggestions:

- ✔ **Checklists:** You can implement a system of annual, monthly, weekly, and daily checklists to keep yourself on track and measure your progress. Audit your lists at the end of each period to determine how well you've done, and then set more challenging goals moving forward.

- ✔ **Success journal:** Make daily or weekly entries in your journal to keep track of what's working and what's not.

- ✔ **Idea-of-the-week book:** Into this book, jot down your idea of the week. If the idea is worth pursuing, give it a shot and then log the results.

- ✔ **Lifetime-achievement book:** Think of this as the equivalent of a profit-and-loss statement. Instead of listing your financial profits and losses, you can describe your achievements and setbacks. Over time, the book comes to represent a measure of your success and can point you in the right direction.

Regardless of whether you have a boss, a manager, or a supervisor, as a power seller, you're ultimately your own boss and should be more demanding of yourself than any boss could ever be. The responsibility for achieving your goals sits squarely on your shoulders. It's up to you to hold yourself accountable. If you're not qualified to hold yourself accountable, consider taking on a personal partner, as explained in Book VII, Chapter 3.

Drawing up the perfect sales plan and executing it to perfection doesn't necessarily guarantee success. In some cases, you may fall short of your goals. In more fortunate situations, your success exceeds your wildest imagination. Whatever the result, you usually have to revisit your sales plan regularly to see where you've ended up and what adjustments are required to get back on track or change your direction to achieve even loftier goals.

The following sections reveal the importance of revising your sales plan to accommodate unexpected shortcomings and take advantage of unanticipated success.

You're better off aiming too high and missing the mark than always achieving less ambitious goals. If you fall short of a goal, you can always extend the time frame, but if you constantly meet unchallenging goals, you'll never achieve your full potential.

Book VII

Becoming a Power Seller

Assessing your progress . . . or lack thereof

You set your goal and specified a time frame for achieving it. When time expires, revisit the goal to determine whether you've accomplished it. Assuming you set a measurable goal, you should come to one of three conclusions:

- ✔ You met your goal.
- ✔ You exceeded your goal.
- ✔ You didn't quite get there.

If you met your goal, kudos for you! Reward yourself and collect your bonus; then return to the beginning of the chapter and set new goals. If you missed your goal or exceeded it, you have more work to do, as explained in the following sections.

Correcting for wrong turns

When you miss your goal, identify the cause:

- ✔ **The goal and time frame were unrealistic.** Perhaps you were too ambitious. That's perfectly understandable. As long as you're making progress, extending your deadline can put you back on track.

- ✔ **Your plan was flawed.** Plans don't always work. What's important is that you realize the plan was flawed before you pour any more time, money, or effort in it. You may have to dump the plan entirely, start over, or make some adjustments.

- ✔ **You failed to execute your plan properly.** If you dropped the ball during the execution of the plan, you can blame only yourself. It's okay to beat yourself up, but don't beat yourself down. Admit your shortcomings, do what's required to correct them, renew your commitment, and forge ahead.

Although you may need to dump your plan entirely, avoid dumping something that works. A single triumph can be the seed that grows into a hugely successful new sales plan. Cut what doesn't work and build on whatever's working.

The journey to success is like sailing across the ocean. A minor change in course early in your journey can make a huge difference in where you ultimately end up. You don't always have to make sweeping changes.

Building on success

When your plan exceeds your expectations, why not just celebrate and give high fives all around? Because sometimes, success can be more devastating than failure. Imagine that the plan you put in place to increase sales is a resounding success. Product is flying off the shelves — great! Unfortunately, inventory is running low and you don't have another supplier lined up or you can't ship product fast enough to meet demand or you don't have the support staff in place to keep all your new customers happy — not so great; you can do better.

When you check your progress toward accomplishing a particular sales goal, be prepared for situations in which your success exceeds your expectations. An inability to change course to take advantage of unforeseen success can negatively impact sales and is certain to leave you with a missed opportunity.

Discovering New Sales Techniques

To be a power seller, you must continually educate yourself and be open to picking up new strategies and techniques from other salespeople. The following sections point out some of the best continuing education opportunities for salespeople.

You don't really know whether you're good at something until you know about that something and take it for a test drive. Sales books, CDs, seminars, workshops, and other educational resources expose you to different sales strategies and techniques you may not have been aware of and may be really good at. To remain at the top of your game, continue to seek out educational opportunities.

Book VII

Becoming a Power Seller

Reading up on new selling strategies

In addition to this book, which provides various high-octane ways to boost sales and maximize your exposure to sales opportunities (a whole series of strategies is included in Book II, Chapter 2 and Book VIII, Chapter 2), you'll also want to explore other sales strategies, including solution selling, SPIN selling, and question-based selling.

Every expert on the topic of selling has a slightly different approach. By reading widely instead of buying into a single strategy, you can form your own unique sales strategy that fits best with your personality and approach.

Tuning into sales tapes and CDs

Books are great for providing detailed information, but nothing can replace hearing the impassioned voice of a sales coach providing verbal instruction. Tapes, CDs, and other recordings of books have one added advantage — you can listen while you're on the road.

Attending sales seminars and workshops

Books and audio recordings are certainly informative, but mastering a new technique, particularly when it runs counter to something you've been taught in the past, requires practice and feedback. Seminars and workshops provide you with a more dynamic venue in which you can ask questions and perhaps even rehearse new techniques.

Attending a seminar or workshop may require a significant investment of time and money, especially if you have to travel very far, but the return on your investment is usually worth it. In addition to obtaining practical sales training, you have the opportunity to meet other top salespeople, pick up additional techniques from them, and establish valuable professional connections and perhaps even identify partnership opportunities.

Of course, not all seminars and workshops are of equal value, so choose carefully and look for those that feature a combination of the following:

✔ **Panels of top producers:** You want to learn from the best, not those who may someday be best.

✔ **Big-name keynote speakers:** In addition to giving you the chance to rub elbows with success, this shows that the organization presenting the seminar has spent some money invested in it.

✔ **A wide variety of breakout sessions:** Selling is a multifaceted art form, so hone your skills in as many areas as possible.

✔ **Networking time:** Seminars expand *what* you know, but they also expand *who* you know. You often discover more in the hallways and at lunch than you do during the actual sessions. Meet the other attendees and as many of the presenters as possible. If possible, meet each presenter early on and obtain their materials, so you can determine which sessions to attend.

One-day motivational seminars are great if you're in bad need of a pep talk, but don't rely on them exclusively. Look for seminars that have more substance and provide you with educational opportunities to upgrade your skills.

Test-driving new techniques

Salespeople are notorious for not following advice. They read a book on a great new sales technique and a week later they're delivering the same sales pitch they've been using for the last five years. They hire a personal coach to train them, pay $300 an hour or more, and then simply fail to put any of the training into practice.

A very effective way to begin implementing a new sales technique is to first rehearse the technique with a colleague: One of you plays the salesperson, and the other pretends to be the buyer. Consider switching roles, so you

each have a chance to play salesperson and buyer. Some salespeople claim to learn more by playing the role of buyer. Keep in mind that mastering a new technique may require several role-playing sessions and considerable practice to work out the bugs.

Tip: Some sales techniques require you to master subtle tactics. Consider hiring someone who has mastered the technique to provide training, supervise role-playing sessions, and offer expert feedback. Role playing with peers or a boss also can be very effective.

Swapping secrets with colleagues

One of the bonuses of working in sales is that most salespeople love to talk . . . or maybe they just love to *hear* themselves talk. Whatever the case, they're usually willing to share what they've picked up in the course of their career. Get connected with as many salespeople as possible and pick their brains. Even if they sell in a completely different industry, they can offer tips and suggestions that can stimulate your own creativity.

Book VII

Becoming a Power Seller

Keeping pace with your industry

A good salesperson can sell anything — cars, houses, insurance, video games, computers, shoes, you name it. A power seller loves what she sells. Assuming you love what you sell, this next bit of advice is something you'll have no trouble putting into practice: Keep pace with your industry. Subscribe to your industry's top magazines, journals, and newsletters; bookmark leading industry websites and visit them regularly; and share information with others in the industry.

A great way to keep up on late-breaking industry news is to sign up for Google News Alerts. Go to Google News (http://news.google.com) and perform a search. Scroll to the bottom of the search results, click the link to create an e-mail alert for the keyword or phrase you searched for, and follow the on-screen instructions. Whenever Google detects a news story that matches the keyword or phrase you entered, Google notifies you via e-mail.

Keeping up on changes in the industry is much easier than having to catch up later. Be proactive in gathering information. In highly competitive markets, falling behind for even a short time can lead to disaster. By keeping up with the latest news and developments in your industry, you become a much more valuable resource person for your customers and can better understand their needs and the issues they face.

Setting the Stage for an Unlimited Upside

As an entrepreneurial salesperson, getting stuck in a dead-end job doesn't seem likely to happen. After all, when you're earning commissions, you can earn as much as you're willing to work, right? Well, maybe not. Salespeople can still get stuck in dead-end jobs by boxing themselves in — picking the wrong product, service, or company; pursuing business from customers who demand too much attention; working for an uninspired company; or refusing to delegate tasks that others are perfectly capable of handling.

Limit your upside, and you can achieve only a limited level of success. It's like buying an 8-foot ladder when you own a two-story house. That ladder isn't going to get you on the roof.

Yet if you maximize your upside, you can discover unlimited opportunities. You can continually expand and ramp up your efforts with additional resources and personnel. You never feel cramped, you always feel driven by a new challenge, and your dreams become more and more expansive.

This section introduces the main limitations to a salesperson's upside and then reveals strategies for overcoming these limitations and maximizing your upside.

Replacing the wrong product or service with one that's right

If possible, steer clear of products and services with a limited upside. Here are some red flags to watch out for:

- ✔ **Something you don't like:** If you can't get excited about the product or service or you're selling a product or service you don't believe in, consider selling something else.

- ✔ **Fad item:** Don't jump on the bandwagon whenever a fad rolls into town. Sales are likely to go from boom to bust in a hurry, and eventually all the resources you invested in building a brand around that fad are going to be wasted.

Be aware of the difference between a *fad* (short term) and a *trend* (long term). Mistaking a trend for a fad could keep you from capitalizing on a lucrative opportunity. Beanie Babies and Pet Rocks were clearly fads, for example, but blogging (which you can read more about in Book VII, Chapter 7) is a revolutionary change that's here to stay.

✔ **Poor quality:** A market always exists for second-rate products and services at low prices, but selling shoddy products and services ultimately harms your reputation.

✔ **One-time purchases:** Avoid selling anything that a person buys only once during her life, such as cemetery plots. Houses, cars, candles, computer software, and IT servers that have a three-year lifecycle are examples of products that require renewal. When you sell things like this, you can afford to invest time and resources in establishing long-term relationships with clients.

✔ **Saturated market:** Some products are merely commodities, and competition is based solely on who can offer the lowest price. Competing on low price may work for some mega-giant retailers, but it usually means you're scraping the bottom of the barrel.

When you're looking for ways to boost sales, product selection must factor in. If you're selling a product that has a narrow appeal, the market is saturated, or you're simply facing superior competition, you may be fighting a losing battle. Part of being a power seller is knowing how to pick a winner — a product or service with an unlimited upside, as the following sections explain.

Book VII

Becoming a Power Seller

Listing products and services packed with potential

Chances are good that if you're selling for a fairly large company, the company has already performed the necessary research and is aware of the product's market potential. If you're running your own business or trying to pick a company to work for that has products or services with the most potential, make sure those products and services have the following qualities:

✔ **Universal appeal:** The larger the market, the bigger the upside. Focusing on a niche market is fine, as long as that market has more consumers than you can possibly reach in the course of your career.

✔ **Opportunities for repeat sales:** Anything that people buy more than a couple times over the course of their lives is a candidate, including houses, cars, computers, phones, and bottled water.

✔ **Reliable consumer base:** A reliable consumer base is one that's not likely to disappear after a short period of time. In other words, don't chase fads. The more reliable the consumer base, the longer you can expect to be in the business of selling that product or service.

✔ **Something you won't tire of selling:** If you have to convince yourself that you like what you're selling, you're probably selling the wrong thing.

Pick a product you can build a career around — houses, cars, computers, productivity software, power tools, or something else that people are going to always need. Becoming a power seller requires that you build a brand identity. Even if you sell branded products, you still want your clients thinking about *you* as their go-to guy or gal who represents the company. Whenever a customer thinks of the product you sell, she should immediately think of you. Pick a product with an unlimited and long-term upside, so you don't waste time building brand identity with a product that's destined to drop off the radar a few months or years down the road.

Assessing multimedia marketing opportunities

Some products have limited media potential; they may play well in TV ads but not in print or on the radio, or they may play well in print but not transition to TV. You're not likely to see a huge boost in sales by advertising a specialty software program on TV, for example.

When looking for products and services with an unlimited upside, lean toward those that you can advertise and market effectively in as many media as possible — print, TV, radio, websites, blogs, direct mailings, e-mail, and so forth. With more ways to reach prospective customers, you have more ways to expand your market.

Upgrade to better customers

If you operate in accordance with the credo that "the customer is always right," you're making a big mistake. Customers are often wrong, and when a customer is wrong, serving them can quickly become a costly full-time operation. Unless you can settle them down in a hurry and get their expectations in line, your best move may be to cut them loose.

Identify your worst customers and consider giving them *less* attention rather than *more* attention (which they demand). This strategy may seem counterintuitive — the squeaky wheel is supposed to get the grease — but in sales, pulling back from a bad customer is a no-lose situation. The bad customer either goes elsewhere (to burden your competition) or decides to cooperate and become a more profitable and less burdensome source of revenue.

Even when you're dealing with the worst customer in the world, remain respectful and polite, and let the customer down easy. Remain professional at all times. Refusing to serve a customer at your restaurant because she never leaves a tip, for example, can destroy your business. (This actually happened in a small town in Indiana.)

To identify your best and worst customers, determine how profitable each customer is. Gross sales is only one consideration. Also, factor in the amount of repeat business the customer represents, the amount of time the customer requires, frequency and size of returns, payment issues, referrals you receive from that customer, how your relationship with that customer affects your status in the industry, and so on. Consider ranking customers and then work on finding replacements for the customers at the bottom of your list.

Bottom line: It's up to you to decide who qualifies as a best customer. In the business world, "best customer" usually equates with "most profitable" customer, but profitability can be a little tough to pin down. When creating your list of credentials for a best customer, consider the following traits:

- ✔ **Places you first:** When the customer thinks of a product or service you offer, she thinks of you first.

- ✔ **Pays a fair price:** Customers who value the product and service you offer are willing to pay the going rate. Those who don't value what you have to offer are constantly low-balling you on price.

- ✔ **Challenges you:** When customers constantly raise the bar, requiring you to expand your knowledge, improve or add new skills, increase productivity, and so on, they're improving your business.

- ✔ **Allows you to do what you do well:** Customers should know your business sufficiently to ask you to perform in areas where you excel rather than pushing you into areas outside your realm of expertise.

- ✔ **Exposes you to new opportunities:** Your best customers are collaborators — people or companies with whom you develop mutually beneficial relationships. These customers steer business your way and may even offer some cross-marketing opportunities. We value this quality more than any of the others.

Book VII

Becoming a Power Seller

Acquiring the support and resources you need

Ideally, you're self-employed or you work for a company that nurtures an entrepreneurial mindset among its salespeople. In the latter case, your company and manager encourage you to set goals, establish your own sales plan and strategy, and provide you with the resources required to put your plan into action.

Unfortunately, not everybody works in such an enlightened or supportive environment. If you're not thriving in your current work environment, the reason may be that it's not the right place for you. Assess your current company, being particularly sensitive to warning signs like lack of support, lack of training opportunities, and an overbearing manager — one who's obsessed with sales quotas, disregards your opinions, berates you, or undermines your authority with customers or clients.

If you find yourself in a less-than-ideal situation, you have a couple options, as the next sections explain.

Convincing management to invest in your success

How do you go about convincing management to get you what you need? The best approach is to act as though you're starting your own business and trying to convince a bank executive to approve a small-business loan:

1. **Draw up your sales plan (refer to the earlier section "Charting Your Road Map to Sales Success").**

2. **Meet with your sales manager to review your plan, highlighting the potential boost in sales and profits.**

3. **Provide your manager with an itemized list of tools, supplies, and other resources required to properly execute your plan, along with an estimated total cost and ideas for implementing your plan.**

   Include enough supporting documentation to convince management to say "yes." Remember, agreeing is easier if you can hear, see, and possibly test-drive the plan first. Show and tell all the way to close.

In most well-run companies, new sales associates receive plenty of training and support. When training and support aren't provided, they're usually readily available upon request. Don't automatically assume that your company is unsupportive just because management doesn't take the initiative to offer resources. You may simply need to ask.

Before you can expect to receive any additional support from management, establish yourself as a talented and hard-working salesperson. Show up at sales meetings and training sessions with an eagerness to improve. Be willing to shadow an expert you want to emulate. By showing up and acknowledging that you're ready, willing, and able to learn, you're more likely to get the support you need. Nobody can support your efforts to improve sales if you're not doing your part.

If your supervisor shoots down your plan, do what you normally do when you're trying to sell something — head on up to the decision maker. The higher you climb the ladder in the business world, the more likely you are to connect with someone who's entrepreneurial by nature and values people who have goals and plans.

Finding a company that's a better match for you

If you've followed the advice in this book, you have a strong work ethic, and you've tried to get the support and training you need, but your sales still aren't where they should be, it may be time to find a company that's a better match.

Don't quit your current position without careful deliberation. By implementing the strategies suggested throughout this book, you're likely to discover that the job, your company, and your supervisor weren't the cause of your lackluster sales. If you're doing everything this book recommends, and your sales are still less than stellar, then the company you work for (or its products or services) may not be the right fit. In that case, maybe it's time to begin your search for a company that treats its salespeople right.

Abandoning the I-can-do-it-all mentality

Salespeople tend to be control freaks, but trying to do everything yourself is a sure way to cap any hoped-for increase in productivity.

Do the math. You're only one person. You have 24 hours in a day and seven days in a week. You can boost your productivity with software and other tools, but time still limits how much you can do by yourself. To dash those limitations, delegate less critical tasks to others.

The fact that your job description includes a list of tasks doesn't mean that you're personally responsible for performing those tasks. You don't have to do everything. You're responsible for making sure everything gets done. To maximize your earnings potential, focus on the tasks you do best and that bring in the money; then delegate any tasks that meet one or more of the following conditions:

- ✔ Someone else can do it just as well for less money. If you earn $50 an hour, don't cut your grass if you can get it cut for $10 . . . unless, of course, mowing the lawn is therapeutic.
- ✔ Someone else can do it better or faster.
- ✔ You don't like doing it — the task drains your energy and motivation.

Chapter 2

Getting in Step with Your Customer

. . . .

In This Chapter

▶ Brushing up on sales psychology

▶ Riding the waves of the buying cycle

▶ Exploring sales strategies and techniques

▶ Sharpening your skills

. . . .

Selling is like ballroom dancing. To avoid stepping on your dance partner's toes, you learn the steps. You practice to get a feel for how your partner moves and make your movements more natural and fluid. Assuming you and your partner have mastered the steps and practiced sufficiently, you move effortlessly and gracefully across the dance floor, never missing a beat. Onlookers can't tell who's leading and who's following.

Selling requires a very similar finesse. With selling, the dance steps are the basic selling techniques you employ. Over time, you practice these techniques until they become effortless and fluid. To avoid stepping on your customer's toes, you get a feel for your customer — what your customer needs and how she goes about making a purchase decision. Done right, the process of buying and selling takes on the appearance of a graceful dance. You take the lead and guide your customer to making the right decision, but as you interact, neither of you seems to be leading the other.

Although this is certainly an overly romanticized description of the sales process, it illustrates the three key factors for selling effectively: knowing your customer, knowing how to sell, and practicing to the point at which selling feels natural. This chapter focuses on the key factor of knowing your customer, giving you an inside look at how customers generally make purchase decisions, revealing several proven strategies, and showing you how to practice your skills until you're the Fred Astaire or Ginger Rogers of sales.

Knowing Why Buyers Buy

Knowing why people generally buy stuff — especially your stuff — can assist you in making your customers more sensitive to their wants and needs. Until you know what your prospective clients want or need, you're in no position to sell them anything. All you can do is present the product and describe its features. When you know what the client is looking for, however, you can *pitch* the product to the client's wants or needs and have a much more effective presentation. In the following sections, I reveal the seven key buyer motivations and then show you how to identify these motivations as they play out in the marketplace.

Looking at the seven buyer motivations

Sure, you're selling a product or service, but your customer buys to solve a problem or meet a need. Early on, focus more on your customers and figuring what their motivation to buy is. So why do people buy stuff? For the following reasons:

- **Need/problem:** Customers you contact may already be well aware that they have a need or a problem, but many others are totally clueless. Until your customer is aware of the problem and realizes that viable solutions are available, she sees no need for the product or service you're selling. Early in the process, either through advertising or your interview, raise your customer's awareness of the problem and pique her interest in seeking solutions. Only then are you prepared to lead your customer through the process of analyzing available solutions.

- **Desire for more:** Numerous products and services are designed to assist people in making more money. If you're in corporate sales, that's pretty much all you sell, because businesses are in the business of making money. If what you're selling can make people more productive, if it can boost revenue or cut expenses, then you have a product you can sell by playing to your customer's desire to make money.

- **Fear:** Fear sells. Some claim that fear sells better than sex, and they may be right. Just think of all the advertising invested in marketing products that protect us from real or perceived threats: satellite communications systems for cars (giving you a lifeline no matter where you go), home alarm systems (providing early warning of break-ins or fire), bottled water (who really knows what's in tap water?), and so on.

- **Pleasure:** If you're selling in a feel-good industry, such as vacation travel, spas, hobbies and handicrafts, or home décor, marketing to your customers' pleasures is paramount. But even in industries in which pleasure isn't the central focus, you can often sell luxury-class items by focusing on the pleasure they're likely to provide for the consumer.

When a customer is in the market for an $80,000 car, for example, she's wanting something more than a comfortable ride to work. If you want to learn how to cater to pleasure, go to a boat show.

✔ **Vanity:** People not only want to feel good, they want to look good, and they generally want other people to think they look good, too. Whether you're selling cosmetics, clothing, jewelry, accessories, hair care products, plastic surgery, or a host of other personal care products and services, your marketing and selling strategies need to target the customers' need to look good.

✔ **Impulse:** People often buy stuff because everyone else is buying it. You don't need to be a great salesperson to take advantage of a hot trend, because people know what they want and often purchase impulsively. Success depends more on distributing the product and placing it in high-profile locations where purchase is more convenient.

✔ **Fatigue:** Pushy salespeople can be very successful simply by wearing the customer down, but think twice before taking this approach. It may work for a door-to-door salesperson who wanders from town to town, but bullying tactics are counterproductive when you're trying to build a reputation that secures future business.

Identifying motivations for buying your product or service

Selling requires an ability to get inside your customer's head and figure out why that person is likely to want or need the product you're selling. Of course, you don't really know what motivates your customer to buy until he tells you, but you can get a general idea by examining what your products and services have to offer:

1. **Jot down a list of products or services you're selling.**

2. **Next to each item, list all the motivations that a customer may have to purchase the product or service.**

   You may find that the primary motive is to solve a problem or alleviate a fear, but secondary motivations may also come into play.

3. **Rank the motivations in order of strength.**

   Which motivation is most common and likely to convince your customer to make a purchase decision?

4. **Use the motivation rankings to assist your prospective customer in making the right purchase decision.**

   Read on for additional details on how to assess a prospect's needs and then pitch your products to those needs.

Book VII

Becoming a Power Seller

Collaborating on the Purchase Decision

Regardless of what you're selling and your customer's possible motivation for buying it, your customer follows a predictable pattern when making a purchase decision. The more aware you are of this pattern, the more effective you can be at teaming up with the customer to arrive at a mutually beneficial purchase decision. Regardless of what your customer's buying, she generally takes the following four steps in making a purchase decision:

1. **Identifies a problem or need, either on her own or with the assistance of someone in marketing or sales . . . not necessarily you.**

2. **Searches for and compares products or services that meet her needs.**

3. **Compares prices of comparable products and services.**

4. **Measures the risk of purchasing or not purchasing the product or service.**

Although customers often follow this step-by-step process in order, the decision-making process can take some rapid and unexpected turns, and the longer the customer takes to decide, the more jumbled the steps become. After assessing the risks of purchasing a product or service, for example, a customer may decide not to purchase and skip back to Step 2 or Step 3, so be prepared to make adjustments on the fly.

The following sections describe each step in the purchase decision process and highlight what you should be doing at each stage to guide your customer in making the right decision.

Calling attention to the problem or need

As a salesperson, you essentially solve problems or serve people's needs. In most cases, however, your customer doesn't even realize that he has a problem or that the need exists. During this stage of the process, you're assisting the prospective client in identifying a need, and you can do it in either of two ways:

✓ **Advertising:** On its surface, advertising may appear to push a particular product or service, but the underlying message of almost all advertisements is that the customer has a need that's not being sufficiently met.

✓ **Interviewing:** If you sell by contacting customers directly, your early conversations are or should be centered on identifying your customer's needs or problems. In other words, you should be asking lots of questions directed at rooting out problems, needs, or concerns that the prospect may or may not be aware of.

Ask questions before pitching what you're selling. You don't know what your customer needs or wants until that customer tells you, and once you know, you can more effectively pitch your product or service to your customer's needs. The more excited you are about your product, the more you must avoid the temptation to start reciting a litany of product features. Early in the buying process, your goal is to gather information and understand the customer's needs. (See the section "Asking questions to draw out the information you need," later in this chapter for details.)

Identifying possible solutions

To be the best salesperson you can be, stop selling. Don't think of yourself as a salesperson. Think of yourself more as a friend or colleague who's helping his buddy solve a problem. If your friend came to you with a problem, you'd probably listen first to gather as much pertinent information as possible. You may even ask your friend whether she tried any solutions and, if she did, what the results were. You probably wouldn't simply dive in and start offering advice before you knew what was going on.

At this point, you should have identified the prospect's wants or needs (as explained in the preceding section). Now you can shift the interview to asking questions like the following, which identify possible solutions and determine whether what you're selling meets your customer's needs:

- **What do you do now?** Instead of launching into a long-winded description of what your company does and what you have to offer, shift the focus to the customer's situation.

- **How are you currently doing it?** Your customer may already have a system or products in place. By understanding the customer's current solution, you're in a better position to demonstrate how your products and services can better meet those needs.

- **What are you trying to do?** Encourage your customer to present what she thinks would be the ideal solution or at least her vision of the results that would follow if the ideal solution were in place. The answer to the first question "What do you do?" tells you where the customer is right now, while the answer to this question tells you where the customer wants to be tomorrow.

- **What can I do for you?** After you know where the customer is and where the customer wants to be, this question flows naturally. You're essentially asking the customer, "How do you see me assisting you in getting from point A to point B?"

Book VII

Becoming a Power Seller

You may need to reword these questions so they're more applicable to what you're selling. If you sell houses, for example, instead of asking "What do you do?" and "What are you trying to do?" you may ask, "Where do you live?" and "Where do you want to live?" Someone selling computers may ask, "What do you use your computer for now?" and "What do you think you'd like to be able to do with your computer?"

Prospective customers often dismiss problems, convincing themselves that no satisfactory solution exists or that the solution is too costly or time consuming to pursue. When talking with the customer at this point, consider asking whether she has considered or even tried other solutions. By discussing these other solutions, you get a better feel for what the customer *doesn't* want.

Weighing costs and benefits

Knowing that a solution is available, customers proceed to analyze the costs — more specifically, they analyze the costs versus the benefits. This is where the scales begin to teeter-totter and where sticker shock begins to set in on big-ticket items or large-scale solutions.

At this stage in the decision-making process, you can be very successful by focusing the customer's attention on the consequences of not purchasing the product or service. If you're in corporate sales, for example, you may ask the customer how a decision not to move forward is going to affect production or plans for expansion. In real estate, you may ask a couple who's thinking of purchasing a more affordable house how much that's going to save them in the long run, if "more affordable" means "one that needs substantial work" or "one that's smaller than they hoped for."

When customers are assessing the costs and benefits, remain in question mode. Don't simply point out the negative consequences. Ask questions that draw the customer's attention to the negative consequences of not moving forward.

Second-guessing the decision

After people decide to purchase something, especially an expensive something, they begin to have second thoughts. They start talking to colleagues, relatives, friends, neighbors, their hairdresser, you name it, and begin wondering whether they really need it, whether they can get it cheaper somewhere else, or whether the salesperson is trying to pull a fast one over on them. Whatever the situation, the customer gets a case of what's technically known as *buyer's remorse* or, more commonly, *cold feet,* and you'd better be ready with a pair of warm socks.

At this stage in the purchase decision process, you're essentially addressing customer concerns, fielding objections, and trying to keep the customer calm. In real estate, for example, the buyer is excited about the home, and then comes the home inspection, when buyer's remorse can easily set in. If you're an agent, make sure you're there during the inspection to resell, confirm that the buyer is making a great decision, and overcome any obstacles with suggestions of how to resolve potentially deal-busting decisions.

In corporate sales, you also have to remain engaged with the prospect, especially if your company follows the hunter-farmer sales model — that is, the person who lands the deal (the hunter) is ultimately not the person who services the account (the farmer). In this situation, the hunter needs to continue to remain engaged with the client to ensure quality service and continuity.

Your ultimate goal is not to sell but to assist prospective clients in choosing the solution that's the best fit for them, even if this means not getting the sale. When you're not selling for commissions or bonuses but to satisfy your customers, you're doing it right, and the commissions and bonuses start flowing your way.

Brushing Up on a Few Power-Selling Techniques

Book VII

Becoming a Power Seller

Some people seem to be born to sell. They have personality plus. Anyone would buy anything they were selling. If you're one of these people, lucky you. You can safely skip this section and tend to other ways of increasing your sales and revenue.

For the rest of you who weren't quite born to be salespeople, there's still hope. By acquiring a few basic skills along with some turbocharged techniques, you can take your game to the next level and begin selling like a seasoned pro.

Dealing with the decision maker

You can waste a lot of time and energy selling to people who don't have the power to make the final decision. This is a bigger problem in corporate sales, where your initial contact is likely to be lower on the chain of command, but you may also encounter this problem if you're selling high-priced items, such as houses, cars, or insurance, to couples.

Whenever you're selling, sell to the decision maker; otherwise, you're not selling — you're simply negotiating your way past the gatekeepers. The following sections show you how to spot the decision maker and work your way up to the person you should be selling to.

Spotting the decision maker

Identifying the decision maker is fairly easy. Look for the person who has the most power and control. If you're dealing with a couple, the decision maker is the one who typically exhibits the following qualities:

- Sits in the front seat when driving out to look at houses.

- Speaks on behalf of the couple. (When you ask a question, the non–decision maker looks at the decision maker.)

- Is the one who directs and is willing to adjust which features are important, based on the type of product they're purchasing.

Even though you may be consciously pitching the product to the decision maker, don't make the non–decision makers feel like second-class citizens. Treat everyone equally — not the same, but equally. Otherwise, you could lose the sale.

In corporate sales, spotting the decision maker can be much more challenging, because that person may be hiding behind a host of other managers, employees, voicemail, and e-mail. When you find the person, however, the signs of power are similar to those you observe when selling to couples or families. The decision maker is the person to whom all others defer.

Working your way to the decision maker

When you're selling to companies, the path to the decision maker is likely to be strewn with blockades and detours. In most cases, you first have to get past the automated gatekeepers — voicemail, caller ID, and e-mail. Then, if you're lucky enough to contact an actual human being, you're likely to find that the person isn't actually the decision maker.

To take some shortcuts to the decision maker in a business setting, consider the following tips:

- **Find out how purchasing decisions are typically made in the industry you're working in.** Do companies typically have a purchasing department? Does the CEO or CFO make the purchasing decisions? Are decisions handled by individual department heads? You can look at the company's website to find the names of department heads and other managerial personnel.

- ✔ **Use the time-crunch technique.** When meeting with prospective clients whom you suspect are not the decision makers, ask when they would like to have this solution implemented. If they say something like "two months," you can follow up by saying, "Two months? That's okay, but it's pretty aggressive. Who's involved in the decision-making, so I can assist you in meeting your timeline?"

- ✔ **Network with current and former employees, customers, and suppliers of the company.** See whether any of your contacts can personally introduce you to the decision maker.

- ✔ **Introduce yourself to the receptionist and ask who's in charge of (fill in the blank)?** For example, "Who's in charge of IT?" or "Who's in charge of printing?"

If you're not talking to the decision maker, you should be working your way up to that person. Don't waste time pitching your products and services to people who can't decide to buy them.

Mastering the meet and greet

Your first meeting with a prospective client can set the entire tone of your relationship. Following are some guidelines to ensure that your relationship has a positive start:

- ✔ **When meeting the client at her home, knock on the front door instead of ringing (just in case someone's sleeping), and take your shoes off at the front door.**

- ✔ **Shake hands and introduce yourself first.** A firm, friendly handshake is best.

- ✔ **Maintain eye contact without getting into a staring match.**

- ✔ **Pay attention to seating arrangements.** When meeting a couple at their home or apartment, try to move them to the kitchen table. The living room is for company; the kitchen is where friends and family typically feel most comfortable. If meeting in a public place, try to arrange it so that your back is facing a wall, so that you receive the full and undivided attention of your clients.

- ✔ **If the client offers you a nonalcoholic drink, accept it or ask for water.**

- ✔ **Some small talk can break the ice and establish you in the eyes of your client as not only a salesperson but a human being.** Don't force it, though, and always avoid discussing sex, politics, religion, or schools.

Book VII

Becoming a Power Seller

No matter how badly your day has gone, how tired you feel, or how much you'd rather be somewhere else, pump yourself up and pump some energy into the conversation. By boosting the energy in the room, you put your client more at ease, jump-start his positive thoughts, and improve your chances of achieving your sales goal.

Asking questions to draw out the information you need

Asking questions is a critical part of selling effectively, because it enables your customer to feel more in control of making the purchase decision while providing you with the information you need to guide your customer in the right direction.

Realize, however, that all questions are not created equal. If you ask a yes/no question, and the answer is "No," the conversation is pretty much over. The following list offers suggestions on how to phrase your questions in a way that keeps the conversation going and provides you with the information you need.

When phrasing your questions, consider asking customers how they *feel* about something rather than what they *think* about it. The purchase decision is often an emotional choice, so knowing how your customer feels can give you a better idea of what the customer really wants.

✔ **Ask thought-provoking questions.** The best questions are those that provoke thought and compel your customer to offer up details rather than yes/no answers. These questions may also demonstrate your understanding of the customer's situation or business and your genuine interest in discovering solutions that are best for them. For example:

> **Poor:** "Do you like the neighborhood where you're living?" (Requires a simple yes or no answer.)

> **Better:** "What are some of the best things about the neighborhood where you're living?" (Makes the person think and offer details about what she's looking for in a neighborhood.)

✔ **Answer a question with a question.** Customers can trap you with their own targeted questions. If you're not careful, you can actually un-sell your product by giving the wrong answer. When you're not completely sure from the way a customer asks a question what answer she's looking for, consider answering the question with a question of your own.

For example, if you sell real estate and the buyer asks how big the yard is, you have only a 50/50 chance of giving the right answer if you don't know whether she wants a big yard or a small yard. If you respond with the question, "How big of a yard are you looking for?" you can then phrase your own answer more effectively. If she wants a big yard, you can say, "This house has one of the largest yards in the neighborhood." If she wants something smaller, you can say, "The lot is pretty average for this area." Same lot, but you're framing the customer's perspective, and perspective is reality.

✔ **Use yes/no questions tactically.** Ask yes/no questions sparingly and only when you're almost certain that the client's answer is going to be "yes." You can even stack these questions as a way to get the client in the rhythm of saying "yes" and then finish the series by asking for what you really want. For example:

"Is it okay to put a for sale sign on your front lawn?"

"Is it okay to schedule an open house?"

"Can we put a lockbox on your door, so other agents can show your home to more buyers?"

"Can we add your house to multiple listing services to generate more interest?"

And so on, until you can present the contract and say something like, "Great, let's get started. This is a listing contract. . . ."

Mirroring your customer

Your customer is likely to feel more comfortable in your presence if he feels that you're on the same level with him. To evoke a sense of camaraderie in your clients, use a technique called *mirroring*. If your client talks loudly, raise your voice. If the client speaks softly, lower your voice. If your client prefers talking on the phone over meeting in person, make more phone calls than visits. If your client seems a little timid, tone down your presentation.

Looking for win-win opportunities

The more successful your customer is, the more successful you're likely to become, so throughout the decision-making process, your focus should be on doing what's best for your customer. What's best for your customer is what's best for both of you. Strive to make transactions mutually beneficial.

If your product isn't right for your customer or your customer can't really afford it, selling it to him anyway may book you one commission, but it'll hurt you in the long run.

Changing "no" to "know"

Salespeople are no strangers to the word *no,* but when a customer says "no," try to hear "know," as in the customer doesn't yet *know* enough to say "yes." If the customer really means "no," then you should certainly back off, thank the customer for her time, and move on. Customers often say "no," however, when they're having second thoughts and require a little additional information. Be patient and persistent.

Customers are inclined to be more cautious just prior to making a purchase decision — just before signing on the dotted line. Plus, when they're considering buying from one of several salespeople, they often become most negative with the salesperson they're most likely to purchase from. These are positive signs: The key is to realize that this resistance is actually a sign that they're getting closer to closing the transaction and not get discouraged.

Knowing when to stop

Some salespeople become so excited when the customer finally decides to make the purchase that they keep selling, going on and on about how happy the customer is going to be, what a good decision she made, blah, blah, blah. What they fail to realize is that this places them at an increased risk of losing the sale. When the customer has decided to make the purchase, whether it took you 20 minutes or 20 days to make the sale, stop selling and seal the deal. (For information on how to close, refer to Book V, which offers closing strategies for a variety of situations.)

Practicing Your Sales Presentation

A sales presentation is only as good as it is natural, and to make it natural requires practice. Just think how stiff a group of actors would be staging a play after only a few rehearsals. The more you practice, the smoother your delivery and the better able you are to ad-lib when your customer throws you a curveball. Here are some ways to get much more out of your practice sessions on or off the job:

 ✔ **Watch and listen to yourself work.** Audiotape your presentation and listen to it later. If you hold sales presentations in your office, you may also consider videotaping a few presentations and watching them later. By hearing and perhaps listening to both yourself and your client, you can develop a clearer sense of what you're saying and the effect it has on a client. You can then adjust your presentation accordingly.

After a presentation, most salespeople have an overly negative view of their performance. They may have done quite well but walk away feeling as though they "blew it." Keep this in mind when you start to feel as though you blew a sale. You probably did much better than you think.

✔ **Team up with a trainer.** If you're fortunate enough to work for a company that provides training for its salespeople, take full advantage of the trainer. If you do most of your sales over the phone, you may be able to record your sales calls (with the client's permission, of course), and then review those calls with your trainer to determine what you can do more effectively. If you meet clients in person, the trainer may be able to sit in on the meeting and provide feedback later. (If your company doesn't offer a trainer, consider asking a colleague you admire to provide some coaching or going outside the company and hiring a sales coach.)

Former salespeople often make lousy trainers. They often have big egos fueled by the belief that becoming manager was a huge promotion. They can't stop selling and insist on stepping in when they think you're about to lose a sale. These intrusive trainers can actually undermine your credibility with a client. A good trainer remains as invisible as possible and provides feedback to you later . . . in private.

✔ **Role-play.** Sales consultants often recommend role-playing with a colleague. Although this technique can be of some use, especially if you're brand-new to the company or to sales and you want a little practice before heading out to meet with real customers. But don't rely on it solely; you're much better off practicing new skills in an actual sales setting with a real customer.

In sales, the most important place to practice is in front of the customer. It's no secret — the more you do it, the better you get at it. Real sales experiences, good or bad, make you a better salesperson.

Book VII

Becoming a Power Seller

Chapter 3

Teaming Up for Success with Personal Partnering

● ●

In This Chapter

▶ Identifying skills you want to improve

▶ Developing a personal improvement plan

▶ Selecting a personal partner

▶ Evaluating and celebrating your mutual success

● ●

*Y*ou probably have one or two nagging goals that, for whatever reason, you haven't been able to achieve. Maybe you want to run a marathon, learn a foreign language, or play a musical instrument. Maybe you've even tried a couple times but became distracted by something that seemed more important. Ten years later, you're kicking yourself for not following through.

But what if you had shared your plan for achieving that goal with someone else — someone you had teamed up with, with the intent of holding each other accountable for actively pursing your individual dreams? Both you and your partner would have significantly improved your chances of achieving your individual goals. This is what personal partnering is all about.

In this chapter, you discover the personal partnering process — a personal change technique developed by Terry Wisner, founder of Partnering To Success, LLC. You can use this approach to effect positive changes in your career. Here you find out how to team up with a personal partner to prioritize your goals, support one another's efforts, and celebrate your achievements on your way to mutual success.

Flagging Areas for Improvement

Like any serious effort to make a positive change in your life, changing the way you sell begins with an honest assessment of your current skill set. Until you admit that you could be doing something better and then identify that something, you have no idea what you need to work on.

Of course, assessing your sales skills sounds a lot easier than it really is. It requires that you admit your own shortcomings and take a step back to see yourself as others see you. This section shows you how to gather the information required to identify areas for improvement. Consider these your "lesser strengths."

Performing a self-assessment

When trying to identify areas for improvement, start with yourself. What do you feel you could be doing or doing better to boost sales? You may, for example, feel as though you're not very good at talking on the phone, or maybe you think you need to develop computer skills. Look for your lesser strengths.

Here are some key areas to examine:

- ✔ Communicating over the telephone
- ✔ Communicating in person
- ✔ Obtaining high-quality leads
- ✔ Improving efficiency through technology
- ✔ Meeting clients for the first time
- ✔ Asking for referrals
- ✔ Developing product expertise
- ✔ Researching the competition
- ✔ Networking and building productive relationships
- ✔ Finding out more about your customers

Throughout this All-in-One, you discover strategies, skills, and techniques that can make you a more effective salesperson. As you come across new sales tools and methods you'd like to try, add them to your list.

Taking a sales skills assessment test

A sales skills assessment test can assist you in evaluating your knowledge of the selling process and identifying your strengths and weaknesses. If your company doesn't offer a skills assessment test of its own, use your favorite Internet search engine to look for "sales skills assessments." Most of the assessments require that you complete a questionnaire online. The assessment service analyzes your answers and delivers a report highlighting your strengths and weaknesses.

Look for assessment tools that offer what is called *360-degree feedback* — perspectives from your customers, your peers, your boss, and yourself. You recommend the raters you want to assess you, and the company gathers information from these people. By seeing yourself from different perspectives, you can build a skill set that enables you to improve relationships with all those people who have a vested interest in your success. The Booth Company (www.boothco.com) offers several assessment programs.

Gathering insight from colleagues

Other salespeople you work with may witness your interactions with clients, either over the phone or in person, and they usually form opinions of how you handle various situations. If they're polite, they may keep their comments to themselves, but this discretion doesn't help you identify areas for improvement.

To break the ice, encourage your colleagues to open up by asking them to provide you with honest feedback. Tell them that you're trying to sharpen your sales skills and that you would appreciate any insights or recommendations they have to offer. Maybe you sound a little too abrasive on the phone. Perhaps you talk too much and listen too little. Whatever the case, these are things you should be aware of.

Don't kill the messenger. No matter how harsh the criticism, accept it without holding a grudge against the person who offered it. The person who cares for you is the one who tells you when you have something stuck in your teeth or quietly slips you a breath mint when you really need it, not the person who looks the other way.

Book VII

Becoming a Power Seller

Collecting customer feedback

Customers see you as nobody else sees you — from the perspective of someone who's going to purchase something from you. They can usually purchase whatever they want from three or four other people, but they chose you (or didn't choose you) for some reason, and you should know why.

Whether someone chooses to buy from you or not, try to find out what went into the purchase decision and how your sales presentation affected that decision. Avoid yes-or-no questions, such as, "Are you satisfied with the purchase?" Instead, keep your questions open-ended to encourage customers to identify areas for improvement.

Here are some questions you may consider asking:

✔ "What factors did you consider in making your purchase decision?"

✔ "What made you decide to choose the product you chose?"

✔ "What could I have done better?"

✔ "Why did you choose to purchase from the other company?"

Customers who are also in sales often provide the most insightful feedback. Getting feedback from salespeople who buy your products is like getting coaching from a professional golfer instead of some weekend duffer. Seek feedback from those who are most qualified to give it.

Listening to the boss

Regardless of whether your boss has sales experience, she may have valuable feedback to share concerning how well you're doing relative to other salespeople and information about you that clients have shared. When receiving your regular evaluation, remain receptive to any criticism or suggestions. In addition, seek out additional feedback if you think that your boss can offer valuable insight.

Seeking improvement is a sign of strength, not an admission of weakness.

The quality of feedback from a manager or supervisor can range from totally clueless to remarkably perceptive, so no one's telling you to blindly follow your manager's advice. You should, however, listen to what your manager has to say. He could be right, particularly if you've heard the same feedback from someone else.

Your manager's compensation is probably tied directly to the success of his sales force, so everyone's best interest is served through collaboration. Consider discussing your proposed personal improvement plan with your boss and requesting your manager's support in achieving your goals.

Targeting Key Skills

People who achieve excellence in a particular field are those who act with singularity of purpose. They focus on a few things, or perhaps just one, and pour all their energy and resources into achieving whatever they decide is most important. In short, they know how to prioritize.

 You can work on identifying and prioritizing goals or areas of improvement alone or with your partner. If you think your personal partnering experience would be more productive if you spent some time alone to contemplate and prioritize your goals, follow the process outlined in these steps before you team up with someone else. If you're having trouble getting started, however, you may want to find a partner first; skip to the following section, "Teaming Up with Your Personal Partner," and then come back to this section later.

To target the sales skills you want to work on first, follow these steps:

1. **List 100 (or so) sales skills you would like to sharpen.**

   List as many as you can think of.

2. **Underline the top seven skills you feel are most valuable and in need of development.**

   If you had only a month to significantly boost sales, which seven skills do you feel would need the most work?

3. **Highlight one big thing on the list.**

   You already know that if you try to do too much, nothing gets done right, so pick one skill you want to focus on: your product knowledge, computer knowledge, overall business knowledge, competitive knowledge, listening skills, whatever. Pick only one!

4. **Pick a couple easy things.**

   Achieving small goals that have a positive impact on your selling skills — buying a BlackBerry, sending thank-you notes or birthday cards to customers, or jotting down a to-do list first thing every morning, for example — keeps you engaged in the change process.

Book VII

Becoming a Power Seller

5. Write down your plan.

What you don't write down doesn't get done, so develop a plan and write it down.

Make sure that your personal partnering plan is SMART:

- **Specific:** Provide enough detail to explain how the efforts will culminate in the desired change.

- **Measurable:** Include intermittent goals, so you can track progress.

- **Actionable:** Specify tasks you're going to accomplish and the steps required to complete those tasks.

- **Realistic:** Set realistic objectives, to avoid frustration and disappointment.

- **Timed:** Set deadlines for accomplishing each task and achieving the planned objective.

Balance is key to long-term success, so when you're prioritizing your goals, make sure they include your personal goals as well. If you achieve your professional goals without achieving your personal goals, or vice versa, you're likely to be disappointed overall, which is a sign that you're not truly successful. Balance enables you to achieve your full potential in all areas of your life.

Teaming Up with Your Personal Partner

Personal partnering takes more than merely connecting with someone you know, making a few promises, and then going your separate ways to pursue your dreams. It requires that you work closely together, support one another, and meet regularly to track progress and make any necessary adjustments. You need to find a compatible partner, share your priorities and your plan, set down the rules, and then team up to execute your plans.

This section shows you how to locate a suitable partner and launch your partnership in the right direction.

Finding a good match

Personal partnering is effective with just about any two or three people who are dedicated to one another's success, but it works much better when you share common interests and goals. Teaming up with someone in sales, who is probably more aware of what you're trying to accomplish and the challenges you're facing, is likely to be more productive than dealing with someone who just doesn't get it.

Knowing what to look for and what to avoid

When you're in the market for a personal partner, look for someone who fits the following profile:

- A salesperson, ideally in the same or a related industry and with a skill set comparable or superior to yours
- A goal setter who shares the goal of improving her skills and who would like to see you become more successful
- A person you like and respect and who likes and respects you
- A person already with a plan or a willingness to develop such a plan
- An honest individual who won't pull punches

Some of the most productive partnerships arise when partners have complementary skill sets or resources. When you and your partner review one another's lists, look for opportunities to barter one another's skills and resources to your mutual benefit.

When choosing a personal partner, avoid the following:

- **Clients or customers:** Although you may have a productive client/server relationship, mixing personal matters with business could strain the relationship.
- **Competing co-workers:** Internal competition in sales teams often can create an environment not conducive to personal partnering. If you find yourself in a situation like this, consider looking for a partner who sells in another district or region or for a different company altogether.

What happens between you and your partner stays between you and your partner. Sharing goals requires a certain level of intimacy and trust and may reveal some vulnerabilities. Discuss this issue with your partner and commit to communicate in confidence. Don't fall into the common trap of being overly positive and constantly patting each other on the back. Try to surround yourself with people who don't hesitate to tell the truth.

Agreeing on a partnering style: Collaborative or cooperative

Although your partner should have a plan for improvement, you don't necessarily need to be working toward the same objective. In fact, your goals can be totally different. What's important is that you and your partner support one another in your efforts to improve. And you can do this in either of two ways — through collaborative or cooperative partnering:

✔ **Collaborative partnering:** In a collaborative effort, partners share a common goal. Collaborative partnering is the most common arrangement for co-workers who are striving to achieve a common goal, such as host an event, build a website, or attend a conference together.

Working collaboratively does not necessarily mean that you and your partner are performing the same tasks. If you're attending a conference together, for example, you may split up to maximize your networking opportunities and attend different training sessions. If you're hosting a promotional event, one of you may be working on invitations, while another is lining up a caterer, and a third partner is developing marketing materials.

✔ **Cooperative partnering:** With cooperative partnering, partners don't share a common goal. Each partner is free to pursue her own goals but is still accountable to her partner, and partners must encourage and support one another in their individual pursuits.

Sharing your priorities and your plan

Sharing your priorities and your plan with your partner is the unveiling of your vision for future success. Assuming you're both passionate about the journey you're embarking on and believe in the individual plans you're sharing, your first meeting is likely to be positive and brimming with energy.

During this meeting, you want to examine each other's plan in as much detail as necessary to clarify key points. As you review your own plan and your partner's plan, ask yourself and each other questions such as the following, which are designed to flesh out each plan and make them more concrete:

✔ Why is this so important to me?

✔ What will happen if I don't accomplish this?

✔ How will I know when I've met my goal?

✔ Who else, if anyone, needs to be involved?

✔ How are we going to celebrate after we both achieve our goals? As an incentive to support one another, you celebrate only after you've *both* achieved your goals. (See the section "Celebrating your success," later in this chapter, for details.)

The idea is to support and hold each other accountable to make the planned improvements. This feedback is essential in both finalizing the plan and communicating it to your partner.

Setting the ground rules

Although you can certainly formalize your personal partnering agreement by drawing up a contract and signing it, you can forgo the formalities and take a more casual approach, but you should always schedule a follow-up meeting and have a plan for tracking one another's progress. Specifically, you and your partner should come to an agreement that lays out the following ground rules:

- ✔ Frequency of follow-up contacts
- ✔ Method of following up (in person, via phone, via e-mail)
- ✔ Guidelines for judging success
- ✔ Rewards for achieving stated goals
- ✔ Consequences for not achieving stated goals
- ✔ The support role that each person must fill

Support and encourage one another's growth — don't criticize or ridicule. You can't force your partner to implement her plan. Your role is part cheerleader, part taskmaster, and part facilitator. Your partner's desire to achieve her goals and to honor her commitment to you and to herself should be motivation enough to keep her on track.

Book VII

Becoming a Power Seller

Collaborative competition

When you're teaming up with a colleague to achieve a goal, collaborative competition can keep you both on track. Suppose that you and your partner share the goal of making ten additional cold calls per month. You agree to keep each other posted on your weekly progress. After three weeks, you both observe the following pattern:

Week 1 Extra Cold Calls: You 3, Partner 1

Week 2 Extra Cold Calls: You 3, Partner 0

Week 3 Extra Cold Calls: You 2, Partner 2

By the end of the third week, you have eight new cold calls to your partner's 3. Your partner, who happens to be committed to your mutual success, can plainly see that she needs to get her booty in gear to meet her quota, and you realize that you need to offer some support. At this point, you may want to give your partner a call and offer some tips on how you go about generating cold calls.

Keeping each other on track

Personal partnering is effective only if you and your partner remain in contact, communicate clearly, provide the necessary encouragement and support, and hold one another accountable. The following sections walk you through the process of staying in touch and keeping one another on track.

Tracking progress

Staying on course is a lot easier than getting back on course after a long detour, and the best way to stay on course is to follow up with your partner frequently, particularly early on. You can follow up with actual face-to-face sessions, via telephone calls, through e-mails or instant messaging, or through whatever other communication channels you have available.

Follow-up schedules vary, depending on your and your partner's preferences, whether you're in the initial stages of executing your plans, and the specific tasks that your plans entail. If you plan on making one extra sales call per day, for example, your partner may check your progress daily for the first week, once a week for the next month, and then monthly for the rest of the year. If your objective is to average 30 lead-generating phone calls per month, you may consider scheduling feedback sessions on a weekly basis for the first month and then monthly after that.

Time your feedback sessions to accommodate both your plan and your partner's plan. The goal is for both of you to succeed.

Providing BACKUP

Throughout the personal partnering process, both you and your partner need to support and encourage each other by offering BACKUP:

Be empathetic toward each other.

Actively listen to one another.

Constantly focus on the other's goals.

Keenly watch for nonverbal signals.

Understand — you may not know everything.

Pursue the other's thoughts and feelings.

Sharpening your listening skills

Listening to your partner isn't like listening to background music. Give your partner your full, undivided attention. Here are some tips for becoming a more active listener:

- ✔ **Create a positive environment.** Turn off cellphones and get away from external distractions as much as possible.

- ✔ **Ask first.** By asking your partner to go first, you show that you're genuinely interested in what she has to say. Doing so elicits the same courtesy from your partner.

- ✔ **Take brief notes.** Jot down key points and any questions you have.

- ✔ **Listen attentively.** Sit with your body relaxed and facing your partner, and establish eye contact.

- ✔ **Communicate nonverbally, too.** Use appropriate facial expressions to indicate that you're listening and hearing what your partner is saying. Be careful not to overdo it, though.

- ✔ **Ask probing questions.** Open-ended questions elicit more thought and deeper connection within the discussion. They also reveal that you're interested in hearing more.

The ability to ask intelligent questions and process what the other person has to say are critical sales skills. Use your feedback sessions with your partner to practice these skills.

Reviewing, celebrating, and building

Party time! When your relationship with your partner culminates in some level of mutual success, it's time to review your overall performance, celebrate, and draw up plans to build on that success. This section shows you how to work on your endgame and enjoy the fruits of your labor.

Reviewing your overall performance

As you execute your plans, you have many opportunities to review your progress, and when you're about to wrap it all up, you have one final opportunity to review your overall performance. At this stage, you and your partner should sit down and run through the following questions:

- ✔ Did my objectives force me to stretch far enough? Were my objectives challenging enough?

- ✔ Was I fully engaged in this change process?

- ✔ Did we meet our goals?

- ✔ What are some other self-improvements I can make?

- ✔ Could I have been more helpful to my partner?

- ✔ How helpful was the personal partnering process?

Take a few moments together and discuss your responses with your partner. Try to quantify the results in numbers. Has this experience resulted in a boost in sales volume? Has it increased gross sales or decreased expenses? Has it improved your overall job satisfaction?

Celebrating your success

During the planning phase (covered in the earlier section "Sharing your priorities and your plan"), you and your partner discussed how to celebrate when you both achieve your goals. Here are some suggestions:

- ✔ Dinner at a fine restaurant
- ✔ A trip to the spa
- ✔ A weekend fishing trip
- ✔ A day at the races
- ✔ A shopping spree

Team up with your partner to plan a celebration suitable for the success you've both achieved, and don't worry too much about the expense. Your future success will more than pay for it.

Building on past success

After you've wrapped up your review and celebrated your success, jump back to the beginning of this chapter and launch a new improvement plan right away. The success of your previous plan and the positive energy that flows from that success is just the momentum required to make self-improvement a habit rather than a one-time event.

Chapter 4

Embracing Change as a Growth Strategy

In This Chapter

▶ Adjusting to changes in the way customers shop

▶ Tuning in to what's happening in your industry

▶ Taking the lead to improve products and services

▶ Shifting your strategy to seize fresh opportunities

The old saying "The only constant is change" has never been more true. The rate of change is accelerating at a phenomenal pace, fueled primarily by technology but also by the age of ideas and information. Each day delivers innovations in products and services, how they're marketed, where they're sold, how they're paid for, and how they're used. Changes in technology, society, politics, and other areas have revolutionized everything from what we eat and where we eat it to how we elect our government representatives. These same changes probably already have influenced the way you sell.

When change occurs, you essentially have three options: resist it, accept it, or seize it. Resisting a positive change typically results in falling victim to it. As soon as your competitors implement the change, you lose ground. Accepting the change keeps you in the running. Seizing the change and making it work to your advantage enables you to reap its full benefits and grow both personally and professionally.

In this chapter, you discover how to embrace change as a growth strategy. Here, you find various ways to keep up on changes inside and outside your industry that affect the way customers shop for products and services. With the information in this chapter and the right attitude, you're well positioned to ride the next big wave of change to the shores of success.

Working on Your Business

Capitalizing on change often hinges on how well prepared you are when change and its twin sibling, opportunity, come your way, but many salespeople are so busy working *in* their business that they forget to work *on* their business. They're too busy trying to earn a living or make a sale and earn that next commission, so they don't invest the time required to make their business more successful. You have to think, anticipate change, plan ahead.

Joseph Kennedy, Sr., purchased thousands of acres of land surrounding the oil fields of his days. Everyone knew that there was oil on the land, but they thought that the oil was too deep to reach. Kennedy bought up the land for cents on the dollar because everyone else saw it as worthless. He believed that American ingenuity would eventually produce an oil drill that could dig deep enough to tap into those fields. Obviously, he was right.

You need to develop the same foresight and belief in the future that Joe Kennedy exhibited with his investments in those oil fields. Be willing to take a risk. Otherwise, you'll spend your entire life scrambling for the next sale. Get involved with the industry leaders, so you know what's coming around the bend and can remain on the leading, bleeding edge.

Keeping an Eye on How Customers Buy

Top-producing salespeople seem to have a knack for staying one step ahead of their customers. When retail shoppers started flocking to the Internet, the most successful retailers were already there. The next tier of successful retailers got there in a hurry. The few who resisted the change are still suffering the consequences, if they're not already out of business.

Of course, not every fad turns into a trend and eventually becomes tradition. Some fads simply fade. Remaining on top, however, requires that you tune yourself in to your customers' needs and how they research and ultimately purchase the products and services you sell. Use the following sections to get yourself geared up for changes in the ways that your customers find and buy your products and services.

Getting a handle on the basics

Effective marketing and selling require a coordinated effort that communicates to the buyer throughout the entire purchase-decision cycle. As explained in Book VII, Chapter 2, a buyer typically takes the following four steps when deciding to purchase a product or service:

1. **Identify a problem or need.**

2. **Search for products or services.**

3. **Compare prices.**

4. **Measure the risk of purchasing or not purchasing.**

These steps rarely occur in a single place over a set period of time. A consumer may view a TV commercial for toothpaste, for example, research different brands of toothpaste on the Internet, and then compare prices and other products at the grocery or pharmacy before ultimately deciding to purchase a specific product.

Asking the right questions

To create an effective selling strategy, you need to identify the various ways that your customers arrive at a purchase decision and then develop a well-coordinated marketing and selling strategy that communicates your message to the customer at every step in the decision-making process. To get started, answer the following questions:

- ✔ **Where is my customer likely to first discover the problem or need?** Pharmaceutical companies market in doctors' offices and medical facilities, where customers are likely to hear first about a problem. They also market on television and in magazines to people who may have been diagnosed but are unaware of new treatment options or have certain symptoms but no diagnosis. In some cases, you may be the person who first reveals the customer's problem or need.

- ✔ **Where is my customer likely to search for additional information?** The world is packed with resources for assisting people with their purchase decisions — magazine articles, websites, product comparison charts, store clerks, and so on. Identify the top sources that customers turn to when making a purchase decision, and make sure you have some input in what the sources say about your products and services.

✔ **Where can my customer go to check prices?** You should have a pretty clear idea of what your competition is charging and what they're offering at that price, but you should also know where your customers go to check prices. Do they compare prices online or at the store? Do they usually just ask you? Know where they're going to check prices and make sure your prices are included. If you're charging a little more, explain why. If you offer something extra, say so. Give the customer a reason to buy from you instead of from one of your competitors.

✔ **When customers have doubts about purchasing or not purchasing the product, where can they find assistance in resolving those doubts?** The final stages of the purchase decision are critical, and you want to be there when the customer is wringing her hands. Unfortunately, this is the time in major purchase decisions when friends and relatives commonly get involved and raise the prospective buyer's level of doubt. Keeping in touch with the customer during this time is key to closing the sale. Contacting the customer via phone or e-mail is often best, but if your customers commonly seek reassurance elsewhere, find out where and establish a presence there, if possible.

Staying on top of changes

The way customers buy changes over time. Twenty years ago, nobody would ever have considered purchasing beer through the mail, but thousands of beer lovers are now beer-of-the-month subscribers who can go online to select the brands they want to try. Home buyers are spending more time researching homes on the Internet. People may even discover a new product by purchasing some totally unrelated other product. You can stay on top of these changes by working ahead of your customer; check out the following ideas to get started:

✔ **Use references and testimonials.** References or testimonials from other customers often can assist you when customers have doubts about purchasing or not purchasing products or whether to purchase from you or someone else. The more you can do to establish trust throughout the purchase decision-making process, the less likely your customer will be to bail out at the last minute.

✔ **Just ask!** Don't hesitate to ask customers how they found out about you and how they ultimately decided to purchase a product from you. When you notice a change in the way your customers shop, be prepared to change the way you sell. Every change you make is an opportunity for growth — a way to sell more effectively and gain a competitive edge.

Following the Sears lead

The story of Sears, Roebuck & Company provides a perfect example of how a company managed to make successful transitions to adapt to its customers' changing shopping habits.

Sears started out in the early 1890s, when Richard Sears decided to launch his own mail-order company, selling mostly watches and jewelry. At the time, most people in the United States (38 states at the time), were shopping at local general stores and paying steep prices for merchandise. Sears figured he could compete with these stores nationally without having to set up his own stores all across the nation.

In 1893, Sears met Alva Roebuck, and they teamed up to establish Sears, Roebuck & Company. By 1894, they had a 322-page catalog and were selling a wide selection of merchandise, including bicycles, sewing machines, and sporting goods. By 1908, Sears was even selling mail-order homes — complete kits for building your own home. They actually sold over 100,000 homes by 1940, when they stopped selling the kits.

In 1925, Sears opened its first department store. Marketing itself to America as the working man's place to shop, Sears department stores became hugely successful.

After many years of expansion and diversification, Sears hit some hard times in the '80s and '90s and nearly closed under bankruptcy.

Everyone was migrating from shopping at department stores to shopping in specialty stores. This was the era of the gourmet of products.

In 1993, Sears started to turn it around. They realized that they were known primarily for their quality Craftsman tools and that people were beginning to forget about all the other merchandise they carried, including kitchen appliances, jewelry, and apparel. To attract the customers they lost, Sears launched one of its most successful ad campaigns ever, inviting customers to "Come see the softer side of Sears."

In 2004, Ty Pennington joined forces with Sears, adding his flair for style and design. Pennington and Sears leveraged the power of the multimedia marketplace and tapped into the popularity of reality TV with the show *Extreme Home Makeover.* With more and more women becoming do-it-yourselfers and the engaging personality of Ty Pennington, Sears was again able to increase its market appeal, this time showing people shopping at Sears for products and using Craftsman tools.

By remaining sensitive to the way its customers were shopping and even where they were being introduced to new products and brands, Sears was able to stage a comeback in a very competitive retail market. And Sears retains a strong and growing presence today.

Book VII

Becoming a Power Seller

Changing the Way Customers Buy

As new ways of shopping and gathering information become available, customers naturally adapt to the methods and tools that make the purchase experience faster, easier, and more satisfying. As a salesperson, you have to adapt to remain in sync with your customers, but this is a more reactive approach to dealing with the ever-changing market.

You also can choose to become more proactive by introducing new ways of marketing and selling your products that enhance the shopping and buying experience. The following sections show you how to become a more innovative salesperson and create a unique buying experience for your customers that can perhaps lead to additional revenue-generating opportunities.

Looking for cross-selling opportunities

Cross-selling provides you with a great opportunity to stay ahead of your customers by anticipating needs that may coincide with what you already provide.

In the late 1970s, along with buying and selling real estate and owning a sports bar, Ralph R. Roberts decided to open an arcade. A building next door to his bar became available. Ralph bought it and installed video games. He was amazed at the number of kids who streamed into and out of the building . . . and at the number of quarters that rolled his way. Ralph had quarters galore. Business was so good that when another nearby building became available, right behind the arcade, he bought it and opened up a hand car wash. Parents could eat lunch at the sports bar, and kids could hang out at the arcade while the family's car was being cleaned. Ralph took $20 customers and turned them into $75 to $100 customers simply by increasing the number of services he offered. Today that's called *cross-selling*. Back then, Ralph was just trying to stay ahead.

To begin thinking of ways to add products or services to your current lineup, start by asking yourself these questions:

- ✔ **What other products and services do these customers enjoy that complement what I already provide?** For instance, if you own a coffee shop, it makes sense to sell some baked goods alongside a cup o' joe.

- ✔ **What other products and services do customers enjoy that fit their needs while they're shopping with me or taking advantage of my services?** Okay, two words here: vending machines. When you're at a hotel, waiting for an oil change, or at work, you often overpay for cans of sodas or bags of chips because they're conveniently located nearby. Discover your own rendition of a vending machine.

- ✔ **How can I make my customers' experience with me easier?** Several grocery stores have carts that you can pile a gaggle of youngsters into, but the smart ones provide grocery carts that look like cars, animals, and other shapes that may even play cartoons while you shop. A grocery cart isn't a product or service you purchase at a grocery store, but some creative thinking by grocery-store chains made the connection that people would probably shop longer if the kids were occupied!

✓ **What products or services can enhance the use of the product or service my customer just bought or uses regularly?** An obvious example of this is a warranty. Warranties cost a little extra but give customers the peace of mind that they have recourse if something goes wrong; it also shows customers that you're confident in the workmanship of your product or service.

✓ **What services or products do my customers often use immediately after using my products or services?** Think batteries here. Toy stores and electronic stores always carry a full line of batteries for the products they sell. They know you're going to need batteries for all those battery-operated toys and gadgets and that you'll eventually need to replace those batteries. A business that creates marketing materials for businesses within its area can add a courier service to its line of services, making some extra money every time those materials have to be delivered to local businesses . . . don't forget rush charges!

Identifying new selling methods

Innovations are often born from problems — as the saying goes, "Necessity is the mother of invention." Use some standard problem-solving strategies to start generating ideas:

Book VII

Becoming a Power Seller

1. **Jot down a list of problems that you believe are preventing you from reaching your sales goals.**

2. **Jot down a list of customer complaints and suggestions.**

   Your customers' problems are your problems. Any problem is fair game, regardless of whether you think it's getting in the way of increased sales. You never know where your inspiration will come from.

3. **Arrange your list of problems in order from most serious to least serious, and then pick the top five.**

4. **Brainstorm solutions to the selected problems.**

5. **Pick the top solutions for each problem and begin to implement them.**

   Far too many salespeople trip on the last step. They come up with brilliant ideas on how to make the purchase process easier and more enjoyable for their clients, and that's the end of it. Put your ideas into action!

When you're trying to invent new ways to sell, think less about the end result (increased sales) and more about the buying experience. Ask yourself what you could possibly do to make the experience more valuable and satisfying for your customer.

Identifying revenue-generating opportunities

New ways to sell don't have to cost you more money. Some innovations can actually save you time and money or even lead to additional revenue-generating opportunities.

You may notice several businesses that are actually two or more businesses combined. Auto supply stores, for example, often have a service department. They know that many prospective customers aren't qualified to work on their own cars. By adding a service department, they can sell more parts and supplies, and the parts and supplies store can refer more customers to the service department.

A few years ago, a major computer and appliance store added onsite computer technical support as one of its services. Management realized that customers often had problems with the computer equipment they purchased and were reluctant to bring the equipment in for service. By adding onsite technical support, which customers were willing to pay for, the store solved a major headache for customers while adding a second revenue stream.

Don't give away valuable services unless you absolutely have to. If your customers are willing to pay extra for education, training, superior customer support, or any other services you can offer, use your ideas to generate additional revenue streams.

Prepping your customers for the coming changes

Your customers may not appreciate some of the changes you try to implement, especially if they're stuck in their old ways of doing business, but if the change you're promoting is truly better for your customers, it's a change worth fighting for, and the best time to fight is before the fight even starts.

Before implementing a radical change in the way customers shop or buy, get some buy-in:

- ✓ **Float the idea past a few customers to see what they think.** You may be able to improve on the idea.

- ✓ **Take it for a test-drive.** Don't unleash your idea on all your customers at once. Test it on a select group of customers and work out the bugs first.

- ✓ **Keep your customers posted.** If you're not sure how your customers are going to react, prepare them in advance to avoid the shock. If you're sure that your customers are going to love it, a little shock can be a good thing.

Serving the savvy consumer

Today's consumer is a new breed. The average consumer is tech savvy, well informed, and pretty good at tracking down information. To serve today's consumer, you'd better know your stuff. Phony sales pitches and fluff no longer work. Provide the information and resources your customer needs to make a well-informed purchase decision, and back it up with impeccable customer service after the sale. (For information on generational differences and advice on how to reach customers in each category, refer to Book II, Chapter 5.)

Real-estate agents, for example, have relied on the Multiple Listing Service (MLS) for years. The MLS contains descriptions of all the properties listed through real-estate agents. Buyer's agents can read through the listings to find homes that may appeal to their clients. Years ago, the MLS was a thick book, published weekly. Although the information was supposed to be confidential, most top agents bought several copies of the book and passed them around to clients.

Next came "Boris," an MLS that distributed listings over phone lines, similar to the way a fax or teletype machine works; you could request the information you wanted. Then came the Internet, which allowed agents or members to access the information. Now, just about anyone can go on the Internet, find homes for sale, and compare prices. Check out www.realtor.com to see this in action.

Tweaking Your Current Marketing and Sales Strategy

You always can achieve a higher level of success, but not if you stick with the status quo. Top-producing salespeople are constantly tweaking their packaging, marketing, advertising, and sales presentations to experiment with what they hope are more productive methods. Even a subtle change can dramatically boost sales.

In the following sections, you discover how to ruthlessly evaluate your sales strategies and techniques, toss everything that's not working, and experiment with other strategies and techniques that hold more promise.

Although you may have to drop everything you're doing and change direction 180 degrees, give each idea careful consideration before moving forward and then implement your changes incrementally. You may very well discover that changing course a couple degrees at a time is enough to revolutionize the way you sell over the course of your career.

Keeping score: What works? What doesn't?

Refrigerator magnets. Every real-estate agent has tried those, and they're probably still giving them away in the hopes of gaining a coveted high-profile spot on every refrigerator in the neighborhood. Yet handing out all those magnets doesn't correlate to much of a lift in sales. Agents have tried personalized pens, too, with similar results — and chip-bag clips and jar openers and, well, you name it. The problem isn't trying new things (many of which are actually pretty useful); the problem is moving from one thing to another without stopping to evaluate whether that thing is actually producing the boost you're looking for.

When you're looking for ways to freshen up your marketing program, make one change at a time and keep score as much as possible to see what works and what doesn't. If you run a television commercial, check to see how much new business it generated. Was it worth the cost? If you try a direct-mail campaign, compare your sales figures before running the campaign against sales figures from the month you ran the campaign and the month following the campaign. Make sure you're getting your money's worth, and if you're not, try something else.

Sales extinction exhibit

With all the products and sales methods that have fallen by the wayside, you could almost start your own sales museum, complete with a huge extinction exhibit. Here are some of the items that you'd probably see in such a museum:

- ✔ **The door-to-door salesman . . . made extinct by the Home Shopping Network and the Internet:** Who would have ever thought that you could tune into your TV to watch product demonstrations or order products online and have them shipped right to your house?

- ✔ **The corner candy store . . . replaced by grocery stores, pharmacies, and gas stations:** Nowadays, you can buy candy anywhere.

You still see some high-end candy stores, but most kids can't afford the specialty chocolates they offer.

- ✔ **Telemarketers . . . not extinct yet, but the National Do Not Call Registry has certainly put a dent in the population.**

- ✔ **Eight-track tapes . . . replaced by cassettes.**

- ✔ **Cassettes . . . replaced by CDs.**

- ✔ **CDs . . . replaced by MP3 players.**

Don't get added to the list. By riding the waves of change, you don't have to face extinction. In fact, you can evolve to usher in the era of a new species of salespeople.

Don't completely dismiss a new idea just because it didn't work the first time. A television commercial may fail for any number of reasons. Perhaps it wasn't aired at the right time or it was a lousy commercial. Gather some feedback, try to figure out why it didn't work, and then make some adjustments to improve it. If it still doesn't work after you've made the necessary changes, then consider dropping it.

Finding the "why" behind your customer's "no"

A customers usually has a pretty good reason for walking away without purchasing a product, and you need to know what that reason is, particularly if the reason is due to something you said or did or didn't say or do. If a sale falls through and you don't understand why, start asking questions and doing a little soul searching:

- ✔ **Consider asking the customer directly.** You might ask, "So I can do a better job in the future, may I ask why you chose someone else?" or "What could I have done differently to have earned your business?"

- ✔ **Ask yourself whether you did something to scare off the customer.** If you get feedback, for example, that some people are turned away by your energy level, you may have to ratchet it down a notch by mirroring your customers. (For more about the mirroring technique, check out Book VII, Chapter 2.)

- ✔ **Ask yourself whether your pace was too fast or too slow.** If you tend to go too fast, you're making it impossible for some customers to keep up with you. Go too slow and your customers may grow impatient for the end — and hurry it along with a "No, thanks."

Don't always assume that the customer's decision to buy from someone else is your fault. In real estate, for example, your client may be lured away by an agent whose strategy is to build up the seller's expectations (a technique called "buying the listing") to win the client away from you. As a salesperson, take the high ground. You're better off letting down a customer today and winning her trust and respect for potential future sales and recommendations than dazzling her today and disappointing her tomorrow by failing to sell her home.

Personalities don't always mesh. Don't beat yourself up just because a few customers don't appreciate your style — they may come back to you, and if they don't, you have another group of buyers who are probably going to love your style.

Book VII

Becoming a Power Seller

Leaving a proven product alone

If you're selling products that require constant updating, such as computers, software, or video games, your company has no choice but to constantly seek to improve those products. In other cases, however, the product is perfectly fine. If it has a proven track record, leave the product alone and try changing everything else. Frequently, a subtle adjustment in packaging, marketing, or even your sales presentation can transform a mediocre-selling product into a smash hit.

In 1957, Tang was first introduced in the United States and received a lukewarm welcome. Sales didn't really take off until 1972, when Apollo flights were associated with the product. The manufacturer changed the packaging by including a map of the moon on the label and ramped up its marketing. The product became a huge seller without a single change to the product itself.

Sometimes you have to be brutally honest when analyzing what works and what doesn't. Now is the time to call up the harshest critics and creative thinkers. Toss everything that doesn't work and replace it with something that holds more promise.

Capitalizing on Changes in the Industry

Nowadays, an entire industry can undergo a transformation that seems to happen overnight. Remember the video arcades of the early 1980s? As soon as game systems became readily available for homes, video arcades disappeared from the landscape. Rising oil prices influence car-buying decisions. Rising or falling interest rates affect the housing market.

Although you're often powerless to stem the tide of changes in the industry, you need to remain well informed and sensitive to changes that may affect what you sell and the way you sell it. Keep your finger on the pulse of the industry and any factors outside the industry that may trigger changes:

- ✔ **Read widely.** Changes in politics, the economy, or related businesses can affect your industry. In addition, reading widely often can open your mind to new ideas that boost sales.

- ✔ **Read industry publications.** Subscribe to at least one trade publication and then read it. All too often, people subscribe to journals or magazines and then just stack them in the waiting room.

✔ **Attend conferences.** When you want to hear the buzz, attend conferences and network with your peers. You often can spot upcoming trends long before they appear in the trade publications.

✔ **Research online.** Visit the websites of the industry leaders and look for clues as to what's coming around the bend. If they have a newsletter, subscribe to it.

✔ **Stay connected.** Talk with others inside and outside the industry. In addition to gathering valuable information, you often can find that chatting it up with other professionals sparks creativity and innovation.

Sales visionaries

Industry leaders often are visionaries who demonstrate how to capitalize on changes in the industry. Here are some stories of some of these visionaries:

✔ Dave Liniger, founder of RE/MAX, envisioned a national brand for real-estate agents. He began a program for training agents and was the first to create real-estate conventions. His first convention attracted only 16 participants. Now, the conventions draw over 10,000.

✔ Walt Disney saw that the car would become more affordable to more families, and the day would come when families would want to drive to a single vacation spot that would offer something for kids of all ages.

✔ Guthy-Renker envisioned a multimedia marketplace in which coordinated marketing through TV, radio, the Internet, and direct marketing could transform individuals into brands that could drive sales of various products.

✔ Ralph J. Roberts, Comcast founder (no relation to Ralph R. Roberts, an author of this book), popularized cable television. In 1963, Roberts purchased a 1,200-subscriber cable television system in Tupelo, Mississippi, that he eventually grew into one of the world's leading media, entertainment, and communications companies.

Consider adding your own name to this list of visionaries. You may think you're just in sales and that you're not a corporate mogul like these folks, but when you think about it, these people were selling, just like you. As they were selling and trying to make a living, they just happened to notice an opportunity. Instead of simply daydreaming about it, they seized the opportunity and made it happen. You can, too!

Book VII

Becoming a Power Seller

Chapter 5

Branding Yourself through Shameless Self-Promotion

In This Chapter

▶ Discovering your marketable assets and putting them down on paper

▶ Giving your marketing materials a uniform look

▶ Making a name on the Internet

▶ Grooming yourself to become a recognized expert

Typical salespeople target markets, customers, and clients. Top-producing salespeople become the target — they market themselves. They build a strong brand presence so prospective customers and clients seek them out whenever they become aware that they need the product or service the salesperson represents. By investing some time, talent, and energy into building a brand presence or persona, you become a much more efficient and effective salesperson. Prospective customers and clients call you. Cold calls become warm calls. And because you've already established trust, you no longer need to convince prospective customers and clients that you're trustworthy.

This chapter leads you through the process of finding something unique about you that you can market and shows you how to log all your assets on paper to simplify the process of marketing those assets. This chapter also reveals several different ways you can market yourself to build a brand identity that your customers — past, present, and future — won't be able to forget.

Discovering the You in Unique

What is it about you that people will remember? What would you like them to remember about you? Whatever that something is, that's what you want to promote.

A real-estate agent in Montgomery, Alabama, Sandra Nickel, is known far and wide as "The Hat Lady." She wears a distinctive hat wherever she goes. Her hat logo appears on her business card, on all her correspondence, and even on her website (www.hatteam.com). She has a solid team of real-estate professionals who handle the daily business. She functions as the rainmaker, ensuring that the phones keep ringing and the Internet remains abuzz with the voices of interested buyers and sellers. She tells the story of Midtown Montgomery volunteers working tirelessly to improve the community. In the process, the Hat Lady attracts a lot of attention . . . and a lot of business.

Whatever you choose to be known for, make sure it's something you can be comfortable with for your entire career. As long as Sandra wants to remain the Hat Lady, she has to wear a hat. So, pick something you want to be known for. This could be a hat, tie, fancy shoes, the car you drive, a childhood nickname, a physical trait, or anything else on which you can focus your personal marketing campaign on promoting.

You don't have to and probably shouldn't do the same things other salespeople do. Instead, find a way to promote yourself that fits with your personality. What fits a very outgoing, gregarious personality is different from what would fit a more reserved personality. (If you're extremely shy, however, that's something you're going to have to overcome.)

In real estate, agents love to add their pictures to everything. Some even go so far as including their wives, children, and dogs in their marketing mug shots. Before you start using family portraits for promotion — even as remarkable as your family undoubtedly is — think about safety considerations and keep your spouse and children out of your marketing efforts.

Shameless self-promotion stresses "self." Sure, you may put your company logo and name on your business card and correspondence, but You, Inc., is ultimately the company you're promoting. You, Inc., is the central focus of your marketing campaign.

Changing your name?

Unique is good, but if your name is so unique that people can't pronounce it or so common that you sound just like any other Tom, Dick, or Harry, then you may want to consider changing it. You don't have to go to extremes like Marion Michael Morrison did — he chose a different name entirely and became John Wayne. Instead, consider a nickname or your middle name.

You certainly don't have to change your name to make your name into a brand, but if your birth name poses too great of a challenge to pronounce or remember, you may want to consider using something more simple.

Crafting a Unique Selling Point

Why should your customers do business with you instead of one of your competitors? That's the question that your unique selling point (USP) needs to answer. Think of a USP as a sort of résumé or curriculum vitae that's focused less on your knowledge, experience, and accomplishments and more on how your customers can benefit from your knowledge, experience, and accomplishments.

You may or may not decide to share your USP with prospective customers, but having a USP, in writing, serves three important purposes:

- ✔ It enables you to spot weak areas where you can improve.

- ✔ It reminds you of the value you deliver to customers so you can remind them of it.

- ✔ It provides you with written content you can use in other marketing materials you develop.

The following sections show you how to get started on your USP, flesh it out with additional details, and then use it effectively in your marketing and sales campaigns.

TIP

Check out the USP at www.ralphroberts.com; once there, just click the About Ralph link. This USP may be a little on the long side, but it demonstrates how to structure and word a USP in a way that focuses more on benefits and solutions and less on features.

Book VII

Becoming a Power Seller

Moving from features to benefits to solutions

REMEMBER

Your USP is not about you — it's about what you can do for your customers that your competitors cannot or will not do. In your USP, you're selling yourself, but keep in mind that when you're selling anything, you're always selling to a customer. You need to prove to your customer that nobody can serve their needs better than you.

To focus your USP on addressing your customers' needs and providing solutions, begin connecting what you have to offer (features) to your customers' needs. Next, develop a list of benefit statements and then apply those benefit statements to the solutions you offer. The following steps show you how:

1. **Divide a sheet of paper into two columns — what you have to offer on the left and your customers' needs on the right.**

2. **In the left column, list your education, experience, skills, and anything else you have to offer.**

3. **In the right column, list your customers' needs.**

4. **Draw lines to connect each customer need with what you offer that best serves that need.**

5. **Write at least one benefit statement for each skill-need combination that expresses how you are uniquely qualified to serve the customer's need.**

   If, for example, you're a certified computer technician, you're selling computer equipment, and your customers often need technical support, one of your benefit statements may be "Specialized training in computer service and repair make me uniquely qualified to answer any questions you may have regarding the setup and upgrading of your computer."

6. **Group related benefit statements into logical categories.**

   These categories should represent solutions to common problems that you solve for your customers.

After completing this exercise, you should have the content you need to actually put together your USP, as explained in the following section.

Crafting your personal-professional unique selling point

Your USP is essentially *[Your Name] For Dummies*. Consider it a brochure that lays out exactly why your customer would want to buy from you rather than from any other salesperson on the planet. Your USP should include the following elements:

✔ **Your name:** You're marketing yourself, so your name is the title of your USP.

✔ **Your photo:** Obtain a professional photograph that has you looking professional. This is the image that you want to tattoo on your customers' brain cells.

✔ **A one-line summary of your USP:** This is a single phrase or sentence that describes your unique selling point.

✔ **Section headings:** Use plenty of headings to break down the material into easily digestible chunks.

✔ **Detailed information:** Go easy on the paragraphs, opting for lists, wherever possible, but provide plenty of detail below each heading, so your reader is fully informed.

Include testimonials from other customers or clients, if you have testimonials. Including positive statements from other customers is a big plus. Just be sure to obtain written permissions from your clients before quoting them.

Implementing your unique selling point in marketing and sales

You don't have to use your whole USP in your marketing materials, but you'll probably find that you're often copying and pasting paragraphs and lists when you create proposals and presentations. Take the most pertinent information, paste it where needed, and then make a few modifications, if necessary, to blend it with the other material.

You also can use your USP to remind yourself before sales calls and presentations exactly what you offer your customers that nobody else in your area can or will offer. Never forget your USP, and never let your customers forget it, either. That's why they buy from you.

Designing a Consistent Look and Feel for Your Brand

Even the most creative salespeople can have a tough time creating a brand presence. They get bored with having everything look the same. Their instinct tells them to use a completely different design for their business card, stationery, website, brochures, and so on. When creating a brand presence, however, consistency is exactly what you want. (For more about creating a brand presence, check out *Branding For Dummies* by Bill Chiaravalle and Barbara Findlay Schenck [Wiley].)

Giving all your marketing materials a unique look would be like dressing up in a different disguise every day of your life — your customers wouldn't be able to recognize you. To create a strong brand presence, use the same basic design, colors, fonts, and logo on all your marketing materials, including the following:

- ✔ Business cards
- ✔ Stationery
- ✔ Brochures
- ✔ Pamphlets
- ✔ Newsletters
- ✔ Press releases
- ✔ Websites
- ✔ Blogs

Unless you're a talented designer, don't trust your instincts. Hire a professional. Find some marketing materials you like and contact the company that sent them out to find out who did the design. Or head down to your local full-service print shop and ask whether they know of any designers. After you settle on a design, color scheme, font, and logo, get some feedback from your better, honest customers before forging ahead. After you pick a design, you need to stick with it, so make sure you're going to be happy with it three or four years from now.

You're not a shameless self-promoter if you don't have a billboard. If you sell to the general public, get your photo pasted on a billboard along with a short, catchy slogan and your phone number, e-mail address, and web address. Thousands of people are likely to drive past the billboard daily, and most of them are likely to take notice. If you're in corporate sales, the billboard idea may not be right for you, but you should still be looking for other opportunities to get your face in front of prospective clients — perhaps by taking out an ad in an industry publication.

Tossing business cards

Many salespeople treat their business cards like hundred-dollar bills. They stick them in their wallets or purses and hand them out only to the people they regard as top candidates.

Instead, you should treat your business cards like rice at a wedding. If you go to a sporting event, when the crowd goes wild, lean over the railing and toss a handful of business cards up in the air. Some people may actually pick them up, stick them in their purses or wallets, and

call you when they need the product or service you're selling. And how fun would it be to ask someone, "So, how did you hear about me?" and hear the reply that they caught the card flying through the air at a Pistons game.

Carry a stack of business cards with you wherever you go. Leave them on the counter at the local diner. Tack them up on the bulletin board at your local grocery store. Hand them out to everyone you meet.

Establishing Brand Presence on the Internet

Your marketing materials may work great to establish a brand presence in the real world, but you also need to consider that other world — the Internet. With more and more people shopping or at least seeking out additional product information on the web, establishing a brand presence online is essential.

Establishing a presence on the Internet isn't quite as effective in building customer trust as having a bricks-and-mortar business with a phone number and mailing address. The stronger your presence online, however, the more likely it is that your customers will feel as though they're dealing with a legitimate business.

In Book II, Chapter 4, you discover how to take advantage of the multimedia marketplace and additional details on how to create your own website and blog. Here's a checklist of what's required to build a brand presence on the Internet:

- ✔ **Register your own domain name.** (A domain name is a text-based address of a computer on the Internet. In www.dummies.com, dummies.com is the domain name. The domain name is also the part of an e-mail address that comes after the @ sign.) The reason you want your own identifiable domain name is the same reason you want your own telephone number and address: It tells your customers exactly where to find you. If you start selling for another company, having a unique domain name enables your customers to follow you.

- ✔ **Build your own website.** Well, you don't actually have to build it yourself. You can hire someone to do it, but you really should have your own website with a design that's consistent with the look and feel of your other marketing materials.

- ✔ **Build and maintain your own blog.** Regardless of whether you have a website, a blog enables you to join the blogging community. Establishing relationships in a community (online or off) is key to long-term sales success. If you're not blogging, start now. For more about blogging to sell, see Book VII, Chapter 7. For a lot more about blogging in general, check out *Blogging For Dummies,* 4th Edition, by Susannah Gardner and Shane Birley, and *Buzz Marketing with Blogs For Dummies,* by Susannah Gardner (both published by Wiley).

When posting material on your blog or on other online gathering places, such as Facebook and Twitter, remain professional. Too many people post questionable material and fail to realize that what they say is going to follow them for the rest of their lives. The same is true for adults, especially people who are in business. Before posting a message on your site, think about how that message reflects on you as a person and how it may affect the perception that future customers may have of you.

✔ **Contribute to other online communities and social media venues.** Even if you have your own blog, you should establish a presence in other online communities, including Facebook, Twitter, LinkedIn, and possibly even YouTube. Contribute to other peoples' blogs and answer questions posted in message boards. Where appropriate, you can mention your own website and blog to drive traffic from these other communities to your landing pads on the web.

✔ **Publish an e-newsletter.** An e-newsletter, which you can distribute via e-mail or by posting it on your website, enables you to contact your customers regularly with valuable information and promotions without seeming to be just another pushy salesperson.

Make sure to heed the CAN-SPAM Act, and send newsletters only to people who give you permission to do so. Also, always allow recipients an option for easily opting out. For more on the CAN-SPAM Act, see `http://business.ftc.gov/documents/bus61-can-spam-act-compliance-guide-business`.

✔ **Add a signature to your e-mail messages.** Every e-mail program has an option to add a signature to outgoing messages. Include in your signature your name, contact information, and a list of your accreditations, titles, and websites. Here's a sample signature :

Ralph R. Roberts GRI CRS

Author of *Flipping Houses For Dummies*

Phone: 586-751-0000

E-mail: `ralphroberts@ralphroberts.com`

Web: `www.ralphroberts.com`

Establishing a presence on the Internet is not a one-time deal. Don't simply set up a website and then leave it to stagnate. Unless you keep fresh content coming, people are going to stop visiting. If necessary, draw up a schedule to freshen the content regularly — at least once a week, but preferably twice or more.

Boosting Your Street Cred

When you find someone who knows what she's talking about, your natural inclination is to seek out that person whenever you need assistance with something in her area of expertise. If you find an excellent restaurant server who knows everything on the menu and how it's prepared and is attentive to your needs, you want to sit at that server's table every time you eat at that restaurant. If a certain financial advisor is known as the most successful and trustworthy in your area, that's the person you want handling your money.

Become an expert in your industry. You don't have to be an expert on everything, but be an expert on something. Then get out there and prove to the world that you're the expert you say you are. In the following sections, you find out where to go to start establishing yourself as the resident expert.

When you're getting started, you may have to actively seek out speaking gigs and other opportunities to prove yourself the expert. After you get the ball rolling, however, you can pretty much stop looking, because people will seek you out. All you have to do then is make yourself available.

Speaking to local groups

Local groups, including church groups; philanthropic organizations, such as Kiwanis, Rotary, and the Lions Club; the chamber of commerce; and schools are always on the lookout for speakers with expertise on a wide variety of topics. Many of these groups begin their regular meetings with a 15- to 20-minute speech, and the meetings often are packed with community and business leaders.

These venues give you the opportunity to get your face and message in front of many of the decision makers without having to make a heavy-handed sales pitch. If you do meet with these people later in a sales situation, they already feel as though they know you, making your job that much easier.

The following list provides some tips on how to get your start as a local public speaker. For additional public-speaking tips, tricks, and techniques, read *Public Speaking For Dummies,* 2nd Edition by Malcolm Kushner (Wiley):

- ✔ **Hone your public speaking skills.** Many salespeople who are comfortable speaking to individuals and small groups are terrified of delivering a speech to a large group of people. To overcome anxiety about public speaking, consider joining Toastmasters, an international club devoted to assisting its members in developing their public speaking and leadership skills. Toastmasters groups typically consist of 20 to 30 members who meet once a week for about an hour to acquire new skills and take turns practicing those skills and evaluating one another. To find out more about the organization and locate a group near you, visit www. toastmasters.org.

- ✔ **Assess the PR value of local groups.** Brainstorm a list of organizations and local groups in your area, and then prioritize the list. Highlight the groups that are most likely to put you in front of the movers and the shakers — these are the people who can open doors for you.

- ✔ **Get your foot in the door.** Selling yourself as a speaker is just like selling products, but first you need a product to sell. Write a 15- to 20-minute speech, complete with a one- to two-page handout demonstrating that you have something to say. Shop it around to the leaders of the groups you want to speak to. Better yet, join the group, establish relationships with the group's leaders, and let them know that you're interested in addressing the group.

✔ **Make sure your speech hooks your audience.** Whenever you speak to a group, you should have three goals: to engage, to entertain, and to educate. Try to hook your audience from the very beginning, keep them laughing or crying, and pass along some valuable information or a bit of wisdom. Another way to encourage people to remember you is to offer them a gift — a handout with speaking points, a copy of an inspirational book, or some other token that they can look at later. Whatever you choose to give, make sure it reinforces your brand presence and includes your name, contact information, web address, and so on.

✔ **Stick around afterward.** After delivering your speech, hang around for the rest of the meeting and linger for a while after the meeting. Attendees are most likely to seek you out following the meeting and introduce themselves. Be ready to hand them your business card or brochure.

You don't have to speak on a business-related topic. You can talk about whatever interests you — a hobby, marriage, the challenges of raising teenagers. As long as you're engaging, entertaining, and have something to say, you and your speech are likely to leave a lasting impression.

Volunteering your time and expertise

As a salesperson, you have a unique gift to offer just about any nonprofit organization on the planet — your ability to sell and generate revenue. Every organization needs at least one salesperson to contribute to its fundraising efforts. If you want to take a break from selling, you can use your communication and organization skills in any number of ways.

Several sales gurus recommend that you "give to get." I prefer the "give to give" approach. Give for the sheer pleasure of giving. If you expect something in return, you're setting yourself up for disappointment. You may be so busy waiting for the expected return on your investment that you completely miss what you actually receive.

When you're shopping for a nonprofit organization, try to find one that's a right fit for you and your business. If you sell real estate, for example, you may decide to volunteer your time and expertise to Habitat for Humanity or a local organization that revitalizes urban spaces. If you sell invisible fencing, you may decide to volunteer with the Humane Society or local animal shelters or rescue organizations.

Don't just write a check — participate. Participating enables you to interact with community leaders. *Remember:* Branding is about more than giving yourself a high profile on the shelf. It's about earning a reputation as someone who is sincerely committed to building better communities, and that means volunteering your time and expertise.

Becoming the resident expert

Nobody likes a know-it-all, but everyone appreciates someone who really knows her stuff. By establishing yourself as the resident expert in a specific area, you become much more than a face and a logo — you become the go-to guy or gal, the person other people seek out when they have a question or a problem.

The first step — actually becoming an expert — is often the hardest. After overcoming this initial challenge, you're ready to build credibility by doing any (or preferably all) of the following:

- ✔ Publishing articles magazines and journals, or even writing a book. (If you can't find a publisher, self-publish. Books are like business cards on steroids.)
- ✔ Granting interviews to local reporters or being interviewed on radio. Why not try hosting your own radio show?
- ✔ Appearing on television in both advertisements and news stories.
- ✔ Giving speeches to local groups or national organizations.
- ✔ Publishing a website or blog where you provide valuable information and guidance.

See Book II, Chapter 3 for additional details on tapping the full power of the multimedia marketplace.

Posing as an expert when you're not truly an expert is a sure way to lose whatever credibility you have. Do your homework and become a true expert before you proclaim yourself one.

Mastering the 10/10/20 technique

One of the not-so-secret secrets to sales success is to build on past success, and the best time to practice shameless self-promotion is when those successes are still fresh. One technique, called the 10/10/20 technique helps you do that.

The 10/10/20 technique is a way that you can spread the news of your latest sale to about 40 other people easily and with relatively little time commitment. Here's how this technique works when applied to selling real estate (and why this book refers to it as the 10/10/20 technique): When you list or sell a house, knock on the 10 doors to the left and right of the house you just sold and the 20 doors across the street and distribute your postcard with a handwritten note letting the neighbors know that you've listed or sold their neighbor's home. That's it. That's all it takes to start generating new clients. Distributing these cards takes less than an hour. Most of the neighbors are not going to want to talk with you at length. In less than an hour, you have the potential of reaching 10,000 people.

Whoa! Where did that 10,000 number come from? Every person knows at least 250 other people. By contacting 40 people in the area, you indirectly contact nearly 10,000 more, and everyone in sales, particularly in real estate, knows that selling is all about meeting people and building relationships.

But you don't have to be in real estate to make the 10/10/20 technique work for you, because the key principle is applicable to many different areas. If you just sold a car to a nice couple, for example, you can have another salesperson take a picture of you and your customers in front of the car and put the picture on a postcard. Ask permission to send the postcard to your customers' neighbors, and give them a stack of postcards to hand out as well.

If you're in corporate sales, tweak the technique. On your client's birthday, show up with a cake, introduce yourself around the office, let everyone know about the birthday, and present the birthday cake to your client. How many salespeople does your client know who would remember her birthday and do something to celebrate it? Your client will always remember you, and so will everyone else in the office. Take a photograph of your client and her co-workers, upload it to your blog with a brief message, and e-mail your client a link to the page. You don't even have to wait for your client's birthday — simply show up to celebrate a "Just Because" day.

Chapter 6

Putting the Latest Technologies to Work for You

In This Chapter

▶ Confronting your tech phobias

▶ Gathering the tools of the sales trade

▶ Empowering yourself on the web

▶ Harnessing powerful communication technologies

*W*ith each passing year, technology changes more rapidly. You may feel as though someone's cranking up the speed on your treadmill when you're already having a tough time keeping pace. And here we go telling you that you have to do even more!

Although new technology may seem overwhelming at first, it often opens the doors to new opportunities and improved efficiency. Resist the latest technological advances, and you find yourself working harder and harder just to keep up. Embrace technology, and you soon discover that you're far ahead of the pack — and you don't even have to break a sweat to stay there.

This chapter shows you how to put the latest technologies to work for you in generating a host of new clients and ever-expanding opportunities.

Overcoming Resistance to New Technology

Technology can be pretty scary, especially if you were born prior to Generation X (that is, prior to 1965; Book II, Chapter 5 has more on generational differences). Most people can handle a smartphone and even fumble their way through the process of typing a document or crunching numbers in a basic spreadsheet. The newer, more challenging technologies, however, can seem somewhat overwhelming at first. Communication is no longer driven primarily by telephones and the mail carriers. To remain competitive, sales-people now have to juggle e-mail, texting, social media (including blogging, Facebook, and Twitter), and other communication tools and technologies.

If you get hot flashes every time you think about having to master some new technology, the following sections may be able to calm you down.

Assuming a playful attitude

The absolute worst time you can start learning how to use a new gadget or software package is when you need to use it. You have a presentation to give tomorrow, and you just installed PowerPoint, thinking that this is going to make your job a whole lot easier. Now you have two problems: figuring out how to present the material and wrestling with a fairly complicated piece of software. It's like trying to read your new car's owner's manual while you're weaving through city traffic.

Try to approach new technologies when you don't need them. Pretend that you just bought yourself a new toy. When you have some free time, play around with it. Try it out on something that doesn't really matter. Show your friends and family some of its coolest features. The more the technology feels like a toy, the more your work is going to seem like play.

Carry around the instruction booklet with you so that, when you're waiting in a doctor's office or for some other appointment, you can glean one new piece of information to help you with the technology. Don't try to swallow the entire manual; consume the information slowly, one bite at a time.

Optimizing your technological tools

When you adopt a new technological tool, explore all its features. By sticking with the features you need most and using what you already know, you may be able to stay on track, but to excel, you have to reach beyond your grasp.

Thinking you're too old for the new technology is just nonsense. All you have to do is start. Spend 15 minutes to a half-hour per day trying something new. Before you know it, you'll discover that you've acquired a whole new skill set.

Overcoming objections to the cost

As a salesperson, you have to buy stuff as a professional courtesy to all the other salespeople out there who are trying to make a living. If that's not a good enough reason to shell out some cash for the latest technologies, then consider some of the potential benefits in terms of sales and productivity:

- ✔ Increased sales as the new technologies generate leads
- ✔ Enhanced productivity, giving you more time to deal directly with customers or pursue other interests
- ✔ Increased opportunities as you discover innovative uses for new technologies
- ✔ Improved visibility as technologies including web pages and blogs draw the attention of customers online
- ✔ Increased ability to recommend new technologies to your clients as another way of giving back to your clients and demonstrating your genuine interest in their success

As a top seller, try not to focus solely on how much a product or service costs. Also consider how much revenue it's going to generate. If it has the potential for a good return, it's worth the investment.

Consult with someone in your industry who is tech savvy. The last thing you want to do is arrive at a conference thinking you've adopted the latest, greatest technology only to discover that you should have purchased something better — you've blown all your money on cutting-edge technology and have nothing left to invest in bleeding-edge technology.

Getting over the feeling that it's unproven

One school of thought promotes the idea that you should always wait until a technology has proven it has legs before making it a part of your daily business. If you follow this suggestion, you may miss the advantage that new technology can give you over your more hesitant peers. Instead, analyze the technology on your own to determine whether it can do any of the following:

- ✔ Save you time or money
- ✔ Make you time or money
- ✔ Attract positive attention

If a technology can do any one — or preferably all — of those things, then that's all the proof you need to become an early adopter.

Feel free to tap into the expertise of your more technically gifted colleagues to determine whether the technology can do these things for you.

Pumping Up Your Productivity with Computers and Software

Computer technology enables you to accomplish more in less time. You can push your sales into overdrive and eventually attain warp speed. You can instantly pull up a list of thousands of contacts, complete with notes about birthdays, anniversaries, and names of spouses and kids; e-mail thousands of contacts with a single click of a button; and broadcast articles, audio, and video across the country and around the world for the cost of a few pennies.

A computer equipped with the right software can significantly increase your productivity, reduce errors, and boost sales. The following sections describe the equipment and types of software that no salesperson should live without.

When you show up with the latest technology in tow and demonstrate that you can use it, you project an image of competence. Clients want to work with a salesperson who is both old-school personable but also new-school tech savvy.

Becoming a road warrior

Salespeople make up a fair percentage of the road warriors in the business world, and if you're part of this crowd, you carry your office with you. Make sure that your traveling office is properly equipped by purchasing and mastering the following essentials:

- **Notebook or tablet PC:** A high-quality notebook or tablet PC is a must for delivering presentations on the road, carrying your most important digital documents along with you, and staying connected with the home office and your other clients. If you're in a business in which you or your clients may need to sign documents, seriously consider a computer that enables you to sign on-screen using a stylus.

- **Portable printer:** Even if you do everything on the computer and send it back to the office, pack a portable printer, just in case one of your clients is more comfortable looking at marketing materials on paper or requests a paper copy of a contract.

- ✓ **Wireless Internet access:** Many hotels, coffee shops, and offices have Wi-Fi (wireless Internet access), and most computers have the capability to access it when it's available. But having your own wireless Internet service is a good idea. Shop carefully to choose a service with coverage in the areas where you most commonly travel.

- ✓ **Smartphone:** For times when you don't need to lug around your full-featured notebook or tablet PC, a smartphone, such as an iPhone or BlackBerry, enables you to keep in touch without weighing you down.

- ✓ **Digital projector:** If you deliver presentations to only one or two clients at a time, you can forgo the digital projector. Your clients can easily watch your presentation on the computer screen. If you need to deliver presentations to rooms full of people, then a digital projector is a must. To choose the right projector, you typically have to make some trade-offs in terms of image quality, price, and weight.

- ✓ **Ethernet cable:** Although most hotels are going wireless, some still require a cable to connect to the Internet. Carry an Ethernet cable just in case.

- ✓ **Power adapter for a car:** A power adapter that plugs into your car enables you to charge your computer's battery while you travel from one client to another. Make sure you get the right adapter. Visit your local electronics store and explain exactly what you'll be using it for.

- ✓ **Power strip:** Carry a power strip. A power strip not only enables you to plug several devices into a single outlet, but it also functions as an extension cord, so you can reach an outlet a little easier.

  If you find yourself using your power strip at the airport, consider sharing it with others who are waiting for flights; it's an excellent tool for networking with people in need.

- ✓ **Digital audio recorder:** Use a digital audio recorder to take note of any ideas that pop into your head and to record your presentations so that you can review them and improve on them later.

- ✓ **Digital camera:** You never know when you may be presented with a photo op. Some of these cameras are so tiny now, you can practically pack them as easily as a credit card. Better yet, get a smartphone that has a digital camera built right into it; some of these smartphone cameras can even record short video clips.

- ✓ **iPod or MP3 player:** Don't waste a moment acquiring knowledge. If you're not reading a book, you can be listening to a book on tape . . . or get pumped up for your next presentation by listening to your favorite tunes. This is another area where you can lighten your load by buying a smartphone that has digital recording capabilities.

✔ **Headset:** If you have Skype or some other VoIP (Voice over Internet Protocol) phone service, carry a headset so you can plug into your computer to talk on the "phone." Some of these services can even push the signal directly to your smartphone so that you don't have to lug around a headset.

✔ **Your copy of *Selling All-in-One For Dummies*:** Hey, you're going to need something to read on the plane and in the hotel room. This book can also be a great conversation starter that assists you in meeting new prospects.

Draw up a checklist of everything you need to pack. If you plan on delivering a sales presentation on the road, make sure you have all the equipment you need and that your equipment is working properly prior to departure and as soon as possible after you reach your destination. You don't want to discover just minutes before giving your presentation that you forgot the cable that connects your notebook PC to your digital projector. If your client has promised to provide the equipment you need, call ahead to remind them and show up early to test everything.

Mastering a contact management program or customer relationship management system

Every salesperson should have a way to track customers and prospects. The ideal solution is a dedicated customer relationship management (CRM) system, such as Sage ACT! (www.act.com) or NetSuite CRM+ (www.net suite.com/portal/products/crm/main.shtml). A sophisticated CRM system enables you to track customer interactions at all points of contact with your business online and off, so all departments, including sales, marketing, and customer support, are better able to coordinate their customer-service efforts. In addition, CRM systems typically enable you to launch and manage online marketing and sales campaigns and provide analytics, so you know what's working and what's not.

At the very least, you should use a contact management program, such as Microsoft Outlook, to gather and record as much personal information about your clients as possible, including the following:

✔ Name and contact information

✔ Birthday

✔ Spouse's name and birthday

✔ Wedding anniversary

✔ Children's names and birthdays

✔ Hobbies and favorite pastimes

Whenever you contact a customer, you want to make a good impression and an emotional connection. Show your clients that you care enough about them personally to remember details about the things that are most important to them. Of course, although you should gather details about your customers, don't make your calls sound like interrogations. Gather the information slowly and naturally during the conversation.

Read up on the program or system you choose. Peruse not only the literature that comes with the program but another how-to manual as well. Doing so ensures that you're tapping into all the features your contact management program offers, and not just highlights offered by the manufacturers' "Getting Started" guides.

Knowing your way around a presentation program

When you're delivering a presentation to prospective clients, you want your presentation to look as professional as possible, and there's no better way to do that than to create it and deliver it with a presentation program, such as PowerPoint.

PowerPoint and other presentation programs almost force you to use your words sparingly and communicate with clients in a more audiovisual format. You can even create notes pages to leave with your clients and post your presentation online so that your more tech-savvy clients have ready access to it. Perhaps best of all, you can simply adjust a presentation you already created for a different client instead of starting from scratch. (For instructions, tips, and tricks for using PowerPoint, check out *PowerPoint 2010 For Dummies*, by Doug Lowe [Wiley].)

If you're still putting together your presentations in a word-processing program or relying on printed marketing materials, one of the first software programs you should pick up is a presentation program. Clients are often mesmerized by a presentation on a computer screen that would otherwise put them to sleep, especially if they get to click through at their own pace.

Always have a backup plan in place. Technology is great when it works, but sometimes it doesn't, and when it doesn't, you still need to be able to function. When giving presentations to clients, a backup plan is even more important. The show must go on, even if your computer won't turn on. Back up your presentation and store the backups in multiple places: on your server, on two CDs that you keep in different pieces of luggage if you're traveling, and so on. Although you can usually find someone to borrow a computer from, you can't find someone who has your presentation.

Tapping into the Web

The Internet is one of the more powerful and intriguing technologies from which you can benefit as a salesperson, because it's an entirely different world — a digital, virtual, multimedia world where clients and prospective clients not only passively absorb your message but also interact.

In some ways, selling on the Internet in the 21st century is more like selling from a corner store during the 1950s than like selling in the 1990s. The Internet is turning the entire world into a small town in which customers base their purchase decisions more on recommendations from peers than on marketing and advertising. To appeal to these 21st-century customers, you'd better have an online presence.

The following sections reveal several ways to leverage the power of the web to boost sales.

Researching customers and competitors

One of the main benefits of the migration of sales from the real world to the virtual world is that you now have easier access to information about your customers and competitors. Your competitors probably have websites or blogs. Customers who use your products and services may have their own websites or blogs and probably hang out in communities like Facebook and Twitter.

If you're marketing online, you need to establish a presence on the web, but another way to leverage the power of the web is to use the information it contains to your advantage, as discussed in the following sections.

Hanging out with your clientele

Go online and hang out where your customers hang out. Get to know them. Become part of the community by contributing to their blogs and message boards. Get involved in their discussions, and offer your expert insights and advice. You don't have to give your sales pitch; in fact, doing so may harm your reputation in the community. By contributing something of value to the discussion, however, you begin to establish a solid reputation online as a knowledgeable and trusted source.

Contributing to the community means giving something of value. A real-estate agent, for example, may contribute by publishing articles that offer tips to homeowners and people looking to buy a home. Search the web for questions related to your area of expertise and post answers to people's questions. Publish articles to assist other professionals in your field. If you sell cars, you may post a newsletter with tips on caring for your car or how to choose the right car. If you sell computer software, you may post articles or messages on how to use some little-known feature of the program or troubleshoot a common problem.

Checking out the competition

When you want to know what your competitors are up to, go online and find out. You can check out their websites, see what they're promoting and how they're promoting it, and gather all sorts of ideas on how to promote your own products and services (and yourself).

You want to lead, not follow, so check out the competition, but avoid the temptation to mimic others.

Gathering leads

If you've already established a strong presence on the Internet, you may not need to rely on professional lead-generation services to steer business your way, but if you don't have a strong online presence or you need additional leads, check out some of the Internet lead-generation services.

Assessing the benefits of lead-generation services

Lead-generation services offer several benefits to you as a salesperson, including the following:

Book VII

Becoming
a Power
Seller

- ✔ **Advertising:** Lead-generation services often do the marketing and advertising for you, so you can focus more resources on following up with motivated customers than trying to find them.

- ✔ **Screening:** The service commonly weeds out any less-promising prospects, so you deal only with serious candidates who have shown an interest in your product or service.

- ✔ **Gathering leads 24/7:** While you're performing other tasks, eating, sleeping, or even on vacation, a lead-generation service continues to gather leads for you and deliver them on demand.

Before choosing a service, find out how many other salespeople are receiving the same leads, how old the leads are, and how the leads are screened. Bad leads are worse than no leads, taking up precious time and resources you could be spending on more profitable pursuits.

Making the most of your lead-generation service

A lead-generation service is only as good as you make it. Many salespeople claim that services sell the same leads to more than one salesperson, making it too difficult to actually get that person's business. While you should certainly shop for a service that provides higher-quality leads and less competition, you have to do your part as a salesperson to make the most of the leads you receive.

Here are some tips on how to optimize the leads you get:

- **Qualify those leads.** Your lead-generation service may qualify some leads for you to screen out the worst of them, but you should have your own system in place for ranking prospects. Spend the most time on the top prospects.

- **Be the first to call and offer the best service.** The Internet is like a fast-food restaurant — patrons are looking for instant gratification and immediate contact. Even slight delays can result in lost opportunities.

- **Follow up with a welcome e-mail message.** Have some information about you and your company and services prepared well in advance, so you can deliver it without delay.

- **Add the customer to a drip e-mail campaign.** A drip campaign may send the prospect a different message once a week or so to remind them of you. If prospects don't hear from you, they can find plenty of other salespeople to deal with.

- **Treat your lead like a customer.** Too many salespeople expect leads to be willing buyers. You still have to sell. Treat the prospect well, and you can turn the prospect into a customer. Continue to follow up, even after the sale, so that the person becomes a customer for life.

Every system, even lead-generation systems, have drawbacks, but if you put a system in place, make a plan, and then work the plan, you'll have more business than you know what to do with.

Claiming your "place" listings

People rarely use standard phone books or Yellow Pages to "let their fingers do the walking" and find local businesses anymore. Now they typically use online directories, including Google Places (www.google.com/places) and Yelp (www.yelp.com). Chances are pretty good that your business is already listed in one or more of these directories. If it is, you can and should claim the listing and flesh it out with additional details (like your hours of operation, your address and phone number, and so on). If your business isn't listed, you can add it.

In addition to providing your business with another location on the web where customers and prospects can more easily find you, these online directories typically enable you to add your business's web address, which people can click to obtain additional information. Many people search these directories from their smartphones while they're out and about, so be sure you're where they're likely to look.

Soft-selling through social media

Social media consists of information generated through social interactions that occur on sites like Facebook and Twitter. As people interact in these online venues and others, they may share information about you, your business, the products and services you sell, and your competitors. In addition, people who hang out in these venues may search for information that relates to you or what you sell. Because of this, you really should establish a presence in all the most popular social media venues. In this book, that means Facebook, Twitter, YouTube, and LinkedIn (see Book VII, Chapter 7 for details).

Tapping the power of pay-per-click advertising

To be a top salesperson in your industry, you'd better be advertising and marketing on the web, no matter what you sell.

In Book VII, Chapter 5, we encourage you to set up your own website or blog as a form of soft-sell, self-promotion. You also should be looking into other ways of advertising your products and services and driving traffic to your website or blog.

Most of the major Internet search tools, including Google, offer affordable online advertising in the form of pay per click (PPC) and pay per thousand (PPM — the *M* stands for mil or thousand) ads. When someone searches for a word or phrase associated with your product or service, up pops a link to where you want the person to go. With PPC, you pay for the ad only if someone clicks the link. PPC ads aren't foolproof. You really need to study up on them before you dive in, but the online advertising service you choose should have plenty of information to help you get started. (Check out *Building Your Business with Google For Dummies,* by Brad Hill [Wiley].)

Networking with colleagues online

With more and more people, especially salespeople, setting up shop on the Internet, you're likely to find colleagues from all over the world online. Every colleague is an opportunity to develop a new relationship, gather strategies and tips, share information, and open yourself to new sales and business opportunities.

Book VII

Becoming a Power Seller

To get in touch with the top people in your industry, join one or more professional organizations in your industry and check out what they offer online in terms of message boards, blogs, and other features where you can meet and share information with colleagues. Try to obtain phone numbers and e-mail addresses, and follow up by personally contacting the people you meet online.

Most of the top salespeople in any industry have their own website or blog, complete with their contact information. Visit their sites, and if you like what you see, give them a call or send them an e-mail message introducing yourself.

Discovering new sales "secrets"

Although some salespeople are very protective of their secrets of success, top salespeople are so proud of their achievements that they can't help but broadcast them all over the Internet. Take advantage of this immense, free school of sales.

The real reason that top salespeople are so willing to share their "secrets" is usually because everybody already knows the secrets. The real secret of top salespeople is that they actually put into practice what every salesperson knows she *should* be doing.

Tuning in with the Latest Communication Tools

Twenty years ago, relatively few communications media were readily available — typically a phone and hand-delivered mail. Now you have access to fax machines, smartphones, e-mail, instant messaging, teleconferencing, online seminars, blogs, conference call centers, voicemail, call forwarding, and text messaging. With all these options, you can remain in contact with your customers 24/7 — assuming, of course, that you take advantage of these technologies.

In the following sections, we fill you in on the communications technologies you should explore and some tips on how to maximize their effectiveness.

Optimizing the power of your phone system

If you finally traded in your pager for a smartphone, congratulations. You're one step closer to having the phone capabilities that customers expect in order to contact you at a moment's notice. You can do much more, however, to pump up the power of your phone system and use it to generate more sales. The following sections reveal some options you may want to consider.

Giving customers a toll-free number

Don't discourage customers who live in other states or countries from calling you by having them pay long-distance charges. Set up a toll-free line, so they can call for free. This is particularly important if you're a retailer. Giving customers a quick and easy way to contact you builds trust and makes customers more comfortable placing an order with you.

One of the best features of a toll-free number is that it rings through to your business number, so you don't need a separate phone line. In addition, this allows you to take the toll-free number with you if you move your business.

Implementing automatic call forwarding

Just because you're on the road doesn't mean you're out of touch. With call forwarding you can have any incoming calls routed to whatever phone number you choose — your home phone, smartphone number, or even the hotel where you're staying in Fiji.

Call your phone company to ask about call forwarding and other services they offer. Phone companies are constantly developing new communications technologies and may have something available that you haven't yet heard about.

Making your voicemail greeting more personal

When customers call or prospective customers return your calls, leave the impression that their call is important to you by playing a special voicemail greeting. Change the greeting daily or at least every week. Instead of using the standard, "Hello, you've reached Plackard Industries, please leave a message after the tone," say something like, "Happy Valentine's Day!" (or whatever day it is), let them know where you are, what you're doing, when you'll be back in the office, and how they can contact you or someone who's covering for you in the meantime.

If you change your greeting daily, include detailed and timely information like what your schedule is going to be for that day. Are you going to be out of the office or at a lunch meeting? Share that info. You also can say when the best times to call are and give a number where you can be reached or an alternative contact in case of emergency.

In addition to recording an upbeat and memorable voicemail greeting, work on the greeting you use when you answer the phone. "Hello?" doesn't cut it. If the caller's name appears, greet the caller by name. Smile when you answer, so you sound happy to hear from the person. Deliver a greeting that the person is unlikely to hear from other salespeople, such as, "Mrs. Dithers! Thanks for returning my call. What can I do for you today?"

Book VII

Becoming a Power Seller

Text-messaging customers and clients

Text-messaging is a great way to enable your customers to leave you a message — especially if your customers are more inclined to type than talk.

With text messaging, your customers or clients can send you a message using their cellphones or instant messaging software on their computers. They simply type the message and instead of sending it via e-mail, they send it to your phone. Some smartphones even include an app that enables users to speak their message and then send it as a text message, something you may want to look into.

Text messaging is sort of a combination of e-mail and instant messaging for cellphones. On a cellphone, when you receive a text message, the phone typically rings a special tone to indicate that you've received a text. You can then select a special menu option for checking text messages, read the message, and respond to it using the buttons on your cellphone's keypad or screen.

Always accommodate your customer's preferences, particularly in respect to how they prefer to communicate. Some people love talking on the phone, and others hate it. Some prefer texting over voice, and others hate getting text messages from anyone but friends or family. As a salesperson, you should be comfortable with all communications media and cater to your customer's preferences. If you don't know which communications medium a customer prefers, ask.

Adding a conference-call center

A conference-call center is a great way to meet with clients and colleagues via phone. Depending on the system you choose, you may even be able to record the conference calls and have them transcribed or simply file them in case the calls generate ideas that you may want to follow up on later. You can meet with one or more clients over the phone, engage in workshops or coaching sessions, and even bring others into the discussion to troubleshoot problems or address issues that arise during the call. Callers simply dial the central number, enter a secret code on their phone, state their name, and join in the meeting.

To find out what's available, contact your phone company or search the web for "conference-call service providers."

Improving e-mail efficiency

You probably know how to send and receive e-mail messages, but you may not be aware of all the fancy features your e-mail program has that can make your life easier, including the following:

✔ **Filters:** You can set up e-mail filters to have messages automatically sorted for you into separate folders. You can then prioritize the messages you want to answer first. You can even *filter out* messages that will only waste your time by having them sent to the trash.

✔ **Groups:** If you find yourself frequently sending the same messages to the same people, consider creating a group that contains everyone's e-mail addresses. Instead of entering each address separately, you can send a message to the group to have it distributed to everyone in that group.

Don't disclose other people's e-mail addresses without their consent. When e-mailing more than one person, enter the recipient's e-mail address or the group name in the BCC (blind carbon copy) field instead of in the To or CC field.

Send something of relevance and value to everyone in your e-mail address book at least once a month. You may want to notify recipients of a special offer, share a tip for making the most of a product you sell, or even send a link to an inspirational web page or video.

Hopping on the smartphone bandwagon

Smartphones have led the charge of what's called Sales Force Automation (SFA). Equipped with wireless e-mail and phone service, voicemail, GPS, and other features, SFA enables companies to store information about customers in a central location and provide remote access to that information to everyone in the company, particularly the sales force. It also allows management to track its salespeople in the field.

Salespeople often resist any attempts by management to automate sales. They don't like having to hand over their client portfolios and share the information they spent so much time gathering. They hate the fact that management can trace their movements in the field via GPS. And many salespeople simply don't want to spend time learning how to use a new gadget — time they could be using to make sales and earn commissions.

However, the benefits far outweigh the potential drawbacks:

✔ You can carry your contact information with you.

✔ You can send and receive e-mail on the road.

✔ You can surf the web without having to open your notebook computer.

✔ If a customer fails to show up for a meeting, you can connect to your central office and find another prospect in the area to visit.

✔ You can compare your performance to other salespeople at your company and discover areas where you need to improve.

✔ You can find the closest Starbucks in the area — you can even get directions to it. Okay, maybe not essential, but for some of us, it's pretty darn important!

Keeping in touch with instant messaging

Many salespeople who sell primarily from their computers find that instant messaging (or IMing) is an excellent communications tool for keeping in touch with clients.

With an instant messaging program — such as Google Chat, AOL Instant Messenger (AIM), Yahoo! Messenger, Facebook Chat, or iChat — you can communicate via computer and the Internet with someone anywhere in the world instantly (assuming you both have computers and compatible instant messaging programs). These programs have become sophisticated enough to handle not only text messages but also voice and video.

You can continue working on your computer with your IM program running in the background, and when a customer sends you an instant message, you're automatically notified of its receipt. You can then type and send the person a message, call the person on the phone, or even teleconference with the customer, as explained in the following section.

Teleconferencing over the Internet

Teleconferencing hasn't quite achieved the promise it had in *The Jetsons,* but with the Internet, it's getting closer and closer. With your computer, a high-speed Internet connection, and the right software, you can now teleconference with clients and colleagues from all around the world.

Teleconferencing technology varies in cost, quality, and performance. For basic teleconferencing, you can use a webcam and Skype (www.skype.com) or even one of the instant-messaging programs described in the previous section. *Web-conferencing* systems enable conference participants to share a whiteboard and other presentation tools.

Telepresence is a step up, designed to create a more realistic encounter — as if you're sitting in the same room right across the table from other conference participants. Telepresence systems combine technology and environmental elements, including elaborate room design, acoustics, lighting, and specific network engineering to ensure high performance and project life-size images.

To see what's available, research "teleconferencing," "web conferencing," and "telepresence" online. For more on video conferencing, head to Book III, Chapter 3.

Chapter 7

Tapping the Power of Word-of-Mouth Advertising through Social Networking

....

In This Chapter

▶ Understanding the marketing power of social media and social networking

▶ Building a high profile online with blogs

▶ Using your blog as a lead-generation tool to boost sales

▶ Mixing it up in social-networking communities

....

People have an infinite selection of channel-surfing opportunities — hundreds of TV and cable channels, radio stations, satellite radio stations, newspapers, magazines, movies (at theaters, on DVDs, and through pay per view), websites, blogs, instant messaging, and social-networking sites like Facebook. In addition, people can find out almost anything on the Internet for free, and it's interactive, on demand, and available 24/7.

This is good news and bad news for people in sales. The good news is that you have a host of new opportunities to market products. The bad news is that you have a host of new opportunities to market products — you can't just advertise on prime-time TV anymore and think that you're reaching a majority of your target consumers.

Various factors, the biggest of which is perhaps the Internet, are fragmenting the delivery of media, marketing, and communication. Traditional media channels are not engaging consumers and prospects as they once did. Increasingly, consumers are tuning out traditional messages and tuning in to new communication channels to fill the void.

As a salesperson, you need to connect with clients and prospects in a whole new way to get your message across to them. Social media and social networking are the newest and most effective communication media. This chapter shows you how to harness their power and start rubbing elbows in the vast online network of social media and networking.

Grasping the Concept of Social Media

Every day, millions of Internet users commune on sites like Facebook (to network with friends, family, and colleagues), YouTube (to share video), Twitter (to share brief messages called *tweets*), and LinkedIn (for professional and business networking), to name only a few of the more popular online destinations.

With more and more prospective customers spending more and more time online, the most successful salespeople are establishing a presence online where their prospects and clients hang out. They're replacing their traditional marketing toolkits with 21st-century marketing tools, as shown in Table 7-1.

Table 7-1	Marketing Tools for the 21st Century
Old Media Marketing Toolkit	*New (Social) Media Marketing Toolkit*
TV/cable	Online video, such as YouTube
Radio	Podcasting
Magazine	Blogs
Newspaper	RSS (Really Simple Syndication)
Consumer groups	Social networks, including Facebook Pages and Places
Direct mail	E-mail drip campaigns
Telephone directories	Online directories, such as Google Places and Yelp
Video games	Social gaming, smartphone apps
Billboards	Online properties, including blogs, landing pages, and social properties including Facebook Pages
Telemarketing	Opt-in social marketing, including Facebook and Twitter

Most of these new era tools are social-media and social-networking sites and services that enable you to improve and expand sales by building a community and interacting with its members to meet their needs.

The following sections reveal the differences between the most popular social-media and social-networking offerings and explain the overall approach to incorporate these tools properly in your online marketing efforts.

Exploring the social-media and social-networking landscape

Early in the development of the Internet, websites were fairly static. People visited them, but they didn't quite interact with the sites. For users, the web was pretty much an information kiosk — you could get something out of it, but you couldn't put anything back in. If you wanted to interact, you did it through discussion forums or online chat.

The social-media ball got rolling with the invention of blogging. Blogs combine the simplicity of the web with the social-networking aspect of discussion forums. Although some "blogs" are nothing more than static websites that look like blogs, a *blog* is really an attractive, robust, discussion forum. For many businesses, blogging is the cornerstone of their social-media and social-networking efforts. Their blog functions as their social center, where they have more influence over the content and direction of discussions. From this center hub, they can more easily branch out to other social venues, such as Facebook, Twitter, YouTube, and LinkedIn, and drive traffic from those venues back to the blog. (For more about blogging, see the section "Drawing Attention to Yourself with Blogs," later in this chapter.)

Other social-networking sites, like Facebook, Twitter, and YouTube, provide free and paid features to help businesses promote themselves and their products and services. On these sites and others like them, you have to remember that you're no longer on your own turf. You're just another member of the community, where the unwritten rule is "No soliciting."

 Keep in mind that social marketing is not about selling. It's about establishing a credible presence in communities, interacting with the community, and providing the community with something of value — information, entertainment, whatever. Ideally, you want to build a loyal community around your brand and have communities sell to one another and expand your reach.

Book VII

Becoming a Power Seller

Applying social media to marketing and advertising

In the old days, advertising could be characterized as "repeated messages that emphasized a product's or service's desirable qualities in such a way that captured the consumer's attention and aroused within them the desire to buy." The goal was *mass appeal* — targeting the biggest potential markets.

Those days are over. Mass is out. Niche is in. The consumer has become the real advertiser. In social media, you build a partnership with your consumer. You build a relationship in which your client is so excited about you and your product that she spreads the word for you, calling attention to your products, services, and brand. Your online content strategy can achieve what's known as a *franchise in the mind* — a collective, community consciousness that ripples around the world through the underlying currents of the Internet.

Another major shift has been from *push marketing* to *pull marketing*. In the old days, marketing was (and still is, in traditional media) all about *pushing* messages at targeting audience. With push marketing, the marketer is telling the consumer, "Whether you like it or not, I'm going to tell you what I think you want to hear." Pull marketing draws people in with something of interest or value and invites them to explore, attend, discuss, or otherwise get engaged in a community of people with shared interests.

One of the most attractive aspects of social-media marketing is that it's so affordable. Initially, you may have a substantial investment of time and money creating a low-level buzz, but after the buzz begins, it catches on like a wildfire with very little effort on your part. You start the buzz, and your clients convert that buzz into brand presence or a franchise in their minds.

Putting the "social" in marketing media

Although traditional marketing and advertising center around product and service, social-media marketing gathers its energy from personality, values, and community.

Most salespeople try to build a brand on a single feature or benefit, such as experience, knowledge, education, or service. But creating a strong emotional appeal by focusing on features and benefits is nearly impossible. The best branding campaigns are built on a personality, philosophy, or a set of values. These qualities are inherently emotional and, when used consistently, give you a huge competitive advantage in the marketplace over time.

Social media puts the social and emotional back into marketing. It enables you to establish a strong positive rapport with your community of clients and prospects and, over time, build the trust that makes clients comfortable buying whatever you're selling.

For 21st-century salespeople looking to engage hundreds or thousands of prospects and customers, social media provides a powerful solution for creating, organizing, managing, and distributing your content online.

Assessing the pros and cons of social media and networking

Putting yourself and your company out there on the Internet can be a little scary at first. After all, the Internet is the consummate democracy — total freedom, almost to the point of anarchy. Say the wrong thing at the wrong time, and somebody is likely to pick it up and use it against you. Hordes of prospects and clients may inundate your site with questions, complaints, and outright attacks. This can potentially do more harm than good.

Still the potential benefits far outweigh the potential drawbacks, both of which are covered in the following sections. Armed with this information, you can decide for yourself whether to use social media as part of your sales arsenal.

The overriding reason that every salesperson should be engaged in online communities is that prospects and clients want it. If you don't do it and your competition does, you've already conceded a good slice of the pie to your competitors.

Book VII

Becoming a Power Seller

Considering the benefits of social media and networking

The following list highlights ten key areas where social media and social networking can benefit your marketing efforts:

- ✔ **Search engine marketing:** Being engaged in social-networking communities, especially through your own business blog gives you an increased presence on major search engines like Yahoo! and Google. Some search engines pick up new blog content in as little as five minutes. One veteran blogger put it this way, "BLOG stands for *Better Listings On Google.*"

- ✔ **Direct communications:** Social media and networking provide a way for you to speak directly and candidly with customers and prospects so you can collaborate with them to develop and deliver the products and services in highest demand.

- ✔ **Brand building:** Social media and networking serve as other channels to put your brand in front of the customer and keep shaping its identity in real time.

- ✔ **Competitive differentiation:** You gain the opportunity to tell your story over and over and set yourself apart from the competition. Over time, you build brand awareness and increase customer loyalty.

- ✔ **Relationship marketing:** Blogs and other social media and networking tools enable you to build personal, long-lasting relationships with your customers that foster trust. Your prospects and customers come to know you personally. Over time, you develop lifelong relationships with your customers.

- ✔ **Niche marketing:** Social-media sites, including blogs, Facebook Pages, and YouTube Channels, are very niche-specific. You can use them to penetrate underserved niche markets.

- ✔ **Media and public relations:** The mainstream media relies on social media and networking, particularly in the form of blogs, for source material. As a result, journalists call you, not your competition.

- ✔ **Lead generation:** Social-networking tools offer a more personal form of lead generation in that they enable you to establish rapport with readers, which fosters trust. When you finally contact a prospect directly, the contact is warm instead of cold and is more receptive to what you have to say.

- ✔ **Expert positioning:** Social media and networking enable you to articulate your viewpoints, knowledge, and expertise on matters pertaining to your industry, your local community, and other areas of interest to you, your clients, and your prospects.

- ✔ **Customer referrals:** Social media and networking foster customer loyalty while creating a mini lead-generation service for you. Loyal customers become "brand evangelists," promoting your brand to family, friends, and associates and demanding little, if any, additional effort on your part. For additional details, check out the following section on word-of-mouth marketing.

Creating buzz with word-of-mouth marketing

Word-of-mouth marketing, often referred to as *viral marketing,* is the best marketing that ever was, is, and likely will be. On the Internet, social media and networking are like word of mouth on steroids. You can't assign a dollar figure to the value of having others talk positively about you, your company, and your products and services, but you can certainly see the results.

Not only do clients and prospects interact with you via your social-media platform, but they also talk to one another — for good or bad. The people in your social network can become your best brand-building evangelists, spreading your message and your presence throughout their networks.

Instead of artificial, biased commercial messages, people can now get genuine advice and answers from their peers on anything they're looking for.

Word-of-mouth marketing derives its power from the ability of consumers to influence one another when making purchasing decisions. Blogging and other social-media and social-networking activities enable consumers to create an informal consumer's digest for recommending products and services. Consumers are placing less trust in the marketing messages that corporate America has been spewing out for years and taking ownership of the buying process, relying more on the word on the street to decide where to spend their hard-earned money.

Sizing up the potential drawbacks

Social media and networking is not all positive. It adds transparency, which is always a little dangerous. If you're phony, somebody is going to spot it and cry foul. If you upset a customer, that customer is likely to post a critical comment on Facebook or Twitter or even on your business blog. If you write in the wrong tone, a sensitive individual can take issue with what you said. In other words, people are going to react to what you say and how you say it and talk about you, good or bad.

Some other potential drawbacks, especially relating to blogging are these:

- ✔ Social networking requires a time commitment to create posts, monitor comments, answer questions, and respond to the messages that others post.

- ✔ People can vandalize your social properties by posting obscenities, vulgarities, or racial epithets or by hacking into an account.

- ✔ Someone may try to use your blog to advertise his own products and services.

- ✔ Competitors can pose as clients and post nasty messages.

You can minimize the effects of potential drawbacks by knowing what you're doing or hiring a professional to create and manage your blog. You can draw up an editorial schedule and compose a post once every week to ease the burden of creating content, or take on guest bloggers to write content for you. Vandalism can be controlled by putting the proper security checks in place, monitoring posts, and automatically censoring obscenities. Blogging platforms, such as WordPress, also enable you to install plug-ins that can help secure your blog and filter out undesirable comments.

Don't throw the baby out with the bath water. Just because you have a concern about a particular aspect of social media or networking, don't let that spook you. You can usually find a solution or compromise to address your concern.

Drawing Attention to Yourself with Blogs

Blogs are consumer magnets, primarily because search engines, such as Google and Yahoo!, love blogs. Keep in mind that when people start searching for information on the Internet, they use a search engine. The higher your website or blog ranking, the higher the profile it has. Blogs do a much better job than standard websites at feeding search engines what they're hungry for — fresh content and relevant links. Although you may create a small website and attract a small amount of traffic, a comparably sized blog can attract huge crowds.

The following sections show you how to keep your blog on center stage by updating its content regularly and populating it with relevant links that attract attention.

Add a Google Site Map to your blog to improve its ranking with Google and other search engines. To create a sitemap, create a sitemap file and copy it to the directory on your domain server where your site is stored. Then, sign into Google and tell Google the location of the sitemap file. For additional details about Google Site Map, visit www.google.com/webmasters/sitemaps. If you're not technically inclined, check our *Blogging For Dummies,* by Brad Hill (Wiley), or hire a web designer.

Updating your blog with fresh content

More than anything else, search engines value unique content. When a search engine visits a website or blog, it looks for content that it hasn't "seen" since the last time it visited the site. Sites that are constantly updated with new information tend to get higher rankings, so freshen up that content regularly. When a search engine discovers a site that hasn't been changed in weeks or months, it "assumes" that the information is older or that nobody cares about the site.

When posting to your blog, carefully select the words you use in post titles and the bodies of the posts. Search engines look for repeated *keywords* and *phrases* to index. Think of very descriptive words or phrases that apply to the content on your site and that the people you want to visit your site are most likely to search for, and use them repeatedly. Over time, this teaches the search engine what your site is about.

Don't overuse keywords, because search engines may lower your site's ranking for doing so. Think about using keywords and phrases to label the content on your site, not as an artificial means to raise its importance.

Another way to include fresh content on your blog is to get other people to freshen the content for you — encourage visitors to post comments.

Populating your blog with relevant links

Search engines also love websites and blogs that are "well connected," meaning the site has plenty of links pointing to other sites and plenty of other sites pointing to it. This interconnectedness sends a message to the search engine that the site is a credible member of a community of websites and blogs, and not just some fly-by-night operation.

The following items suggest a few ways you can use a search engine's preference for well-connected sites to your advantage:

- ✔ **Cross-market your website and blog.** Insert links in your blog entries to your company website and link to your blog from your company website. The more links into and out of your blog, the more "Google Juice" you produce and the higher your search engine listings.

- ✔ **Populate your blogroll with relevant listings.** Woven into the fabric of blogging are lists of blogs called *blogrolls* — links to other relevant blogs and websites. Think of them as mini-directories to other sites in the niche-neighborhood. Blogrolls enable search engines to better understand the site's primary focus. In addition, as a blog gains credibility, other bloggers link to the site, creating a wealth of inbound links from other relevant sites that raise the blog's credibility.

- ✔ **Add relevant links to posts.** In addition to labeling your blog posts with relevant keywords and phrases, add links to your posts that point to other high-profile websites and blogs with content that's related to yours. In addition to drawing attention to your blog, this raises the profile and credibility of other websites and blogs in your community.

 Google offers a free tool called Google Analytics that can automatically track and report on traffic streaming into your blog or website. It tracks the number of visitors, which site directed them to your site, which pages they viewed most, the amount of time spent on each page, and much more. All you do is copy a small script that Google creates for you and paste it on every page of your blog or website. In a blog, all you have to do is paste it in one location, and every page you create contains the tracking code. For details, check out Google Analytics at www.google.com/analytics.

Getting your blog discovered on Technorati

Technorati (www.technorati.com) is one of the most popular blog *aggregators* — it gathers posts from thousands of blogs in a variety of categories, including entertainment, business, sports, technology, and living. You can "claim" your blog to add it to Technorati's blog directory in whichever categories you choose. Claiming your blog is another way to raise its profile and expand its reach.

Book VII

Becoming a Power Seller

The process for claiming your blog on Technorati is fairly straightforward. Visit www.technorati.com, register to become a member, click your profile name or photo (or photo placeholder), scroll down to and then click inside the Start a Blog Claim box, type your blog's web address, click the Claim button, and follow the on-screen instructions to complete the process.

Consider registering your site with Google Blog Search at http://blog search.google.com.

Distributing your content with RSS

Are you wondering what that orange button is that you've seen on blogs and other websites? It represents something called RSS, which stands for *Really Simple Syndication,* among other things. RSS provides Internet users with a way of gathering and organizing content from websites and blogs through a syndicated feed. It essentially allows users to create their own custom online newspapers that pull news and other information from a wide selection of websites and blogs. If someone subscribes to your feed, whenever you update your blog, the person automatically receives the new content.

This is called *permission marketing,* and it creates connections with consumers and clients that are much stronger than spam e-mail and other unsolicited forms of marketing.

Most blogging platforms, including WordPress, have integrated RSS feeds or an RSS widget you can add to one of your blog's sidebars. After adding the widget, access your blog's home page, and click the RSS link to view the feed. The feed's address appears in your browser's address bar. Use this address to register your blog's RSS feed with news aggregators such as NetworkedBlogs (www.networkedblogs.com).

For additional details about creating RSS feeds, go to the source. Visit Feedburner at www.feedburner.com or Newsgator at www.newsgator. com. You can also read *Syndicating Websites with RSS Feeds For Dummies,* by Ellen Finkelstein (Wiley).

Enabling users to distribute your content

One of the best ways to distribute your blog content is through the people who read your blog posts. You've probably seen content on the web followed by icons that let users "like" the content on Facebook or share it on Twitter. You can easily add this feature to your blog by installing a plug-in designed for this purpose.

Blogging platforms, including WordPress, typically have a plug-ins page where you can search for and install plug-ins. After you've installed the plug-in, it automatically adds icons for one or more social-networking sites to every post, so users can share your posts with a single click.

Converting blog traffic into sales

Attracting Internet traffic is nice, but it's not an end in itself. At the end of the day, a blog is a website, and any website can attract visitors. It's what becomes of the visitors when they arrive at the site that matters most. A marketing website, whether static or dynamic (like a blog), has two goals:

- ✔ **Establish credibility in the marketplace or industry.** You establish credibility by offering valuable information and resources. Credibility leads to trust, and trust leads to sales.

- ✔ **Capture leads to promising prospects.** Web surfers are not looking for blogs for blogs' sake; they're looking for pertinent, useful content. Sites that provide valuable content generate interest, comments, and leads. By positioning your blog as a site with valuable content, you automatically get more opportunities to capture leads owing to your increased visibility in search engines.

The ultimate goal of your blog is to turn traffic into business. In the world of sales and marketing, this is called *lead generation*. In Internet parlance, it's called *conversions*. It does little good to have traffic unless that traffic translates into something more tangible, such as an e-mail contact, phone call, or other type of actionable item with the potential for generating additional business transactions.

Traditional lead-generation systems are designed to highlight comparisons and give readers the opportunity to compare features and benefits of different products, services, and companies. This approach is a *competitive perspective*. An effective blog, however, establishes meaningful relationships with its readers. The sole purpose is to create a substantive bond based on qualities of trust, goodwill, respect, mutual appreciation, and open communication.

Establishing a Presence in Virtual Communities

Building relationships on the Internet freelance style by setting up your own blog is like having your own booth at a sales convention. Clients and prospects can choose to visit if they want to and if they can find you through Internet search engines or perhaps links from other websites and blogs.

Another way to rub elbows online is to establish a presence in virtual communities, such as Facebook, Twitter, YouTube, and LinkedIn. Each community has its own culture that attracts a unique crowd, so you may find one community a better fit for you than another.

The following sections lead you on a guided tour of some of the more popular virtual communities, to assist you in choosing a hangout that's best suited to you and what you sell and optimize its marketing potential.

Your ultimate goal is to sell, but don't actively try to sell on Facebook and other social venues. Your goal is to establish a presence and build relationships. You do that primarily by offering users something of value — valuable information, opportunities to communicate with people of interest or have fun, special deals, and so on. Relegate your traditional advertising to the actual advertising features the social venue offers.

Engaging the Facebook community

Although Facebook is primarily a social venue, it's also a great place to promote products and services, and Facebook provides several features to do just that.

Creating a Facebook page

Your first order of business is to set up a base of operations on Facebook — a business page. To set up a Facebook page, take the following steps:

1. **Scroll to the bottom of the Facebook screen you're on (down to the footer) and click Create a Page.**

2. **Choose the type of page you're creating.**

3. **Click the checkbox next to "I agree to Facebook Pages Terms."**

4. **Click Get Started.**

   Facebook creates and displays your page and presents six steps to getting started.

5. **Follow the on-screen instructions to flesh out your page.**

After creating your page, you can return to it to make changes. To return to your page, click Home (in the top menu), then Pages or the name of the page (in the left menu).

Note: During the writing of this book, Facebook seemed to be transitioning Pages to a new feature called Places, so the options for creating a Page or Place and managing it may differ.

Post updates or other content at least twice a week to attract "likes" and keep users engaged.

Feeding blog entries to your Facebook page

Assuming you have a blog, you don't have to perform double-duty by posting to both your blog and your Facebook page. To save time, feed your blog entries to your Facebook page. To set up a blog feed on your page, take the following steps:

1. **Display the page on which you want the feed to appear.**

2. **Click Edit Page, near the upper-right corner of the page.**

3. **Click Apps, in the left column.**

4. **Under Notes, click Edit Settings.**

5. **On the Tab line, click Add next to Available, and then click Okay.**

6. **Click Go to App (below Notes).**

7. **Click Edit Import Settings, near the bottom of the left column.**

8. **Click in the Enter a Website or RSS/ATOM Feed Address box and type the address of your blog or its RSS feed.**

9. **Click the checkbox next to By Entering a URL.**

10. **Click Start Importing.**

11. **Check the preview of your feed, and if it looks right click Confirm.**

    If it doesn't look right, click Cancel and try again.

Getting a vanity URL

When your Page has a 25 fans, you can claim a vanity URL for your page — a web address that more clearly and simply reflects the page title. Go to Facebook.com/username, click Set a User Name for your pages (below the box that allows you to set a username for your profile), and follow the on-screen instructions.

Advertising on Facebook

Although you shouldn't do any heavy advertising or selling on your Facebook page, advertising on Facebook is perfectly acceptable, especially if your advertisement offers something of value, such as a two-for-one sale. To find out what's involved, scroll to the bottom of any Facebook page and click Advertising. From this page, you can click the Create an Ad button to have Facebook step you through the process of creating an ad and a budget for your advertising campaign.

Book VII

Becoming a Power Seller

Claiming your Facebook place

Facebook Places is a feature that enables you to take advantage of location marketing — presenting content to customers and prospects that's relevant to their current geographical location. Customers can check in to your Facebook place to find out more about it and access any promotional deals you decide to offer.

To claim your Facebook place, access the Facebook app from your smartphone or go to `http://touch.facebook.com`, and then select the Places tab. Or, if you're using Facebook on a computer, click in the Search box in the top menu and search for your business by name. If your business isn't listed as a Place, add it:

1. **Access the Facebook app on your mobile device or use your web browser to go to** `http://touch.facebook.com`, **and then select the Places tab.**

2. **Click Check In.**

3. **Click the Add button and follow the on-screen cues to complete the process.**

If Facebook already has a place for your business, claim that place so you can customize it. When you're ready to claim your place, access its Place page, click I Certify That I Am an Official Representative of Your Business Name, click Proceed with Verification, complete the Claim Place form, and click Submit. (Facebook verifies your ownership of the business by calling your business phone number and prompting you to enter the PIN it provided or checking the documentation you submitted as proof of ownership.)

After you've claimed your place, go to it using your smartphone's Facebook app or through `http://touch.facebook.com`, click Merge with Existing Page (in the left menu), and follow the on-screen cues to merge your place with your page, so you have a single Facebook property to maintain.

Offering check-in deals

Facebook enables businesses to offer promotional check-in deals to Facebook members. With a check-in deal, a customer who's physically present at the business, such as a store or restaurant, checks in to the business's Facebook Place and receives a special offer if such an offer is available. The customer may need to check in a certain number of times to receive the offer, just like those special deals where you have to get a card punched a certain number of times to get a free beverage. If an offer is available, instructions appear on the screen telling the customer how to redeem the offer — typically, by showing the screen to the server or clerk.

Weaving your own spider web

Successful social networking hinges on your ability to weave your own spider web to snare clients. It's all about making contacts. Build strategic contact points on the Internet wherever your clients and promising prospects tend to gather and then cross-promote these contact points (your websites, blogs, and social-networking pages). This creates a mini spider web that can begin to expand both organically and exponentially.

The most effective online salespeople create multiple *participation points* — places where clients and prospects want to interact and engage. By testing these new social-media tools you can determine which ones have participants who appreciate innovative, new approaches and the opportunity to connect with salespeople who are people first and salespeople second.

Your prospects and clients need to feel empowered to search and find the information they're looking for without being pressured. They need interaction, participation, and the approval of the online community to buy your products from you. Social networking provides them with all this and more.

During the writing of this book, Facebook's Deals feature was a work in progress and available only in certain cities. To find out more about deals, log in to Facebook, click Account, Help Center, Browse Help Topics, and then below Ads & Business Solutions, click Deals.

For more about marketing and selling on Facebook, check out *Facebook Marketing For Dummies,* by Paul Dunay and Richard Krueger (Wiley).

Book VII

Becoming a Power Seller

Tweeting on Twitter

Twitter is another popular social venue where you can and should keep in touch with your clientele. With Twitter, you send tweets, which consist of no more than 140 characters, including spaces. Although these tweets enable you to distribute only snippets of content, they can help drive traffic to your blog, where users can find more information. To find out more about Twitter, including how to get started, visit http://support.twitter.com.

Whenever you publish a blog post, tweet about it and include a link to that post. If you installed a share plug-in, as explained previously in this chapter in the section "Enabling users to distribute your content," you can simply click the Share on Twitter icon following the post to go to Twitter and post your tweet. An easier solution is to use a service like Twitterfeed (www.twitterfeed.com) to automatically feed your blog posts to your Twitter account.

To find out more about how to use Twitter for marketing and sales, check out *Twitter Marketing For Dummies,* by Kyle Lacy (Wiley).

Getting some air time on YouTube

YouTube (www.youtube.com) became a cultural phenomenon seemingly overnight, allowing anyone with a creative imagination and a digital camcorder to produce and distribute his own short video clips online. Commercial applications of YouTube in marketing, advertising, and sales, however, are still in their early stages. Corporations have dipped their toes into online video as a new advertising vehicle, but success stories from salespeople are still anecdotal.

Nevertheless, some salespeople are able to harness the power of YouTube and put it to work for them in boosting sales. The biggest opportunities for driving sales with YouTube come in the form of soft-sell videos, such as the following:

- ✔ Educational videos that show how to use a new product or one of its more complicated features

- ✔ Entertaining videos that contain some mention or appearance of the product, perhaps even a video that makes fun of the product

- ✔ Third-party testimonials, in which a YouTube member posts a video clip of herself singing the praises of a particular product or company

Stay away from posting any obviously commercial ads on YouTube. They're likely to drive away more customers than they can possibly attract. If you find a video on YouTube, however, that promotes a product or service you sell, consider linking to it, adding it to your marketing materials, and *tagging* it (adding a search term to it, so clients and prospects can easily find it by performing a search).

Dig it, man, Digg it!

Looking for a way to generate links to your business website or blog, drive traffic, and increase search engine rankings? The social news site Digg (www.digg.com) may be the answer you've been looking for. Digg is a site where regular folks can submit stories for consideration. Other users read the stories and "digg" them. That's Web 2.0 nomenclature for rating a story. If your story receives enough diggs, it gets promoted to the front page.

Claiming your business listings

You may have business listings on the web and not even know about them, but you should know about them and claim them, when possible, so you can customize those listings. Claiming a listing typically consists of notifying the service that you own or represent the business and then confirming your ownership in some way. To confirm ownership, the service usually provides you with a PIN when you submit your claim and then calls the business phone number that's in the listing and prompts the person who answers to enter the PIN.

Search for your business on the following sites, claim your listings, and then use whatever tools the service offers to customize your listings:

- Google Places at `www.google.com/places`

- Yahoo! Local at `http://local.yahoo.com`

- Yelp at `www.yelp.com`

- Bing at `www.bing.com/business portal`

The site, which averages 1.5 million visits per day, utilizes the "wisdom of crowds." In other words, no editorial staff is at work screening stories and deciding on what makes the headlines and what gets buried. It's all up to you and your peers to make the news.

What are the marketing benefits? Say you write an informational article and post it to your website or blog. By submitting it to Digg, which you can do with a single click if you install Digg on your blog, you leverage the chance of that article getting linked to by a large number of readers, including other bloggers.

Digg facilitates viral marketing. The end result is that many more people may read the article than would otherwise read it, more people are likely to visit your blog, and search engines see this activity and reward you for it. All in all, Digg provides an excellent means by which your quality content can get read, linked to, and ranked in the search engines. As always, remember not to be overtly selling in your blog posts. You may send those posts to Digg, but no one else is going to dig 'em.

Cross-promoting your blog and social properties

To spread the word about your blog and social properties, use them to promote one another. On your social properties, be sure to edit your profile or page to include your blog's address. When you post on your social properties, such as Facebook, Twitter, and YouTube, be sure to link back to your blog or website. After claiming your business listings, make sure they include a link to your website or blog.

Likewise, use your blog or website to promote your social properties:

✔ On Facebook, you can create different types of badges to add to your website or blog. Facebook provides the HTML source code to paste on your site for displaying the badge. For more about creating badges, visit www.facebook.com/badges.

✔ On Twitter, you can create a Follow button to add to your site. After logging in, scroll to the bottom of the right pane and click Resources. This takes you to a page where you can create a Follow button, Tweet button, or Widget to add to your website or blog.

✔ To link your Twitter and Facebook accounts, log in to both accounts in separate browser windows or tabs, go to http://apps.facebook.com/twitter, and when asked "Would you like to connect your twitter and Facebook accounts?" click Allow.

✔ To link your site to your YouTube account, head to YouTube's Creator's Corner at www.youtube.com/t/creators_downloads, where you can find YouTube buttons and Banners.

Book VIII
The Book of Tens

The 5th Wave   By Rich Tennant

"Here at Don's, we seal a deal with a straight
look, a handshake, and a reverse Step-Over
Toe-Hold."

In this book . . .

Throughout this All-in-One, you find strategies, advice, techniques, and more that can help you perform better and smarter in just about every aspect of selling. That's great, but, let's face it: It's a lot of reading.

If you're in the mood for some quick and easy advice, Book VIII has just what you need. Consider it the donut-hole book: Good stuff in bite-size pieces. Here you can get advice on how to avoid the ten biggest mistakes most salespeople make, ten can't-lose strategies for becoming a power seller, ten tips on how to break out of a sales slump, and more.

Chapter 1

The Ten Biggest Sales Mistakes

Everyone knows about baseball great Babe Ruth's 60-home-run season, but few people realize the staggering number of times he struck out to earn that record. Failure has happened, is happening, and will continue to happen to all of us. Failure is inevitable, but it isn't something to fear. Too few people realize that. In fact, fear of failure is one of the greatest causes of failure in the world! Although no one expects you to embrace failure as a friend, you can learn and profit from the experience.

This chapter gives you a brief look at the ten most common mistakes every salesperson makes and tells you how to avoid falling into these traps.

Undervaluing Prospecting

Prospecting is absolutely critical to building a successful sales career. To be a successful salesperson, you have to make sales, and to make a lot of sales you have to prospect. Yet you'd be amazed at the lack of attention salespeople pay to this key step in the selling cycle. Some salespeople pass by opportunities to make sales every day.

Real professionals learn the right way to find new leads for business. Professionals keep on learning and applying what they learn until they become real champions.

For all the prospecting information you need — including advice on how to overcome any hesitation you may feel about it — head to Book II.

Not Taking Charge or Responsibility

You've worked the phone, mailed the letters, and exploited all the social media venues you know of. You're working really hard, and you're just not finding qualified potential clients. Lots of people work hard. The world is full of salespeople who put in long, hard hours and who aren't even close to living up to their potentials. It's sad but true that many of them will blame their poor results on everything — the economy, their product, their territory — but themselves and their lack of skills.

The ability to sell isn't a gift from that magic genie in the bottle. It's a skill that anyone can learn as long as he has the drive to learn it and is willing to make the effort. If you aren't living up to your full potential, maybe the challenge isn't your skill level but your attitude. Be enthusiastic. Set goals. Get some sales knowledge — this entire tome is chock-full of ideas — and then apply your skills and strategies. That's how things get better.

Talking Too Much

People with the "gift of gab" tell great stories and can keep an audience engaged and listening. But spinning tales, although great around the campfire, is death to the salesperson. You just can't buttonhole someone, turn on the charm, barrage her with friendly words, and think you're making a sale. Why? Because when you're talking, you aren't listening!

Selling is a skill that requires careful questioning so you can glean useful information while you listen. An interested introvert wins out every time over an interesting extrovert because the center of attention for the introvert isn't himself — it's his potential client. He'll ask more questions and better questions, which means he gets more and better information. The interested introvert has the buyer properly evaluated and qualified, while the extrovert is chasing his buyers away with every word he utters.

Using the Wrong Words

So, what are wrong words? The answer depends on the situation, the nature of the business, the people involved, and a thousand other factors. Take overfamiliarity, for example. Using a first name before asking permission to do so is one way to use the wrong word. Cursing, even mild profanity, is clearly out of place. Using language that shows cultural, gender, or racial biases is also a no-no. Using jargon your client doesn't understand, poor grammar, inappropriate slang, and incorrect references to the individual's business are other examples of the wrong word in the wrong place. All these words undermine your ability to communicate effectively with your potential client.

Book III, Chapter 4 has advice on how to avoid these situations.

Not Practicing What You Learn

You read and study skills and strategies. You rehearse them with your family and friends. You know how to approach a potential client (refer to Book II), how to share information about your product in a way that keeps the buyer listening and engaged, how to lead the client to a close. Finally, the big day arrives. You gear up, knock on that door, and say, "You wouldn't want to buy a motor home, would you?" Bang! You're dead.

 REMEMBER

Selling, which is part art and part science, isn't an inborn trait; it's a skill that you can learn. All you have to do is learn the principles and apply them. The techniques in this book have been tested, proven, and improved for decades. Not only do they work, but they work very well. Trust them, use them as you're supposed to, and you can become a master salesperson.

Not Asking for Referrals

Too many salespeople blow chances for referrals. Forgetting the basic tenet of asking for referrals is easy to do in the excitement of making a sale or during the fear of a cold call. Make yourself remember. If you forget, you're just hurting your own success. Somebody, sometime is going to close those very buyers you never bothered to get.

Book VIII

The Book of Tens

The best time to ask for referrals is right after you've closed the sale. Even when you're cold-calling and the answer is a polite "thanks, but no," you can ask that person whether she may know someone else who would be interested in your product or service. Getting referrals can be done. It must be done. Like lightning, it's elemental. (Book IV, Chapter 8 has details.)

Lacking Sincerity

To buy from you, people have to like and trust you and believe that what you're saying is to their benefit. If they see dollar signs in your eyes, they know immediately the person you want to benefit the most is you. But by being sincere and showing a genuine commitment to serving the needs of your potential clients, you'll find more clients, make more presentations, close more sales, and build a more successful and prosperous life.

Being sincere is impossible when you try to interest someone in a product or service that you know is not for his benefit. A professional is dedicated to finding the people who can truly benefit from her product or service so she can best serve their needs with a product that is truly good for them.

Ignoring Details

Sloppiness has no place in the professional world. Stalling on the phone while you look for the name of the person you just called or misspelling a word in a follow-up letter marks you as somewhat less than professional. Not following up or checking in with a client who invested in your product or not doing something you said you'd do are hallmarks of your lack of attention. Having a lax attitude about the details tells your potential clients and existing clients that you really aren't interested in their benefit — and if they believe this, they'll look for someone who is interested in serving them.

Look around your office or over your shoulder. Who's busy staying in touch or double-proofreading a follow-up note? It should be you.

Falling into a Slump

Everybody has highs and lows, good days and bad days. If you were to chart that cycle for a year, it would look something like a wave pattern. You can make similar charts quarterly, monthly, and weekly to measure your performance. Like an annual sales diagram, such a chart can tell you not only when to expect the highs, but when to anticipate the lows. For example, if you're really hot Monday and Tuesday after the weekend, but finish poorly at the end of the week, plan some activity Wednesday to recharge your batteries and avoid the Thursday–Friday slump. Being able to see a slump coming gives you the time and opportunity to head it off.

Not Keeping in Touch

By asking the right questions during your qualification of a potential client, you can learn what services she's likely to need, even if she doesn't need them today. Then, by following up at regular intervals, you can ensure that your name is the one she thinks of when the time comes. The key is to get permission to keep in touch with potential clients and then do it according to your promises.

In your follow-up call, you can reintroduce yourself with something like this:

> Mrs. Jones, this is Richard Row of The Richard Rowboat Company. We spoke last fall. You gave me permission to contact you again in the spring. I was wondering what your thoughts are today about that 10-foot aluminum model I discussed with you and your husband.

A few seconds per call is all it takes. You won't even notice the time away from the rest of your schedule. Isn't a few seconds of your time worth a potential sale from someone who already knows you and perhaps even likes and trusts you or the brand you represent?

Book VIII

The Book of Tens

Chapter 2

Ten Power-Selling Tactics and Techniques

*E*very salesperson needs a toolbox packed full of strategies, techniques, and tips to place prospective clients at ease and make them more receptive to sales presentations. In this chapter, you find ten tools to stock your own toolbox. Feel free to personalize these methods for your own use. You don't want to look and sound like some other sales rep who just met with these same clients.

Focus on Relationships, Not Sales

Chances are, you know people who call only when they need something from you, and these folks probably make you a little uncomfortable or even bitter. You may even avoid them and screen their calls.

Customers and clients are the same way with salespeople, because salespeople usually call when they want something, namely for the customer to buy something. This is why building relationships is so important. Beyond all the advice about building mutually beneficial relationships with customers that you can find throughout this book, here are a few more:

- Develop and implement a customer relationship program that puts you in regular contact with customers *without* selling them anything. This should include regular phone calls, e-mail messages, newsletters, and a blog that they can visit at their leisure.

- Arrange business development meetings with existing, past, and prospective clients on a regular basis.

- Conduct focused seminars and workshops of interest for your target markets.

- Arrange speaking engagements with your target market's industry and professional organizations.

- Network, network, network!

Generate Positive Publicity for You and Your Company

In addition to targeting prospective customers, become a high-profile target by generating positive publicity for yourself and your company:

- Create at least one blog for your business.

- Create at least one community-based blog to support your community.

- Write articles for professional and trade publications on current topics of interest to your target markets.

- Regularly publish and distribute a press release announcing something important and of current interest.

- Get involved in the communities in which you work and live. Give, give, give.

Implement an Hour of Power

Set aside an Hour of Power every day of the week, during which you commit to placing a certain number of phone calls to people in your address book just to keep in touch. Here's a quick overview of how to conduct an Hour of Power:

1. **Pick a group of 100 people in your address book you want to contact.**

2. **Think of something engaging to say that's *unrelated to selling*.**

3. **Let everyone in the office know when your Hour of Power is about to begin and tell them not to disturb you during this time.**

4. **Lock yourself in your office and start placing the calls.**

Keep a log sheet of how many calls you make per day. You can start out slow, with maybe 10 or 25 calls per day, with a goal of making 100 calls per day. One hundred seems to be the optimum number for success.

Work Your Way to the Decision Maker

Salespeople often get screened out by receptionists or other employees who are a little lower on the totem pole than the company executives — the decision makers. Here's a trick to work your way past these sales screeners.

When you call someone, even if he has no idea who you are, say, in the most authoritative voice you can muster up, "Hi! This is *<your name>*!" and then keep the conversation going in a way that emphasizes your confidence and complete expectation that, of course, the person you're trying to reach would be anxious to talk to you. Chances are, the gatekeeper will put you through to the person in charge.

Be Yourself

Before customers are going to buy from you, they have to buy *into* you. So you'd better look, act, and sound genuine. Even though you step it up when you're selling (infusing a little more energy in the relationship than you do when you're not selling), always be yourself. That way, people will know what they're getting.

Some people won't like what you have to offer, but if you're going to have any staying power in sales, you'd better be real and true to yourself. Trying to act the way you think others *want* you to act will only exhaust you.

Book VIII

The Book of Tens

Focus on Ends and Let the Means Fall into Place

Far too many salespeople get so wrapped up in planning their success and worrying about how they're going to achieve it that they never take the first step to attaining their goals. Those who ultimately succeed set their eyes on the prize and then deal with issues as they arise.

Remember back to when you were first learning how to ride a two-wheeler (without training wheels). You knew that balance was the key, but you probably were so focused on balance that you forgot to pedal and would keep falling down or teetering at best. Your dad or mom or whoever was training you probably held the bike and ran alongside you to give you the confidence you needed and to keep your mind off the balancing act. Then the person would let go so you'd think he still "had" you. Pedaling is the secret to keeping your balance — you have to keep moving forward with your eyes on the goal and not worry so much about how you're going to get there. Same in sales.

Prioritize Your Customers

Being a salesperson often seems like being a farmer: busy during the planting season and when the crop is ready to harvest, but in between, business is dead. To keep this from happening; you may be tempted to over-commit, taking on too many clients and being unable to provide them with quality customer service.

In the best of all possible worlds, you'd have a steady stream of business, but that's a pipe dream — it's probably not going to happen. The next best thing you can do is prioritize your customers:

- ✔ **A customers (the most dollar-productive customers):** Paying customers receive your full attention when they demand it. These people are the ones who are going to continue to drive business, leads, and opportunities in your direction. Keep them happy.

- ✔ **B customers (top prospects):** These people may be existing customers who aren't exactly in the top bracket or prospects who you strongly believe could reach that upper bracket. These are the people you want to spend the most time nurturing.

- ✔ **C customers (good prospects):** These prospective customers are very promising candidates with whom you want to spend sufficient time and resources to nurture.

- ✔ **D customers (for "deleted"):** These people are existing customers or prospective customers who are going to drain you of time and resources, offering little, if any, return on your investment. You want to let these people go or refer them to some other salesperson down the road.

List your top 5 customers, your top 25 customers, and your top 100 customers, and then assign them to your slots — A, B, and C. These are the customers you want to focus on, in that order.

Ask for Referrals

When you've earned a customer's satisfaction, don't hesitate to ask the customer to refer you to others who may need your products or services. Supply your customer with a stack of business cards and ask him to hand them out freely and call you if he needs more.

Better yet, ask for the names and contact information for two or three people your customer knows who may be in need of what you're selling. If your customer can't think of anyone right off the top of his head, ask whether you can call back in a couple days. You may even offer the person some incentive to provide you with referrals, perhaps a discount or rebate of some sort.

The best time to ask a customer for a referral is when the person thanks you for going above and beyond the call of duty. The person says "thank you" probably because he has no better way of showing his appreciation. Give him that better way by asking for a referral. For information on getting referrals, head to Book IV, Chapter 8.

Stay Put Instead of Job Hopping

The temptation to change jobs whenever the commissions splits are unsatisfactory or your company seems unsupportive can be overwhelming. But job hopping is generally counterproductive. You waste a great deal of time and energy getting reestablished.

What you may not realize is that, during the change, you go back to focusing on the basics, but when you achieve success, you attribute it to the new job, and not the likely cause of the success: your getting back to the basics. If you had focused on the basics before you left your old job, you could've gained success without the interruption and probably achieved an even higher level of success.

Book VIII

The Book of Tens

Of course, sometimes you have to jump ship. Don't put up with a company that constantly sets you up for failure. If your current company can't deliver on the promises it expects the sales team to make or can't pay commissions or sets unrealistic quotas resulting in a high-pressure environment, you may be better off moving on.

The most important resources you have at your disposal are not the external resources that your company offers you but your own internal resources — your skills and your determination to succeed. Sell more, earn more, and your boss is likely to be very eager to negotiate better splits with you. You have to take the first step, and it doesn't have to be a step out the door. I'm not saying that you should always stick with a job no matter what. Sometimes, you have to walk, but try negotiating with your supervisor before making a final decision.

Just Do It!

The one huge mistake that all mediocre or lousy salespeople make is that they don't follow through. They pay for books, seminars, tapes, classes, coaching, and everything else they need to know to succeed, and then they fail to follow through on one single thing they've learned.

Whenever you pick up a new tip, discover a new technique, or hear about a great technology that can make you more productive, try it out — put the idea into action. Even if you don't see positive results immediately, keep at it. Even if, after giving it a good shot, it doesn't work for you, you've made some progress. You now know more than before you tried it. And if it works, all the better. You now have one more tool in your sales arsenal.

Chapter 3

Ten Ways to Break a Sales Slump or Avoid It Entirely

In This Chapter

▶ Dodging a sales slump before it happens

▶ Giving yourself even more reasons to sell

▶ Flexing your marketing muscle

▶ Seeking inspiration from mentors and family

*E*ven power sellers have slow days . . . or weeks or months. The trick is to keep working and, more important, keep networking, marketing, and pounding the pavement to pull yourself out of that slump. This chapter offers ten proven methods for cranking up sales after a slowdown — or even a meltdown — and a few tips for keeping that momentum flowing.

Steering Clear of Sales Slumps

The key factor in avoiding a slump is knowing what usually triggers it. Here are some common triggers and other causes to look out for:

✔ **Making the sale:** When you make a sale — especially a big sale you worked hard on — the tendency is to breathe a big sigh of relief and celebrate. That's great, but don't party too long.

✔ **Focusing too much on the present and not enough on your future:** You may lull yourself into thinking that just because you don't have a client or prospect to deal with, you have nothing to do. Turn downtime into productive time.

✔ **Getting distracted:** Even a minor distraction can derail you. Either ignore the distraction or deal with it and then get back to what you were doing.

✔ **Being able to pay your bills:** If you're highly motivated by commissions, you may tend to ease up whenever all your bills are paid. To keep this from happing, work ahead. Have a goal to save up a certain amount of money, so you're not selling in "feast or famine mode" — working too hard when bills stack up and not hard enough when times are good.

You also may experience slumps regularly due to the nature of your business. In real estate, for example, people buy and sell fewer homes over the winter and more in the spring. Recognize the timing of these slumps and plan for them.

Don't worry or fret about slumps, because worry is a sure way to kill future sales. Keep a confident and positive attitude.

Motivating Yourself with Added Incentives

When you feel your motivation sliding (or if you're someone who struggles with motivation in general), try dangling a carrot in front of yourself. Plan a vacation. Go car shopping. Look at new houses. Find something that you really want to work for, and use that reward as your proverbial carrot. Sometimes a little added incentive is all it takes. Eventually you find that you don't work for things anymore — you work for the thrill of the deal. Putting a deal together and knowing that you ultimately helped someone is a real hoot and a great motivator.

A reward doesn't always have to be a possession. You may want to set the goal of spending more quality time with your family, setting aside more time to volunteer in the community, or even earning some extra money for your favorite charity. Anything that gives you a purpose to sell is fair game.

Steering Clear of Negative People and Situations

When your entire office or the entire industry is experiencing a sales slump, all the Negative Nancys start crawling out of the woodwork to whine about how bad it is, berate management, and complain. Don't get caught up in this downward spiral of negativity. It will suck the positive energy right out of you.

Avoid the break room, coffee room, lunchroom, water cooler, and wherever else the negative people congregate. Seek out the positive people and spend time with them, planning how to pull yourselves and your company out of the current slump. You may be able to turn a negative person positive, but don't expend too much energy on such pursuits, and never let someone drag you in the same hole he's in.

Starting Right Now

One way to quit smoking is to pick a date on which you're going to be smoke-free. Theoretically, this gives you a few final days to indulge yourself prior to making an all-out commitment to stop. What often happens, however, is that people indulge themselves over the weekend, manage to make it through Monday, and then start back on Tuesday with the goal of quitting again the next Monday.

 Instead of setting a date on which to begin doing something positive or stop doing something negative, start now. Even if you take the tiniest step toward your goal, you're making progress. Don't put it off until tomorrow. Tomorrow never comes.

Recommitting Yourself to Success

A sales slump is often a sign that you're operating off-plan. You made a commitment to success, carefully drew up an effective plan, worked your plan for a few days or weeks or months, and then became so busy that you completely forgot about your plan. You're now back to where you started. Even worse, you may begin to think the *plan* failed.

Get rid of any thoughts you may have of ditching your plan. If your plan for success really didn't work, tweak the plan and try again. If you simply drifted off-plan, then regroup and recommit to getting back on-plan.

A failed plan also can indicate that you're spending too little time on real business and too much time on monkey business. Get rid of the time wasters and back to dollar-productive activities. Stop the feel-good stuff and get on to the business of business.

Ramping Up Your Lead Generation

When you're selling little or nothing, that usually means people have forgotten about you. Unfortunately, far too many salespeople mistakenly think it means that they need to sit by the phone and wait for it to ring.

When sales slip, you have much more time on your hands to shake the bushes for business. Ramp up your marketing efforts by exploring a marketing medium you haven't tried yet. Book II, Chapter 3 is packed with ideas. Also, check out Book II, Chapter 5 for tips on how to explore opportunities in other markets. You could be in a sales slump because you're doing all the wrong stuff. Go back and see what worked before, revisit the basics, and then get creative.

After your increased marketing efforts pull you out of your current slump, keep at it. Salespeople who ignore marketing when sales are brisk and attend to it only when sales taper off discover that their sales slumps are deeper, longer, and more frequent. Market in good times and bad, especially in bad times. When you find yourself thinking, "I can't afford to advertise," you're probably at a point where you can't afford not to.

Revisiting Your Relationships

One of the best sales prospecting tools you have are the relationships you've nurtured with customers, colleagues, and other people you've bumped into as a part of your networking activities. When business tapers off, use the extra time to rekindle old relationships and begin new ones.

Make a habit of keeping in touch with your contacts and strengthening your relationships over the course of the year. When you're in a sales slump, contacting these people for assistance or leads won't feel as though you call only when you need something. When you make a habit of keeping in touch with contacts over the course of your career, you soon discover that your sales slumps become more shallow and less frequent.

Reviewing Your Records

To easily identify why you're experiencing a slow time, keep impeccable records and then review those records when you've had a string of what appears to be bad luck or good luck. You often can spot patterns in what you're doing or not doing that correspond to the hills and valleys you're experiencing. The only catch is that you need good records. If you don't already keep a journal, day planner, or some other log of what you're doing to improve sales — the number of prospecting calls you make each day, the number of follow-up communications you make, and so on — start today.

Consulting an Expert

Even though you're a professional salesperson, you may not have a clear, unbiased view of your sales technique. To get such a view, consult an expert.

Ask another salesperson whose opinion you respect or ask your mentor, coach, supervisor, or personal partner for some advice. Describe your current situation in detail, including what you were doing when sales were good, what you were doing when the slump started, and what you're doing now. Ask your sales doctors for their diagnoses and treatment plans, and then sit down and consult with them to find a cure.

Book VIII

The Book of Tens

Outside experts may not be able to offer any real solution, but even so, they often can make you feel less isolated and offer a compassionate ear that may be enough to help you work through the problem yourself.

When you're in a rut, falling off the face of the earth is too easy. Keep in touch with people. Call a positive friend and go out to lunch. Get jazzed up. You know what gets you motivated, so do it.

Getting Friends and Family Involved

Your family holds a significant stake in your sales success, so get them involved in motivating you and generating ideas. Make a contest out of it. Tell your family that if you become the top salesperson for the month, you all can go on a mini-vacation. Set a sales goal for the week, and when you achieve that goal, you all can go out to dinner and a movie.

Get your family excited about your success. The more excited they become, the more they can motivate you with their support and suggestions. Enthusiasm is contagious!

Chapter 4

Ten Advanced Closes

When you've mastered the closing strategies in Book IV and you're ready to move ahead, here are ten additional closes that have proven successful.

The Wish-Ida Close

When you know what you're offering is truly good for your prospective client, and your buyer has agreed but just doesn't seem to want to make a decision, the Wish-Ida close is perfect. It's lighthearted, yet it makes a valid point:

I understand how you feel, Bill. We're all members of the Wish-Ida Club. Wish Ida stayed in my first house and paid it off. Wish Ida invested in gold 20 years ago so I'd be rich today. Wish Ida grabbed a chance to gain an exclusive advantage. Wouldn't it be great to get rid of at least one Wish Ida by saying yes to something you really want?

The "No" Stall Close

When potential clients are hemming and hawing about making a buying decision, sometimes you need to be a little more direct. This strategy helps you remind them why they starting talking with you in the first place — to fulfill a need or to resolve a challenge.

You have your clients' best interests in mind, so deliver the following words with warmth and sincerity.

> John and Mary, I can appreciate what you're saying. In fact, it could be a nice way of saying "no." I look at *no* as the first two letters of the word *nothing*. By that I mean, if you say "no" today, nothing will happen and things will stay pretty much the same. You'll still have the same concerns: _____. [Summarize all the challenges or needs they've told you they have.] However, if you say "yes" to what our research shows, all those things will change for the better. You'll have _____. [Summarize the benefits they'll receive.] So, based on that truth, does the word *no* still seem best to you?

This strategy is somewhat of a last-ditch effort to give them a brief overview of everything discussed up to this point. If these folks are on the fence, this strategy may be enough to help them move on over to the buying side.

The Best-Things-in-Life Close

Everyone wants to have the best things in life. Everyone wants to believe that he has made some of the best decisions when considering major purchases or investments. The best-things-in-life close gets the potential client's mind off the money objection and onto the enjoyment of benefits, which is what ownership is really all about:

> Isn't it true that the only time you've ever really benefited from anything in your life has been when you said yes instead of no? You said yes to your marriage. (*Optional:* And I can see how happy you are.) You said yes to your job, your home, your car — all the things that I'm sure you enjoy. You see, when you say yes to me, it's not really me you're saying yes to, but all the benefits that we offer, and those are the things you really want for your family, don't you agree?

This strategy gets the potential clients hearing the word *yes* several times. It also conjures mental images and positive feelings about past benefits they've enjoyed by going ahead with a buying decision.

The No Close

When you've given your best presentation and your buyer still says "no," you have little to lose by saying the following words and putting your shoes on your client's feet. The following example is for life insurance, but it works for any type of product.

Mr. Johnson, there are many salespeople in the world, and they all have opportunities that they're confident are good for you. And they have persuasive reasons for you to invest with them, don't they? You, of course, can say no to any or all of them, can't you? You see, as a professional with ABC Company, my experience has taught me an overwhelming truth: No one can say no to me. All he can say no to is himself and his own peace of mind knowing that his family will be taken care of financially should something unforeseen happen to him. Tell me, how can I accept this kind of no? In fact, if you were me, would you let Mr. Johnson say no to anything so critical to his family's future?

You must speak the preceding words with sincerity and empathy for your potential client's situation.

The My-Dear-Old-Mother Close

Tom Hopkins learned this strategy from the incredible Zig Ziglar. This technique can be your salvation when you find yourself involved in a series of silences as you roll from close to close with the same potential client. How, you ask? If you have a clever way to break tension, pressure turns into humor — explosive laughter sometimes. Lots of people can handle pressure, but laughter will pop them wide open. So, when the pressure has been on for several seconds after your last close and it's getting heavy in the room, suddenly grin from ear to ear and say, "My dear old mother once said, 'Silence means consent.' Was she right?"

Because you should never tell your buyers anything that's untrue, the next time you talk to your mother or grandmother or someone else's mother, ask her whether she's ever been in a situation in which silence means consent. If she has, ask her to say those words to you. Now you can honestly use that line as a close. If she hasn't heard of such a situation, simply ask if she believes it can happen. Then, adjust how you say this so you speak the truth.

The Sharp-Angle Close

The sharp-angle close is best used when a potential client states a condition of the sale. This might include requiring a certain delivery date or color of your product. If you help people get involved with services, they may need a certain start date so there's no gap in service between the company they're using now and yours. Rather than quickly stating that you can meet their requirements, the words you'll use will move you one step closer to having them make a commitment.

CLIENT: If we decided to go with your service when our agreement with XYZ Company ends next month, we wouldn't want to have any gaps in coverage. Your team would have to be on-site and up to speed by November 1. Could you handle that?

YOU: If I provide you with a guarantee in writing on our agreement that we can meet those needs, are you willing to approve the paperwork today?

The client has thrown down a gauntlet of sorts. You accept the challenge, but wrap it into a closing question to make the sale. The key here is to be so well prepared that you know whether you can make the promises the client is requesting of you and your company.

The Buyer's-Remorse Close

When people make major decisions, you can expect them to have second thoughts about things afterward. That's why so many contractual agreements for large-ticket items have a 72-hour clause that allows buyers to change their minds. Champion sellers understand this and figure out how to address the issue before they leave a new client with these words (fill in the blank with the name of your product or service):

John, Mary, I feel good about the decision you've made tonight to get involved with _____. I can tell you're both excited and somewhat relieved. From time to time, I've had people just like you who were positive about the decision they made until they shared it with a friend or relative. The well-meaning friend or relative, not understanding all the facts and maybe even being a little envious, discouraged them from their decision for one reason or another. John, Mary, please don't let this happen to you. In fact, if you think you may change your mind, please tell me now.

The Secondary-Question Close

As the name suggests, with this strategy, you state the obvious major decision but follow it immediately with a minor question. The answer to the question is something the decision maker needs to make a decision about if she intends to move forward with the purchase.

As I see it, Ms. Carter, the only decision we have to make today is how soon you'll start enjoying the increased profits this new service will bring your company. By the way, are you going to use it in both locations or start with just the main office here?

When Ms. Carter answers your secondary question, she's already thinking ahead to the usage of your service. When she mentally and emotionally assumes ownership, the actual process of approving an agreement is not far behind.

The Take-It-Away Close

No one wants to be thought of as not good enough for something. As a child, if you knew you could play ball, but someone said you may not be good enough for the team, you probably wanted to be on the team more than ever. By subtly inferring that you have to see whether your prospect qualifies before she can own the product, she may change her tune from playing hard to get to trying awfully hard to get it. This close works especially well for products that involve financing or insurance (which may require the client to meet a certain health standard).

Well, Ms. Franklin, I understand your concerns about going ahead with this new equipment. Before we can place an order with our supplier abroad, however, we need to go through the financial process to be certain your company can qualify for such a large investment. Let's proceed with that aspect of the purchase first, shall we?

The Lost-Sale Close

If you've done everything and your prospect still doesn't go ahead, admit defeat. Pack up your visual aids and prepare to head for the door. Then use the lost-sale close. More often than not, it reopens conversation enough that your prospect will give you something to grasp onto to tell you if he may say "yes."

Pardon me, Mr. Johnson. Before I leave, may I apologize for not doing my job today? You see, if I had been a bit more eloquent, I might have said the things necessary to convince you of the value of my product. Because I didn't, you and your company will not be enjoying the benefits of my product and service and, believe me, I am truly sorry. Mr. Johnson, I believe in my product and earn a living helping people own it. So that I don't make the same mistake again, will you please tell me what I did wrong?

If you speak those words sincerely and with a somewhat defeated look, many potential clients will tell you what their real concern is. In many cases, it will be something that just didn't come up during the sales process or something they were hesitant to share with you. Grab onto it and move back into selling mode.

Chapter 5

Ten (Or So) Ways to Sound Like a Pro on the Phone

*I*f you're a sales professional, you may not consider yourself to be in *telephone* sales — maybe because your job title isn't "telemarketer" or because you don't work in a call center. But in today's world, *all* salespeople rely on the telephone to be successful in their work. In any sales scenario, the first contact with a potential customer, for example, is likely to be via the phone, even if follow-up is face to face.

So, when you're on the phone to a prospective client, remember that just because the person on the other end of the phone can't see you doesn't mean your image doesn't come across loud and clear. When you *sound* professional, you're *seen* as a professional — even if the prospect never meets you. Conveying that image takes a little more than dressing for success. This chapter can help you be the professional that you are.

Always Use a Headset

The act of putting on a headset is a psychological trigger to prepare for business — it's game time! A headset also frees your hands so you can take notes. By making a record of important information, you're better set to confirm, review, summarize, and follow up on all critical points.

When you're not concentrating on keeping the receiver between your ear and shoulder, you're free to focus on the prospect. Using a headset also reduces neck fatigue *and* eliminates the risk of dropping the phone while talking to a prospect; blasting the prospect's eardrum with a thud on the desktop is *not* professional.

Stand Up and Be Heard

Ever notice that singers always *stand* when they perform? That's no coincidence. They know that their voice carries more resonance, range, and power when their diaphragm isn't folded over.

You can use the singers' secret for sounding more authoritative and self-assured when speaking to prospects on the phone by performing a little practice exercise. First, stand tall and say what you would to a prospective client. See the energy and enthusiasm that pours forth? Now slump into your desk in a question-mark curve and repeat the sales pitch. Feel the conviction (or lack thereof) seep out of your voice? Even if you did somehow manage to maintain the same level of enthusiasm, did you notice how much more energy it takes to generate the power and exuberance when you're slumped over?

Spice Up Your Delivery

In order to keep your prospect's attention, don't put him to sleep. Avoid speaking in a flat, monotone voice. Instead, vary the delivery of your speech to grab attention. Play with the following three vocal elements to vary your speech:

✔ **Tone:** Your speaking voice consists of several qualities, including rhythm, intonation, and inflection, resulting in a one-of-a-kind vocal personality. You can think of this vocal fingerprint as *tone.* Although your tone is what makes your voice *yours,* you can optimize your phone communication by paying some attention to it. Make sure your tone conveys the message you want it to.

✔ **Volume:** No, not the volume on your headset but the decibel of your own voice. Talk too quietly, and you generate lots of "Could you repeat that?" requests. Speak too loudly and the prospect must hold the receiver at arm's length. Keep your volume within a reasonable range, but be sure to vary it to hold the prospect's attention and emphasize key points.

✔ **Pace:** Most telephone salespeople are guilty of speed talking. Chalk it up to enthusiasm, nervousness, or desire to get in the sales points before the recipient hangs up. At any rate, you want to avoid this sport. Slow talking can be just as bad; you'll have people wanting to finish your sentences for you. Moderate the pace of your speech, occasionally varying it for effect or emphasis.

Talk Less and Listen More

The more you listen to *others* talk, the more you find out about them. If you do all the talking, you're not going to hear anything you don't already know.

 Start by asking a question or two and then let the other person talk. Tune in to discover more about the prospect, the company, its needs, and its priorities and values. You just may find that, by giving the prospect a chance to talk, you discover the best way to answer those needs and meet those priorities and values. And as a bonus, the prospect hangs up marveling at how smart and knowledgeable you are! (For more on listening, check out Book II, Chapter 2.)

Limber Up Your Body

To sound better and be more effective in telephone sales, do some warm-up exercises to limber and loosen your body. Trust me, you may spend a good part of your day connected to clients by voice only, but telephone sales is a full-contact sport!

 Do facial exercises before your first call. Tighten and then relax your face muscles, and clench and relax your teeth several times. Slowly yawn to limber up your cheeks, muscles, and skin. Balloon out your cheeks a few times. Loosen your neck and shoulders by shrugging and relaxing. Rotate your neck slowly to loosen the muscles. A few full-body stretches aren't a bad idea either. Stretch your quads, hamstrings, and calves as if you were preparing for a run.

Warm Up Your Voice

Your voice, like your body (see preceding section), needs warming up to perform at its best. Start out in the shower by humming a tune (no matter what others in the household may say about your operatic potential). Humming is an outstanding warm-up for your vocal chords. For that matter, croaking like a frog is another excellent vibration exercise to strengthen your chords.

 Get some talk time in before your first sales call. Synchronize dinner plans with your spouse. Ask the kids what's on tap for their day. Chat with a co-worker at the water cooler. And as a bonus, you may just warm up a few relationships, too.

Put in Pre-Call Practice Time

Every salesperson benefits from rehearsing base scripts and dialogues before picking up the phone. Try to get at least 15 minutes of practice before each calling session. Doing the drill out loud is preferable. Don't be put off by teasing colleagues; they won't be laughing when you lead the sales board soon. Practice it all: your opening statements, prospecting scripts and dialogues, appointment objection handling, lead follow-up scripts, and closes.

Sneaking in a follow-up practice session at the end of the day doesn't hurt. Find a supportive co-worker, supervisor, or friend to work with you. If you regularly put in the time to improve your phone-sales skills, you're sure to come across in any phone conversation as the consummate professional you are.

Bundle Your Calls

For maximum effect and optimal impact, plan your call schedule to group calls by type. For example, make all prospecting calls within one block of time, such as the first two hours of the morning, and then follow with a session devoted to lead follow-up calls.

Make at least ten similar calls in a row. By focusing on a type, you find yourself more "in the zone," zeroed in on the skills and strengths you need to tap into for a successful call outcome. And as you tick off the calls, one by one, you find that with each call, you get better.

Tape and Replay Your Calls

Not only do you create a reliable record of the phone conversation when you tape your calls — one that you can refer back to as often as you need to — you also create a valuable tool for self-evaluation. Did you speak too fast? Talk too much? Sound too aggressive? Come across as unprepared? Hear yourself as your prospect hears you, and you're bound to discover ways that you can improve and fine-tune your sales skills on the phone. As long as you're recording the call for training purposes, you don't need to announce that you're doing so.

Index

Notes

Notes

Notes

Apple & Macs

iPad For Dummies
978-0-470-58027-1

iPhone For Dummies,
4th Edition
978-0-470-87870-5

MacBook For Dummies, 3rd
Edition
978-0-470-76918-8

Mac OS X Snow Leopard For
Dummies
978-0-470-43543-4

Business

Bookkeeping For Dummies
978-0-7645-9848-7

Job Interviews
For Dummies,
3rd Edition
978-0-470-17748-8

Resumes For Dummies,
5th Edition
978-0-470-08037-5

Starting an
Online Business
For Dummies,
6th Edition
978-0-470-60210-2

Stock Investing
For Dummies,
3rd Edition
978-0-470-40114-9

Successful
Time Management
For Dummies
978-0-470-29034-7

Computer Hardware

BlackBerry
For Dummies,
4th Edition
978-0-470-60700-8

Computers For Seniors
For Dummies,
2nd Edition
978-0-470-53483-0

PCs For Dummies,
Windows
7 Edition
978-0-470-46542-4

Laptops For Dummies,
4th Edition
978-0-470-57829-2

Cooking & Entertaining

Cooking Basics
For Dummies,
3rd Edition
978-0-7645-7206-7

Wine For Dummies,
4th Edition
978-0-470-04579-4

Diet & Nutrition

Dieting For Dummies,
2nd Edition
978-0-7645-4149-0

Nutrition For Dummies,
4th Edition
978-0-471-79868-2

Weight Training
For Dummies,
3rd Edition
978-0-471-76845-6

Digital Photography

Digital SLR Cameras &
Photography For Dummies,
3rd Edition
978-0-470-46606-3

Photoshop Elements 8
For Dummies
978-0-470-52967-6

Gardening

Gardening Basics
For Dummies
978-0-470-03749-2

Organic Gardening
For Dummies,
2nd Edition
978-0-470-43067-5

Green/Sustainable

Raising Chickens
For Dummies
978-0-470-46544-8

Green Cleaning
For Dummies
978-0-470-39106-8

Health

Diabetes For Dummies,
3rd Edition
978-0-470-27086-8

Food Allergies
For Dummies
978-0-470-09584-3

Living Gluten-Free
For Dummies,
2nd Edition
978-0-470-58589-4

Hobbies/General

Chess For Dummies,
2nd Edition
978-0-7645-8404-6

Drawing
Cartoons & Comics
For Dummies
978-0-470-42683-8

Knitting For Dummies,
2nd Edition
978-0-470-28747-7

Organizing
For Dummies
978-0-7645-5300-4

Su Doku For Dummies
978-0-470-01892-7

Home Improvement

Home Maintenance
For Dummies,
2nd Edition
978-0-470-43063-7

Home Theater
For Dummies,
3rd Edition
978-0-470-41189-6

Living the
Country Lifestyle
All-in-One
For Dummies
978-0-470-43061-3

Solar Power Your Home
For Dummies,
2nd Edition
978-0-470-59678-4

Available wherever books are sold. For more information or to order direct: U.S. customers visit www.dummies.com or call 1-877-762-2974.
U.K. customers visit www.wileyeurope.com or call (0) 1243 843291. Canadian customers visit www.wiley.ca or call 1-800-567-4797.

Internet

Blogging For Dummies,
3rd Edition
978-0-470-61996-4

eBay For Dummies,
6th Edition
978-0-470-49741-8

Facebook For Dummies,
3rd Edition
978-0-470-87804-0

Web Marketing
For Dummies,
2nd Edition
978-0-470-37181-7

WordPress
For Dummies,
3rd Edition
978-0-470-59274-8

Language & Foreign Language

French For Dummies
978-0-7645-5193-2

Italian Phrases
For Dummies
978-0-7645-7203-6

Spanish For Dummies,
2nd Edition
978-0-470-87855-2

Spanish
For Dummies,
Audio Set
978-0-470-09585-0

Math & Science

Algebra I
For Dummies,
2nd Edition
978-0-470-55964-2

Biology For Dummies,
2nd Edition
978-0-470-59875-7

Calculus For Dummies
978-0-7645-2498-1

Chemistry For Dummies
978-0-7645-5430-8

Microsoft Office

Excel 2010 For Dummies
978-0-470-48953-6

Office 2010 All-in-One
For Dummies
978-0-470-49748-7

Office 2010 For Dummies,
Book + DVD Bundle
978-0-470-62698-6

Word 2010 For Dummies
978-0-470-48772-3

Music

Guitar For Dummies,
2nd Edition
978-0-7645-9904-0

iPod & iTunes For
Dummies, 8th Edition
978-0-470-87871-2

Piano Exercises
For Dummies
978-0-470-38765-8

Parenting & Education

Parenting For Dummies,
2nd Edition
978-0-7645-5418-6

Type 1 Diabetes
For Dummies
978-0-470-17811-9

Pets

Cats For Dummies,
2nd Edition
978-0-7645-5275-5

Dog Training For Dummies,
3rd Edition
978-0-470-60029-0

Puppies For Dummies,
2nd Edition
978-0-470-03717-1

Religion & Inspiration

The Bible For Dummies
978-0-7645-5296-0

Catholicism For Dummies
978-0-7645-5391-2

Women in the Bible
For Dummies
978-0-7645-8475-6

Self-Help & Relationship

Anger Management
For Dummies
978-0-470-03715-7

Overcoming Anxiety
For Dummies,
2nd Edition
978-0-470-57441-6

Sports

Baseball
For Dummies,
3rd Edition
978-0-7645-7537-2

Basketball
For Dummies,
2nd Edition
978-0-7645-5248-9

Golf For Dummies,
3rd Edition
978-0-471-76871-5

Web Development

Web Design
All-in-One
For Dummies
978-0-470-41796-6

Web Sites
Do-It-Yourself
For Dummies,
2nd Edition
978-0-470-56520-9

Windows 7

Windows 7
For Dummies
978-0-470-49743-2

Windows 7
For Dummies,
Book + DVD Bundle
978-0-470-52398-8

Windows 7 All-in-One
For Dummies
978-0-470-48763-1

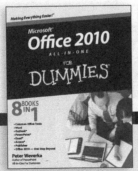

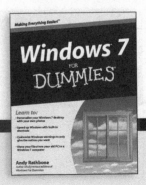

Available wherever books are sold. For more information or to order direct: U.S. customers visit www.dummies.com or call 1-877-762-2974.
U.K. customers visit www.wileyeurope.com or call (0) 1243 843291. Canadian customers visit www.wiley.ca or call 1-800-567-4797.